M000022236

PSYCHOLOGY

STUDYING THE BEHAVIOR OF PEOPLE 2E

A. Christine Parham
San Jacinto College, Pasadena, Texas

Published by
SOUTH-WESTERN PUBLISHING CO.
CINCINNATI WEST CHICAGO, IL CARROLLTON, TX LIVERMORE, CA

by SOUTH-WESTERN PUBLISHING CO.
Cincinnati, Ohio

ISBN: 0-538-16110-8

Library of Congress Catalog Card Number: 87-62836

3 4 5 6 D 2 1 0

Printed in the United States of America

BRIEF CONTENTS

CONTENTS

PREFACE

A study of psychology takes an individual into a realm of knowledge that is fascinating, challenging, and enjoyable. Fascinating to those who are curious about why people think, feel, and behave as they do; challenging because of many technical terms, concepts, principles, and theories to be mastered; and enjoyable when self-understanding and personal psychological growth occurs and a sense of wonder is felt about human processes taken for granted as ordinary. I have attempted to convey my own enthusiasm for psychology through the writing of this text.

CHANGES IN THIS EDITION

PSYCHOLOGY: Studying the Behavior of People, 2d edition, is a major revision of a first edition titled *Basic Psychology for the Work Life.* In addition to the title change, new content has been added in the form of two chapters on developmental psychology, a chapter on states of consciousness, a chapter on behavioral disorders and treatment, an updating of the chapter on physiological psychology, and an inclusion or expansion of the topics of moral development, human sexuality, aggression, stress, altruism, attribution, and personality theory. The study guide has been incorporated into the text; therefore, a more detailed opening chapter outline, objectives, essay questions for review, a list of key terms and concepts, a self-test, and applications have been added to each chapter, and a note to students suggesting a way to study has been added to the preface. Focus questions in wide margins, many more visual aids in the form of photographs, a four-color insert, graphs, and diagrams, and more color have been added. A test bank and transparency masters also are provided with this second edition.

Influences on human behavior are so numerous and the study of human behavior is so broad and includes so many areas that only an introduction to psychology is intended. *PSYCHOLOGY: Studying the Behavior of People,* 2d edition, contains the standard content and essential elements for an introductory psychology course, and it presents the content in a manner that makes the text suitable for a first course in psychology whether it be taken in a senior or junior college; business, trade, technical, or vocational college; high school; or special training program.

PHILOSOPHY AND GOAL

My primary goals while writing *PSYCHOLOGY: Studying the Behavior of People,* 2d edition, have been to provide knowledge of the basic psychological concepts, principles, theories, methods, and approaches of psychology and to show the application of this knowledge in life experiences. In providing this knowledge, an attempt has been made to present the major approaches to studying and understanding human behavior—psychoanalytic, behavioral (learning), cognitive, humanistic, developmental, and biological—to avoid giving the reader a biased perspective. An unbiased perspective enables an individual to see issues and attack problems from a variety of approaches and to use what seems to fit the situation best rather than seeing and attacking problems from a single approach or relying on memorized, quick, easy, general solutions. This kind of knowledge can help an individual (a) develop critical thinking with regard to generalities and tentative hypotheses, (b) broaden the scope of his or her knowledge beyond specific skill areas, (c) develop practical insights that bridge the gap between theory and practice, and (d) provide a background that will increase the meaningfulness of many courses such as those in management, marketing, personnel management, organizational behavior, and organizational development. The individual who learns and applies principles of psychology may experience immediate as well as long-range, lifetime benefits by being able to (a) deal more effectively with people; (b) be more successful in a career; (c) adapt better to change; (d) become more successful in predicting, understanding, and influencing behavior; (e) dispel myths about human behavior; (f) cope better with stress; (g) find deeper satisfaction in work and life experiences; and (h) enjoy better overall physical and psychological health.

Knowledge of psychology is especially relevant to people in the world of work. A successful work experience depends to a great extent on the development of the ability to understand the self and others and the ability to adjust or adapt to environmental conditions as well as on the development of the skills necessary for the work. If through the study of psychology a person develops a greater understanding of the behavior of people and the ability to deal more effectively with life's problems and stresses and becomes a better decision maker and problem solver, that person will be happier, more effective, and more likely to advance up the career ladder. Statistics indicate that more workers do not apply for higher level jobs, are not employed, are dismissed from their jobs, or are overlooked for promotions because of ineffective human relations and poor adjustment than because of lack of skills.

FEATURES

Perhaps the most unique feature of *PSYCHOLOGY: Studying the Behavior of People,* 2d edition, is the extensive use of examples and illustrations taken from work settings and my attempt to combine the theoretical approach with the practical approach. Psychology may be presented in a theoretical framework or in an applied or practical framework and may be applied to many specific settings. A theoretical text may not make practical applications, and an applied text may not expose the theories, research, concepts, principles, and theories for understanding behavior. Because almost everyone is either in a work setting with people or will be, this text is intended to be applicable to almost everyone.

A special attempt has been made to organize the chapters in such a way that the student is guided in study according to psychological principles of learning and remembering—specifically, the SQ3R method (survey, question, read, recite, and review) introduced first by Frank P. Robinson in 1941. To aid in surveying, each chapter begins with an outline and a list of learning objectives. Additional aids for surveying include a list of new terms and a summary at the end of each chapter. To aid in questioning, focus questions appear in the margins, a self-test at the end of each chapter may be used as a pretest before reading the chapter, and students may transform topic headings into questions of their own. Questions are intended to motivate reading and to increase concentration, comprehension, and interest during the reading process. To facilitate reading with understanding, learning, and remembering, an effort has been made to keep the language nontechnical and the reading level as low as is feasible. Also, each chapter contains examples, illustrations, photographs, boxes, activities, and applications. Visual materials and color add variety and clarification to the presentation. New psychological terms are boldfaced and defined as they are introduced. Pronunciation of very difficult to pronounce or uncommon but significant names and terms is given in parentheses immediately following the first use of the name or word. To elicit reciting, essay questions and a self-test consisting of objective questions are included for each chapter. A summary at the end of each chapter presents the main ideas of the chapter in a concise form for reviewing.

Another feature of this second edition is that chapters are organized according to areas of psychology and written in such a manner that each can be read and understood independently of the preceding chapters; however, the chapters are arranged in a logical sequence that will enhance understanding if studied in the sequence presented. This feature allows for flexibility in using the text by permitting the omission of chapters considered to be of lesser importance in a particular course and by permitting adaptation of the course to various lengths of allotted time. Integration of material is accomplished by references being made to a previous or later discussion.

Other significant features of this text are the inclusion of enrichment material in annotated suggestions for further reading for use in (a) developing and applying higher level thinking skills, (b) providing background information, (c) adapting instruction to varying levels of student abilities, and (d) providing more in-depth treatment of some topics. Two case studies with discussion questions are provided for each chapter to stimulate discussion and aid in relating concepts to real life situations. A cumulative, alphabetized glossary, a subject index, and a name index are continued in this edition.

ORGANIZATION

PSYCHOLOGY: Studying the Behavior of People has 14 chapters and is divided into four parts. The first chapter is an introduction that describes the nature of psychology, the approaches to explaining behavior, and the methodology of psychology. Part One—Physiology and Development includes chapters concerned with biological psychology, heredity and early development, and later stages and other areas of development. Part Two—Mental Behavior includes the chapter concerned with sensation, perception, and consciousness and the chapters about learning, remembering and thinking, and intelligence and creativity. Part Three—Individuality of Behavior includes the chapters concerned with motivation, emotions, stress, and adjustment, personality, and psychological disorders and treatment. Finally, Part Four—Social Behavior includes the chapters concerned with attitudes and social relationships and group processes. Statistical methods and procedures are included in the Appendix.

INSTRUCTOR'S MANUAL

A Manual containing, for each chapter, definitions of new terms, objectives, a brief overview, a detailed outline, answers to questions for review, the self-test, and applications, activities for classroom use, an annotated listing of films, and suggested readings is provided. Additionally, the Manual provides a detailed listing of other resources, suggestions for evaluation of grading, suggested course outlines, and a sample course syllabus. Using the Manual materials can save time and provide the new and/or overburdened instructor with valuable source materials.

A test bank for each chapter, also available in computerized form, that contains multiple-choice, true/false, and completion questions not previously used in the study materials is provided in the Manual. A programmed review that may be used as a test, as a review worksheet, or as a self-test follows the test bank in the Manual. Two transparency masters for each chapter that may be used to provide handouts for students or to make transparencies for use with overhead projectors during lectures also are provided.

ACKNOWLEDGMENTS

PSYCHOLOGY: Studying the Behavior of People, 2d edition, is the result of much help from many people. First, an expression of thanks and deep appreciation goes to the following academic reviewers who critiqued portions of the text and improved my presentation of psychology:

Gerald Biberman—University of Scranton
George Cooper—Madison Area Technical College
William S. Rholes—Texas A&M University
M. Aaron Roy—Ashland College
David G. Tinsley—Craven Community College
Fredric T. Williams—Madison Area Technical College

To the many people at South-Western who have exhibited dedication, professionalism, and efficiency in the publishing of this text, particularly the editor who guided both the first and this second edition through the writing and production process, I am most grateful and indebted. And finally, to those who made it all possible, my family who provided loving support and a friend who conceived in my mind the idea of such a project and nurtured the growth of the idea to fruition by instilling confidence and giving encouragement, I dedicate this book and express sincere appreciation.

TO THE STUDENT

Often a student believes that all an individual needs to do to master a subject is read the textbook once, like a novel, and the information will be passively absorbed, permanently stored, and easily squeezed out at examination time. This belief is sometimes referred to as the "sponge theory." Research in the psychology of learning and remembering has confirmed that learning and remembering is accomplished more efficiently when particular techniques are used. Proper use of material in this text should increase the effectiveness of study by providing a framework and overview, by focusing on the key concepts, by providing an opportunity for self-assessment, and by preparing for evaluation. Provisions for active student participation, feedback, and the SQ3R study method (survey, question, read, recite, and review) are incorporated in the following recommended procedure for study of each chapter.

1. Read the short outline on the opening page of the chapter, the chapter headings and captions, the glossary definitions for each new term, the learning objectives, and the summary to provide an overview or survey of the chapter.
2. Read the self-test and questions for review at the end of the chapter and the focus questions in the margins, formulate some questions of your own, and look for answers as you read.
3. Beginning with the first main topic heading of the chapter, read carefully each sentence to the next main topic heading.
4. As you read, pay attention to boxed materials, photographs, diagrams, illustrations, and tables and do any activities suggested or that are suggested by the instructor.
5. Before reading the next topic, try to answer the questions you formulated earlier, the focus questions in the margin, and the questions for review related to this topic and retell the content of the topic in your own words.

6. If the questions are difficult to answer or if the topic cannot be retold satisfactorily, reread the material in the text and try again.
7. Once the questions can be answered satisfactorily and the topic retold satisfactorily, go to the next main topic heading and repeat the process until the entire chapter is read.
8. Read the summary at the end of the chapter again for review.
9. In order to evaluate your comprehension and memory of the material, look at the list of key terms and concepts and try to define each one. Check your definition by using the glossary.
10. For further self-evaluation, a programmed review may be provided by the instructor from the Manual. Put a card or sheet of paper over the answers in the right margin and fill in the word or words you think should go in each blank. Check your answers by sliding the card down to expose the correct answer.
11. Next, take the self-test and determine a percentage grade by comparing your answers with the answers provided in the back of the text. If a lower grade than is desired is achieved, reread the chapter and repeat steps 3-5.
12. To prepare and review for examinations, read again the pages in the text for each chapter to be included on the examination and especially read the summary again.

Although research has established a general procedure that usually facilitates learning and remembering, all students do not acquire knowledge and understanding in exactly the same way; therefore, by experimenting you may develop variations of the procedure suggested above that may be better suited to your abilities and personality.

CONCLUSION

Being a psychologist, counselor, teacher of both business and psychology courses, author of a previous text, author of a newspaper column called "Bits of Psychology", and employed in business corporations and governmental institutions provides a background that has enabled me to produce a text that meets the needs of those involved in training others for life and work and of those who are in training for life and work. If those reading and using this text find it enjoyable and personally rewarding, my goal will be realized.

A. Christine Parham

CHAPTER 1

INTRODUCING PSYCHOLOGY

Objectives

When you have completed your study of chapter 1, you should be able to:

1. Give the explanations of behavior that existed before the emergence of psychology.
2. Define psychology.
3. Specify the major specialized areas of psychology.
4. Differentiate between early views of psychology or approaches to explaining behavior.
5. Differentiate between contemporary approaches to explaining behavior.
6. Describe scientific methods of observation.
7. Give an example of the experimental procedure and use the basic terminology of the procedure with understanding.
8. Explain the role of statistics in psychology and use the basic statistical terminology with understanding.

So you have decided to study psychology—to study about the behavior of people, yourself and your friends, coworkers, peers, juniors, and elders. Although you may not plan to become a professional psychologist, gaining a knowledge of psychology and applying the principles can enhance your ability to deal more effectively with the problems and stresses you encounter throughout your life. In addition, understanding and applying the principles of psychology can improve efficiency in accomplishing tasks in the easiest and least expensive way. A knowledge of psychology can also be helpful to you in making adjustments to inevitable changes that occur during your lifetime. For example, estimates indicate that the majority of jobs that will be available in the year 2000 do not exist today.

Why study about behavior of people?

Because you will be involved with people throughout your lifetime, the importance of understanding the behavior of people and building the best possible relationships cannot be overemphasized. Most experts agree that people who concentrate on good human relations get the best jobs. Human relations is more important to the worker today than 40 or 50 years ago for several reasons: (a) Businesses today are larger, more complex, and require more group effort; (b) more people today are employed in service occupations where customer relations determine the future of the business; (c) more supervisors are being trained in human relations and are therefore more aware of the behavior of the workers they supervise; and (d) employees in an organization today may be from a variety of cultures and personalities (see Figure 1–1). For these reasons, interest in the subject of psychology has increased in recent years.

Figure 1–1. Employees in an organization today may be from a variety of cultures and personalities.

THE NATURE OF PSYCHOLOGY

Can you define psychology as a discipline in today's world in contrast to its early origins? Are you aware of the approaches used by psychologists to study the behavior of people? Do you have some understanding of the methods psychologists use to study and explain human behavior? These are the basic questions that will be answered in this chapter.

Early Ideas About Human Behavior

Although psychology as a discipline is only about 100 years old, the notion of psychology is perhaps as old as humanity. Throughout history, attempts have been made to explain the behavior of people by assigning a source or cause based on the best available knowledge.

How did people in the earliest ages explain and treat problem behavior?

Demonology. Evidence indicates that some half million years ago during the Stone Age, cavemen performed operations on human beings who exhibited behavior problems. With crude stone instruments, they would chip a circular hole through the skull of the individual to allow the evil spirits, believed to be causing the behavior, to escape. Spirits were believed to possess a person's body and to direct behavior. A revival of this ancient explanation of behavior in people referred to today as **demonology** reoccurred, with some modification to conform to religion, during medieval times. Good and evil spirits were replaced by God and Satan (the devil). **Exorcism,** which involved using techniques such as noisemaking, drinking horrible concoctions, starving, flogging, and burning to drive out evil spirits, was the primary treatment for changing the behavior of a person.

Do you have some knowledge of mythology?

Gods and Goddesses. Another ancient belief about human behavior was that supernatural beings were responsible for every thought and action. The heavens became filled with mythical gods and goddesses thought to be controlling almost everything—war, love, fertility, worry, marriage, the dead, and even drunkenness. However, activities became more complex as civilization advanced, and some people began to realize that the idea of gods and goddesses controlling every behavior was a myth.

Philosophers. The source or cause of human behavior was a topic of great concern to early philosophers. Later, after the Middle Ages, philosophers developed opinions and beliefs that have influenced modern approaches to explaining behavior. René Descartes' (pronounced *day KART*) **mechanism,** the view that the physical aspect of humans obeys mechanistic laws, assumed that behavior can be explained, at least in principle, if enough can be learned about the physical systems to determine the laws. **Hedonism** held that behavior is determined by the desires to avoid pain and seek pleasure.

Have you studied philosophy?

John Locke (1632-1882), a British philosopher, originated the philosophy of **empiricism,** the view that the mind at birth is a blank tablet and that environmental experiences determine the behavior of the individual. Human behavior is the result of conscious intentions and reasonings according to the philosophical idea of traditional **rationalism.** Free will is assumed in rationalism in that an individual consciously chooses a behavior. **Dualism** holds that human behavior is controlled by complex interactions of both the mind and the body, either of which may initiate behavior. Dualists assume that God creates humans in such a way that the mind guides behavior to satisfy bodily needs. According to dualism, the source of behavior is God; behavior is instinctive in nature. Charles Darwin (1809-1882) theorized that evolution is a continuous process for man and other animal species and that behavior is instinctive. Many of the questions of psychology today originated in philosophy.

What is the root meaning of the word *psychology?*

The Word *Psychology*. The word *psychology* was coined near the end of the sixteenth century and first appeared in the dictionary near the end of the seventeenth century. The word actually comes from two Greek words—**psyche** meaning soul, spirit, life, or mind and **logos** meaning logic, study, or wisdom.

How did the word *psyche* come to mean soul?

In mythology, Psyche was a beautiful young woman who fell in love with Cupid, the god of love. Cupid's mother, Venus the goddess of love, did not like Psyche because she was human; therefore, she separated the lovers and imposed hardships on Psyche. Psyche's love for Cupid was so strong that it impressed the other gods and goddesses, so they turned Psyche into a goddess, thus making her immortal, and the lovers were reunited for eternity. To the Greeks, true love was the highest achievement of the human soul, and so Psyche became the symbol of the human soul. The word *psychology* originally meant the study of the soul as contrasted with its present definition—the scientific study of behavior.

Contemporary Ideas About Psychology

Although the goals of psychology have remained constant, what psychologists study, their methods of study, and their terminology have varied over time. In this section, contemporary psychology will be described.

Can you define psychology?

Definition. The definition of psychology has not remained constant throughout history. Originally, psychology was a study of the soul, next a study of the mind, and later a study of behavior. Today **psychology** is defined as the scientific study of behavior and mental processes and the application of knowledge gained through that study.

What is behavior that psychologists study?

The term **behavior** refers to any movement or activity of an organism in **response** to a specific **stimulus** or set of stimuli. A stimulus may be any physical event either internal, such as a pain or a thought, or external, such as something heard, seen, felt, or smelled. Because behaviors or responses consist of mental, physical, or internal and external activities or movements, and because such a vast array of stimuli can be presented, you can see that psychology as a study of behavior is a rather broad field. Behavior is anything you do.

What are the two major prongs of psychology?

Note that psychology is defined as "scientific study" and "application." Psychology may be classified as either **pure psychology** (theoretical) or **applied psychology** (practical). Sometimes psychologists are primarily concerned with acquiring or developing knowledge, and other times they are more concerned with the application of knowledge to current problems.

Goals. Psychology as a discipline has goals. One goal is to describe or define behaviors and stimuli objectively or operationally in such a way that they can be measured. **Operational definitions** and measuring devices are not always equally good. Because they are not always completely valid, psychology seeks better descriptions and measuring devices for more accurate measurement. Often many possible operational definitions may be given. Job performance might be described as a score on a job sample test, a supervisor rating, the average number of units produced during several time periods, or the number of units produced during one randomly selected time period. Intelligence might be described as a score on the Stanford-Binet Test, a score on the Wechsler Adult Intelligence Scale, or the speed of learning some particular task. Describing and measuring events and responses is essential in drawing conclusions about behavior scientifically.

Can you differentiate between a theory, a law, and a principle?

Another goal of psychology is to explain behaviors — to understand the underlying mechanics of a behavior, to know causes of or reasons for a behavior, and to present a model of how a behavior occurs. Perhaps explanation is really what psychology is all about — providing laws, principles, and theories of behavior. A **theory** is a tentative explanation of a phenomenon based on present knowledge. A theory explains known facts and shows relationships among concepts and observations previously not related. A **law** is a theory that is generally accepted, very strongly supported, and somewhat precise. A **principle** incorporates a law into a more general and extensive statement that applies to a large range of instances.

Do you ever make predictions about future behavior of a person?

Present or past measurements of behavior may be used by psychologists as a basis for predicting the future occurrence of behavior. A third goal of psychology is to make predictions about behavior. College entrance exams may be used to predict success in a particular college. A score on a mechanical aptitude test may be used to predict how well a factory worker may do on a particular assembly line. A vocational interest test may be used to predict the likelihood of job satisfaction for an individual by comparing his or her personality traits and characteristics and likes and dislikes with those of other individuals who have been successful and satisfied in that occupation (see Figure 1–2).

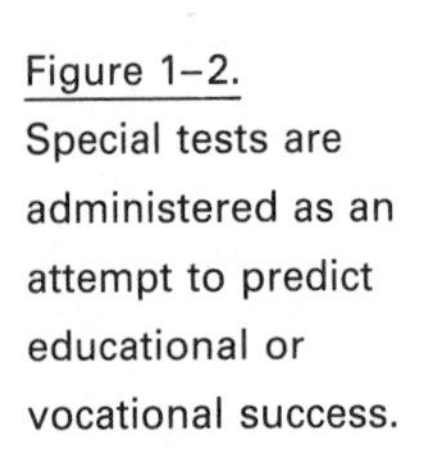

Figure 1–2.
Special tests are administered as an attempt to predict educational or vocational success.

Being able to predict behavior often allows for intervention and control of behavior. To be able to control or influence behavior is the ultimate goal in some areas of psychology. Controlling behavior goes beyond predicting behavior and is concerned with causing a behavior to occur, to be maintained, to cease, or to change in form, intensity, or rate of occurrence. Psychology is concerned with applying knowledge in a beneficial manner and in improving the present or future circumstances of individuals and society. Intervention could possibly prevent behaviors a person does not desire or produce behaviors a person does desire. An employer may be engaged in modifying the behavior of employees, a psychotherapist may be engaged in modifying a patient's behavior, or an individual may be engaged in modifying personal behavior. Once you understand the mechanics of a behavior, you can make predictions about the behavior and oftentimes intervene and control the behavior. Of course, safeguards must insure against the unethical use of such knowledge to modify and control behavior of others for one's own end such as brainwashing.

Scientific Study. Because psychology is defined as the scientific study of behavior, an introduction to psychology should familiarize an individual with the characteristics of such study. You may associate white lab coats, test tubes, and beakers with scientific study; however, these do not qualify a study to be scientific. The manner in which investigations are planned and carried out, the procedures employed in collecting data, and the way findings are interpreted are the criteria for scientific study.

How does the way a psychologist draws conclusions about human behavior differ from the way you draw conclusions?

Scientific study employs the **empirical approach,** which is the pursuit of knowledge through observation and experimentation. The empirical method of science deals with information that is available to the senses and can be validated and confirmed by other individuals. In this approach, methods are used to improve and extend observation and to improve on the design of experiments to avoid the pitfalls of speculation. Psychologists have two things in common—an interest in behavior and an insistence on evidence.

Scientific study goes beyond personal experience (see Figure 1–3). If you recall dreaming only rarely, you may conclude that people dream very little; however, many studies of dreaming indicate that people dream every night. Often we just have no remembrance of the dreams that occurred during the sleep period.

Saying that something makes sense, meaning that it is believable, does not necessarily mean that it is factual. **Common sense assumptions** are ideas one holds to be true without any proof that

Are all common sense assumptions false?

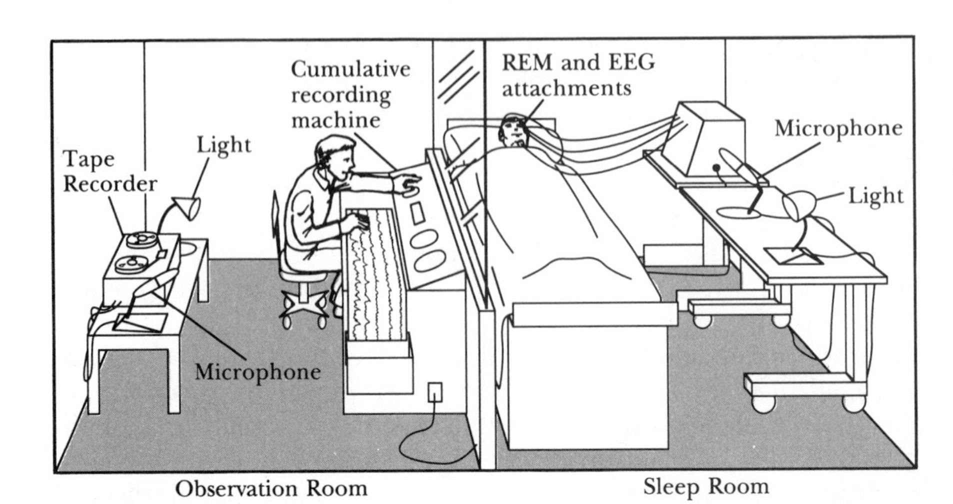

Figure 1–3.
Scientific study goes beyond personal experience.

they are true—statements that are taken for granted. People can easily agree on the plausibility of these assumptions. Sometimes common sense assumptions about behavior are not correct or are only partially correct. Consider these common sense statements: (a) "Absence makes the heart grow fonder" and "Out of sight, out of mind" and (b) "Never too old to learn" and "You can't teach an old dog new tricks." Much of what passes for common sense is inconsistent and vague. Science cannot tolerate such inconsistencies. All common sense assumptions are not false, but they can act as blinders which can prevent you from seeking information that would verify the truth. Whether an assumption is true or false is simply not known without a systematic scientific study.

Areas of Psychology

Because the study of psychology is so broad, intermingles with other disciplines, and includes both theory and the application of theory, psychology as a profession offers a variety of work activities in several special areas. Some knowledge of the work of psychologists will help you to understand psychology and will provide information to use in making occupational choices. Although psychology is subdivided into a number of separate specializations, these areas overlap, so a psychologist may work in several different areas. The findings in one area concerning some behavior may directly relate to studies of behavior in another area. Furthermore, work activities may be common to more than one area of specialization. For example, a psychologist in any area may teach or conduct experimental research.

Clinical and Counseling. Probably the most familiar area of psychology is in applied psychology and is referred to as **clinical psychology.** Psychologists engaged in clinical work are concerned with helping individuals achieve psychological well-being and thus are involved in diagnosing and treating psychological disturbances. Clinical psychologists use a wide variety of diagnostic techniques and therapeutic treatments.

What differences exist between a clinical psychologist, a psychiatrist, a psychoanalyst, and a counselor?

The difference between psychology and psychiatry is often confused. **Psychiatrists** are medical doctors who specialize in the treatment of psychological disorders. Psychiatrists have completed medical school and have followed it with 3 to 5 years of specialized schooling in psychological disorders. A clinical psychologist usually holds graduate degrees—usually a PhD (Doctor of Philosophy) and an MS (Master of Science), having earned those degrees from a psychology department in a college or university other than a medical school. Clinical psychologists may have completed more courses in psychology, conducted more psychological research, or done more psychological testing than a psychiatrist; however, psychologists cannot prescribe any kind of medication, perform surgery, or refer patients for surgery or shock therapy. A **psychoanalyst** may be either a clinical psychologist or a psychiatrist whose approach to treatment is based on psychoanalytical theory or Freudian views (see page 16). A **counseling psychologist** or counselor may or may not have a PhD and works primarily with people who have less serious problems—perhaps problems associated with educational and vocational choices, individual and family adjustment problems, or problems of living with fear and anxiety. Those who work in the area of clinical psychology usually work in clinics or hospitals or have private practices. More psychologists are classified as clinical psychologists than as specialists in any other area of psychology (see Figure 1–4).

What area of psychology has the largest number of psychologists classified in that area?

Industrial and Organizational. Industrial and organizational psychology is an area of psychology that specializes in applying psychological principles in work-related situations and in conducting research to expand knowledge of psychological principles that are applicable in business, industry, and other organizational settings. These psychologists are concerned with such areas as personnel selection, training programs, morale, supervision and management, productivity, job classification, and job satisfaction (see Figure 1–5). Industrial and organizational psychologists often serve as consultants for government agencies and private industry.

What kinds of work do industrial and organizational psychologists do?

MAJOR SPECIALTIES AND WORK SETTINGS OF DOCTORAL LEVEL PSYCHOLOGISTS

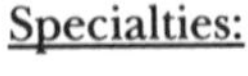

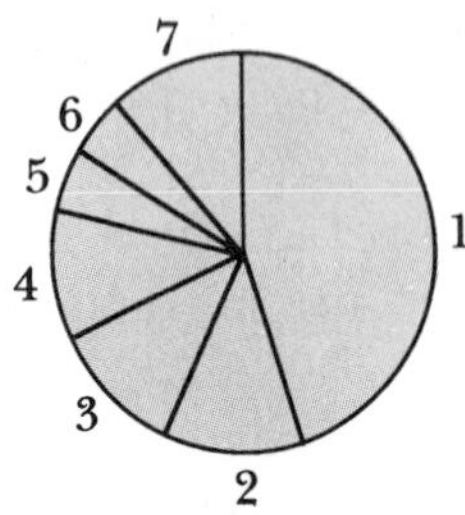

Work Settings:

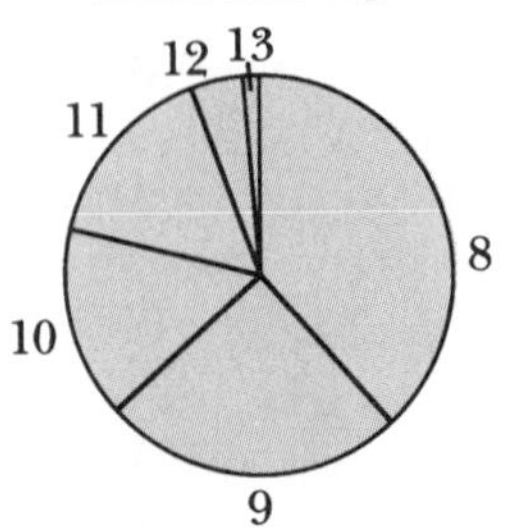

1 Clinical 45%
2 Counseling 12%
3 Personality, developmental, social 11%
4 School and educational 11%
5 Experimental 5%
6 Industrial and organizational 5%
7 Other 11%

8 Colleges and universities 38.1%
9 Hospitals, clinics, and other human services 25%
10 Business, government, and other settings 16%
11 Independent practice 15.8%
12 Schools and other academic settings 4.1%
13 Setting unspecified 1%

Figure 1–4.
A greater number of doctoral psychologists work in colleges and universities than in any other setting, and more identify themselves as being in the area of clinical psychology than in any other area (Stapp & Fulcher, 1981, 1983).

Industrial and organizational psychologists may focus on behavior at various levels. They may focus on an employee's needs, abilities, values, and interests and how these relate to absence, turnover, grievances, theft, individual productivity, career progress, or job attitudes. Or group behavior may be the concern with the focus on communication, conflict within the group or between groups, cohesion of the group, structure and size of the group, de-

Figure 1–5.
An industrial/organizational psychologist may discuss an employee's personal problems, management problems, or the effectiveness of a training program.

cision making, leadership, and group productivity. Often the industrial and organizational psychologist is involved with global or environmental behavior, which might include analyzing the effects of factors such as the employment level in a community, the stability or instability of a community's population, or the political attitudes (liberal versus conservative) within a community.

What are some specialties that have emerged in the area of industrial and organizational psychology?

The area of industrial and organizational psychology has become so broad that a number of specialized concerns have evolved. **Engineering psychology** specializes in the discovery and application of information about the relationship between human behavior and machines, tools, jobs, and work environments. The primary focus is on designing equipment, tasks, work places, and work environments to best match worker abilities and limitations. **Personnel psychology** involves the study of individual differences in performance, methods to assess such differences, and the application of psychological principles to management and employee training. **Consumer psychology** is a study of the dynamics underlying the purchase and consumption of particular products or brands and the utilization of particular services (see Figure 1–6). An emerging specialty is legal or **forensic psychology,** concerned with applying knowledge of human behavior to such matters as jury selection, methods of cross-examination, reliability of eyewitness testimony, construction of personality profiles of criminals, crowd control, and kidnapping and hostage taking.

Figure 1–6.
Consumer psychology employs motivation research to determine why a consumer chooses to buy a particular product or brand.

Organizations are finding that the application of psychological principles can be helpful in increasing productivity, decreasing employee turnover and absenteeism, and resolving work-related problems. Industrial and organizational psychology is presently one of the most rapidly expanding areas of psychology.

Developmental. Developmental psychology is an area in which psychologists are concerned with the growth and development of a person from the beginning of life until death (see Figure 1–7). Behavior and behavioral changes characteristic of each period of development are studied. The periods of development include the prenatal period, infancy, early childhood, later childhood, adolescence, adulthood, and old age. Developmental psychologists work in a wide variety of settings that may include serving as consultants to children's television programs, childcare centers, homes for the aged, or schools. Developmental psychologists may also work with children who have learning problems, or they may work in institutions where they do psychotherapy with emotionally disturbed children.

What periods of life do developmental psychologists study today?

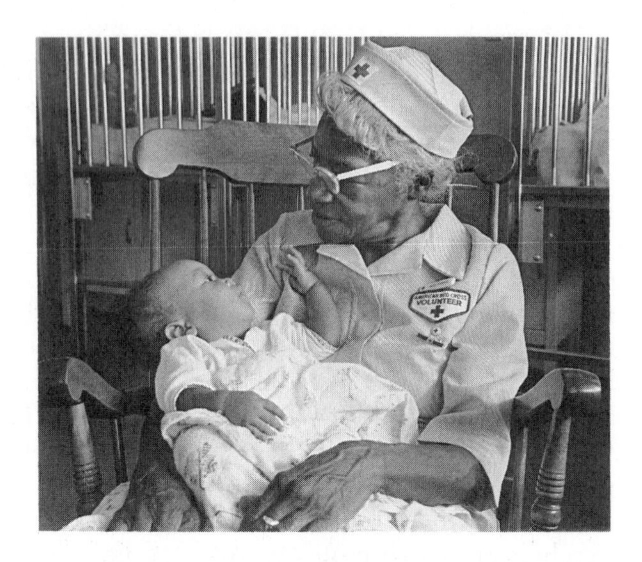

Figure 1–7.
Developmental psychology is concerned with all stages of development.

Do you know a school counselor or school psychologist and what his or her work activities include?

Educational. The area of **educational psychology** is concerned with increasing the efficiency of learning in school. Educational psychologists may work in teacher-training institutions or school settings to develop further knowledge about the process of learning, but they primarily apply their psychological knowledge in school settings to improve learning. Psychologists in education may administer psychological tests, evaluate learning and emotional problems, advise parents and teachers on how to improve academic performance and social adjustment, organize training programs to help teachers, teach psychological principles, conduct research to answer questions of practical significance, or study teacher morale. Educational psychologists often serve as consultants to school systems.

Figure 1–8.
A social psychologist focuses on behavior of people in groups such as family relationships.

Social. The area of psychology that deals with the behavior of people in groups is called **social psychology.** Social psychologists are concerned with how other people influence an individual's behavior. The interactions or relationships among people in families (see Figure 1–8), peer groups, professional groups, and cultural groups are of special interest. Social psychologists focus on such topics as attitude formation and change, group pressures, interpersonal relations, and socially deviant behaviors. Friendship formation, romantic attraction, bargaining, and the effect of violence in the mass media on aggressive behavior may also be topics of study.

Experimental. Another area of psychology, referred to as **experimental psychology**, uses rigorous research methods to experimentally investigate basic psychological processes, usually in laboratory settings (see Figure 1–9). Experimental psychology applies the scientific method to the study of behavior in the strictest sense. Psychologists labeled as experimental psychologists design research projects and have a specialized knowledge of the methods and logic of the scientific approach. Answers to questions that contribute to the practical areas of psychology are provided by experimental psychology. A relatively small number of psychologists label themselves experimental psychologists (see Figure 1–4 on page 10), but all areas of psychology include some experimental psychology because some scientific research is necessary to all psychological investigations. These psychologists are usually based at a university where they combine research with teaching. They often receive grants from agencies to do research concerning particular topics.

Are very many psychologists labeled as experimental psychologists?

Figure 1–9. Experimental psychology uses rigorous research methods, usually in the laboratory, to study behavior.

Physiological. Physiological psychology is an area in which behavior is studied as a function of physical changes in the body, especially in the brain, the nervous system, and the biochemistry of the body. Psychologists in this area study the underlying physical mechanisms that control behavior. To explain behavior, they also investigate the contribution of inherited characteristics. Physiological psychology is the area closest to the biological sciences, and often the decision to label a problem as biological or psychological is arbitrary.

Which area of psychology is very closely related to biology?

APPROACHES TO EXPLORING BEHAVIOR

When did psychology have its beginning?

Psychology became a scientific discipline of its own and joined other sciences in establishing research laboratories late in the nineteenth century (1879). Prior to this time, there had been no separate discipline called psychology and no one with the title psychologist. Throughout psychology's history, researchers have had different views of what to study and how to approach the study of human behavior.

Figure 1–10.
Wilhelm Wundt.

Early Approaches

The earliest views of what to study and how to approach that study are described in this section. Some of these were merely additions to and extensions of presently held views; however, some produced much controversy in the field of psychology, the new science that was emerging.

What was Wilhelm Wundt searching for?

Structuralism. Believing that the elements of the mind could be found just as scientists had found elements of matter and the elements of an organism—cells, Wilhelm Wundt (see Figure 1–10) set up a laboratory in Leipzig, Germany, in 1879 hoping to find the structure of the mind. Because of this emphasis on structure, Wundt's approach or theoretical view became known as **structuralism.** The structuralists studied sensation and used **introspection** to investigate the contents of the mind; i.e., a person would be asked to describe his or her experience of the stimulus presented. The structuralists had difficulty arriving at a set of basic sensations because what was loud to one individual was not loud to another, or what was pleasant to one was unpleasant to another, and what was loud or unpleasant one day might not be on another day. Wundt wrote a book called *Principles of Physiological Psychology* that presented the idea that the mind must be studied just as other natural laws then under investigation were being studied. Structuralism is significant in the history of psychology primarily for the emphasis on careful and precise methods of observation rather than for what was learned about human experience.

Figure 1–11.
William James.

Functionalism. William James (see Figure 1–11), a young American physiology professor at Harvard, turned to philosophy, traveled to Europe, and became a student of Wilhelm Wundt. When James returned to Harvard, he combined physiology and philosophy into a course he called psychology. Out of this course came his book in 1890 called *The Principles of Psychology*. In 1889,

William James changed his title to psychologist and set up the first laboratory for psychological experimentation in the United States.

Who was the first person to use the title *psychologist?*

William James felt that the structuralists were on the wrong track. He believed that the mind consists of the abilities to make decisions and to adapt to environmental situations—that the mind is not just a collection of building blocks. This view extended the study of psychology to include such phenomena as learning, motivation, and emotion. Because James and his followers emphasized the functioning of the mind, the view became known as **functionalism.**

Which early view of psychology focused on perception—interpreting sensation?

Gestalt Psychology. In Germany, Max Wertheimer (see Figure 1–12) and his followers argued that each experience is a complete and organized whole, perceived according to a specific pattern, and that the characteristics of all the various parts of that experience are determined by that pattern. Behavior should, therefore, be studied as an organized whole rather than as separate individual parts. These psychologists focused on how people interpret or perceive a three-dimensional object such as a table from the experience of the pattern of impulses arriving in the brain from the physical energy in the environment via the senses. They used such phenomena as the one discovered in 1832 by the Swiss mineralogist L. A. Necker to demonstrate how two different realities may be perceived from the same physical information (see Figure 5–6, page 161). These psychologists further illustrated their position by pointing out that most people perceive the patterns in Figure 1–13 as a line, a triangle, and a square rather than merely as dots. The views of Wertheimer and his followers became known as **Gestalt psychology,** since **gestalt** is a German word meaning form, pattern, or whole.

Figure 1–12.
Max Wertheimer.

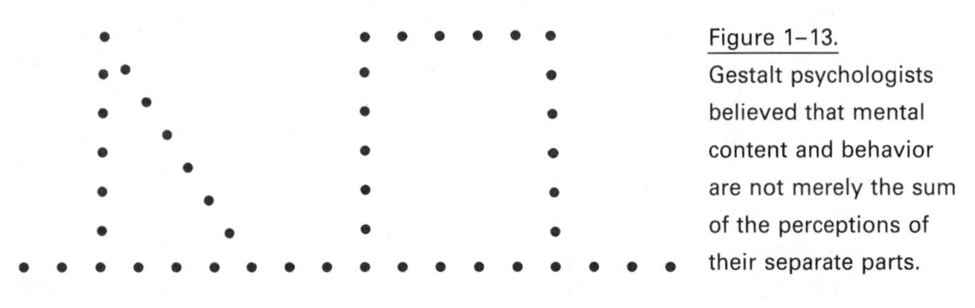

Figure 1–13.
Gestalt psychologists believed that mental content and behavior are not merely the sum of the perceptions of their separate parts.

Psychoanalytic Psychology. During this period, another approach to explaining human behavior, **psychoanalytic psychology,**

Figure 1–14.
Sigmund Freud.

Why is the iceberg often used as a model of the mind according to the psychoanalytic view of psychology?

was developing in the field of medicine. Sigmund Freud (see Figure 1–14), an Austrian physician, proposed that, based on clinical observation, a vast amount of human behavior is the result of unconscious forces hidden within the person. He believed that sexual and aggressive motives, usually unconscious to the person, are the source of behavior. This model of human behavior is sometimes referred to as the "iceberg" model (see Figure 1–15) because only a small part of a person's mind is conscious or exposed to view by the person. The unexposed part of the iceberg represents the unconscious part of the mind—events, thoughts, memories, conflicts, needs, or desires that are repressed because they are threatening in some way to the person, anxiety producing, or forbidden by society. He also believed that most of a person's behavior is caused by unconscious forces and that most adult personality problems can be traced back to early childhood experiences.

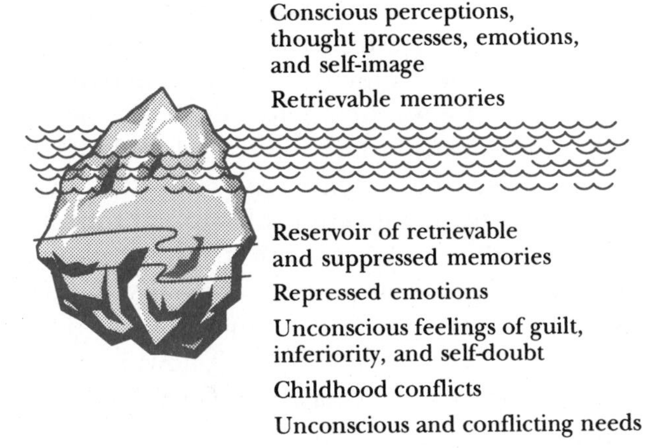

Figure 1–15.
The iceberg is often used as a model to represent the psychoanalytic view of the mind.

The process of discovering repressed forces unconsciously causing a behavior is called **psychoanalysis,** and it may involve free association or daydreaming, analysis of night dreams, and hypnosis. Freudian theory had a tremendous impact on psychology; it laid the foundation for psychotherapy and contributed particularly to the study of personality (see Figure 1–16).

Behaviorism. The Gestalt psychologists were not the only ones who disagreed with the structuralist position. Another group, the behaviorists, disagreed with both the structuralists and the functionalists because they both relied on introspection, which is not a very objective or reliable method of securing information. John B.

Figure 1–16.
The psychoanalytic approach focuses on probing the unconscious part of the mind to explain a behavior.

Watson (see Figure 1–17) was troubled by this lack of objectivity and reliability and by the limitations of the method of introspection. Introspection was limited to normal human adults, and it excluded from study young children, animals, or insane individuals who could not report or describe their sensory experience or answer questions about it. Because behaviors (responses) and environmental events (stimuli) are observable, definable, and verifiable, Watson argued that the only thing that psychology could study was the relationship between directly experienced external or overt stimuli and responses. He believed that behavior is elicited or brought forth by a stimulus as a result of learned relationships. Watson's and his followers' view became known as **behaviorism.** Because they were not concerned with the mind, or internal (covert) stimuli and responses, they emphasized the study of animal behavior as a means of understanding human behavior. The behaviorists are sometimes referred to as stimulus-response (S-R) psychologists.

Figure 1–17.
John B. Watson.

The behaviorists' position of eliminating the structure and functioning of the mind entirely from the concern of psychology produced controversy with both the structuralists and the functionalists. The behaviorists did not deny the mental processes. For example, a person may learn, feel emotion, or be motivated, but these mental states can only be inferred by observing behavior or responses that give psychologists something to study empirically and objectively. Because originally psychology was a study of the soul and then a study of the mind, some psychologists said that first psychology "lost its soul," and now it was "losing its mind."

Why did some psychologists say, "Psychology is losing its mind," when the behaviorist approach began?

Psychology became a full-fledged science, and behaviorism became the most popular viewpoint in America.

Later Approaches

What happened to the early approaches to psychology?

Behavioral and psychoanalytic views are still major approaches to psychology; however, they have undergone some modifications. Structuralism, functionalism, and Gestalt psychology no longer are considered major approaches although some of the principles have been incorporated into newer views. Today psychology has several newer approaches to explaining the behavior of people.

Do psychologists today still believe sexual and aggressive motives are the source of all behavior?

Contemporary Psychoanalytic View. Psychoanalysts today adhere to Freud's view of the unconscious mind; however, they put more emphasis on the conscious mind and less emphasis on repression than did Freud. Motives other than sex and aggression also are believed to provide motivation for behavior.

Contemporary Behaviorism. Behavioral psychologists today are not as radical as John B. Watson in that they do consider mental processes such as thoughts and emotions to be stimuli and responses, whether internal or covert. They do not confine their attention to relationships between directly experienced, observable stimuli and responses, and they involve people more in research than did early behaviorists. Although learning as experience in the environment continues to be emphasized in explaining and controlling behavior, it is now extended to include social learning, learning by observation and imitation of other people (see Figure 1–18), and insight learning.

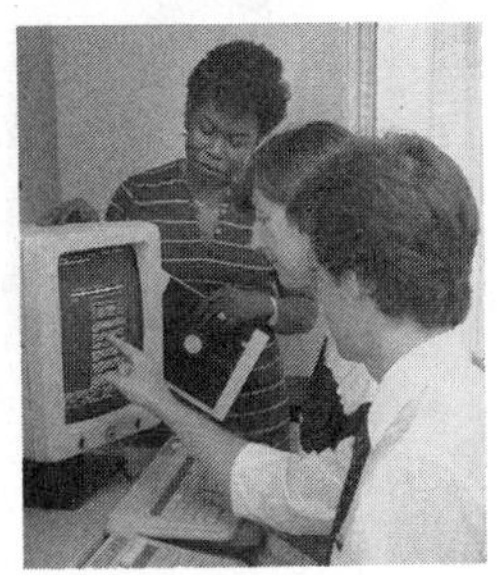

Figure 1–18.
Behaviorists today include learning by observation and insight (mental processes) in explaining and controlling behavior.

Do people grow and reach their potential psychologically as well as physically?

Humanism. The view that people have an inborn tendency to grow and improve, **humanism,** emerged during the 1950s and 1960s. Humanistic psychologists tend to be less objective than behaviorists in their scientific study because many of the topics of importance to them, such as free will, innate goodness of people, and motives that stimulate behavior, are difficult to investigate objectively. They prefer to emphasize subjective experience, such as self-esteem and self-actualization, and psychological needs, such as the need for love, achievement, or creativity. This approach has been important in work on personality and psychotherapy although it has not produced a great deal of research. Psychologists using this approach are basically interested in solving human problems and helping a person achieve more personal growth and freedom from external control. While psychologists using other approaches tend to search for general principles and laws that apply to humans as a species, the humanists are concerned with the uniqueness of a person's personality and the ability of a person to assume responsibility for his or her own behavior. Carl Rogers and Abraham Maslow were the two theorists who led the way in the development of this viewpoint. Humanistic psychology is applied when psychological tests are administered and used in therapeutic techniques in order to help people solve problems and achieve personal psychological growth.

Figure 1–19.
Mental behavior or activity is occurring when one makes comparisons and decisions.

Cognitive Approach. The cognitive approach to psychology is based on the view that the human mind knows more than just the information it takes in directly from the environment. The mind processes or acts on information by producing new thoughts, drawing conclusions, making comparisons, remembering, and making decisions (see Figure 1–19). Basically, **cognitive psychology** is concerned with information processing, that is, with the mind as an information-processing system that takes in information and creates reality for the individual. Psychologists adhering to this approach study the way perception influences behavior and the way experience influences perception. They explain behavior through the thought processes, emphasizing the role of memory, which is at the core of thought. According to this view, conscious cognitive or mental processes are more important in the determination of behavior than unconscious processes, learning, or psychological growth.

Existentialism. The existential view of psychology, or **existentialism,** is the product of a loosely organized group of European theorists, and like humanistic psychology, the evidence for the view is more philosophical and subjective and less scientific and objective in nature than behaviorism. Existential psychologists stress that human existence is in the here and now. The past and future are relevant only to the extent that they affect immediate existence. The focus in explaining behavior is on the person's immediate experience, current feelings, attitudes and values, and efforts toward finding meaning in life. Victor Frankl, an early leader in existentialism, and his followers emphasized that the goal of therapy is not to eliminate anxiety but to give it meaning to enable the person to deal with it more constructively. Existential views are applied when psychologists conduct group sensitivity sessions to examine feelings, attitudes, values, and common experiences (see Figure 1–20).

Figure 1–20.
Group therapy is an application of existentialism.

Biological View. Some psychologists believe that the explanations for behavior are to be found in the biological functioning of an individual. They search for relationships between physiological conditions and behavior. For example, the electrical and chemical activity in the brain is studied to determine behavior, and hormones released by glands and other biochemical activities are studied in terms of their effect on behavior. The findings from this approach have been important in many aspects of psychology such as perception, learning, memory, motivation, emotion, and psychotherapy. When treatments such as diet for hyperactivity, relaxation for reducing anxiety, the mineral lithium for depression, or a psychoactive drug for schizophrenia are used, the biological approach to explaining behavior is being applied.

What is meant by an eclectic approach?

Eclectic Approach. Each of the approaches previously described views psychology somewhat differently. A psychologist who accepts one approach may see most issues and attack most problems differently from a psychologist who accepts another approach. For example, an existential psychologist may use a therapeutic technique for changing a person's problem behavior that is totally different from the technique of psychoanalysis used by a psychoanalytic psychologist. Psychologists in applied areas seem to be becoming more and more **eclectic;** they select from each of the many approaches available and use what seems to fit the situation.

METHODOLOGY

How do psychologists investigate behavior?

Psychology is a science, and psychologists search for truth about human behavior using scientific methods in their investigation. Their investigation involves three steps: (a) The **hypothesis,** or statement to be evaluated, is formulated, (b) each term of the hypothesis is operationally defined, and information relevant to the statement is gathered, and (c) the information is analyzed, and an evaluation is made about the probable truth of the statement based on the collected evidence. Some of the methods most commonly used by psychologists to collect evidence and evaluate hypotheses are described in this section.

Observational Methods

A person usually thinks of the formal experimental method of study when the topic of scientific investigation is mentioned. There are a number of other scientific observational methods; however, the experimental approach is the most complex and is the basic method used by psychologists to explain behavior. The experimental procedure and four other methods are identified on the next few pages.

Naturalistic Observation. Methods referred to as **naturalistic methods** involve the careful observation and recording of behavior in a natural setting with little or no interference by the investigator (see Figure 1–21). An observation of the number of days absent from work per year for an employee or the number of complaints made to a supervisor per week are naturalistic observations. Observing the behavior of children in classes, of teenagers at parties, of strangers in an elevator, and of men and women in management positions are other examples of this method.

Figure 1–21.
A one-way mirror is sometimes used in naturalistic observation.

Survey Method. In the **survey method,** questions are usually prepared to which answers are obtained through a direct interview, by mail, or by telephone. A survey is usually an investigation of attitudes, feelings, traits, opinions, or behaviors that cannot be observed directly. This method may be used to obtain information from a large number of people in a relatively short period of time by using self-report. Public opinion surveys such as those conducted by Gallup are probably familiar because the results are regularly reported on television, in newspapers, and in popular magazines. Market research predicts buying preferences on the basis of consumers' answers to questions obtained in surveys. Data concerning the attitudes and perceptions of employees toward some aspect of the organization for which they work may be obtained by the survey method. Because computers are available to analyze the data from the large number of responses, the survey method is used extensively.

Have you ever responded to questions asked in a survey?

Case Study Method. When a single case is intensively investigated resulting in a large amount of information, the psychologist is using the **case study method.** The information may include personality traits, social relationships, important life events, academic and vocational data, and other biographical or biological information. Information may be collected to understand an individual or an event, or it may be used for more general purposes in exploring the nature and causes of behaviors. By examining a number of case histories, some significant general factors may possibly be noted.

Do you know that Sigmund Freud used the case study method of observation in his study of behavior?

Correlational Observation. The **correlational method** is an investigation of the relationships between measurable events. The researcher determines whether a relationship exists between two sets of information collected about an individual. For example, one might be interested in the relationship between an individual's score on a finger dexterity test and the number of pages typed per day or the number of hours of training completed and supervisor rating of job performance.

Does finding a link or relationship between two variables indicate a causal relationship?

Any characteristic, attribute, or event that can vary in amount when measured or that can be present or absent is referred to as a **variable.** Correlational observations identify relationships between variables. A correlational study does not explain, though, why a relationship exists between variables. For example, a researcher might find that the number of cigarettes smoked per day is inversely related to some measure of job performance; however, anxiety might be a third factor accounting for both an increase in cigarette smoking and a decrease in productivity. Or a relationship might be found to exist between palm width and reading ability of elementary school children, but this does not mean that palm width has a causal effect on reading. Another factor, growth, may be affecting both simultaneously.

The correlational method has been especially useful in predicting behaviors. If a high correlation has been found to exist between two variables and one of the variables is known, the other variable can be predicted with a known probability of accuracy. If some measure such as an IQ score is found to correlate with a job performance measure, then by knowing the IQ score of job applicants, a human resource director can predict which applicant would perform best on the job.

For what purpose would a correlational observation be used?

Experimental Observation. The **experimental method** of observation is the method of investigation that seeks to determine cause-and-effect relationships. It is the most precise method psychologists use to collect evidence to draw conclusions regarding hypotheses, and it is a powerful tool for the psychologist seeking to understand causes of behavior—to explain behavior.

Which method of observation is used to explain behavior?

Using the experimental method of observation is not a simple matter. The experimental observation must be planned with great care to control for various factors, and it must be planned in such a way that the evidence collected can be mathematically analyzed. A primary difference between this method and previously mentioned methods is that the researcher controls and manipulates variables. The scientist intervenes in a situation in order to control the various components and examine effects from a single variable separately. In naturalistic observations, many things may be happening simultaneously in unplanned combinations so that cause and effect cannot always be determined.

What is the primary distinguishing feature of the experimental method of observation?

Experimental Procedure

Because the formal experiment is the basic research tool used to test hypotheses explaining behavior, some understanding of the procedure is relevant in an introduction to psychology. The essence of the experimental procedure is controlling variables to obtain equivalency of groups, manipulating a variable, and looking for some effect on behavior. The variable that the researcher manipulates is referred to as the **independent variable.** The variable that is measured in order to observe the effect of the manipulation is referred to as the **dependent variable.**

Can you differentiate between the independent and dependent variables in an experimental study?

The Logic. The logical reasoning for this approach is that if the only difference between two groups is the variation of the independent variable, then any difference in the measured behavior between the two groups is likely to have been caused by the independent or manipulated variable. A group that receives the experimental treatment, that is, receives the independent variable, is called an **experimental group.** A **control group** is a group in the experiment that does not receive the experimental treatment. Having a control group in the experiment for comparison helps insure that the independent variable accounts for any observed differences in behavior between the groups rather than the variables of being observed in an experiment or expectancy of outcome. Usually, an experiment is thought of in terms of manipulating only one variable and measuring only one behavioral response in two groups, one experimental and one control. However, with modern methods of analyzing data, the experimenter may manipulate a number of variables, measure the effect on more than one behavioral response, and have several experimental groups receiving varying degrees of the variable being manipulated (the independent variable).

What is the purpose of a control group?

Control Methods. Researchers utilize various methods to control variables. Random selection of the participants or subjects in the experiment is one way to control differences in variables and obtain equivalency of groups. By **randomization,** selecting subjects by chance, various traits and characteristics will be distributed equally or in an unbiased way. If a large number of subjects is randomly selected from the total set of all the possible cases and the subjects are then randomly assigned to the groups, only chance differences in measurable variables are assumed to exist between groups to be contrasted or compared. The set of subjects selected to participate in the experiment is the **sample.** The total set of all possible subjects referred to in the hypothesis is the **population.** If the hypothesis is some statement about females, the population is all females. If the hypothesis is a statement about female managers, the population is all female managers.

When randomization is not possible, equivalency may be obtained by matching the subjects in each group according to relevant variables. For example, if age is the relevant variable to control, placing a subject 20 years of age in one group would require choosing a subject of 20 years of age to be placed in the comparison group.

Figure 1–22.
If these subjects do not know which ones are getting a drink with caffeine and the person measuring alertness one hour later in these subjects does not know which ones had a drink with caffeine, it is known as a double-blind technique.

Equivalency may be obtained by using the same subjects for each of the comparison conditions. A pretest or measure may be made on the behavior to be studied prior to the manipulation of the independent variable. Then a measure may be made after the test to determine if manipulating the variable produced a change in behavior for the different conditions.

A blind technique may be used to control possible behavior changes in subjects who may respond a particular way due to the knowledge of experimental treatment. In this technique, the subjects in the experiment would not know whether they were receiving the experimental treatment. For example, to study the effects of a particular motion picture on changing a group of people's attitude, each group would view a film—one group a neutral film and the other group the film hypothesized to change an attitude. Because neither group would know which film is the one being studied, subjects' reactions would not be influenced by what they thought the experimenters expected. This blind technique may also be used to control bias in recording and measuring the behavioral response (see Figure 1–22). If a researcher expects a subject to behave in a particular way due to the experimental treatment, evaluation and perception of the response may be altered and unconsciously biased. In using the blind technique, the person measuring and recording the behavioral response would not know whether the subject received the experimental treatment.

Why is the Hawthorne effect phenomenon called Hawthorne?

The Hawthorne Effect. Psychologists first became aware of the special attention effect and the need to use methods of control for this variable in the 1920s. The effect on a subject's responses during research is labeled the **Hawthorne effect.** Studies to test the effects of light intensity on productivity at the Hawthorne plant of the Western Electric Company began in 1924 (Pennock, 1930). Productivity increased when a group had the light intensity increased.

However, in a later study with another group, a decrease in light intensity also increased productivity. Realizing that something other than light intensity, the variable being manipulated, was causing the increase in productivity, two groups were then randomly selected with the control group participating in the study, being observed and measured, but experiencing no change in the light intensity. When this group increased in productivity as well as did the experimental group, the conclusion was drawn that merely participating in an experiment, being observed, and receiving attention may cause a change in behavior.

The Pygmalion Effect. Psychologists have become aware of a need to control for expectancy in recent years. In 1968, Rosenthal and Jacobson wondered whether students' IQ scores would change if their teachers expected a change. They conducted an experiment in an elementary school for a period of one school year and reported that those children for whom the teachers expected greater gain did indeed show a greater gain in IQ. Many studies, some yielding conflicting evidence, have since been conducted on self-fulfilling prophecy, known as the **Pygmalion effect** (pronounced *pig MAY lih un*). The effect gets its name from Greek mythology (see the boxed insert below). Sometimes, in a process not completely understood, a person's expectancies, beliefs, and perceptions of reality turn into realities. The Pygmalion effect is the tendency of an individual to act, perhaps unconsciously, in such a manner as to insure the expected or desired outcome. The effect does seem to exist in some circumstances but not always. Often the effect is referred to as the placebo effect. This is because a **placebo,** a substance that has no effect on the person such as a sugar pill or saline solution, may cause the person to feel better or get well if the person believes the substance is a medication and expects to feel better or get well (see Figure 1–23).

Figure 1–23.
If a person expects to feel better after taking a substance, he or she may indeed feel better.

PYGMALION

In Greek mythology, a sculptor of Cyprus named Pygmalion carved a statue of a woman from ivory. Because he did not like any of the women who lived in his town, he did not fall in love with or marry any of them. The statue-woman he carved was so beautiful that he believed her to be a real woman and fell in love with her. Venus, the goddess of love, took pity on Pygmalion and breathed life into the statue, and the woman became his wife.

Can you design or plan a simple experimental study?

A Sample Experiment. An imagined sample of the experimental procedure might be as follows. You may believe typists perform better on typing tasks when the noise levels are lower (hypothesis). Typing performance may be operationally defined as the average number of correct words typed per minute (dependent variable). Noise level may be operationally defined in decibels (independent variable). You may randomly select a sample of 100 typists from the population of typists and randomly assign (randomization) 50 typists to be in the experimental group, which is to be exposed to high noise levels of 80 decibels. The remaining 50 typists comprise the control group, which is to be exposed to low office noise levels of 30 decibels. Each group is assigned to type in two different rooms without knowing that the noise levels will be different (blind technique). All other conditions (extra variables) that might affect the typing such as average typing speed, brand of machines, condition of machines, temperature and size of the room, or illumination are planned to be the same, as nearly as possible, for each group. The scorer of the typing tests may not know which typists had been in the experimental group (blind technique). If a **significant difference** is found in the average performance of the two groups, then the difference may be reasonably attributed to the noise level because all other relevant variables were controlled to be about the same in each group (logic). A significant difference means that the difference between the groups, computed by a mathematical formula, is so great that it is unlikely to be due to chance factors. Obviously, the average words typed per minute by each group will not be identical to the nearest hundredth. A difference of 15 or 20 words per minute, however, probably will be significant and therefore not attributed to chance. If a significant difference occurs, a more logical conclusion is that the difference is due to the noise level difference rather than to chance.

How does a "significant difference" differ from just a "difference"?

Statistics

Psychologists use standardized procedures for organizing and summarizing the evidence they collect and for testing the validity of a hypothesis. By using a set of formal rules, the decisions made are more precise and quantitative and freer of bias than are ordinary decisions, and thus they are considered to be made scientifically.

The Concept. Statistics is a body of scientific methods consisting of mathematical ways of handling **data.** The data, often called scores, are the observations collected by the researcher usually consisting of a large number of items presented in numeric form that represent a characteristic or a phenomenon. The data, or scores, are handled mathematically to draw a conclusion about the truth of a hypothesis (see Figure 1–24). Statistics is also a term used to refer to a collection of numeric facts that have been gathered through observation or from other numeric data such as averages, tables, and graphs.

Figure 1–24.
The computer is an invaluable asset in statistics.

The question to be answered becomes whether the differences between an experimental group and a control group in the measured variable, the dependent variable, are great enough to be attributed to the manipulation of the independent variable rather than to chance factors. For a more detailed discussion of statistics, see the Appendix.

What are some procedures used in descriptive statistics?

Descriptive Statistics. Because of the large number of observations, some organization and summarization of the data is needed in order to describe the observations. The methods and formal rules applied to accomplish this task are referred to as **descriptive statistics.** Doing any of the following things with the data involves using the methods of descriptive statistics. The data may be arranged in some particular order such as in a hierarchical order. All like scores or scores that fall into a particular category such as 70 through 74 may be grouped together and a determination made of how many items of data fall into that category. A table showing the number of items falling in each category is a **frequency distribution.** Graphs of the data may be prepared. A **measure of central tendency,** a representative point or score for a set of data that tends to be near the middle of the score range, may be determined. An example of a measure of central tendency is the familiar arithmetic average known as the **mean.** A **measure of variability** may be computed in several different ways to describe the spread, dispersion, or typical distances of scores from the mean. The **range,** the difference between the highest and lowest items of data in the set, is the simplest measure of variability. The **standard deviation** is a more stable and accurate measure of variability that is usually used by researchers. It considers every score in the set of data and is calculated by using the deviation from the mean for each of the scores and then finding a type of average deviation.

Mathematical formulas may be used to calculate a **correlation coefficient**—a descriptive statistic expressing numerically the predictive relationship between two or more variables. A correlation coefficient may range from 0 to 1.00 (as one variable goes up in value, the other one also increases) or from 0 to -1.00 (as one variable goes up in value, the other one decreases) as in the case of an inverse relationship. The higher the absolute value of the correlation coefficient, the higher the degree of relationship. The higher the degree of relationship, the more accurately one variable in the pair can be predicted from the other known variable. If the correlation coefficient for the relationship between a score on a mathematics aptitude test and some measure of a job performance is found to be .90, the test score may be useful in predicting with a high degree of accuracy which job applicant will perform best in the job. A correlation coefficient of 1.00 would be required for correct predictions in 100 percent of the cases. In the behavioral sciences, such perfect relationships are seldom found. If a correlation coefficient is found to be 0, no relationship exists at all, and using one of the variables to predict the other variable produces no higher percentage of accuracy in prediction than chance. When a correlation coefficient of .30 exists, predicting one variable from knowing the other variable produces only a slightly higher percentage of accuracy than random guessing.

What kind of correlation coefficient would be required to make a perfect prediction every time?

Inferential Statistics. Two of the basic concerns of **inferential statistics,** methods used to draw conclusions, are making assumptions about or estimating population characteristics and testing hypotheses. Because it is usually impossible or impractical to measure an entire population, the data collected from a sample group are used to estimate the mean and the standard deviation of the population. Mathematical formulas are used to make the estimates. The method of selecting samples randomly from all possible members of the population is crucial. Also, mathematical ways exist to estimate how large a sample is needed for a given level of accuracy.

What are the procedures of inferential statistics designed to do?

The logic and methods of inferential statistics are more complex than the logic and methods of descriptive statistics. You will find further discussion of inferential statistics in the Appendix.

SUMMARY

1. Attempting to explain behavior of people has a long and varied background—demonology, gods and goddesses, philosophy, and Satanic possession.
2. The word *psychology* comes from two Greek words, *psyche* and *logos,* meaning study of the soul, although today psychology is usually defined as the scientific study of behavior, including mental processes, and the application of knowledge gained through the study.

3. The goals of psychology are to define or describe, explain, predict, and control behavior.
4. Scientific study implies the empirical approach, the pursuit of knowledge by observation and experiment, rather than the common sense approach, which is often vague, inconsistent, false or only partially correct.
5. Psychology is subdivided into areas of specialization: clinical and counseling, industrial and organizational, developmental, educational, social, experimental, and physiological.
6. Psychiatry is an area of specialization in the field of medicine.
7. Industrial and organizational psychology specializes in applying psychology in work-related situations, and it is so broad that specialties such as engineering psychology, personnel psychology, consumer psychology, and forensic psychology have evolved.
8. Early views of psychology and leaders of each view are as follows: structuralism—Wilhelm Wundt; functionalism—William James; Gestalt psyhchology—Max Wertheimer; behaviorism—John B. Watson; and psychoanalytic—Sigmund Freud.
9. Behaviorism, which emphasizes learning and the relationship of stimuli and responses, and the psychoanalytic view, which stresses the unconscious part of the mind, are still major approaches to psychology. Some other later views and approaches to psychology are: (a) cognitive, which emphasizes the role memory plays in the thought process; (b) humanism, which focuses on personal psychological growth; (c) existentialism, which is concerned with giving meaning to immediate experience; (d) biological, which focuses on the brain, nervous system, endocrine glands, and heredity in explaining behavior; and (e) eclectic, which is using a combination of these approaches.
10. Scientific study involves formulating hypotheses and operational definitions, making systematic observations and analyzing them, and evaluating hypotheses.
11. Methods of systematic observation include observing in natural settings, taking surveys, doing case studies, investigating correlations to make predictions, and conducting experiments to determine cause-and-effect relationships for explaining behavior.
12. The essence of the experimental procedure is controlling variables to obtain equivalency between the experimental group and control group, manipulating the independent variable, and measuring the dependent variable.
13. Using random selection for equal distribution of traits in comparison groups, using a control group to control for the Hawthorne effect (effect on behavior of being observed), and using blind techniques to control for the Pygmalion effect (effect of expectancy on behavior) are important control methods.

14. Statistics is a body of scientific methods consisting of (a) mathematical ways to organize, describe, and summarize recorded observations (descriptive statistics) and (b) mathematical ways to draw conclusions about population characteristics and hypotheses (inferential statistics). Statistics also refers to a collection of numeric facts.

KEY TERMS AND CONCEPTS

Demonology
Exorcism
Mechanism
Hedonism
Empiricism
Rationalism
Dualism
Psyche
Logos
Psychology
Behavior
Response
Stimulus
Pure psychology
Applied psychology
Operational definitions
Theory
Law
Principle
Empirical approach
Common sense assumptions
Clinical psychology
Psychiatrists
Psychoanalyst
Counseling psychologist
Industrial and organizational psychology
Engineering psychology
Personnel psychology
Consumer psychology
Forensic psychology
Developmental psychology
Educational psychology
Social psychology
Experimental psychology
Physiological psychology
Structuralism
Introspection
Functionalism
Gestalt psychology
Gestalt
Psychoanalytic psychology
Psychoanalysis
Behaviorism
Humanism
Cognitive psychology
Existentialism
Eclectic
Hypothesis
Naturalistic method
Survey method
Case study method
Correlational method
Variable
Experimental method
Independent variable
Dependent variable
Experimental group
Control group
Randomization
Sample
Population
Hawthorne effect
Pygmalion effect
Placebo
Significant difference
Statistics
Data
Descriptive statistics
Frequency distribution
Measure of central tendency
Mean
Measure of variability
Range
Standard deviation
Correlation coefficient
Inferential statistics

QUESTIONS FOR REVIEW

1. What are seven significant views that existed even before the emergence of psychology, and what is the essence of each view of human behavior?

2. What are the goals of contemporary psychology? Briefly explain each goal.
3. In what ways do the various specialized areas of psychology differ?
4. In the area of clinical and counseling psychology, how does a clinical psychologist differ from a psychiatrist, a psychoanalyst, and a counselor?
5. Who was the first American psychologist, and what views did he hold about psychology as contrasted with other views that emerged in the world at about this same time period?
6. What is the basic premise of each of the seven contemporary approaches to explaining behavior?
7. How do psychologists observe or collect evidence to evaluate hypotheses? Describe five methods.
8. What is the logic of the experimental procedure, and how is equivalency of groups obtained?
9. What is a hypothesis? Formulate a hypothesis and identify the independent variable, the dependent variable, the sample, the population, and the experimental group.
10. What are descriptive statistics? Name six descriptive statistical procedures.

TEST YOURSELF

1. During the time of demonology, what was the primary treatment for changing a problem behavior in a person?
2. A computer seen in an office is referred to as (a) a stimulus (b) a response (c) a behavior (d) an action.
3. Answering the telephone when it rings is for that person (a) a stimulus (b) a response (c) a reflex (d) both a and b.
4. Scientific study implies the pursuit of knowledge through observation and experimentation, which is referred to as the ________________ approach.
5. A psychologist who is involved in diagnosing and treating people with psychological disturbances and helping people achieve psychological well-being is in the field of (a) psychiatry (b) clinical psychology (c) industrial and organizational psychology (d) developmental psychology.
6. ________________ psychology is concerned with the dynamics underlying decisions and behavior regarding the acquisition, use, and disposition of products and services.
7. A school system would most likely employ a psychologist who has specialized in the area of ________________ psychology.
8. Physiological psychologists (a) search for relationships between physiology and behavior (b) study heredity as a factor of behavior (c) study

biochemical conditions in terms of their effects on behavior (d) all three: a, b, and c.

9. The "birth" or beginning of psychology is said to have occurred in ________________ in the year ________________.
10. What method did Wundt use in his laboratory to look for the elements of the mind?
11. ________________ set up the first laboratory for psychological experimentation in the United States, wrote the first psychology textbook, and changed his title at Harvard University from physiologist to psychologist.
12. The view that stated that a vast amount of human behavior is the result of unconscious forces hidden within the person and that focused on the process of discovering these repressed forces became known as ________________ psychology.
13. Humanistic psychologists are basically interested in solving human problems and helping a person to achieve more psychological growth. T or F
14. A belief, hunch, or tentative statement that has not been proven or disproven is called a (a) theory (b) hypothesis (c) falsehood (d) scientific idea.
15. In a study to determine the effect of room temperature on alertness, one group of people is given a test to measure alertness while working in a room with a temperature of 90 degrees; another group is given the test while working in a room with a temperature of 65 degrees. What is the dependent variable in this study?
16. A psychologist who polls 2,000 people to obtain information about their opinions of flexible scheduling to test the hypotheses that more workers under the age of 35 prefer flexible scheduling than workers age 35 or older would be using which of the following methods: (a) experimental (b) survey (c) naturalistic (d) correlational.
17. The ________________ group is used for a comparison group to insure that the variable of special attention shown to the subjects of an experiment is controlled.
18. A blind technique is used to control (a) cheating by subjects (b) possible behavior changes in subjects who may behave a particular way due to their knowledge of the experimental treatment and expected results (c) the subjects' interacting or talking with each other during the experiment (d) fear and worry in the subjects.
19. The higher the absolute value of a correlation coefficient, the (a) lower the degree of relationship (b) more positive the relationship (c) the higher the degree of relationship (d) more negative the relationship.
20. If a set of observations for a dependent variable for a group is found to be 9, 4, 7, 2, 9, 3, 1, the mean for the group is ________________.

APPLICATIONS

A. From casual observation, Dr. John B. Barnabus, psychologist for Modern Industrial Corporation, believed that a one-day seminar in stress management, including relaxation techniques for lowering anxiety, would result in improved job performance. In a scientific investigation of this belief, he randomly selected 20 workers to attend seminars. Ten were randomly assigned to attend the stress management seminar, and the remaining 10 were assigned to attend a history seminar. Dr. Barnabus defined job performance as the average number of units produced in a 40-hour work week. Job performance was measured for each participant for the week preceding the seminar and again for the week following the seminar. The changes in job performance for workers attending the stress management seminar were as follows: 8, 1, -2, 6, 0, 2, 5, -1, 7, 4. The changes in job performance for workers attending the history seminar were as follows: 1, 0, -1, 2, 0, 1, 1, -2, 0, -2.

1. What is the mean change in production for the experimental group and for the control group?
2. What method of observation did Dr. Barnabus use to gather the set of observations?
3. Dr. Barnabus is most likely classified as being in what specialized area of psychology?
4. What is the independent variable, and what is the dependent variable?

B. Satasia Smith interviewed a psychologist, Dr. Maone Silter. She has an office in a downtown office building and is listed in the Yellow Pages of the telephone directory as a psychologist specializing in the treatment of phobias. In her treatment procedures, she spends considerable time on earliest and significant memories of her client and on dreams the client is having. She administers some tests such as "The Word Association Test," which consists of giving a word to the client and the client saying the first word that comes to mind. She believes a phobia is often the result of some inner conflict that produces so much anxiety that the conflict is repressed from consciousness.

1. Dr. Silter is most likely classified as being in what specialized area of psychology?
2. Her philosophical view or approach to explaining behavior is probably what?
3. In which treatment technique does she probably have special training?

SUGGESTIONS FOR FURTHER READING

American Psychological Association. (1986). *Careers in psychology.* Washington, DC: Author.

A 30-page pamphlet that describes psychology and answers questions of students who are considering a future in the field of psychology. Also included is a description of the American Psychological Association and its services and a list of related organizations and sources of information. One copy may be obtained free by writing to APA, Order Department, P.O. Box 2710, Hyattsville, MD 20784.

American Psychological Association. (1981). *Ethical principles of psychologists.* Washington, DC: Author.

An 11-page pamphlet that contains the current APA code of ethics. One copy may be obtained free by writing to APA.

Schultz, D. P. (1981). *A history of modern psychology* (3rd ed.). New York: Academic Press.

A history of psychology that emphasizes the views of psychology popular in the late nineteenth and early twentieth centuries.

Stapp, J., & Fulcher, R. (1983). The employment of APA members: 1982. *American Psychologist, 38,* 1298-1320.

A journal article describing the employment of members of the APA, the trends in employment, and the outlook for the future based on data collected through APA's 1982 Human Resources Survey.

Steininger, M. P., Newell, J. D., & Garcia, L. T. (1984). *Ethical issues in psychology.* Homewood, IL: The Dorsey Press.

The major purpose of this text is to develop in students an awareness of ethical issues in psychology and to provide conceptual tools for thinking about them. An overview of psychology as a whole is presented by describing what psychologists do.

Tageson, C. W. (1982). *Humanistic psychology: A synthesis.* Homeward, IL: The Dorsey Press.

A text that provides a single source of information to the entire field of humanistic-existential psychology. The author identifies seven major themes addressed by humanistic psychologists and summarizes their thought on these themes.

White, L., Tursky, B., & Schwartz, G. E. (Eds.). (1985). *Placebo theory, research, and mechanisms.* New York: The Guilford Press.

A book that explores placebos in psychobiological terms providing insights into how placebos can aid the treatment of a wide range of physical and emotional disorders. The mechanisms, clinical applicability, and limitations of the phenomenon are discussed.

PART ONE

PHYSIOLOGY AND DEVELOPMENT

CHAPTER 2

BIOLOGICAL PSYCHOLOGY

I. NERVOUS SYSTEM
   A. Neurons
      1. Structure
      2. Types by Function
   B. Other Structures
      1. Glial Cells
      2. Nerves
   C. Neural Impulses
      1. Axonal Transmission
      2. Synaptic Transmission
   D. Divisions
      1. Peripheral Nervous System
      2. Central Nervous System

II. BRAIN
   A. Organization and Functions
      1. Hindbrain
      2. Midbrain
      3. Forebrain
   B. Neocortex
      1. Areas and Functions
      2. Hemispheric Specialization
      3. Sex Differences
   C. Systems
      1. Limbic
      2. Reticular Activating
   D. Biological Rhythms
      1. Known Cycles
      2. Popular Biorhythms

III. ENDOCRINE GLANDS
   A. Secretions
      1. Hormones
      2. Peptides
   B. Glands
      1. Pituitary
      2. Thyroid
      3. Parathyroids
      4. Pancreas
      5. Adrenals
      6. Gonads

IV. APPLICATION OF BIOPSYCHOLOGY
   A. Food
      1. Neuronutrition
      2. Malnutrition
      3. Special Diets
   B. Exercise
      1. Stress and Illness
      2. Brain Function
   C. Air
      1. Positive Ions
      2. Negative Ions
   D. Common Drugs
      1. Alcohol
      2. Nicotine
      3. Caffeine
   E. Brain Tissue Transplants
      1. Disease
      2. Aging

SUMMARY

KEY TERMS AND CONCEPTS

QUESTIONS FOR REVIEW

TEST YOURSELF

APPLICATIONS

SUGGESTIONS FOR FURTHER READING

Objectives

When you have completed your study of chapter 2, you should be able to:

1. Describe the neuron in terms of its structure and the function of its various parts.
2. Differentiate between the types and functions of neurons.
3. Explain how neural messages are transmitted along the axons of a neuron.
4. Explain how neural messages are transmitted across synapses.
5. Identify and give the function of neurotransmitters and neuromodulators.
6. Identify and explain the function of the divisions of the nervous system.
7. Name and locate the major structures in the brain, and explain the most important known function of each.
8. Describe the functional organization of the neocortex and cite examples of hemispheric specialization.
9. Identify types of secretions and give names, locations, and functions of major endocrine glands.
10. Understand the relationship between biological functioning and behavior and make application in such areas as diet, exercise, obesity, sleep, drug use, and illnesses.

Any behavior you exhibit, from opening a desk drawer to solving a complex management problem, depends on biological processes. Much of human behavior and mental functioning cannot be explained or fully understood without some knowledge of these processes. Without a nervous system, you could have no behavior. You would be like a table or other inanimate objects, incapable of awareness of your environment and unable to respond to stimuli in your environment. The brain is the most complex piece of matter in the known universe. Through its neural and chemical connections, your brain monitors activity in every cell of your body and controls your body via the nervous and endocrine systems. The secretions from your endocrine glands have enormous effects on your behavior by changing the body chemistry and thus the functioning of the nervous system. Although much is still not known about these biological mechanisms, research findings have provided explanation of certain human behaviors. A brief overview of biological processes fundamental to behavior is presented in this chapter.

NERVOUS SYSTEM

The human body is composed of billions of cells. Each cell is a separate entity enclosed by a membrane and contains the main cell body and nucleus where most of the complex chemical reaction occurs that keeps the cell alive and functioning. Although all the cells of the body have the same general organization and the same biochemical mechanism, they vary in size, shape, appearance, and unique features according to the specialized jobs they perform. For example, cells of the nervous system, blood cells, bone cells, and skin cells are different to perform different functions.

Neurons

The specialized cells of the nervous system that enable a person to be aware of the environment and to have behavior are called **neurons.** The human brain is thought to consist of about 10^{11} (100 billion) neurons (Stevens, 1979). These cells are at the foundation of human behavior and mental functioning.

Can you describe the various parts of a neuron?

Structure. Dendrites are short, delicate, branchlike extensions that protrude from a neuron's main body. Dendrites receive messages or impulses from neighboring cells and conduct that information to the main cell body.

The **axon** is a slender, tubelike fiber extending away from the body of the neuron. Axons vary in length from a few thousandths of an inch to 2 or 3 feet. They carry messages out from the cell, either passing them on to other neurons in the nervous system or to cells in a muscle or gland. Many branching axons may extend from the main axon of a neuron. As shown in Figure 2–1, some axons

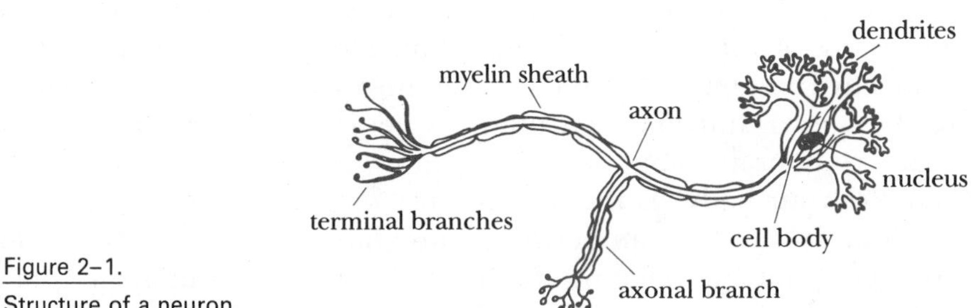

Figure 2–1.
Structure of a neuron.

(long ones in the peripheral nervous system) are covered with fatty nodules called a **myelin sheath** that allows messages to travel faster. The impulse seems to jump to the next tiny gap or space left between the nodules without delay.

At the end of axons are small fibers called **terminal branches.** A knob at the end of each terminal branch releases chemical substances when an outgoing message reaches the end of the branch in order to transmit the message to another neuron.

How do afferent neurons, efferent neurons, and interneurons differ?

Types by function. Neurons have different characteristics depending on their specialized functions. An **afferent neuron** (pronounced *AF er ent*), sometimes referred to as a *sensory neuron,* receives input directly from cells in the sense organs (the input function). The cells in the sense organs are activated by some stimulus in the environment (inside and outside the body) and send messages to the afferent neurons in the nervous system. An **efferent neuron,** sometimes referred to as a *motor neuron,* carries messages out from the brain and spinal cord to cells in muscles that control outward external movement as well as to the smooth muscles that control glands and internal organs (the output function). **Interneurons,** sometimes referred to as *association neurons,* carry messages to and receive messages from other neurons in the brain and spinal cord (the throughput function). These neurons generally have shorter axons that are not covered by a myelin sheath. Color Figure 2–2 illustrates these three types of neurons.

What three functions are carried out by neurons in the nervous system?

Other Structures

The nervous system is composed of structures other than neurons. Two such structures important in explaining behavior are glial cells and nerves.

What kind of relationship exists between glial cells and neurons?

Glial Cells. Each neuron is surrounded by **glial cells,** nonexcitable cells that protect and nourish the neuron. Unlike neurons, glial cells continue to divide and seem to play a role in directing the growth of a neuron and the neuronal pathways or interconnections. They are also believed to play a general role in the metabolism of the nervous system. About 10 times as many glial cells are present in the nervous system as neurons, and they proliferate or reproduce in great numbers after injury to neurons, filling any spaces left by damage.

Are nerves and neurons the same thing?

Nerves. A **nerve** is a bundle of axons from many neurons, much like a telephone cable that consists of many wires, that carries impulses between body parts and the central nervous system. Some nerves are composed of axons that serve an input function, some are composed of axons that serve an output function, and some are composed of axons of both afferent (input) and efferent (output) neurons.

Neural Impulses

A person is aware of the external and internal environment only from the messages or impulses received in the brain. Behavior is exhibited only as a result of these messages or impulses carried by the neurons in the nervous system to the muscles and glands. The impulse must move through neurons traveling along the axons of neurons as well as move from one neuron to another neuron. Because neurons are not physically joined together, the impulse must cross a **synapse,** a small space where one neuron communicates chemically with another neuron. The transmission of neural impulses, therefore, consists of both axonal transmissions and synaptic transmissions.

Is there a special name for the space across which one neuron communicates with another neuron?

Axonal Transmission. The movement of the impulse along the axon of the neuron is electrical. The cell membrane separates two fields of electrically charged **ions,** particles formed when a neural atom or group of atoms loses or gains one or more electrons. **Electrons** are negative charges of electricity that are present in all atoms. When a neuron is in the resting state with no impulse being transmitted, the area outside the cell membrane is composed primarily of positively charged sodium ions, and the area within the cell membrane is composed primarily of negatively charged potassium ions. Because the interior of the neuron is richer in negatively charged ions than the exterior, the neuron itself is said to be negatively charged. Although many substances may permeate through the porous membrane of the neuron while it is in the resting state, positive sodium ions are not allowed to enter, maintaining a stable electrical charge known as a state of **polarization.** Figure 2–3 is a diagram of the electrical activity of a neuron.

How does a message travel through the axons of neurons?

When a place on the membrane of the neuron is adequately stimulated by a substance in the surrounding environment, usually a chemical substance, channels in the cell membrane open and allow sodium ions to enter the neuron. When the balance of electrical charges between the interior and exterior of the cell is altered, the cell is said to be in a state of **depolarization.** Once the balance is altered at a point, channels in the cell membrane at the next point to open are triggered and the process is repeated along the entire length of the membrane. This process of depolarization is the traveling of the message or the neural impulse. Normally impulses move in one direction, from dendrites through the cell body, along the axon to terminal branches.

What is meant by the all-or-none principle?

The neural impulse follows an all-or-none principle in that once the process is triggered, it is repeated along the entire length

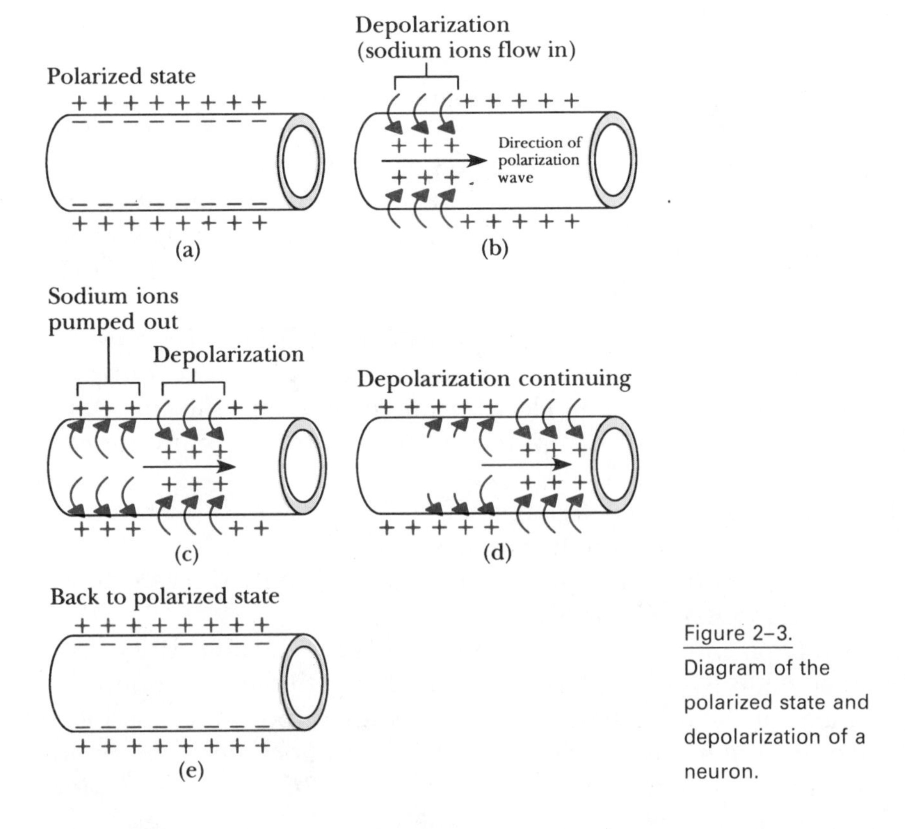

Figure 2–3.
Diagram of the polarized state and depolarization of a neuron.

of the membrane. The strength of the transmission does not decrease or increase as the impulse moves along, and neither does it stop until it reaches the end.

How fast does a neural impulse travel?

The impulse travels at a speed from about 2 to 200 miles per hour, depending on a number of factors. A minimum of about a thousandth of a second with strong stimulation is required to restore the neuron to the polarized state. With weak stimulation, 10 to 15 thousandths of a second is required for the neuron to be able to send another message. Thus, a stronger stimulation may produce more impulses in a given amount of time, resulting in more impulses to muscle cells and a larger response.

How long does it take for a depolarized neuron to return to the polarized state?

Synaptic Transmission. The classic view of synaptic transmission is that the transmission of the message across the synapse is chemical in nature. Thus, the entire process of transmission of the neural impulse is electrochemical. When a neural impulse reaches the knobs on the ends of the terminal branches (see Figure 2–4), chemical substances are released from the knobs into the space that separates the neuron from the surrounding neurons. These substances that are released when the neuron depolarizes and that

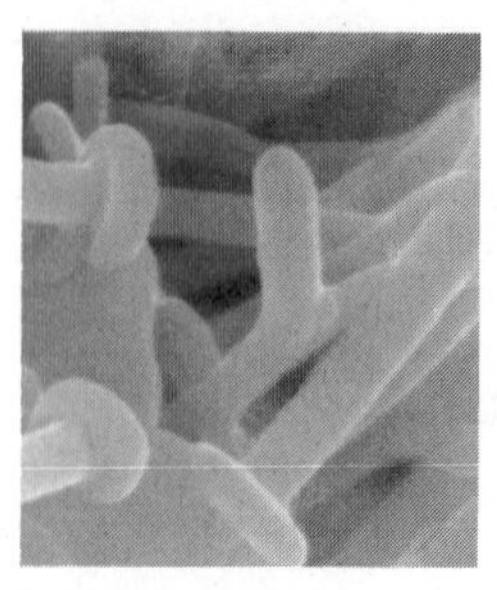
Figure 2–4.
A photograph of terminal branches magnified many thousands of times that shows the knobs on the ends.

may be taken up at **receptor sites,** or matching hookups, are referred to as **neurotransmitters.** Receptor sites are places or parts on a neuron that respond to stimulation or "take up" a substance, allowing it to have an impact on the neuron. Generally, a synapse is where the terminal branches of one neuron terminate on the dendrites of another neuron (see Color Figure 2–5). A typical neuron (see Color Figure 2–6) may have as many as 10,000 synapses and may receive information from 1,000 or more other neurons (Stevens, 1979).

What takes place in synaptic transmission is far from understood; however, in recent years progress has been made with the use of powerful tools. The electron microscope and the following methods of generating computerized images of the brain are examples:

1. **computerized axial tomography** — a method of computing images in three dimension of a basic structure such as the brain based on X-ray photographs—commonly referred to as a *CAT scan* (see Color Figure 2–7).
2. **positron emission tomography** (Mintun, Raichle, Kilbourn, Wooten, & Welch, 1984)—a method of generating a computer image of the brain based on the emission of positrons that indicate where a radioactive form of glucose goes while the brain performs—commonly referred to as a *PET scan* (see Color Figure 2–8).
3. **magnetic resonance imaging** (Bottomley et al., 1984)—a method of computing an image based on magnetic fields and radio frequencies, used mostly as a brain scan, that shows the presence and location of certain chemical elements—commonly referred to as an *MRI image* (see Color Figure 2–9).

Neurotransmitters probably work something like keys, fitting into specific receptor sites that act as locks. Each receptor site accepts stimulation from transmitters of a particular molecular structure (shape) that must match the molecular structure (shape) of the receptor site (lock) (see Color Figure 2–5).

Do neurotransmitters taken up at receptor sites of a neuron always cause depolarization?

A stimulated neuron may be affected in either of two ways by neurotransmitters. Some transmitters have an inhibitory effect; they counteract the excitatory chemicals that would cause depolarization of the neuron. Others have an excitatory effect; they cause depolarization of the neuron, and the message or impulse is transmitted along the neuron to continue through the nervous system.

Acetylcholine (pronounced *AS e til KO len*), an excitatory chemical, was the first neurotransmitter to be identified. Discoveries indicate that each knob on terminal branches contains this chemical, which is released into the synaptic area when depolarization of the neuron occurs. After the release, the knob is quickly refilled for future release. The released acetylcholine seems to be destroyed by other chemicals present in the environment of the synapse. Some chemicals such as those in pesticides and nerve gas that enter the bloodstream and then the environment of the synapse are thought to prevent this destruction of acetylcholine and to interfere with the transmission of the neural impulse (Kimble, 1977).

Other well-known chemical transmitter substances released from the knobs of the terminal branches of neurons are **norepinephrine** (pronounced *NOR ep i NEF rin*), **dopamine** (pronounced *DO pah men*), and **serotonin** (pronounced *SE ro TOE nin*). Norepinephrine and dopamine are closely related. After being released, they are taken back into the knobs on the terminal branches. Amphetamine drugs stimulate the release of these transmitters and block their breakdown after being released, allowing an impulse to be transmitted over and over again through a neuron. Cocaine has much the same effect because it prevents reabsorption (Carlson, 1980). The drug reserpine (pronounced *RES er peen*) has an opposite effect, causing the knobs to leak the norepinephrine out before depolarization, which allows for its early breakdown. This drug is often used as a relaxant in the treatment of high blood pressure. Dopamine is thought to be related to the mental illness known as schizophrenia. A current treatment consists of drugs to block dopamine receptor sites. Serotonin is a factor in the behavior of sleep and the activities associated with sleep such as dreaming. Neuroscientists now believe there are perhaps as many as 200 of these neurotransmitters in the nervous system (Snyder, 1980).

How do amphetamine drugs affect the neurotransmitters called norepinephrine and dopamine?

What is a current treatment for the mental illness known as schizophrenia?

Neuromodulators are chemicals secreted by cells much as glands secrete substances. Neuromodulators have now been discovered that are produced in various places in the body, sometimes produced and released into the bloodstream by neurons (a special type of neurotransmitter) and sometimes produced and released outside the nervous system and carried to it by the bloodstream. These chemicals float around in a synaptic area rather than being released into a synaptic area. Their action is not as fast as that of neurotransmitters, but they may have an effect for a longer period of time. They interact with neurotransmitters and affect the way they function. A neuromodulator may have a molecular structure

In what way does a neuromodulator differ from a neurotransmitter?

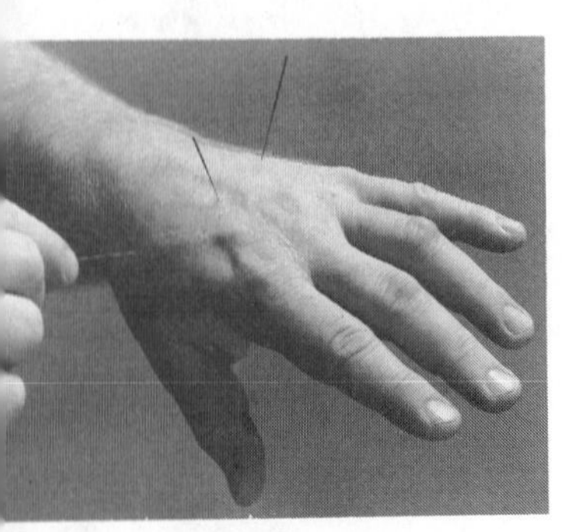

Figure 2–10. Acupuncture is believed to be effective by stimulating the release of endorphins in the brain that suppress pain.

similar to that of a neurotransmitter and can, therefore, occupy a receptor site that is normally occupied by a neurotransmitter. The investigation of neuromodulators such as **endorphins** (internal opiates), which control pain, and other *peptides* (see page 58) is currently one of the liveliest areas of research in neuroscience. The most powerful pain killer produced by the brain, beta-endorphin, has been manufactured and given to human subjects (Zimbardo, 1985). Hypnosis and acupuncture (see Figure 2–10), used as methods of reducing pain, are believed to be effective because they in some manner stimulate the release of the chemicals in the brain that suppress pain (Cotman & McGaugh, 1980). Regular, vigorous exercise is also believed to stimulate the release of endorphins that cause a person to feel better generally.

What are local circuits?

A constant chemical interplay is occurring at a synapse that determines whether a neuron will receive adequate stimulation (be pushed over its threshold) to depolarize and continue the message. This is the classic view and is typically true, but recent studies indicate that synaptic activity can occur in small areas of the dendrites by very weak stimulation that is below the threshold for depolarization of the cell. This discovery of weak electrical interactions has led to the realization that neurons contain **local circuits,** tiny areas only a few millionths of a meter across, where branches of dendrites from several cells may have weak electrical interactions with each other even though stimulation is not of a sufficient strength to cause depolarization of the cell.

The human nervous system is complex. Some psychologists believe that most human behavior will become explainable at the biological level as more is known about the synaptic transmission of the neural impulse.

Divisions

What two main divisions of the nervous system comprise the central nervous system?

Although all its parts are interrelated, the nervous system is divided structurally into several divisions. The two main divisions are the **peripheral nervous system** composed of all the nerves outside the brain and spinal cord that travel to all parts of the body and the **central nervous system** consisting of the brain and spinal cord (see Figure 2–11). Figure 2–12 charts the overall structural organization of the nervous system.

Peripheral Nervous System. All nerves carrying messages to and from the brain and spinal cord and that go out to all parts of the body comprise a subsystem of the nervous system referred to as the peripheral nervous system. Primarily, this system is composed

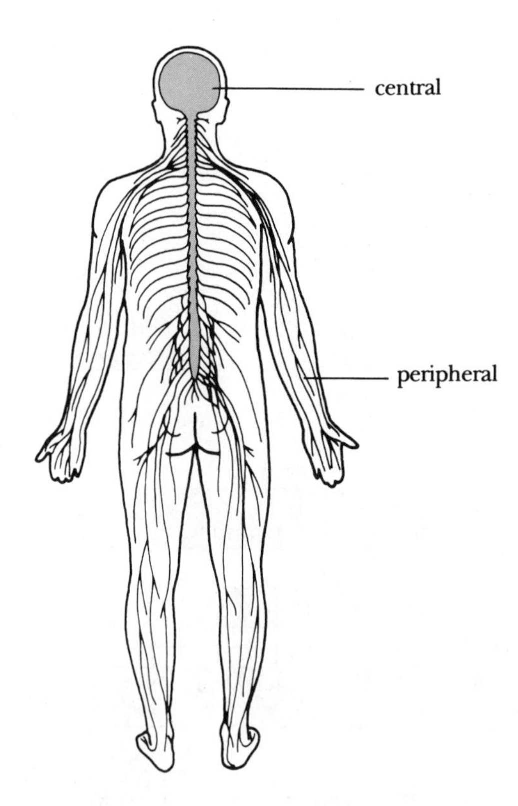

Figure 2–11.
Two main divisions of the nervous system.

of afferent and efferent neurons and carries out the input and output function of the nervous system by taking messages to and from the central nervous system. This system is further divided into two parts, the somatic nervous system and the autonomic nervous system.

The **somatic nervous system** consists of the spinal nerves and the cranial nerves such as the auditory nerve and the optic nerve. These nerves carry messages about the external and internal environment from the sense organs to the central nervous system, and they carry messages from the central nervous system back to muscles of the body where action is initiated. The somatic system mainly serves the voluntary muscles of the body.

How do the somatic nervous system and the autonomic nervous system differ?

The **autonomic nervous system** serves the involuntary muscles involved in behavior of internal body organs such as the heart, stomach, and glands. Internal organs send messages to and receive messages from the central system. This autonomic system consists of two subsystems: (a) the **parasympathetic system,** which is activated in the normal maintenance of life support functions; and

What is the function of the parasympathetic nervous system?

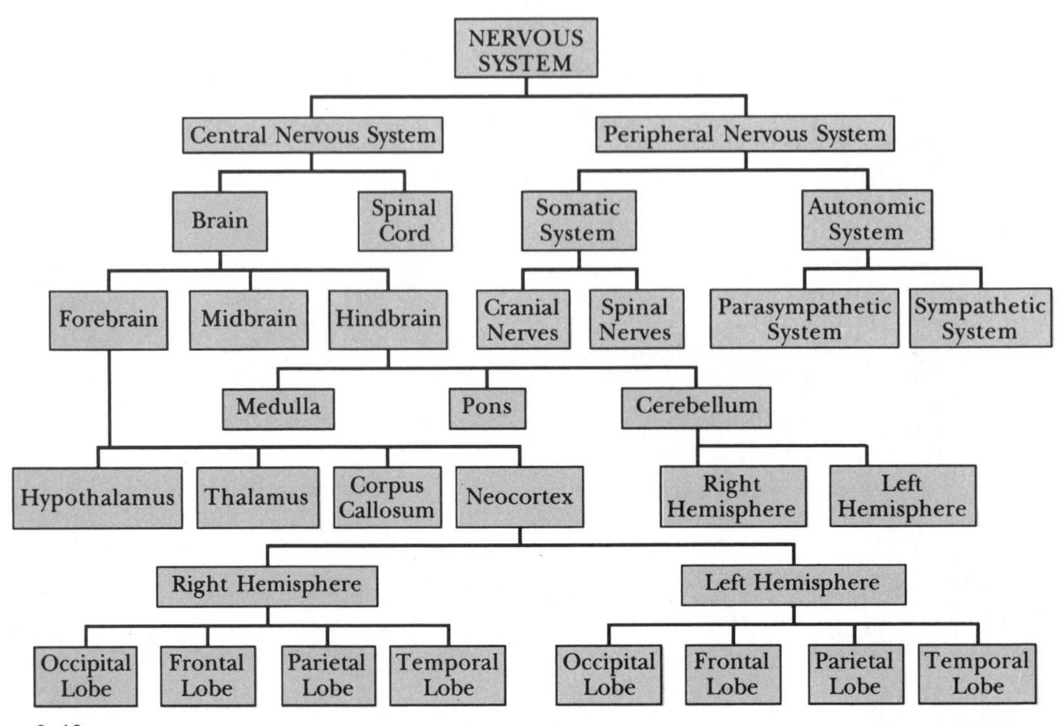

Figure 2–12.
Structural organization of the nervous system.

(b) the **sympathetic system,** which is activated in response to stress and takes over in emergency situations, emotional experiences, threatening situations, and adaptation to changes, whether physical or mental. The sympathetic system prepares the body for action.

What is the function of the sympathetic nervous system?

The parasympathetic and sympathetic systems work together but achieve different results. Generally, the two systems have opposite effects on an organ or gland (see Color Figure 2–13) much like the two sets of voluntary muscles in the arm produce opposite effects, for example. The two sets of arm muscles work together to bend and unbend the elbow—opposite behaviors. In much the same way, the sympathetic system arouses the body to handle stress placed upon it, and the parasympathetic system sends relaxation messages instructing the body to resume normal functioning. The sympathetic system acts more as a unit affecting all the internal organs simultaneously, whereas the parasympathetic system tends to affect only one organ at a time. Normally, as the stress or emotion increases in intensity, the the bodily effect becomes greater. A constant interplay is occurring as the body switches back and forth from one system to the other just as the two sets of arm muscles work together in the bending and unbending of the elbow. However, sometimes one system tends to dominate in a person. Some people seem to be uptight more of the time, and some people seem to be calm and relaxed more of the time.

Central Nervous System. The central nervous system is the body's master control center. It consists of the brain and spinal cord. The spinal cord has two primary functions, one of which is the regulation of reflex behaviors. In a reflex response, a message for a specific body movement may be processed in the spinal cord or in the subconscious part of the brain before the message reaches the conscious part of the brain. The second function of the spinal cord is to carry messages from nerves in the peripheral nervous system to the brain and from the brain back to nerves in the peripheral nervous system. The connective function in the central nervous system is performed by interneurons (see the organizational chart of the nervous system in Figure 2–12).

What are the two primary functions of the spinal cord?

BRAIN

The brain weighs about 3 pounds, consumes about 20 percent of the oxygen used by the body while in a resting state, and is the most active, energy-consuming organ of the body. It is composed of three basic divisions—the hindbrain, the midbrain, and the forebrain.

Does the brain consume very much oxygen?

What are the three basic divisions of the brain?

Organization and Functions

The brain is a difficult organ to study. However, by using a variety of techniques, scientists have learned the basic anatomy of the brain and much about the functioning of the brain. One of the techniques used to learn about the organization and function of the brain involves electrical stimulation of parts of the brain to observe their specific function. Also, studying people who have brain damage from injury, tumors, strokes, and the like has provided information about brain functioning.

Hindbrain. The **hindbrain** is the lower part of the brain that merges with the spinal cord. This division of the brain includes the **medulla,** the part adjoining the spinal cord that controls reflex behaviors such as breathing and heart rate and helps maintain upright posture. The **pons,** positioned just above the medulla, contains fibers that connect the higher and lower levels of the brain and the two hemispheres of the **cerebellum,** also in the hindbrain. Body movement messages are relayed from higher levels of the brain to the cerebellum, which is involved in the control of motor behavior, especially balance and coordination. Color Figure 2–14 shows the location of some of the major parts of the brain.

Midbrain. The **midbrain** is located between the hindbrain and forebrain near the center of the brain. The midbrain, which has many functions, plays a major role in hearing and seeing. For example, areas controlling eye movements and reflexes such as dilation of the pupils are located in the midbrain, which sends out three different pairs of cranial nerves to eye muscles.

Forebrain. The **forebrain** is the upper portion of the brain, above the midbrain, that includes such structures as the neocortex, corpus callosum, thalamus, and hypothalamus. The lower portion of the forebrain controls hormonal release, autonomic nervous system functions, and emotional and motivational processes, whereas the upper part is associated with consciousness. The **thalamus** functions as a relay station for messages coming in from the sense organs and directs the messages to particular areas of the brain. The **hypothalamus** functions as a thermostat for the body and plays an important role in controlling hunger, thirst, body temperature, and endocrine activity in order to maintain the needed balance for survival. In addition, the hypothalamus seems to have some control over the autonomic nervous system. During physical or mental stress, the hypothalamus sends messages to activate the autonomic nervous system. Also in the forebrain is the **neocortex** (cerebral cortex or simply cortex), which is a mass of cell bodies and unmyelinated axons that covers the two hemispheres of the brain, forming an "umbrella" over the structures in the center of the brain (see Color Figures 2–15 and 2–16). The two hemispheres are connected by the **corpus callosum,** a large mass of fibers that allows the two sides of the brain to communicate with each other. By studying individuals who have had the corpus callosum severed, psychologists have learned much about the functioning of the two hemispheres of the brain.

What part of your brain functions as a relay station?

What part of your brain functions as a thermostat?

Figure 2–17.
Roger Sperry.

THE "SPLIT BRAIN"

A radical and usually a last resort treatment for severe epilepsy in humans that involved severing the corpus callosum was introduced by Roger Sperry (see Figure 2–17) and his colleagues (1982). Because the corpus callosum is the connection between the two hemispheres of the brain, the two hemispheres cannot communicate. In 1981, Sperry, of the California Institute of Technology, was awarded

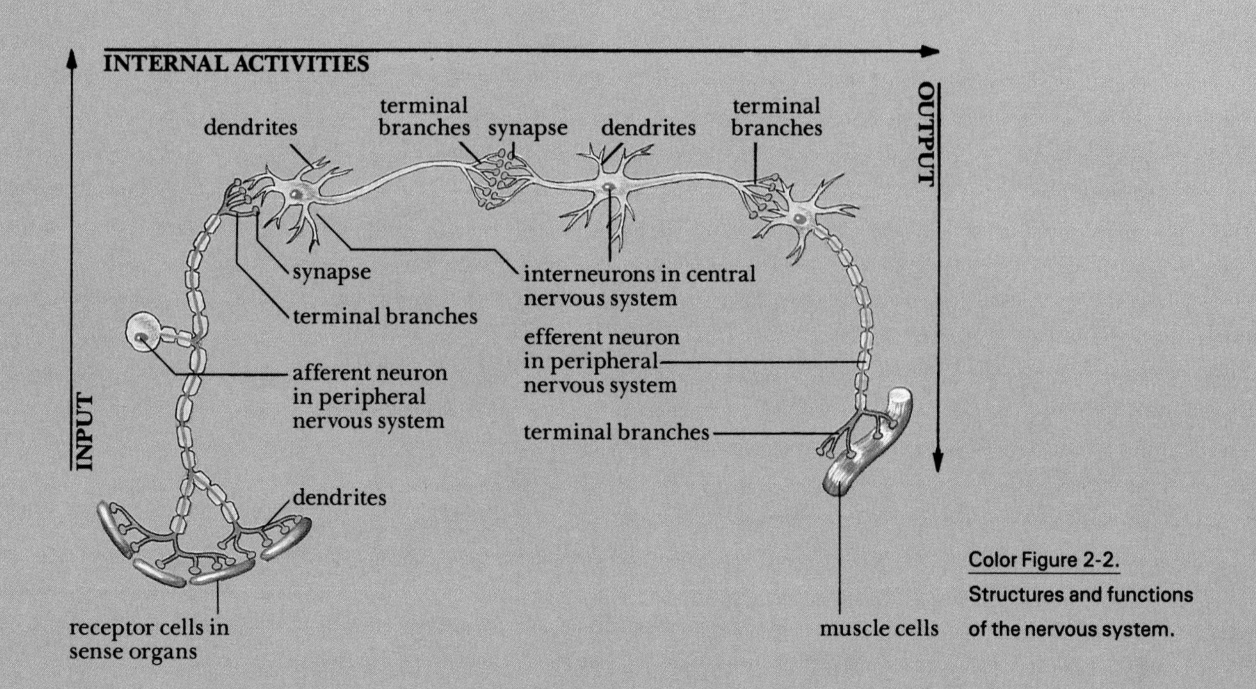

Color Figure 2-2.
Structures and functions of the nervous system.

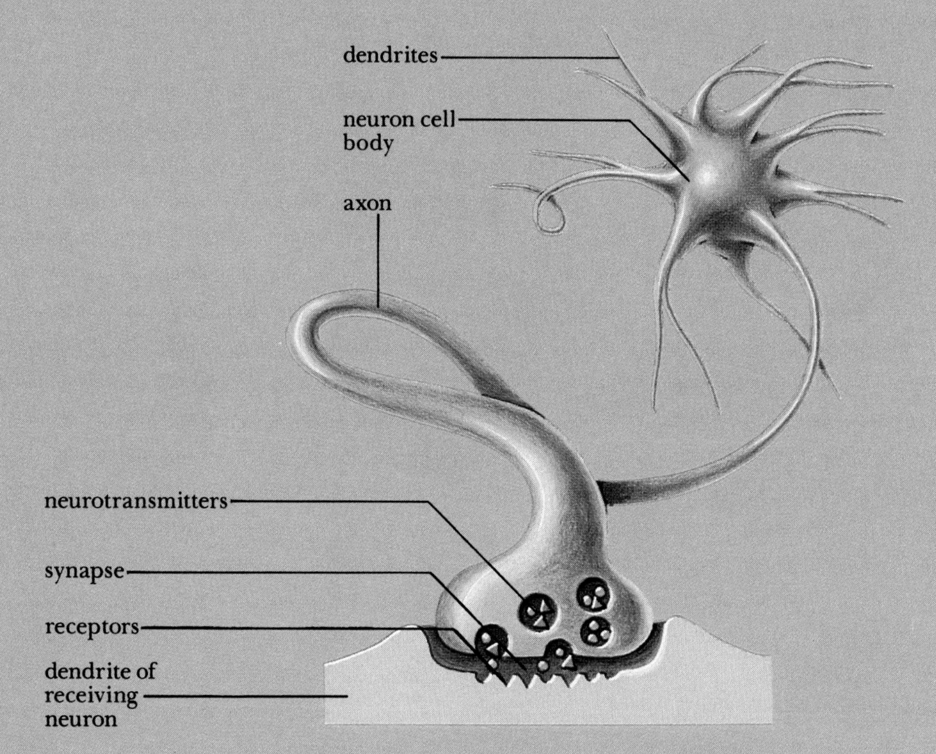

Color Figure 2-5.
Neurotransmitters are released into the synapse and may be taken up at receptor sites on other neurons.

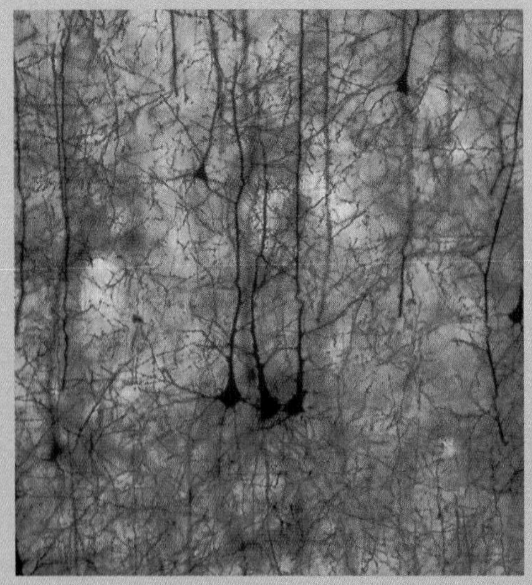

Color Figure 2-6.
A typical neuron may have as many as 10,000 synapses.

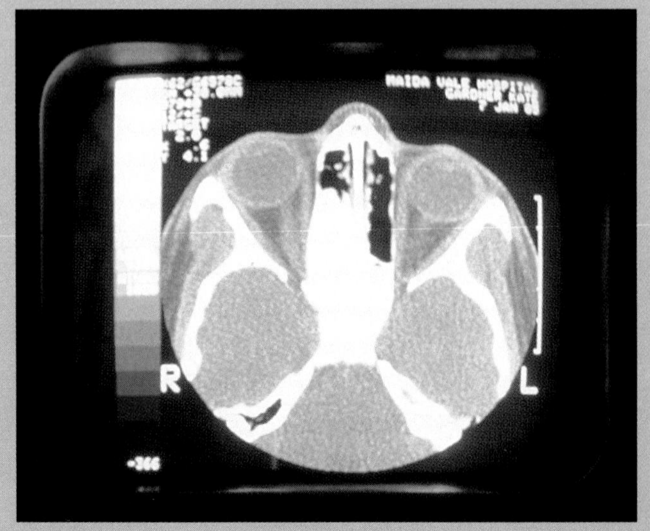

Color Figure 2-7.
A CAT scan of a human brain.

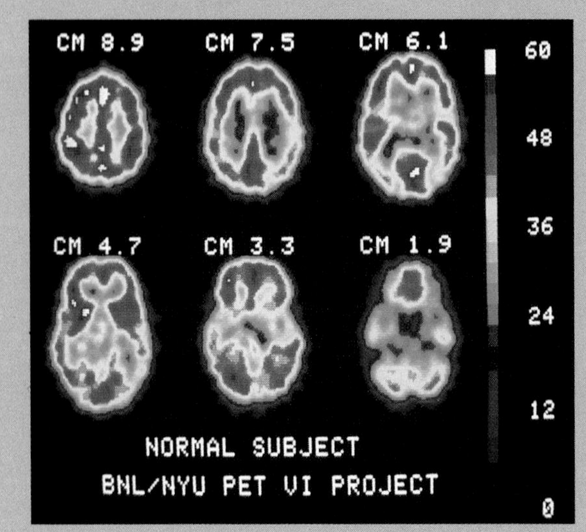

Color Figure 2-8.
A PET scan of a human brain.

Color Figure 2-9.
An MRI image of a human brain.

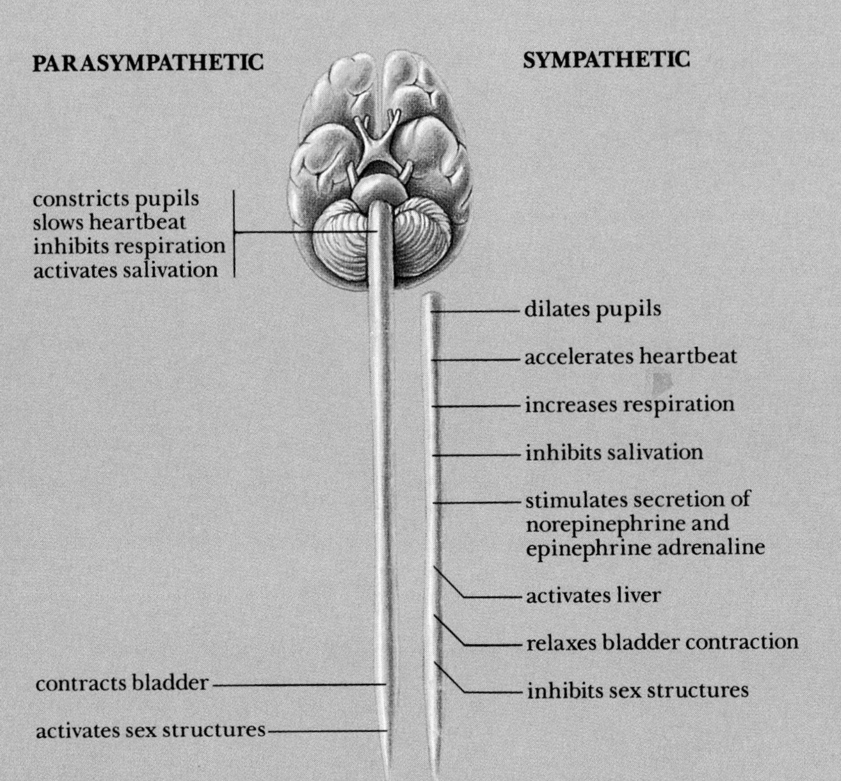

Color Figure 2-13.
The autonomic nervous system.

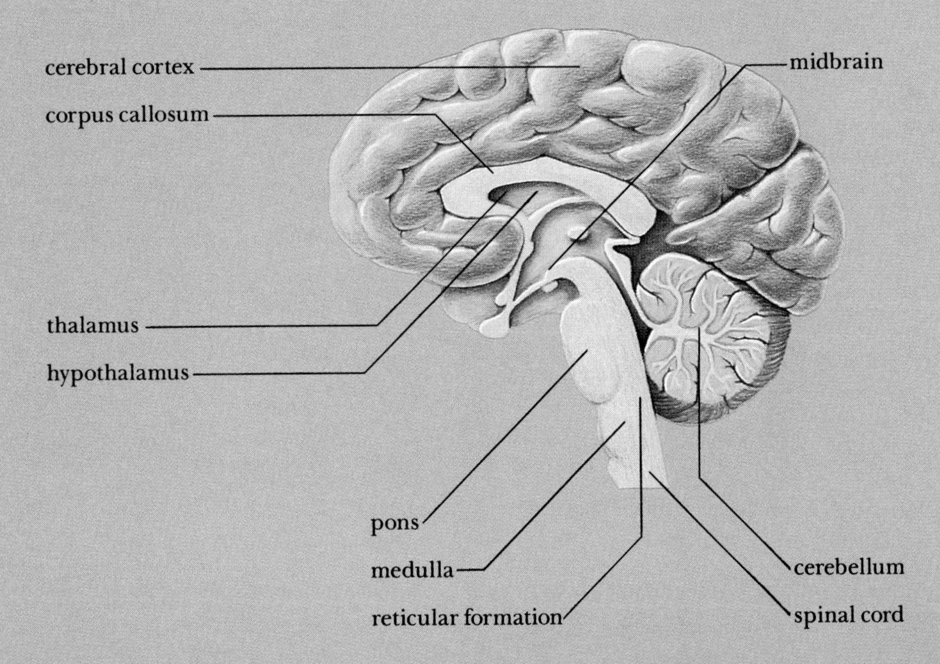

Color Figure 2-14.
The right hemisphere of the brain (medial view).

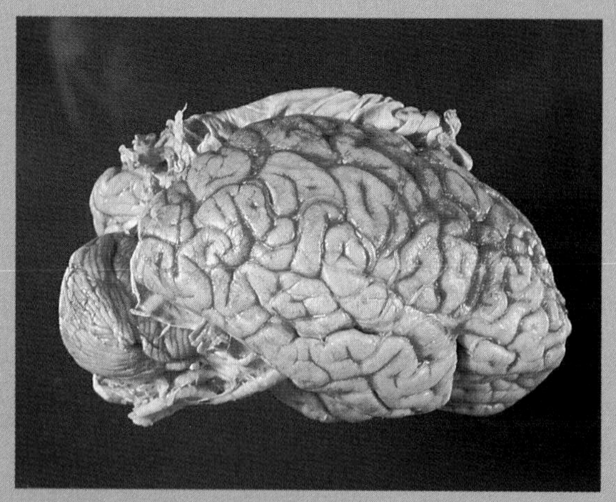

Color Figure 2-15.
A side view of the neocortex of the human brain.

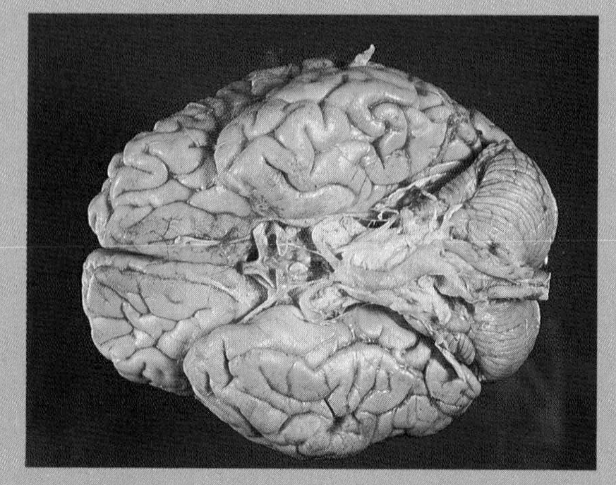

Color Figure 2-16.
A top view of the neocortex of the human brain.

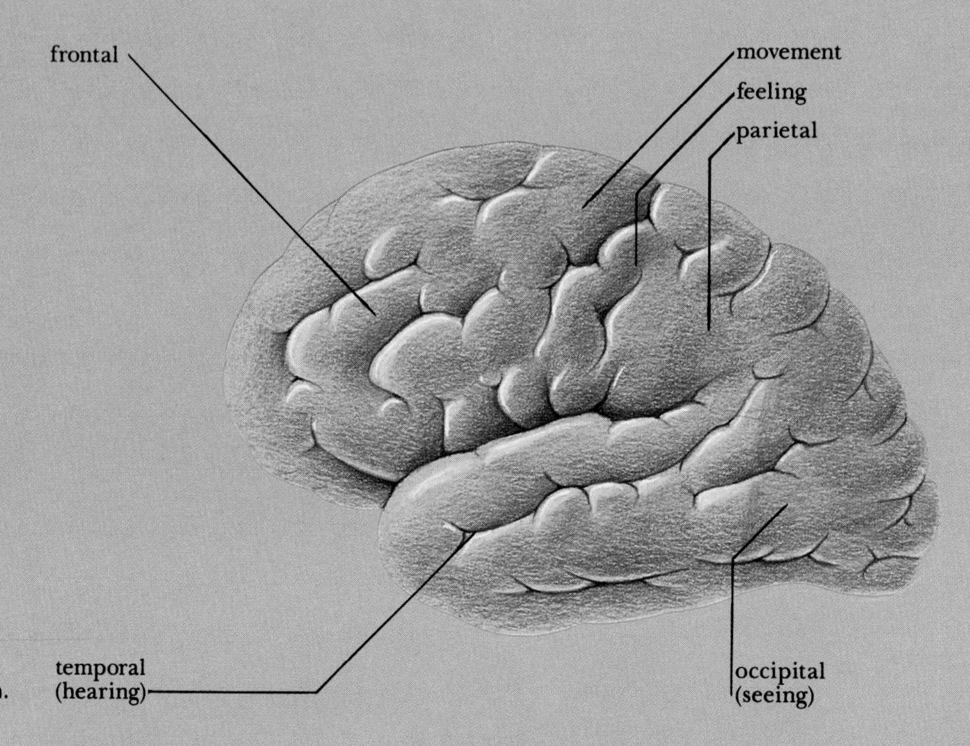

Color Figure 2-18.
The lobes of the brain.

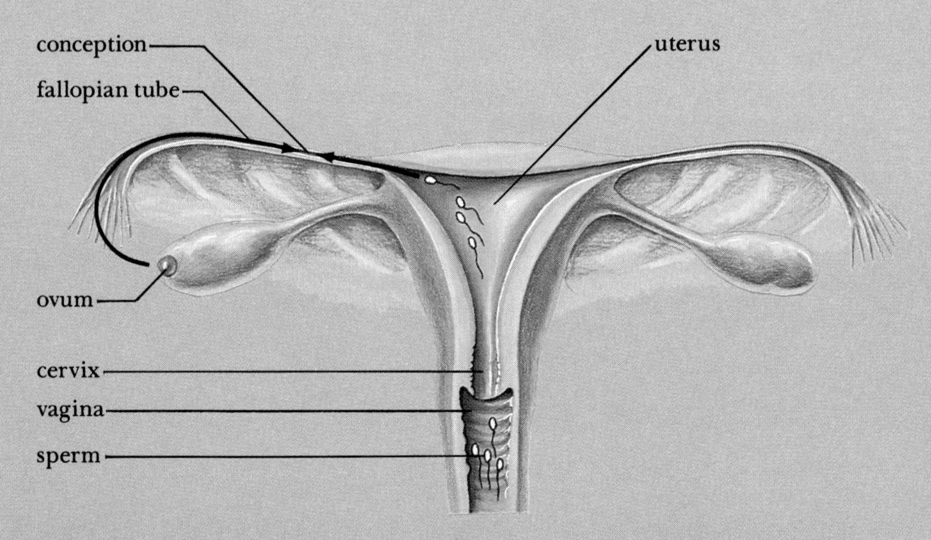

Color Figure 3-3.
Schematic diagram of the female reproductive system showing how conception occurs.

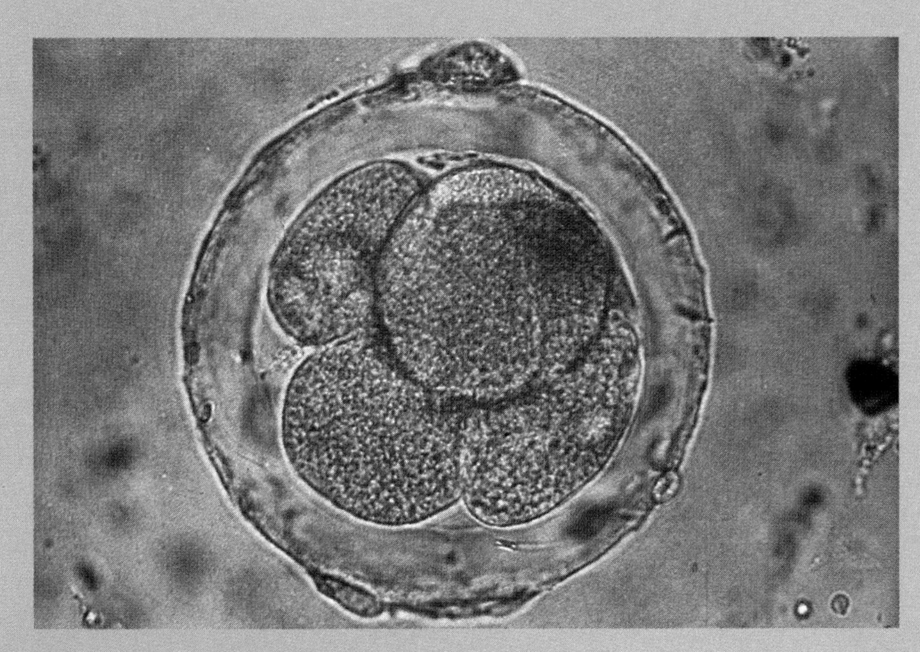

Color Figure 3-4.
Within a few days, a fertilized egg has formed a cluster of cells.

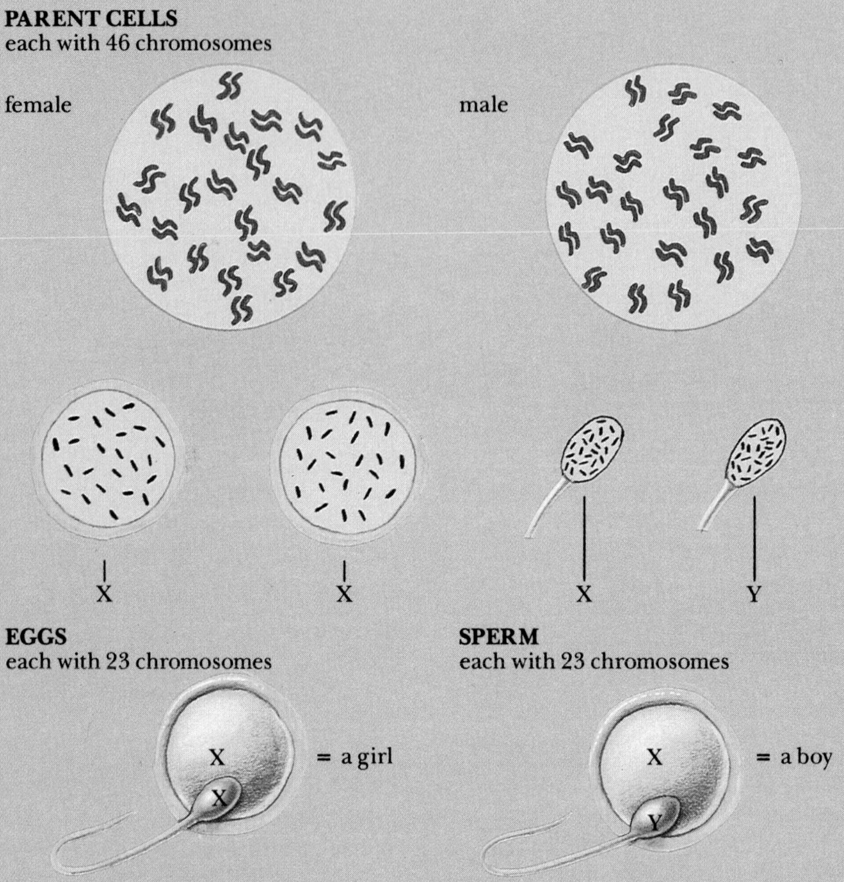

PARENT CELLS
each with 46 chromosomes

female

male

X

X

X

Y

EGGS
each with 23 chromosomes

SPERM
each with 23 chromosomes

X
X
= a girl

X
Y
= a boy

Color Figure 3-6.
Hereditary mechanisms determine an individual's sex.

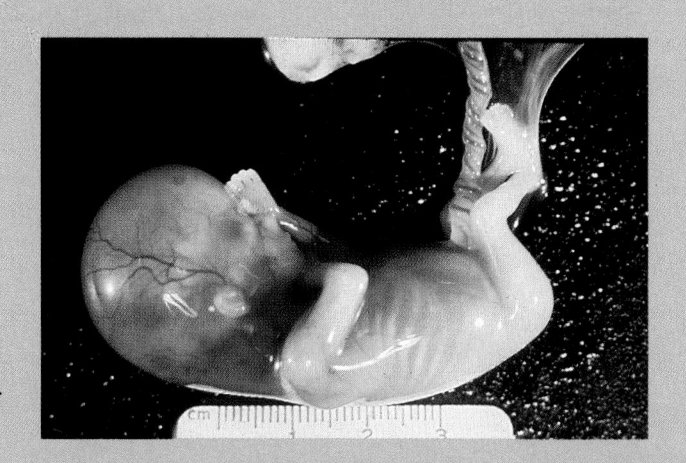

Color Figure 3-12.
An embryo 8 weeks after conception.

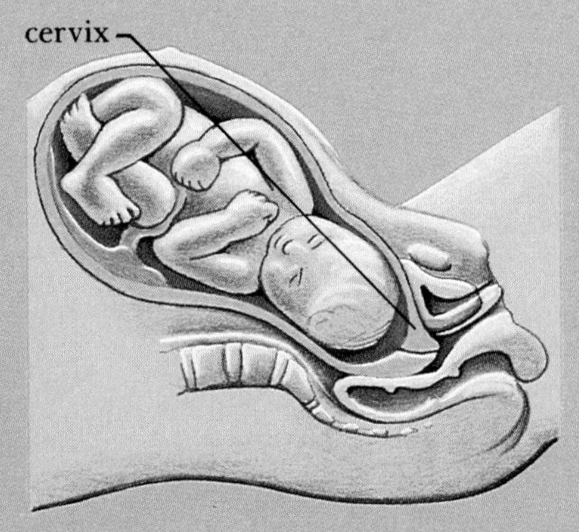

before birth
(cervix closed)

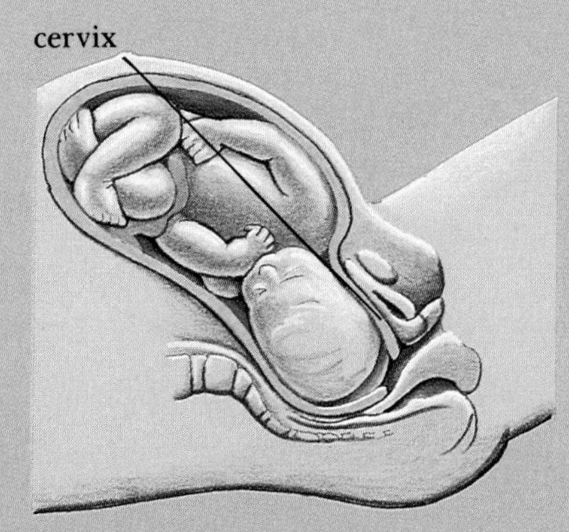

early part of Stage 1
(cervix opening)

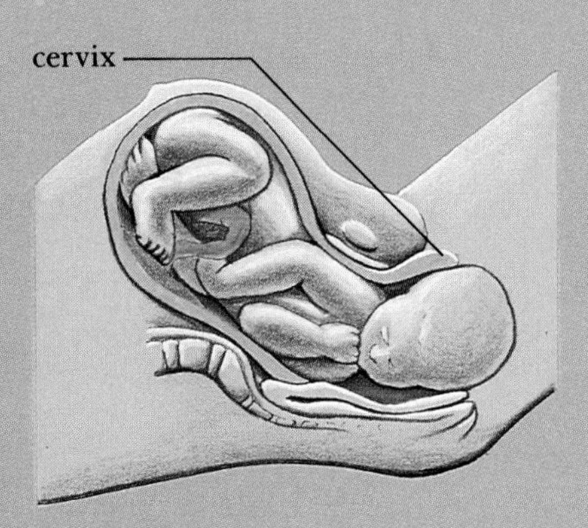

last part of Stage 1
(cervix opening more)

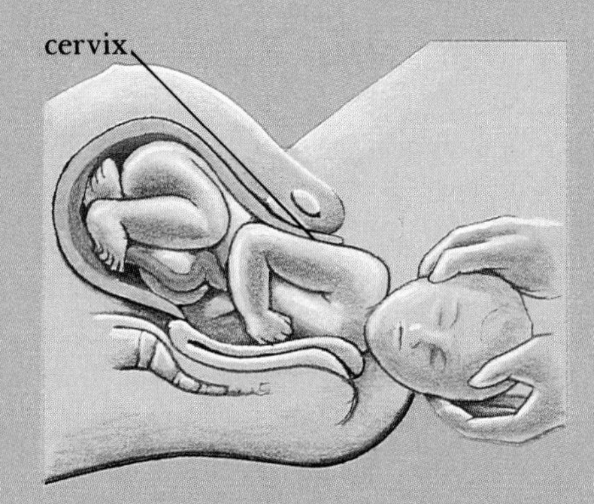

Stage 2
(passage from mother)

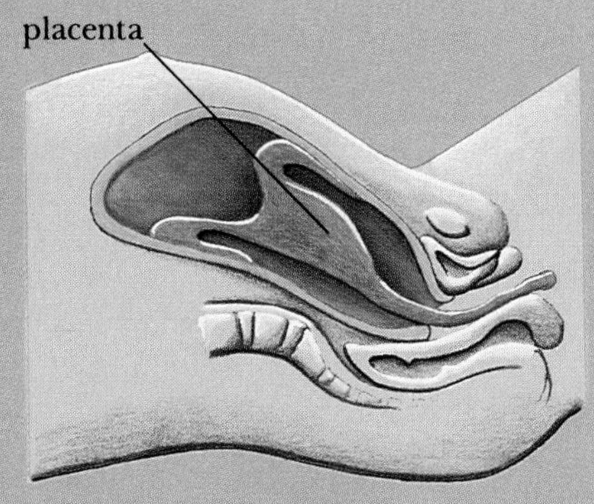

Stage 3
(passage of placenta)

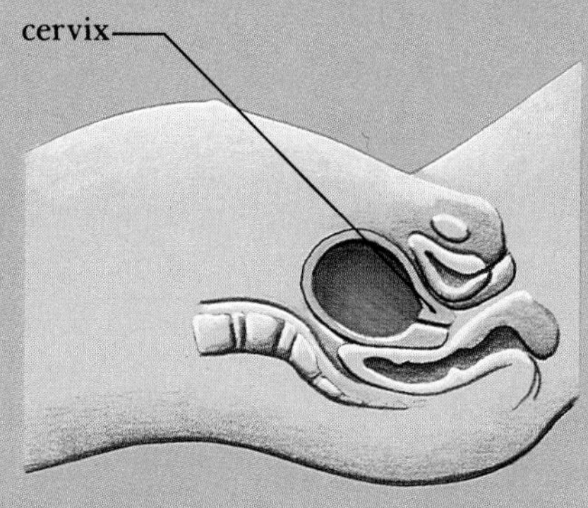

after birth
(cervix closed)

Color Figure 3-16.
The sequence of steps during birth.

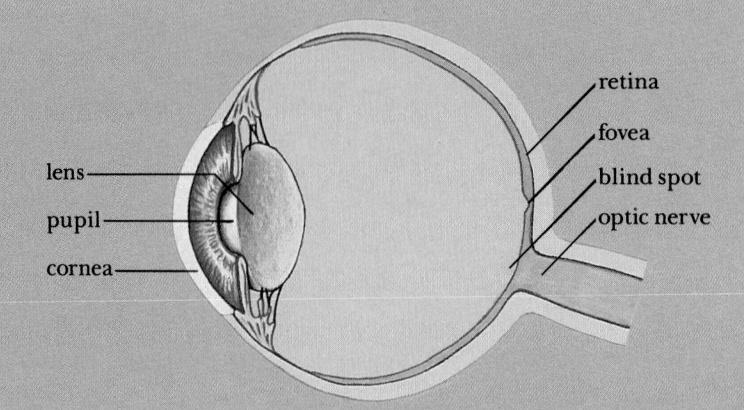

Color Figure 5-1.
A cross section of the human eye.

Color Figure 5-2.
Stare at the dot in the middle of the green, black, and yellow flag for about 30 to 40 seconds, and then look at a blank, white sheet of paper. As the activity level of stimulation reverses (decreases), your brain interprets the message as the opposite color and produces an image of a red, white, and blue flag.

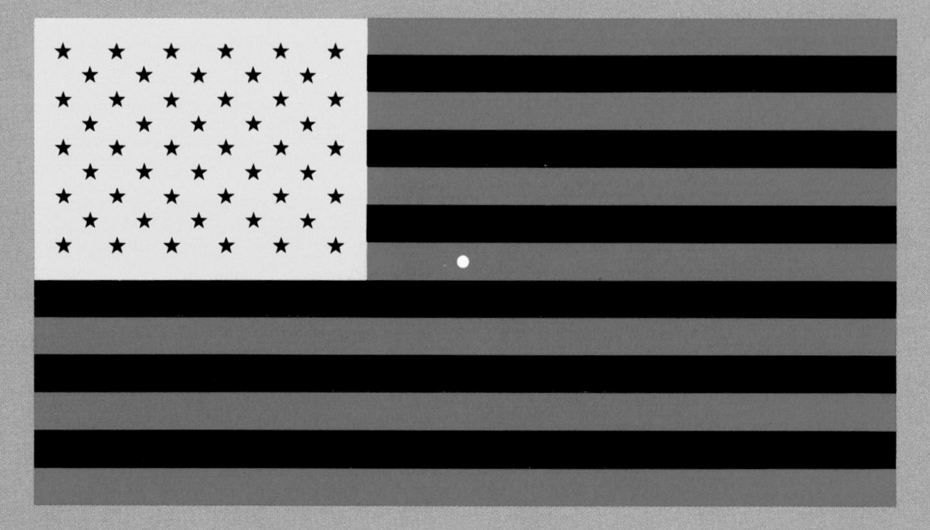

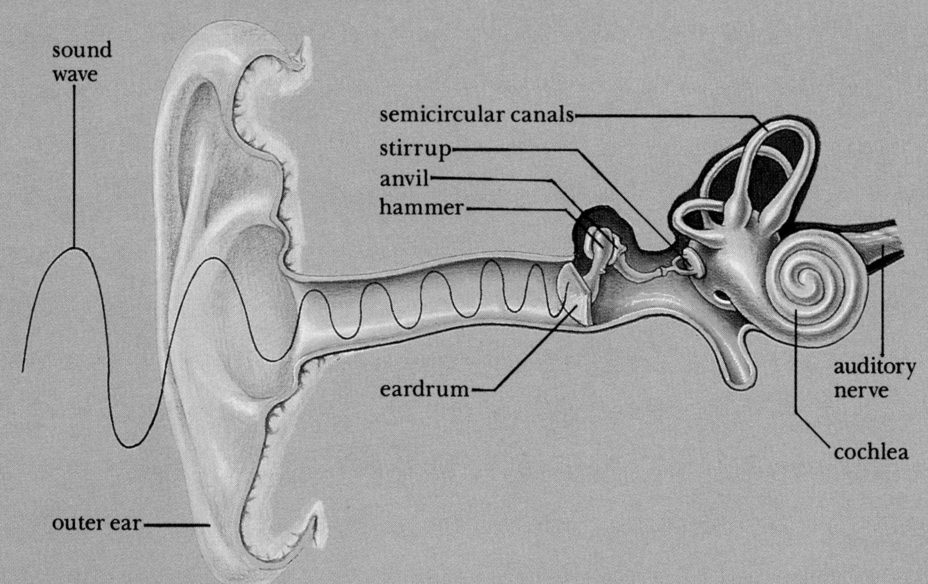

Color Figure 5-5.
The human ear.

half of the Nobel Prize for his research on hemispheric functioning in the brain.

People who have had the split-brain surgery seem to lead rather normal lives, but psychologists have been interested in studying them by setting up precise psychological tests to help understand how the hemispheres operate in normal conditions. When an object such as a key is placed in the dominant right hand of a recipient of the split-brain surgery, it is identified by touch and the person can verbally name the object. But if the key is placed in the left hand and the person cannot see it, he or she cannot identify it by verbally naming it. Split-brain surgery persons can identify the object by pointing with the left hand to a card in a group of cards with the word *key* written on it or by pointing to the object in a group of objects. Each hemisphere of the brain is capable of learning and remembering. After listening to a story, split-brain surgery recipients can recall the main details verbally, but they tend to confuse the order and leave out parts of the story.

Neocortex

The neocortex is wrinkled and crumpled into folds, a little like a wadded-up piece of paper, to fit inside the skull. If it were spread out smoothly, it would cover 2 or 3 square feet of surface area. This part of the brain has "the consistency of Jell-O and the color of day-old slush" (Begley, 1983, p. 40).

What does the neocortex look like?

Areas and Functions. Each hemisphere of the brain consists of four large areas—hunks or lobes (see Color Figure 2–18)—each of which has a specific responsibility. The **temporal lobes,** located on each side of the two hemispheres, control hearing. The **occipital lobes** (pronounced *AHK sip uh tuhl*), located at the back of the hemispheres, receive and interpret impulses from the eyes. The **frontal lobes,** the large front portions of the hemispheres located behind the forehead and least understood of the four lobes, are considered to be the site of mental processes uniquely characteristic of humans such as worrying, self-awareness, planning, and willful and purposeful choosing. These lobes also handle information about body movement and seem to be involved in keeping track of past and future movements (Stuss & Benson, 1984). The **parietal lobes** (pronounced *puh RIGH uh tuhl*), located at the top of the hemispheres between the occipital and frontal lobes, integrate sensory input and contain the part of the cortex involved in feeling

Each hemisphere of the neocortex has how many lobes?

(sensitivity to touch). The functions of some parts of the lobes of the brain are not completely understood yet.

Sensory projection areas are areas for specific functioning localized on the cortex. At least one region has been identified for each of the senses except taste and smell. In the motor projection area at the back of the frontal lobe, there is a specific area for receiving and sending messages related to the movement of each specific body part. In the projection area for touch at the front of the parietal lobe, there is a specific area for sensitivity for each place on the body. Some of these areas for movement and feeling are larger in proportion to the body size than others. For example, the area for movement for the fingers is larger than the area for the hip because the fingers are involved in more movement in a person's behavior than the hip, and the area for feeling for the lips is larger than the area for feeling in the forearm (see Figure 2–19). Particular areas on the body that are especially sensitive to touch for individual survival or sexual arousal for reproduction have larger areas on the cortex in proportion to places on the body not especially sensitive to touch. A person may have a very specific disability as a result of brain damage in a specific place in these areas. For example, one part of the body such as a finger, arm, or leg may be paralyzed and have no movement or sensitivity to touch. Or one's vision or hearing may be impaired.

Is there more area on the cortex for impulses from the movement of large body parts such as the shoulder than for smaller body parts such as the thumb?

Other specific areas located at various places on the cortex combine impulses from different senses to create meaningful impressions. These areas are involved in interpreting our world, language, speech, and thought. A person may have a very specific disability as a result of a disorder in one of these specific areas. For example, a person may lose the ability to understand the meaning of words, to use language to express thoughts, to understand complex pictures, or to remember even a well-traveled route. Recently, a neurosurgeon identified the parts of the cortex involved in naming objects and doing arithmetic (Ojemann, 1983).

Is there a specific area on the cortex for such specific things as naming objects?

Hemispheric Specialization. The two hemispheres of the cortex are referred to as the right and left hemispheres. In general, the left hemisphere governs the functions of the right side of the body, and the right hemisphere governs the functions of the left side of the body. The two hemispheres look about identical, but there are significant differences. Although each hemisphere seems to handle specific tasks, communication is going on between them constantly, and they seem to cooperate in an integrated fashion.

The left hemisphere governs the functions of which side of the body?

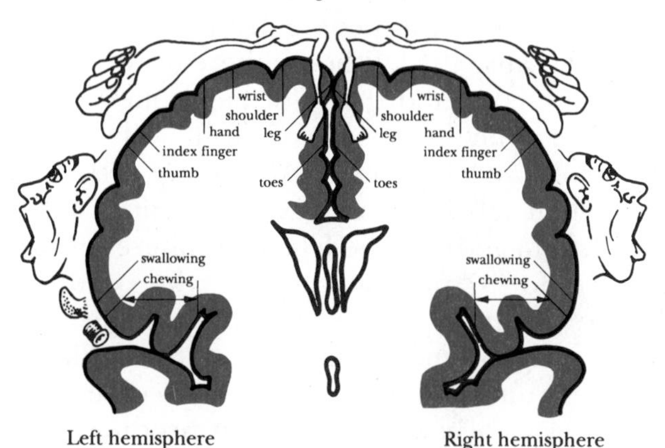

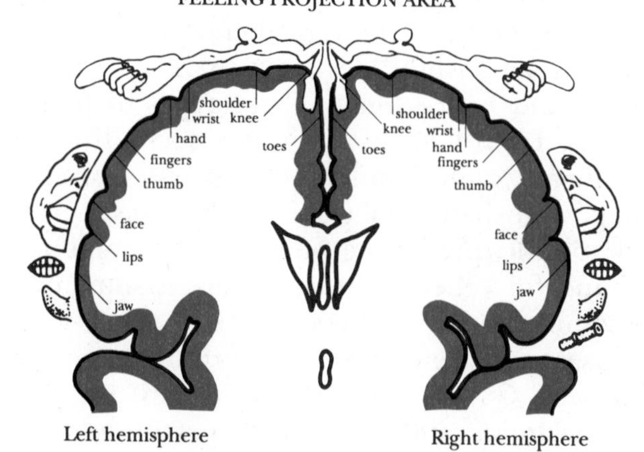

Figure 2–19.
Location and amounts of cortex devoted to movement and feeling.

The left hemisphere is normally the center for language control and analytical thought; the right hemisphere governs artistic and spatial abilities and is generally believed to be responsible for creative thinking. Nonverbal sounds such as melodies are believed to be represented primarily on the right hemisphere. Kinsbourne (1982) suggests that negative feelings are processed primarily in the right hemisphere and positive feelings in the left hemisphere. Thus, if a person has damage to the right hemisphere, he or she possibly may appear only happy and cheerful; damage to the left hemisphere would leave the person feeling perhaps only angry, gloomy, and depressed.

In general, the control centers for what functions are located in the left hemisphere?

Most people show right or left dominance in their behavior. For example, about 90 percent of the people are right-handed, left-hemisphere dominant because the left hemisphere of the brain controls the right side of the body and the right hemisphere controls the left side. There is no one theory to account for why about 10 percent of the population are left-handed. Also, there is a wide variation in characteristics of left-handers. Sixty percent of left-handed people produce language from the left hemisphere just as most right-handed people do (97 percent). People who produce language from the left hemisphere can be identified by the way they write. People who are right-handed and write with the hand straight produce language from the left hemisphere. People who are left-handed and write with a hooked hand also produce language from the left hemisphere. Right-handed people who write with a hooked hand and left-handed people who write with a straight hand produce language from the right hemisphere of the brain (Pines, 1980). Some relationship does seem to exist between organization in the brain and handedness. Three types of hemispheric organization are found in left-handers according to Ornstein (1985): (a) similar to right-handers, (b) reverse of right-handers, and (c) language and spatial abilities in both hemispheres. Some people are hand specific, preferring one hand for some activities and the other hand for other activities. There is some evidence that heredity accounts for handedness, but there is no clear explanation. In some cases, experience in the environment seems to account for handedness. Corballis and Beale (1976) suggest there is a hereditary factor and a random factor. A person inherits either a tendency toward dominance, in which case language centers are on the left and the right hand is dominant, or a person inherits a tendency toward symmetry, in which case randomness takes over and language may be produced from either the left or right hemispheres of the brain and either the right or left hand may be dominant.

What group of people are right brain dominant for language?

Sex Differences. Some sex differences have been found in the hemispheres of the cortex of the brain. Analytical and sequential thinking is thought to be represented more predominately in the left hemisphere of males than females. McGlone (1980) found that damage to the left hemisphere interfered more with these abilities in males than in females. Also, physical differences in males and females are indicative of different functioning in the brain. In maturation, boys have been shown to have earlier development of the

Are there any differences in the hemispheres of the brain for males and females?

right hemisphere (Witelson, 1976), whereas girls showed earlier left hemisphere development (Bryden, 1973).

Systems

The brain has systems involving several parts to perform some functions. Two such systems are the limbic system (see Figure 2–20) and the reticular activating system (see Figure 2–21).

Limbic. The **limbic system** is an interconnection of several structures in the center core of the brain, including parts of the thalamus and hypothalamus. It is related to motivation and emotional behavior, especially aggression, and it includes the pleasure centers of the brain. Another structure included in the limbic system, the **hippocampus,** seems to be related to learning, recognizing novelty, and remembering (Thompson, Berger, & Madden, 1983).

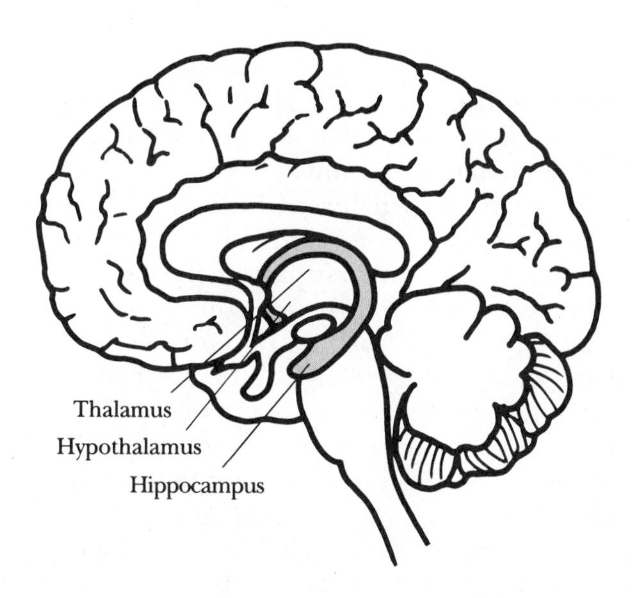

Figure 2–20.
The limbic system, an interconnection of several structures in the center core of the brain.

Reticular Activating. The **reticular activating system** consists of a netlike bundle of neurons that extends through the hindbrain, midbrain, and into part of the forebrain. The primary function of this system is to arouse the individual. When impulses reach this region, they can send messages that prompt reactions throughout the brain because some ascending neural tracts connect to this system. The reticular activating system is important in sleep and attention or levels of awareness. Both the existence and intensity of consciousness are controlled by this system, which seems to serve as

Which system controls the existence of consciousness or awareness?

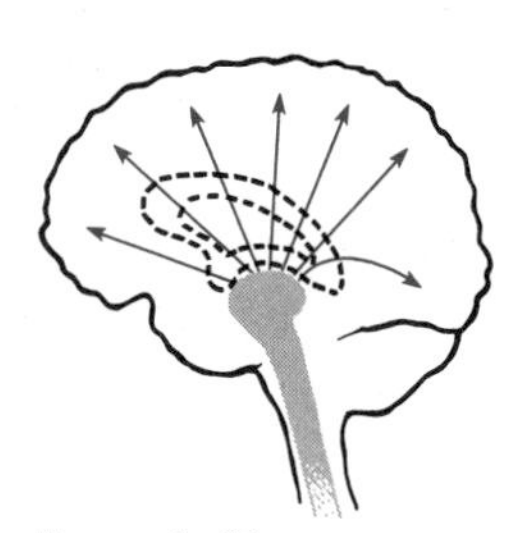

Figure 2–21.
The reticular activating system, a netlike bundle of neurons that extends through the hindbrain, midbrain, and into part of the forebrain.

the gateway to the brain, letting in the most urgent messages and keeping out distracting messages. Anesthetics work mainly by slowing down or disengaging this system.

Biological Rhythms

Humans as well as animals experience cycles in a number of biological processes. Built in biological "clocks" producing rhythmic activity are an intriguing and not yet fully understood part of an individual's makeup.

Known Cycles. Some body cycles are well-known such as the 28-day menstrual cycle in females, the sleep cycle, and the temperature cycle. As a result of the rhythm of biological changes, body temperature increases from about 8:00 a.m. to about 8:00 p.m. and then drops to its lowest point about 4:00 a.m. Sleep is part of a 24-hour biological cycle also and does not seem to depend on the sun for timing. All sorts of metabolic and physiological functions such as levels of substances in the blood and levels of various chemicals in the urine show a 24-hour cycle. There are rhythms in the nervous system and in the secretions from glands. Job performance seems to be related to these biological rhythms.

Are you a "day person" or a "night person"?

Biological rhythms may vary for different individuals, even though they are on a 24-hour cycle. Some individuals are more active at night and less active during the first part of the day. As a result, a person is sometimes labeled as a "day person" or a "night person." People who engage in shift work or fly from one time zone to another may have their biological rhythms disturbed and their job performance affected. Sometimes a person may have the sleep rhythm disturbed and experience difficulty in sleeping. Biological rhythm disturbances are believed to be related to serotonin, the major neurotransmitter regulating the functioning of a part of the brain that affects blood sugar and body rhythm (Turkington, 1986). Most likely the brain is the master controller of all body rhythms.

Popular Biorhythms. Biorhythms is a popular notion today. The term **biorhythms** refers to biological cycles such as emotional, intellectual, and physical cycles that are believed by some scientists to begin at birth, rise and fall at different rates, and have a small but significant part in the explanation of human behavior. The evidence on biorhythms is weak because rhythms are approximations and do not remain constant from birth. Illness or drugs, for example, can disrupt body rhythms.

BIORHYTHMS

The idea of biorhythms is a popular view that claims that many kinds of body rhythms exist that begin at birth and rise and fall at different rates. Three cycles—emotional, intellectual, and physical—have been charted, but the only scientific proof of their existence is statistical. The physical cycle is 23 days, the emotional cycle is 28 days, and the mental cycle is 33 days. Critical days occur when one of the cycles is at its lowest point. Double or triple critical days occur when two or three of the cycles are at the lowest point simultaneously. Critical days are not predetermined as dangerous; they only give an idea of the energy potential. Energy potential is highest when the three cycles are at the highest point simultaneously.

Industry is paying attention to biorhythms. Johns-Mansville Manufacturing Corporation, United Airlines, and Denver Yellow Cab are among those who have made use of biorhythms to reduce accidents and increase efficiency (Frazier, 1977).

ENDOCRINE GLANDS

The body has two major interacting biological systems for integrating and coordinating behavior—the nervous system and the endocrine system. The endocrine system consists of several glands located throughout the body. These glands manufacture and secrete chemical substances into the bloodstream. The discussion in this section will focus on the major endocrine glands, their secretions, and their relationship to behavior.

Secretions

Some glands of the body empty secretions into a cavity of the body. The salivary glands empty secretions into the mouth; tear glands secrete into the eye cavity; and digestive juices are secreted into the stomach. The **endocrine glands,** however, are ductless glands that secrete chemical substances directly into the bloodstream.

Hormones. Hormones, chemical substances secreted by endocrine glands, function as neuromodulators to have an effect on an individual's behavior. Because the endocrine glands secrete directly into the bloodstream, they have a widespread and immediate effect on behavior. The hormones, carried by the bloodstream to specific locations where they fit the intended receptor sites, are larger molecules than neurotransmitters. Working through a feedback system, hormones are secreted to help maintain a physiological balance in the body. Some hormones affect many organs, some affect only one organ, and some affect other endocrine glands. An endocrine gland may secrete many hormones, or it may secrete only a few or only one hormone.

Peptides. Of great interest currently in the study of human behavior is the finding that an endocrine gland in the brain and also the hypothalamus in the brain manufacture and secrete large protein molecules that are made up of long chains of various amino acids. The chains are then separated by enzymes into pieces of varying lengths called **peptides.** These peptides can be of perhaps hundreds of different varieties, each having a specific effect on specific neurons in the nervous system. Many of these peptides are found throughout the body and seem to work like hormones as neuromodulators, being manufactured in one part of the body and carried by the bloodstream to other parts of the body for action. Sometimes they may travel across synapses in the same manner as neurotransmitters. Several of these peptides have been identified, and new ones are being found regularly. Endorphins, now well-known peptides, are similar to morphine and have the ability to control pain. There is now evidence to suggest that perhaps there may be peptides for controlling other behavioral systems such as eating, drinking, sexual activity, and fighting.

Does your body manufacture its own narcotics?

Glands

Several endocrine glands are located in various places in the body. Figure 2–23 shows the names and location of the endocrine glands. In this section, the function and behavioral effects of insufficient or excessive secretions are pointed out.

Figure 2–22.
Hormones produced by the pituitary gland control the timing and amount of growth of the body.

Pituitary. The **pituitary gland,** the master gland of the body located in the brain, produces more hormones than any of the other endocrine glands and even produces peptides. One group of hormones produced by the pituitary controls the timing and amount of growth of the body (see Figure 2–22). Another group of hormones produced by the pituitary controls other endocrine glands. The relationship between the pituitary gland and the hypothalamus provides a good example of the interdependence of body systems. Certain hormones produced by the pituitary gland (part of the endocrine system) stimulate the hypothalamus (part of the nervous system) in the brain, which results in a chemical change in the bloodstream. The chemical change stimulates the release of hormones from other endocrine glands, which further changes the

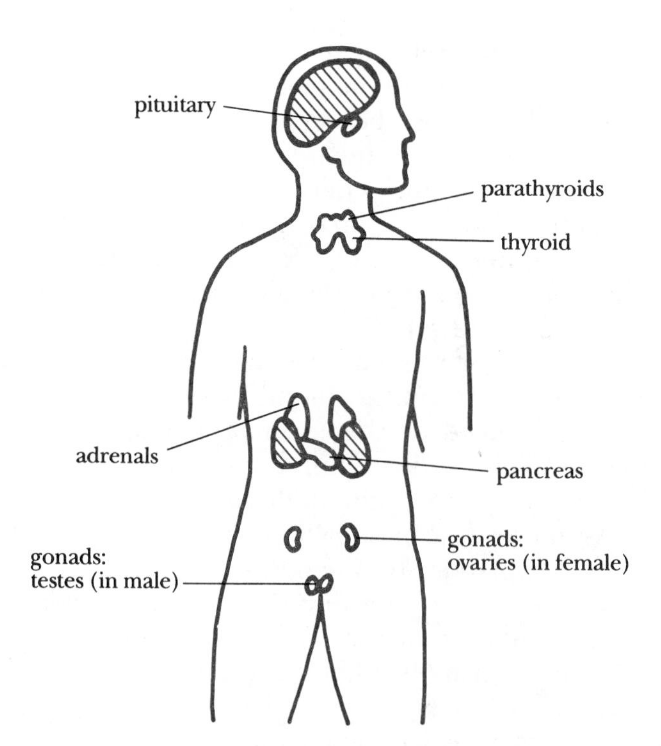

Figure 2–23.
Endocrine glands.

chemistry of the bloodstream and causes the pituitary gland to release more hormones.

Thyroid. The **thyroid gland** secretes a hormone that regulates the rate at which energy is produced and used by the body. A person with an overactive thyroid may be excitable, tense, nervous, and underweight. A person with an underactive thyroid may be overweight, inactive, slower, and prone to sleep more.

Can an underactive thyroid gland cause an individual to be overweight?

Parathyroids. The **parathyroids,** embedded in the thyroid, release a hormone that controls the calcium and phosphate levels in the blood. Calcium and phosphate affect the excitability of the nervous system. Muscle spasms or twitches may result from insufficient secretions of this hormone. Secretion of too much of this same hormone may produce drowsiness.

Pancreas. The **pancreas** secretes two hormones that work against each other to control the level of sugar in the blood. Improper functioning of the pancreas may produce conditions commonly referred to as sugar diabetes and low blood sugar with such behavioral effects as moodiness, chronic fatigue, irritability, or decreased mental activity.

What are some symptoms of sugar diabetes and low blood sugar?

What bodily changes occur when the adrenal glands secrete epinephrine and norepinephrine in response to stress?

Adrenals. The **adrenal glands** release epinephrine (adrenalin) and norepinephrine (noradrenalin) into the bloodstream, resulting in a number of important changes in the body, all of which prepare it for action. For example, heart rate and blood pressure are raised, stored sugar is released for quick energy, the muscles tense and receive more blood, the blood is prepared to clot more quickly, the blood vessels in the peripheral parts of the body constrict, all the body tissues become generally more tense, digestion stops, and the pupils of the eyes become larger. Other hormones are produced by the adrenal glands that regulate the sodium potassium level in the bloodstream. In addition, hormones that enable the body to resist stress are produced by the adrenal glands, which help prevent the depletion of the body's natural immune system, a condition that would leave the body vulnerable to infection and disease. Prolonged stress, however, can deplete the system.

Do males and females secrete the same hormones in the same amounts?

Gonads. The **gonads,** sex glands, are the **ovaries** in the female and the **testes** in the male. Hormones produced by the sex glands stimulate the reproductive organs to mature and are a factor in the distribution of the body fat. Hormones known as **androgens** are secreted primarily by the male sex gland and trigger the development of secondary sex characteristics such as beard growth and deepening of the voice at puberty. Hormones known as **estrogens** are secreted primarily by the female ovaries and play a role in such secondary sex characteristics as breast development. **Progesterones,** also secreted by the ovaries, create the menstrual cycle and prepare the female body for pregnancy, childbirth, and nursing of the newborn infant.

Hormones secreted by the ovaries may have a direct effect on a woman's moods. Androgens have an influence on sexual motivation. In most animals, hormones totally control sexual motivation; they serve as a driving force. In humans, sex hormones serve to sensitize people to erotic stimuli.

Because the size and development of the endocrine glands and the way they function may vary from person to person and because the glands sometimes malfunction due to disease or injury, hormone output may differ for individuals and may account for some of the variability in behavior of people.

APPLICATION OF BIOPSYCHOLOGY

Knowledge of the biological processes in the nervous system, the brain, and the endocrine system can be meaningful in everyday work-and-play behavior. In this section, a few instances will be considered.

Food

Research suggests that the brain is much more affected by its internal environment (the blood) than has been thought, and even the last meal may affect its environment. Diet has been demonstrated to have striking short-term effects on behavior.

Neuronutrition. Acetylcholine is found especially in the hippocampus, which plays a role in memory. Choline, used to make acetylcholine, is present in egg yolks, meat, fish, cereals, and legumes. Serotonin levels and levels of another neurotransmitter that affects sleep behavior are increased by a high-carbohydrate diet (Kolata, 1982). Lack of serotonin causes insomnia. Because serotonin inhibits the transmission of neural impulses, a lack of it allows for faster sensory transmission, and transmission may even be so fast that it leads to malfunction of normal perception. A chemical is found in many foods that is used in making norepinephrine, which controls blood pressure and may be involved in depression. What people eat does seem to have some affect on how much or how well they sleep as well as on their dreaming, their blood pressure, and their perception of the environment. This discovery explains why drinking a glass of warm milk and eating a lot of turkey have been named as activities that cause an individual to be sleepier.

Malnutrition. Malnutrition can be a factor in brain development affecting both the growth and sophistication of the nervous system. Experimental studies have shown distortions and shrinkage in brain structures in undernourished rats. Malnutrition can be a factor in mental retardation. Severe malnutrition, particularly during the first year or two of development, causes a brain to be smaller than it would be normally and causes structural changes that slow down the transmission of impulses and interfere with the processing of information. Because a child's brain has attained 75 percent of its adult size by 2 years of age, what the mother eats during prenatal development may give an individual an intellectual advantage or disadvantage.

Why is good nutrition especially important during prenatal development?

Special Diets. Understanding more about the chemistry of behavior has led to the formulation of many different special diets to control particular behaviors. Newborn babies are tested at birth to determine if they have the inherited inability to metabolize a specific protein (phenylketonuria—PKU), a condition that may result in mental retardation. If such a condition is found, mental retardation can be prevented by dietary restriction of specific proteins.

Special diets are sometimes effective in minimizing hyperactive behavior (Rimland, 1983). Additives in foods have been implicated in hyperactivity and allergies, and sometimes eliminating foods with such additives from the diet is effective in the control of such behaviors. Even an "anti-jet lag diet" has been developed at the Argonne National Laboratory, designed to fool the biological rhythmic activity built into the nervous system. The diet, which grew out of studies of body rhythms, helps an individual counteract the effects of a rhythmic dysfunction often referred to as jet jag that is experienced by some people when they travel long distances across several time zones. The diet includes eating lightly the day before a long flight and then eating foods such as eggs, cottage cheese, fish, salads, and fruit, all of which are low in both calories and carbohydrates. There may be more truth to the old adage, You are what you eat, than was once believed.

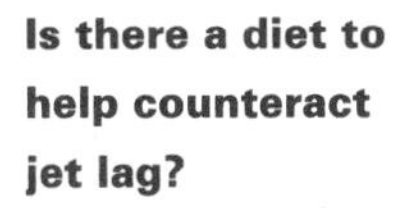

Is there a diet to help counteract jet lag?

Exercise

Exercise is a popular technique used today by many people to help cope with stress, improve cardiovascular and metabolic capacity, and experience an elevation in mood. The exercise needs to be strenuous for a long enough period of time to put an overload demand on the body. Such endurance or aerobic conditioning exercises include hiking, jogging, brisk walking, running, swimming, bicycling, calisthenics, and active sports.

Figure 2–24.
In general, people who exercise vigorously on a regular basis are less likely to develop heart disease and various other illnesses.

Stress and Illness. One way exercise seems to have an effect on behavior is by reducing the levels of epinephrine and norepinephrine in the bloodstream generally. Exercise accomplishes this by training the adrenal glands to respond to stress more efficiently. Recent research with previously nonrunning students indicates that pushing the heart and lungs to their maximum capacity by doing aerobic exercise for a semester causes the adrenal glands to respond with higher levels of epinephrine and norepinephrine in a stressful situation (Dienstbier, 1982). This response enables the person to deal with the stress without depleting the body's immune system as much. People who exercise on a regular basis are less likely to develop heart disease or diabetes and have fewer heart attacks and less severe heart attacks than people who are not active (see Figure 2–24). Some studies are even indicating a link between cancer and how a person responds to stress. Thus, there is some evidence that a person who exercises a lot will be ill less often.

What is speculated to account for the "runner's high"?

Brain Function. Endorphins have been shown to rise in the nervous system during a long-distance race (Colt, Wardlow, & Frantz, 1981), and it appears that regular, vigorous exercise increases endorphin levels even more. Because endorphins are the body's own pain killers working like morphine, people who exercise on a regular basis usually report that they feel better generally, experience more freedom from pain, have the ability to withstand more pain, and experience more peak experiences of exhilaration than when they do not exercise regularly. It has also been speculated that the "runner's high" may be caused by a temporary shift from left hemisphere dominance to right hemisphere dominance (Sachs, 1984).

Air

The air that we breathe in the environment, which is filled with gaseous molecules that have electrical charges (ions) attached, can also affect brain function. These ions may be negatively or positively charged. When negative ions predominate, the air is said to be negatively ionized, and when positive ions predominate, the air is said to be positively ionized.

Positive Ions. The air breathed seems to have an effect on neurotransmitters. Ionization of the air has a direct effect on the level of serotonin in the brain (Krueger, 1978). Hot, dry winds filled with a greater amount of positive ions have often been associated with outbreaks of suicide and violence, according to Krueger (1978). Krueger (1978) also states that negative ions seem to disappear in enclosed spaces and in crowded, polluted, urban areas.

Figure 2–25.
A person's mood seems to elevate as negative ionization increases.

Negative Ions. Air filled with a greater amount of negative ions such as air around waterfalls, beaches, and clean mountains has a refreshing and stimulating effect (see Figure 2–25). Krueger (1978) further notes that a person's mood seems to elevate as negative ionization increases. The implication is that the environment in which you work and live can have an effect on your behavior and may even explain short-term changes in behavior.

Common Drugs

Because a drug may be defined as any substance that alters the structure or functioning of the body when ingested, there are many drugs. In this section, only a few common drugs are brought to attention. Medications will not be discussed in this text. Drug abuse will be addressed further in later chapters in sections related to altered states of consciousness and substance abuse disorders.

Is alcohol a stimulant or a depressant?

Alcohol. Learning more about the biological functioning of the nervous system has provided a better understanding of how drugs affect behavior. Alcohol, an easily available and socially accepted drug, has profound effects on the mind. Almost all of the alcohol consumed enters the bloodstream directly without being digested. When it enters the stomach, about 20 percent of it passes through the stomach lining and enters the bloodstream. About 75 percent of it is absorbed into the bloodstream as it passes through the small intestine. The bloodstream carries the alcohol to the central nervous system where it slows down the reticular activating system, which results in a lessening of inhibitory control mechanisms in the cortex. Although alcohol may appear to be a stimulant because the release of normal inhibitions may produce a happy or euphoric feeling, it is a depressant. As the concentration of alcohol in the bloodstream increases, the drinker may gradually become sleepier; as other areas of the brain are affected, feelings of depression, nausea, and unhappiness may occur.

How does alcohol affect perception?

Alcohol in the bloodstream has varying effects on perceptual and judgmental functions. Perception of dim lights is heightened; perception of differences between brighter lights, colors, and depth is impaired. Even a small amount of alcohol interferes with the ability to discriminate between different pitches and rhythms; however, perception of loudness is not affected. Alcohol affects perception of time, causing time to seem to pass more quickly. Alcohol in the bloodstream also diminishes smell and taste perception. Excessive use may lead to the perception of things that are not really in the environment (hallucinations) either while alcohol is being consumed or during withdrawal. Even small amounts in the bloodstream cause dilation of the pupils, slight increases in blood pressure, and temporary elevation of blood-sugar levels. The effects of alcohol vary with the amount of alcohol in the bloodstream and with the weight and gender of the user (see Table 2–1).

Is one hemisphere of the brain more sensitive to alcohol than the other?

Studies on alcoholism using computerized axial tomography (CAT scan) to do a density analysis of the brain indicate that the left hemisphere of the brain is more sensitive physiologically to alcohol than the right hemisphere and that even in young, chronic alcoholics the left hemisphere of the brain already reveals significant changes (Alcoholics, 1981). A question to be answered by a firm is, Can a person who avoids alcohol function more efficiently on the

Table 2–1
Relationships between alcohol consumption and blood level, by gender and weight.

Absolute Alcohol (oz.)	Beverage Intake in 1 Hour	BLOOD ALCOHOL LEVELS (MG/100 ML) Female (100 lbs.)	Male (100 lbs.)	Female (150 lbs.)	Male (150 lbs.)	Female (200 lbs.)	Male (200 lbs.)
½	1 oz. spirits[a] 1 glass wine 1 can beer	.045	.037	.03	.025	.022	.019
1	2 oz. spirits 2 glasses wine 2 can beer	.090	.075	.06	.050	.045	.037
2	4 oz. spirits 4 glasses wine 4 cans beer	.180	.150	.12	.100	.090	.070
3	6 oz. spirits 6 glasses wine 6 cans beer	.270	.220	.18	.150	.130	.110
4	8 oz. spirits 8 glasses wine 8 cans beer	.360	.300	.24	.200	.180	.150
5	10 oz. spirits 10 glasses wine 10 cans beer	.450	.370	.30	.250	.220	.180

[a]All spirits are assumed to be 100 proof.

Note. Reproduced by permission from: Ray Oakley, *Drugs, Society, and Human Behavior* (p. 168), St. Louis, 1983, The C.V. Mosby Co.

job than if he or she consumes alcohol? A number of firms have established formal alcohol control programs.

How does nicotine affect the body?

Nicotine. Nicotine, a drug in cigarettes, seems to act both as a stimulant and as a depressant on the central nervous system. It seems to be able to act as a stimulant when a person is drowsy and as a relaxant when a person is tense (Stepney, 1983). It elevates heart rate and blood pressure, increases stomach activity, and constricts the peripheral blood vessels, and a person can become dependent on it. Evidence now suggests that a person who does not smoke or breathe secondary smoke from others who do smoke is healthier than if he or she did smoke or breathe secondary smoke. Thus, it is reasonable to assume that people will be able to perform better in work situations if they do not take nicotine into the body regularly.

How does caffeine affect the body?

Caffeine. The most widely used stimulant drug is caffeine found in coffee, tea, chocolate, and many soft drinks. It acts as a stimulant, raising the general level of activity in the nervous system. A stimulant produces an effect similar to that of a stressful event or threat, activating the sympathetic part of the nervous system to prepare the body for action. Some activation of the sympathetic nervous system may enhance performance, but people who consume too much caffeine may experience tremors, rapid heartbeat, overactivity, restlessness, or nausea.

What is one of the problem areas of industrial and organizational psychology?

People take many drugs—in medications of a nonprescription nature or medications prescribed by a physician. And of course, there is the illegal use of drugs. One of the problem areas of industrial and organizational psychology is the detection, management, control, and correction of ineffective work performance due to drug use or abuse.

Brain Tissue Transplants

Gaining more knowledge about the brain and nervous system is providing hope for people with brain disorders where previously there was no hope for a cure. Until recently the idea of reconnecting delicate brain tissue to the millions of neurons or doing a brain tissue transplant was unthinkable. Recent experiments with brain tissue transplants in rats are yielding promising results with aging and diseased brains.

Disease. Most of the initial research with brain tissue transplants has been aimed at Parkinson's disease, which involves the gradual loss of control over movement of the body parts. Researchers produced symptoms similar to Parkinson's disease in rats by destroying the part of the brain that produces the neurotransmitter dopamine involved in the control of movement. When the researchers transplanted cells taken from this part of the brain of unborn rat fetuses into the "diseased" rats' brains, the abnormal movement symptoms of Parkinson's disease were greatly reduced (Freed, Cannon-Spoor, Krauthamer, Hoffer, and Wyatt, 1983).

Has a brain tissue transplant ever been done successfully on a human?

In 1983, at the University of Lund in Sweden, Dr. Anders Bjorklund performed a tissue transplant on a human patient suffering from Parkinson's disease who reportedly was so paralyzed by the disease that she could only lay in bed "stiff as a board." Dr. Bjorklund took dopamine-producing cells from the adrenal glands and placed them in the patient's brain. The patient showed some improvement in movement ability after the transplant (McKean, 1984).

Aging. Experiments in which brain tissue from rat fetuses was implanted into the brains of old rats whose ability to learn certain tasks was very poor because of their aged brain resulted in a significant improvement in ability to learn the tasks (Gage, Bjorklund, Stenevi, Dunnett, & Kelly, 1984). Perhaps in the next few years brain deterioration from aging, injury, disease, or malfunctioning neurons can be alleviated or even cured through such transplants. And scientists are even imagining a far-off future when entire lobes of the brain might be transplanted from a donor to a person.

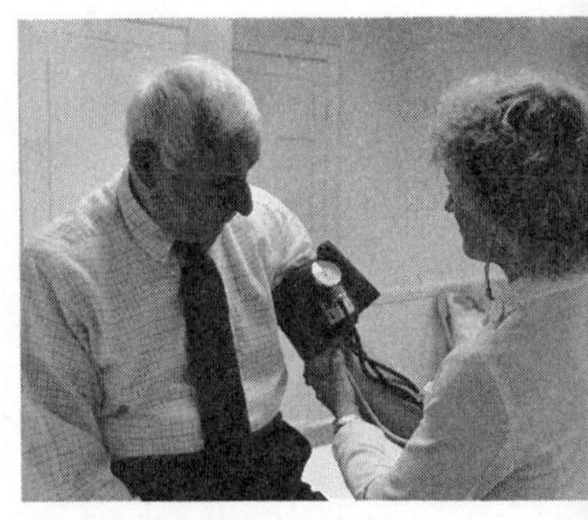

Figure 2–26.
The worker's physical functioning is important to the employer. Many companies provide medical examinations for employees.

Biological processes have an impact on behavior and need to be understood to explain people's behavior (see Figure 2–26). Although much new knowledge of the basic functioning of the nervous and endocrine systems has been gained during the last few years, much of what is important about the brain and its interrelated systems still remains to be learned. Many questions about human behavior cannot be explained until more of the incredible complexities of the brain are understood. Research on the human brain is the new frontier in the study of human behavior.

SUMMARY

1. The nervous system is composed of billions of specialized cells called neurons that are surrounded and protected by 10 times as many glial cells.
2. In addition to the nucleus, the main cell body, and the membrane that encloses the main cell body (common to all body cells), a neuron

contains (a) dendrites to receive messages, (b) an axon and branching axons to carry messages through the cell, (c) terminal branches to send the messages out to other neurons, and sometimes (d) a myelin sheath to speed along the messages.

3. Afferent neurons are close to cells in sense organs and receive input from the environment directly from those cells. Efferent neurons are located close to cells in muscles and send messages to the muscles that elicit behavior. Interneurons carry messages to and receive messages from other neurons in the brain and spinal cord.
4. Neural impulses are received in a neuron at receptor sites and are transmitted through neurons by depolarization of the cell (axonal transmission). Neural impulses are transmitted across the synapse from one neuron to another by chemical substances released by the terminal branches of the neuron called neurotransmitters (synaptic transmission), according to the classic view.
5. Some neurotransmitters have an excitatory effect and others have an inhibitory effect. Acetylcholine, dopamine, norepinephrine, and serotonin are well-known neurotransmitters.
6. Neuromodulators are chemical substances, often called peptides, produced in various places in the body and released into the bloodstream to interact with neurotransmitters and affect the way the neurotransmitters function.
7. The two main divisions of the nervous system are the peripheral system, which is made up of the somatic and autonomic nervous systems, and the central system, which is made up of the spinal cord and brain.
8. The two subsystems of the autonomic nervous system are the parasympathetic system and the sympathetic system, which work together but achieve different results. The sympathetic system prepares the body to react to stress, and the parasympathetic system tells the body to return to normal functioning.
9. Some of the brain structures in the hindbrain are (a) the medulla, which controls reflex behaviors such as breathing and heart rate, (b) the pons, which serves a connective function, and (c) the cerebellum, which is involved in control of motor behavior.
10. The (a) thalamus, which functions as a relay station, (b) hypothalamus, which functions as a thermostat, (c) corpus callosum, which serves a connective function, and (d) neocortex, which covers the two hemispheres of the brain, are structures in the forebrain.
11. The neocortex consists of (a) a right and a left hemisphere each containing a temporal lobe with the sites for hearing, (b) an occipital lobe with the sites for vision, (c) a frontal lobe with the sites for uniquely human mental processes, and (d) a parietal lobe with the sites for integrated sensory input.

12. The neocortex has specific areas for specific responsibilities such as (a) the motor projection areas at the back of the frontal lobes, (b) the feeling (sensitivity to touch) projection areas at the front of the parietal lobes, and (c) the areas located at various places on the cortex that combine impulses from different senses to create meaningful impressions such as in speech, language, and thought.
13. In general, the left hemisphere of the brain is dominant and governs the right side of the body and handles language and analytical thought; the right hemisphere governs the left side of the body and handles nonverbal sounds, artistic and spatial abilities, and creative thinking.
14. Three types of hemispheric organization are found in left-handed people: similar to right-handers, reverse of right-handers, and language and spatial abilities in both hemispheres.
15. The brain sets up systems involving several parts to perform functions; the limbic system is related to motivation and emotion, the reticular activating system is related to level of awareness, and the biological rhythms system is related to body cycles.
16. The pituitary, thyroid, parathyroids, pancreas, adrenals, and gonads (sex glands consisting of the ovaries in the female and the testes in the male) are endocrine glands that secrete hormones into the bloodstream, have a very direct and immediate effect on behavior, and help to maintain the chemical balance necessary for the proper functioning of the nervous system.
17. The pituitary gland, as does the hypothalamus, manufactures and secretes peptides (neuromodulators) into the bloodstream, endorphins being well-known peptides.
18. The thyroid gland regulates the rate at which energy is produced and used; the parathyroids control excitability of the nervous system; the pancreas controls blood sugar levels in the blood; the adrenals prepare the body for action; and the gonads stimulate development of reproductive organs and secondary sex characteristics and control the processes of reproduction.
19. Relationships between food, exercise, environment (air), and drugs and behavior are being explained through a knowledge of the biological functioning of the nervous system. Brain tissue transplants offer new hope to people with brain disorders.

KEY TERMS AND CONCEPTS

Neurons
Dendrites
Axon
Myelin sheath
Terminal branches
Afferent neuron
Efferent neuron
Interneurons
Glial cells
Nerve
Synapse
Ions

Electrons
Polarization
Depolarization
Receptor sites
Neurotransmitters
Computerized axial tomography
Positron emission tomography
Magnetic resonance imager
Acetylcholine
Norepinephrine
Dopamine
Serotonin
Neuromodulators
Endorphins
Local circuits
Peripheral nervous system
Central nervous system
Somatic nervous system
Autonomic nervous system
Parasympathetic nervous system
Sympathetic nervous system
Hindbrain
Medulla
Pons
Cerebellum
Midbrain
Forebrain
Thalamus
Hypothalamus
Neocortex
Corpus callosum
Temporal lobes
Occipital lobes
Frontal lobes
Parietal lobes
Limbic system
Hippocampus
Reticular activating system
Biorhythms
Endocrine glands
Hormones
Peptides
Pituitary gland
Thyroid gland
Parathyroids
Pancreas
Adrenal glands
Gonads
Ovaries
Testes
Androgens
Estrogens
Progesterone

QUESTIONS FOR REVIEW

1. Name and describe the function of four structures unique to a neuron.
2. How do afferent, efferent, and interneurons differ?
3. Explain how the neuron depolarizes.
4. Summarize what is known about the chemical activity at a synapse and synaptic transmission.
5. What are the two major divisions of the nervous system, their subsystems, and the function of each?
6. What are the three divisions of the brain, and what is the name, location, and function of each of the major parts in each division?
7. What is the name of and the function of each of the four lobes of the neocortex?
8. How do the right and left hemispheres of the brain differ in both right- and left-handed people?
9. Name the endocrine glands, give their locations, and describe the major function of the hormone or hormones secreted by each of the glands.
10. How have food, exercise, air, alcohol, nicotine, and caffeine been found to affect the mind?

TEST YOURSELF

1. The specialized cells of the nervous system are called ________________.
2. When activated by energy in the environment, the cells in the sense organs send messages that are received directly by (a) afferent neurons (b) efferent neurons (c) interneurons (d) muscles.
3. The part of the brain that functions as a relay station for messages coming in from the sense organs and directs the messages to particular areas of the brain is the ________________.
4. Which part of the brain functions as a thermostat for the body and plays an important role in maintaining the needed balance for survival?
5. Generally, the left hemisphere of the neocortex governs the functions of the ________________ side of the body and ________________ and ________________ thought.
6. The limbic system (a) is an interconnection of several structures in the center core of the brain (b) is related to motivation and emotion (c) includes the pleasure centers of the brain (d) a, b, and c.
7. Which lobe of the brain is the site for receiving and interpreting messages from the eye?
8. Which endocrine gland is located in the brain and often referred to as the master gland of the body because it produces hormones that control the other endocrine glands?
9. The main effect of alcohol is on the brain, and it (a) increases activity in the nervous system (b) decreases activity in the nervous system (c) affects only motor functioning (d) affects the lowest area of the brain, the medulla, first.
10. The central nervous system is composed of (a) the sympathetic and parasympathetic systems (b) the brain and spinal cord (c) the somatic and autonomic nervous systems (d) a, b, and c.
11. The transmission of the message across the space that separates the terminal branches of a neuron from the dendrites of the next neuron is referred to as ________________ transmission.
12. The ________________ nervous system, a subdivision of the ________________ nervous system, arouses the body to handle either mental or physical stress placed upon it.
13. The part of the brain that is related to levels of awareness and is important in sleep and attention is the ________________ system.
14. Mood seems to elevate as the air is filled with a greater amount of negative ions. T or F
15. The first neurotransmitter identified was (a) acetylcholine (b) serotonin (c) reserpine (d) cocaine.
16. Endorphins and other peptides are called ________________ because they float around in the bloodstream after being manufactured

and released from some place in the body and interact with and modulate the way neurotransmitters function.

17. Synaptic activity can occur in small areas of dendrites from very weak stimulation that is below the threshold for depolarization of the cell. T or F
18. Most left-handed people have language areas on the right hemisphere of the brain. T or F
19. Exercise seems to have an effect on behavior by training the ________________ glands to respond to stress more efficiently, thus affecting the levels of ________________ and ________________ in the bloodstream and lessening the likelihood of many illnesses.
20. The cerebellum, which is involved in the control of motor behavior, especially balance and coordination, is located in the (a) forebrain (b) midbrain (c) hindbrain (d) neocortex.

APPLICATIONS

A. Bindra and Jack Block, a married couple, do not get along very well. He has a job at a company that requires him to be at work at 7:30 a.m. Jack has a problem with getting up and getting to work on time. Bindra must "nag, nag, nag" every work morning to get him up to go to work. She accuses him of being irresponsible and lazy. At night, however, he is wide awake, alert, and active—wants to go out or stay up late. Bindra is tired by nightfall and likes to go to bed early. He accuses her of just not wanting to be with him. They also quarrel a lot about setting the thermostat for the temperature in the house to be comfortable.

Bindra and Jack live in a part of town that is old, crowded, and has several manufacturing plants nearby, and the air is known from testing to contain a heavy concentration of positive ions. Since Bindra feels so tired, exhausted, and depressed by nightfall, she usually has a glass of wine. They also have problems in making family decisions. Jack reasons logically and can logically and mathematically show the advantages and disadvantages of particular decisions. Bindra seems to make decisions based more on intuition and feeling. Bindra is creative, artistic, excels in playing the piano, and likes to listen to music. Jack is good at speaking and often gives talks publicly. Bindra is left-handed and writes with a straight hand below the line. They generally feel irritable and depressed.

1. Is there any psychological evidence to suggest that Jack may not be irresponsible and lazy, and that he might function better on a job that offered flexible scheduling or a later work shift? If so, what?
2. Is there any psychological evidence to suggest that if Jack and Bindra moved to a different location, perhaps near a large body of water, they might be in a better general mood? If so, what?

3. Is having the glass of wine a good thing for Bindra to pep her up and help her be more active during the evening?
4. Which hemisphere of the brain do you think is probably dominant for Jack? for Bindra?

B. Curt Card is having trouble on the job. He can't concentrate, and his thinking seems to be slowing down. He is uptight, restless, and always hurrying around in a frenzy. Often, he has trouble going to sleep at night and stays wide awake for hours. In fact, he even experiences tremors occasionally and often feels nauseous.

Curt is primarily a vegetarian, eating eggs or meats only rarely. He doesn't like fish and positively cannot stand to eat liver. He doesn't care much for beans or legumes of any type. Early in the morning he doesn't have much of an appetite and anyway he doesn't have time to eat, so he usually grabs a cup or two of coffee. In fact, he is drinking more and more coffee all through the day in an effort to keep going and make it through the day. He does not set aside a regular time each day for exercise and is so busy he never finds time for an hour of exercise. Anyway, he just doesn't feel like exercising. He tries to avoid all foods high in carbohydrates, especially late in the day, as he is very weight conscious.
Assuming Curt has no medical problems:

1. Would you recommend to Curt that he change his vegetarian diet? Why or why not?
2. Do you think the coffee is helping Curt make it through the day? Why or why not?
3. Do you think Curt's logic that he doesn't have time for exercise and doesn't feel well enough to exercise is good logic? Why or why not?
4. Would you recommend any diet changes that might help Curt's insomnia? If so, what?

SUGGESTIONS FOR FURTHER READING

Bloom, F. E., Lazerson, A., & Hofstadter, L. (1984). *Brain, mind, and behavior.* New York: W. H. Freeman.

Written to accompany the 1984 Public Broadcasting System television series "The Brain," it focuses on recent discoveries related to the brain and is prolific with illustrations, drawings, and color photographs.

The brain (Special issue). (1979). *Scientific American, 241* (3).

The entire issue consisting of 11 articles is devoted to the discussion of the structure and function of the brain and nervous system. An excellent overview with discussion of future applications.

Davis, J. (1984). *Endorphins: New waves in brain chemistry.* New York: Doubleday.

A discussion of the function of endorphins in human behavior that is written with the student and general reader in mind.

Hunt, M. (1982). *The universe within: A new science explores the human mind.* New York: Simon and Schuster.

Many aspects of the mind such as physiology and evolution of the brain; thinking, remembering, and problem solving; and artificial intelligence as compared to human intelligence are discussed in this book written for the layperson.

Kolb, B., & Whishaw, I. Q. (1985). *Fundamentals of human neuropsychology* (2nd ed.). New York: W. H. Freeman.

The entire field of neuropsychology is summarized quite well in this book.

Levinthal, C. F. (1983). *Introduction of physiological psychology* (2nd ed.). Englewood Cliffs, NJ: Prentice-Hall.

Although most topics general to physiological psychology are covered, hormones, neurotransmitters, and chemistry of the nervous system receive particular attention.

Teyler, T. J. (1984). *A primer of psychobiology: Brain and behavior* (2nd ed.). New York: W. H. Freeman.

A nontechnical explanation of the brain is given in this introduction to biological psychology.

Springer S. P., & Deutsch, G. (1985). *Left brain, right brain* (2nd ed.). New York: W. H. Freeman.

A revised edition of an award-winning book that is easy to read and gives a thorough and interesting survey of the latest research related to the similarities and differences of the two hemispheres of the brain.

CHAPTER 3

HEREDITY AND DEVELOPMENT

Objectives

When you have completed your study of chapter 3, you should be able to:

1. Describe, using proper terminology, genetic materials, processes by which new cells and gametes are produced, fertilization, and how a person's sex is determined.
2. Discuss maturation as to what it is, trends, and alteration.
3. Explain what is meant by and give an example of a dominant, recessive, codominant, polygenic, and sex-linked characteristic.
4. Give several examples of characteristics resulting from defective genes and chromosomal abnormalities.
5. Describe the three stages of prenatal development and the impact of specific teratogens on prenatal development.
6. Discuss birth as to setting, stages, and types.
7. Describe the appearance, behavior, and capacities of the normal human newborn.
8. Give some milestones in the pattern of physical and motor development in infancy and childhood.
9. Briefly trace the early pattern of the development of sensation, perception, and language.
10. Identify the psychological tasks to be mastered, according to Erikson, from birth through the childhood years, and give the approximate age for achievement of each task.

What is to be gained by studying human behavior?

The biological factors influencing behavior are numerous. Some of these were discussed in the preceding chapter, but in addition, hereditary endowment, growth, and maturation are significant factors in personal development and in the shaping of behavior. These factors must be considered when attempting to understand the behavior of people. Understanding the normal processes of development will help you put your own life into perspective and help you understand others who are older or younger or different in some way. Also, both as a society and as individuals, much time, effort, and money is directed toward the rearing and developing of children because they are the adults—the workers, the managers, the decision makers, the teachers, and the parents—of tomorrow. By knowing more about human development, perhaps we can assure that a better future world will evolve.

The role of heredity and early development in a person's characteristics is the focus of this chapter. Specifically, the mechanics of individual heredity are explained, and the **prenatal** (from conception to birth), **perinatal** (during birth, which includes shortly before and immediately after birth), and **neonatal** (newborn) periods of life are described. The latter part of this chapter includes a discussion of the concept of development during the **postnatal** (after birth until death) period especially as it relates to infancy and childhood. Special attention is given to physical growth and motor development, development of sensation and perception, language development, and psychological tasks to be mastered in infancy and childhood. Other aspects of the postnatal period and areas of development are discussed in chapter 4.

HEREDITY

A human being can be viewed as having an evolutionary heredity extending back to the first traces of life, thus having a kinship with all other organisms. Also, a person can be viewed as having a species heredity in that people are the potential possessors of all the limitations and capacities with which humans are endowed. For example, people cannot fly through the air or breathe under water without equipment, but people do have a nervous system that enables them to invent ways of adapting to the environment. Most important to the psychologist, however, is a person's own individual heredity. People inherit from their parents specific structures, characteristics, capacities, and limitations that account for their physical characteristics and that have a profound effect on their behavior throughout life.

Which part of a person's heredity is most important to the psychologist?

SOCIOBIOLOGY

Sociobiologists claim that much human behavior is rooted in preservation of the genes, which are the carriers of heredity. Most people do not like to think that their genes control their behavior, but that is what sociobiologists claim. Sociobiology is defined as the systematic study of the biological basis of all social behavior (Wilson, 1975). Sociobiologists today point out that it is the survival of the genes, not the survival of the individual, that matters. For example, acts of self-sacrifice for others are explained in terms of their benefits to the survival of one's own gene pool. Some psychologists do not accept this theory and feel that more research is needed.

Human Reproduction

Reproduction is the mechanism by which the thread of life is sustained. It is the process by which a single cell duplicates its genetic

Figure 3–1.
Reproduction, the duplication of genetic material, allows for growth and repair.

material. As illustrated in Figures 3–1 and 3–2, this duplication of genetic material allows for growth and repair of an organism, and it is also the means by which genetic material is passed from generation to generation to maintain the life of the species.

Genetic Material. Human reproduction involves the uniting of a **sperm** from the male with an **ovum** (egg) from the female. Because the sperm and the ovum each possesses 23 **chromosomes,** their union forms a cell of 46 chromosomes. The chromosomes are the carriers of heredity. A chromosome is a complex structure composed of thousands of **genes** threaded together like a string of beads. Each gene, the basic unit of heredity, is composed of a biochemical substance called *deoxyribonucleic acid (DNA),* which carries chemically coded instructions that determine physical appearance, body functioning, and growth. Chemically, DNA is composed of

Figure 3–2.
Reproduction is the means by which genetic material is passed from generation to generation.

What constitutes the genetic code that determines a person's physical appearance, body functioning, and growth?

four chemical bases that may be arranged in an almost infinite number of ways. The particular arrangement that exists in a given chain of DNA molecules is thought to constitute the genetic code responsible for the creation of a particular hereditary characteristic. The particular variations in the arrangement of these four chemical bases account for differences in living organisms.

Fertilization. When a sperm penetrates an egg's membrane, **conception** or fertilization is said to have occurred. The usual means of human fertilization is by sperm being released from the penis of the male into the vagina of the female and then the sperm migrating to an ovum (egg) in the fallopian tube (see Color Figure 3–3). Sperm cells and egg cells (with only 23 chromosomes) are called **gametes.** The newly formed cell containing 46 chromosomes in 23 pairs, formed by the union of the sperm with its 23 single chromosomes and the ovum with its 23 single chromosomes, is called a **zygote.**

Mitosis. In a process called **mitosis,** the zygote divides within a few hours to form two new cells of 46 chromosomes, each cell having identical genetic material to that of the original zygote. The strands of DNA pull apart in the middle where two chemical bases are connected, much like the unzipping of a zipper. Each chemical base then picks up a new matching chemical base from the surrounding material that is identical to the one from which it separated. In a few hours, the process is repeated with the two newly formed cells dividing in the same manner to yield four new cells, and in a few more hours these four cells divide to yield eight cells. The cells stay together to form a cluster (see Color Figure 3–4) resembling "the clustered seeds of a berry" (Harris, 1986). Mitosis continues on and on to form eventually the body of a person containing billions and billions of cells. In the case of identical twins, something unusual seems to happen in the first division of the zygote that causes the two new cells not to remain clustered together, so a cluster then forms from each of them. Identical twins develop from one single fertilized egg and thus have identical chromosomes (see Figure 3–5).

Figure 3–5.
Identical twins develop from one and the same fertilized egg.

Meiosis. To produce the sperm and ova, specialized reproductive or germ cells that are already present at birth divide in a special way in a process called **meiosis.** During meiosis, the chromosomal material in the cell makes a copy of itself as in mitosis, and then the original 23 pairs (46 chromosomes) migrate to one end of the cell as the duplicated 23 pairs (46 chromosomes) migrate to the opposite end. As the migrating pairs move close together, genes may cross over from one chromosome to another before the cell completely divides. In a second division, one of the chromosomes in a pair moves to one end of the cell while the other chromosome of the pair moves to the other end, and the cell divides to form two new cells of 23 single chromosomes each—half the full number needed for a zygote. Thus, in a two-step process four gametes are formed from a germ cell.

Theoretically, the 23 chromosomes in a sperm coming from the father can occur in one of 2^{23} or 8,388,608 different combinations, and the same can be true of the 23 chromosomes coming from the mother. Thus, the same male and same female theoretically can produce 64 billion genetically different offspring without even considering the crossing over of genes. The chance that there will ever be two people exactly alike genetically, except for identical twins, is almost nil.

Who produces more gametes—a male or a female, or do they produce about the same number?

Immature sperm cells and egg cells are present in male testes and in female ovaries at birth. When an individual reaches puberty and adolescence at about 12 years of age, hormones stimulate the maturation of the gametes. The genetic material then divides, and in males about 200 million sperm are produced each day throughout adulthood and stored in the testes. About 250 to 500 million sperm may be released in one ejaculation. In females, mature ova are produced in the ovaries, and one egg is released from one of the ovaries about every 28 days, to possibly be fertilized by a sperm, until menopause. Sometimes two or more eggs may be released by an ovary rather than one as is the norm. If two eggs are fertilized by sperm, two zygotes are formed and nonidentical twins develop. Because these twins develop from two separate fertilized eggs, they do not have the same genetic material even though they develop simultaneously.

Does the genetic material from the mother or from the father determine the sex of a child?

Sex Determination. The chromosome from the male and the chromosome from the female that form a pair in a zygote are alike except for those labeled the 23rd pair. This pair carries the genes that determine an individual's sex and may consist of two different types—X and Y chromosomes. Males have one of each type with the 23rd pair consisting of an X chromosome and a Y chromosome, whereas females have two X chromosomes. All ova (eggs) then contain an X chromosome, but a sperm may contain either an X or a Y chromosome. If a sperm containing a Y fertilizes an egg, the newly formed cell or zygote will have an X chromosome and a Y chromosome and a male will develop. If a sperm containing an X fertilizes an egg, the zygote will have two X chromosomes and a female will develop. Color Figure 3–6 illustrates the mechanics of heredity that determine the sex of a person.

Maturation

What is meant by the term *maturation*?

Changes occur in people's appearance, capacities, and behavior as they grow older. In this section, the role of heredity in these changes will be clarified.

The Concept. The chemically coded instructions in the DNA composition of the genes serve as a biochemical blueprint for the construction of the person—the size, shape, and functioning of every part of the body. These instructions determine physical characteristics such as eye color, and they even influence nonphysical processes of development such as personality and intelligence. **Maturation** refers to the control that the genes exert over the unfolding of biological events from conception to death. Maturation produces changes in the nervous system and other bodily structures that in turn make possible the appearance of certain behaviors. For example, the development of physical abilities is related to the maturation of the skeletal, muscular, and nervous systems. The maturation of the cortex of the brain is related to language and growth of intelligence as well as the development of motor skills and other behaviors. The voice change in the male and the graying of the hair are examples of maturation. Maturation refers to bodily and behavioral changes that are brought about by the action of inborn mechanisms, growth, and the passage of time rather than by learning or environmental experience.

General Trends. Three identifiable trends are observed in maturation. One general trend is seen in the head-downward progression in physical growth and purposeful movements. The head develops sooner in proportion to the lower part of the body, and head movements come under control before movements of the legs and feet (see Figure 3–7). Another general trend is the center-outward progression. The center portions of the body develop and come under control before the peripheral parts. For example, the heart develops physically before the arms. Children can control the trunks of their bodies enough to turn over or sit up before they can control their fingers enough to write. Another general trend is the progression from massive, global, and undifferentiated responses to specific, integrated responses. An infant's response to anger may involve the entire body, but an older child's response to anger may be limited to striking or shouting.

Interaction. Although some hereditary differences appear from the time of birth, the development of many behavioral characteristics depends on the interaction between heredity and envi-

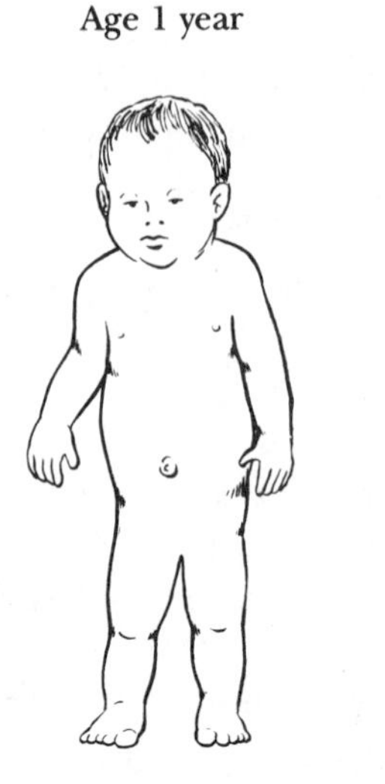

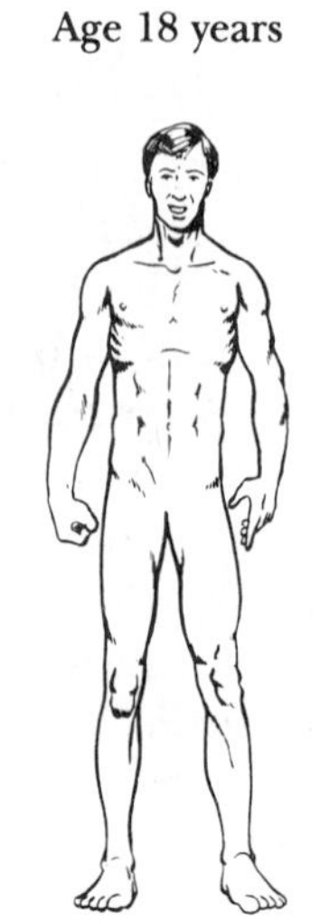

Figure 3–7.
Growth occurs in a head-downward progression so that the head reaches full growth sooner than the legs. This accounts for the change in body proportions.

ronment and the time when the environmental experience occurs. Heredity seems to provide a framework for physical and behavioral development by providing personal potentials and limitations that are altered by environmental factors such as learning, nutrition, disease, or culture. Physical characteristics such as height, bone structure, hair color, and eye color depend more on heredity than environment. Psychologists are particularly interested in the degree to which psychological characteristics such as ability, temperament, and emotional stability are inherited and the degree to which the environment or experience accounts for these characteristics. The environment can be altered or manipulated to bring about particular results in development. The controversy over heredity versus environment as determinants of human behavior has been particularly intense over the years and has now evolved into a concept that considers their interaction.

What is meant by a critical or sensitive period in an individual's life?

Sometimes environmental conditions will have a greater effect on a behavior at a particular time or affect the behavior of an individual if and only if the conditions occur at certain times in the maturational process. These periods, referred to as **critical periods** or sensitive periods, exist when a set of environmental conditions has an optimal effect. For example, a specific skill may be learned at a later time but with more difficulty than if mastered during a critical period. Critical periods usually correspond to times of rapid growth or change. A readiness for learning requires maturation. Physical structures must be mature before practice will establish a skill.

Laws of Heredity

The 23 pairs of chromosomes from the father and mother produce gene pairs, each with biochemical instructions for the formation of a particular physical characteristic or behavior. An interesting phenomenon about genetic mechanisms is what happens when the two genes of a pair do not give the same instructions for the development of a characteristic.

Dominant and Recessive Genes. A gene may be a **dominant gene,** meaning that it predominates another gene, or it may be a **recessive gene,** meaning that it defers to the dominant gene. If a person has two dominant genes or one dominant and one recessive gene, the characteristic controlled by those genes will reflect the dominant gene. Only if two recessive genes are paired will the recessive gene determine the characteristic (see Figure 3–8). Examples of dominant characteristics are dark skin color, dark hair color, dark eye color, full lips, dimpled cheeks or chin, freckled face, premature grayness, high cheekbones, narrow nose bridge, and abundant body hair. Examples of recessive characteristics are light skin color, blonde or red hair, straight hair, attached earlobe, blue eyes, thin lips, and broad nose bridge. Sometimes two genes can be codominate as when the offspring of a Negro parent and a Caucasian parent has light brown skin.

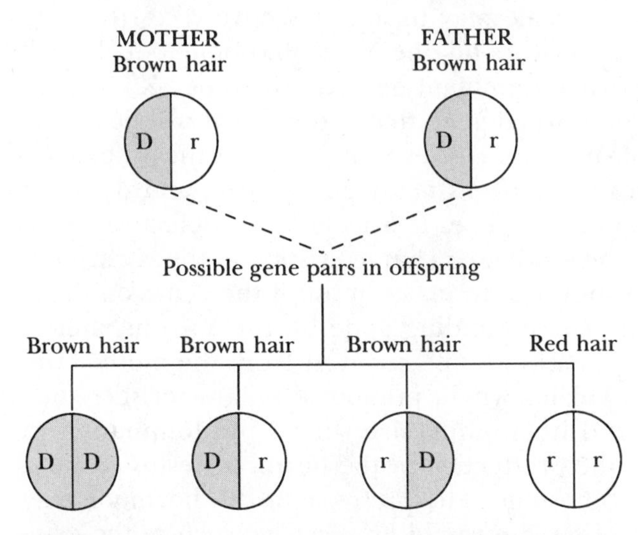

Figure 3–8.
Transmission of hair color by dominant and recessive genes.

Can some traits be determined by the interaction of several genes?

Some characteristics may be influenced by a variety of genes operating in a complex interaction. Important human characteristics such as intelligence, personality, temperament, physical structure, and probably also susceptibility to some forms of mental illness are predominantly **polygenic**—they are the result of the interactive effects of many genes. These traits are likely to show continuous variations from one extreme to the other rather than fall in distinct categories as do single-gene-determined traits. A number of studies (Buss & Plomin, 1975; Vandenberg, 1967) suggest that there is a hereditary basis for at least three aspects of temperament—activity, emotionality, and sociability. Some people have higher levels of activity and are more energetic and vigorous as they go about life. People differ in how aroused they become by events and how much emotion they feel. Some people desire the company of others and seem to enjoy interacting with people more than other people. Of course, environmental factors and experience may influence these characteristics.

Why are some recessive faulty gene traits found primarily in males?

Sex-Linked Characteristics. The 23rd pair of chromosomes contains the genes that determine sex and other characteristics that are referred to as **sex-linked characteristics.** For example, the genes necessary for the formation of the cells of the eye that make color vision possible are carried by the sex chromosomes. The gene related to hemophilia, a disease that prevents blood from clotting, is also on this pair. A female may have a defective recessive gene for one of these characteristics on one X chromosome, but she will most likely have a normal dominant gene on the other X chromosome of the pair. The normal gene that is dominant will be active, so the defect will not show up. However, in the male the Y chromosome is shorter, does not have as many genes on it, and does not provide a normal dominant gene. If a male has a defective recessive gene for one of the sex-linked characteristics on the X chromosome, the defect will show up. In males, most of the genes on the X chromosome have no corresponding gene on the Y; thus, almost all the genes on the X chromosome received from the mother will be expressed. This explains why a number of characteristics such as color blindness and hemophilia are found predominantly in males. The gene for the production of the hormone testosterone is present on the Y chromosome. The presence of this hormone may stimulate genes that otherwise would be recessive such as the gene that determines baldness. Thus, baldness is primarily a male trait (see Figure 3–9).

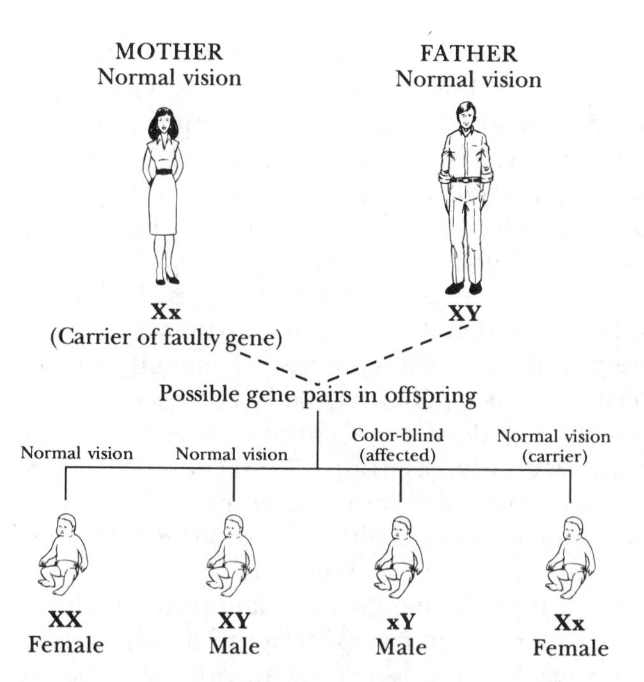

NOTE: There is no gene for a sex-linked trait on the Y chromosone. This chart applies for any sex-linked trait. There is a 50% chance for a male to be affected or a 50% chance to be normal. There is a 50% chance for a female to be a carrier or a 50% chance of not being a carrier.

Figure 3–9.
Diagram of how inheritance of sex-linked traits work.

Disorders. Occasionally, a recessive gene that may produce an undesirable trait such as albinism—a condition in which an enzyme needed to form the substance that pigments the skin, hair, and eyes is lacking—may be handed down. Other examples are the gene that prevents tasting certain bitter substances and genes that produce deformities such as more than 10 fingers or toes. PKU—inability to metabolize a specific protein, sickle-cell anemia—abnormal blood cells, Tay-Sachs—inability to metabolize fats, and diabetes—production of insufficient insulin to metabolize sugar are also the result of undesirable recessive genes.

Some disorders are caused by an abnormal number of chromosomes. Most of the time in meiosis, the pairs of chromosomes divide perfectly and all gametes have 23 single chromosomes.

Is it possible for a person to have only one chromosome or three or more chromosomes in a chromosome pair?

Occasionally, however, an error occurs and a gamete may have an extra chromosome or be one short. A few individuals have only a single X chromosome instead of a pair of sex chromosomes, so they have only 45 chromosomes instead of the usual 46 in their body cells. The external genitals are female, but the internal female organs are poorly developed and conception may be impossible. A few individuals have three sex chromosomes, such as XXY or XYY. The external genitals of an XXY person are male, but the individual may exhibit some female traits such as breast development and smooth-textured skin. Some degree of mental retardation usually is associated with the X0 and the XXY chromosomes. About one in 1,000 males has the extra Y chromosome. Early studies (Jacobs, Brunton, Melville, Brittain, & McClemont, 1965) showed that these males were taller on the average and that they showed up in prison populations in slightly disproportionate numbers. Mental retardation was not noted, however.

Figure 3–10.
An individual with Down's syndrome.

Down's syndrome, a type of mental retardation in which the individual has distinctive facial features (see Figure 3–10), is commonly referred to as *mongolism* and is associated with the presence of an extra chromosome. Down's people have 47 chromosomes in their body cells instead of the normal 46, the extra one being on the 21st pair (see Figure 3–11). The likelihood of Down's syndrome increases with the age of the parents. Seemingly, the genetic material in older reproductive cells is more likely to divide improperly. Down's syndrome is the most common of all birth defects with more than 5,000 children being born with this condition annually (Harris, 1986).

Genetic Therapy

Can a person find out if he or she is a carrier of some recessive faulty gene?

Genetic therapy, particularly counseling, is now available to prospective parents. Blood tests can determine whether or not a person is a carrier of some recessive genes. Probabilities can be computed concerning the appearance of particular characteristics. Some genetic disorders can be diagnosed after pregnancy occurs, and advances are being made in the ability to modify genetic material.

Counseling. Genetic counseling is becoming more common as knowledge of inheritance patterns increases. For those who are known carriers of defective or undesirable genes or who are suspected to be at high risk as carriers, counseling can be very helpful in enabling them to make informed decisions concerning child-

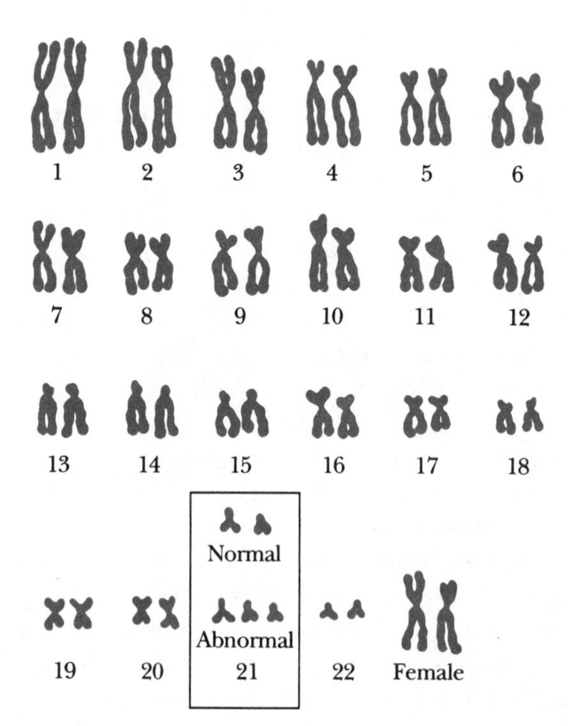

Figure 3–11.
Down's syndrome is caused by an extra chromosome being on the 21st pair.

bearing. When carrier or high-risk parents elect to have a child, a genetic diagnosis can be made by studying cast-off cells taken during pregnancy. The 16th week of pregnancy is the optimal time for such a study. Many genetic abnormalities can be diagnosed by counting the chromosomes to determine whether the fetus has a normal number. Of course, further counseling may be needed in making the decision as to whether to continue the pregnancy if genetic abnormalities are found.

Can parents find out before a child is born, even soon after conception, if there is a chromosomal abnormality?

Genetic Engineering. Advances made recently in the fields of genetics and medicine indicate that the ability to modify an individual's genetic makeup by direct intervention and manipulation may soon be possible. **Genetic engineering,** the ability to modify an individual's heredity, is now a distinct possibility. In 1973, scientists found that they could alter the genes of animals by adding to or removing part of the DNA using recombinant DNA techniques. The most successful work in recombinant DNA with humans has been the addition of genes for making hormones and antibodies. Currently, fetal surgery (operating on a developing child before birth) is being performed, but the procedures are far from simple and still somewhat experimental, and major issues confront the surgeons (Fletcher, 1981). Fetal surgery has been done to correct urinary tract obstruction and the accumulation of fluid on the brain. Because techniques of fetal surgery have been developed, it is hoped that recombinant DNA surgery soon can be done during the prenatal period of development. Does this mean that a parent may soon be able to choose characteristics desired for a child and have genes manipulated to produce those characteristics? Many factors complicate such a procedure. First, genes are complex structures, and being able to manipulate for exact outcomes is most unlikely. Overshooting or undershooting the goal even minutely could be disastrous. Instead of adding 3 or 4 inches of height, gigantism or abnormal growth may result. Second, genes do not always function in isolation, so a change in one gene may affect other genes. Decreasing a gene variety might create a risk of extinction of the human species. Also, moral and ethical questions are raised as to what is a desirable or undesirable trait—such as skin color, straight or curly hair, or blue or brown eyes. Genetic engineering does offer hope of curing or preventing genetic disorders such as mental retardation, hormonal deficiencies, and sickle-cell anemia. Such an ability could have profound social consequences.

What problems are associated with the technology of modifying an individual's genetic makeup?

FROM CONCEPTION TO INFANCY

The months from conception through birth constitute an extremely important time in a person's life because experiences during this period can affect an entire lifetime. Much development occurs during this period, and as a result neonates are more than passive creatures. They are capable of learning, behaving, and expressing some emotion, and they are aware of the world around them. This section will be particularly concerned with environmental influences during conception through birth and the characteristics of the newborn. The substages of this period from conception to infancy will also be identified.

Prenatal Development

A person's development begins at the time of fertilization when the zygote from which he or she evolves is formed. Growth proceeds and change occurs very rapidly during the prenatal period.

Stages. As described in the discussion of mitosis earlier in this chapter, the original fertilized egg first undergoes divisions. The first 2 weeks of prenatal development are known as *the period of the* *ovum.* The formation of the zygote marks the beginning of the period, and the attachment of the mass of cells to the wall of the **uterus,** the organ in the female in which the young develops, marks the end of the period.

About 2 weeks after the ball of cells has attached to the uterus, the cells begin to differentiate according to their various functions. Although the genetic material of each cell remains identical, various cells take on different shapes, characteristics, and functions. This specialization of cells continues during the following 6 weeks. Once attachment occurs, the mass of cells is called an **embryo.** The period of time from attachment until the last of the specialized cells (bone cells) have their beginning (about the end of the 8th week) is known as *the period of the embryo.* Precisely coded genetic instructions direct the formation of the various special kinds of cells and the major body systems and body organs.

By the end of the period of the embryo, the eyes, ears, nose, mouth, hands, fingers, feet, toes, and sex organs are clearly recognizable (see Color Figure 3–12). The internal organs are also formed well enough that organs such as the liver, kidneys, and heart as well as the nervous system are functional. The kidneys are capable of moving uric acid from the bloodstream, and the heart begins to beat by three 3 weeks after fertilization. By the end of the 8th week of development, the embryo is two million times larger than the zygote from which it evolved; however, it weighs only about an ounce and is only about one inch long.

Also during the period of the embryo, important structures that support the ball of cells develop. These structures include (a) the protective membrane that forms a sac in which the mass of cells grows, (b) the fluid that fills the sac to protect the developing child from injury and heat loss and to allow for unrestricted movement, (c) the **placenta** that forms at the site of implantation to permit the exchange of nutrients and waste products between the mother and developing child, and (d) the umbilical cord that extends from the placenta to the navel of the developing child to transport nutrients and oxygen from the mother and waste products from the child to the mother. These supporting structures are shown in Color Figure 3–12.

During the remainder of the prenatal period, growth, maturation, improvement, and perfection of the body systems and parts that had their beginning during the time of cell specialization continues. From the 9th week after fertilization until birth, the developing organism is referred to as a **fetus,** and the time period is labeled *the period of the fetus* or fetal period. During this time the body systems develop to prepare for life outside the mother, and anatomical details such as hair, fingernails, eyebrows, and eyelashes are added. Between the 10th and 16th week after fertilization, the approximately 100 billion neurons develop. The glial cells begin to develop about the 20th week and continue to develop until about 2 years after birth; however, the process slows down considerably after about 28 to 32 weeks into the prenatal period. Body movements are usually strong enough in the 4th prenatal month that the mother is aware of them. By the 5th month the behavior includes sleeping and waking, and the remaining months even include such behaviors as thumb sucking, hiccuping, sneezing, crying, tossing, and turning as well as the development of most of the reflex response patterns. Much of the weight gain in the last month is due to fat deposited under the skin of the fetus. As growth increases, movement becomes more restricted due to a cramped environment.

How long does it take for a human to develop from a zygote to normal-term birth size?

The normal amount of prenatal time for humans to develop in order to live outside the mother is generally considered to be 9 calendar months or, more precisely, 10 cycles of 28 days (280 days). The average prenatal time for newborns may be less for various reasons, so development is considered to be to normal term if the prenatal period is as much as 267 days (Harris, 1986).

What are teratogens?

Environmental Influences. Although the developing organism is under direct genetic control, its external and internal environments can have an impact. The external environment is the fluid in the sac that surrounds the organism. The internal environment consists of the continuous flow of oxygen, nutrients, hormones, chemicals, and other substances from the mother's bloodstream carried by the umbilical cord to the organism. The internal environment also includes the proteins and enzymes manufactured within the organism. Environmental factors that have a negative effect on prenatal development are called **teratogens** (*te RAH to jenz*). Researchers are continually identifying factors that are or have a potential to be teratogens. These factors are classified into six categories: (a) disease or illness agents; (b) drugs; (c) nutrition; (d) stress and emotional factors; (e) radiation; and (f) chemicals, toxins, and pollutants.

If a mother has the "three-day" measles (rubella), can the virus affect the embryo or fetus she is carrying?

Some disease agents that are known to be passed to the developing child and have an undesirable effect are measles (both rubeola and rubella, the "three-day" or German measles), syphilis, diphtheria, influenza, typhoid, chicken pox, herpes simplex II, and acquired immunodeficiency syndrome (AIDS) (Jackler, 1986). Viruses particularly seem to be teratogens. Rubella is most likely to affect the ears, eyes, and heart—all of which are developing rapidly during the first 3 months of prenatal development, which is the most critical time for a deleterious effect. Syphilis may cause visual and hearing impairment, physical deformities, or brain damage that results in mental retardation. Herpes simplex II, presently incurable although treatment may relieve symptoms and prevent worsening, may cause premature delivery, infant death, vision disorders, and nervous system disorders.

What are some drugs known to be passed from the mother to the developing embryo and fetus that have negative effects?

Because many prescription and nonprescription drugs have been identified as having a negative impact on prenatal development, no medications should be taken during the prenatal period except as directed by a physician. The drug thalidomide marketed in Europe in the late 1950s produced abnormal limb development if taken during the first few weeks of pregnancy when the limbs were developing. Diethylstilbestrol (DES), a synthetic hormone used to prevent miscarriage, was found to be a factor in a rare form of vaginal cancer. This discovery, made in the 1960s, occurred 20 years after the introduction of DES. In 75 percent of the cases studied, the girls' mothers had taken DES during pregnancy (Herbst, 1981). Sex hormones such as androgens and progesterones in birth control pills, if taken during pregnancy, may affect the size of the genitals or the body size of the developing child (Schardein, 1980). Addictive drugs rapidly cross the placenta, and fetal addiction occurs. Withdrawal symptoms are seen in 60 to 90 percent of infants born to drug-addicted mothers (Larin, 1982).

Social drugs such as alcohol and the nicotine in cigarettes have been found to be teratogens. A newborn with the fetal alcohol syndrome may be smaller than normal, have a smaller brain and show mild to moderate mental retardation, have smaller eye openings, and be uncoordinated. Infants born to smoking mothers are likely to be smaller than average, to have increased fetal heart rate, to be hyperactive, or to be born prematurely. Another social drug now suspected of being capable of having deleterious effects on prenatal development is the caffeine found in regular coffee, many soft drinks, and many over-the-counter drugs.

The unborn child is completely dependent on the mother for nutrition. The fetus is most susceptible to the effects of prenatal malnutrition during the last 3 months of fetal development. Effects include death before birth, low birth weight, and increased likeli-

Figure 3–13.
The unborn child is completely dependent on the mother for nutrition.

hood of death during the first year of life as well as the development of fewer connective links between neurons and slower than normal development of the myelin sheath on neurons. The main long-term consequences of inadequate nutrition are lower intelligence and poorer school performance than normal. Specific dietary deficiences such as insufficient protein are associated with the development of fewer neurons. On the other hand, it is almost impossible to overdose on natural food (see Figure 3–13). For example, it would take many bushels of carrots consumed in a day to overdose on vitamin A. Vitamins and minerals taken in pill form by the mother, however, and the overall diet of the mother should be guided by a physician. Too much vitamin A is associated with birth defects such as cleft palate, and too much vitamin D taken throughout pregnancy may cause mental retardation.

In what ways can severe or prolonged emotional stress in a mother affect the unborn child?

Evidence also exists that hormones released into the mother's bloodstream during stress and emotion can possibly affect the unborn child. When the mother is stressed, the unborn child may be stressed also. The children of mothers who are subjected to severe or prolonged emotional stress during pregnancy are more prone to be hyperactive, to be irritable, to have feeding problems, and to have digestive disturbances. High and persistent anxiety in the mother is also associated with prematurity and complications during birth.

High levels of radiation have been associated with lack of proper growth, changes in chromosomes, leukemia, and mental deficiences in exposed offspring (Brent, 1980). Some chemicals, toxins, and pollutants have been identified as teratogens. Methylmercury poisoning from contaminated fish, grain, and meat, which can cause such neuromuscular disorders as cerebral palsy, epilepsy, and mental retardation, is one example. Breathing lead-based paint fumes in an unventilated area for a substantial length of time during pregnancy is suspected to be a source of mental retardation in the unborn child. Very limited data and few scientific studies exist on environmental pollution such as pesticides, lead contamination, and exposure to many other chemicals. Chemical exposure during pregnancy sufficient to have deleterious effects on the unborn child is most likely to occur in industrial settings or laboratories.

Birth and the Newborn

The physical and psychological events related to birth are a focus of this section. Also, an attempt is made to acquaint the reader with the product of the process of birth—the newly arrived individual called a neonate.

The Birth Setting. In many instances, options are available concerning the birth setting. One option may be whether to have the birth occur at home, usually under the supervision of someone trained in home birth called a midwife; in a hospital; or in a birthing room. Until about 45 or 50 years ago, the traditional setting was in the home. For the last 3 decades or so, the traditional setting has been in a hospital delivery room. Today many hospitals have a birthing room or birth center designed to be very much like home (see Figure 3–14). This room or center is an alternative to a home birth or a hospital birth but has the advantages of both. First, it provides a more normal and relaxing atmosphere where siblings, fathers, and other relatives or friends may be present with the mother, if desired. Second, the birth is physician supervised, and there is immediate access to emergency facilities should complications arise. The arguments for home or birthing room deliveries are psychological in nature—the experience can be less traumatic for the mother, and emotional attachment or bonding of mothers, fathers, and siblings to the newborn is facilitated. Because of psychological research findings, most hospitals now allow fathers to be present in the delivery room, allow for natural childbirth (without anesthesia or other medical interventions unless necessary) if desired, and allow "rooming in," that is, newborns may stay in a crib in the room with the mother (see Figure 3–15).

Figure 3–14.
Now birthing rooms give mothers another option for the birth setting.

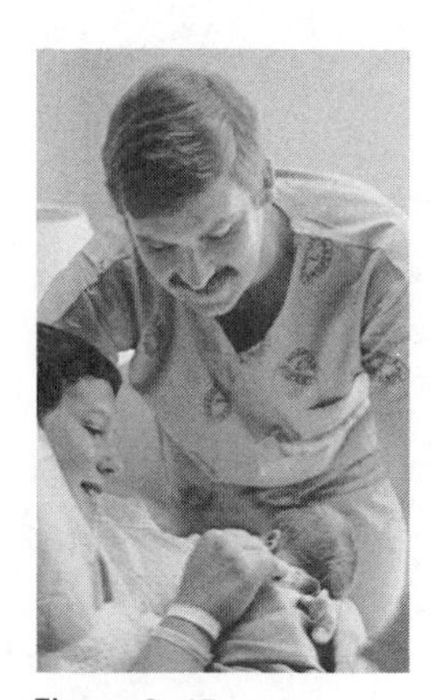

Figure 3–15.
Most hospitals now allow fathers in the delivery room and allow "rooming in."

Stages and Types of Birth. The birth process is believed to be triggered by hormonal changes in the mother, the fetus, or both.

How is a baby born?

There are three broad stages in the normal birth of a child. The first stage involves the head of the unborn child pushing against an opening, the **cervix** of the uterus (see Color Figure 3–16). Bee (1981) likens this to a person pushing his or her head through a turtleneck sweater that is too tight. Eventually, the neck of the sweater is stretched wide enough that the largest part of the head passes through. The second stage is the actual passage of the child through the cervix and out of the mother's body. Because the head is the largest part, the remainder of the infant's body follows easily. The third stage of the birth process is the pulling away of the placenta from the uterus and its passage, a process that may take 5 to 30 minutes. Ninety-five percent of births are head first. Occasionally, bottom, feet, or shoulder may be presented first. When normal delivery may endanger the mother or the child for any of a number of reasons, the child is delivered surgically in a process called a **Cesarean section** (or simply a C-section), so named because Julius Caesar was supposedly delivered this way. In a Cesarean section, the baby is removed from the uterus through an incision in the abdominal wall.

What is meant by a gentle birth, and is it needed?

Frederick Leboyer (1975), convinced that traditional hospital delivery was traumatic for the baby, introduced his method of "gentle" birth. A few hospitals and birthing centers now offer this method of birth as an option. In the Leboyer method, the lights are lowered, everyone speaks as quietly as possible, and the temperature in the delivery room is raised during the birth. The umbilical cord is not cut after birth until natural breathing is established, perhaps as long as 15 to 30 minutes. Instead, the baby is placed in a curved position across the mother's abdomen for a period of time, and then the baby is placed in a pan of warm fluid simulating the fluid the fetus was in before birth. The question is, Are babies really traumatized at birth by the traditional method? Are "gentle" births needed? Opinions differ on answers to the question. The Leboyer procedure is intended to reduce the shock of gravitational pull, temperature loss, bright lights, and unmuffled sounds experienced for the first time. Berezin (1980) reports that gentle-birth babies breathe well, cry less, and seem more alert and attentive than babies born by the more traditional hospital delivery.

Because of various conditions, some babies are born prematurely—before the 267 days that are required to complete the normal prenatal phase of development have elapsed. The lower the birth weight, the higher the risk of death of these infants because they are not as ready for life on their own as are full-term babies. Premature babies are more likely to experience respiratory problems in the first few days and weeks after birth due to immature lungs, to be more vulnerable to infection, to be less alert and responsive, and to be slower in motor development over the first few years of life. If these babies are given special care soon after birth and experience a stimulating environment (see Figure 3–17), they usually catch up to normals by school age. The more environmental stimulation they have, the stronger and healthier these prematures usually become.

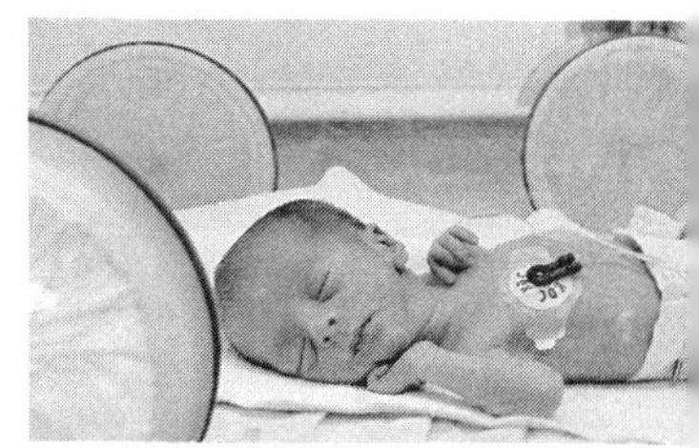

Figure 3–17.
Given special care soon after birth and a stimulating environment, prematures usually catch up to normals in the preschool years.

The Newborn. One minute after birth and again 5 minutes after birth the overall condition of the newborn is evaluated by the child being given the Apgar test (1953), named after Dr. Virginia Apgar who developed the test. Table 3–1 shows the behaviors and characteristics that are tested and how the score is derived. A score of 7-10 points indicates good condition, 4-6 points indicates fair condition, and 0-3 points is indicative that the child is either dead or in very poor condition and needs immediate emergency attention.

What's the first test given a child after birth?

	Score		
Sign	0	1	2
Heart rate	Absent	Slow (less than 100)	Over 100
Respiratory effort	Absent	Slow, irregular	Good, crying
Muscle tone	Flaccid	Some flexion of extremities	Active motion
Reflex irritability	No response	Cry	Vigorous cry
Color	Blue, pale	Body pink, extremities blue	Completely pink

Table 3–1
Apgar test of overall condition of newborn.

The normal newborn has disproportioned body parts compared with the adult—a larger (about one fourth the total body size) and misshapen head; shorter arms, legs, and neck; and narrower shoulders. The average weight and length of newborns is 7 to 7.5 pounds and 19 to 21 inches respectively (see Figure 3–18). A newborn usually loses at least one-half pound during birth and the first 3 or 4 days after birth. Most babies regain this loss and are back to

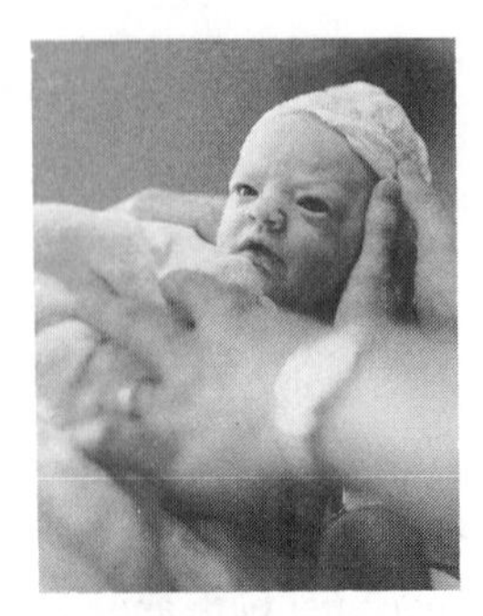

Figure 3–18.
A normal newborn.

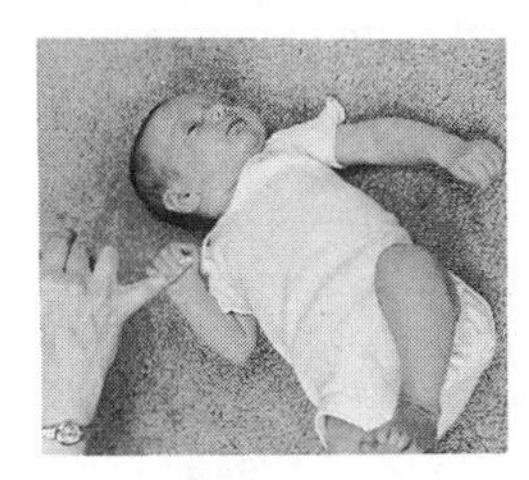

Figure 3–19.
The infant grasping reflex.

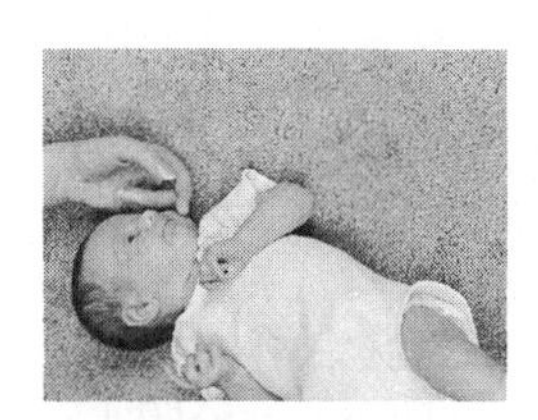

Figure 3–20.
The infant rooting reflex.

birth weight within 2 weeks. This regain marks the end of *the period of the neonate* or neonatal period. On the average, newborns sleep about 18 hours a day. They can cry, which serves several purposes. Crying improves lung capacity, helps to organize the workings of the heart and respiratory system, and communicates distress.

The neonate shows a host of reflexive behaviors. Some behaviors seem to play a role in survival, and some, such as the grasp reflex, seem to be remnants from evolutionary ancestors. These behaviors disappear in the early months after birth when they are not used in adapting to the environment (see Figure 3–19). Also, many reflexes such as the sucking reflex disappear when other areas of the brain develop and other behaviors are learned so that these reflexes are no longer used in adapting to the environment. Of course, many reflexes that are used in adapting to the environment and in survival such as the eye blink are maintained throughout the lifetime. Because nervous system development is related to the presence and disappearance of some of these reflexes, they are often used in diagnosing neurological dysfunction. Table 3–2 lists the names and description of a few major reflexes in the neonate. In addition to the major reflexes mentioned in Table 3–2, at least 15 other reflexes are present in the child at birth that serve protective, defensive, or survival functions. These include the swimming reflex, several reflexes of the eye, and the cough, sneeze, yawn, and gag reflexes (Helms & Turner, 1976).

The neonate's sensory systems are functional at birth; however, some are more mature than others. All parts of the body are sensitive to touch, and normal, full-term infants respond to painful stimuli by grimacing, moving, or crying. Newborns may respond to the direction of a sound by changing their gaze or posture, becoming quiet to low-frequency sounds, or becoming alert and active to high-frequency sounds; and as early as 2 weeks of age they may even stop crying and attend to the sound of a human voice. Al-

Table 3–2
Major reflexes present in the neonate.

Reflex	Stimulus	Response	Comments
Rooting (see Figure 3-20)	Touch on cheek	Head turns in direction of touch	Important in survival. In feeding, head turns toward touch by nipple and this brings lips to nipple.

Reflex	Stimulus	Response	Comments
Sucking (see Figure 3-21)	Touch on lips	Sucking motions	Important in survival. Insures feeding because neonate sucks on whatever is put in mouth.
Grasping	Object placed on palm	Hand grasps firmly	Absence in newborn indicates neural depression. Lost by 6-12 months of age.
Moro	Loud noise or sudden loss of support	Both arms go outward, back arches, legs draw up, fingers spread out	Brain damage or immaturity indicated by absence. Basic reflex lost 3-6 months after birth.
Babinsky (see Figure 3-22)	Touch on foot	Toes spread out	Failure to disappear by 4-6 months of age indicates lack of myelination or other nervous system malfunction.
Stepping (see Figure 3-23)	Touch of foot to floor when held in upright position	Walking or stepping movements of feet and legs	Persistence beyond 4 months of age is often associated with neuromuscular complications.

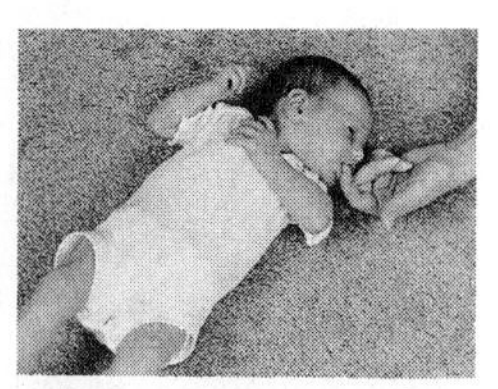

Figure 3–21.
The infant sucking reflex.

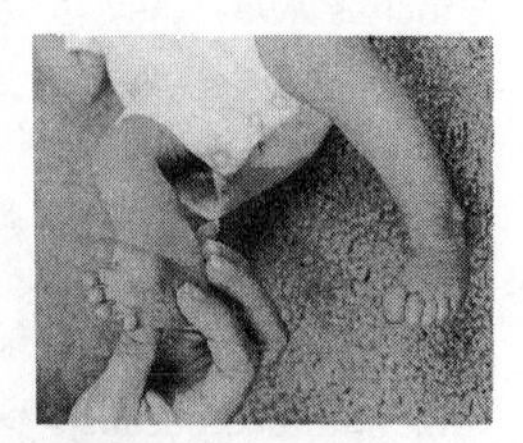

Figure 3–22.
The infant Babinsky reflex.

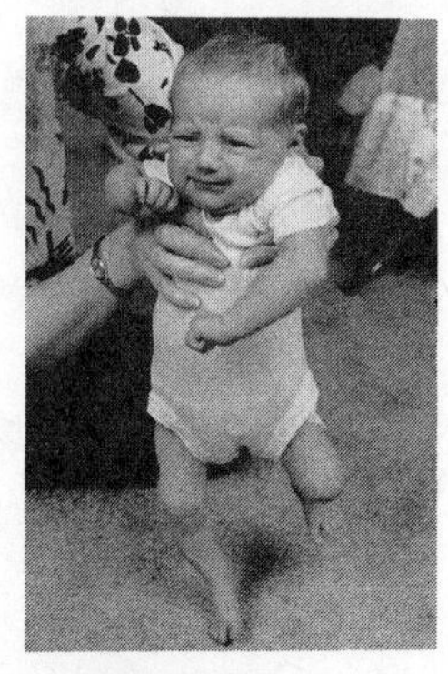

Figure 3–23.
The infant stepping reflex.

though research on the sense of smell is sparse, indications are that newborns can discriminate odors because they react to strong odors, and breast-fed infants can differentiate the odor of their mother's milk from that of another mother's milk. Newborns demonstrate a preference for a sweet-tasting liquid and pucker, turn away, or cry when given sour or bitter liquids. Although the eye is structurally mature at birth, the muscles controlling the eyes are not. Babies at birth can, however, scan (primarily the horizontal axis) and focus for 4 to 10 seconds on high-contrast, moving ob-

Figure 3–24.
When you hold newborns in your arms and look down at them and your face is about 8 inches away, they can focus on your face and are attracted to your eyes and mouth (probably their first perceptions), as you look and talk, because of the movement and contrast.

jects at least one-fourth inch in size that are about 8 inches away and in the center of their visual field (see Figure 3–24). Research is not clear on whether the newborn perceives color.

EARLY DEVELOPMENT

People change from day to day, their behavior changes, and these changes are noticeable. You may hear such expressions as the following: "Billy started walking today." "I see you have grown a little taller." "Tasia is more proficient in her job than she was a year ago." "Halsey is not as shy as he was in high school." This section addresses the general characteristics of development and the changes that occur during infancy and childhood in the areas of physical growth, motor development, sensation and perception, language, and psychological development.

The Nature of Development

As noted earlier in this chapter, heredity (maturation), environment (experience and learning), and time (critical or sensitive periods) interact to determine development. In our culture, the human life span is typically divided into early development (which includes prenatal development and the stages of infancy and childhood), adolescence, adulthood, and old age.

Psychologists who study development are most concerned with what information?

Definition. The changes that occur in a person and in that person's behavioral capabilities are referred to as development. Developmental psychology is that branch of psychology committed to the study of these changes that occur throughout the life span, of the processes through which change is effected, and of the conditions that bring about change. Psychologists who study development are most generally concerned with information on behavior at different ages, on behavioral changes as people grow older, on environmental events that influence behavior, and on variations among individuals in their development.

What are some generally agreed on characteristics of development?

Characteristics. Although maturation, experience, and a particular time may each be a factor influential in overall development, one factor may be more or less influential at different stages of the life span in different specific areas of development. Researchers have generally found, however, that development is orderly, directional, to a large extent cumulative, and increasingly differentiated and complex in organization. Much of developmental psychology has focused on determining as precisely as possible the sequential milestones in very specific areas of development.

The sequential milestones in some specific areas of development seem to follow a smooth, gradual, continuous pattern analogous to walking up a ramp, and some specific areas seem to follow a discontinuous pattern of stops and starts analogous to walking up steps. Whether the sequences proceed in a continuous fashion or in a discontinuous way as a series of abrupt changes, called stages, is a controversial issue. Flavell (1982) states that a majority of the recent research suggests that development is more likely to be gradual and continuous. Stage theories are useful descriptions, however, of the changes that occur in some areas of development.

Does development occur in a smooth, continuous pattern or in a step fashion in a discontinuous pattern?

Rate. Although the sequences of development that individuals progress through are relatively constant, the specific ages when these sequences occur are not. Remember that when an average age for the emergence of a particular behavior such as walking is given, it is a mathematical computation used to represent a group, not a particular individual. Infants may begin walking as early as 8 months of age or as late as 18 months of age with the average age cited as 13 months (see Figure 3–25).

Figure 3–25.
Infants may begin walking as early as 8 months of age or as late as 18 months of age with the average age cited as 13 months.

Also, there is variation in the way an individual progresses through the sequences. For example, progression through the sequences may be rapid or slow for different behaviors for different individuals, or progression through the sequences of a particular behavior may vary between rapid and slow at different stages for an individual. A rapid rate of early physical growth in infancy does not mean the individual will be unusually large in adulthood. Or a slow rate of preschool intellectual development does not always mean that the child will also develop slowly through the sequences of intellectual development in elementary school.

Development is considered to be cumulative; however, some controversy exists concerning the impact of early environmental stimulation. The controversy is related to whether certain experiences are necessary for normal development. In other words, can later experience make up for a lack of earlier experience? Is early experience crucial or necessary in determining whether an individual reaches full hereditary potential? Some psychologists are concerned that too much early environmental stimulation or pressure, pushing for early achievement of the next step in the developmental sequence, may set up the individual for later failures (Langway, 1983). Psychologists are generally agreed on the positive effects of early environmental experience, particularly where a deficit exists or a disadvantaged condition exists. Also, psychologists agree that

Should a very young child be given a lot of sensory experience (seeing, hearing, and touching)?

early environmental experience is especially important for later development and in reaching optimum development in some areas, but a deficit in early stimulation does not necessarily set the individual on an irrevocable course.

Infancy and Childhood

Although each individual is unique, there are certain broad similarities in the life stages of infancy and childhood. Some broad similarities in physical, motor, sensation, perceptual, and language development and in psychological tasks achieved are described in this section.

Physical Growth and Motor Development. Overall, physical stages of growth continue to be rapid during the first 3 years of life. By 5 years of age, children have doubled their birth length and increased to about five times their birth weight. Birth weight usually doubles in the first 5 months and triples in the first year. About half the adult height is reached by age 2. Comparisons of present-day averages with those of 100 years ago show that Americans today are taller and develop earlier. Improvements in environmental conditions such as nutrition and medical care are thought to account for this phenomenon.

Are the average height and the average age for reaching physical maturity the same for Americans today as were the averages 100 years ago?

Physical rates of growth are much slower during the middle years of childhood (5 or 6 years to approximately 9 years of age); however, rapid advancement is made in motor skill abilities that require both large-muscle and fine-muscle movements and coordination. The ability to perform a voluntary motor task depends on maturation of the skeletal, muscular, and nervous systems. Figure 3–26 shows the stages in the development of the ability to maintain the upright position and walk.

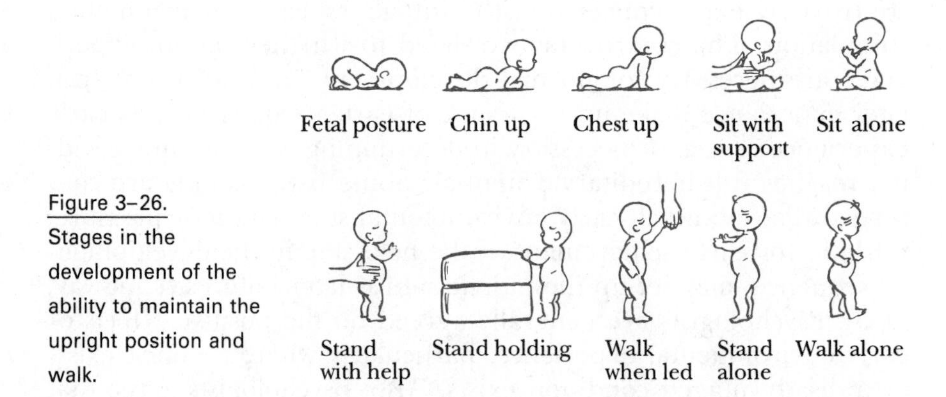

Figure 3–26. Stages in the development of the ability to maintain the upright position and walk.

By 5 to 6 years of age, the body fat layer is about half as thick as at age 9 months because fat cells are formed primarily in the last prenatal month and the first year after birth. Another period of rapid formation of fat cells occurs during adolescence. The head has attained 90 percent of its adult size by the 6th year.

Figure 3–27.
The 20 temporary teeth have usually erupted by 3 years of age.

Development of the teeth, known as dentition, and bone development are also aspects of physical growth and development. The set of 20 temporary teeth has usually erupted by 3 years of age, and the permanent teeth begin to replace them by about age 6 or 7 (see Figure 3–27). The last of the permanent teeth do not appear until adolescence or even early adulthood. Bones develop in three ways. They may increase in number, become longer and larger, and grow harder.

Development of Sensation and Perception. The ability to see and identify something that is 20 feet away as well and as clearly as the average normal adult (20/20 vision) is not reached until about 11 or 12 years of age. The ability to hear and respond to a wider range of frequencies and to determine the location of a sound in space also continues to improve steadily until adolescence. The senses of taste and smell are fully developed in the preschool years. In fact, the young child has more taste buds than an adult and thus has a sharper sense of taste and may react more vigorously to the taste of something. The sense of touch is highly developed at birth.

Although by age 5 or 6 a child normally can coordinate the senses of touch, vision, and hearing as well as an adult, shifts in preference may occur at different ages. The sense of touch seems to be the preference at 2 to 4 years of age. By ages 5 and 6, vision begins to be the preference. Sharp contrast and movement attract the attention of infants up to about 2 months of age, and then the features begin to attract attention—individual parts of an object are the visual preference, and scanning occurs, although the scanning is very unsystematic. By 5 months of age, the child can perceive parts, note similarities in objects, and begin to note discriminations in patterns. A pattern that is discrepant from an experienced pattern then begins to attract attention. During the 3rd and 4th years, the child focuses more on color and size, and then by age 6, the child focuses more on shape as do adults. The amount of time a child focuses on an activity increases with age, and children generally become less impulsive and more reflective with increased age. Children also get better at selecting relevant features to attend to, focusing attention on a single aspect, and ignoring irrelevant information.

What is perception, and how does it differ from sensation?

In a broad sense, perception is the construction of meaning—the process of building on sensation. Gradually the child is better able to organize and interpret or give meaning to the raw information received through the senses, to fill in and smooth over incomplete or ambiguous sensory information, and to add information from memory.

Although both past experience and heredity play a significant role in the development of perception, the extent of the effect of heredity and environmental experience is not agreed upon by all psychologists. Psychologists do agree that perception is an integration of heredity and experience. Because the organization of some neural impulses seems to be predetermined by heredity, some perceptual constructions such as perception of space, events, and form are apparently innate. They appear to be built into the nervous system.

Evidence for the role of heredity in perception is the ability to organize sensory information in such a way as to locate a sound in space at birth. Also, most crawling infants refuse to crawl across a glass surface where a simulated drop-off or visual cliff appears even when the mother beckons (see Figure 3–28). Because babies cannot be tested on the visual cliff until they can move voluntarily on their own will, the findings are inconclusive as to whether depth perception is present at birth. However, when animals that are

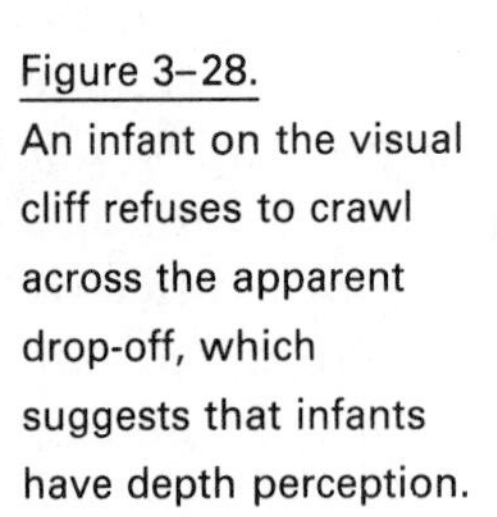

Figure 3–28.
An infant on the visual cliff refuses to crawl across the apparent drop-off, which suggests that infants have depth perception.

mobile at birth such as chicks, kids, and lambs were tested immediately after birth, the same results were found as those found with crawling human babies. Human babies as young as 2 months of age show a significant variation in heart rate between their position on the cliff or non-cliff side of the visual cliff. Thus, there appears to be some innate perception of space.

Others have demonstrated that experience in the environment affects the development of perception. One psychologist (Kohler, 1962) had people wear goggles that inverted the visual world. Although very clumsy at the beginning, by the end of a month they could generally perform visual motor tasks such as bicycling or fencing as well as before beginning to wear the goggles. When the goggles were removed, the individuals were clumsy again and had to relearn motor behaviors. Studies of adults whose vision was restored by surgery after being blind from birth indicated that the patients could not identify simple, familiar objects by sight until they had several weeks of training. They could, however, distinguish figure from background (Senden, 1960). This evidence suggests that perceptions develop gradually beginning with an innate perceptual construction, and the perceptual construction becomes more accurate and more detailed with learning (see Figure 3–29). Studies of perception consistently show that environmental experience is essential to perceptual development. Heredity seems to provide the prewired organizations of the sensory receptors, the brain, and the muscles. However, the child must have sensory input or experience and must respond physically to it—activity or movement is essential. Perception is sensory-motor integration; it is

What is essential, in addition to sensation, for perceptual development—for organizing, interpreting, and responding appropriately to messages received in the brain from the environment?

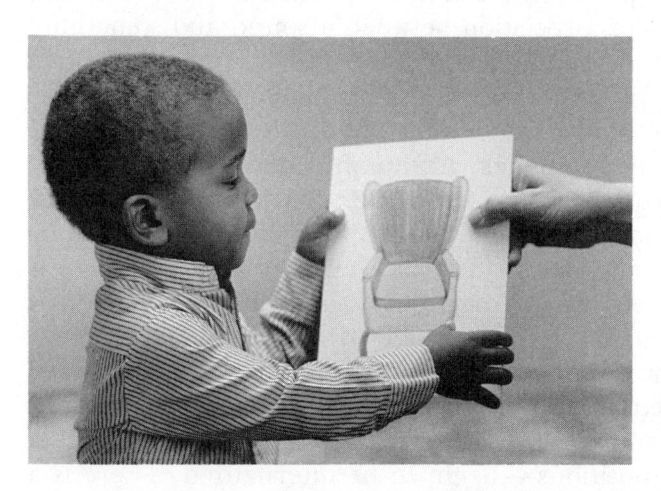

Figure 3–29.
Will this child identify this picture as a chair because of inherited characteristics (maturation), experience in the environment (learning), or a combination of the two?

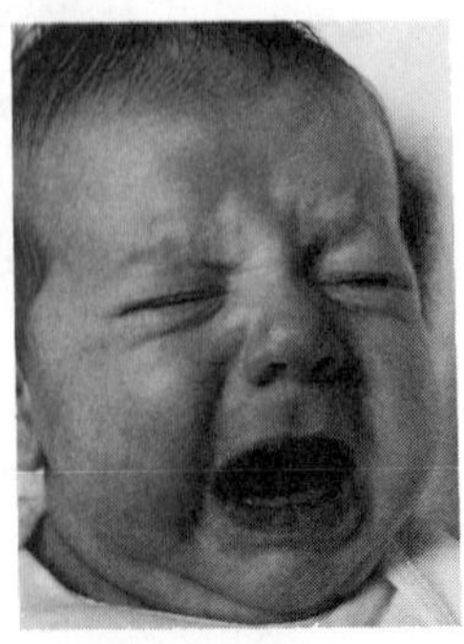

Figure 3–30.
Speech is the means of communication that develops naturally in humans. The newborn infant makes a sound as soon as it is born (the birth cry—a reflex response to fill the lungs with air).

the development of appropriate responses to incoming sensory messages.

Language Development. Transmission of a message from a sender to a receiver is called communication. Language is communication by means of a system consisting of a set of symbols that are put together in an almost infinite variety of ways to represent things that exist in the environment, to express ideas, and to communicate messages. Speech, the use of a system consisting of a set of sounds, seems to be a means of communication that normally develops in humans (see Figure 3–30). Of course, various sets of sounds may comprise a system, thus various languages such as English, German, Spanish, or French may be spoken. Whether the set of symbols consists of sounds, visual symbols (letters of the alphabet for a written language or hand signs [see Figure 3–31] that can be seen by the deaf), or shapes (that can be felt with the fingers by the blind), language development follows the same sequence and pattern.

During the prelanguage phase, or before the child speaks the first words, sounds are produced involuntarily. The human neonate cries (makes a sound) as soon as it is born. The infant adds gurgling and cooing sounds during the 1st to 3rd months of age, inadvertently producing vowel and consonant sounds as he or she cries, breathes, and swallows. Early cooing sounds are primarily vowels. Between the 3rd and 7th months of age, babbling occurs. This is the repetition of combinations of vowels and consonants. Every sound that exists in any language can be produced, and babies all over the world can produce the same sounds and follow the same sequences in producing them. As sounds acquire meaning and children learn an association between a sound and something in the environment, the sounds common to their culture are practiced. Those not practiced drop out. The smallest distinguishable units of sound, the individual sounds that are used in a particular language, are called **phonemes.** Although a few babies may produce their first words intentionally (i.e., voluntarily produce a sound or combination of sounds with meaning attached) as early as 8 months of age or as late as 2 years of age, the average age is about 12 to 13 months. A unit of sound with meaning attached to it is a **morpheme.** During the next stage of language development the **syntax,** rules or grammar of the language—the order in which words are combined, the order for question asking, the addition of suffixes, plurals, and the use of various parts of speech such as pronouns and prepositions—begin to be internalized. There is a

Figure 3–31.
Various language systems follow the same sequences and pattern of development.

particular sequence in which this occurs. For example, prepositions are the last part of speech to begin to be used.

The **semantics** of the language is the formation of concepts or word meanings—the relationship between sound and significance. A word may be in the child's vocabulary; however, the meaning associated with the word may not be completely or accurately formed. Feelings and images associated with a word may vary among individuals. By age 5 or 6, a child's spoken language is very much like that of the adult except for size of vocabulary (semantics) and sentence length (complexity of sentence structure such as the use of more phrases, clauses, and compound sentences). Thus, language development is a product of both maturation and experience in the environment (see Figure 3–32).

Figure 3–32.
A social environment in the form of hearing oneself and others talk enhances language development.

Psychological Tasks to be Mastered. Erikson (1963) divided development into eight life stages, four of these being in infancy and childhood. He described a major task to be mastered at each stage. During the first year of a child's life when the child is completely dependent on others for safety and comfort, the task is to develop a sense of trust in the predictability of the world and his or her own ability to make things happen. Improper or unpredictable care as a child by those who are unloving and rejecting may account for insecurity, suspiciousness, or inability to relate to others later in life.

During the 2nd and 3rd years of life, the task is to develop a sense of independence (autonomy). Walking, grasping, dressing the self, and feeding the self lead to free choice and to learning control. Whether a child is encouraged to climb, touch, explore, and do things rather than be criticized, teased, or ridiculed when he or she falls, spills something, or fails and whether the child is consistently overprotected is significant (see Figure 3–33).

Figure 3–33.
Erikson believes the trait of independence (autonomy) or dependence is developed between the ages of 1 and 3.

The task to be mastered by the 4- and 5-year-old child is initiative. At this age the child usually wants to conquer the world—to try to do everything including fix things, cut one's hair, and vacuum the house. To develop intiative, children need to be encouraged to engage in activities with supervision and to be allowed the freedom to choose activities, use imagination, and ask questions. If consistently a child is not permitted to try new activities and is not directed to permissible and acceptable activities, he or she may be overwhelmed by guilt and shame.

From the 6th to the 12th year of life, children's attention turns from play more toward work as they learn the skills of their culture. They learn to read, write, do arithmetic, use tools, and

Figure 3–34.
Children can discover their powers and limitations through work experiences.

accomplish tasks. The basic task to be mastered is industry—to win approval through productivity. If children fail to accomplish industriousness during these years, they will develop a sense of inferiority. Because work is one of the best ways to achieve a sense of mastery, children can discover their powers and limitations through work experiences. Children may perform physical work such as mowing lawns, delivering papers, or running errands (see Figure 3–34). Early work experiences help by developing skills, providing a model for behaving as an adult, and allowing children to rehearse work abilities before they are actually needed for self-support.

The physical and psychological tasks of childhood are too numerous to cover in this text. Biological and environmental factors and the interaction of the factors in development are also numerous. Therefore, only a brief introduction to what psychologists have learned about heredity and development has been presented in this chapter. Human development is complex, and it is a complicated area to study.

SUMMARY

1. The life stages may be delineated as prenatal, perinatal, neonatal, and postnatal. Postnatal includes the stages of infancy and childhood, adolescence, adulthood, and old age, each stage representing a step in physical maturation and psychological development.
2. By mitosis and meiosis, a human being develops from one cell, a zygote formed at the time of conception that has 23 chromosomes from a sperm provided by the father and 23 chromosomes from an ovum (egg) provided by the mother. Sperm and ova are gametes formed by germ cell division in a process called meiosis.
3. A chromosome is made up of many genes composed of chains of DNA molecules. DNA consists of four chemical bases in various arrangements that constitute a genetic code for the creation of a particular characteristic.
4. An individual's sex and certain sex-linked characteristics are determined by the 23rd pair of chromosomes. The individual receives an X chromosome from the mother and either an X or a Y chromosome from the father, so that an XX combination forms a female, an XY combination forms a male, and the resulting sex-linked characteristics are determined.
5. Inherited characteristics are those determined by the genetic materials present at the moment the person is conceived. Development

refers to the sequence of structural and behavioral changes that occur in a person as he or she matures as a product of heredity, environment, and time.

6. Maturation, the control that genes exert over the unfolding of biological events from conception to death, follows some general trends as seen in the head-downward, center-outward, and massive-to-specific progressions.
7. Some behavioral characteristics may be a result of heredity, and some may be a result of the environment; however, most depend on the interaction between heredity and the environment with heredity providing potentials and limitations that may be altered by the environment.
8. A critical or sensitive period refers to a time in the developmental period when an environmental condition will have an optimum effect on the behavior of an individual.
9. The two genes for a specific characteristic (one from the father and one from the mother) may both be dominant, both be recessive, or one may be dominant and one recessive with dominant genes predominating over recessive genes. Some characteristics are determined by a single gene, some by an interaction of both genes, and some, said to be polygenic, are determined by a variety of genes operating in a complex interaction.
10. Abnormal or undesirable traits may result from an abnormal number of chromosomes in the zygote and thus in all the cells of the body. For example, 47 chromosomes instead of the usual 46 causes Down's syndrome. Also, defective genes can cause undesirable traits such as albinism.
11. Advances are being made in genetic counseling and genetic engineering in evaluating the probability that a child born to carriers of a defective gene will inherit the gene, in diagnosing in the early prenatal stage of development, and in modifying genes or chromosomes.
12. The three stages of prenatal development in sequence are the period of the ovum (the first 2 weeks while attachment to the uterus of the mother is occurring), the period of the embryo (the next 6 weeks while specialization of cells is occurring), and the period of the fetus (from 8 weeks after conception to birth while the body systems prepare for life outside the mother).
13. Materials present in the mother's bloodstream have an effect on the prenatal processes. Factors that may have a negative effect (teratogens) are disease or illness agents, drugs, improper nutrition, radiation, stress and emotional factors, and environmental, chemical, and toxic pollutants.
14. The usual options for the birth setting are the home under the supervision of a midwife and the hospital delivery room or birthing room under the supervision of a physician; the new hospital birthing room

is designed to give the advantages of both the home and the hospital delivery room.

15. Birth triggered by hormones progresses through three broad stages—the head of the unborn child pushing the cervix open, the passing of the unborn child from the mother through the cervix, and the passing of the placenta.
16. The method of "gentle" birth proposed by Leboyer is used by a few physicians although its advantages are controversial. A Cesarean section is the surgical removal of the baby from the uterus of the mother.
17. Although 280 days is generally considered to be the length of time required for prenatal development, babies born after 267 days of development are considered to be to normal term.
18. A newborn's condition is evaluated by the Apgar test. The neonate with an average weight and length of 7 to 7.5 pounds and 19 to 21 inches is capable of exhibiting a host of reflex behaviors, has functional sensory systems, sleeps about 18 to 20 hours a day, cries, and has disproportioned body parts compared with an adult.
19. In general, development is orderly, directional, cumulative, and increasingly differentiated and complex in the sequential milestones of specific areas of development; however, individual differences exist in the rates of progression through the sequences.
20. As illustrated by the tripling of birth weight in one year and the reaching of half the adult height in 2 years, physical growth continues to be especially rapid the first few years after birth. Then physical growth slows down during middle childhood as rapid advancement is made in motor-skill ability.
21. Although the senses of taste and smell are fully developed in the preschool years and the sense of touch is highly developed at birth, the senses of seeing and hearing continue to improve until adolescence.
22. Perception, the process of building on sensation to construct meaning, begins to develop rapidly soon after birth and seems to be a product of both heredity and experience. Perception is the integration of sensory and motor experiences directed by maturation of the nervous system and organizations built into the nervous system.
23. Speech, the language or communication system that normally emerges in humans, like perception seems to be a product of both maturation and experience and develops rapidly during the first 4 or 5 years of life.
24. Erikson divided development into eight life stages, and the characteristics or tasks to be mastered at each of the four stages of infancy and childhood are 1st year, basic trust; 2nd and 3rd years, autonomy; 4th and 5th years, initiative; and 6th to 12th years, industry.

KEY TERMS AND CONCEPTS

Prenatal
Perinatal
Neonatal
Postnatal
Sperm
Ovum
Chromosomes
Genes
Conception
Gametes
Zygote
Mitosis
Meiosis
Maturation
Critical periods
Dominant gene
Recessive gene
Polygenic
Sex-linked characteristics
Down's syndrome
Genetic engineering
Uterus
Embryo
Placenta
Fetus
Teratogens
Cervix
Cesarean section
Phonemes
Morpheme
Syntax
Semantics

QUESTIONS FOR REVIEW

1. What genetic materials make up a chromosome, how is a zygote containing 46 chromosomes formed, and how is a person's sex determined? What is mitosis? Meiosis?
2. What is maturation, and what general trends are observed in maturation?
3. Explain what is meant by and give an example of a dominant, a recessive, a codominant, a polygenic, and a sex-linked trait.
4. What is the basis for the development of a male, a female, nonidentical twins, and identical twins?
5. Name and describe the three stages of prenatal development and the six classifications of teratogens.
6. Describe three stages of normal birth, three usual options for the birth setting, and the two methods of birth called the Cesarean section and the Leboyer gentle birth.
7. What is the newborn human baby like in appearance, behavior, and sensory capacity?
8. Describe a few milestones in the patterns of physical and motor development in the areas of height, weight, head size, walking, and prehension and in the development of sensation and perception during infancy and childhood.
9. Describe the pattern of the prelanguage phase and three other phases of language development.
10. According to Erikson, what four psychological tasks are to be achieved in infancy and childhood, and at about what age?

TEST YOURSELF

1. Gametes are (a) sperm (b) ova (c) both sperm and ova (d) embryos.

2. The process of division of reproductive or germ cells that produces sperm and ova is ________________.
3. A male develops from a zygote containing an ________________ combination of chromosomes for the 23rd pair.
4. What is the most common birth defect, occurring in more than 5,000 children annually, that is caused by an extra chromosome being with the 21st pair in the zygote?
5. Critical or sensitive periods usually correspond to (a) times of slow development (b) times of rapid development (c) the time when an environmental condition has an optimal effect on development (d) both b and c.
6. If a gene pair for a single-gene-determined trait consists of a dominant gene and a recessive gene, the characteristic that develops will be determined by the ________________ gene.
7. Both genes of a gene pair as well as many genes from other gene pairs may be active and influence the development of some characteristics in an individual. T or F
8. Specialization of cells and the formation of the major body systems and organs occurs during the (a) period of the ovum (b) period of the embryo (c) period of the fetus (d) period of the neonate.
9. Environmental factors that may have a negative effect on prenatal development such as alcohol, the rubella virus, or hormones produced from stress are called ________________.
10. Although development is orderly, directional, and to a large extent cumulative, the rate of development in individuals and in particular areas of development may vary considerably. T or F
11. The spreading out of the toes stimulated by a touch on the neonate's foot is the ________________ reflex.
12. The first stage of birth is the pulling away of the placenta from the uterus and its passage from the mother. T or F
13. Maturation is the (a) same as development (b) change in behavior that occurs from academic learning in the home or school (c) change in behavior that occurs from sensory experience in the environment such as seeing, hearing, touching, tasting, and smelling (d) change in behavior that occurs as a result of biological changes controlled by the genes.
14. Development is a product of (a) heredity (b) environment (c) time (d) the interaction of heredity and environment over time.
15. As a general rule, by 5 years of age children have ________________ their birth length and increased their birth weight by about ________________ times.
16. The ability to see and identify something that is 20 feet away as well and as clearly as the average normal adult (20/20 vision) is reached by about 5 years after birth. T or F

17. Perception is the (a) same as sensation (b) organizing, integrating, and giving of meaning to sensation (c) reflex response to a stimulus (d) same as memory.
18. Give the correct sequence for the appearance of the following in language development: phonemes, syntax, crying, morphemes, babbling, and gurgling and cooing.
19. Early sensory stimulation from the environment (a) is not recommended because of possible damage to the sense organs of the infant (b) does not seem to have a significant effect on development (c) may result in retardation (d) is generally agreed by psychologists to have positive effects for later sensory functioning and for reaching optimum development in some areas.
20. According to Erikson, between the ages of 6 and 12 children develop either (a) a sense of industry or a sense of inferiority (b) a sense of autonomy (independence) or a sense of dependency (c) a sense of trust or a sense of mistrust (d) a sense of initiative or a sense of shame and guilt.

APPLICATIONS

A. Ann, who holds an administrative position in a large corporation, and her husband, Bob, have just learned that conception has occurred and prenatal development of their first child is taking place. Bob and Ann both have dark brown hair, and Ann's father is color-blind. Ann does not smoke cigarettes; however, in the office area where Ann works, several coworkers smoke almost constantly. Ann does drink alcoholic beverages regularly when she takes customers and potential customers to lunch and dinner and when she and Bob go out with friends and to parties, which they do frequently. Because she experiences considerable pressure in work, she usually has some type of alcoholic drink when she gets home in the evening to help her relax.

Bob thinks Ann should ask her coworkers not to smoke in the office work area now, and that she should refrain from having alcoholic beverages. Ann doesn't want to ask her coworkers to stop smoking in the office unless there is some real justification for it. Also, she thinks that it will be difficult to avoid alcohol and that it will appear that she is not sociable. Bob and Ann are both wondering whether they will have a boy or a girl and whether the child will have any defects.

1. Is it possible that Ann and Bob's child could have red or blonde hair since they both are brunettes? Why or why not?
2. What will determine whether Bob and Ann have a boy or a girl, and will the probability of the child being color-blind be the same whether it is a boy or a girl? Explain your answer.

3. Is Bob just overreacting and worrying for no reason about Ann's drinking and breathing cigarette smoke? Why or why not?
4. If their child should happen to have Down's syndrome when it is born, what would have caused the defect?

B. Lucy and Tom have two young children—Billy, age 1 month, and Sarah, who is now 34 inches tall and just had her 2nd birthday. Lucy has given up her position with the XYZ Corporation to stay home and care for the children for a couple of years. She wants to get Billy started off right, so she asked Mrs. Toner, her next-door neighbor who has reared four children and now has grandchildren, for advice. Mrs. Toner told Lucy, "Don't pick Billy up when he cries and hold him, rock him, or carry him around. Feed him on a strict schedule, and if he seems to want to eat before it is feeding time, just ignore him and let him cry. Otherwise, he will become spoiled. He needs to learn right in the beginning months of life that crying doesn't bring attention and get him what he wants."

Lucy is especially protective of Sarah because she is a girl, is her first child, and was born about 3 weeks prematurely. She tries to do everything for Sarah—feeds her, dresses her, and carries her around. She is afraid that she will get hurt or get some germs that will cause her to become ill. Anyway, it is easier to feed her than to clean up the mess she makes feeding herself. Lucy doesn't have time to let Sarah attempt to dress herself, and it is easier to hold on to her than to follow her around and watch her. She is so anxious for Sarah to be perfect in behavior that she is critical of her if she spills her food, falls down, or tries to touch or play with anything in the house other than her toys. Lucy believes in keeping her home attractive with lots of nice and expensive accessories and just teaching Sarah not to touch them.

1. Do you agree with Mrs. Toner's advice to Lucy about how to care for Billy? Why or why not?
2. According to Erikson, what personality trait will Sarah probably develop during the 2 years her mother is staying home from work to care for her that will probably persist as a personality trait during the remainder of her life unless specific action is taken to change it?
3. How tall do you think Sarah will be when she reaches her full adult height?
4. What stimuli in the environment attract Billy's attention now, which sense is fully developed, and which two senses will not be fully developed until about the beginning of adolescence?

SUGGESTIONS FOR FURTHER READING

Berezin, N. (1980). *The gentle birth book: A practical guide to Leboyer family-centered delivery*. New York: Simon & Schuster.

An excellent description of the Leboyer method.

Harris, A. C. (1985). *Child development.* St. Paul, MN: West Publishing Company.

An interesting and current child development text that combines research and applied experience and is easy to understand.

Lamb, M. E. (Ed.). (1981). *The role of the father in child development* (2nd ed.). New York: Wiley.

Written by leading researchers on the impact of the father on the developing child, this book is the most thorough collection of information currently available.

McClearn, G. E., & DeFries, J. C. (1973). *Introduction to behavioral genetics.* San Francisco: W. H. Freeman.

An introductory textbook for the field of behavior genetics that is understandable and a good starting point.

Nilsson, L. A. (1981). *A child is born: The drama of life before birth.* New York: Dell.

Many photographs of prenatal development are included in this book prepared especially for parents-to-be.

CHAPTER 4

DEVELOPMENT: LATER STAGES AND OTHER AREAS

Objectives

When you have completed your study of chapter 4, you should be able to:

1. Describe the adolescent life stage in terms of physical and psychological changes that occur and the psychological tasks to be mastered.
2. Describe the life stage of adulthood and the psychological tasks to be mastered.
3. Give Super's sequential stages of career development.
4. Discuss old age in terms of characteristics, stereotypes, adjustment to change, and stages of development in progressing through the final stage of life—death and dying.
5. Summarize Piaget's theory of the development of intelligence, including his successive stages of cognitive development, approximate ages for reaching the stages, and characteristic behaviors of each stage.
6. List and describe the stages of progression in moral development according to Kohlberg.
7. Identify milestones an individual reaches when following the patterns of social development.
8. Discuss emotional development in terms of attachment and the development of specific emotions.
9. Identify sequential stages in the development of the concept of self and recognize the impact on personality.
10. Give milestones in the development of an individual's sexuality in the acquisition of sex-role behaviors as well as in physiological development.

People's appearance, behavior, thinking, concept of right or wrong, relationships with other people, ability to experience emotion, and concept of the self may change as they grow older. Brim and Kagan (1980) point out that although the early years of development are the formative ones, people have a remarkable capacity for change across the entire life span. This chapter examines development from adolescence on to the end of life and focuses on the sequences and stages of development in the areas of intellectual, moral, social, emotional, concept of self, and sexual development.

LIFE STAGES FROM ADOLESCENCE ON

Johnny, a teenager, is growing a beard. Sally and her adolescent peers are planning to go to a rock concert to see their "idols" in person. The Brands, a couple with two children, go to work for a large corporation from early in the morning until late in the afternoon 5 days a week. The Sanders are retired grandparents who spend much of their time visiting with the grandchildren, doing volunteer work, and traveling. And the Sanders' parents, in their late 80s and 90s, are not moving around as fast or seeing and hearing as well as they did 20 years ago. Some typical characteristics, changes that occur, and tasks that are to be mastered in adolescence, adulthood, and old age are pointed out in this section.

Adolescence

What is the basis for much of the frustration and conflict that produces stress during adolescence?

In the United States, adolescence is a time of pulling away from the family—of becoming independent both economically and emotionally and becoming capable of structuring life's activities. Much frustration is experienced as an adolescent strives to achieve independence and at the same time cling to the security of dependence. Conflict is experienced as the adolescent becomes capable of perceiving others' points of view and tries out different roles in various settings. At the beginning of adolescence, the individual is still very much a child; physical development is far ahead of psychological development. By the end of adolescence, the psychological development as well as the physical development is very much adult.

Physical Development. Adolescence begins with **puberty**—the period of time from the beginning of development of the primary and secondary sex characteristics until the physiological achievement of sexual maturity around age 13. Adolescence ends when a person becomes economically and emotionally independent and establishes an identity apart from the parents. It is difficult to attach a specific age to the end of adolescence because people assume adult roles at various ages. They usually assume them, however, between the ages of 18 and 25 with 18 being the legal age for becoming an adult. Early adolescence (puberty) is marked by a rapid physical growth spurt. An adolescent may grow 4 to 6 inches taller in a single year, and the body proportions change from child to adult dimensions. Sexual maturity follows the growth spurt.

Psychological Development. Young adolescents are usually critical of their parents and society. They can imagine ideal possibilities because they are now capable of abstract logic. Their parents' actual beliefs and behaviors may differ from these imagined ideals. Adolescents can argue endlessly about minute details of parental errors, prejudices, and perceived foolishness. This typical activity seems to serve the purpose of loosening bonds between the parent and child, thus helping the child become more independent. It also helps adolescents bring into focus ideas about the kind of person they do and do not want to become and provides an opportunity for them to try out new ideas in a safe environment (see Figure 4–1).

Figure 4–1.
Arguing with parents seems to serve the purposes of loosening parent-child attachments and providing an opportunity for the adolescent to try out new ideas in a safe environment.

Young adolescents are usually also very critical of themselves and are easily shamed and embarrassed. Because their thoughts are often focused on themselves, they believe others' thoughts are similarly focused on them; young adolescents, then, are psychologically egocentric (see Figure 4–2). If they dislike their looks or behaviors, they are sure everyone else is similarly critical; and if they are pleased with their behavior or appearance, they are sure everyone else admires them as well. As adolescents mature and reach adulthood, they become less egocentric and realize that others do not necessarily share their thoughts and feelings. This realization is necessary if they are to form mutual relationships and to perceive another person's needs.

Tasks to be Mastered. Much of the unsettled behavior that occurs during adolescence is an attempt to arrive at a consistent and satisfying identity. Adolescents try out different ways of behaving. They shift from job to job, relationship to relationship, and life-style to life-style. Identity formation is not a process of which adolescents are totally conscious. By isolating select features from various models and combining them into a unique identity, adolescents develop a sense of self that is different from anyone else yet shares many characteristics with others. According to Erikson, the task to be mastered during adolescence is the development of a sense of identity.

Figure 4–2.
Young adolescents are psychologically egocentric.

Adulthood

Adulthood is marked by decision making—about advanced education, occupation, intimate relationships, and marriage—and the shift in concern from wanting to be liked by everyone to needing to love and be loved by one special person (see Figure 4–3). Later adulthood is marked by commitment beyond the self—to family, community, work, and even society as a whole and the future world. Individuals who are adults physically but who are still adolescents psychologically may have difficulty in parenting or succeeding in a vocation.

Figure 4–3.
In adulthood, a shift in concern occurs from wanting to be liked by everyone to needing to love and be loved by one special person.

Description. Adulthood is the time period when people are usually in the process of establishing themselves financially, rearing children, taking their place in the community, and making progress in their jobs. Older adults are usually more established than young adults and reap the consequences of their earlier years. Adulthood essentially coincides with a person's entrance into the world of work. It begins with the termination of a person's continuous schooling and ends with a retirement. Work consumes more of an adult's waking hours than any other activity.

Super (1957) views the process of engaging in a career as developmental in nature. He proposes five sequential stages. During Stage I, the Growth Stage, careers are thought about in terms of fantasy, interests, and capacities. This stage lasts up to about 14 years of age. During Stage II, the Exploration Stage, careers are explored through self-awareness and role experimentation provided by school and part-time work (see Figure 4–4). This stage lasts from about age 15 to age 24. A commitment to a permanent job within a particular career occurs during Stage III, the Establishment Stage, which lasts from about age 25 to age 44. Stage IV, the Maintenance Stage, is from about age 45 to age 65. It covers

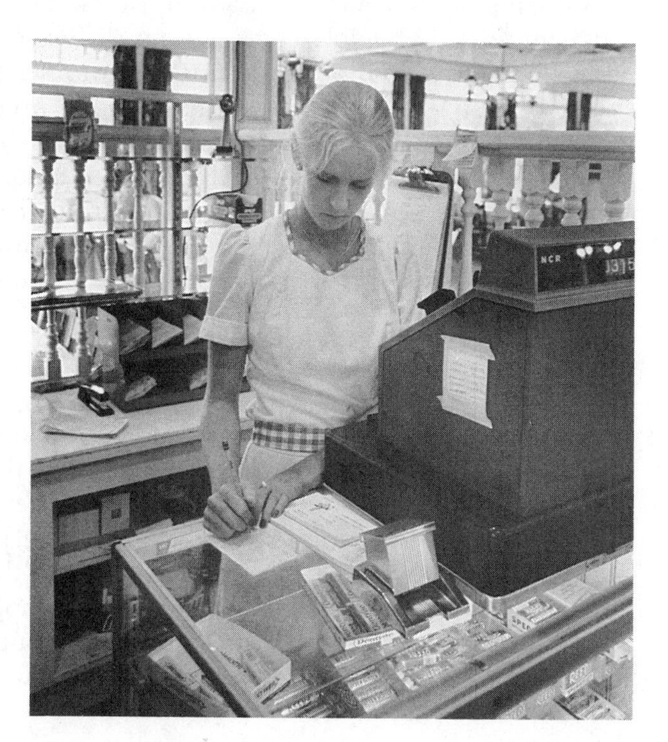

Figure 4–4.
During Super's Stage II, the Exploration Stage, from about 15 to 24 years of age, careers are explored through part-time work.

the time when a person does whatever is needed to continue or maintain a career. During Stage V, the Decline Stage, from about 65 years of age and older, the pace and demands of the job may change, and retirement will require new patterns of adjustment. Sometimes adults may shift career directions and orient themselves toward new goals; however, vocational interests tend to be rather stable throughout the adult period (Troll, 1975).

Occupational status largely determines social status, which in turn relates to a person's values, customs, and expectations. Jobs determine many things such as where people live; how often they move; who cares for their children; the number of hours they spend working, eating, or sleeping; their evening and weekend activities; their participation in organizations; and the amount of money they have to spend. Vocational choice and vocational development exert a great influence on an adult's life.

Figure 4–5.
Erikson considers the development of a meaningful love relationship or deep friendship to be the major achievement of early adulthood.

Tasks to be Mastered. Erikson considers the major achievement of early adulthood to be the development of a meaningful love relationship and/or deep friendship with others (see Figure 4–5). Failure to establish intimacy, i.e., the ability to care about others and to share experiences with them, results in isolation. In later adulthood, fulfillment is achieved through productive or creative work, by guiding one's children, or by helping others—all of which broadens one's energies to include society in general. Erikson called this task generativity.

Old Age

The concern of old age revolves around an attitude toward life in general, particularly one's own life, and the meaning and purpose of life. This attitude can be strikingly different for a person who has mastered the psychological tasks at each stage of development than for a person who is psychologically still a child or an adolescent, or who has failed to form intimate emotional relationships and to succeed in the world of work as an adult.

What are some typical physical characteristics of old age?

Characteristics. Although some people are old at 65, some much sooner, and some much later, the common retirement age is considered to be 65 and is seen as a dividing line between adulthood and old age. Physical changes that may accompany old age are dry and wrinkled skin, impaired strength and agility, brittle bones that break easier and mend slower than in earlier years, white hair that becomes thinner, and a bowing spine. Less time is usually spent in deep sleep, and more naps may be taken during the day. A general slowing down of behavior usually becomes one of the noticeable effects of old age. Also, the sensory processes may become less acute. Older people have a varied course of development. Some remain actively engaged in work, family, and society while others retire to a quiet, uninvolved life; still others are plunged into poverty and isolation by forced retirement and social neglect.

What is ageism?

Ageism refers to discrimination or prejudice on the basis of age. The older person is often stereotyped, especially by the media, as being senile, meddling, lonely, dependent, unattractive, and incompetent. Youth may be stereotyped as being fresh, attractive, energetic, active, and appealing. Ageism applies to people of all ages and can affect young as well as old people. For example, a person applying for a job may be considered too old or too young to adequately perform the job even though he or she may not be told that age is a factor. Many people refuse to accept stereotyped images of themselves. One of the best ways older people can combat ageism is to counter stereotypes with facts.

Figure 4–6.
The developmental tasks of the aged are to adjust to change and to develop a sense of integrity.

Adjustment to Change. The developmental tasks of the aged are to adjust to change and to develop a sense of integrity (see Figure 4–6). Two principle theories have been proposed to explain successful adjustment to the changes of aging. The **disengagement theory** assumes that as people grow older, withdrawal from their social surroundings should occur because withdrawal is seen as a natural part of aging that has psychological benefits. The aged welcome disengagement because it relieves them of roles and responsibilities they have become less able to fulfill. Society benefits from disengagement because younger people with new energy and skills fill positions vacated by the aging people.

Figure 4–7.
Proponents of the activity theory believe that as people grow older they should remain active in order to retain the satisfaction that work brings.

In contrast to the disengagement theory, the **activity theory** assumes that activity is the essence of life. As people grow older, they need to maintain the activities of their earlier years and their work responsibilities for as long as possible and then seek other activities to replace work in order to maintain a high level of activity and not lose the satisfactions that work brings (see Figure 4–7). Society benefits from their experience and ability to think reflectively. Whether older people meet the challenges of life by withdrawing from some activities or by taking up new ones seems to be an individual matter according to some researchers (Elias, Elias, & Elias, 1977); however, the majority of studies conducted on aging support the activity theory (Barrow & Smith, 1979). According to Erikson, whether a person successfully achieved the tasks of each of the preceding developmental periods determines whether that person develops a sense of integrity or despair in old age. Old age is a time of reflection.

Death and Dying. If a person can look back with a sense of satisfaction and acceptance and develop a sense of integrity, aging and death may be faced with dignity; otherwise, the aged person may fall into despair, and aging and death may be faced with fear and depression (see Figure 4–8). Based on extensive study of terminally ill patients, Elizabeth Kubler-Ross (1969) theorizes that a dying person progresses through five psychological stages: (a) *denial,* when the person denies that death is impending; (b) *anger,* as frustration builds; (c) *bargaining,* when the person pleads with God, doctors, and others for postponement of death; (d) *depression,* when death is imminent; and (e) *acceptance,* when the person is almost void of feelings and seemingly ready for life on earth to end.

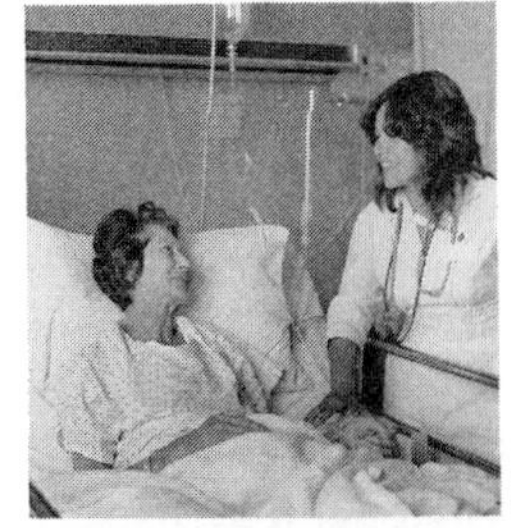

Figure 4–8.
Based on extensive study of terminally ill patients, Elizabeth Kubler-Ross theorizes that a dying person progresses through five psychological stages.

COGNITIVE AND MORAL DEVELOPMENT

Understanding the thinking, cognitive, and intellectual capabilities of a person and the way a person reasons about right and wrong at various ages and stages of development has important practical applications in the business world as well as for parents, teachers, and other individuals. Because a large proportion of the population of our nation is under 12 years of age, designing and marketing products to fit the intellectual needs and capabilities of children is big business. For example, consider the toy industry, the book-publishing business, television programming, or advertising. Recognizing the level of development of thinking and of moral reasoning in a person can help a manager to have more realistic expectations of an employee, to better understand an employee's behavior, and to be able to deal with an employee more effectively. The most influential theoretical approach to the study of the development of thinking and the theory on which virtually all the recent research on moral reasoning has been based are presented in this section.

Are there practical applications of the theories of cognitive and moral development?

Intellectual Development

The child's logic changes and becomes more and more like an adult's. Jean Piaget (pronounced *Pea ah ZHAY*) (1896-1980) (see Figure 4–9) concluded from his many observations that attention needs to be shifted from looking at the quantity of intelligence or problem solving to looking at the quality of thinking in problem

Figure 4–9.
Jean Piaget.

solving in order to understand an individual's behavior. Furthermore, he concluded that children of different ages have a distinctive, characteristic way of thinking and solving problems. This qualitative view of intelligence and the stages of cognitive development—the development of thinking and the intellectual processes used in problem solving—are explained on the next few pages.

What point of view did Piaget take?

Piaget's Views. Piaget, one of the most influential psychologists of this century, believed that cognitive development—the development of thought, knowledge, and understanding—has its roots in the biological makeup of the individual. However, he also believed experience in the environment (learning) is a necessary component. Piaget took an interactionist point of view and theorized that cognitive development progresses through a sequence of stages. Biological development of the nervous system guides the sequence, but special training and experience progresses the individual to the next stage, provided a certain level of maturation has been reached. The forces of maturation interact with an individual's experiences in the environment. This interaction results in action patterns (**schemes**) and thought structures (**operations**) that enable the individual to adapt to the environment, to act and think in a particular way.

In Piaget's view, intelligence can be defined as the ability to adapt to the environment and to new situations. The order of the stages of intellectual development for the development of thought remains constant; however, the rate of progression through the stages varies for different individuals. An individual's schemes and operations (i.e., the ways he or she responds to a stimulus situation, thinks, understands, and adapts to the environment) proceed through a series of qualitative changes by the processes of assimilation and accommodation.

In Piaget's view of intelligence, what is assimilation?

In the process of **assimilation,** a person adapts to new situations by applying existing action patterns and thought structures (schemes and operations). For example, the newborn has a reflex action pattern to turn the head toward the touch of the nipple on the cheek for feeding. Babies will make this same response to any new object that touches the cheek. Or an individual may have an action pattern for turning the lid to open a bottle. When presented with a bottle never encountered before, the individual will apply the same action pattern. Or a worker may have the thought structure for solving distance, rate, and time problems for automobile travel by the formula $d = rt$. If presented problems in distance, rate, and time with trains, the worker can solve them with the same operation. Assimilation is a horizontal expansion of intelligence.

In Piaget's view of intelligence, what is accommodation?

In the process of **accommodation,** a person adapts to new situations by changing or modifying existing schemes and operations. For example, the individual mentioned earlier may encounter a new bottle with a lid that must be pressed down at the same time that it is turned in order to open the bottle. The action pattern must be changed or modified to fit the new situation. Or if the worker mentioned earlier is presented with distance, rate, and time problems of airplanes or boats, the formula may have to be modified to account for the wind speed or the rate of the water current. Changing ways of thinking and acting is a vertical expansion of intelligence and is the way a person moves up to the next stage. Therefore, new experiences in the environment must be encountered that do not fit the existing ways of acting and thinking for intellectual growth to progress to a higher level.

Stages of Cognitive Development. The **sensorimotor stage** of intelligence, which consists of approximately the first 2 years of life, is the stage that occurs prior to the development of language and involves sensation- and motor-response relationships. One intellectual achievement during this period is the ability to exhibit goal-directed, intentional behavior. Another achievement during this period is the ability to coordinate and integrate information coming in from the different senses. A third important achievement during this stage is understanding that objects are permanent and exist even when not seen (see Figure 4–10). In other words, during this period children become capable of mentally perceiving objects and events not present in their environment.

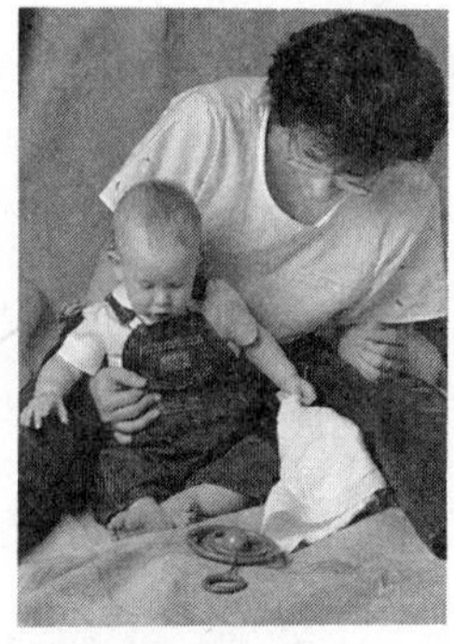

Figure 4–10. Searching for and finding an object becomes possible during infancy.

During the **preoperational stage,** the period from approximately 2 to 7 years of age, the child becomes increasingly able to represent objects and events symbolically. This development is exhibited in the child's use of language and mental imagery as when the child uses a stick to represent a gun or a doll to represent a baby. The preoperational child is egocentric; the child cannot recognize any role or viewpoint other than his or her own. If asked, "Why does the sun shine?", the response may be, "To keep me warm." Or if asked, "What are TV sets used for?", the response may be, "To watch my favorite cartoons." Also, the preoperational child tends to center—to focus attention—on a single aspect of a visual stimulus, ignoring other relevant attributes. For example, in the glass problem in Figure 4–11, the preoperational child cannot

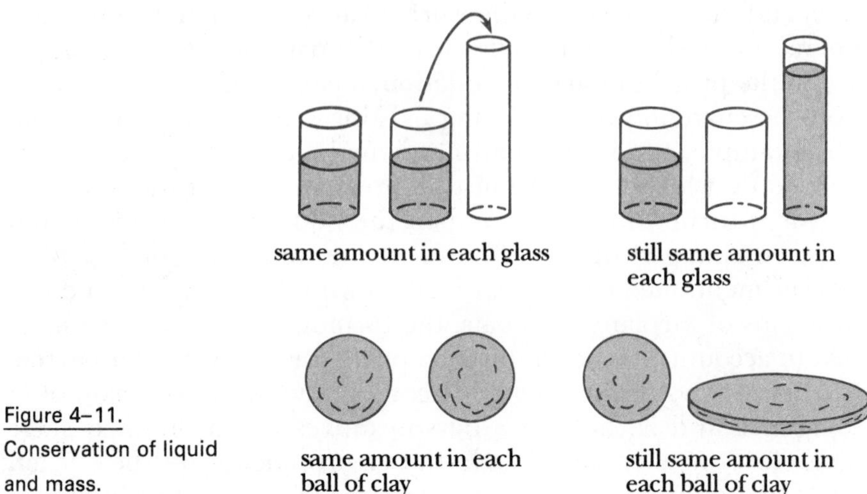

Figure 4–11.
Conservation of liquid and mass.

focus on height and width simultaneously; and in the clay problem, he or she cannot focus on both size and shape at the same time. A third important characteristic of a child in this stage is the inability to reverse the thought processes or to **conserve.** For example, a child in this stage thinks that a ball of clay when flattened contains more mass because the flattened clay takes up more surface area than the original ball of clay. The child cannot mentally roll the flattened clay back into the round ball and realize that if it were rolled up again it would be the same amount of clay because nothing was taken away or added. The child in this stage also has difficulty differentiating between objects and living creatures and injects human qualities and feelings into inanimate things (animistic behavior). For example, the preoperational child may believe that a chair will hurt if it is kicked or that boats sleep at night.

What is meant by the ability to conserve?

The child develops the capacity to reason and solve problems in a logical manner during the **concrete operational stage,** the period from about 7 to 11 years of age. Classification systems develop during this period so that a hierarchical relation of classes and subclasses is established. For example, if six yellow apples (three large and three small) and four red apples (one large and three small) were placed in view, the child could correctly respond to the question, Are there more yellow apples or more large apples? The preoperational child could answer the question, Are there more yellow apples or more red apples? but could not answer the preceding question. The ability to reverse thought processes or to conserve is characteristic of the concrete operational stage. Piaget's writing discusses conservation of numbers, length, liquid, mass, weight, area, and volume. Conservation of mass is illustrated when the child understands that changing the shape of the ball of clay does not change the amount of clay. Conservation of liquid is illustrated when the child understands that the amount of liquid remains the same whether it is poured into a tall, thin glass or a wide, low glass. During the concrete operational stage, a child is capable of understanding how a solid can be transformed into a liquid and changed back again to the original state.

The **formal operational stage** follows the concrete operational stage and is characterized by the ability to do abstract thinking, to consider all possible combinations of events in problems presented, and to exclude those that are irrelevant. The capacity to consider hypothetical situations is also characteristic of this stage. Imaginal representation in the younger child was limited to the child's experience; now hypothetical events or combinations that the child has never actually experienced can be imagined. The child can now think about how things could be rather than how they are—logical deductive reasoning. This ability is necessary for formulating hypotheses for scientific inquiry (see Figure 4–12). The formal operational stage is also characterized by the ability to deal with abstract philosophical principles such as the meaning of life. In summary, in the formal operational stage, the individual can do a mental operation on a mental operation.

Figure 4–12.
Formal operational thinking enables an individual to consider hypothetical situations and do logical deductive reasoning necessary for scientific inquiry.

Moral Development

Figure 4–13.
Lawrence Kohlberg.

Moral development is the process of internalizing standards of right and wrong—of internalizing a culturally defined set of rules whereby behaviors are personally classified as good or bad, acceptable or unacceptable. People develop a set of values and a conscience that results in feelings of guilt when transgression of the behaviors labeled good or right occurs or, in other words, when violation of the conscience occurs. A person's morality is his or her system of learned personal beliefs and thoughts used to evaluate situations or behaviors. A person's morality may change and may develop throughout life. Lawrence Kohlberg (see Figure 4–13), inspired by the work of Piaget, proposed a stage theory of moral development. The stages of moral development that an individual progresses through according to Piaget and Kohlberg will be examined in this section.

What are the three parts into which moral development can be divided?

Issues. Moral development can be divided into three parts: (a) moral behavior, what the individual actually does; (b) moral feelings, how the person feels when the behavior is a transgression of the value system; and (c) moral reasoning, the rationale or type of thinking used to justify the rules for ethical conduct.

A person's behavior does not always follow moral reasoning, and ultimately it is moral behavior that socialization seeks to influence. Social learning theory, which is concerned with the processes of reinforcement, punishment, and imitation, is most concerned with the moral behavior part of moral development. Social learning theory is presented later in chapter 6.

Moral feelings are assessed through measures of guilt. Guilt may be conscious, but it is primarily unconscious and is related to anxiety and personality disorders. The psychoanalytic view of psychology is particularly concerned with this part of moral development. Attention is directed to guilt, anxiety, and the feeling part of morality in chapters 11 and 12 on personality theories and psychological disorders.

On which part of moral development did Piaget and Kohlberg focus?

Piaget and Kohlberg focused on the cognitive element of moral development—moral reasoning or thinking. According to Kohlberg (1969), moral behavior is guided by consistent moral thought. Juvenile delinquents have lower moral reasoning scores than nondelinquents, and a person with a high level of moral reasoning is less likely to cheat or harm another individual in a contrived situation at the request of an experimenter. How an individual thinks influences how he or she acts and feels. According to both Piaget and Kohlberg, moral feelings and behaviors are mediated by changes in cognitive development. As cognitive development progresses, thinking becomes more complex and more consistent in a logical sense, and thus moral reasoning can change and affect moral behavior and moral feelings. Moral reasoning is the part of moral development to which attention is directed in this chapter.

Piaget's views. To develop his general theory of cognitive development in children, Piaget observed children in game playing and tried to understand the way they think about and use the rules of the game. He also talked to children to understand how they think about such ethical concepts as stealing, cheating, lying, punishment, and justice. Piaget concluded that until about age 3 (during the sensorimotor stage) the child has no understanding of rules.

Piaget further concluded that preschool (or preoperationally thinking) children progress through a distinct stage of moral development. When rules are first internalized, the rules are believed to be absolute and unchangeable, and coming from an external authority such as parents or God. Another feature of this stage is a belief that if a rule is broken, punishment will automatically be meted out immediately. A young child may look around worriedly after violating a rule, expecting some automatic punishment to follow. If a child accidentally tears a page in a book and immediately falls down and bruises the knee, the child reasons that it is punishment for bad behavior. Also, if a child is running and falls down and bruises the knee, running is reasoned to be bad because it was followed by punishment. A third feature of this stage is that the child judges the level of goodness or badness of the behavior mostly on the consequences rather than on intentions. For example, a child who accidentally drops a tray and breaks *four* cups while helping set the table has exhibited worse behavior than a child who intentionally and deliberately throws a cup at a person to hurt the person and breaks *one* cup.

A shift occurs in moral reasoning about the time a child reaches the concrete operational stage of thinking, when the child realizes that punishment is meted out socially by people and is not automatic. The child realizes that punishment occurs only if witnessed by a relevant person, and that punishment in fact may not always occur. In this stage, the child can define a set of acceptable rules and play cooperatively (see Figure 4–14). Rules are viewed now as

Figure 4–14.
After a child reaches the preoperational stage of thinking, he or she can define a set of acceptable rules and play cooperatively.

the product of mutual consent; however, rules are still viewed as invariant, and everyone must follow the same rules. Because children's knowledge of the details of the rules may be unclear, different versions of the rules may be applied at various times. Also, the intentions of the person begin to be taken into account in judging the badness of a behavior.

According to Kohlberg, through how many stages of moral reasoning may an individual progress?

Kohlberg's Views. Kohlberg agreed with Piaget's view. However, he believed that the process was more complex and progressed on through many more stages throughout a person's lifetime than Piaget had proposed. By interviewing and studying responses of people to moral dilemmas (see box on page 131), Kohlberg concluded after 20 or so years that there are three main levels of moral reasoning and two substages within each level. Thus, there are six distinct stages in the progression of moral development. Kohlberg argues that these stages are universal and follow the same sequence in all cultures. He believes each stage is built on the one preceding it so that a new stage of moral reasoning does not emerge until the preceding one has been mastered.

What is the relationship between cognitive development and moral development?

According to Kohlberg, the cognitive structures in the brain must reach a particular level of maturity for a particular stage of moral reasoning to be reached, but the social environment provides the raw material on which the thinking operates. Peer interaction is considered to be of major importance. Authority figures may impose rules, but the mutual give-and-take in peer interaction provides the individual with an opportunity to take the view of another person. Reciprocal discussion with others, group encounters, education, travel, and the encountering of other cultures provide opportunities for an individual to take the view of another person also (see Figure 4–15). Social isolates were found to have less advanced moral reasoning than those who interacted frequently with a group (Kohlberg, 1958). Leadership in groups is thought to be a factor in the development of moral reasoning because boys and girls who had been leaders in extracurricular group activities were found to be at a higher Kohlberg stage of moral reasoning than those who had not been leaders (Keasey, 1971).

Figure 4–15.
Reciprocal discussion with others, group encounters, education, travel, and the encountering of other cultures provide opportunities for an individual to take the view of another person.

The fourth stage is the stage most commonly found in adults. Only a very few adults ever reach the final stage of moral thought. Just because an individual reasons at a particular stage in one behavioral domain does not mean he or she reasons at that stage in all domains of behavior. For example, 20 percent of an adult's moral reasoning may be at the fifth stage, 70 percent at the fourth stage, and 10 percent at the third stage. The adult would be considered to be at the fourth stage of moral development because it is the most typical of his or her type of moral reasoning.

Kohlberg was not interested in whether an individual should or should not exhibit a particular behavior. Instead, his objective was to analyze the reasoning and to understand the guidelines used to make the decision. The box on page 131 shows examples of responses to a dilemma presented that have been coded at the six different stages of moral development.

Kohlberg's Levels and Stages. The three levels of moral development and the two stages within each level that people progress through according to Kohlberg are only briefly summarized here. Level I, called **preconventional morality** because the conventions or rules of society are not yet known and understood, is typical of children up to about 9 years of age. At this level, moral value resides in external happenings, in actions, or in needs rather than in a person and in standards. Moral behavior is under external control rather than internal control. Because the child is egocentric and thinks in terms of the self, what is evaluated as good or bad is in relationship to the self. Stage 1 of Level I moral development is specifically characterized by a punishment orientation. Behavior that is punished is bad, and behavior that is not punished is good. Moral behavior is exhibited to avoid punishment. When moral development progresses to Stage 2, the orientation is on reward or

In Stage 1 of moral development, what determines whether a behavior is good or bad?

In Stage 2 of moral development, what determines whether a behavior is right?

the satisfying of needs. A behavior is judged to be right if it satisfies one's own need or involves an even exchange—reciprocity. Moral behavior is exhibited to bring some sort of benefit in return.

Level II, known as **conventional morality,** is typical of 9- to 20-year-olds. Morality at this level is called conventional because moral value resides in what is conventional or typical behavior or in the rules of the society. Stage 3, which is in this level, is often called the good-boy/good-girl stage. Behavior is judged to be right if it pleases or impresses others, conforms to stereotyped images, keeps everybody happy, and maintains goodwill. Moral behavior is exhibited for praise, acceptance, and approval by other people. Conforming behavior leads to an internal awareness of rules, and in Stage 4 identification shifts to institutions of society such as church, school, and government. Moral value resides in authority and maintaining social order. This stage is characterized by an orientation to fulfilling duties, showing respect for authority, and abiding by the laws. Behavior that is fulfilling agreements, obeying laws, obeying an authority figure, or contributing to society, the group, or the institution (community service) is judged to be good or right behavior. Moral behavior is exhibited to maintain the social order—to show respect for God, others, and authority.

In Stage 3 of moral development, what determines whether a behavior is judged to be good?

In Stage 4 of moral development, what is used to judge behavior as right or wrong?

Level III, **postconventional morality,** is believed not to occur until after the age of 20 and then in only a small proportion of the population. This level is called postconventional because morality goes beyond or past internalizing and understanding rules to understanding and internalizing principles. Level III is a principled morality. Moral value resides in conformity by the self to standards or duties that protect the rights of individuals such as the right to life and liberty, not just blind obedience to authority; this conformity is sometimes referred to as mutual agreement.

Stage 5, which is in Level III, is characterized by recognition that laws are changeable. A person in this stage may devote time and energy to getting laws changed for the betterment of society as a whole. Stage 5 is a social-contract orientation and is a shift to a larger viewpoint. Kohlberg believes that this stage emerges when a person recognizes that there are some issues that can't be resolved by relying on fixed laws. Right behavior is reasoned to be what accomplishes the greatest benefit for the greatest number of people. Generally, right behavior is what conforms to the rules, laws, and authority, but these are considered relative and must be balanced with rights, fairness, or appropriateness.

Stage 6 is an orientation to universal ethical principles that transcend the authority of law. Right behavior is following self-chosen ethical principles (following one's own conscience) when laws violate these principles. Right behavior is behavior that respects the dignity of the self and all humans. Thus, moral development is a movement from external control to internal control.

A POPULAR KOHLBERG DILEMMA

In Europe a woman was near death from a special form of cancer. There was one drug that the doctors thought might save her. It was a form of radium that a druggist in the same town had recently discovered. The drug was expensive to make, but the druggist was charging ten times what the drug cost him to make. He paid $200 for the radium and charged $2000 for a small dose of the drug. The sick woman's husband, Heinz, went to everyone he knew to borrow the money, but he could only get together $1,000. He told the druggist that his wife was dying and asked him to sell it cheaper or let him pay later. But the druggist said, "No, I discovered the drug, and I am going to make money from it." So Heinz became desperate and broke into the man's store to steal the drug for his wife.

SIX STAGES OF RESPONSES TO THE HEINZ DILEMMA

Stage 1—Punishment orientation
Pro He should steal the drug. It is not really bad to take it. It is not as of he did not ask to pay for it first. The drug he would take is only worth $200, so he is not really taking a $2,000 drug.
Con Heinz shouldn't steal; he should buy the drug. If he steals the drug, he might be jailed and have to return the drug anyway.

Stage 2—Reward-exchange orientation
Pro Heinz should steal the drug to save his wife's life. He might be sent to jail, but he'd still have his wife.
Con He should not steal it. The druggist is not wrong or bad, he just wants to make a profit. That is what you are in business for, to make money.

Stage 3—Good-boy/good-girl orientation
Pro He should steal the drug. He would only be doing something that is natural for a good husband to do. You cannot blame him for doing something out of love for his wife, but you could blame him if he did not love his wife enough to save her.
Con He should not steal. If his wife dies, he cannot be blamed. If she dies, it would not be because he is heartless or because he did

not love her enough to do everything that he could do legally. The druggist is the selfish or heartless one.

Stage 4—Maintaining-social-order orientation

Pro He should steal the drug. When you get married, you take a vow to love and cherish your spouse. Marriage is not only love, but it's an obligation. It's like a legal contract.

Con He should not steal the drug. It is a natural thing for Heinz to want to save his wife, but it is still always wrong to steal. He knows he would be stealing and taking a valuable drug from the man who made it.

Stage 5—Social-contract orientation

Pro He should steal the drug. The law was not set up for these circumstances. Taking the drug in this situation would not be right, but it would be justified.

Con He should not steal the drug. You cannot completely blame someone for stealing, but extreme circumstances do not really justify taking the law into your own hands. You cannot have people stealing whenever they are desperate. The end may be good, but the end does not justify the means.

Stage 6—Universal-ethical-principles orientation

Pro He should steal the drug. This is a situation that forces Heinz to choose between stealing and letting his wife die. In a situation where this kind of choice must be made, it is morally right to steal. He has to act in terms of the principle of preserving and respecting life.

Con He should not steal the drug. Heinz is faced with the decision of whether to consider the possibility of other people who need the drug just as badly as his wife. Heinz ought to act not according to his particular feelings toward his wife but in consideration for the value of all the lives involved.

Note: From *Handbook of Socialization Theory and Research* (pp. 379-380) by D. A. Goslin (Ed.), 1969, Chicago: Rand McNally. Copyright © 1969 by Rand McNally. Adapted by permission.

SOCIAL AND EMOTIONAL DEVELOPMENT

The nature of an individual's relationships with people and the emotions experienced change over time. In this section, significant aspects of these areas of development will be highlighted.

Attachment

Ainsworth (1972) defined **attachment** (sometimes referred to as *affection*) as an emotional tie or bond that develops between a person and another specific individual—a psychological need for the physical presence and emotional support of that individual. When an emotional tie exists, there is an effort to be near or maintain contact in some way. Attachments may exist between children and adults and between children as well as between adults.

Figure 4–16.
The first and probably the most important social relationship formed is the one between the parent or caregiver and the infant.

Parent-Child Attachments. The first and probably the most important social relationship formed is the one between the parent or caregiver and the infant (see Figure 4–16). The caregiver first forms an attachment to the child, which ensures that the child will be nurtured and protected. Sometimes attachment occurs even before birth or at the time of birth when the infant is seen, but the ties are strengthened by repeated contact and interactions with the child.

Attachment of the child to the caregiver follows a predictable pattern. Up to about 3 months of age, attachment behaviors are directed indiscriminantly to any human. About 3 to 5 months of age, the infant is able to discriminate the primary caregiver from others, if they have had repeated contact, and to respond to that particular person with behaviors such as smiling, gesturing to be held, or following the person's movements with the eyes. By about 6 or 7 months of age, the first meaningful attachment has occurred and the infant actively seeks contact with the caregiver (see Figure 4–17). Attachments to others with whom the child has frequent contact may also occur. Although attachments are usually made to people, it is not uncommon for attachments to be made to objects such as a blanket or a familiar toy (see Figure 4–18).

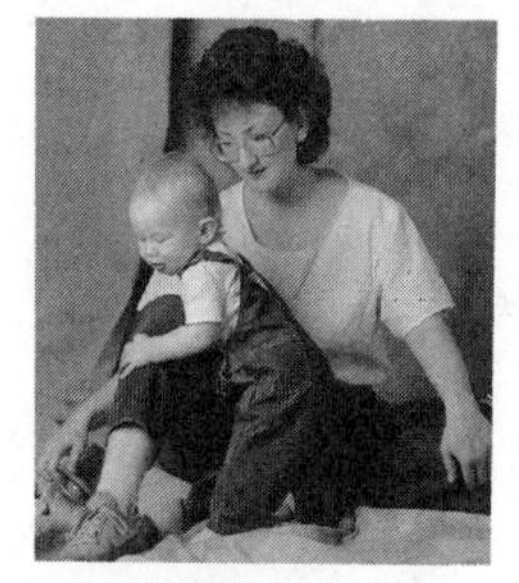

Figure 4–17.
By about 6 or 7 months of age, the first meaningful attachment has occurred and the infant actively seeks contact with the caregiver.

Sometimes for various reasons this natural system of bonding fails or is not as strong as it needs to be for the well-being of the child. Factors that may have a negative effect on the attachment of the parent to the child are (a) unwanted pregnancy; (b) disappointed expectations about such things as sex, physical characteristics, or behavior (the infant is expected to require little attention, for example, and very seldom cry, but the baby does cry and requires a great deal of attention); and (c) unresponsiveness on the part of the infant, perhaps because of some abnormal condition that may cause the parent to feel rejected by the infant. If the parent or caregiver is not securely attached to the infant, he or she gradually may withdraw from the child, and child abuse can in some instances result. Oftentimes it is possible to intervene therapeutically and help an unattached caregiver become more attached.

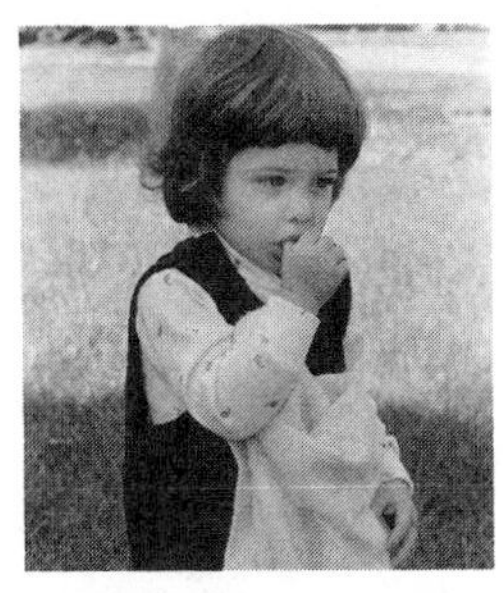

Figure 4–18.
It is not uncommon for attachments to be made to objects such as a blanket or a familiar toy.

An infant may not attach to a person during the first few months because of maturational deficiencies, because contact has not been maintained with one caregiver long enough for attachment to form, or because of unresponsiveness on the part of the caregiver. Caregiver style and personality of the infant both influence the security of the attachment. Caregivers of securely attached infants are more supportive of their infant's independent play, more sensitive to the infant's needs, and more expressive than caregivers of insecurely attached infants.

According to Bee (1981), researchers have been finding that the first social relationship (attachment) has an effect on later adjustment, and links have been found between early attachment to the caregiver and later success with peers, with school tasks, with taking the lead, with curiosity, and with ego maturity (concept of self). As more and more mothers of young infants enter the work force, the impact of day-care centers on attachment has become a concern. After many studies in various settings, researchers have concluded that day-care centers do not necessarily weaken the emotional bonding between parent and child (see Figure 4–19).

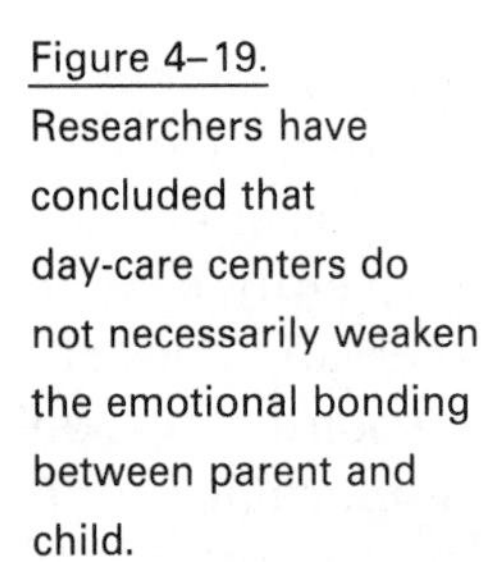

Figure 4–19.
Researchers have concluded that day-care centers do not necessarily weaken the emotional bonding between parent and child.

When the care given by the center is of optimal quality, even for infants one year of age the effect can be advantageous and be an enriching and stimulating experience (Harris, 1986). Of course, day-care centers can be physically and emotionally devastating to a child. Two features of day-care that emerged as being significant in the National Day Care Study (Ruopp, Travers, Glantz, & Coelen, 1979) were (a) training—whether or not the child was cared for by a caregiver who had specific training in the area of child development; and (b) group size—whether or not the child was cared for in a small group of 15 or less.

Do emotional bonds with parents or caregivers remain the strongest relationships throughout life?

Peer Attachment. The strongest emotional bonds for the first few years are with parents or other caregivers, but other children (peers) gradually become more and more important. By adulthood primary attachments are to peers—friends, lovers, or spouses. During the first year of life, babies begin to interact with each other by looking, imitating actions, and smiling. From 1 to 2 years of age, children spend more time looking at each other, may exchange toys, or may say something to each other such as, "hi." The more time a child spends with peers the more social the child becomes. Mildred Parten (1933) described five stages of peer interaction or play: (a) solitary play, playing alone and independently; (b) on-looker play, watching other children play and asking questions; (c) parallel play, playing beside but not with another child; (d) associative play, playing with another child, talking about common activities, borrowing and loaning toys, but not sharing a goal; (e) cooperative play, sharing to achieve goals, cooperating to produce some product, and dividing the labor. The stage of cooperative play is usually reached by school age.

What are the stages of the development of play?

As young as age 3 or 4, children begin to have special attachments or emotional bonds with another child—friendships (see Figure 4–20). Friendship formation too progresses through stages and tends to increase in number over the school years. During elementary school, friendship groups begin to form almost exclusively of the same sex. In adolescence, the groups become closer knit, more significant, and more segregated along social class than in elementary school. The groups also shift to include both sexes.

Figure 4–20. As young as age 3 or 4, children begin to have special attachments or emotional bonds with another child—friendships.

In a study of popularity (Asher, Oden, & Gottman, 1977), it was found that children chosen most frequently as playmates or leaders of groups had the following characteristics: friendly, outgoing, successful in school, physically attractive, excellent at some task valued by the group, and physically mature for their age (see Figure 4–21). The families of children who are popular seem to have some common characteristics also. They discourage aggression and antisocial behavior, do not frustrate the child, punish very little, like their children and tell them they do, and foster secure attachment in the first years of the child's life. It seems that children who feel good about themselves (like themselves) are liked by others.

Figure 4–21.
Popular children have been found to be friendly, outgoing, successful in school, physically attractive, excellent at some task valued by the group, and physically mature for their age.

Figure 4–22.
In older children and adults, two kinds of social relationships are needed—an emotional attachment to one special other person and social ties to a network of friends.

In older children and adults, two kinds of social relationships are needed—an emotional attachment to one special other person and social ties to a network of friends (see Figure 4–22). The need for emotional attachment to one particular person seems to develop from the infant's attachment to the caregiver. It makes available a sense of comfort and security. Social ties to a network of friends provide a sense of group identity and integration. Thus, there are two kinds of loneliness: (a) emotional, due to loss or absence of an emotional attachment; and (b) social, due to loss or absence of social ties (a network of friends).

Love has been defined in many ways. Rubin (1970) defined love as an attitude held by one person toward another consisting of three components—attachment (which has already been defined), caring, and intimacy. Caring is the feelings of concern and responsibility for the life and growth of another person. Intimacy is the desire for close and confidential communication with the person—the desire to share thoughts and feelings more fully than with anyone else. Intimacy may be psychological, physical, or both.

Development of Emotions

A child's emotions become increasingly differentiated as cognitive development advances. And negative emotions as well as positive emotions develop because both are needed for an individual to be well prepared for life.

For best psychological adjustment, should an individual experience only positive emotions?

Positive Emotions. Emotional balance needs to be maintained to avoid a distorted outlook on life. An individual should not become so dependent on everything being rosy that unpleasant emotions cannot be tolerated when they arise. But neither should one be so dominated by unpleasant emotions that a disagreeable, sullen, sad disposition develops that interferes with good social adjustment.

A child at birth is capable of experiencing general, undifferentiated excitement; however, very soon feelings of delight and distress are differentiated. Then between 6 months and 1 year of age, delight is differentiated into elation and attachment (or affection) for adults, which become emotional experiences of the child. By 18 months of age, a child is experiencing affection or attachment to other children, and by 2 years of age a child can experience joy and milder forms of joy such as pleasure and happiness. Humor also is being experienced by 2 years of age, although what is humorous changes with age.

Negative Emotions. Distress is differentiated into the emotions of anger, disgust, and fear by the time a child is 6 months of age and into jealousy soon after reaching 1 year of age. With the child as with the adult, empathy parallels emotion recognition. A young child may feel sympathetic distress when another person is sad or angry, but he or she may not have the ability to assume the differentiation of the emotion perceived by that person.

Are fears innate or are they learned?

Fears are learned from experience in the environment and are important for survival. Fear becomes differentiated as cognitive development progresses. Anxiety begins to be experienced first in the form of stranger anxiety by about 6 months of age. Shyness is an almost universal form of fear at this early age due to uncertainty as to how a person will react. A child does not begin to feel embarrassment until standards of behavior are learned and does not experience worry until the concept of future is learned. What is feared is related to age. Imaginary, irrational fears are typical of the preschool age child such as fear of the dark, of being alone, or of imaginary creatures. Fears become more realistic with school age such as fear of school failure, of rejection, or of physical injury. Fears gradually decrease as an individual gets older, but anger tends to increase.

What are some sources of anger?

Anger begins to be experienced first in response to physical discomfort, then in response to interference with possessions or when goal-directed activity is added, and later in response to faultfinding, teasing, thwarting of desires, and lecturing. Anger arouses aggression that is directed towards objects or persons. The form and amount of aggression changes with age. The peak of physical aggression is at about age 4. Verbal aggression begins about this time, and as verbal aggression increases, physical aggression decreases. Children who are reinforced for aggression, who are rejected, who are permitted to be aggressive and then punished for it, and who watch a lot of violence on TV seem to show heightened aggression. The most consistent findings in sex differences in social relationships is that boys are more aggressive than girls. To enhance the development of good interpersonal or social relationships leading to good psychological and emotional adjustment, children need to be taught assertive behavior and reinforced for assertive behavior, which is distinguished from aggression in that it is not aimed at hurting the other person. When the anger is turned inward and aimed at hurting the self, submissive behavior is the result.

What is the difference in aggressive, assertive, and submissive behavior?

Another negative emotion that develops rapidly during the preschool years is jealousy. Feelings of resentment toward a brother or sister is an early form of jealousy caused by feelings of insecurity, most likely fostered by a decrease in warmth and attention on the parent's part toward the child and an increase in the number of prohibitions imposed on the child (Kendrick & Dunn, 1983).

The way a child learns to cope with these emotions when they first appear sets a pattern that influences behavior and personality throughout life. An individual learns to cope by trial and error, by imitation of a model, and by reinforcement and punishment of response patterns.

DEVELOPMENT OF A CONCEPT OF SELF AND SEXUALITY

Although a newly born infant is a separate person physically and is physically male or female, the infant has no perception of the self as an individual or as a member of a particular sex. These perceptions develop over time and have a great impact on the personality of the individual as an adult.

The Concept of Self

The concept of the self consists of three parts—a self-image, a self-concept, and self-esteem. The development of these aspects of the self and the feelings associated with them affect a person's happiness and functioning throughout his or her lifetime.

Patterns of Development. The **self-image,** a recognition of the self, begins to develop first. The first stage in the development of the concept of self is the recognition of being separate from others.

Newborn infants appear to consider the mother or caregiver and the self to be a single unit, not recognizing that their own body parts such as the hand or foot are a part of the self. By age 18 to 20 months, the child recognizes his or her image in a mirror and can point to the self in photographs (see Figure 4–23). By age 3 or 4 the child shows possessiveness about objects and people—things belong to "me." Recognition of self as being separate from others is then clearly established, and a self-image has emerged.

Figure 4–23.
By age 18 to 20 months, the child recognizes his or her image in a mirror and can point to the self in photographs.

The next stage in the development of a concept of self is perceiving the self as a changing and developing entity. This stage develops parallel to the development of object permanence, and thus the self-image continues to be recognized as growth and change occur. During the preschool years, the child begins to identify dimensions by which people differ such as age, size, and gender and locates the self in these same dimensions. The self-image is thus expanded, and it continues to expand during the child's lifetime as more and more complex and abstract dimensions are identified. The image may include such abstract traits as curiousness or indecisiveness and may be somewhat realistic or may be more or less distorted.

Are people's self-concepts always realistic?

As children begin to act independently, they find out what they can do. The **self-concept** is a perception of one's capacities and abilities. The self-concept is not fixed and changes over time as capacities and abilities change because it is heavily dependent on current tasks and relationships. How a child performs in school during the school age is a primary factor in the development of the self-concept. The self-concept, like the self-image, may be realistic or may be distorted in varying degrees. Beliefs about the self's abilities influences actions. When individuals believe they can accomplish a task, they act differently than if they believe they cannot accomplish the task.

What is self-esteem?

Self-esteem is the value an individual places on the self—how important he or she feels to significant others or how much he or she "counts." This also begins to develop during the preschool years and continues throughout a lifetime.

Positive Versus Negative Concepts. As the concept of self develops, emotions and feelings are associated with it. One may like or dislike his or her image; one may be pleased or displeased with what he or she can do; and one may value or devalue the self. Putting all of these perceptions together as a composite, a person has in general and in varying degrees either a positive or a negative concept of the self.

Figure 4–24. Other people give feedback that is influential in forming one's concept of self. Thus, the home and school, early social environments, are important determiners of the concept of self.

Whether a positive or a negative concept of self emerges depends on a number of factors because the concept of self grows out of social encounters. Just as the mirror gives feedback about the physical self, other people give feedback that is influential in forming one's concept of self. Thus the home and school, early social environments, are important determiners of the concept of self (see Figure 4–24). By 5 years of age, a child already seems to have formed an overall general attitude of liking or disliking the self—a positive or negative concept of the self. Socioeconomic status, rate of development, and child-rearing practices also have considerable influence on the concept of self. A satisfying and supportive relationship with parents seems to be crucial to learning to like the self. Success with current relationships and tasks may alter this concept somewhat as development continues. The overall child-rearing practice most favorable to the development of a positive concept of self has been found to be the participative (also referred to as democratic) approach rather than the authoritarian (dictatorial) or permissive approach. Also, the ideal concepts formed by the child are an important influence. Instead of forming realistic ideal concepts for comparison, an individual may form and compare the self with ideals that are unrealistic—too high or too low. The media and society, as well as parents, are important in the formation of the ideal concepts. The development of a positive self-image, a good self-concept, and high self-esteem indicative of an overall positive concept of the self, is considered by most psychologists to be the most important predictor of personal happiness and effective functioning for an individual. Individuals with a positive concept of self handle or cope with anger in an assertive manner. Individuals with a negative concept of self cope in a number of ways. They may use an aggressive manner to belittle others or boast and brag in an effort to deny the negative feelings. Individuals with a negative concept of self also may cope by being shy and quiet to avoid attracting attention and letting others see how unacceptable they are. Or they may be submissive and not get their own needs and desires met because they do not feel they are important enough to count.

What is the single most important predictor of personal happiness and effective functioning?

Sexuality

Sexuality is the whole of an individual's sexual behavior. It includes the development of the gender concept as well as the biological development necessary for the physiological response to sexual arousal for reproduction.

The Gender Concept. A child's concept of gender begins to develop around age 2 and gradually becomes clearer over time. Gender identity begins to occur first and then is accompanied by sex-role stereotyping and sex-role behaviors. The stereotyping and behaviors become clearer as gender identity advances. The child goes through three distinct stages in the development of the gender concept (Slaby & Frey, 1975). First, around 2 to 3 years of age, the child can discriminate males from females and label the self as male or female (gender identity). By about 4 years of age, children conclude they always have been and always will be this sex (gender stability). And third, by about age 5, children figure out that a person's sex will not change even if the person changes in appearance to look like the opposite sex (gender consistency). To help determine if a child has gender identity, ask the child if he or she is a boy or a girl. To help determine if a child has gender stability, ask the child if he or she will be a boy or a girl when grown up or was a boy or girl when a baby. To help determine if gender consistency has developed, have a familiar person dress up to appear as the opposite sex and ask the child if that person is a boy or a girl.

What are the stages in the development of the gender concept?

Various theories have been offered to explain how the gender concept forms and thus how the formation of opposite sex sex-role behaviors occasionally occurs rather than same sex sex-role behaviors. Some psychologists argue that sterotyping and sex-role behaviors are learned by the child being reinforced for doing sex-appropriate things and for imitating same-sex models. Some argue that the process of developing sex-role behaviors is cognitive in nature; once the child is capable of discriminating between two sexes, information is stored on behaviors by sex, rules are generalized, and conclusions drawn. The Freudian view holds that the process occurs at the unconscious (subconscious) level through a process of identification with the parent and others of the same sex. Some psychologists argue that physiological differences, such as in hormonal pattern and in organization of the brain, are the primary factors in development of sex-role behaviors. None of these views seems to be able to explain all the data on sex-role development. No doubt each process contributes to some extent in an interactive way in the development of the gender concept.

Is there one theory that explains the development of sex-role behaviors?

Research studies indicate that individuals who are high in both masculine- and feminine-stereotyped traits are better psychologically adjusted than those individuals high in only one. Examples of traits stereotyped as masculine are strong, assertive, and independent. Examples of traits stereotyped as feminine are warm, expres-

Is androgyny considered to contribute positively or negatively to psychological adjustment?

Figure 4–25.
Teaching as well as other professions requires both masculine- and feminine-stereotyped traits.

sive, and nurturing. During the adult years when a person embarks on a career, many occupations require both the masculine and feminine traits. Teaching and medical professions are examples of careers that require independence, dominance, and assertiveness and also sensitivity and nurturing (see Figure 4–25). Sandra Bem (1975) coined the term **androgyny** (pronounced *an DRAHG e ne*) for a self-concept that allows a person to engage in both feminine- and masculine-stereotyped behaviors. There is evidence today that children are being encouraged to develop both masculine- and feminine-stereotyped traits.

Sexual Development. As gender discrimination and gender identity are forming during the preschool years, children seem to be especially curious about the appearance and function of the genitals. Parents need to be sensitive to the child's needs to know, and they need to be comfortable enough with their own sexuality to answer the child's questions frankly. Parents need to teach socially acceptable behaviors in a manner that does not transmit negative feelings about the body or the genitals. Attitudes formed at this time, such as that the genitals are filthy or dirty or the association of the genitals with punishment, can affect sexual behavior in adulthood. Parents' responses to questions and situations not only influence children's attitudes toward sexual behavior but also influence whether the child will continue to approach parents with sex-related questions and concerns. For example, the child may not continue to approach the parent with questions if the parent shows embarrassment, sends the child to the other parent, or tells the child he or she will find out later. Whether sex education should be taught to children of school age in the home, the school, the church, all three places, or not at all is controversial.

Whether the child has sex education or not, at the age of puberty there is a rapid development of primary and secondary sexual characteristics. The **primary sex characteristics** are the structures essential to reproduction such as the ovaries and the vagina in the female and the testes and penis in the male. The **secondary sex characteristics** are physical characteristics that develop that are not part of the reproductive system such as body hair or breast tissue. The normal age for the onset of menstruation (pronounced *MEN stroo a shun*), the most clearly defined sign of sexual maturity in females, is 10 to 15 years of age. The normal age for the ejaculation (pronounced *e JAK u LA shun*) of semen, the most clearly defined sign that male reproductive organs have become mature, is between 12 and 16 years of age (Helms & Turner, 1976).

What are the most clearly defined signs of physical sexual maturity?

SUMMARY

1. Adolescence, which begins with puberty, is a psychological and physical pulling away from the family and is the time during which sexual maturity, an adult-size physical body, and a sense of identity are attained.
2. Adulthood, marked as beginning with the termination of continuous schooling and ending with retirement, is characterized by decision making related to advanced education, occupation, marriage, and commitment beyond the self to family, community, and work.
3. Super proposed five sequential stages in the process of engaging in a career: growth (up to age 14), exploration (15-24 years of age), establishment (25-44 years of age), maintenance (45-65 years of age), and decline (65 years of age and older).
4. Old age, often accompanied by stereotyping and considered to begin about age 65, involves adjusting to change and developing a sense of integrity, which is dependent on the successful achievement of the tasks of each of the preceding periods. Two conflicting theories have been proposed to explain successful adjustment to old age—the disengagement theory and the activity theory.
5. Elizabeth Kubler-Ross theorizes that a dying person progresses through five sequential psychological stages: denial, anger, bargaining, depression, and acceptance.
6. Piaget theorizes that cognitive development progresses through a sequence of four stages guided by the interaction of a person's biological maturation and environmental experiences. The stages in sequence are sensorimotor, preoperational, concrete operational, and formal operational.
7. According to Piaget, a person's intelligence or cognitive development occurs through the processes of assimilation (applying existing schemes and operations to new situations) and accommodation (modifying existing schemes and operations to fit new situations).
8. Inspired by Piaget, Kohlberg theorizes that moral reasoning, the process of internalizing standards of right and wrong, progresses through three levels (preconventional, conventional, postconventional) consisting of six stages—two stages in each level.
9. According to Kohlberg, Stage 1 of moral reasoning is punishment oriented; Stage 2 is reward-exchange oriented; Stage 3 is a good-boy/good-girl orientation; Stage 4 orientation is to maintain the social order; Stage 5 is a social-contract orientation; and Stage 6 is a universal-ethical-principles orientation.
10. Attachment, an emotional tie or bond that normally develops between parent or caregiver and child but can fail or be affected by various factors, is the first and probably the most important social relationship an individual experiences. Attachment of the child to the

caregiver and the child to other children (peer interaction) follows a predictable pattern.

11. Day-care centers of optimal quality have not been found to weaken emotional bonding between parent and child, and they can provide an enriching and stimulating experience.
12. Children who are popular seem to have some common characteristics, and the families of popular children have common characteristics as well. Popular children tend to be friendly, outgoing, successful in school, physically attractive, excellent at some task valued by the group, and physically mature for their age. Popular children's families tend to discourage aggression and antisocial behavior, do not frustrate the child, punish very little, like their children and tell them so, and foster secure attachment.
13. Older children and adults need two kinds of social relationships—a special emotional attachment to one special other person (thought to stem from the first attachment to the caregiver and to make available a source of comfort and security) and social ties to a network of friends (thought to provide a source of group integration and identity).
14. Both positive emotions such as delight, joy, happiness, love, and humor and negative emotions such as distress, disgust, fear, anger, jealousy, and sadness need to be experienced to prepare a person for life, but emotional balance needs to be maintained to avoid a distorted outlook.
15. Anger arouses aggression, behavior aimed at hurting another person, which at first is primarily physical but gradually becomes more and more verbal in nature. Assertive behavior rather than aggressive behavior should be modeled and taught to an individual to enhance social development and good psychological and emotional adjustment.
16. The concept of self is a composite of the self-image, the self-concept, and self-esteem. It may be realistic or distorted in varying degrees and positive or negative in varying degrees. It follows a predictable pattern in development, and it is probably the most important predictor of personal happiness and effective functioning of an individual.
17. Sexuality is the whole of an individual's sexual behavior including the concept of gender (gender identity, sex-role stereotyping, and gender or sex-role behavior) and biological development of primary and secondary sex characteristics as well as sexual arousal and response to sexual arousal for reproduction.
18. The concept of gender has been theorized to be influenced by learning (both by reinforcement and by modeling), cognitive processes (information processing), identification (subconscious processes), and biological processes.
19. A self-concept that allows a person to engage in both feminine- and masculine-stereotyped behaviors (androgyny) has been found to be

advantageous to an individual's psychological adjustment and well-being.

20. The most clearly defined sign of sexual maturity in females is the onset of menstruation and in males is ejaculation.

KEY TERMS AND CONCEPTS

Puberty
Ageism
Disengagement theory
Activity theory
Schemes
Operations
Assimilation
Accommodation
Sensorimotor stage
Preoperational stage
Conserve
Concrete operational stage
Formal operational stage
Moral development
Preconventional morality
Conventional morality
Postconventional morality
Attachment
Love
Self-image
Self-concept
Self-esteem
Sexuality
Androgyny
Primary sex characteristics
Secondary sex characteristics

QUESTIONS FOR REVIEW

1. What are some typical physiological and psychological experiences of adolescence, and what is the developmental task to be mastered by each according to Erikson?
2. When is the adulthood stage considered to begin and end, what activities primarily constitute adulthood, and what are the two developmental tasks to be mastered according to Erikson?
3. What are the two developmental tasks of old age and the two theories of successful adjustment to aging?
4. Who developed a theory of the psychological stages one progresses through in death and dying, and what are the stages in sequence?
5. Name in sequence and describe the stages Piaget believes a child progresses through in the course of cognitive development.
6. Who developed a comprehensive description of three levels and six stages of moral development? Name and describe the levels and stages in the sequence in which they occur.
7. What is attachment, what are some milestones in the attachment of child to parent and child to peers, and how does attachment affect personality?
8. What are some positive and negative emotions that begin to develop in the first 2 years of life? Discuss the development of fear, anger, and aggression.
9. How does the concept of self develop, and what does it include?
10. What does one's sexuality include, and what are some milestones in the development of one's sexuality?

TEST YOURSELF

1. Adolescence is characterised by (a) a rapid spurt of physical growth (b) frustration and conflict (c) egocentrism (d) all three: a, b, and c.
2. According to Erikson, the task to be mastered during adolescence is to (a) develop a sense of autonomy (b) establish one's self financially (c) develop a sense of industry (d) develop a sense of identity.
3. According to Erikson, the major achievement of early adulthood is to establish (a) identity (b) intimacy through a meaningful love relationship and/or deep friendships with others (c) autonomy (d) trust.
4. The correct order of the five stages a person progresses through in the process of dying according to Kubler-Ross is (a) acceptance, anger, bargaining, depression, denial (b) bargaining, anger, denial, acceptance, depression (c) acceptance, depression, bargaining, anger, denial (d) denial, anger, bargaining, depression, acceptance.
5. The correct order of Super's five sequential stages of making a career choice is (a) exploration, maintenance, decline, growth, establishment (b) growth, exploration, establishment, maintenance, decline (c) establishment, exploration, maintenance, growth, decline (d) maintenance, establishment, decline, growth, exploration.
6. The majority of studies conducted on aging support the (a) activity theory (b) disengagement theory (c) reflection theory (d) integrity theory.
7. Piaget's stages of cognitive or intellectual development in correct order are: ________________, ________________, ________________, and ________________.
8. A child is shown two balls of clay that he or she agrees are the same size. The child then observes one ball being flattened to a pancake shape and is asked, "Which one has more clay now, or do they have the same amount of clay?" This would be an experiment to test the child's ability to (a) conserve (b) add classes (c) multiply classes (c) engage in representational thought.
9. Piaget concluded that a preschool-age child reasons that a behavior is good or bad according to the consequence, that rules are absolute and unchangeable coming from an external authority, and that punishment will automatically follow a broken rule or bad behavior. T or F
10. Kohlberg believes that the majority of adults reach Stage 6, the final stage of moral development. T or F
11. ________________ is considered to be of major importance in the development of moral reasoning.
12. Kohlberg's Level II, known as ________________ morality, includes Stage 3, called the ________________ stage, in which behavior is reasoned to be right if it wins ________________ of others.
13. Mildred Parten's stages of play or peer interaction are, in the order in which they develop, as follows: ________________, ________

__________, ______________, ______________, and ______________.

14. The social relationships needed by older children and adults include (a) an emotional attachment to several special other persons (b) a social tie to only one or two friends (c) a social tie to a network of friends but no emotional attachment to any one special person (d) an emotional attachment to one special other person and social ties to a network of friends.
15. A child should be protected from experiencing negative emotions such as anger, fear, or jealousy and ideally for best psychological adjustment in adult life should experience only positive emotions such as happiness, joy, and humor. T or F
16. To enhance the development of good interpersonal relationships and good psychological and emotional adjustment, children need to be taught to be (a) physically aggressive (b) verbally aggressive (c) assertive (d) neither aggressive nor assertive but submissive.
17. The perception that an individual has of his or her value or importance to significant others is referred to as the individual's (a) self-esteem (b) self-image (c) self-concept (d) ego.
18. What is considered by most psychologists to be the single most important predictor of personal happiness and effective functioning for an individual?
19. Gender identity, sex-role stereotyping, and gender behaviors first appear in an individual about (a) the age of puberty (b) 2 or 3 years of age (c) school age (d) adulthood when sexual maturity is complete.
20. The most clearly defined sign of sexual maturity in females is (a) menstruation (b) ejaculation (c) progression through the three stages of the gender concept (d) the development of a self-concept that allows them to be strong, assertive, and independent as well as sensitive and nurturing.

APPLICATIONS

A. Susan Appleside, Jerry Bascom, Mary Dunbar, and Jack Promise work for the ABC Corporation. They are aware that a coworker who is having some financial problems and having difficulty keeping his car from being repossessed took (borrowed without permission or stole) $500 from the company. Each is faced with the dilemma of whether to report the matter to top management.

Susan reasons that it would be wrong to report the incident because the coworker just needs the money to tide him over a temporary situation, it probably will not occur again, and if his car is repossessed he would not be able to get to work. She thinks her coworkers would consider her to be a tattletale and an unsympathetic person and would reject her as a friend if she reported the incident. She thinks that keeping quiet will keep everybody happy and avoid hurt feelings and confusion.

Jerry reasons that it would be right to report the incident to top management because those in management value honest, trustworthy, dependable employees, and he thinks they will consider him to be a good employee they can depend on if he reports the incident.

Mary also reasons that it would be right to report the situation to top management because there was a statement in the employment contract they signed with the company that stealing or taking money from the company is a felony and any knowledge of such is to be reported to management. She reasons that it is a legal responsibility and her duty as a law-abiding employee to report the incident.

Jack reasons that the incident should not be reported because the contract that he signed contained a statement to the effect that he would always act in a manner he believed to be in the best interest of the company. Since he believes this to be a one-time incident and that the coworker will repay the money, he believes he has a legal obligation not to create a scene and cause any disruptions in production.

1. At what level of moral reasoning, according to Kohlberg, are all four of these employees? Why do you think so?
2. Susan and Jerry are at what stage of moral reasoning? Why do you think so?
3. Mary and Jack are at what stage of moral reasoning? Why do you think so?

B. Gertie Roman, Bill Hall, and Marcie Ginnis are employees at Mr. Jersey's place of business. On different occasions, Mr. Jersey has called on each of them to hold a piece of machinery while he hammers it back into place, and each time he missed and hit the employee's finger when he first began hammering.

Gertie reacted by continuing to hold the piece in place for him, being afraid he would be displeased with her work and with her as an employee if she refused; however, she did beg him to please be careful because it hurts when her finger gets hit and even complained that she was afraid he would miss again.

Bill reacted by refusing to hold the piece any longer for Mr. Jersey, told him he was incompetent, boasted that he could hammer better than that, and insisted that Mr. Jersey hold the piece and let him hammer. Bill missed once deliberately just to get even with Mr. Jersey and show him how it felt when he had missed and hit his finger. Bill and Mr. Jersey had "words" and parted in a huff without getting the job done.

Marcie reacted by taking action to protect herself from getting hurt and to get the job done without being critical or degrading or doing anything to hurt Mr. Jersey. She used her mental capacities for effective problem solving, asking Mr. Jersey to wait a moment for her to get a pair of pliers with which to hold the piece of machinery in place. The job got done, no one got hurt physically or psychologically, and a positive social relationship was maintained.

1. Which one of the employees displayed aggressive behavior?
2. Which one of the employees displayed assertive behavior?
3. Which two employees do you think have a low concept of the self? How can you tell?

SUGGESTIONS FOR FURTHER READING

Bee, H. L., & Mitchell, S. K. (1984). *The developing child* (4th ed.). New York: Harper & Row.

A basic general text, well written and easy to understand, that covers topics in this chapter in more detail.

Geer, J., Heiman, J. & Leitenberg, H. (1984). *Human Sexuality*. Englewood Cliffs, NJ: Prentice Hall.

An in-depth coverage of topics covered in this chapter and an excellent overview of the entire field of human sexuality.

Kubler-Ross, E. (1969). *On Death and Dying*. New York: Macmillan.

The five steps by which one comes to terms with death are presented in this book by the scientist best known for helping call attention to the needs of the terminally ill.

Maccoby, E. E. (1980). *Social development: Psychological growth and the parent-child relationship*. New York: Harcourt Brace Jovanovich.

A review of the literature on the parent role in socialization.

Phillips, J. L., Jr. (1975). *The origins of intellect: Piaget's theory* (2nd ed.). San Francisco: W. H. Freeman.

An introduction to Piaget's theory of intellectual development that is easy to read.

Sheehy, G. (1976). *Passages: Predictable crises of adult life*. New York: Dutton.

A best-selling book about adult development that describes psychological crises people encounter during their middle years.

Wallerstein, J. S., & Kelly, J. B. (1980). *Surviving the breakup: How children and parents cope with divorce*. New York: Harper & Row.

A readable presentation of the long-range effects of divorce on children and on their parents based on the first major study of this topic.

PART TWO

MENTAL BEHAVIOR

CHAPTER 5

SENSATION, PERCEPTION, AND CONSCIOUSNESS

Objectives

When you have completed your study of chapter 5, you should be able to:

1. Explain the concepts of transduction, threshold, and adaptation.
2. Describe the basic anatomy, concepts, and experiences of vision and hearing.
3. Name the other senses possessed by humans, and describe how a person has the sensations.
4. Explain the concept of perception.
5. Name and describe the patterning and stabilizing principles of perception, and explain illusions.
6. Relate ways in which experience and conditions influence perception, and explain distortion in perception.
7. Cite the functions, structures, and varieties of consciousness.
8. Name and describe patterns of naturally occurring changes in consciousness—the alternate states of sleep and dreaming.
9. Name and describe the induced altered states of consciousness known as hypnosis and meditation.
10. Identify the main categories of consciousness-altering substances, name some drugs in each category, and give the effect of each drug on individuals.

People need reliable and specific information about the outside world in order to adequately function in it. Without information about the outside world and a means of processing, interpreting, and acting on it, people would be like inanimate objects. The sense organs extract information from the environment. In this chapter, the kinds of information people obtain and the way the information is obtained through the senses is examined. Sensations or messages transmitted by the sense organs have little or no meaning of their own. They must be organized, interpreted, and given meaning in the central nervous system in a process called *perception*. Some aspects of the development of perception in infancy and childhood were discussed in chapter 3. In this chapter, the basic principles of perception and factors affecting perception are discussed. Attention will be given to special kinds of perception—illusions, distortions, person perception, hallucinations, subliminal perception, and extrasensory perception. Innumerable stimuli reach the senses, and innumerable messages are sent by the sense organs to the nervous system. Even though much information about the environment is filtered out by the sense organs and by the processes of perception, people still cannot be conscious of all the available information. The most important information to attend to at any given moment must be selected. The information a person is attending to at any given moment and the perceptions he or she is aware of at any given moment is said to be *conscious* or *in consciousness.* Because needs and situations change continually, consciousness changes continually. The functions, structure, and varieties of consciousness will also be a focus of this chapter. Finally, techniques for altering consciousness—meditation, hypnosis, and the use of consciousness-altering substances—will be discussed.

SENSATION

Sensation was one of the earliest topics of interest to psychologists. Because information about the outside world comes through the senses and all of the senses do not function in the same way, basic research on sensation is concerned with what a sense organ responds to and how the sense organ registers information and transmits it to the nervous system. This understanding then leads to applied research, relating capabilities of humans to task requirements.

Basic Concepts

Three basic concepts related to sensation that are important to understanding human behavior are transduction, threshold, and adaptation. These concepts will be described in this section.

What is transduction?

Transduction. All living systems carry out three functions—inputs, internal activities (throughputs), and outputs. In the human organism, the sense organs of the body serve the function of input. Sense organs translate energy in the environment such as warmth, cold, pressure, light rays, sound waves, chemicals, movement, and gravitational pull into a common kind of energy the nervous system can understand. **Transduction** is this translation or changing of energy from one form to another form. The energy received from the environment is translated at the sense organ level and relayed to the peripheral nervous system. In the nervous system, the information is carried to the central nervous system and processed, and then decisions are made and orders given. The nervous system serves the function of throughput. The muscular system serves the function of output. The level of a person's awareness of the environment is directly related to how well his or her sense organs carry out the function of transduction.

Thresholds. Stimulus thresholds, sometimes referred to as absolute thresholds, are the minimum levels of energy that are required for transduction to occur. Different species have different thresholds for transduction to occur in a particular sense organ. For example, a dog can hear sounds a human cannot. There are also variations in thresholds within a species. For example, one person's threshold for hearing might be 18 decibels, and another's might be 20 decibels. One person may not hear, see, smell, or feel something in the environment that another person does. Some things exist in the environment of which most people are unaware unless the energy is magnified to the threshold level for transduction to occur. For example, germs cannot be seen except when they are magnified in size under a microscope, and radio signals cannot be heard without amplification.

How do stimulus thresholds and difference thresholds differ?

The senses also have **difference thresholds**, the minimum levels of energy change required for a stimulus difference to be detected from changes in such stimuli as brightness, loudness, temperature, taste, or pressure. As with stimulus thresholds, different people may not have the same difference thresholds. Thus, one person may detect a change in a stimulus that another person may not be able to detect.

Adaptation. People's thresholds do not remain constant. When the cells in sense organs are exposed to a constant level of energy from the environment, the cells become less sensitive and thus the threshold is raised. This process of desensitization is referred to as **adaptation.** Adaptation is a fundamental biological principle that is important to survival in a hostile environment. Adaptation explains why a person may not experience the same stimulus in the environment in the same way at different times. The principle of adaptation also explains why some people have a different awareness of the environment. For example, an individual may adapt to a particular odor, such as that of cigarette smoke or of some industrial chemical, and not smell it. Or an individual may adapt to certain noises, such as a loud office environment, the sound of a pounding hammer, or the sound of trucks passing, and not be aware of them.

How does adaptation function to be important to survival?

The Senses

The senses often have been referred to as the "five senses"—seeing, hearing, feeling, smelling, and tasting. There are really

Can you name all the human senses?

more than five senses. In this section, the human senses will be named and described.

Vision. The major parts of the human eye are shown in Color Figure 5–1. In the eye, the cells responsible for transduction are located at the back of the eyeball on the **retina** (pronounced *RET n ah*). The retina contains receptor cells that are activated by light rays. Light rays enter first through the transparent cornea of the eye and then pass through the *pupil,* a small hole in the front of the lens of the eye. The pupil enlarges and contracts to control the amount of light entering the eye. Muscles connected to the lens tighten to increase the curvature of the lens, thus focusing the image as it is projected onto the retina.

Are all receptor cells in the eye alike?

The retina contains two general types of receptor cells called rods and cones. The cells called **rods** are sensitive to brightness or differences in light intensity and are involved in night vision. If only rods were in the retina, people would see only in black and white, not in color. The cells called **cones** respond to differences in wavelength of light rays and light intensity. In bright light, these cells are extremely sensitive to wavelengths. Cones are involved in color vision and are concentrated in the **fovea,** an area on the retina. Only cones are found in the fovea. The fovea is the most sensitive part of the retina because it contains a greater number of receptor cells than surrounding areas. Therefore, vision is sharpest when the image is projected on this area.

Is there part of the image from the visual field that is not received by the eye and thus not received by the brain?

The place where the optic nerve leaves the retina to carry the neural impulse to the brain has neither rods nor cones. Light rays in the visual field falling here will not stimulate a neural impulse, and the brain receives no information of that part of the visual field. This area of the retina is referred to as the **blind spot.** Usually a person does not notice the blind spot because there are two retinal images (one from each eye). The part of the image that is not received by one eye will be received by the other eye. The box that follows shows how to locate the blind spot.

One explanation of how a person sees in color is the Young-Helmholtz trichromatic theory. According to this theory, there are three different kinds of cones, and each kind responds to light wavelengths corresponding to a different primary color. All the different colors a person sees are the result of different combinations of stimulated cones.

A later theory proposed that the three different kinds of cones do not respond to just three separate primary colors, but rather

LOCATING THE BLIND SPOT

Close your right eye and stare at the cross with your left eye. While doing this, move the book to about 12 inches from your face. Bring the book closer and closer until the circle disappears. When the circle disappears, it has been projected onto your blind spot.

they respond according to an opponent process. This opponent process theory assumes that each type of cone is capable of responding to either color of a pair of primary colors that oppose each other. But the cone cannot respond to both colors at the same time because stimulation by one color is associated with inhibition by its opposite. One kind of cone responds to blue-yellow stimulation, another kind to red-green stimulation, and a third kind to black-white stimulation. Another explanation of the opponent process in color vision proposes that the level of electrical activity, or the rate of neural impulses in a cell, may be increased or decreased by a color (see Color Figure 5–2). For example, a blue-yellow cone might send a message that is interpreted as yellow with increased activity, and when the level of electrical activity reversed (decreased), it would then send a message that is interpreted as blue. Or a red-green cone might send a green message with increased activity, but when electrical activity reversed (decreased activity), it would send a red message (Hurvich & Jameson, 1974).

What is the visual experience of color-blind individuals like?

Individuals who have all three kinds of cones have normal vision and are called **trichromats.** Individuals who are missing either the red-green or the blue-yellow cones or both do not perceive color normally and are said to be *color-blind.* Those individuals who have one type of cone missing, either the red-green or the blue-yellow cones, are called **dichromats.** Those who have two types of cones missing (both the red-green and blue-yellow cones) are called **monochromats.** A monochromat sees only blacks and whites or grays. His or her visual experience is much like a television picture with the color turned off. A dichromat with red-green color blindness is only partially color-blind, unable only to differentiate between red and green. His or her visual experience is much like a television picture with the blue and yellow turned on and the red and green turned off. A dichromat with blue-yellow color blindness has a visual experience similar to a television picture with the red and green turned on and the blue and yellow turned off.

Hearing. The stimulus in the environment that causes transduction to occur in the ear is a sound wave, or vibration, in the air (see Figure 5–3). In a sound wave pattern, one cycle is the distance from the beginning of one wave to the beginning of the next wave.

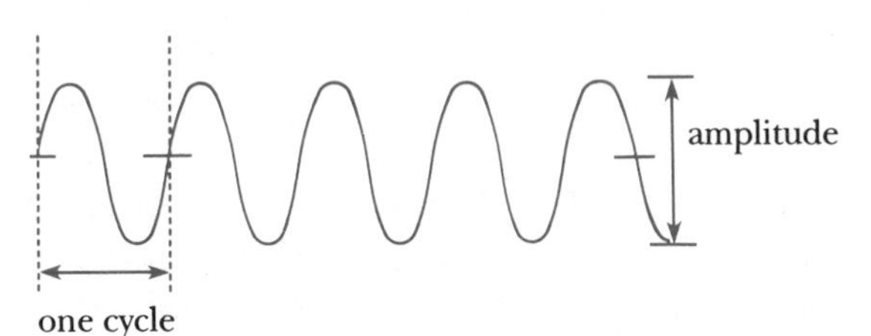

Figure 5–3.
The sound wave.

Sound waves are perceived in terms of loudness, pitch, and timbre. The **frequency** of the waves (how many cycles or waves arrive per second) determines the **pitch** of the sound—how high or how low it is. The **amplitude** (height of the cycle or wave) determines the loudness. The **timbre** (quality or texture of the sound) is determined by a complex pattern of overtones that are produced by accompanying sound waves that are different multiples of the basic frequency (see Figure 5–4).

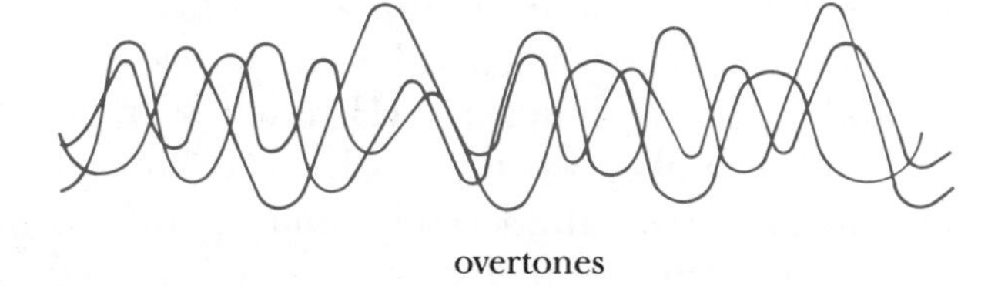

Figure 5–4.
Overtones determine the quality (timbre) of the sound.

Where are the receptor cells for hearing located?

Sound waves are collected by the outer ear and channeled through the ear canal where they hit the eardrum and cause it to vibrate. The eardrum vibration puts three tiny bones, commonly called the *hammer, anvil,* and *stirrup,* into sequential motion. See Color Figure 5–5 for a diagram of the structure of the ear. The eardrum vibration moves the hammer, which is attached to the anvil, and the anvil is attached to the stirrup. The stirrup is connected to a membrane in such a way that when the stirrup moves, the membrane also moves or vibrates. This membrane covers part of the snail-shaped cochlea in the inner ear. Fluid inside the cochlea is moved with the vibration of the membrane. This movement of the fluid stimulates tiny hair cells located on a membrane inside the cochlea where transduction occurs. Afferent neurons in the auditory nerve are depolarized, and the patterns of neural impulses relayed to the brain by axonal and synaptic transmission are interpreted or perceived as loudness, pitch, and timbre.

What are the four skin senses?

Other Senses. The sensations of pressure, warmth, cold, and pain are produced by the stimulation of different kinds of cells in the skin. Light pressure applied to the skin moves hairs on the skin, some of which are too fine to be seen without a microscope. The movement of the hairs stimulates the cells of the nerve endings that are wrapped around the base of the hairs to start the neural impulse. Heavy pressure disturbs capsules beneath the surface of the skin that contain nerve endings. The disturbance of these capsules stimulates cells and fires a neural impulse that travels through the nervous system. The impulses originating from the movement of hair on the skin or the disburbance of the capsules beneath the skin are perceived as touch or pressure.

Two kinds of cells in the skin respond to temperature. One kind of cell responds to temperatures above body temperature. Impulses originating from the stimulation of these cells are perceived as warmth. The other kind of cell responds to temperatures below body temperature. Impulses originating from the stimulation of these cells are perceived as cold. One may be able to locate cells that transmit impulses perceived as cold by touching various places on the inside of the bend of the elbow or on the forearm with the lead of a pencil, which is cooler than body temperature.

Is pain perceived from only one type of receptor cell?

The sense of pain functions differently from the other senses. Any of the cells in any sense organ, if overstimulated, may produce impulses that are perceived as pain. Different types of cells that respond to different types of pain have not been found, but two kinds of nerve fibers have been found that seem to carry different pain messages—fast, sharp, and more localized pain or pain that is slow, aching, widespread, and of a longer duration (Liebeskind & Paul, 1977). A network of free nerve endings in the layers of the skin is thought to send pain messages to the brain. More variation among individuals seems to exist for pain than for any of the other senses. One theory proposes that there are neurological pathways with areas that either refer pain to other pathways or stop pain by

Which sense seems to have more variation among individuals than any of the other senses?

a flood of impulses from another pathway. These areas function as gates to let through or block out impulses perceived as pain (Melzach & Wall, 1965). This gate control theory explains the experience of arm pain during a heart attack and how acupuncture works. As was pointed out in chapter 2, recent research provides evidence that the body manufactures chemical substances in some areas of the brain and spinal cord that suppress pain impulses—endorphins (Snyder, 1977).

Where are the receptor cells for the sense of equilibrium or balance located?

The inner ear is responsible for more than the sense of hearing. Additional hairlike cells are located in the semicircular canals of the inner ear (see Color Figure 5–5). The movement of fluid in the semicircular canals stimulates the hairlike cells, which send neural impulses to the brain. Impulses originating from these cells provide an awareness of body position or balance, called **equilibrium,** which makes it possible to maintain an upright posture.

Do people have receptor cells in muscles and joints?

The muscles and tendons of the body have some cells that respond when a muscle is expanded or contracted. These cells also respond to changes in angles of position of the body. These cells enable an individual to be aware of the movement and position of the different body parts, referred to as the **kinesthetic sense.**

Chemical substances stimulate cells in some sense organs. The cells that start neural impulses that are perceived as taste are located inside the taste buds on the tongue. One type of cell responds to bitter substances, another to sweet substances, another to salty substances, and another to sour substances. Taste is not the same as flavor, which is perceived from a combination of impulses from the skin senses, taste, and smell. When chemical substances come in contact with the tiny hairlike cells in the taste buds, transduction occurs and starts a neural impulse through the nervous system. The hairlike cells in taste buds are replaced with new ones about every 7 days. The number of receptor cells in taste buds tends to decrease with the age of the person. This may account for differences in sensitivity to taste of some foods among children, adults, and elderly people and for the differences in sensitivity at various times for a single individual.

For which of the senses are the receptor cells located in the brain?

The cells where transduction occurs for smell are located high above the nasal cavity in an area of the brain about half the size of a postage stamp. It is not known exactly how the sense of smell functions, but is is thought by some to be related to the distinctive size, shape, or electrical charge of the molecules of various chemicals in the air. The molecules fit into one or more of some basic types of socketlike holes in the smell part of the brain just as a key fits into a lock (Amoore, Johnston, & Rubin, 1964) and, therefore, are differentiated and perceived as different odors.

PERCEPTION

An individual constructs a three-dimensional world filled with objects and events referred to as reality. In this section, the concept of perception is explained, and the patterning and stablizing principles involved in this construction or perception of the world are identified. Also, experiential factors that influence perception are pointed out, and unrealistic perceptions such as illusions, hallucinations, and distorted perceptions receive attention. Finally, some controversial perceptions are pointed out.

The Concept of Perception

Perception is an active process, not just a passive reception of information directly from the outside world. In a broad sense, perception is the construction of meaning (Pylyshyn, 1973).

Construction of Reality. Reality is constructed from sensations, the raw information or evidence that is transferred to, organized, and interpreted by the brain. The construction of reality from sensation is influenced by heredity, predetermined organizational processes carried out in the brain, and the environment or experience, such as memory of previous constructions, motivations, expectations, and environmental conditions. Perception is like guessing or hypothesizing about what is out there in the world; it is a process of building on sensation. In the process of perception, incomplete or ambiguous sensory information may be filled in and smoothed over; sensory information may be changed by the addition of information from memory; parts of sensory information may be amplified or may recede into the background; or sensory information may be noted and attended to or ignored. The perception of a cube from the flat lines printed on a flat piece of paper is an illustration of how meaning may be assigned to the sensory information and judgments and integrations made. Figure 5–6 demonstrates how two different realities may be constructed from the same sensory information. This phenomenon was discovered in 1832 by the Swiss mineralogist L. A. Necker.

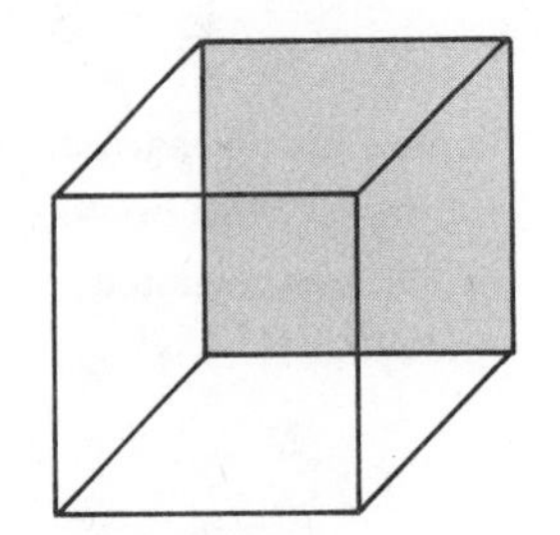

Figure 5–6.
The Necker cube. The shaded surface can appear as either the top surface or the back surface of a transparent cube.

Hallucinations. Sometimes signals or neural impulses originate within the nervous system rather than from the environment through the sense organs. Meaning is constructed from the signals in the same manner as if they originated from an environmental source of energy. Thus, one may have a perception of something that is not really in the world, a **hallucination.** Seeing a person, hearing voices, or feeling a hand on the shoulder when in reality such is not present in the environment is a hallucination. Generally, only people with psychological or medical disorders or those who are under the influence of a hallucinogenic drug or hypnotic suggestion experience hallucinations. When this phenomenon occurs during sleep, it is called *dreaming*. The need for stimulation of the brain seems to be so important that if an individual is deprived of sensation from the environment through the sense organs, there is a backup system for impulses to be sent internally to stimulate the brain. Experiments with sensory deprivation in the waking state indicate that the need for sensory stimulation is so strong that visual sensations like dots and geometric forms and eventually hallucinations begin to occur as a result of deprivation (Heron, 1957).

What conditions produce hallucinations?

Feature Analysis. Feature analysis, a theoretical explanation of how perception occurs, explains perception as an active, hypothesis-testing process. Context (sensation) and experience interact with the fixed, inherent structure of the nervous system whereby the individual seems to abstract features of the signal or neural impulse and compare them with patterns stored in long-term memory. The abstracted features seem to pass through a series of stages. At the first stage, the features of the incoming neural impulses are recorded. In the next stage, specific features of the signal or pattern of neural impulses such as lines, curves, or angles are focused on. In the third stage, the pattern of the features rather than the individual features is focused on. In the next stage, the pattern of the features is compared with the patterns stored in long-term memory, and recognition of the stimulus occurs. In the last stage, special features of the pattern are compared with special features of stored patterns that are similar. This last stage is a high-level task that enables a person to discriminate between patterns that are very similar. Each stage is a higher level mental task than the previous stage.

What and how many stages are in the process of perception?

Is perception learned primarily from books or from experience (practice)?

Perceptual Learning. Perceptual learning is a type of cognitive learning that has been defined by Eleanor Gibson (1969) as "an increase in the ability to extract information from the environment as a result of experience or practice with the stimulation coming from it" (p. 3). Focusing attention is important in perceptual learning. Skill in many occupations is based on the ability to perceive slight discriminations in sensory information. People who are trained can perceive distinctions that untrained people cannot. For example, a trained person may be able to distinguish the calls of birds, sounds of motors, or textures of rocks. Perceptual learning usually comes from experience rather than from books.

Organizing and Interpreting Principles

Perception is organized along principles called the *laws or rules of perceptual organization* by the Gestalt psychologists who first studied perception and identified the principles. Stabilizing processes seem to make possible dependable interpretations of sensory input under different environmental conditions. These principles of organization and processes of stabilization and the reliability with which they operate are the focus of this section.

Figure 5–7. A reversible figure-ground drawing. The vase may stand out as the figure, or the two faces may stand out as the figure.

Patterning. Patterning or grouping puts together large amounts of information quickly and integrates the elements into meaningful wholes. The processes are referred to as **perceptual organization.** The principles or rules of grouping apply to stimuli from all the senses, not just the visual sense.

The tendency to perceive a figure with a defined contour and boundary as being in front of a ground that flows around the figure, the **figure-ground rule,** is very strong and is a basic rule of perceptual organization. In a bar of music, for example, the melody may be the figure and the chords the ground. Sometimes the figure and ground may exchange roles and a different perception is constructed. In Figure 5–7, the vase may stand out as the figure, or the two faces may stand out as the figure.

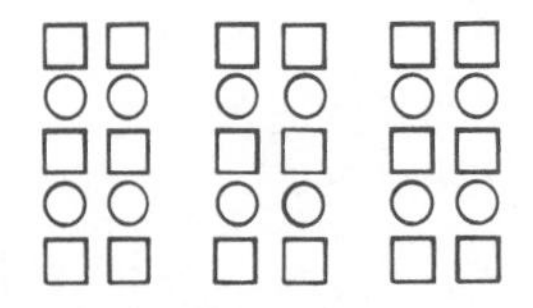

Figure 5–8. The rule of proximity is illustrated when three pairs of two columns each are perceived.

Other grouping principles are the rules of proximity, similarity, continuity, closure, and common fate. Parts seem separate or grouped together depending on how close together they are—the **proximity rule.** The rule of proximity is illustrated in Figure 5–8 when pairs of columns are perceived. The **similarity rule** is illustrated in Figure 5–8 by the similar patterns being grouped together so that horizontal rows of circles and horizontal rows of squares are perceived. The **continuity rule** states that continuous contours are grouped together. Seeing a wavy line and a straight line in Figure 5–9 illustrates the rule of continuity. Missing pieces of a familiar pattern are automatically filled in according to the **closure rule.** Figure 5–10 is perceived by most people as a circle rather than three separate arcs, which illustrates the principle of closure. The **common fate rule** is the tendency to perceive parts as a single whole if they move together. Perceiving a star or some

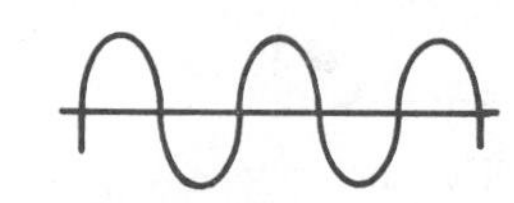

Figure 5–9. Seeing a wavy line and a straight line illustrates the rule of continuity.

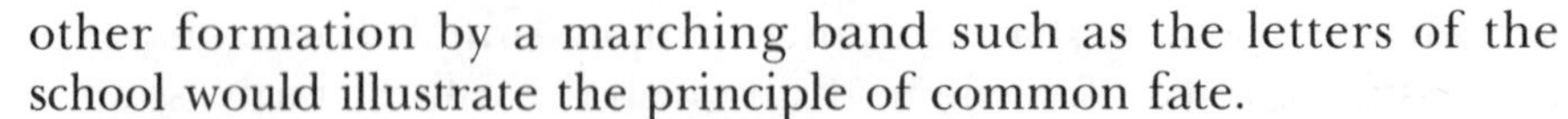

other formation by a marching band such as the letters of the school would illustrate the principle of common fate.

Figure 5–10.
The closure rule of patterning or grouping is illustrated when a circle is perceived from the three separate arcs.

Stabilizing. The stabilizing principles that provide a standard, dependable way of interpreting sensation are referred to as **constancy principles.** The constancy principles are interpretative rules for judging occurrences that involve a decision or tendency to stabilize the moving, changing objects in the world rather than to follow the movements. Although the actual size and shape of the image of an object on the retina of the eye changes with its distance from the eye and with its movement to another position, the object is perceived as remaining the same size and shape. The actual change in the size of the retinal image is perceived as distance away, and the change in the shape of the pattern is perceived as orientation in space.

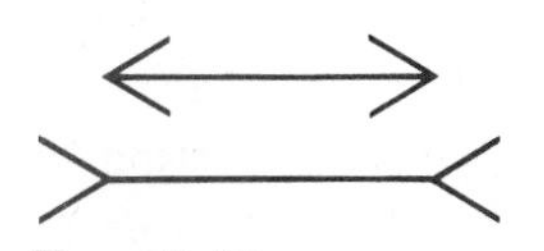

Figure 5–11.
The Muller-Lyer illusion. Although the length of the two lines is the same, the lower one is perceived as being longer.

Illusions. The patterning and stabilizing principles interact to interpret the world, and they operate so reliably that they sometimes misinterpret or produce a misleading or invalid perception of reality called an **illusion.** Figures 5–11 and 5–12 are examples of constancy illusions. Constancy illusions are the products of experience or learning. When the perception is distorted and fails to correspond to reality, interpretations or judgments of the sensory input are at fault, not the senses.

Patterning principles also produce the illusion of movement, which every person seems to experience when watching a motion picture. This illusion depends on the principles of closure and proximity. The blank spaces between the still pictures on the film are filled in, and the still pictures are flashed rapidly enough that they appear so close together that grouping persists and is not switched off.

Influences on Perception

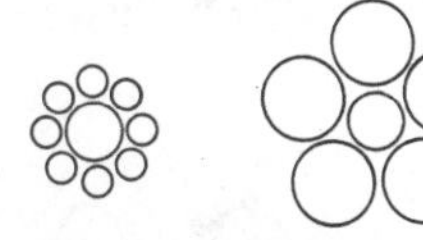

Figure 5–12.
The Ebbinghaus illusion. The inner circles are the same size although the one on the left is perceived as the larger.

Perception is clearly a product of both inherited characteristics (organization of neural impulses in the brain) common to all humans and sensory experience from the environment (learning), which is different for different individuals. Several factors are known to influence an individual's perceptual experience such as culture, needs, interests, values, expectations, temporary conditions, and body size. Perceptual set, conditions, and characteristics that influence an individual's perception will be discussed in this section.

Perceptual Set. A **perceptual set** is a predisposition to perceive something in the environment in a particular way—realistically, unrealistically, or distorted—as a result of prior experiences, suggestions, expectancies, or motivations. People have great power over their own perceptions, seeing (or hearing, feeling, tasting, or smelling) what they expect or what fits their preconceptions of what makes sense. For instance, when proofreading, an error may not be seen due to a perceptual set. Figure 5–13 is a set of drawings designed by B. R. Bugelski (1971) to demonstrate perceptual set. After looking at the left column from top to bottom, most people perceive the last figure as that of an old man; a people set occurs. After looking at the right column from top to bottom, most people perceive the last figure as a rat even though it is identical to the last figure in the left column; an animal set occurs.

Figure 5–13.
After looking from the top down the left column, describe the last drawing. Then look down the next column and describe the last drawing. These sets of drawings were designed by Bugelski (1971) to test the establishment of perceptual set in children.

Perceptual set may occur in **person perception,** the perception a person has of other people. Differences in relationships that exist among people at work are often related to perception. Sometimes people make erroneous judgments that result in distorted perception of others. Two people, for example, may say the same words in the same harsh tone of voice. If one is perceived to be good-natured or is expected to be in a good humor, he or she may be perceived as joking. If the other one is perceived to be grouchy and is expected to be in a bad humor, he or she may be perceived as hostile and angry.

The **halo effect** is another example of distorted perception of others. In the halo effect, a favorable impression of an individual created by one characteristic overshadows other characteristics so that virtually everything the individual does is judged in a favorable light. When the halo effect occurs, the error is in assuming or expecting the presence of many positive traits from the existence of one favorable trait.

Logical error is the tendency to see different traits as belonging together when they logically do not. A person may be assumed or expected to have a certain trait or traits because of a particular characteristic the person does have, because of the person's relationship with another person, or because of the person's physical attractiveness. A person may be perceived as honest because of physical attractiveness or dishonest because of physical unattractiveness. A person may be assumed to be honest because he or she is a friend of an acquaintance who is an honest person. Or a person may be assumed to be a liar because he or she steals.

The influence of expectation (or the Pygmalion effect), based on prior information, may shape not only first impressions but future interactions with a person. Just as a stereotype of a group of people may be formulated, a stereotype may be developed that can be applied to a single person. Stereotypes act as cognitive shortcuts that may produce selective bias in information processing and storing. They cause one to see only the evidence that fits the stereotype and to ignore evidence that is contrary to the stereotype. If a supervisor expects employees to be unproductive, they most likely will be unproductive; and if the supervisor expects the employees to be highly productive, they most likely will be—at least as perceived by the supervisor, who will possibly see only the evidence that fits the belief or expectation.

Conditions and Characteristics. A number of conditions in the environment and characteristics of the individual can influence perception. For example, the perception of a time period may be long or short depending on whether the activity is interesting or boring. Also, objects tend to be perceived in relationship to one's body size; therefore, a room may have been perceived as larger or a hallway longer when a person was 4 years old than when the person is adult size. These changes in perception will not be noticed if the stimulus is seen regularly so that the change is gradual as the body size slowly changes. The remembrance of some childhood stimulus may be noticeably quite different from the later adult perception if the stimulus has not been experienced since childhood.

Temporary conditions such as background, size of nearby objects, and lines may influence perception. A person may dress in a solid, dark color or in something with vertical lines to be perceived as being taller or smaller. A person of average height may be perceived as short if standing by a very tall person or as tall if standing by a short person. If two circles about 5 inches in diameter are cut from the same gray sheet of construction paper and one is placed on a black sheet of construction paper and one on a white sheet, one circle will appear to be a darker shade than the other one.

Do you think food looks more appetizing and tastes better to a hungry person than to a person who has just eaten a huge amount of food?

Researchers have demonstrated that needs influence perception. For example, hungry people have been found to perceive an ambiguous picture as being a picture of food more often than people who have just eaten (McClelland & Atkinson, 1948). Sexually aroused men have been found to perceive women as more attractive than unaroused men perceive the same women (Stephan, Berscheid, & Walster, 1971). Children from poor families have been found to estimate the size of coins to be larger than do children from rich families.

Some differences in perception among cultures have been found. In a major cross-cultural study consisting of 1,878 persons from 14 non-European cultures plus an American sample, it was found as predicted that cultural experience with broad plains and open spaces increases susceptibility to the horizontal-vertical illusion. Cultural experience without such openness as with forest dwellers was found to decrease susceptibility to the illusion (Segall, Campbell, and Herskovits, 1966). The horizontal-vertical illusion is demonstrated in Figures 5–11, 5–14, and 5–15.

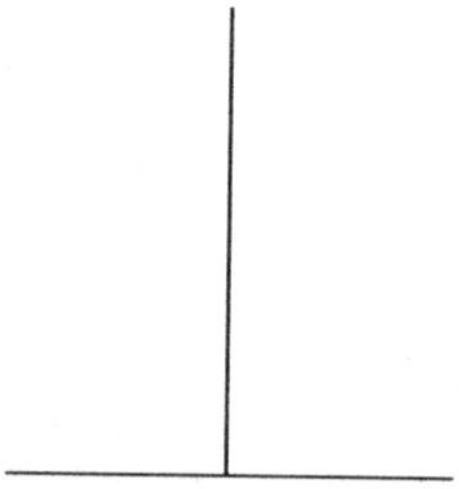

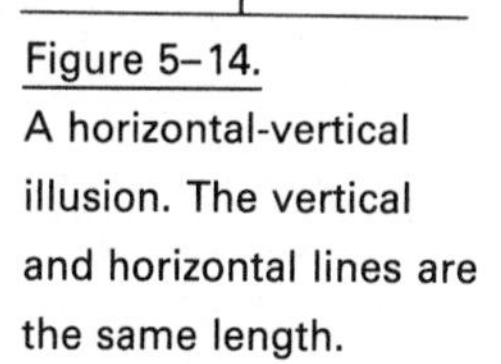

Figure 5–14.
A horizontal-vertical illusion. The vertical and horizontal lines are the same length.

Although many of the ways in which people organize and interpret sensation are inborn and common to all humans, there are many factors that influence the process of perception that insure that an individual's perceptions of the world are somewhat unique. Some people's perceptions may be more realistic than some other people's perceptions. Sometimes an individual's perceptions may become so distorted that the individual may have difficulty functioning effectively.

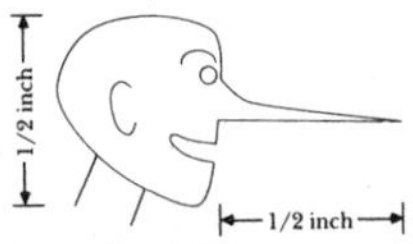

Figure 5–15.
A vertical-horizontal illusion. The length of the nose is the same length as the height of the head.

Controversial Perceptions

Much controversy erupted about subliminal perception after a report in 1957 that movie theater audiences were being influenced to drink Coca-Cola and eat popcorn by advertisements flashed on the screen so briefly the people in the audience had no conscious perception of them. Also, there is much controversy about whether there are forms of perception that occur without sensation. These two issues will be addressed in this section.

Can a person perceive something in the environment without knowledge of the perception?

Subliminal Perception. Another word for threshold is *limen,* and *sub* means below; therefore, levels of energy in the environment that are below the stimulus (or absolute) threshold required for transduction and conscious perception are referred to as subliminal stimulation. **Subliminal perception** refers to the possibility that there may be unconscious perception of these weak, below-threshold stimulations in the subconscious part of the mind. The question is whether an individual is or can be affected by stimuli that are subliminal. One problem that arises in answering this question is that the absolute threshold of an individual varies, and what is thought to be subliminal may in fact not be. Another problem is that sometimes people may deny having perceptions of a stimulus, but when asked to make perceptual judgments, they do better than random guessing.

Recent experiments hint that under certain conditions there may be such a phenomenon as subliminal perception. In one experiment, geometric figures flashed regularly one at a time for

.001 of a second each (not long enough to be perceived) to a group of University of Michigan students. These geometric figures were later chosen as being liked more than other figures in the group that were being viewed for the first time (Kunst-Wilson & Zajonc, 1980). The experiment was repeated with similar results with another group of students at Wesleyan University (Seamon, Brody, & Kauff, 1983). Subjects who were flashed words so briefly that they couldn't even guess whether or not the flash contained a word retained some meaning from the word when tested. When the subjects guessed the correct response rather than the wrong response, they reported it just felt right (Marcel, 1983; Fowler, Wolford, Slade, & Tassinary, 1981). Myers (1986) points out how this might be: "Stimuli too weak to cross our thresholds for conscious awareness may nevertheless trigger a small response in our sense receptors, a response that may even be transmitted to the brain and cross some threshold for feeling or meaning, though not for conscious awareness" (p. 142).

Is subliminal perception being used in an attempt to influence behavior?

Subliminal stimulation is reportedly being used by a few merchants in an effort to decrease shoplifting by the use of an inaudible voice warning of being watched and of the consequences. Also, some advertisers are using subliminal visual stimulation in pictures in magazines. Experimental evidence indicates that an individual's brain does process much information without conscious awareness. Subliminal persuasion or learning, however, is probably a myth because as Myers (1986) points out, in experiments an individual's attention is focused on the subliminal stimulus. In real life situations, however, an individual's attention is not focused on the subliminal stimulus but on stronger stimuli that command attention and are consciously overpowering any effect of subliminal stimuli.

Do you believe in ESP?

Extrasensory Perception. Another question to be answered about perception is whether people can perceive only what is taken in through the senses or whether there is such a phenomenon as **extrasensory perception (ESP)**—perception from some source of stimulation of the brain that comes in some way other than through the known sensory channels. Most Americans, including the college educated, believe in the phenomenon of ESP (Frazier, 1984-85). Although the media is filled with reports of psychics solving police cases and people sometimes have dreams that are fulfilled, research psychologists and prominent scientists are skeptical.

What do parapsychologists study?

Those who study paranormal or beyond normal happenings are known as **parapsychologists.**

Four variations of ESP are claimed: **telepathy**—perception of another person's thoughts; **clairvoyance**—perception of an event too remote to have come through the senses such as perception of an automobile accident 1,000 miles away; **precognition**—perception of an event before it occurs; and **psychokinesis**—ability to influence a physical object or event through thought rather than the muscular system. Most people's beliefs in these varieties of ESP are based on television and stage performances in which the performer controls what the audience sees and hears and not on scientific laboratory experimentation in which the experimenter controls what the psychic sees and hears.

What is the basis for scientific questioning of ESP?

The varieties of ESP have been questioned by scientists chiefly on the basis of unreliable evidence, dishonesty, and inadequate research methods. Skeptics note that an uncritical mind is a gullible mind and that mentalist stage and television performers are simply good magicians performing tricks with the mind rather than tricks with objects such as rabbits. Fernald and Fernald (1985) state that "research findings supporting ESP generally become weaker as the controls against normal sensory awareness is increased" (p. 142). In other psychological research, effects usually grow stronger as extraneous variables are better controlled. Fernald and Fernald (1980) further point out (a) that it is very difficult to apply adequate controls in ESP research because the basic variable is essentially unknown and (b) that no useful theory is in existence to provide a conceptual framework for studying ESP. A prominent British psychologist, Mark Hansel, writes (1980) that "after a hundred years of research, not a single individual has been found who can demonstrate ESP to the satisfaction of independent investigators" (p. 314).

What is partially the basis for some researchers and some individuals believing in ESP?

ESP may exist. Based on statistical probabilities in experiments with large numbers of trials, many researchers assume the phenomenon of ESP does exist, and they are currently trying to discover the situational and personal variables related to ESP. Some of the researchers point out that a scientific laboratory is not conducive to ESP and therefore is an unlikely place to find ESP. And so the controversy about ESP continues.

People seem to believe that ESP exists partly because of mistakes in perception, interpretation, and memory and partly because of a need for wonderment and magic. The human perceptual system has the capacity for organizing neural messages into wonderful sights and sounds. "A century of research has revealed many of the secrets of sensation and perception, but for future generations of researchers there remain profound and genuine mysteries" (Myers, 1986, p. 184).

CONSCIOUSNESS

What is consciousness?

There is no precise definition of consciousness that is universally agreed upon. The literal meaning of the word *consciousness* from Latin is "knowing things together." When first used in the seventeenth century, consciousness was defined as being what passes in a person's mind. Consciousness is a state of awareness, what is in a person's mind presently, or a person's span of attention at the present moment. What is present in an individual's consciousness is only a very small portion of what is available. Likening the mind to a newspaper, Ornstein (1985) calls consciousness the "front page" of the mind. The newspaper has only the most important happenings and things, not everything that could be put in it. What is in the mind that is most important gets present conscious attention (front page).

Nature of Consciousness

The items of highest priority are in consciousness at any given moment—those items most needing action. Because priorities change from moment to moment, consciousness changes from moment to moment. Also, a person may deliberately change or alter consciousness. It is new information and important information that receives an individual's conscious awareness. Actions and patterns that have been repeated many times and are well learned (such as walking) do not need to be in consciousness for processing; they are already stored in the mind and may occur automatically without conscious attention. Both physical skills and mental operations may become automatized, thus freeing a person to bring new information into consciousness. Because the size of consciousness is limited, the process of making room for other and new information in consciousness might be thought of as being automatized.

Function. As was pointed out in chapter 3, most behavior in other species is primarily instinctive or reflexive, requiring no learning. Some human behaviors such as the eye blink are also reflexive, that is, no consciousness or learning is required for the behavior to occur. But having the ability for consciousness allows people to learn, remember, and think, all of which are important to survival. Consciousness serves four main functions for an individual: selection of information, coordination of actions with events, priority setting, and detection of discrepancy. Even after much information is filtered out and simplified through the processes of sensation and perception, more information is left than can be processed. Consciousness is another stage in the process of selecting what information most needs to be processed. Consciousness connects the brain to specific things in the environment to enable an individual to coordinate his or her actions with events. An individual can only consciously act on what is in consciousness. Consciousness has an automatic priority system. Information that is important for survival takes priority. For example, pain stimulation may take priority in consciousness over other stimulation. Or as was pointed out in chapter 3, particular stimuli take priority in consciousness in infants and young children that insure development of the intellectual processes. Consciousness automatically selects information that is different from what is already stored in memory. Thus movement, change, contrast, and unusual or novel stimulation take priority in consciousness.

What takes priority in consciousness?

Structure. Although a number of divisions of consciousness have been proposed, the best known proposal is the division of consciousness into four levels. The **awareness level** of consciousness includes those things noted by a person or those things "we are keeping track of" (Ornstein, 1985, p. 258). Most often people are conscious of what they are aware of, but oftentimes something is in awareness without consciousness of its being in awareness. For example, a sleeping person may be aware of hearing his or her name called or an awake person may be aware of being in the library, and yet the person may not be conscious of being aware of the circumstance. Sometimes an individual may not be conscious that he or she was aware of something until later, suddenly realizing after an event that something happened.

Information that is said to be at the **preconscious level** of consciousness is information that can become conscious as needed—stored knowledge and memories. For example, knowledge of who is the president of the United States or memory of where you ate lunch yesterday would probably be in the preconscious division.

The **nonconscious level** of consciousness functions at a lower level of awareness and includes information of the automatic internal events such as the heart beating or the blood circulating (see

Figure 5–16.
Walking that occurs automatically without conscious attention to it is an example of the nonconscious level of consciousness.

Figure 5–16). Nonconscious information can become conscious, particularly if something malfunctions.

The **unconscious level** of consciousness (sometimes called subconscious) is a still lower level of awareness. This level contains information that is not available to consciousness. The information is in awareness at some level, however, because it can affect behavior, dreams, mannerisms, and speech as in slips of the tongue. This is the level of consciousness that psychoanalysts seek to bring up to a higher level of awareness in an individual. Awareness, then, is considered to exist at various levels of consciousness.

Varieties. Just as there are several divisions of consciousness, there are a variety of states of consciousness. Two general states have been differentiated: the normal state (the awake state in which most of a person's time is spent) and any change from this state, which is referred to as an alternate or an altered state of consciousness. Awake consciousness is not a single state of consciousness, however. Three varieties are differentiated: directed consciousness, flowing consciousness, and daydreaming. Directed consciousness is focused, and attention is directed to absorb information; it is single focused. Probably most of a person's waking state is spent in flowing consciousness—less directed so that awareness continually drifts from one thing to another. Daydreaming is focused as is directed consciousness; however, daydreams are fantasies not bound by logic or reality and consequently are uncensored. Most people daydream many times a day, usually when stimuli in the environment are boring, automatized, or unchanging. A different variety of consciousness occurs between the waking state and the sleeping state. Just before completely entering the state of sleep and just before completely awakening, consciousness is reported to be characterized by vividness, originality, independence of conscious control, and changeability (Budzynski, 1977). Creative insight oftentimes occurs during this variety of consciousness.

During job performance, the individual progresses through cycles of varying levels and states of consciousness that are significant in the explanation of some workers' behaviors. For example, the level or variety of awareness may be a factor in poor job performance, resulting in accidents or in a lower level of production.

Sleep and Dreaming (Alternate States)

A dramatic change in consciousness occurs in sleep; however, conscious experience continues during sleep in the form of dreams.

Sleep and dreaming are **alternate states** of consciousness—states that occur naturally and are different from the normal awake state (see Figure 5–17).

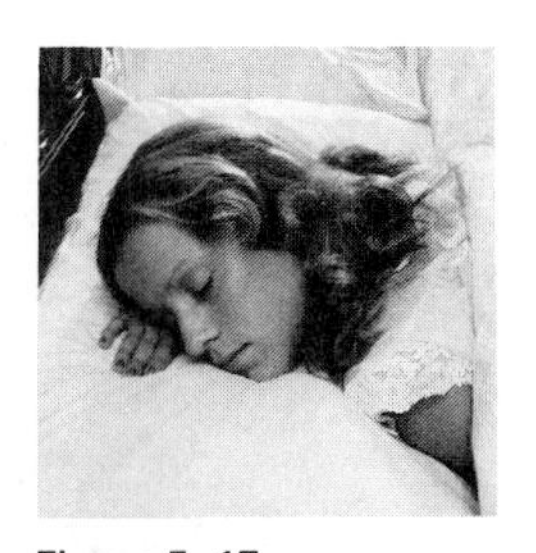

Figure 5–17. Sleep and dreaming are alternate states of consciousness that occur naturally.

Patterns. Five different brain wave patterns (Kleitman, 1963) differentiate five states or stages of sleep, i.e., varieties of consciousness during the sleep state (see Figure 5–18). The typical sleep pattern of a young adult involves about 8 hours. An average of 10 to 15 minutes is spent in each stage, descending from Stage 1 to Stage 4, then ascending back to Stage 1. Stage 1 with **REM sleep** is the stage of sleep in which dreaming characterized by rapid eye movements (REM) occurs. Stage 1 often is not accompanied with REM sleep and is then said to consist of no rapid eye movements (NREM). About $1\frac{1}{2}$ to 2 hours is required to complete a cycle.

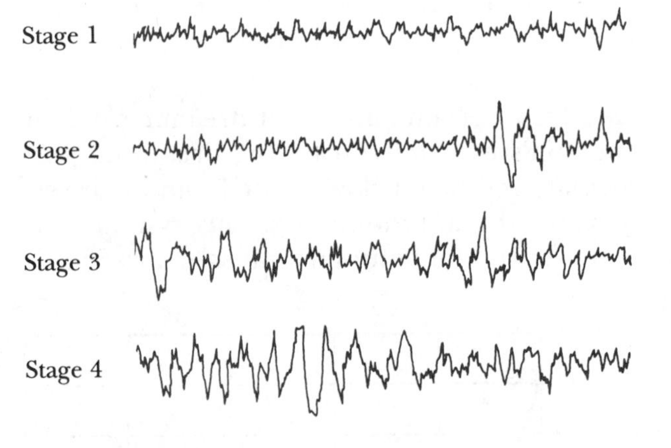

Figure 5–18. The brain wave patterns typical of each of the five stages of sleep.

The cycles continue during the sleep period until about three to five cycles have been completed. The first period of REM sleep is usually no longer than 10 minutes. These periods gradually become longer until they last maybe 30 to 45 minutes so that the average dream time is about $1\frac{1}{2}$ to 2 hours per sleep period (see Figure 5–19). And REM sleep (see Figure 5–20) decreases with age (Roffwarg, Muzio & Dement, 1966). Newborns spend about 8 to 10 hours each day (50 percent of the sleep time) in REM sleep, whereas adults age 60 and older spend only about an hour each day in REM sleep (20 percent of the sleep time).

Dreaming. When an individual has been deprived of REM sleep and is then allowed to sleep undisturbed, the REM (dreaming) periods will be longer to make up for the deprivation; thus,

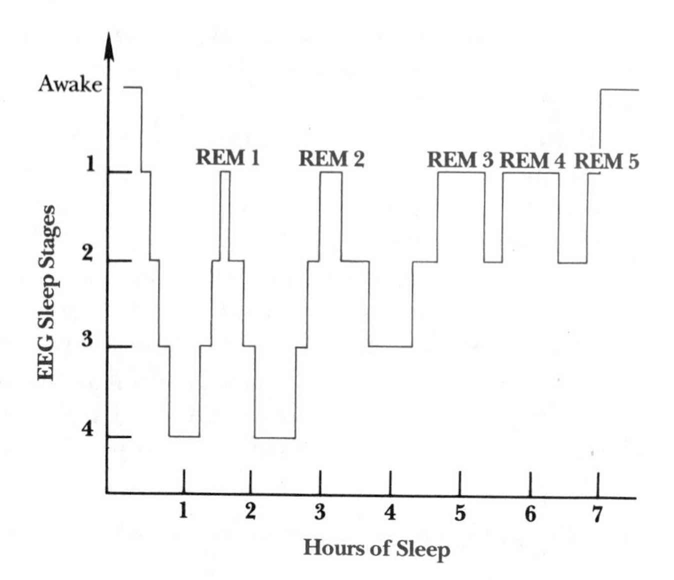

Figure 5–19.
Typical sleep pattern for a young adult.

there seems to be a need for a certain amount of dreaming. When in the REM state, a person's eyes move rapidly, breathing and heart rate become irregular, and blood flow in the brain increases. The involuntary muscles of the autonomic nervous system continue to be activated; however, the voluntary muscles are inacti-

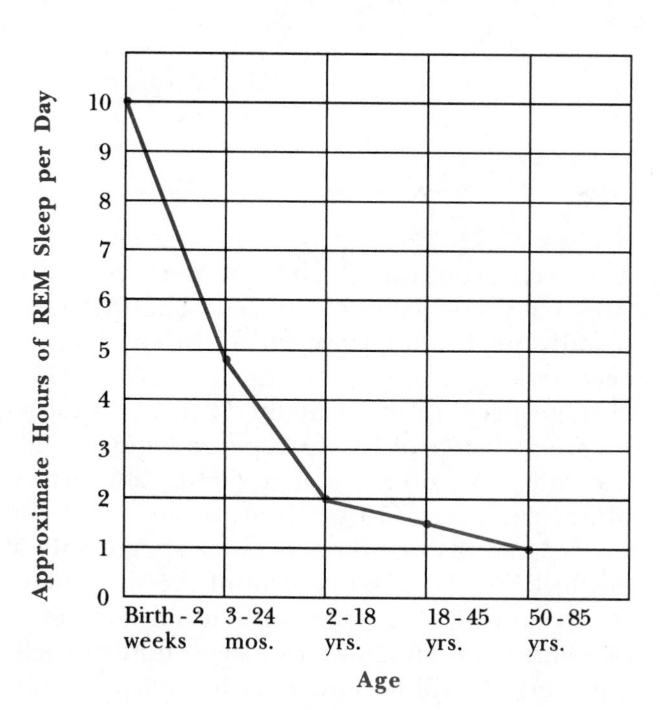

Figure 5–20.
REM sleep decreases with age.

vated (blocked or paralyzed). Thus a person may have a pounding heart from fear experienced in a dream, but the legs do not move during the experience of walking in a dream.

What are some explanations of why a person dreams?

One recently advanced theory explaining dreaming (Hobson & McCarley, 1977) proposes that involuntary mechanisms send impulses to stimulate the brain when impulses are not being sent from sensory stimulation as they are in the waking state. Dreams then are an attempt by the brain to make a coherent interpretation (following the principles of perception) out of essentially incoherent bursts of impulses in the cortex of the brain during sleep. The cortex recalls memories that can be associated with the impulses it is receiving. If no logical connections are found, illogical and remote associations are made, or the gaps are filled with recent memories. According to Sigmund Freud and later psychoanalysts, dreams are symbolic expressions of unconscious desires and serve as sources of wish fulfillment to drain off tensions created during the day.

Another theory of dreams proposes that as non-REM sleep is needed for physical restoration such as cell repair and protein synthesis, REM sleep is needed for mental restoration. REM sleep has been found to increase after human subjects had to learn complex tasks and after experiencing a disturbing and frustrating atmosphere (McGrath & Cohen, 1978). This theory may explain why the amount of REM sleep decreases with age. As less and less new information must be learned, there is less need for REM sleep.

Altered States

Sleep and dreaming are examples of alternate states of consciousness—states that occur spontaneously. Other states of consciousness such as a hypnotic state or trance produced by hypnosis or a highly relaxed transcendental state produced by meditation are examples of **altered states** of consciousness—induced states, or states that do not occur spontaneously and must be deliberately evoked.

Hypnosis. The phenomenon of **hypnosis,** an induced passive state in which there is increased responsiveness to suggestions and commands, has a long history dating back to the 1600s and *mesmerism*— Franz Anton Mesmer's treatments to improve people's health based on the belief that humans could be magnetized like a bar of iron. Only since the 1950s, however, has hypnosis been a phenomenon for scientific investigation. Researchers have not been able to identify physiological differences between hypnotized and nonhypnotized people as they have in the case of sleep and awake people who exhibit different brain wave patterns. The hypnotic state is not the same as sleep; however, hypnotized subjects report dreamlike imagery. In experimental studies, individuals experience a wide range of changes in consciousness while in the hypnotized state. There seems to be no clear dividing line between the hypnotized state and the nonhypnotized state; it seems to be a matter of degree on a continuum. For example, a person may become so engrossed in reading a novel or watching a television show that he or she is in some semblance of a hypnotic trance. Subjects who experience all the suggested effects in the hypnotized state are said to be highly hypnotizable, and those who experience only a few or almost none of the suggested effects are said to be low hypnotizables. Whether subjects are high or low, all do remain aware of who and where they are. Recent research has revealed that highly hypnotizable subjects change from left-hemisphere dominance to right-hemisphere dominance as they enter the hypnotic state (MacLeod-Morgan, 1982).

What are some explanations of how the hypnotic state is produced?

Several different viewpoints of hypnosis exist. There is evidence to suggest that the hypnotized person is in a state of consciousness that is qualitatively different from normal consciousness—a trance state. And there is support for the view that both the hypnotizer and the hypnotized are actors with the subject picking up cues from the hypnotizer and becoming so totally engrossed in the drama and role and believing in it so totally that he or she literally acts out the part. The neodissociation theory (Hilgard, 1973), which grew out of research with the use of hypnosis for pain relief, is based on the divisions of consciousness—various levels. This view holds that there is another level of consciousness or another real world beyond present perceptions, that the pain is felt at some level of awareness, and that the pain is blocked from normal consciousness, similar to the unconscious level. The cognitive-behavioral view holds that hypnosis is really self-induced by a subject's own thoughts; the hypnotizer acts only as a coach to guide the person's thinking (Ruch, 1978).

What are two major uses of hypnosis?

Currently, several practical applications of hypnosis are being made. One primary use of hypnosis is in psychotherapy as an aid in changing maladaptive behaviors. It is also being used in solving crimes as an aid to witnesses' recall; however, using hypnosis to aid recall in solving crimes is not the same as the use of psychic perception (ESP) to aid in solving crimes. Also, a major use is in the relief of pain, particularly in the areas of obstretrics and dentistry and even in major surgery.

If an individual considers hypnosis as an aid in dealing with some problem, only an experienced and reputable practitioner should be consulted. The following sources can help one find or check the credentials of such a practitioner: the local medical society or psychiatry department of the closest university-affiliated hospital; the American Society of Clinical Hypnosis, 2250 East Devon Avenue, Suite 336, Des Plaines, IL 60018; the American Psychological Association, 1200 17th Street, NW, Washington, D. C. 20036.

How can an experienced and reputable practitioner of hypnosis be located?

Meditation. Meditation is a technique for detaching the self from awareness of the stimuli and events of everyday life that activate the sympathetic nervous system and for achieving a state of deep relaxation, inner peace, and heightened self-awareness. As the relaxation response is elicited inhibiting the activation of the bodily emergency system, the "flight or fight" response, certain physiological changes occur such as in blood chemistry, brain waves, and heart rate. The relaxation response is almost the opposite of the bodily emergency reaction of the sympathetic nervous system activated when a person experiences fear, anger, and other strong emotions. The relaxation response consists of bodily responses that include decreased activity in both the sympathetic and somatic nervous systems. Meditation, an altered state of consciousness, seems to transcend normal human experience and is reportedly difficult to describe—a deep sense of peace and unity within the environment.

Figure 5–21. Meditation is a technique for producing relaxation that transcends normal human experience.

There are many varieties of meditation. Meditation is an important part of *yoga,* a form of exercise and relaxation derived from an Eastern religion, and Zen Buddhism. Transcendental meditation is a simple technique introduced by Maharishi Maheah Yogi that produces relaxation, heightened awareness, and more efficient performance of both mental and manual skill tasks. Another method of relaxation devised by Herbert Benson (1977) and his colleagues requires no elaborate training or belief in a religious philosophy (see Figure 5–21). The description of this method appears in the box that follows.

A METHOD OF RELAXATION

1. Sit quietly in a comfortable position and close your eyes.
2. Deeply relax all your muscles, beginning at your feet and progressing up to your face. Keep them deeply relaxed.

3. Breathe through your nose. Become aware of your breathing. As you breathe out, say the word "one"; in...out, "one"; etc. Continue for 20 minutes. You may open your eyes to check the time, but do not use an alarm. When you finish, sit quietly for several minutes with closed eyes and later with opened eyes.
4. Do not worry about whether you are successful in achieving a deep level of relaxation. Maintain a passive attitude and permit relaxation to occur at its own pace. Expect other thoughts. When these distracting thoughts occur, ignore them by thinking "Oh, well" and continue repeating "one." With practice, the relaxation response should come with little effort. Practice the technique once or twice daily, but not within 2 hours after any meal because the digestive processes interfere with the changes in the autonomic nervous system that bring about relaxation.

Note. From "Historical and Clinical Considerations of the Relaxation Response" by H. Benson, J. B. Kotch, K. D. Crassweller, and M. M. Greenwood, 1977, *American Scientist, 65,* pp. 441-445.

Consciousness-Altering Substances

What are the main categories of consciousness-altering substances?

Hypnosis and meditation use experience or environmental events to alter consciousness. Using these techniques modifies the underlying physiology of the individual and thus the functioning of the nervous system in an indirect manner. Drugs, as was pointed out in chapter 2, can directly modify the activity in the nervous system and alter consciousness. Consciousness-altering substances are classified into four main categories: depressants, stimulants, hallucinogens, and psychiatric drugs. These classifications are not mutually exclusive. For example, a psychiatric drug may also be a stimulant or a depressant. In this section, each of the categories will be discussed in terms of examples of drugs classified as being in the category and the effects from use of these drugs.

How do depressants affect the central nervous system?

What are some common depressants?

Depressants. Depressants depress the central nervous system functioning, i.e., they slow down or inhibit the neural functioning. The effects from the depression may range anywhere on a continuum from mild to severe, even leading to death. Depressants may be classified into two general categories: sedatives and analgesics. Sedatives have a calming effect and bring on sleep. Sedatives include barbiturates such as Phenobarbital, Nembutal, and Seconal; minor tranquilizers such as Valium or Librium; nonbarbiturates such as Quaaludes and antihistamines commonly used in products to combat cold and allergy symptoms; and alcohol, which received attention in chapter 2. Barbiturates are commonly prescribed as sleeping pills; however, they stimulate sleep rather than cause natural sleep. They also suppress REM sleep. Although chemically different, barbiturates and alcohol have almost identical effects. The chronic user develops a tolerance, and physiological and psychological dependence can develop. In pregnancy, they can cross the barrier and reach the fetus; hence, babies born to users may already be physically dependent at birth.

What is a difference between sedatives and analgesics?

Sedatives stimulate sleep, but they do not suppress pain stimuli. Analgesics, the opiate drugs such as morphine and heroin, relieve pain, may stimulate sleep, may induce extraordinary dreamlike experiences, and may relieve symptoms of diarrhea and coughing. Opiates are immediately rewarding because they are tension reducing; they dull the senses and relieve psychological distress by blocking so many impulses there may be no awareness of needs such as hunger. Tolerance and dependence can develop.

How do stimulants affect the central nervous system?

What are some common stimulants?

Stimulants. Drugs classified as **stimulants** increase activity in the central nervous system and have the capacity to increase arousal and alertness, elevate mood, and combat tiredness and sleepiness. Larger and larger doses may cause anxiety, irritability, tremors, convulsions, or even death. Amphetamines are stimulants. Caffeine, a stimulant commonly ingested in coffee and soft drinks, was a topic for discussion in chapter 2. Cocaine, an amphetamine-like drug, is also a behavioral stimulant. Cocaine produces a sense of exhilaration and relief from fatigue that lasts for approximately a half hour. Cocaine intoxication is similar to a psychological disorder called mania, which is characterized by an extremely frantic and high mood.

Depressants and stimulants are drugs used primarily for medical purposes. The altering of consciousness from depressants and stimulants, therefore, is usually a side effect from use of the drugs for medical purposes or from an abuse of the drugs.

How do hallucinogens affect an individual, and why are they often called psychodelic drugs?

Hallucinogens. Hallucinogens are drugs that distort perceptions. They alter brain function and mental and behavioral activities. These drugs are often called *psychedelic drugs* because the primary purpose of their use is to change consciousness. Lysergic acid diethylamide (LSD) is the most powerful hallucinogenic drug, acting to reduce levels of serotonin in the brain and thereby causing ordinary and familiar objects and situations to be experienced as significantly different. Major hallucinogens such as LSD induce strong activity in the sympathetic nervous system and in the reticular activating system.

What is the hallucinogenic drug in marijuana?

Tetrahydrocannabinol (THC), a drug in marijuana, may be in different levels of concentration in different preparations. Marijuana is most often used socially at parties for pleasure. At low levels, users report that it enhances sensory experience and elevates mood. A relaxed and drowsy feeling with daydreaming is also reported. At higher levels, users may be loud, boisterous, and easily distracted, and they may feel emotions more intensely. Marijuana smoking has been found to interfere with driving (Klonoff, 1974), with the transfer of information into permanent memory (Tinkleberg & Darley, 1975), and with normal lung functioning (Taskin, Calvarese, Simmons, & Shapiro, 1978). Medical research suggests that long-term use may depress the level of male sex hormones. And unlike alcohol, which is eliminated from the body rather quickly, THC remains in the body for days.

What are some behaviors frequently exhibited by PCP users?

Phencyclidine (PCP), often referred to as "angel dust," originally was used as an animal tranquilizer. It is an anesthetic drug with dangerous hallucinogenic properties for humans. The behavioral effects are variable and unpredictable among individuals and within the same individual. The same dose in different individuals or in the same individual at different times may produce a pleasant, euphoric experience or totally uncontrolled behavior. A person under the influence of PCP may experience euphoric confusion, delirium, agitation and violent behavior toward others, mania, hallucinations, feelings of numbness or insensitiveness to pain, lack of muscular coordination, delusions, a sense of detachment from the environment, a supernatural strength, and spatial disorientation so severe that up and down cannot be differentiated. A PCP user frequently exhibits unconventional behaviors such as going into public places nude, committing suicide, or engaging in extreme, irrational violence.

What medical uses are there for psychiatric drugs?

Psychiatric Drugs. Today a wide variety of drugs are established as being effective in bringing a person's consciousness to a normal state when neurochemical imbalances cause disorders in normal consciousness — psychiatric illnesses. For example, antipsychotic drugs are used in the treatment of schizophrenia and may reduce or eliminate hallucinations, delusions, and other psychotic symptoms. The drug lithium is often used in the treatment of manic-depressive (bipolar) disorders. These psychiatric drugs will be discussed in greater detail in chapter 12 in the section on therapies, which deals with abnormal personality.

Understanding human consciousness involves understanding the functioning of the human nervous system. Inducing altered states of consciousness through the use of drugs involves changing the functioning of the central nervous system, and the central nervous system doesn't repair itself if damaged.

SUMMARY

1. Cells in the sense organs translate energy in the environment, through a process called transduction, into a form of energy that can be relayed through the nervous system as a neural impulse.
2. The stimulus (or absolute) threshold, a minimum level of energy required for transduction, and the difference threshold, the minimum level of energy change required for a stimulus difference to be detected, vary according to species and from individual to individual for a particular sense organ.
3. When cells in sense organs are exposed to a constant level of stimulation, adaptation occurs whereby the cells become less sensitive and the threshold is raised.
4. Cells called rods located on the retina of the eye are stimulated by brightness or differences in light intensity. Cells called cones, also located on the retina, are stimulated by the wavelengths of light rays. Cones are involved in color vision, and rods are involved in night vision.
5. The fovea contains a concentration of cones, and vision is sharpest when the image is projected on this area; the blind spot contains neither rods nor cones, and images projected on this area of the retina are not carried to the brain.
6. The trichromatic theory proposes that different combinations of three kinds of stimulated cones account for how different colors are perceived. The opponent process theory proposes that one kind of cone is capable of responding to either color of a pair of primary colors that oppose each other.
7. Individuals with three types of cones are known as trichromats, partially color-blind individuals with only two of the three are known as dichromats, and color-blind individuals with only one of the three are known as monochromats.
8. Sound waves produce vibrations of the eardrum that initiate a series of motions that eventually stimulate cells in the cochlea of the inner ear to send neural impulses to the brain. These impulses are perceived as hearing.
9. Sound waves are perceived in terms of loudness determined by the amplitude or height of the waves, in terms of pitch determined by the frequency of the waves, and in terms of timbre determined by the pattern of overtones.

10. Various cells in the skin are stimulated by pressure, warmth, and cold. Also, a network of nerve endings in the skin sends impulses that are perceived as pain. The gate control theory and the production of chemical pain killers in some areas of the brain help explain a person's perception of pain.
11. Cells in the inner ear send messages concerning the body's equilibrium or sense of balance. Cells in muscles and tendons enable one to be aware of the movement and position of body parts; this awareness is referred to as the kinesthetic sense.
12. Cells in taste buds on the tongue, which tend to decrease with the age of the person, are stimulated by sweet, sour, salty, or bitter substances for the perception of taste. Transduction for smell occurs directly in a part of the brain in a process not yet completely understood.
13. Perception is the construction of meaning from information received through the senses and involves the filling in of incomplete information and the changing, amplifying, attending to, or ignoring of parts of sensory information.
14. Perception that is constructed from an internal source of stimulation rather than from an external source of stimulation so that the individual sees, hears, feels, or otherwise senses objects or events that are not really in the environment is a hallucination.
15. Feature analysis is a theoretical explanation of how perception occurs and of the stages in perception.
16. Environmental experience prepares one to perceive or misperceive by creating expectancies or sets. Environmental experience results in perceptual learning.
17. The organizing processes of perception (perceptual organization) involve grouping or patterning, which puts together large amounts of information quickly following principles related to figure-ground, proximity, similarity, continuity, closure, and common fate.
18. Stabilizing processes provide a standard and dependable way of interpreting events by providing rules for perceiving objects as constant and for perceiving any change in size, contour, or texture from sensory information such as distance, depth, or location in space.
19. The organizing processes operate so reliably that illusions or misinterpretations may be produced.
20. Research has shown that both heredity and past experience play a significant role in perception. Heredity seems to provide the prewired organization of the sensory receptors, the brain, and the muscles; but the environment must provide sensory input.
21. A perceptual set is a predisposition to perceive something in the environment in a particular way.
22. Principles of perception also apply in one's perceptions of other people. Making inferences rather than relying on facts sometimes leads

to distorted perceptions because of the halo effect, logical error, stereotyping, and expectation.

23. Perception may be influenced by such conditions as interest level, body size, background, size of nearby objects, lines, needs, and culture.
24. Whether perception occurs in the subconscious part of the mind when the intensity of stimulation is below the stimulus or absolute threshold, called subliminal perception, is controversial.
25. Whether stimulation can occur in some way other than through the known sensory channels to produce perception, called extrasensory perception, is controversial. Those who study such beyond normal perception such as perception of another person's thoughts (telepathy), perception of a distant event (clairvoyance), perception of a future event (precognition), and movement of a physical object through thought (psychokinesis) are known as parapsychologists.
26. Consciousness is what is in a person's mind presently, and it includes only those items of highest priority because the size of consciousness is limited.
27. Consciousness serves four main functions for an individual: selection of information, coordination of action with the environment, priority setting, and detection of discrepancy.
28. Four divisions or levels of consciousness are proposed: awareness, preconscious level, nonconscious level, and unconscious level.
29. Consciousness exists in a variety of states: the awake states of directed consciousness, flowing consciousness, and daydreaming; the alternate states of between sleep and awake, sleep, and dreaming; and the altered states such as the hypnotized state, the state of deep relaxation, and drug-induced states.
30. Consciousness-altering substances are classified into four main categories not mutually exclusive: depressants, stimulants, hallucinogens, and psychiatric drugs.
31. Depressants depress the central nervous system's functioning and include sedatives such as barbiturates and alcohol and analgesics such as the opiates morphine and heroin, which also relieve pain.
32. Stimulants increase central nervous system activity and include the amphetamine drugs and such drugs as cocaine and caffeine.
33. Hallucinogens alter brain functioning and produce distorted perceptions. They include the drugs LSD; THC, a drug in marijuana; and PCP, commonly referred to as "angel dust," an anesthetic drug that may have very dangerous and unpredictable effects.
34. Psychiatric drugs help bring a person's consciousness to a normal state when neurochemical imbalances cause disorders in normal consciousness. They include the major tranquilizers as well as other drugs such as lithium.

KEY TERMS AND CONCEPTS

Transduction
Stimulus thresholds
Difference thresholds
Adaptation
Retina
Rods
Cones
Fovea
Blind spot
Trichromats
Dichromats
Monochromats
Frequency
Pitch
Amplitude
Timbre
Equilibrium
Kinesthetic sense
Hallucination
Feature analysis
Perceptual learning
Perceptual organization
Figure-ground rule
Proximity rule
Similarity rule
Continuity rule
Closure rule
Common-fate rule
Constancy principles
Illusion
Perceptual set
Person perception
Halo effect
Logical error
Subliminal perception
Extrasensory perception
Parapsychologists
Telepathy
Clairvoyance
Precognition
Psychokinesis
Awareness level
Preconscious level
Nonconscious level
Unconscious level
Alternate states
REM sleep
Altered states
Hypnosis
Meditation
Depressants
Stimulants
Hallucinogens

QUESTIONS FOR REVIEW

1. What is transduction, a stimulus threshold, a difference threshold, and adaptation?
2. How does a person see and hear, and what are the theories of color vision?
3. What senses are possessed by humans, and how do the sensations other than seeing and hearing occur?
4. What is perception, and what are the stages of perception according to the feature analysis theory?
5. What rules of patterning and what stabilizing principles apply in perception?
6. What are some influences on perception?
7. How is consciousness divided, what purposes does consciousness serve, and what are some varieties of consciousness?
8. What are the patterns of sleep and dreaming and the theories of dreaming?
9. What are hypnosis and meditation? Describe the states.
10. What are the main categories of consciousness-altering substances, some drugs in each category, and general effects of these drugs on individuals?

TEST YOURSELF

1. The translation of a sound wave or any form of energy in the environment into a common form of energy the nervous system can understand is called (a) adaptation (b) transformation (c) gravitational pull (d) transduction.
2. When the cells in a sense organ are exposed to a constant level of stimulation, (a) adaptation occurs (b) the cells become less sensitive (c) the threshold for transduction to occur is raised (d) all of the above.
3. The most sensitive part of the retina, which contains the greatest concentration of cones and is therefore the area where vision is sharpest, is called the ________________.
4. The cells in the eye that respond to differences in wavelengths of light rays and are involved in color vision are called ________________.
5. According to the trichromatic theory of color vision, an individual who is only partially color-blind and cannot differentiate between red and green is a (a) monochromat (b) trichromat (c) dichromat (d) neither a, b, nor c.
6. The frequency, or number of cycles or waves of a sound wave arriving per second, determines the (a) loudness of the sound (b) amplitude of the sound (c) timbre of the sound (d) pitch of the sound.
7. Adults have more cells inside the taste buds on their tongues than children. T or F
8. Four different types of receptor cells respond to different substances; thus an individual can perceive four different types of tastes. T or F
9. Perception (a) is the construction of meaning (b) is the process of building on sensation (c) is influenced by previous constructions of reality, motivation, and expectations (d) all of the above.
10. According to the theory called feature analysis, the third stage of perception focuses on (a) recording the features of the signal (b) comparing special features of the pattern with special features of stored patterns that are similar (c) the pattern of the features rather than the individual features (d) the specific features of the signal or pattern of neural impulses.
11. The rule or principle of perceptual organization whereby parts seem separate or grouped together depending on how close together they are is referred to as (a) proximity (b) common fate (c) figure-ground (d) continuity.
12. In person perception, perceiving the presence of many positive traits from the existence of one favorable trait is referred to as the halo effect. T or F

13. Stabilizing processes referred to as ________________ principles seem to make possible dependable interpretations of sensory input under different environmental conditions.
14. Constancy illusions are the product of (a) neurological damage (b) a genetically determined brain dysfunction (c) prolonged sensory deprivation (d) the reliable operation of patterning and stabilizing principles.
15. Stored knowledge and memories in consciousness that can become available as needed reside in the (a) nonconscious level of consciousness (b) preconscious level of consciousness (c) unconscious level of consciousness (d) awareness level of consciousness.
16. Probably most of a person's waking state is spent in (a) directed consciousness (b) daydreaming (c) flowing consciousness (d) altered consciousness.
17. Five varieties of consciousness occur during sleep. Dreaming most frequently occurs during ________________.
18. Human adults dream about 10 to 15 minutes during a normal 8-hour sleep period. T or F
19. The neodissociation theory of hypnosis holds that (a) both the hypnotizer and hypnotized are totally engrossed actors (b) there is another division or level of consciousness (a trance state) (c) hypnosis is self-induced (d) hypnosis is a state of sleep.
20. Barbiturates, antihistamines, alcohol, morphine, and heroin are (a) stimulants (b) hallucinogens (c) psychiatric drugs (d) depressants.

APPLICATIONS

A. Mr. Apple, who is overly obsessed with neatness, received 15 completed application forms for the position of office manager. John's application form stood out above the others as being exceptionally neat. Mr. Apple selected John to come for an interview and perceived all traits for qualifying for the position to be high in John. John was hired to fill the position.

Vi, who worked under John's supervision, wore so much perfume that it was annoying to others in the office. When John approached her with the problem, she accused him of just making up something for which to critize her because she didn't smell the perfume as strongly.

1. Because Mr. Apple is overly obsessed with neatness, do you think his perception of John's qualifications for the job could have been influenced by the neat application form? Why or why not?
2. Is it possible that Vi really didn't smell the perfume as strongly as the others in the office, or was she just being defensive and denying the criticism because she couldn't accept a criticism? Why or why not?

B. Pert Dannon stayed up all one night and did not sleep. The next night he slept a full 8 hours, but he reported that he had a restless night, dreaming more than usual.

At work, Pert can concentrate and focus his attention on the problem at hand and absorb information related to the problem for a time, but he is continually being distracted by what is happening around him and thoughts of other things going on in his job and in his life. Sometimes while driving home from work in his old work car, he fantasizes about driving a Rolls Royce; and sometimes when he sees a beautiful, young model on television, he fantasizes about being married to her.

Every evening and sometimes during the day, Pert goes through a meditation exercise for a few minutes that produces deep relaxation, a deep sense of peace and unity within the environment, and heightened awareness of the environment. He believes his performance of both mental and manual skills on the job are more efficient when he does this regularly.

1. Do you think Pert really did dream more the night following the night he did not sleep, or was he just overly tired and remembered the dreams better?
2. In what state of consciousness is Pert when he is concentrating and focusing on the problem at hand? when he is distracted by happenings around him and thoughts of other things? when he is fantasizing? when he is meditating? when he is dreaming?
3. Is Pert's fantasizing abnormal? Is it abnormal for Pert to spend very much time in consciousness of surrounding happenings and thoughts of other things while on the job?
4. Do you think it was "all in his mind," or is it possible Pert really is more efficient in both mental and manual skills when he meditates regularly?

SUGGESTIONS FOR FURTHER READING

Benson, H., & Klipper, M. (1976). *The relaxation response.* New York: Avon Publishers.

An easy-to-read book that describes a simple method of relaxation and serves as a guide for controlling anxiety.

Bowers, K. S. (1983). *Hypnosis for the seriously curious.* New York: Norton.

An introduction to hypnosis that focuses on its nature and clinical applications.

Hastorf, A. H., Schneider, D. J., & Polefka, J. (1970). *Person perception.* Reading, MA: Addison-Wesley.

A book about perception of people that should interest psychology students.

Hochberg, J. E. (1978). *Perception* (2nd ed.). Englewood Cliffs, NJ: Prentice-Hall.

A book that is an expanded and rigorous treatment of many topics being studied by psychologists interested in perception.

Ornstein, R. E. (1977). *The psychology of consciousness* (2nd ed.). New York: Harcourt Brace Jovanovich.

A book that brings together much of the literature on consciousness for individuals who wish to study consciousness in depth.

Ray. O. S. (1983). *Drugs, society, and human behavior* (3rd ed.). St. Louis: C. V. Mosby.

A textbook that is a thorough introduction to the effects of psychoactive drugs—both physiological and psychological effects.

Rock, I. (1984). *Perception.* New York: Scientific American Library (Distributed by W. H. Freeman).

Many of the early concerns of perception are treated with excellent illustrations.

CHAPTER 6

LEARNING

Objectives

When you have completed your study of chapter 6, you should be able to:

1. Relate the discovery of classical conditioning and the extension to emotional reactions in humans, and describe how the basic principles were first demonstrated in the laboratory and with a human.
2. Recognize occurrences of and be able to apply principles of classical conditioning.
3. Recognize occurrences of and be able to apply principles of operant conditioning.
4. Appropriately use the terminology of learning theory in context.
5. Describe reinforcement and punishment in terms of effect on behavior, determinants of effectiveness, types, schedules, and side effects.
6. Describe and give examples of two forms of social or observational learning, and cite the determinants of effectiveness in social learning.
7. Define learning sets, insight, and insight learning.
8. Describe and give the steps in behavior modification, and identify some techniques used.
9. Relate practical uses of behavior modification.
10. Explain biofeedback, and tell how it is being used.

A bird builds a nest, a fish navigates, a cat washes it's face, and a spider spins a web. These are innate behaviors, instinctual chains of movements, or fixed action patterns found in all members of the species that allow members of the species to meet the basic needs in their lives without learning. People also have innate behaviors, but they are simpler than fixed action patterns and are called reflexes. A **reflex** is an automatic response to something in the environment such as the dilation of the pupil of the eye in response to decreased illumination, the eye blink in response to a puff of air, or the knee jerk in response to a tap on the knee. Although some learning can occur, most of the behavior of lower animal species consists of reflexes and fixed action patterns. Most of the behavior of the higher species, humans, consists of learning even though some behavior is reflexive. Humans are innately endowed with the capacity to learn to meet their basic needs. Imagining things people could not do if they could not learn will bring forth the realization that learning is involved in nearly everything a person does. Understanding learning, then, is essential to understanding human behavior.

What is learning?

A person can learn, see others in the process of learning, and observe that people respond in different ways as a result of learning. Learning cannot be observed directly, however, because it is an abstraction that is inferred by a relatively permanent change in an individual's behavior that occurs as a result of experiences with people, places, events, or objects. Sometimes reading, studying, or teaching is considered to be parallel to learning; but these activities are only a part of learning. Reflex behaviors and behaviors that result from maturation or from physiological changes arising from illness, fatigue, intoxication, or drugs are not learned. Learning is the process whereby behaviors change to insure survival under changing conditions and to meet the demands of the current environment. Learning is central in developing, modifying, and maintaining knowledge, skills, and attitudes necessary for success in the business world. Several forms of learning that have been identified are described in this chapter. The primary focus is on association learning because insight learning involves remembering and thinking, the topic of chapter 7.

CLASSICAL CONDITIONING

What form of learning was first to be identified?

What is classical conditioning?

Classical conditioning, the first form of learning to be identified, is the shifting of an old response to a new stimulus. Associations are formed when a new event is paired with an event that brings forth a particular behavior. The new event then comes to also bring forth the behavior because it becomes a signal for the event. Thus, classical conditioning is often referred to as *signal learning.* For example, classical conditioning has occurred when an individual responds to the presentation of a blue sheet of paper by blinking the eyes after the blue sheet of paper has been presented immediately before a puff of air into the eyes on several successive occasions. Blinking in response to a puff of air into the eyes is an unconditioned response. When the blue sheet of paper becomes associated with the puff of air and elicits blinking, conditioning or learning has occurred and blinking is a conditioned response. The box on page 193 describes how one may demonstrate classical conditioning by shifting the response of hand raising from one stimulus to a new stimulus. The discovery, application to humans, and basic principles of classical conditioning are topics examined in this section.

Discovery

Who discovered classical conditioning?

Ivan Pavlov (1927), a Russian physiologist, used dogs to study the digestive processes. Because the presence of food in the mouth brings forth the reflex response of salivation, Pavlov inserted tubes into the salivary glands to measure the amount of saliva produced when he fed the dogs. He became perplexed when, after being in the laboratory for a while, the dogs would salivate before they were given food. Pavlov then turned his attention to this phenomenon and demonstrated classical conditioning in the laboratory.

What perplexed Pavlov?

How did Pavlov demonstrate classical conditioning?

Pavlov's Demonstration. Pavlov demonstrated classical conditioning by immediately following the ringing of a bell with the presentation of food to the dogs. Initially, the dogs did not salivate when the bell rang. After following the bell with food several times, Pavlov rang the bell without presenting food. He discovered that the bell alone now produced salivation in the dogs. A form of learning currently referred to as classical (earliest model) conditioning had occurred (see Figure 6–1). The dogs responded differently to an environmental event (bell) as a result of an environmental experience (pairing of bell with food). Originally the bell was neutral; it did not bring forth a specific response in the dog. After the bell became associated with food, it came to signal the presentation of food and to produce the same response as the presence of food in the mouth—salivation. Classical conditioning

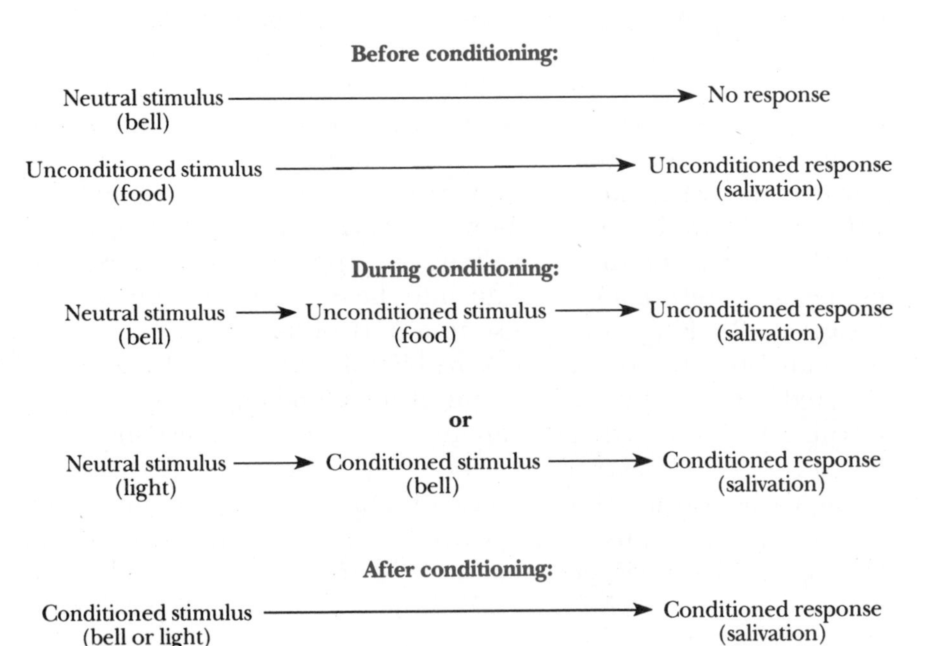

Figure 6–1. Diagram of classical conditioning.

had occurred by associating a neutral stimulus with an unconditioned stimulus.

A **neutral stimulus** is a person, place, event, or object that does not bring forth a specific response from the organism. An **unconditioned stimulus** is some phenomenon that brings forth a specific response, even the first time it is presented—a reflex response. A reflex response is referred to as an unlearned or **unconditioned response.**

Extended Study. Pavlov extended his experiment by turning on a light before ringing the bell. At first, turning on the light did not elicit salivation. However, after turning on the light and immediately following it with the ringing of the bell a few times, the dog would then salivate when the light was turned on without the light being followed by the ringing of the bell. Classical conditioning had also occurred by associating a neutral stimulus (light on) with a **conditioned stimulus** (bell), a learned stimulus. A response brought forth by a conditioned stimulus is referred to as a learned or **conditioned response** (see Figure 6–1).

A DEMONSTRATION OF CLASSICAL CONDITIONING

Instruct a group of people to raise their right hands whenever you raise yours. These instructions establish a reasonably reliable stimulus-conditioned response relationship. Try it a few times to make sure everyone is responding. Then begin to precede the raising of your hand with saying "now" as if to indicate when you are going to raise your hand. Do this for about 15 or 20 trials. Then just say "now" without raising your hand. Several people should be conditioned to raise their hands when you say "now". The word *now* was originally a neutral stimulus for hand raising; it has become a conditioned stimulus for hand raising (VanRijn, 1973).

Emotional Reactions

Who heard about Pavlov's studies with dogs and extended the principle to explain human behavior?

John B. Watson, the American psychologist who developed the behaviorist theory, was attracted to Pavlov's explanation of how old responses are shifted to new stimuli and believed that this could explain most of human behavior. He extended the principle to include emotional reactions such as fear, anger, and love that account for likes, dislikes, and attitudes.

Watson's Views. Watson recognized three innate reactions in humans—fear, anger, and love—as being similar to Pavlov's reflexes, and he proposed that all emotional reactions to stimuli are learned in association with these three. For example, a loud, unexpected noise elicits the startle or fear response reflexively at birth. Anger is experienced first innately in response to physical discomfort, and love is first experienced innately in the form of attachment. Any neutral stimulus immediately preceding a noise may be associated with the noise and will then bring forth fear responses. Any neutral stimulus associated with discomfort brings forth disliking or negative feelings, and any neutral stimulus associated with love and caring brings forth liking or positive feelings.

An electrician may show no signs of fear when handed a particular tool to use. However, if there are loud, explosive sounds somewhere in the building each time that tool is handed to the electrician several times in succession, fear reactions may then occur when that tool is presented even though no loud, explosive sound occurs this time. Or, the director of a project may not experience feelings of anger when a particular worker appears. However, if the director happens to become angry about some incident every time the worker appears for several times in succession, the director may then experience feelings of anger when the worker appears even though there is no incident to elicit anger. Or, if a person to whom one is attached and loves has blond hair, blond hair may become associated with feelings of love and elicit a feeling of liking when meeting a stranger with blond hair.

Figure 6–2.
Albert developed a fear of white rats after a white rat was associated with a loud, frightening noise.

The Classic Demonstration. The classic demonstration of conditioning of an emotional reaction (Watson & Rayner, 1920) was with an 11-month-old boy named Albert who showed no fear of white rats and enjoyed watching them. After the appearance of a white rat was immediately followed by a loud, frightening noise a few times, Albert showed signs of fear when a white rat appeared alone without the noise (see Figure 6–2). Albert also showed signs of fear when a white rabbit and anything white and furry was presented.

If reading about this experiment involving 11-month-old Albert causes concern about psychological research, keep in mind that the American Psychological Association has been interested in ethical practices in psychology since it was founded in 1892 and periodically publishes a revised ethics code for research with human subjects. Any evidence of failure to abide by the code of ethics is grounds for dismissal from the American Psychological Association and for suspension of the psychologist's license to practice psychology. The 10 basic principles of the present ethics code for research with humans as briefly summarized by Bourne and Ekstrand (1985) are listed in the box that follows.

SUMMARY OF ETHICAL PRINCIPLES IN THE AMERICAN PSYCHOLOGICAL ASSOCIATION ETHICS CODE FOR RESEARCH WITH HUMAN SUBJECTS

1. The investigator is personally responsible for the ethical acceptability of the research and should consult others when there is any doubt.
2. The investigator is also responsible for the ethical conduct of all who work with and for him or her, although all involved have ethical obligations.
3. Prospective subjects have a right to be as fully informed as possible about the nature of the experiment—this is known as obtaining the subject's informed consent to participate in the experiment.
4. The investigator should maximize openness and honesty with subjects and minimize deceit. If the true purpose of the experiment must be concealed from the subject, the subject should be fully informed after the experiment as to why this deception was necessary.
5. People may not be coerced into participating, and they must be allowed to withdraw from participation at any time.
6. The investigator must make clear to subjects what agreement is being made between the two parties (subject and experimenter) and must honor any commitments made to the subject.
7. The investigator must minimize discomfort and protect subjects from harm and danger. If any of these are likely to be involved, the subject must be fully informed of the risks. Procedures involving any serious and lasting harm are forbidden.
8. After the experiment, the subject is to be given full feedback about the nature of the study.
9. If any undesirable consequences have occurred, the investigator must detect them and remove or correct them.
10. All information collected must be considered confidential. If this is not possible, the subjects must be so informed beforehand (Bourne & Ekstrand, 1985, p. 26).

Basic Principles

Pavlov demonstrated the basic principles of classical conditioning in the laboratory with dogs. Watson and other psychologists have demonstrated the basic principles in human behavior. In this section, the concepts of extinction, spontaneous recovery, stimulus generalization, and stimulus discrimination are explained.

What is extinction in learning theory?

Extinction. When an old response is shifted to a new stimulus, the new stimulus may not elicit the old response indefinitely. If the new stimulus is presented repeatedly without being paired with the old stimulus, the new stimulus may cease to elicit the response. This phenomenon is referred to as **extinction.**

How did Pavlov demonstrate extinction in the laboratory?

Pavlov demonstrated extinction in the laboratory by conditioning a dog to salivate to the sound of a bell. He then repeatedly sounded the bell without pairing it with the appearance of food. The amount of salivation relative to the sound of the bell decreased until finally no salivation occurred when the bell was sounded. The association of the bell with the absence of food had become stronger again than the association of the bell with the presentation of food (see Figure 6–3).

Can you cite some examples of extinction learning in people?

The electrician previously mentioned may cease to experience fear when handed a particular tool if no further loud, explosive sounds are paired with the presentation of that tool for several consecutive times. The person may cease to blink in response to a

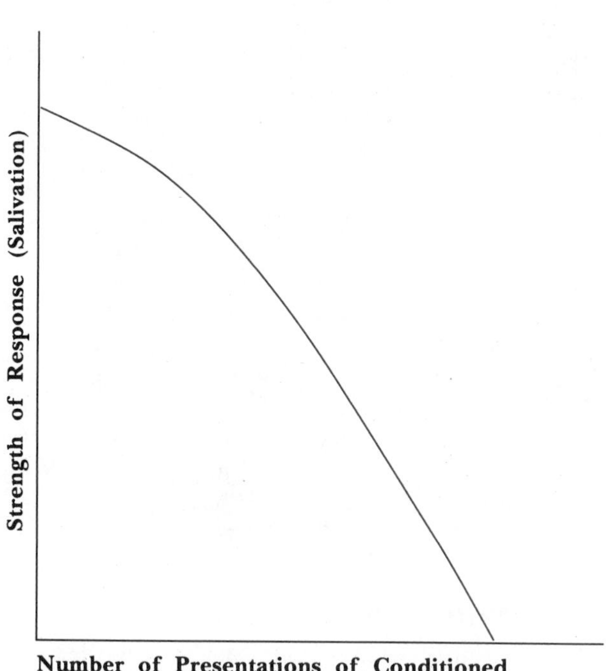

Figure 6–3.
Diagram of extinction.

blue sheet of paper if it is presented for a number of consecutive times without the puff of air. The project director may cease to experience feelings of anger when the worker appears if incidents eliciting anger no longer occur when the worker appears.

Spontaneous Recovery. Sometimes after extinction has seemingly occurred and a period of time passes during which neither the old stimulus nor the new stimulus nor the pairing of them occurs, the new stimulus may be presented and again will elicit the response. This is referred to as **spontaneous recovery.** Several time lapse periods may be required before spontaneous recovery ceases to occur (see Figure 6–4).

What is meant by spontaneous recovery in learning theory?

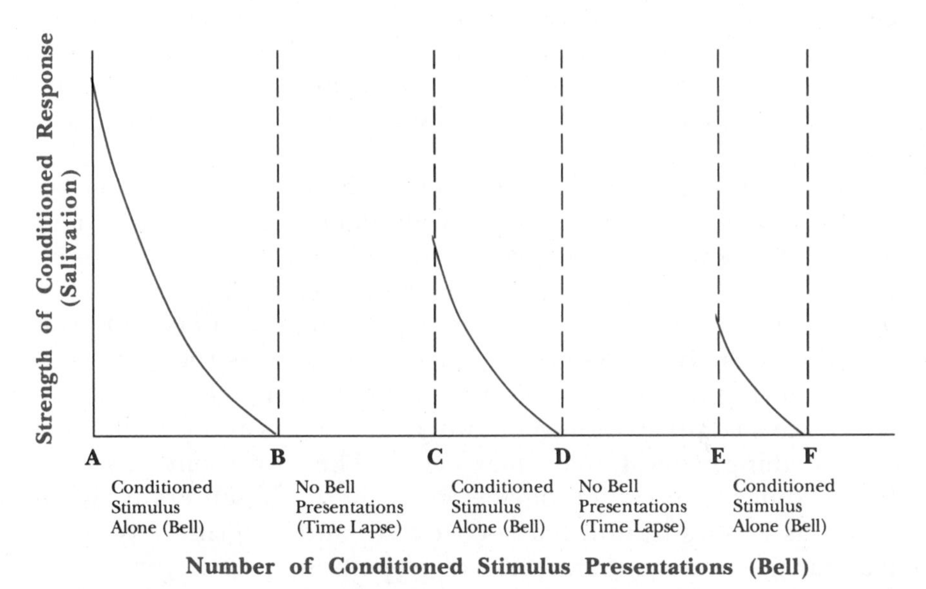

Figure 6–4. Diagram of spontaneous recovery.

Pavlov demonstrated spontaneous recovery in the laboratory by conditioning a dog to salivate to the sound of a bell and then sounding the bell without pairing it with food until extinction occurred. He then put the dog out of the laboratory and into the yard for a period of time. When he brought the dog back into the laboratory and sounded the bell, the dog salivated again even though it had previously ceased salivating in response to the sound of the bell. The association of the sound of the bell with no food had weakened during the time the dog was out of the laboratory, and the association of the bell with the appearance of food was stronger again.

How did Pavlov demonstrate spontaneous recovery?

Can you cite some examples of spontaneous recovery in people?

Spontaneous recovery would be demonstrated by a person who is involved in an automobile accident and continues to drive until extinction of the fear response to driving occurs and then stops driving for an extended period of time and experiences fear again when driving is resumed.

What is stimulus generalization?

Stimulus Generalization. When a new stimulus comes to be associated with a stimulus that already elicits a particular response, any stimulus similar to that new stimulus may also elicit the response even if direct conditioning has not occurred. This is the principle of **stimulus generalization.** Pavlov found that although conditioning a dog took place by pairing a bell of a particular tone and loudness with the presentation of food, the sound of a bell of any tone or loudness elicited the response of salivation. Watson demonstrated that a white rabbit or anything similar to the white rat that Albert had been conditioned to fear also elicited a fear response.

Figure 6–5. Stimulus generalization occurs when an employee likes a co-worker because of a particular feature similar to another person with whom the employee has had a pleasant experience in the past.

Stimulus generalization is an important aspect of learning because most often a person outside the laboratory does not have exactly the same stimulus presented each time (see Figure 6–5). People would not be able to read if the principle of generalization did not apply; no two people have identical handwriting, and print is seldom exactly the same shape, size, or color as the print presented during the original act of learning to read. If an employee walks into a company storeroom with no windows and is frightened by something, conditioning may occur. The storeroom may elicit fear responses in the employee when he or she enters it again. Stimulus generalization may occur also, and entering any room that has no windows may elicit fear responses.

What is stimulus discrimination?

Stimulus Discrimination. Another important aspect of conditioning is learning to react to a specific stimulus and not to respond in the same way to all similar stimuli. Learning to recognize the differences between similar stimuli is referred to as **stimulus discrimination.** The process of stimulus discrimination involves learning to respond to a particular stimulus and to inhibit that response in the presence of other stimuli, even similar stimuli (see Figure 6–6).

How did Pavlov's dogs learn to differentiate very similar stimuli?

Pavlov demonstrated in the laboratory that dogs conditioned to salivate to the sound of any bell could be conditioned to salivate to a specific bell such as a bell of 35 decibels and not to salivate to a similar bell such as a bell of 25 decibels. He accomplished this by pairing the bell of 35 decibels with food and not pairing the bell of 25 decibels with food. After a few trials, the decibel level paired

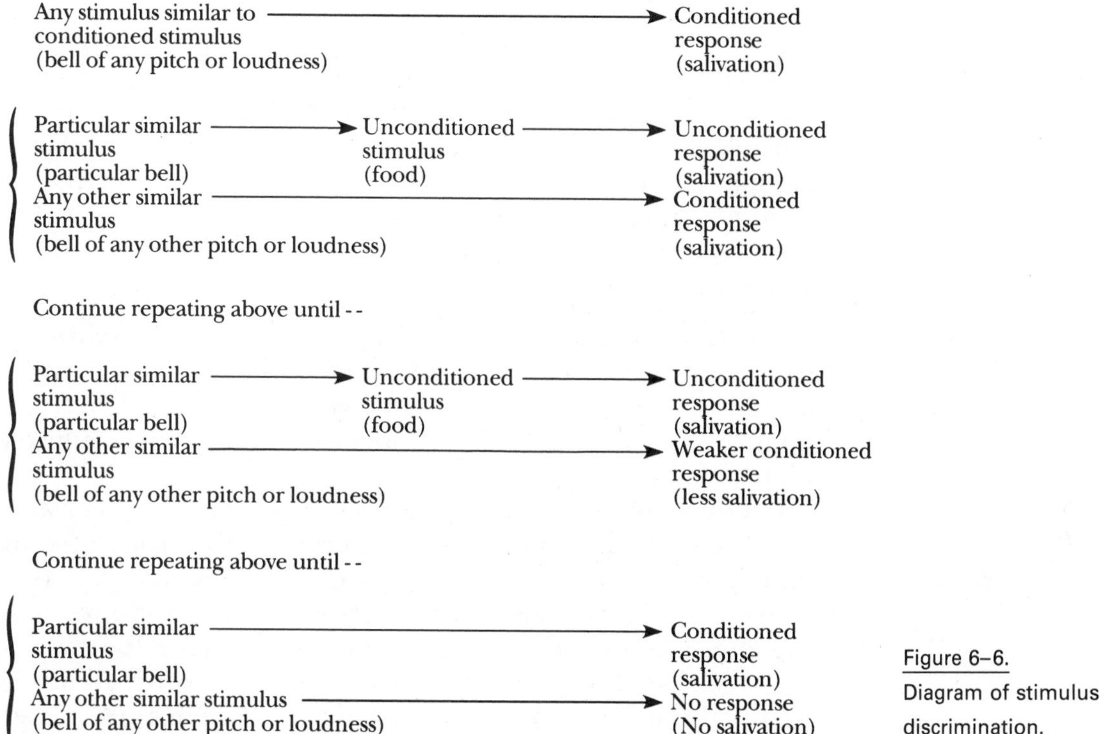

Figure 6–6. Diagram of stimulus discrimination.

with food produced salivation, and the decibel level not paired with food did not produce salivation.

Stimulus discrimination is as important to learning how to read as stimulus generalization. If an individual could not learn to discriminate between similar stimuli, reading would not be possible because the letters *b, d, p,* and *q* would elicit the same response. An automobile mechanic may learn to respond differently to very similar engine sounds. A manager may learn to discriminate between the handwriting of the president of the company and the handwriting of a fellow employee and to respond differently to each person's handwriting.

OPERANT CONDITIONING

Who proposed the theory of operant conditioning, and what is it?

The laws of association explained by Pavlov were extended by B. F. Skinner. Skinner was primarily concerned with *emitted behaviors*

(behaviors involving the voluntary muscles) rather than *elicited behaviors* (behaviors involving the involuntary muscles). Pavlov was concerned with the association of stimuli. Skinner was concerned with the association of a response with the consequence of that response. Skinner considered this association to be another type of conditioning or learning that explains even more of human behavior than classical conditioning. Skinner's theory of operant conditioning and the concepts of reinforcement and punishment are discussed in this section.

Skinner's Theory

In this section, operant conditioning is defined, and Skinner's experimental work is described. Various kinds of consequences are also discussed along with the effect they have on behavior. Additionally, the basic concepts of operant conditioning are given attention.

Concept of Operant Conditioning. Skinner proposed and demonstrated operant conditioning experimentally, primarily with rats and pigeons, using a device referred to as a Skinner box (see Figure 6–7). A Skinner box provides an opportunity for a particular response, such as pressing a bar, and a consequence for that response, such as receiving a pellet of food, to occur. Skinner referred to the situation or setting in which the response is emitted as the **discriminative stimulus.** The spontaneous behaviors that an organism is capable of emitting such as pressing, pecking, turning, making a sound, or moving particular body parts are referred to as

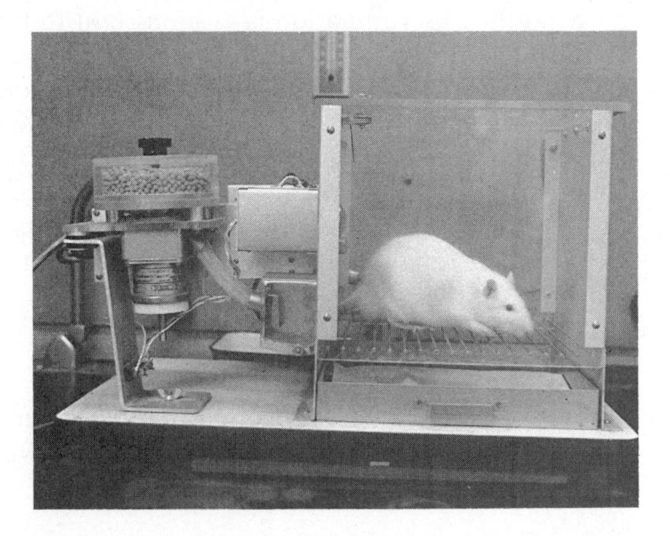

Figure 6–7.
A Skinner box.

operants. They operate on the environment; thus, the term operant conditioning is applied to this type of learning. **Operant conditioning** occurs when a randomly or spontaneously emitted behavior becomes associated with the consequence or effect the behavior has on the environment and increases or decreases in frequency according to whether the effect is desirable or undesirable (Skinner, 1953).

What are the three general categories of consequences of a behavior?

What effect does each general category of consequences have on a behavior?

Consequences. According to Skinner's theory, operants (responses) may operate on the environment to produce either a reinforcing or a punishing consequence, or there may be no operation on the environment and no consequence. A reinforcing consequence increases the frequency of the operant, and a punishing consequence decreases the frequency of the operant. If a response has no effect whatsoever on the environment, the frequency of the response will decrease. For example, turning a door knob is an operant that may be followed by the consequence of the door opening when a person desires to leave the room. This operant will be associated with the opening of the door and will probably increase in frequency when one wants a door open. If an employee criticizes his or her supervisor and is demoted as a consequence, the operant of criticizing the supervisor will probably decrease in frequency. When attempting to start a machine and pressing a particular button has no effect of any kind on the machine, pressing that particular button will decrease in frequency.

What is the difference between positive and negative reinforcement?

Reinforcing consequences may be of two general types. **Positive reinforcement** is something that pleases, rewards, or satisfies the person that it is delivered to following the response. If a person desires a cup of coffee and placing a coin in a machine results in receiving a cup of coffee, positive reinforcement is illustrated. **Negative reinforcement** is a consequence that increases a response and is rewarding because it either removes an aversive discriminative stimulus, provides escape from it, or prevents it from occurring. Negative reinforcement would be illustrated if an employee is dawdling (aversive discriminative stimulus to the supervisor), the supervisor yells in an angry voice (response), and the employee stops dawdling (negative reinforcement for the supervisor). The supervisor's yelling in an angry voice when an employee is dawdling will increase.

What is punishment?

The term **punishment** refers to the delivery of a painful or aversive consequence following the occurrence of a response. Punishment is the delivery of something that is physiologically or psychologically unpleasant or painful to the person that decreases the

Figure 6–8.
Types of punishing consequences.
(a) Time-out: "You exceeded the speed limit; therefore, you must delay driving your car for one week." (b) Response-cost: "You exceeded the speed limit; therefore, your car will be taken away permanently."
(c) Punishment (physiological): "You exceeded the speed limit; therefore, you will do hard labor for one week."
(d) Punishment (psychological): "You exceeded the speed limit, you unreliable, incompetent, uncaring person."

frequency of the occurrence of the response. Physical punishment in a job situation would be illustrated if a worker pushed the red button rather than the green button on a machine, releasing a piece that smashed a finger. Harsh criticism from the manager would be an example of psychological punishment. **Time-out** or **response-cost** refers to a consequence that delays (time-out), removes, or prevents (response-cost) a pleasant discriminative stimulus. If the children are watching their favorite television program (pleasant discriminative stimulus for the children) and the parent turns the TV off as a consequence of their scuffling, time-out or response-cost would be demonstrated. In general, learning through association with punishing consequences involves either the withdrawal of pleasant stimuli (time-out or response-cost) or the administration of unpleasant stimuli (punishment) (see Figure 6–8).

Whether a consequence is reinforcing or punishing depends on the effect of the consequence, not the consequence itself (see Figure 6–9). The consequence might be pleasing, rewarding, or satisfying for one person but not for another, or it might be reinforcing for a person at one time and not at another time. Likewise, the consequence of a response might be unpleasant, aversive, or painful for one person but not for another, or it might be a punishing consequence for a person at one time and not at another time. If the consequence increases a response, it is reinforcing; if the consequence decreases a response, it is punishing. For example, arriving late to work at one company results in being sent to a

Figure 6–9.
Presenting a report may be a pleasant consequence of working on a project for one person. To another person, however, such a presentation would be a painful and punishing consequence.

job site on the east side of the city. One employee might like the consequence because it enables the employee to work with a friend; the frequency of this employee's tardiness would increase. Another employee might not like the consequence because of dislike for the supervisor at the job site on the east side; this employee's tardiness would decrease in order to avoid the consequence.

Can you give an example of extinction, spontaneous recovery, stimulus generalization, and stimulus discrimination in operant learning?

Basic Principles. The basic principles of extinction, spontaneous recovery, stimulus generalization, and stimulus discrimination also apply in operant conditioning just as in classical conditioning. If a response ceases to operate on the environment and therefore no longer is paired with a reinforcing consequence, extinction will occur, and the response will cease to be emitted. For example, an employee may tell jokes that are followed by laughter and attention from others (positive reinforcement). If everyone suddenly ignores the jokes, reinforcement no longer is paired with the response, and the joke telling by the employee will cease—extinction occurs. If the employee is out of the office for an extended period of time but tells a joke again upon returning, spontaneous recovery in operant conditioning has occurred.

Stimulus generalization would be demonstrated if a person learns to emit a particular response in a particular situation or in the presence of a particular discriminative stimulus and then emits the same response in similar situations. For example, a child may be conditioned to respond politely to members of the family in the home. The child may also respond politely to people in other settings. When a person learns to discriminate between similar situations for emitting the response, stimulus discrimination is demonstrated. For example, cursing may occur in frustrating situations with peers on the job but may not occur in a similar situation with a supervisor present who has shown disapproval of cursing.

What is response generalization?

Response generalization is the emission of similar but physically different responses in a particular situation. An individual may always speak a greeting to the manager on arrival to work, but the greeting may be a little different each time—louder, softer, with different words such as *hello* or *good morning*, or with a little or big smile.

What is response discrimination?

Response discrimination occurs when two or more similar but physically different responses are emitted in a particular situation and one response is reinforced but the others are not. When greeting the manager upon arrival at work, saying hello loudly may be reinforced with a return hello and smile, whereas saying hello softly may not be reinforced. The employee learns to say hello loudly. Response discrimination may occur when learning a new behavior such as learning to operate a word processor. When the correct response is made, the word processor operates properly; thus, the correct response is reinforced. When any other similar response is made, the word processor does not operate properly and the similar responses are not reinforced. The use of the correct response will increase, whereas the use of all other responses will decrease or cease even though they may be very similar to the correct response.

How are behaviors shaped?

Most of a person's behaviors would never occur spontaneously. New behavior is created through **shaping** whereby reinforcing different behaviors that are closer and closer approximations of the desired or target behavior is used to gradually change an old behavior. "Operant conditioning shapes behavior as a sculptor shapes a lump of clay" (Skinner, 1953, p. 91). The responses necessary for piloting an airplane do not occur spontaneously. Instead, the responses are shaped by reinforcing closer and closer approximations. One small part of the task may be accomplished and then another until the piloting is attempted under simulated conditions, then with an instructor, and then alone.

Reinforcement and Punishment

Several factors influence the degree of effectiveness of a consequence in increasing or decreasing the frequency of a behavior, and there are many types of reinforcing and punishing consequences. Whether or not the consequence occurs each time the response is made and the type of schedule the consequence is following when it is not occuring each time the response is made also effect the behavior. Skinner emphasized the use of reinforcing consequences, whenever possible, to shape behavior because of the possible side effects of punishment. These topics are addressed in this section.

What four factors determine the effectiveness of reinforcement?

Effectiveness. According to Miller (1975), there are four main factors that determine the effectiveness of reinforcement. These factors are (a) contingency—for maximum effectiveness, the reinforcement must be delivered only if the organism makes the response; (b) immediacy—the more immediately the reinforcement follows the response, the greater the effect; (c) size—the greater the quantity of reinforcement, the greater the effect; and

(d) deprivation — the more deprived an organism is of the reinforcement, the greater the effect.

Correlated reinforcement is reinforcement in which the quantity varies in proportion to the quantity or intensity of the response. Correlated reinforcement is effective because it provides the learner with more information concerning the value of the behavior modification. This then enables the learner to discriminate responses and thus have more control over the behavior (Travers, 1972). Money paid in proportion to the number of pages typed and a grade on a test assigned in proportion to the number of correct responses given are examples of correlated reinforcement.

What is correlated reinforcement, and is it effective?

Types. Although each consequence must be tested to determine if it is a reinforcer for a specific individual, there are types of consequences that are generally considered to be reinforcers. **Primary reinforcers** are those that satisfy a biological need, such as food. Primary reinforcers may lose their effectiveness due to overuse but, subsequently, may regain their effectiveness after a period of deprivation. **Secondary reinforcers** are conditioned or learned reinforcers that gain their effectiveness from association with other reinforcers such as a smile from a person followed by friendly conversation with that person. If this happens frequently enough, the smile may become a reinforcer by being associated with friendly conversation. Or, a good grade may be associated with acquiring a desired job. These secondary reinforcers may lose their effectiveness from either overuse or extinction. **Generalized conditioned reinforcers** are associated with many different reinforcers; therefore, extinction or ineffectiveness from overuse does not usually occur. Some generalized conditioned reinforcers are money, approval, attention, affection, diplomas, and grades.

What kind of needs are satisfied by primary reinforcers?

What type of reinforcers can lose their effectiveness from extinction as well as overuse?

Is there a type of reinforcer that usually never becomes ineffective?

Sometimes responses may be reinforcers. Premack (1965) demonstrated that a behavior that occurs often can be used as a reinforcer of a behavior that occurs less frequently. The **Premack principle** is sometimes referred to as "Grandma's Law" — "eat your spinach, then you may eat your ice cream." A response such as talking with co-workers occurs more frequently for an employee than a response such as writing a report. If the employee is allowed to talk with co-workers only following the completion of a report, report writing would be expected to increase.

Can a behavior be a reinforcer for another behavior?

Intrinsic reinforcers are those internal feelings of satisfaction that people get from a particular behavior (see Figure 6–10). An employee's work may produce a feeling of competency, mastery,

Figure 6–10. Sometimes people engage in certain activities only because those activities are stimulating or satisfying within themselves.

achievement, or self-actualization, which satisfies a need for this feeling and increases the work response. Intrinsic reinforcers have limitations in work situations because managers cannot directly control them. Managers can only hope that the employee will receive a feeling of satisfaction from the work, which will increase productivity. Tangible things that can be used as reinforcers are referred to as **extrinsic reinforcers.** A manager can give extrinsic reinforcers such as money, fringe benefits, promotions, approval, or privileges.

What is the difference between an intrinsic and an extrinsic reinforcer?

Schedules. Consequences can be applied according to many different schedules, and the relationship of these schedules to a response has been investigated (Ferster & Skinner, 1957). Research has been concerned with two general types of schedules: **continuous schedules** in which a consequence follows the response every time it occurs and **intermittent schedules** in which a consequence follows the response only some of the time. Learning is more rapid with continuous than with intermittent schedules. Continuous schedules produce a steady rate of performance as long as the consequence continues; however, the reinforcer may cease to be effec-

In general, how do continuous and intermittent schedules of reinforcement affect behavior differently?

tive rather rapidly from overuse. A continuous schedule leads to more rapid extinction of the response or to weakening of the behavior when the consequence is suddenly withheld. A reinforcer is less likely to become ineffective with intermittent reinforcement. Also, intermittent reinforcement is capable of producing a high frequency of the response that is resistant to extinction. Fishing or gambling are activities that are subject to intermittent reinforcement.

Intermittent schedules may be of many different types. Two general types are **interval schedules** based on a period of time and **ratio schedules** based on number of responses. On an interval schedule a person who repairs television sets might receive reinforcement in the form of praise from the supervisor only after a 3-hour time lapse since the last reinforcement. On a ratio schedule, the person might receive praise following each fifth television set repaired.

What are four classifications of intermittent schedules of reinforcement?

Schedules may be further classified as to whether they are fixed or variable. The preceding examples of praise given the person repairing television sets represent a **fixed interval schedule** (a fixed or set amount of time passage for reinforcement to occur) and a **fixed ratio schedule** (a fixed number of responses that must occur before the reinforcement comes). If the praise is given at variable or random time intervals such as after 1 hour, again after 4 hours, after 8 hours, and after $\frac{1}{2}$ hour, then a **variable interval schedule** is in effect. If the praise is given when a variable or random number of responses is emitted such as when four television sets are repaired, when one is repaired, and when ten are repaired, a **variable ratio schedule** is in effect. If an employee receives a paycheck at the end of each month, a fixed interval schedule of reinforcement is in effect. If an employee is paid $30 on the completion of each 20 pages typed, a fixed ratio schedule is in operation. A commission salesperson probably receives reinforcement on a variable ratio basis—a sale may be made to the fifth person attempted, to the next one, to the tenth one, or to the twentieth one. The slot machines in gambling houses are set up on a variable ratio schedule of reinforcement. Food-dispensing machines are set up on a continuous schedule of reinforcement. A variable interval schedule occurs commonly in the irregular dispensing of promotions to higher level positions within many companies.

How do the classifications of intermittent schedules affect behavior differently?

Different types of intermittent schedules have different effects on the response. Ratio schedules tend to produce a higher rate of response than interval schedules because in a ratio schedule one

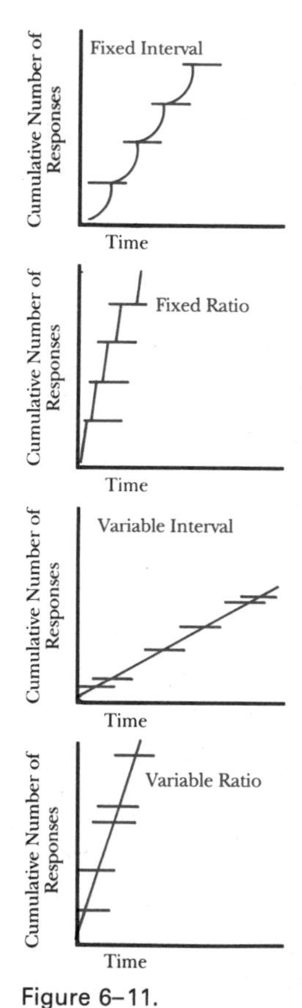

Figure 6–11.
Different schedules of reinforcement affect the rate of responding differently. The steeper the line, the faster the responding is. The dashes across the line indicate when reinforcement is given.

gets the reinforcer faster by making more responses. Ratio schedules also tend to produce steady responding. In a psychology course, if a student is to receive reinforcement in the form of test results every 4 weeks on a fixed interval schedule, the response of studying will probably slow down immediately following the test and increase immediately preceding the next test. Fixed schedules tend to produce an uneven response pattern with a pause immediately following reinforcement (see Figure 6–11). Behaviors being reinforced on a variable ratio schedule are the most difficult of all to extinguish.

A fascinating relationship between a response and reinforcement called **superstitious behavior** may occur when the reinforcement is not contingent on the response. B. F. Skinner (1948) demonstrated that if food is delivered regularly to pigeons regardless of what they do, the pigeons will develop particular behaviors. One pigeon might flap its wings frequently. Another might turn its head to one side frequently or peck the wall frequently even though these behaviors would have no effect on obtaining food. This phenomenon was explained as follows. A random response occurred accidentally just before a food award was delivered. The association caused the response to be repeated again and again. The response frequently coincided with the delivery of food and came to be reinforced on a variable ratio schedule. In a like manner, a person may just happen to wear a particular color on the day he or she has to perform a specific task and may do well on the task. The person may then wear that particular color each time the task is to be performed again because of doing well previously while wearing that color. The person may do well again enough times to receive enough intermittent reinforcement (a variable ratio schedule) to maintain the superstition that wearing this color influences the performance of the task. A salesperson may carry a rabbit's foot on a key chain when attempting to make a sale. Enough coincidences of making a sale when carrying the rabbit's foot may maintain the superstition that the rabbit's foot has an effect on whether or not a sale is made.

Side Effects of Punishment. The use of punishers is not as predictable or desirable as the use of reinforcers in modifying behavior. Even though punishment may suppress a response, various undesirable side effects may occur. One example is that the suppressive effects may generalize to related behaviors. An individual who is punished for inappropriate aggression may become generally unassertive, even in situations in which assertive behaviors would be appropriate. The use of punishment creates an aversive situation, and the punished person may learn a response to avoid the aversive situation (negative reinforcement) rather than learn a response to bring positive reinforcement. For example, a person may learn to avoid criticism by not attempting tasks. Sometimes another inappropriate behavior may be increased that is more debilitating to the person than the response being punished if the behavior removes or avoids the punishment (negative reinforcement). Lying may avoid the punishment for stealing, or physically attacking the punisher may remove the punishment being administered; however, an increase in frequency of lying and attacking may result. Punishment produces frustration and emotional responses, which may disrupt the normal functioning of a person and produce unpredictable behaviors. Also, humanitarian, ethical, moral, and legal grounds must be considered in using punishment. Lastly, in using punishment to modify behavior, even though the inappropriate behavior may be suppressed, if no attempt is made to reinforce an acceptable behavior to replace it, little growth will take place. In general, if punishers are used to suppress a behavior, reinforcers should be used in conjunction with them to shape an acceptable alternative behavior. In too many work situations, feedback is in the form of psychological punishment (hurting the psyche—"here's what you are doing wrong") rather than in the form of psychological reinforcement (building up the psyche—"here's what you are doing right") or a combination of the two.

OTHER FORMS OF LEARNING

Can operant and classical conditioning explain all learning?

Learning occurs in ways other than by classical and operant conditioning. Learning may occur by observing the behavior of others or by insight, two forms of learning discussed in this section. These ways of learning save time and effort. Behaviors that are observed to be reinforced when others perform them can be imitated, and behaviors that are observed to have negative consequences for others can be avoided.

Observational Learning

A larger, more general approach to learning that expands on operant conditioning is the topic addressed in this section. Oftentimes this type of learning is referred to as observational learning or social learning (Bandura, 1977).

Figure 6–12.
Some behaviors are learned by observing a model and imitating the observed behavior.

The Theory. Observational (social) learning is a type of learning described by Albert Bandura (1965) that focuses on modeling whereby a person learns to do something by watching someone else do it (see Figure 6–12). Social learning theory explains how people have the ability to acquire large, integrated patterns of behavior without having to form them gradually through shaping by tedious trial and error reinforcement. And modeling can be more than just learning a specific behavior; it can be learning to govern behavior by the same rules models have been observed to follow. The model may be another person making a response, a picture of a person making a response, or a cartoon character making a response. The model may be imagined with the image being supplied by reading, by hearing verbal descriptions, or by creative imagination.

Determinants of Effectiveness. The prerequisites for observational learning are (a) a model; (b) attention to, recognition, and differentiation of what is distinctive in the model's response; and (c) storing of what is distinctive in the model's response in memory.

What determines the extent to which the behavior of a model will be imitated or the extent to which identification will occur?

The effectiveness of modeling in learning depends on whether the modeling is reinforced, because the principles of operant conditioning apply to learning from a model. Therefore, the consequence following modeling is central to whether the modeling will increase or decrease. If followed by punishment, the modeling will decrease. If the modeling is not reinforced, extinction will take place. If the modeling is reinforced, the imitation will increase. Also, schedules of reinforcement affect modeling by determining the amount of time necessary for acquisition, maintenance, and extinction of the behavior. The greater (a) the similarity between the learner and the model, (b) the need for the reinforcement anticipated, (c) the expertise of the model, (d) the number of models observed, and (e) the more prestigious the model and the more the model's behavior is seen as being reinforced, the greater the likelihood that the behavior of the model will be imitated.

In learning theory terminology, is there any difference between imitation and identification?

Forms. Many personality traits are a product of observational or social learning. Sometimes the modeling is conscious, and sometimes it is unconscious. **Imitation** is the conscious mimicking of a model's behavior. **Identification** is the unconscious mimicking of a model's behavior. Often an individual is not consciously aware of modeling such as in sex-role identification. The attitudes and dispositions of parents, friends, teachers, or others may be unconsciously modeled. In identification, when words and actions of parents are contradictory, most children model the actions of their parents rather than behave as they are told. The same could possibly be said concerning adults and models such as when a worker identifies with the supervisor or fellow workers. What happens to models as a result of their outbursts of emotion, expressions of affection, openness, or secrecy with others may be being unconsciously mimicked by others.

Insight Learning

Some human behavior is difficult to account for without introducing the cognitive or thought processes. Contemporary cognitive psychologists believe that the development of learning capacities consists of stages and that each stage requires previous learning.

Can learning occur through thought?

Description. Learning abilities seem to build on a hierarchy of past learning and learning sets. **Learning sets** are specific approaches that have been learned that may be used in solving new but similar problems. Learning sets are formed when a person encounters problems or tasks based on the same principle. A correct solution or learning of a task provides reinforcement for the manner in which the problem was solved or the task was learned. When new problems or tasks with a common principle underlying their solutions or learning arise, the person already has a "set" or a "learned way" to solve the problem or to learn the task.

What are learning sets?

Insight. A sudden awareness of how a problem can be solved without any trial and error preceding it or awareness or knowledge of a fact from inference without any direct input preceding it describes insight. **Insight learning** is learning that occurs in the thought processes and includes both learning sets and insight. To illustrate insight learning, arrive at the solution to the problem in Figure 6–13 using cognitive processes. The solution may be found at the end of this chapter on page 225. If you solved the problem on your own, it probably suddenly struck you that you could go beyond the boundaries of the square. If so, that realization was an insight. Without it, you might never have solved the problem. Insight occurs when the solution to a problem suddenly becomes completely clear. Insights that are less dramatic seem to occur frequently in ordinary thought processes that affect or give direction to a person's behavior. At this stage of learning, the complexity of the processes has reached a point where learning can be discussed more easily under the heading of *thinking* (see chapter 7). Insight does seem to be another kind of learning that occurs without obvious reinforcement and can occur in a single trial or without any trials at all.

Figure 6–13.
Connect all the dots with only four straight lines without lifting your pen or pencil from the paper or going through any dot more than once.

APPLICATION OF LEARNING PRINCIPLES

The principles of learning are now being applied in management situations of all kinds, in teaching, in self-control, and in the medical field. The systematic use of learning principles, or learning technology, to shape behavior in order to accomplish desired goals is becoming more and more common. In this section, the focus is on the application of principles of learning, known as behavior modification and biofeedback.

Behavior Modification

What is behavior modification?

Behavior modification is the application of learning theory to modify or change people's behavior, whether individually or as a group. Although behavior modification was originally associated with B. F. Skinner and operant conditioning, it does not involve any one set of learning principles. Today, behavior modification may involve the use of a variety of learning principles—classical conditioning, observational or social learning, and the thought processes as well as operant conditioning—with emphasis on goal setting to achieve target behaviors and on the measurement of behavior change.

What are the steps in a behavior modification program?

Steps. Generally, programs of behavior modification using positive reinforcement follow a series of steps as follows:

1. *Identify a specific target behavior.* Work with a single behavior and define the behavior in such a way that everyone involved is referring to the same behavior. For example, job behavior may be defined as number of units produced.
2. *Devise a way to measure the behavior, and identify how much of the target behavior currently exists.* For example, job behavior as defined above might be measured in terms of average number of units produced per hour, and the average number currently being produced per hour may be four.
3. *Determine and state the desired target behavior in terms of goals or objectives.* This is often done in organizations with employee participation. Think of the desired target behavior as composed of several interrelated units. For example, the goal of increasing production to 100 units might be broken down into subunits of increasing from the current response of 75 units per week to 80 units the 1st week, to 85 units the 2nd week, to 90 units the 3rd week, to 95 units the 4th week, and to 100 units the 5th week. This would be an application of the learning principle called shaping.

4. *Design and apply positive reinforcement.* (See Figure 6-14.) Be sure to reinforce the behavior immediately after it occurs, not to demand too much effort for too little reward, to reinforce each successive approximation to the target behavior when first beginning, and to shift to an intermittent schedule once the target behavior is acquired in order to maintain it.
5. *Monitor and record on a continuous basis the behavior that is to be modified.* Measurement of the behavior after beginning a program of reinforcement is essential if the effectiveness of the program is to be evaluated.
6. *Change the program.* Target behaviors, reinforcers, and schedules should be changed as necessary based on whether or not the plan is working.

Figure 6–14.
Positive reinforcement in the form of feedback, praise, or recognition has been found to be effective in changing work-related behaviors in industrial/organizational settings.

These general steps apply to any behavior modification program whether it is intended to modify individual behavior or group behavior in industrial/organizational settings (see the box on page 216), homes, prisons, schools, or mental institutions; or whether one individual is managing the contingencies to alter the behavior of someone else or to control his or her own behavior. Individuals sometimes perform better when they plan and choose the behaviors to perform and the reinforcement to receive rather than having these behaviors and reinforcements imposed on them. In the final analysis, external control is really just a means to achieve self-control. Some behaviors can be modified only by self-control because they are not always accessible to others. These behaviors might include such private events as thoughts, fantasies, or images.

What are some techniques used in behavior modification programs along with reinforcement?

Techniques. Several different techniques may be used in behavior modification. Physical restraint is the technique whereby the individual places physical restrictions in order to achieve a particular end, such as not having any sweets in the house to avoid eating sweets.

Stimulus control is a technique in which the environment is designed so that certain cues (descriminative stimuli) increase the likelihood that specific behaviors are performed. Selecting a place to relax where there are few cues associated with work or selecting a place to study, such as a particular room or a particular desk that is used only for studying, are examples of stimulus control.

In the alternate response technique, a person engages in responses that interfere with or replace the response to be controlled or eliminated. For example, learning to relax controls tension because relaxation and tension are incompatible, chewing gum controls eating or smoking, or increasing smiling decreases frowning because these behaviors cannot occur simultaneously.

Other techniques include self-monitoring and recording, self-instruction, and observation. Self-monitoring and recording works on the premise that becoming aware of the behavior sometimes controls that behavior. Most people are not aware of the extent to which they engage in some behaviors. Self-instruction, a technique that encourages individuals to make specific comments or suggestions and direct language toward themselves, has often been used to develop self-control. Observation of others who have achieved the goal and modeling what they do may be used in self-control. Remember that once a goal is set, shaping may be used to start moving toward it. Sometimes in self-control an individual may need to engage another person to administer the reinforcers if cheating cannot be resisted (see Figure 6–15). Those who succeed in self-control seem to try longer and tend to use more techniques than those who fail; therefore, one should try several techniques (Watson, 1978).

Figure 6–15.
The main problem with a person administering his or her own reinforcement is cheating.

Uses. The use of behavior modification in psychotherapy is addressed in chapter 12, and its use in self-control is addressed in the immediately preceding topics—steps and techniques. Behavior modification is also used in training and instructional programs.

How can learning principles be applied to training programs?

Training programs consist of organized experiences used to develop or modify knowledge, skills, and attitudes of people in the organization; therefore, learning principles may be applied to the variety of training programs that are conducted in industrial/organizational settings. Training programs have goals. The main question in a training program is whether the employee's goals are the same as the planner's goals. For example, if the planner has the goal of producing the maximum units of a given quality in a given time and the trainee has the goal of producing just enough units to keep from losing the job, the training program may not be as effective as it could be if the planner and trainee were working toward the same goal. An employee's personal goals will affect learning in an orientation training situation. If personal goals are long-range, the individual will be likely to learn all that is possible. If personal goals are short-term or immediate, the individual will be likely to learn only enough to stay on the payroll.

A training program should recognize which reinforcers are operative and most effective in a particular situation. The satisfaction of a basic physical need is seldom an important reinforcer. Social reinforcers such as approval or recognition from others for a job well-done seem to be more important. Also, a personal feeling of accomplishment, self-satisfaction, information about progress and achievement, or monetary reward may be effective. Too often money is used as a reinforcer when other, less tangible reinforcers are more important.

Why is participation important in training programs?

The principle that an individual learns best through participation is important in training programs. Participation allows for immediate feedback and immediate reinforcement of the response. Some techniques used to obtain active participation in supervisory or managerial programs are discussion meetings, role playing, and games such as management games, which provide simulated situations.

Active participation is achieved in some training and instructional programs by employing a technique called programmed instruction, which B. F. Skinner was instrumental in developing.

What is programmed instruction?

Programmed instruction presents the learner with a small segment of information and then calls for a response to make sure the material is learned before a new segment is presented. As soon as the response to the question (which may be multiple-choice, fill-in-the-blank, true-false, or something similar) is made, the learner checks the correctness of the answer immediately with the correct answer, which is usually printed in a second column or on the next page for immediate feedback—reinforcement. In addition to being in textbook form, such programmed instruction may be designed for teaching machines and computers—computer-assisted instruction (CAI)—that automatically provide feedback before presenting the next segment of information. Programmed instruction is based on the principle of shaping because the learning of each segment of information in the sequence moves the learner closer and closer to the final objective of the course of study.

What are some ways in which achievement of goals in training programs may be measured?

Achievement in training and instructional programs should always be measured. This measurement may take different forms. Often, because the objective of training programs is increased productivity, important measurements are statistics concerning output such as the number of items produced per hour or day, the percentage of workers meeting an established standard, or the amount of time required to complete a job. More indirect measures may relate to the number of rejects or the decrease in costs and breakage. Even more indirect measures may be changes in absenteeism or employee turnover. If the goal is gaining information, as in some orientation training programs, measures used may be similar to those used in school classrooms. The most difficult training programs to evaluate are those in the area of human relations skills such as supervisory and managerial training programs.

BEHAVIOR MODIFICATION IN INDUSTRY

Edward J. Feeney was a pioneer in the application of behavior modification principles to the business environment (Hilts, 1974). At age 22, he took a job with Emery Air Freight Corporation. After taking a course in behavior modification, Feeney began to apply behavior modification principles at Emery. Probably his dock-loading project is best known. A performance audit showed that packages headed for the same destination were not being sent with maximum efficiency. Forty-five percent of the time these packages were sent separately to the same destination rather than more efficiently sent together in one large container. The employees and supervisors on the dock, however, thought their performance was good. Training was not the answer, Feeney decided, because the employees knew how and when to use the containers. It was a matter of behavior modification. Feeney devised a plan whereby reinforcement was given in the form of checklists that allowed the employees to keep track of their own performance and thus receive immediate feedback. Reinforcement was also given in the form of graphs of group performance placed on bulletin boards and through praise and recognition by supervisors for performance improvement. Container use jumped from 45 to 95 percent in offices all over the country and has been maintained for several years by continued use of feedback and reinforcement. Savings from this program alone for one year were $650,000.

Figure 6–16.
Biofeedback is used for training a person to regulate internal processes.

Biofeedback

Biofeedback is a method of training people to regulate internal physiological states such as heart rate, blood pressure, brain wave pattern, glandular and muscular activity, and temperature. This method uses an electronic recording device that provides immediate feedback, usually in visual or auditory form, on one or more physiological acts such as breathing differently, thinking particular thoughts, or concentrating or relaxing at different levels (see Figure 6–16). Normally, these behaviors and the physiological consequences of these behaviors are nonconscious. Biofeedback brings the response and the consequence into consciousness, allowing for learning (operant conditioning) principles to operate.

Is learning theory used in the medical field in the treatment and prevention of illness?

Behavioral Medicine. Because this method of changing biological functioning does not include drugs, it is free of the side effects that some patients experience from some medications. Some physicians are now using this technique to treat some medical problems. Early experiments with rats and later experiments with humans demonstrate that biofeedback can be effective in regulating such human physiological problems as pain, headaches, drug abuse, asthma, blood pressure, and epilepsy (King & Montgomery, 1980; Miller & DiCara, 1967; Miller & Brucker, 1979; Qualls & Sheehan, 1981). In biofeedback, instead of doctors doing things to patients such as administering drugs, patients learn to do things to help themselves.

Biofeedback holds promise, and its use is expanding in an area of psychology in the field of medicine called **behavioral medicine**—the application of learning theory to the treatment and prevention of illness. The initial expectations for biofeedback, however, seem to have been overestimated (Miller, 1985). This application of operant conditioning is not a cure for all of a person's physical problems, and people are not able to gain mastery over the function of the involuntary muscles that control the visceral organs in the same specific way that they learn to control the voluntary muscles that operate the skeletal parts of the body such as the fingers or legs. The learning seems to occur without the individual knowing how he or she does it. Oftentimes the learning is accomplished through a shaping technique, and biofeedback is most frequently used in combination with other treatments.

How is biofeedback useful in psychotherapy?

Psychotherapy. More and more psychotherapists are using biofeedback in therapy with clients. Because immediate visual or auditory feedback is given electronically concerning the internal reactions to feelings, thoughts, and other stimuli, biofeedback is useful in psychotherapy in several ways. The therapist can see emotional arousal in response to particular stimuli in a more objective way than having to depend on the client's statement of whether he or she experiences emotional arousal or on body language. When a client's feelings are repressed and unconscious, the client is more likely to accept from the machine that he or she is emotionally aroused by some particular stimulus than from the therapist. The use of biofeedback seems to shorten the time required in therapy. Biofeedback is very useful in teaching a client how to relax to reduce stress and tension. The use of biofeedback often builds up self-confidence in a client. The therapist can vividly show the client that he or she can control the bodily reactions to stress, anxiety, and various other feelings. In psychotherapy, as in behavioral medicine, biofeedback is used most frequently in combination with other therapeutic techniques.

SUMMARY

1. Learning is an abstraction that is inferred by a relatively permanent change in behavior that occurs as a result of an experience. Behaviors resulting from reflexes, maturation, illness, fatigue, intoxication, or drugs are not learned.
2. Classical conditioning, discovered by Pavlov in laboratory experiments with dogs, concerns the association of stimuli whereby a new stimulus comes to elicit a response by being associated with an old stimulus that elicits the same response.
3. Emotional responses such as feelings of fear, anger, and love that account for likes, dislikes, and attitudes may be learned according to principles of classical conditioning.
4. Operant conditioning, demonstrated by B. F. Skinner, concerns the association of a response with the consequence that follows it. Conse-

quences may be reinforcing—either positive or negative reinforcement—and increase frequency of a response, or they may be punishing—either punishment, time-out, or response-cost—and decrease frequency of a response.

5. Extinction, spontaneous recovery, stimulus generalization, stimulus discrimination, response generalization, and response discrimination are basic principles of classical and operant conditioning.
6. Most behaviors do not appear suddenly full-blown but are shaped in small steps by reinforcing different behaviors that are closer and closer approximations of the target behavior (goal).
7. The effectiveness of reinforcement is related to contingency, immediacy, size, and deprivation. Correlated reinforcement is especially effective because the size of the reinforcement varies in proportion to the size of the response.
8. Primary reinforcers are those that satisfy a biological need; secondary reinforcers are conditioned ones that satisfy a learned need. Intrinsic reinforcers are those that elicit internal feelings of satisfaction; extrinsic reinforcers are those tangible things that satisfy a need.
9. Reinforcement may have different effects depending on whether it is continuous, occurring each time the response is made, or is intermittent, occurring only part of the time. Reinforcement schedules are classified as fixed ratio, fixed interval, variable ratio, or variable interval.
10. A continuous reinforcement schedule results in more rapid learning and faster extinction than occurs with an intermittent schedule. Ratio schedules tend to produce a steady and high rate of responding, whereas fixed schedules tend to produce an uneven response pattern with pauses immediately following reinforcement. Behaviors being reinforced on a variable ratio schedule are the most difficult of all to extinguish.
11. Reinforcement rather than punishment is better to use for behavior control whenever possible because results are more predictable, undesirable side effects are less likely, an acceptable behavior is learned, and reinforcement is more humane.
12. Learning may occur from observation of a model. Whether imitation and/or identification occurs depends on the perceived consequences, schedules of reinforcement, similarity between the learner and the model, the need for the reinforcement anticipated, the expertise and prestige or status of the model, and the number of models observed.
13. Insight learning occurs in the thought processes and includes learning sets and insight.
14. Behavior modification is the application of learning theory to modify an individual's (including the self) or a group's behavior. Behavior modification involves identifying the behavior to be modified, devis-

ing a way to measure it, setting goals, applying reinforcement, monitoring and recording progress, and changing the program as needed.
15. Techniques used in behavior modification include physical restraint, stimulus control, alternate response, self-monitoring and recording, and observation of others.
16. Learning principles may be applied to training programs through goal setting, reinforcement, active participation, programmed instruction, and evaluation of achievement of goals.
17. Use of biofeedback as reinforcement has been demonstrated to be a promising form of operant conditioning in behavioral medicine and psychotherapy in teaching a person to regulate internal physiological states such as heart rate, blood pressure, brain wave pattern, glandular and muscular activity, and temperature.

KEY TERMS AND CONCEPTS

Reflex
Classical conditioning
Neutral stimulus
Unconditioned stimulus
Unconditioned response
Conditioned stimulus
Conditioned response
Extinction
Spontaneous recovery
Stimulus generalization
Stimulus discrimination
Discriminative stimulus
Operants
Operant conditioning
Positive reinforcement
Negative reinforcement
Punishment
Time-out/response-cost
Response generalization
Response discrimination
Shaping
Correlated reinforcement
Primary reinforcers
Secondary reinforcers
Generalized conditioned reinforcers
Premack principle
Intrinsic reinforcers
Extrinsic reinforcers
Continuous schedules
Intermittent schedules
Interval schedules
Ratio schedules
Fixed interval schedule
Fixed ratio schedule
Variable interval schedules
Variable ratio schedules
Superstitious behavior
Observational (social) learning
Imitation
Identification
Learning sets
Insight learning
Behavior modification
Programmed instruction
Biofeedback
Behavioral medicine

QUESTIONS FOR REVIEW

1. How did Pavlov demonstrate in the laboratory and Watson demonstrate with a human the various principles of classical conditioning?

2. Define and give an example to illustrate each of the basic principles of classical conditioning.
3. Who developed the theory of operant conditioning, and what is a discriminative stimulus, an operant, and a Skinner box?
4. What are the basic principles of operant conditioning? Give an example of each.
5. What are the types of possible consequences and schedules of consequences of operant conditioning, and how does each affect the response?
6. Define the various types of reinforcers, give the factors that determine the effectiveness of reinforement, and explain why punishment is generally not as effective as reinforcement.
7. Who focused on observational learning—modeling? Differentiate between imitation and identification, and cite the determinants of effectiveness in social learning.
8. What is meant by learning sets, insight, and insight learning?
9. What are the steps, some techniques, and some applications of behavior modification?
10. What is biofeedback, and how is it being used?

TEST YOURSELF

1. Classical conditioning is a form of learning in which (a) a new event is associated with an event that brings forth a specific behavior, and the new event comes to signal that event and brings forth the same behavior (b) a model is observed and imitated (c) the consequence of a response is associated with the response (d) reasoning and thinking produce the learning.
2. Ivan Pavlov, a Russian physiologist, used dogs in the laboratory studies he conducted in formulating the principles of ________________ conditioning.
3. If the supervisor's angry yelling frightens you, the supervisor's face becomes flushed and red just prior to the yelling, and in the future any flushed and red face frightens you, ________________ conditioning and ________________ generalization has occurred.
4. With reference to the situation described in item 3 above, if the supervisor changes jobs and you no longer hear angry yelling immediately following seeing a flushed, red face and a flushed, red face no longer frightens you, ________________ has occurred.
5. If after you have learned to respond to a buzzer by going to take dictation from X, another buzzer is installed to signal you to take dictation from Y and you learn to respond to the slightly different sound by going into Y's office instead of X's office, ________________ has occurred.

6. Which of the following is most closely associated with the formulation of the principles of operant conditioning? (a) Ivan Pavlov (b) Albert Bandura (c) B. F. Skinner (d) John B. Watson
7. A response made by an individual may operate on the environment and produce a reinforcing consequence that increases the frequency of the response. T or F
8. A consequence that increases a response by removing, providing escape from, or preventing the occurrence of an aversive stimulus is known as ________________.
9. Punishment refers to negative reinforcement. T or F
10. Because most of an individual's behaviors do not occur spontaneously, reinforcing different behaviors that are closer and closer approximations of the desired behavior until the desired behavior occurs may be used. This process is called ________________.
11. According to Miller, how effective a reinforcing consequence will be depends on (a) immediacy of the reinforcment (b) size or quantity of reinforcement (c) how deprived the person is of the reinforcement (d) all of the above.
12. Reinforcers that satisfy a biological need and may lose their effectiveness due to overuse but may regain their effectiveness after a period of deprivation are referred to as (a) secondary reinforcers (b) conditioned reinforcers (c) generalized reinforcers (d) primary reinforcers.
13. Making smoking a cigarette for a chain smoker who seldom says something complimentary to someone contingent on saying something complimentary to someone is an example of the ________________ principle to increase a behavior.
14. An internal feeling of satisfaction such as a feeling of competence, achievement, or self-actualization that a person gets as a consequence of a response is a(n) ________________ reinforcer.
15. A continuous schedule of reinforcement results in (a) more rapid extinction than an intermittent schedule (b) more rapid learning than an intermittent schedule (c) more rapid loss of the reinforcer's effectiveness than an intermittent schedule (d) all of the above.
16. Ratio schedules tend to produce a higher rate of response than interval schedules. T or F
17. The use of punishment is as predictable as the use of reinforcement and is as acceptable as reinforcement in modifying behavior. T or F
18. Observational learning is associated with Albert ________________, focuses on ________________, and may consist of either imitation, which is conscious learning, or ________________, which is unconscious learning.
19. Today behavior modification involves the use of (a) classical conditioning principles (b) operant conditioning principles (c) observational learning principles (d) all of the above.
20. An operant conditioning technique used to train people to control in-

ternal physiological states such as heart rate, blood pressure, brain wave pattern, glandular and muscular activity, and temperature is known as (a) stimulus control (b) physical restraint (c) biofeedback (d) punishment.

APPLICATIONS

A. Lois Anthony, who works in the shipping department of Zonic, Inc., received a ring from her husband for a birthday gift. About a month later, her husband received in the mail from an elderly relative a ring very similar to the one he had selected and given Lois. It was disclosed that the ring had belonged to his deceased grandmother, and the elderly relative remembered that when he was a young child he was very fascinated with the ring. Because of this, she had decided to send the ring to him as she was dispensing with some of her belongings.

1. Do you think an experience in the environment influenced Lois' husband's choice of a ring? If so, what type of learning is this?
2. What basic learning principle is illustrated?
3. What is the conditioned or learned response, and what is the conditioned or learned stimulus?

B. A manager at T & W Corporation is concerned about the large number of employees arriving late to work—about 50 percent of the staff on any given day. The manager wants to reduce this to at least 3 percent and decides to use behavior modification to change this behavior.

1. For best results, would you recommend that the manager use a punishing consequence for being late or a reinforcing consequence for being on time? Why?
2. What techniques will probably be used if the manager decides to reinforce being on time?
3. If the manager decides to use reinforcement, what can be done to get maximum effectiveness from the reinforcement?
4. Once the goal of tardiness being reduced to 3 percent occurs, what type of schedule would be best to employ in giving reinforcement to avoid either extinction of the behavior of coming on time or eventual ineffectiveness of the reinforcement?

SUGGESTIONS FOR FURTHER READING

American Psychological Association. (1982). *Ethical principles in the conduct of research with human participants.* Washington, DC: Author.

A 64-page guide that outlines the responsibilities and provides a thorough discussion of the principles essential for a psychologist's ethical conduct during the course of research with human participants.

Grasha, A. F. (1978). *Practical applications of psychology.* Cambridge, MA: Winthrop Publishers.

A book that stresses applications and provides many exercises to illustrate particular concepts and to personally involve the reader with the information.

Hilts, P. J. (1974). *Behavior modification.* New York: Harper's Magazine Press.

An interesting and easy-to-read book about behavior modifiers—what they do, how they do it, and what it means.

Kazdin, A. E. (1975). *Behavior modification in applied settings.* Homewood, IL: Dorsey Press.

An introduction to behavior modification techniques in applied settings. The major focus is on the application of operant principles, the implementation of behavior modification techniques, and the measurement and evaluation of program effectiveness. The book contains one chapter on self-control.

Lang, P. J. (1970, October). Autonomic control, or learning to play the internal organs. *Psychology Today,* pp. 37-41, 86.

Discusses the use of operant conditioning techniques to control behaviors of the autonomic nervous system such as heart rate and blood pressure and discusses some intriguing possibilities for the future.

Miller, L. K. (1980). *Principles of everyday behavior analysis* (2nd ed.). Monterey, CA: Brooks/Cole.

An excellent book designed to teach the principles of behavior modification to the beginning student. It is simply written and easy to understand, and it uses many everyday examples of behavioral principles. A concept-programmed instruction approach is used to teach the application of conditioning principles.

Miller, N. E. (1985, February). Rx: Biofeedback. *Psychology Today,* pp. 54-59.

A journal article by a leading researcher and pioneer in the use of biofeedback that gives an excellent review of the current status of biofeedback in preventing unnecessary suffering, correcting disabling conditions, and helping people regain control of their lives.

Solution to the problem illustrating insight learning on page 211.

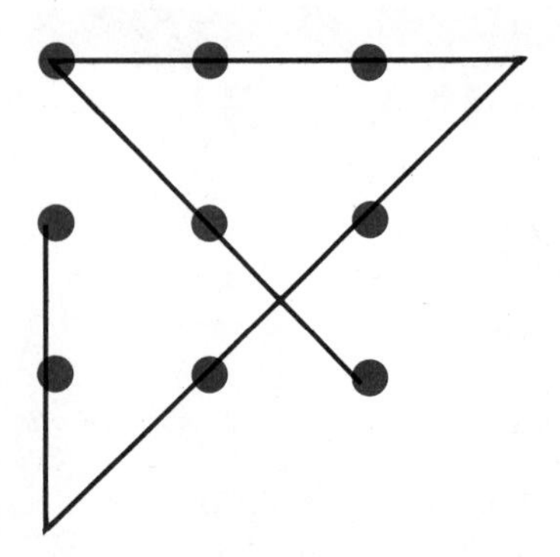

CHAPTER 7

REMEMBERING AND THINKING

Objectives

When you have completed your study of chapter 7, you should be able to:

1. Describe the earliest research on memory, the methods of measurement used, and the contributions made to understanding memory.
2. Discuss the biological explanations of memory.
3. Name, give the characteristics, and give examples of the three major systems of memory storage.
4. Identify, describe, and illustrate the processes involved in storing material in memory.
5. Give several explanations of forgetting.
6. Describe individual personality characteristics that can influence memory.
7. Describe the characteristics of learning materials and learning procedures that affect memory of the material.
8. Name and describe the basic units of thought in the order in which they first appear in thought development.
9. Give the steps and various kinds of thinking involved in problem solving, and identify factors that influence problem solving.
10. Cite factors that affect an individual's thinking in decision making.

The processes of remembering and thinking are essential for human functioning—for working on a job, for positively impressing others, and for communicating with others. Every action that is a result of learning is based on remembering and thinking. Without memory processes and past experience available to consciousness, people would have to begin life anew each moment. Remembering is bringing into consciousness, thinking of or recalling, any experiences with people, places, events, objects, or information. **Memory** is the process of preserving information for later use. It is the persistence of learning over time, for either a few moments or for years. The major approaches to explaining memory—biological, structural, and process—are discussed in this chapter.

Thinking involves manipulation of the world symbolically through mental images, categories, words and signs, and the generation of ideas. These building blocks of thought are also topics of discussion in this chapter. The section on thinking relates to the thinking function in terms of problem solving and decision making.

MEMORY

Who did the first systematic memory experiments?

Herman Ebbinghaus (1885), who was the first person to study memory using systematic experiments, discovered much about memory and contributed to later studies of memory through the experimental techniques he devised (see Figure 7–1). More recent research on human memory has revealed the complexities of the memory process and provided explanations of the memory system. Currently, memory is most often viewed cognitively in a structural and an information-processing framework. The biological approach to the study of memory, however, has contributed to the understanding of memory through explanations of the biological basis of memory.

Figure 7–1.
Herman Ebbinghaus.

Early Studies by Ebbinghaus

The study of memory began when Ebbinghaus conducted a long series of experiments on himself. He learned lists of nonsense syllables. A **nonsense syllable** is a vowel between two consonants that together do not form a meaningful word, such as BAX, JUP, HEB, or LOM. Ebbinghaus used these syllables to avoid any effects on memory related to meaning and to avoid any of the recall being related to something previously learned.

What did Ebbinghaus find out about memory?

Findings. Ebbinghaus found that in recalling a list, those items at the beginning and at the end of the list are recalled more readily than those items in the middle. In addition, Ebbinghaus found that the length of time between initial learning and recall affects the amount of the information remembered. This famous curve of forgetting, shown in Figure 7–2, indicates that much of what a person learns is quickly forgotten. Ebbinghaus found from his experiments that the more time an individual spends on the learning task, the greater the amount remembered. Also, he found that the percentage of recall varies according to the method of measurement. Although Ebbinghaus learned much about memory, perhaps his major contribution was simply to focus the attention of psychologists on the important and fascinating topic of memory.

How can memory be measured?

Methods of Measurement. Ebbinghaus tried measuring memory by several methods that are still used today. In the **free recall** method of measuring memory, individuals are asked to learn and then recall at a later time a list of nonsense syllables

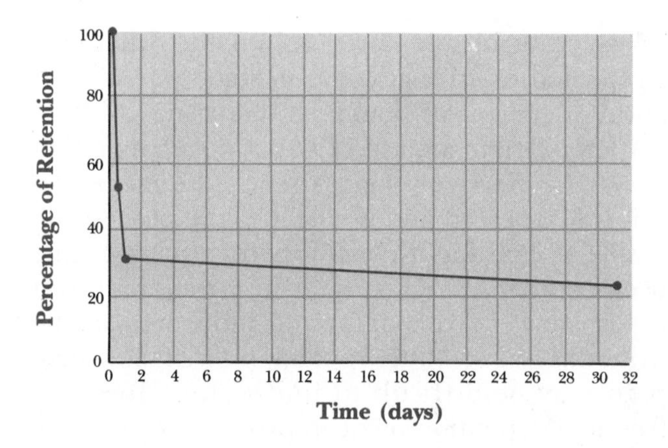

Figure 7–2.
Retention as a function of time (data from Ebbinghaus, 1885). After 20 minutes, 53 percent was remembered; 34 percent after one day; and 21 percent after 31 days.

in any order. In the **serial recall** method of measuring memory, individuals are asked to learn and then recall at a later time a list of nonsense syllables *in the order learned.* The **recognition method** of measuring memory is a method by which individuals are asked to recognize learned material using measurement tools such as multiple choice tests. When the learned nonsense syllables were presented in a longer list of nonsense syllables, Ebbinghaus found that a greater percentage of the learned ones could be remembered through the recognition method than by using the method of free recall; in addition, he found that more could be remembered by using the free recall method than by using serial recall. Finally, Ebbinghaus devised the relearning method for measuring the total amount of retention. In the **relearning method** of measuring memory, the percentage of savings in terms of time or number of trials necessary to recall previously learned material represents the percentage of retention. Ebbinghaus read a list of nonsense syllables until he could recall it perfectly, keeping a record of the amount of time or number of trials needed to do that. Then after a period of time, hours or days, he relearned the list by reading it until he could recall it perfectly. Again he kept a record of the amount of time or number of trials needed to achieve perfect recall. The percentage of savings in terms of time or number of trials required to relearn versus the time or number of trials required in the original learning represented the percentage of retention or the percentage remembered.

Biological Processes

Psychologists have studied memory from a biological approach. Some researchers believe that as information is passed through the brain, a trace or mark is left, probably electrical in nature, that perishes quickly unless repeated or strengthened in some way to lead to a long-term chemical or structural change in the brain.

Memory Trace. A long-term chemical or structural change that occurs in the brain may be relatively permanent. The more frequently the information is repeated and the deeper the processing, the more distinguishable and lasting the memory trace will be. The memory trace has been compared to a path taken through a forest (Morris, 1979). The path may be very faint and indistinguishable after only one or two walks over it (little repetition or shallow processing), and the path may be difficult to find again. However, after many walks (frequent repetition or deep processing) over the path, it may be easy to find again. Some theorists propose that the structural changes that take place in the brain that allow a person to remember something occur at connections between brain cells.

What is a reverberating circuit?

According to Hebb (1949), sensory information coming into the brain travels from one cell to the next until it makes a full round or circuit. When activated by a cue, the circuit will be repeated (memory). A relatively permanent structural change in the brain formed as sensory information travels in the form of a neural impulse from one cell to the next until a full round or circuit is made is called a **reverberating circuit.** A person may have billions of such memory routes or circuits in the brain.

What is an engram?

The physical representation of memory in the brain is often called an **engram,** a general term for a persistent structural change caused by stimulation of living neural tissue. A person's brain is assumed to be packed with billions of engrams that are stored in all different parts of the brain. For example, some experiments indicate that one form of memory, the location of objects, is localized in the hippocampus region of the brain (Olton, 1977). Other experiments have led some researchers to conclude that the site of classical conditioned learning is probably in the cerebellum. When there is a delay between the unconditioned or conditioned stimulus and the neutral stimulus, the hippocampus is also involved (McCormick & Thompson, 1984).

The Structural Change. The structural change that occurs to make memories permanent seems to occur at the synapse. In response to experience, new neural interconnections are either formed, preserved, or eliminated. If there is a lack of the neurotransmitters (chemical messengers) that are required for forming the interconnections, as when blocked by certain drugs or loss of brain tissue that secretes the neurotransmitters, memory storage is disrupted (Davis & Squire, 1984). Thus, neuronal theories view the process of memory as a change in the electrical activity of neurons or in the pattern of synaptic linkages between them.

Some researchers suggest that memory resides in **ribonucleic acid (RNA) molecules**, which control the production of protein similar to the way genetic information is encoded in deoxyribonucleic acid (DNA) molecules (McConnell, 1974). Activity in a nerve cell results in the production of several chemicals, including RNA (Hyden, 1969). Molecular theorists suggest that memory traces are changes in large RNA molecules that are in the nuclei of neurons. Studies on planaria (flatworms) and rats have also shown that when RNA from an animal that has learned to respond in a particular way is transfered to a second animal, the second animal will learn to respond in that way more rapidly than an animal injected with RNA from an animal that has not learned to respond in that particular way (McConnell, 1974). Currently, RNA as a memory vehicle is highly controversial and without validity because the findings could not always be duplicated. The most prevalent view, because interest in neurotransmitters has accelerated, is that the change occurs at the synapse where neurons communicate with one another (Lynch & Baudry, 1984; Meyers, 1986).

What is the molecular view of the memory trace, and why is it highly controversial and without validity today?

Which view of the memory trace is most prevalent?

Cognitive View

The structural approach to explaining memory is part of the cognitive view of memory. Information is portrayed as being stored in the memory system in three types or levels of storage systems (Atkinson & Shiffrin, 1968, 1971). The process approach to explaining memory is also part of the cognitive view. The process approach is concerned with information processing. These two approaches to understanding memory complement each other.

How many types of memory storage does a person have, according to the structural approach to explaining memory?

Structure of Memory. The three memory storage systems or three levels of memory are sensory memory, short-term memory, and long-term memory. New information must pass through the first two levels to get to the third. At the first level, the **sensory memory** level, information flows from the senses into the sensory registers. Information entering these waiting rooms stays for a short time and then is processed further or is lost.

What is sensory memory?

These sensory impressions are held only briefly—generally only a fraction of a second to perhaps a few seconds; but the longer the impression is held, the weaker it gets until it completely vanishes (Klatzky, 1975). Sensory registers have a large storage capacity and take in much more information than a person can process; therefore, only a few of the sensory impressions work their way into conscious awareness. There are too many simultaneous sensory impressions for the brain to be able to process and hold them all in the short-term memory system. Therefore, while the information is held in the sensory registers, attention to it may occur whereby some information is selected for further processing. This information is then passed on to short-term memory in the higher centers of the brain where recognition (perception) and consciousness occur. **Echoic memory,** or auditory memory, is the sensory image or impression of a sound that is held in the sensory register for up to 3 or 4 seconds, making it possible for an individual to rehear information almost like an echo even if attention is elsewhere. In **iconic memory,** a visual image, or icon, is held no more than 1 or 2 seconds. Echoic memory disappears a little more slowly than iconic memory.

Which disappears faster—echoic or iconic memory?

At the second level of the memory system, **short-term memory,** information is in the present consciousness, and the person is presently aware of the information. However, information is usually held there only briefly. Information in short-term memory selected from the sensory registers will disappear or be forgotten in 15 to 20 seconds unless it is repeated over and over or receives some sort of extra attention (Klatzky, 1980; Reed, 1982). For example, when the visual sensory impression of the number *3* is held in short-term memory as an identified number, it is kept in the present consciousness by repetition. The capacity of short-term memory storage is very small—only about seven meaningful units on the average. Short-term memory is an active, working system and is important in thinking. It is where mental operations occur during comprehension, problem solving, and decision making. Partial results and ideas produced in a long mental task are held in short-term memory (Hothersall, 1985). The small capacity of short-term memory places a limit on the number of ideas that can be held in consciousness simultaneously for thinking (Baddeley & Hitch, 1974).

How much information can be stored in short-term memory on the average?

Finally, at the third level, **long-term memory,** information is held in a permanent storage system, but it is not conscious except when brought into short-term memory. Long-term memory has a large capacity because it holds all of a person's knowledge—everything that has been attended to while it was in consciousness for an entire lifespan. Transfer of information to long-term memory storage is accomplished by acting on information while it is held in the short-term memory by using repeating and other forms of processing discussed in the next section (see Figure 7–3).

Figure 7–3.
Repeating the name of a new co-worker several times while it is in short-term memory will help transfer it to long-term memory.

How is semantic memory different from episodic memory?

Endel Tulving (1972) proposed that long-term memory consists of two components. **Semantic memory** is the part of long-term memory that consists of information, facts, and general, non-personal knowledge. It is sometimes said to be like a dictionary or encyclopedia because information is stored semantically in terms of meaning. Semantic memory forms the basis for comprehension, thinking, reasoning, and decision making. Many psychologists believe that semantic memory is stored in a hierarchical network structure (see Figure 7–4). **Episodic memory** is the part of long-term memory that consists of the chronologic record of a person's personal experiences. It is sometimes said to be like the person's diary—an autobiographical record. The requirement for episodic memory is merely to have an experience and form a long-term memory of it. Episodic memory is particularly affected by rehearsal or repetition.

Information Processing. The process approach to explaining memory is concerned with information processing, the mental activities or processes that occur when a person remembers. The learner is an active participant in information processing. For

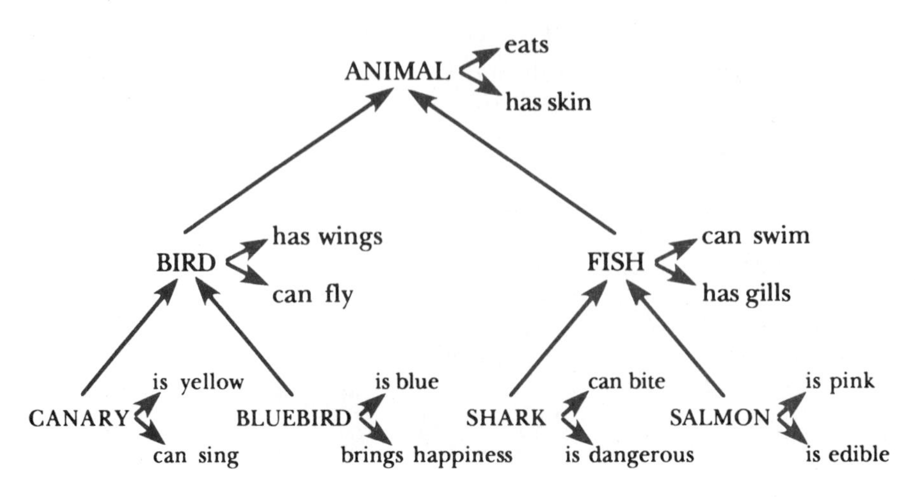

Figure 7–4.
Portion of a hierarchy in memory, showing relationships among the units and properties within the category *animal* as proposed by Collins and Quillian's network model (1969).

Note. From "Retrieval Time From Semantic Memory" by A. M. Collins and M. R. Quillian, 1969, *Journal of Verbal Learning and Verbal Behavior, 8,* pp. 240-247. Copyright © 1969 by Academic Press. Adapted by permission.

example, a person selectively attends to stimuli, employs strategies for storing information, and uses cues to evoke memories. The processes involved in information processing are subdivided into three categories referred to as encoding, storage, and retrieval.

What is encoding?

Encoding is the process of coding, translating, and entering information into the memory system for immediate or later use. For example, if a person is introduced to a new employee at a business meeting, at the encoding stage the sound waves are changed in the ear and passed on to the brain if the name receives attention. The name is then perceived, and features such as syllable sequence and number of syllables are recognized and may be associated with other stored information or physical features of the person. Also, strategies for storage of the name in long-term memory such as repetition may be employed. **Storage** is the process of holding the information in the memory.

Retrieval is the process of locating the stored information and bringing it back into conscious awareness. Retrieval of the employee's name may occur a week after the introduction when the person meets the new employee while walking down the hall and speaks the new employee's name. A **retrieval cue** is anything that helps to retrieve a memory. The appearance of the person and the sight of the associated physical features of the person may serve as the retrieval cue. All three processes—encoding, storage, and retrieval—must work together smoothly for an individual to remember. If any one of the three processes breaks down, the result is failure to remember.

What three processes are necessary for remembering to occur?

More information is available in long-term memory storage than can be retrieved. Most forgetting is the result of the loss of access to the information rather than the actual loss of the information. An analogy is the storage of a particular book in a huge library. The book is available to the person; however, unless the name of the book, the name of the author, or something else is known about the book, it may not be accessible to the individual. What takes place while the information is in conscious awareness (short-term memory) is crucial to whether a cue is available and the information can be retrieved or not. The more encoded features that are stored, the greater the likelihood that a retrieval cue will be available to retrieve the memory. For example, the subheadings and boldfaced words in this textbook may serve as retrieval cues for recalling the information.

Because of the difficulties in trying to make all the complex operations and numerous codes fit the basic structural approach explanation of memory, an alternative explanation has been offered (Craik & Lockhart, 1972). Rather than viewing information as being stored or held for a period of time in a distinct structural storage system (sensory memory, short-term memory, and long-term memory), the information is viewed as passing through deeper and deeper levels of processing ordered along a continuum. The processing may vary in depth from shallow (the analysis of physical aspects) to deep (the analysis of meaning and emotional aspects). For example, in the previous example of a person being introduced to a new employee, processing only the auditory sound features such as the syllables would represent shallow processing. If the new employee's name is Deepwater, analyzing the meaning of the word and imaging the new employee in a deep body of water or associating the name with a frightening personal experience that occurred in deep water would represent deep processing. Research experiments have demonstrated that it is not the amount of rehearsal an item gets in short-term memory and the amount of time an item is held in short-term memory but rather the depth of processing of the descriptive characteristics that is related to retention (Craik & Watkins, 1973). The deeper the processing, the better the retention. According to the depth-of-processing concept, short-term memory is a shallow level of processing, and long-term

How do shallow and deep processing differ?

memory is a deeper level of processing. This concept is consistent with the biological concept of a memory trace referred to earlier in this chapter. Figure 7–5 is a simplified diagram of the cognitive view of memory.

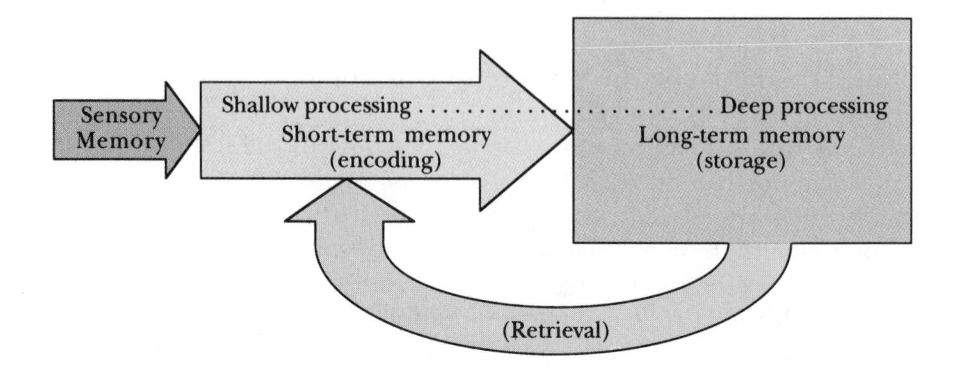

Figure 7–5.
A simplified diagram of the cognitive view of memory.

Explanations of Forgetting

Various explanations have been given for the forgetting of a specific, isolated fact or experience. Each explanation probably accounts for some but not all forgetting.

Trace Decay. The trace decay theory of forgetting proposes that with the passing of time and without repetition, the strength of the memory trace is weakened and therefore the memory itself is less likely to be retrieved. A person may forget a business appointment that is made a month in advance if it is not strengthened by reminders (cued and repeated).

What are the two types of interference that explain some forgetting?

Interference. The interference theory holds that the information gets mixed with other information, which interferes with the storage; thus, the information becomes harder to retrieve. Something previously learned may interfere with remembering something learned more recently (**proactive inhibition**). For example, learning new information in chemistry class immediately prior to learning new information in psychology class interferes with retention of the new information learned in psychology. Something learned later may also interfere with remembering something learned previously (**retroactive inhibition**). Therefore, learning the new information in psychology class interferes with retention of the new information learned in chemistry class. A person may forget a business appointment because a number of events occurred immediately prior to or immediately after the appointment was made. Organizing and coding activity for storage of the appointment in long-term memory may have been lessened due to the processing of either previous or following events. Figure 7–6 outlines the experimental procedure for illustrating proactive and retroactive inhibition.

	1	2	3
Experimental Group	Learn List A of nonsense syllables	Learn List B of nonsense syllables	Recall List B
Control Group	No learning activity	Learn List B of nonsense syllables	Recall List B

Proactive Inhibition

	1	2	3
Experimental Group	Learn List A of nonsense syllables	Learn List B of nonsense syllables	Recall List A
Control Group	Learn List A of nonsense syllables	No learning activity	Recall List A

Retroactive Inhibition

Figure 7–6. Experimental procedure for illustrating interference effects on recall. The experimental group does not recall as many nonsense syllables as the control group due to interference.

Repression. The psychoanalytic explanation for forgetting is repression. In **repression,** a person unconsciously blocks out memories that may be unpleasant, emotionally disturbing, or in conflict with a belief system. Although it is not what Freud had in mind when he discussed repression, a business appointment that is forgotten because the person unconsciously did not want to keep the appointment might be an example of repression. **Psychological amnesia** is the most extreme form of repression. A person's life may have been so frightening or miserable that all memory of personal events is blocked out. People suffering from psychological amnesia may not be able to recall who they are, where they work, anything about their family, or where they live; but they may be able to function on a job or be capable of functioning normally at the present and in the future. Through therapy, the repressed memories may be unblocked.

Is information stored by exact representation?

Reconstruction. The reconstruction theory proposes that events may be distorted in the process of storage and retrieval. Distortion may take place at the time of storage when the general idea is abstracted or summarized for storage. People do not store information passively by exact reproduction as a copy machine does; rather, people actively interpret information as it is received and store the information as it is interpreted. As a result, a specific memory may be incorrect or not available because it was misinterpreted or omitted when the event was stored. An individual may reconstruct an event as it is unconsciously desired to be, or the event may be reconstructed as it seems it should have been. Distorted reconstruction, which explains some forgetting, is illustrated in the box that follows.

DISTORTED RECONSTRUCTION

Read the following list of words: bed, rest, awake, tired, dream, wake, night, eat, comfort, sound, slumber, snore. Close the book and reconstruct the list by writing down as many of the words as you possibly can without looking back at the list. Research indicates that the word *sleep* is included on the reconstructed list in more than half the cases. It seems sleep should have been there even though it was not (Deese, 1958). Including the word *sleep* when recalling the list is an example of distorted reconstruction, which explains the forgetting of the exact words on the list.

Unavailable Cues. Sometimes an inability to retrieve an event or experience may simply be because a cue is not available to trigger the memory. An individual may forget another person's name and later remember it by going through the letters of the alphabet. The letter of the alphabet with which the name begins may serve as a retrieval cue. Emotional states as well as words, events, and places can serve as retrieval cues. Things learned while an individual is in one mood are more likely to be recalled when the individual is in that mood again. When happy, people tend to recall happy events; when sad or depressed, they tend to recall sad or depressing events (see Figure 7–7).

Malfunction of the Brain. Sometimes forgetting may have a physiological basis such as brain damage or some malfunctioning of the brain. Loss of brain tissue from disorders such as Alzheimer's disease or hardening of the arteries may disrupt the

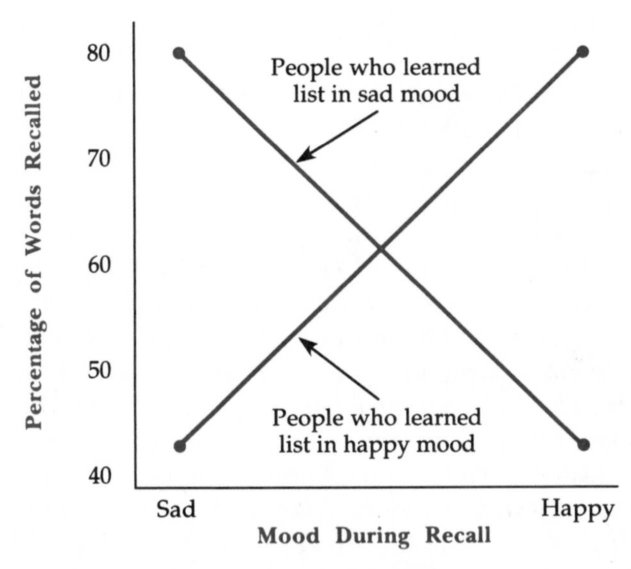

Figure 7–7.
The effects of emotional state on memory are demonstrated by the fact that words learned when sad are best recalled when sad; words learned when happy are best recalled when happy.

Note. From "Mood & Memory" by G. Bower, June 1981, *Psychology Today,* p. 64. Copyright © 1981 (APA). Reprinted with permission from *Psychology Today Magazine.*

memory processes. Evidence suggests that alcohol may interfere with the neurotransmitter serotonin's activity and account for failure to later remember events that occurred while drinking heavily (Weingartner, Rudorfer, Buchsbaum, & Linnoila, 1983). Malfunctioning of the brain might be an explanation for a breakdown in the process of encoding, storage, or retrieval. A breakdown of any one of these could account for a failure to remember an event that had been experienced.

FACTORS INFLUENCING MEMORY

Memory is a function of many factors. Characteristics of the individual as well as characteristics of the material have an effect on memory. Also, the procedure used in learning has been found to influence memory. Some of these characteristics and learning procedures are pointed out in this section.

Characteristics of the Individual

Factors within the individual who is doing the remembering affect what the individual remembers. Some characteristics that have been noted are intelligence, motivation, attention span, anxiety, cognitive style, and use of imagery.

What are some individual traits that may enhance remembering?

Intelligence, Motivation, and Attention. Intellectual or mental ability and motivation have long been recognized as fundamental aspects of remembering. (The concept of motivation is explained in chapter 9.) People vary in their abilities to remember facts or behaviors that are related to the performance of a particular task, sometimes because of varying intellectual ability and sometimes because of varying degrees of motivation. In addition, the ability to selectively attend to certain aspects of the environment while ignoring other aspects of the environment varies among people and is related to retention of an event. The amount of time a person can concentrate attention on a topic also varies among people and affects retention. The size of a person's working memory, or the number of aspects of the environment that can be held in the short-term memory storage systems, varies among people and is a factor related to memory. An average of seven items is the typical size of an adult's short-term memory. However, for some people nine or ten items may be held in short term memory; for others, only three or four items.

Does anxiety affect remembering in the same way in all people and for all tasks?

Anxiety. Anxiety is another factor that has been demonstrated to influence remembering (Tobias, 1979). Some individuals are less anxious than others, and some learn to reduce anxiety more than others by such methods as organizing effective programs of study and preparation. Sometimes the thought of learning something new and retaining it provokes so much anxiety that the person avoids the learning situation altogether. Sometimes when an experience is anxiety producing, the person may escape by daydreaming, watching television, or engaging in social activities with friends (see Figure 7–8). A little anxiety may enhance remembering by providing the motivation to prepare for later retrieval. However, extremely high levels of anxiety seem to interfere with remembering. An example is test anxiety in which a person becomes so anxious that the "mind goes blank" and well-known material cannot be remembered. The level of anxiety for maximum efficiency in remembering varies according to the individual and the nature of the task. Higher levels of anxiety interfere more with remembering a highly cognitive (thinking) or more complex task. The implication is that, for maximum performance, anxiety should be kept at an optimal level for each individual for each task.

Figure 7–8. Sometimes when the experience is anxiety producing, the person may escape by daydreaming and fail to prepare for later retrieval.

Cognitive Styles. In recent years, psychologists have become interested in cognitive styles, which describe differences in the way individuals characteristically perceive events, draw inferences from them, and thus store them for retrieval. One cognitive style that has been differentiated is the dimension of field independence-dependence. A **field-independent** individual seems to depend almost entirely on internal bodily information to make judgments, tends to make judgments analytically, and tends to disregard external environmental information that may affect perception or judgment. A **field-dependent** individual seems to depend more on information in the external environment than on information provided by his or her internal environment. A field-dependent person tends to make global judgments and is less able to ignore external environment information that contradicts the internal bodily information. The rod-and-frame test is often used to test for field independence-dependence. In this test, the individual is asked to adjust a tilted rod that is inside a tilted frame with no other visual information available as to the upright position with respect to gravity. The field-independent person is more likely to move the rod upright with respect to gravity. The field-dependent person is more likely to move the rod to be parallel to two parallel sides of the frame. What a field-independent person remembers about an experience may be different from what a field-dependent person remembers. For example, in a job situation, one manager who is field-independent may tend to remember an employee's productivity more in terms of exact statistics, whereas another manager who is field-dependent is more influenced by external information such as personality or physical appearance of the employee. Some people unemployed 10 years ago may be field-independent and remember the unemployment rate according to facts, whereas others may be field-dependent and remember the unemployment rate as higher than the statistics, their memory being more influenced by the environmental situation of unemployment. In remembering how frequently rain occurs in an area, a field-dependent person may remember the frequency as higher if it is raining at the time the judgement is made than if the sun is shining at the time the judgment is made (see Figure 7–9).

How is a field-independent individual different from a field-dependent individual in remembering an experience?

Memory of past events may be influenced by whether an individual tends to be a leveler or a sharpener in cognitive style. **Levelers** tend to see new stimuli as very similar to what has been previously presented. **Sharpeners** tend to notice differences quickly and accurately between new stimuli and stimuli previously presented. Experimental studies have found sharpeners superior to levelers in recalling stories heard years earlier. Levelers are

How do levelers and sharpeners differ in recall of an experience?

Figure 7–9.
A field-dependent person's memory of past weather is influenced more by current conditions than is a field-independent person's memory.

more likely to simplify the grammatical structure of verbal materials they have been asked to recall (Holzman & Gardner, 1960; Livant, 1962).

How does use of imagery affect memory of an experience?

Which is better for recall: an unusual or an ordinary image?

Use of Imagery. Another factor that influences memory is the degree to which the individual makes use of mental imagery. Before language was acquired, the environment was categorized in terms of mental images. Then with the use of language, imagery became less important. Individuals do, however, continue to use imagery, but they vary in their use of imagery when encoding, storing, and retrieving. Stronger use of imagery is associated with better memory (Paivio, 1974). For example, when introduced to a person, an individual might form a mental image of the name of the person. The name *Rose Doe* might be imaged as a rose bush growing out of a batch of dough on top of the person's head. The more unusual the image, the more effectively it influences memory. A person might remember a list of words by forming an image that chains the words together. Frog, magazine, elbow, missile, and photograph might be imaged as a frog with a magazine under its elbow standing by a missile having a photograph taken. Visualizing such an image improves memory of the list.

Characteristics of the Material

Memory is also related to characteristics of the material to be remembered. Some characteristics discussed in this section include the degree of abstraction, the meaningfulness, and the structure, such as organization, length, association value of key words, and number of high-frequency words.

Degree of Abstraction. Information that contains concrete concepts such as apple, chair, desk, or truck relies more on imagery than information containing abstract concepts such as beauty, anxiety, or attitude. Concrete information is remembered better than abstract information. The difference is thought to be due to the stronger use of imagery (Paivio, 1974). A word high in imagery rating is easier to remember. The imagery rating refers to the degree to which the word can bring to mind a concrete picture.

Is more abstract or more concrete information remembered?

Meaningfulness. The meaningfulness of the information presented also has a profound effect on remembering it. When information is presented in terms of its relationship to other information already stored in memory, it is more meaningful. Knowing the whole picture and understanding how each element fits into it aid in forming a memory of it. An activity to illustrate this is contained in the box that follows.

MEANINGFULNESS AFFECTS MEMORY

Look at the following sentence: "Idi du seth ema ter ialy est erd ay." The sentence is gibberish, without meaning, and difficulty is probably experienced in recalling it. Try to recall it. Now look at the following sentence: "I did use the material yesterday." This sentence is the same as the first sentence except that the letters are grouped in such a way as to produce meaningful combinations. Try to recall it. Much less difficulty is probably experienced in recalling this latter sentence.

Structure. Various things about the structure of the material affect recall of the material. For example, how easily the parts of the material can be grouped or organized in some way and the length of the material are two things. To remember a list of ten bits of information requires about twice as much learning time as is required to remember a list of seven bits of information. Material that can be broken down and organized into smaller units can be remembered more easily (see Figure 7–10).

What is meant by the association value of a word?

The degree to which a word can bring to mind other words is referred to as the association value of the word. The association value of the words in the content of material affects remembrance of the material. For some words, the average person can think of 10 or 12 words in a minute that may be associated with them, while for other words only 6 or 8, 3 or 4, 1 or 2, or 0 words per minute may be associated with them. Words high in association value are easier to remember than words low in association value.

List A	List B
book	dog
key	cat
rat	goat
school	lion
box	
marble	chair
hat	sofa
road	stool
clock	hat
doll	coat
	shirt

Figure 7–10.
Words in List B can be remembered more easily than words in List A because they can be organized into smaller units.

The content of material varies in the frequency with which the words are seen in print or used in speech—the frequency rating of the words. High-frequency words are remembered more easily than low-frequency words. Frequency or repetition enhances memory storage.

Learning Procedures

The procedures involved in placing material in long-term memory storage are also important factors influencing memory. Whether the practice periods (storage periods) are long or short, whether they include all or only parts of the material, and whether they are continued after the material is learned are procedures addressed here.

Massed Versus Distributed Practice. Practicing or repeating material to be remembered for short periods of time with rest periods intervening is called **distributed practice.** Doing all the practice or repetition from start to finish in one long, unbroken time interval is called **massed practice.** Usually distributed practice (Ausubel & Youssef, 1965; Hintzman, 1974) has been found to lead to superior retention for equal amounts of practice time for both verbal and sensorimotor learning (see Figure 7–11). For example, a person will retain more from 6 hours of practice in computer operation by practicing one hour in the morning and one hour in the afternoon for 3 days than by practicing 6 hours consecutively in one day. The practice period should not be so brief that time is not allowed for repetition of a complete set of material; neither should the time between practice periods be so great that much of the learning from previous practices is forgotten (DiVesta & Thompson, 1970).

Figure 7–11.
Studying a little and frequently (distributed practice) may result in more lasting memory than studying the same amount of time in one long period (massed practice).

Part Versus Whole Practice. Whether an individual retains material better when it is learned in small parts or by tackling the whole thing at once has been studied extensively. The topic of part versus whole practice is rather complex, and the findings are not clear as to which type of practice produces greater retention. Early research results tended to favor the whole method because the part method had the problem of putting the pieces together in a meaningful way. However, by using the part method, reinforcement for accomplishment of each part may be very effective. Some guidelines for deciding on learning by the whole or the part method for better retention in proportion to the amount of time spent in learning follow.

What are some guidelines for use in deciding whether to learn by the whole or the part method for best retention in proportion to the amount of time spent in learning?

1. The more intelligent person can probably use the whole method more effectively.
2. The whole method is more effective if distributed practice rather than massed practice is used.
3. The effectiveness of the whole method increases with practice.
4. The whole method tends to be more effective for learning meaningful and highly organized material (McGeoch & Irion, 1952). However, the part method seems to become more preferable as the complexity of the material increases.

Overlearning. Overlearning, which refers to the continuation of practice or repetition of material beyond the point when it has been learned, facilitates remembering (see Figure 7–12). Of course, there is a limit to how much continued repetition will increase remembering. In order to remember a greater percentage

"Even though I know the details of the construction plans, I think I will go over these a few more times just to be sure I can remember them next week."

Figure 7–12.
Overlearning, or continuing to repeat information after it can be repeated perfectly, will increase retention of the material.

of information, repetition of the material should be continued even after it has been learned.

THINKING

What is thinking?

Thinking is the process by which a person manipulates and combines representations or symbols held in the mind of events or things, whether present or physically absent. Thinking is sometimes considered to be communication with one's self. The basic units of thought and thinking in problem solving and decision making are discussed in this section.

Basic Units of Thought

Do people think in terms of motor representations?

The representations or symbols used in thought may be in different forms. The most important units of thought are motor representations, images, words, and concepts. These units of thought are described in this section.

Motor Representation. Thinking may involve motor representations, the reactivating of muscular patterns stored in the mind. These are the first representations or symbols to appear in thought development. For example, young infants cannot separate themselves from the world and the objects within it. The world is what they do with it, and events are defined by the actions they evoke. An infant who drops a rattle may continue to shake the fist as if the action will bring back the rattle (Hall, Perlmutter, & Lamb, 1982). Motor representations or symbols continue to be used for such skills as typing, riding a bicycle, or tying knots. People who gesture with their hands while talking or move their lips while reading are using movement to help their thinking.

Are there images other than visual images?

Imagery. Imagery is believed to be a more efficient type of representation than motor representation. Images are built up in the course of cognitive growth. A person may have a stored internal image of a sound, smell, taste, or touch as well as have a visual image. Stored images are used to evoke a previous experience. Research suggests that an internal image corresponds directly to the physical stimulus. In one study, researchers found that people mentally rotate images of geometric figures to determine whether the figures are alike or different (Shepard & Metzler, 1971). Such research suggests that an internal image corresponds directly to the physical stimulus. An image may be stored in incomplete or distorted form, or it may be stored very vividly or only faintly. Only when a person can form concepts and use language can representations go beyond imagery.

What are concepts, and what do they make possible?

Concepts. Concepts, categories for representing or classifying environmental stimuli according to common characteristics, allow a person to identify a new stimulus and guide action in a new situation. Concepts are a more efficient representation or symbol than motor symbols or images because they make it possible to generalize, discriminate, and abstract events. Concepts vary in their level of abstraction. The concept of an apple is not as abstract as the concept of the category *fruit.* Concepts may sometimes be incomplete and not clearly defined. The formation of concepts is important to an individual's ability to think in terms of problem solving.

Language. Representations in the form of words are transformations of things or events in the world according to a rule, an abstraction, or an inference. Words may be attached to a concept to become a symbol for the concept. Meaningful ideas are exchanged among people through use of language. Human language is generative. An infinite number of utterances can be produced using meaningful units (morphemes) made from a set of elements (phonemes) and a set of rules for combining them (syntax). The fact that words do not physically resemble what they represent allows them to be arranged in an infinite variety of ways to produce ideas. Language symbols are an even more efficient way of defining world events. Although thinking can occur without language, most thought depends on language symbols because language allows the world to be encoded into symbols that are easily manipulated (see Figure 7–13).

Figure 7–13.
Thinking relies heavily on language symbols.

Problem Solving

Problem solving involves thinking and remembering. It is the application of past experience and presently available information. An individual does a vast amount of problem solving each day. It may be as simple as figuring out how to open a door or as complex as figuring out how to double the volume of business in the next year. A person has a problem to solve any time it is recognized that a gap exists between the way things are (the situation) and the way things are desired to be (the goal).

When does a person have a problem to solve?

What is the first step in problem solving?

Steps. The first step in solving a problem is identifying or recognizing the problem. After the problem is identified, the second step is to define the problem. Facts about the problem have to be gathered to develop a reasonable definition. Concepts are used in defining the problem. For example, if the problem is how to open the door, a person must have a concept of *open* and *door* and some facts about doors.

What is the third step in problem solving, and what kinds of thinking may be used in this third step?

The third step in solving a problem is the search or the generating of a number of possible solutions, ideas, plans, or recommendations. With many alternative recommendations, the individual has more choices and a greater possibility of finding the most realistic and reasonable solution. This third step may involve either or both convergent thinking and divergent thinking. In **convergent thinking,** the person retrieves answers or previous solutions already stored in long-term memory. Information related to the problem that is stored in long-term memory is brought together or converged. **Divergent thinking** is the opposite in that new, unusual, or unheard-of solutions are developed. The person uses imagination and combines knowledge and experience in new ways to create new answers. This kind of thinking, creative thinking, may involve thinking at the subconscious level, similar to an incubation period, which may end with a seemingly sudden insight, sometimes referred to as a "bright idea" (see Figure 7–14).

Figure 7–14.
Divergent thinking may lead to a seemingly sudden insight for solving a problem.

The fourth step in problem solving is anticipation and evaluation. This step involves thinking that mentally carries out the alternative recommendations before any are actually carried out. By doing this thinking, the person may anticipate that some of the recommendations will create more problems than they resolve. The recommendation that is evaluated as the best alternative to accomplish the desired goal is then chosen.

What are the last three steps in problem solving?

The fifth step involves the implementation of the chosen recommendation. This step should be followed by a sixth step—the reexamination of the problem at a later date to ensure that the applied actions are accomplishing the goals. The final or seventh step is to restudy the problem if the goals are not being accomplished and make modifications.

"This is the way I've solved problems like this one for the last 20 years, and I'm not going to try anything new."

Figure 7–15.
A set or habit of responding in a certain way to similar problems may aid or hinder problem solving.

Influencing Factors. A number of factors influence problem solving. Short-term memory or attention span places limits on the number of combinations of problem-solving operations a person can keep in consciousness simultaneously. All the facts, words, concepts, and procedures related to a problem cannot possibly be kept in mind at the same instant. Thus, a person with a larger short-term memory has more information available in consciousness to actively work with mentally in a given moment than the person with a smaller short-term memory. Also, the amount of information stored in a person's long-term memory and whether it is retrievable when needed to solve a problem are factors influencing problem solving. Conceivably, the more information available to a person in short-term from long-term memory, the better problem solver he or she should be.

The sets that a person has are also a factor in problem solving. The concept of **set** refers to a habit of responding in a certain way because of experience. A set may serve as a cue for finding a solution to a problem, or it may be a hindrance in that it blinds the person to seeing a more efficient solution (see Figure 7–15). A person who is not rigid and conforming or set in his or her ways is more likely to use divergent thinking and be a creative problem solver.

What is meant by functional fixedness?

Functional fixedness is another way in which experience may affect problem solving. With **functional fixedness,** a person may have difficulty thinking of another function for an object that has previously had a particular function; its function is fixed in the person's mind. For example, if a hammer has been used extensively by the individual to drive nails, the individual may have difficulty recognizing that the hammer may also be used as a paperweight. Or a person with functional fixedness may not think of using a table knife for a screwdriver if a screwdriver is not available to do the task. A manufacturer and distributor of baking soda who displays functional fixedness and thinks and advertises only in terms of baking soda's original intended use in baking as a rising agent may not have as high a sales volume as one who thinks and advertises in terms of additional ways baking soda can be used. For example, baking soda can be used for absorbing odors in the cat litter box and in the refrigerator, for toothbrushing powder, and for a scratchless cleanser that deodorizes as it cleans. People who are divergent thinkers are less likely than convergent thinkers to be inhibited in generating new or unusual solutions in problem solving by functional fixedness.

"My decision is to follow through with Plan B rather than Plan A."

Figure 7–16.
Making decisions is part of many jobs.

Decision Making

A decision is a choice between two or more alternatives. The process of decision making involves thinking. People are constantly faced with making decisions in problem solving in work situations as well as in personal life (see Figure 7–16). Usually a number of possible solutions can be generated. In most instances of decision making, a problem exists for which a decision must be made concerning which possible solution to implement.

What are some factors that influence the effectiveness of decision making?

Factors Influencing Effectiveness. The effectiveness of a decision may depend on a number of factors. One factor, for example, may be whether the decision maker has access to relevant, up-to-date information. Another factor may be the personality of the decision maker. A person with a well-balanced personality who is not too rigid, overly cautious, or too much of a risk taker would be more likely to make more effective decisions.

A person's emotions and feelings influence the decision-making process. A decision to continue to manufacture an unprofitable product may be based on sentimentality rather than rationality. Feelings may influence the decision without the decision maker being aware of the influence. Sometimes how a person believes others will react to the decision affects the choice. Rationality is an ideal that people must strive for in making decisions.

The time allotment for making the decision may be a factor in decision making. Usually people think more clearly when they are not rushed. In some situations, a person does not always have much time to spend in analyzing the alternatives for each decision that must be made. However, a person should attempt to gather as much useful information as possible during the time available before making a decision. More time may be allowed for significant decisions—those decisions that affect more people or have a greater effect on the profits of the business. The more significant the decision, the more serious should be the consideration of each alternative. Some people tend to be impulsive decision makers and use little time, whereas other people tend to be reflective decision makers and use much time (see Figure 7–17).

"I'll go with this option."

"Let me think about this for a while, and I'll give you my choice of an option to go with by tomorrow."

Figure 7–17.
Some people tend to be impulsive decision makers and use little time, whereas other people tend to be reflective decision makers and use much time.

Evaluation of Alternatives. One method of evaluating the alternatives in decision making would be to list each alternative on a separate sheet of paper. Then list side by side the disadvantages and advantages, weighted on a scale from 1 to 10, for each alternative. The advantages may be listed on the left and the disadvantages on the right. The decision maker can then see which alternative has more advantages than disadvantages. Sometimes a disadvantage might be serious enough to outweigh several advantages or vice versa.

Outcomes. Some decisions lead to highly favorable outcomes, whereas some lead to highly undesirable outcomes either economically or personally. When evaluating the outcomes of a decision, a person must consider personal satisfaction as well as economics. Most of the time people tend to make decisions that lead only to a minimum standard of satisfaction. Most decisions are made just to take care of the concern in an acceptable manner rather than to lead to a big breakthrough (DuBrin, 1980).

Some forms of thought such as daydreaming and dreaming at night, alternate forms of consciousness not directed toward a goal, are not subject to problem-solving operations and decision making. They are discussed earlier in chapter 5.

People process information and remember even though the memory may sometimes be distorted, incomplete, inaccessible to consciousness, or lost over time. And even the techniques being used can usually be improved. People interpret, predict, and make decisions; in other words, they think. People have the unique ability to think about the past and the future. They can think what the future will be, what the future might be, and what the future should be. Remembering and thinking are the essence of a person's psychological existence.

SUMMARY

1. The first memory studies, conducted by Ebbinghaus in 1885, consisted of measuring retention levels of nonsense syllables by the free

recall, serial recall, recognition, and relearning methods. Amount of time spent while learning and amount of time elapsed since learning as well as position in the list and method of measuring retention were found to influence the percentage of retention. Ebbinghaus' greatest contribution was to focus attention on memory.

2. Biological theories of memory propose that a permanent structural change or memory trace, which is the physical representation of a memory referred to as an engram, occurs in the connections between brain cells, forming reverberating circuits (neuronal theory), and in the RNA in the nuclei of specific cells (molecular theory).
3. The cognitive view consists of the structural and process approaches to explaining memory. The structural approach proposes three types or levels of storage systems—sensory, short-term, and long-term. The process approach focuses on information processing, which includes the processes of encoding, storage, and retrieval, and defines storage as a continuous memory trace with varying degrees of distinguishability based on depth of processing.
4. Memory at the sensory level is unconscious, has a large storage capacity, and consists of impressions made on the senses that are held onto for only an extremely brief time—sometimes up to 3 or 4 seconds for echoic memory (sound) and 1 or 2 seconds for iconic memory (vision).
5. Short-term memory has small storage capacity (about seven units on the average), consists of what is held in consciousness, and can be held only very briefly (15 to 20 seconds) without repetition.
6. Long-term memory has a vast capacity because it is a relatively permanent storage system of all a person's knowledge. Retrieval is less than the amount that is stored and depends on cues to find information and on the method of organization used when the information was stored.
7. Long-term memory consists of two components: semantic memory, which consists of facts, information, and general knowledge; and episodic memory, which consists of a chronologic record of personal experiences.
8. Explanations for forgetting include decay of the memory trace, interference (proactive and retroactive inhibition), repression (unconscious blocking), reconstruction, unavailable cues, and malfunction of the brain.
9. Memory is influenced by (a) characteristics within the individual such as intelligence, motivation, attention span, anxiety, cognitive style, and use of imagery; (b) characteristics of the material such as degree of abstraction, meaningfulness, and structure—organization, length, association value, and frequency rating of the words; and (c) procedures used during the learning process such as massed versus distributed practice, part versus whole practice, and overlearning.

10. Thinking is the process by which a person manipulates and combines mental representations or symbols of events or things, whether present or physically absent. The representations may be in the form of motor representations, images, concepts, and words.
11. A person has a problem to solve any time it is recognized that a gap exists between the way things are (the situation) and the way things are desired to be (the goal), whether the problem is as simple as opening a closed door or as complex as doubling the volume of business.
12. The steps in solving a problem are to identify the problem, define the problem, search for possible solutions, evaluate the alternatives, choose a solution, and apply the chosen action. Later, the problem should be reexamined and modifications to the chosen action made if the goals are not being accomplished.
13. Short-term memory (attention span) limits, retrievable information, sets or habits of responding in a certain way, and functional fixedness (a set for a particular function of an object) all can affect problem-solving ability.
14. People are constantly faced with the decision-making type of thinking—making a choice between two or more alternatives.
15. The effectiveness of decision making may be influenced by the availability of up-to-date and relevant information, by whether the decision maker has a well-balanced personality, by emotions and feelings, and by whether there is time pressure.
16. Listing and weighting advantages and disadvantages for alternatives may be helpful in significant decision making. Most people make decisions that lead only to a minimum standard of satisfaction rather than to a big breakthrough.

KEY TERMS AND CONCEPTS

Memory
Nonsense syllable
Free recall
Serial recall
Recognition method
Relearning method
Reverberating circuit
Engram
Ribonucleic acid (RNA) molecules
Sensory memory
Echoic memory
Iconic memory
Short-term memory
Long-term memory
Semantic memory
Episodic memory
Encoding
Storage
Retrieval
Retrieval cue
Proactive inhibition
Retroactive inhibition
Repression
Psychological amnesia
Field independent
Field dependent
Levelers
Sharpeners
Distributed practice
Massed practice
Overlearning
Concepts
Convergent thinking
Divergent thinking
Set
Functional fixedness

QUESTIONS FOR REVIEW

1. How did Ebbinghaus measure memory, and what did he find out about memory?
2. What biological explanations of memory have been proposed?
3. According to the structural approach to explaining memory, what are the types or levels of memory storage? Name, describe, and give examples of each.
4. According to the process approach to explaining memory, what are the processes involved in memory? Name, describe, and give examples of each.
5. Why does a person forget?
6. What characteristics within a person and what characteristics of the material to be remembered influence memory?
7. How do massed and distributed practice, part and whole practice, and overlearning affect memory of the material practiced? Give some guidelines for deciding whether part or whole practice is better.
8. What are the basic units of thought? Describe and illustrate each type of symbol or representation.
9. What are the steps in sequence that a person progresses through in solving a problem, and how do set and functional fixedness affect problem solving?
10. In the process of decision making, what are some factors that play a role in the effectiveness, evaluation, and outcome of a decision?

TEST YOURSELF

1. Ebbinghaus used all except which one of the following in his early studies of memory? (a) correlational techniques (b) himself as the subject in his experiments (c) lists of nonsense syllables to remember (d) the recall method of measuring memory.
2. Ebbinghaus found that (a) those items in the middle of a list are recalled more readily than those at the beginning (b) the longer the length of time between initial learning and recall, the smaller the percentage of information remembered (c) the method used for measurement does not reflect a difference in the percentage of recall (d) all of the above.
3. In the structural approach to explaining memory, information that is held in the present consciousness is in the ________________ memory storage system.
4. The long-term memory storage system has one component consisting of facts and general knowledge called ________________ memory and another component consisting of a chronologic record of personal experience called ________________ memory.

5. Encoding is the process of (a) holding information in a system (b) getting at the stored information (c) entering information into a system (d) both a and b.
6. Most forgetting is the result of (a) actual loss of information (b) loss of access to the information (c) an item of information in memory filed under more than one category (d) too much information being stored in long-term memory.
7. The structural change in the brain caused by stimulation that is the physical representation of memory is called a(n) ________________.
8. The repression theory explains forgetting as a function of the passing of time. T or F
9. When previous learning interferes with the recall of newly learned information, it is referred to as ________________ ________________.
10. The reconstruction theory explains forgetting as a function of the unconscious distortion of information to fit one's desires or to fit what it seems it should have been. T or F
11. Anxiety seems to enhance remembering up to a point and then interferes with remembering. T or F
12. Field-dependent people tend to disregard environmental information that may distort their judgment and memory. T or F
13. Experimental studies have found that in recalling details of stories heard earlier, no differences between levelers and sharpeners exist. T or F
14. Stronger use of imagery by a person is associated with better memory. T or F
15. Material that is (a) concrete is remembered better than material that is abstract (b) rated high in imagery is remembered better than material that is rated low in imagery (c) meaningful is remembered better than material that is gibberish or meaningless (d) all of the above.
16. The basic symbols or representations of events used in thought in the order in which they first begin to be used are ________________, ________________, ________________, and ________________.
17. Words low in association value are easier to remember than words high in association value. T or F
18. The third step in problem solving is the search for possible solutions, which may include both ________________ and ________________ thinking.
19. A ________________ refers to a habit of responding in a certain way because of experience.
20. A factor related to the effectiveness of a decision is whether (a) the decision maker is overly cautious, too rigid, or too much of a risk taker (b) the time allotment rushes the decision maker (c) the decision maker has access to relevant, up-to-date information (d) all of the above.

APPLICATIONS

A. A student who is above average in intellectual ability has only 7 hours this week to learn the material in a unit of one class. The unit consists of three chapters. The material is well organized. The student wants to use the 7 hours of study time as efficiently as possible. In other words, the student wants to study and learn the material in a way that will give the best possible retention in order to make the highest possible grade on the test.

1. Should the student study about an hour each day this week or do the 7 hours of study on Saturday?
2. If the student decides to study one hour each day, should a topic be read each session and read over and over until it is thoroughly learned? Or should the entire unit be read over each session?
3. If the student decided to read over the whole unit each 1-hour session and by the 4th day can recall the material in the unit, should the student continue to go over the material on the 3 remaining days?

B. A student decided to conduct a memory experiment at a party. When the guests had all arrived, they were taken to a room and allowed to look for 20 seconds at a table with 50 items on it. Twenty minutes later each guest was asked to recall the items on the table. The guests were divided randomly into three groups, and a different method of recall was used for each group. Group 1 was asked to write down in any order the items they remembered being on the table. Group 2 was asked to write down the items in the sequence in which they were placed on the table. Group 3 was given a sheet of paper with 200 items listed on it that contained the 50 items that were on the table. They were to recall the items on the table by placing a check mark by the name of the items.

1. Do you think each group averaged the same percentage of recall? Why or why not?
2. What was the method of recall used with Group 1? with Group 2? with Group 3?
3. Do you think the first item and the last item in the sequential arrangement on the table had a higher frequency of recall than an item in the middle of the sequence? Why or why not?
4. Do you think the percentage of recall in the groups would have been higher, lower, or the same if the guests had been asked to recall the items 3 hours after seeing them instead of 20 minutes after seeing them? Why?

SUGGESTIONS FOR FURTHER READING

Bower, G. H. (1981). Mood & memory. *American Psychologist, 36,* 129-148.

The relationship between mood and memory is discussed in detail in this journal article.

Higbee, K. L. (1977). *Your memory: How it works and how to improve it.* Englewood Cliffs, NJ: Prentice-Hall.

A practical book that offers suggestions for improving memory. Various mnemonic strategies are described, and how they work is explained.

Klatzky, R. L. (1980). *Human memory: Structures and processes* (2nd ed.). San Francisco: W. H. Freeman.

A detailed overview of memory processes that views memory as a system continuously active in receiving, modifying, storing, and retrieving information. Background information is not necessary for comprehension.

Loftus, E. (1980). *Memory: Surprising new insights into how we remember and why we forget.* Reading, MA: Addison-Wesley.

A discussion of memory that is fascinating and based on research findings.

Lorayne, H., & Lucas, J. (1974). *The memory book.* New York: Stein & Day.

A practical book to help a person read faster and remember what is read. Memory techniques are suggested for remembering things in everyday life such as shopping lists, speeches, or long numbers.

Lorayne, H. (1976). *Good memory—successful student.* New York: Stein & Day.

This book is a guide to remembering what is learned. A memory system is presented to aid in remembering the material of any course with special instructions for particular subject areas.

Neisser, U. C. (1982). *Memory observed: Remembering in natural contexts.* San Francisco: W. H. Freeman.

An edited collection of readings covering diverse and interesting topics related to the phenomena of memory in real-life usage such as testifying in court, performing, and getting things done.

CHAPTER 8

INTELLIGENCE

Objectives

When you have completed your study of chapter 8, you should be able to:

1. Define intelligence and differentiate between aptitude, ability, and achievement.
2. Describe various theories of intelligence.
3. Discuss the roles of heredity and environmental experience in the development of intelligence.
4. Give a brief history of intelligence testing including early contributors and their contributions.
5. Describe the concepts of reliability, validity, and standardization as they relate to psychological tests and identify shortcomings of intelligence tests.
6. Name a few tests used in business and industry to assess intelligence and a variety of specific aptitudes and abilities.
7. Relate some research findings about IQ and job satisfaction, IQ as a predictor of success, and IQ and occupational status.
8. Describe an effective procedure for using testing in selecting successful employees.
9. Describe creativity in terms of characteristics, measurement, and stages.
10. Outline some internal and external environmental conditions and characteristics of workplaces that enhance creativity.

Figure 8–1.
Many activities such as riding a bicycle require motor skills, and other activities such as forming a strategy for a chess game require mental abilities.

Some activities call for motor abilities such as hammering a nail into a board, which calls for eye-hand coordination. Other tasks such as speech making or decision making require mental abilities (see Figure 8–1). In many activities, both motor and mental abilities may be helpful. For example, the speaker may also be able to type the speeches, or a company president may also be able to paint a wall in the office. The focus in this chapter is on mental or intellectual abilities referred to as intelligence. The differences in intelligence among people and the implications of these differences for outcomes in life have received much attention in the field of psychology. First in this chapter, an attempt is made to define intelligence. Then, several views of intelligence—the theories explaining it and the conclusions concerning heredity and environment as determinants—are examined. A review of the measurement of intelligence through testing is presented. The use of intelligence tests in the world of work and the relationship of intelligence to job satisfaction, occupational success, and occupational status is addressed. Finally, creativity, a factor of intelligence, is discussed.

THE CONCEPT OF INTELLIGENCE

Why is intelligence difficult to define?

Intelligence is necessary for mental functioning and for performing work activities; however, intelligence is not easy to define. Because intelligence is a construct, not a pure characteristic, and includes a variety of specialized abilities, it can be defined in many different ways.

Definitions of Intelligence

A variety of definitions have been offered for intelligence. Several of these definitions are given here to provide a better understanding of intelligence than only one definition might give. Although seemingly psychologists disagree on both what intelligence means and on how a person acquires intelligence, each of the definitions is correct to a certain extent. Adapting, responding, coping, performing, and problem solving are somewhat similar; and perceiving, learning, and understanding are essential to these activities.

What is Piaget's view of intelligence?

Adapting. Jean Piaget (1952), the Swiss child psychologist who spent many years researching intellectual development, defined intelligence as the ability to adapt to the environment and to new situations—to think and act in adaptive ways. As pointed out in chapter 4, Piaget theorized that intellectual development occurs through a sequence of stages. The capability to think in a particular way develops as that individual interacts with the environment. The order of the stages remains constant; however, the rate and level of progression through the stages varies for different individuals. Piaget views intelligence in terms of quality rather than quantity.

Is intelligence problem-solving ability or aptitude for general learning?

Problem Solving. A common definition of intelligence is the "degree of availability of one's experiences for the solution of immediate problems and the anticipation of new ones" (Hepner, 1973, p. 336). Thus, intelligence is often used to refer to problem-solving abilities. In general, people with higher intellectual abilities are more likely to identify problems and make good decisions than those of lesser intelligence.

Learning. Some psychologists think of intelligence as the aptitude for general learning. People who can understand instructions and basic principles and can reason and make good judgments are considered to be more intelligent than those who cannot. People who are more intelligent generally are found to be better in academic studies.

Understanding and Coping. To David Wechsler (1975), intelligence involves the ability to exhibit effective behavior as well as to build an inner representation of the world—thinking and performing. He defined intelligence as the "capacity of an individual to understand the world around him and his resourcefulness to cope with its challenges" (p. 139). The scales he developed to measure intelligence reflect his definition. Wechsler's intelligence measures yield both a verbal score and a performance score.

How does David Wechsler define intelligence?

Responding. Because behaviorists do not make assumptions about mental processes or mental abilities, they define intelligence as the responses or behaviors a person is capable of making. Behaviorally oriented psychologists think of intelligence in terms of the types of responses available to an individual. As was explained in chapter 1, the behaviorists eliminated the structure and functioning of the mind from the concern of psychology because the mind could not be observed directly. However, behavior or responses could be observed directly and could provide an objective, empirical, and scientific approach to the study of intelligence.

Who thinks of intelligence as being the types of responses an individual is capable of making?

Perceiving. Combs and Snygg (1959) believe that intelligence is really the effectiveness of perception or perceptual skills—the process of assembling sensations into a meaningful and usable mental representation of the world. Perception determines the way the world looks, feels, smells, tastes, or sounds. Perception provides an individual's immediate experience of the world. Because behavior and thinking depend on perceptions of the world, intelligence is related to how adequate and varied are a person's perceptions. Intelligence, then, is really an individual's ability to adequately perceive the environment.

Is intelligence an individual's ability to adequately perceive the world?

Intelligence Versus Similar Terms

Technically, the term *intelligence* is not exactly the same as the terms *achievement, aptitude,* and *ability.* The differences in these terms are described in this section.

Achievement. Psychologists generally distinguish between achievement and intelligence. **Achievement** is what a person has learned, the knowledge and skills that have been acquired through experience. Achievement presupposes an acquaintance with a specific body of material. For example, achievement in calculus refers to the extent of mathematical knowledge in this area (see Figure 8–2). Achievement in air-conditioning repair and installa-

Figure 8–2.
Some individuals have greater achievement in a particular body of knowledge than do other individuals.

tion requires knowledge of those systems and equipment and refers to the degree or level of this knowledge.

What is the technical difference between ability and aptitude?

Aptitude and Ability. The terms *aptitude* and *ability* are often used interchangeably because the ideas are related; however, the ideas are not identical. **Aptitude** is thought of as an innate or natural capacity for performing or learning to perform some task such as repairing machinery (mechanical aptitude) or for carrying out some mathematical function as in accounting (numeric aptitude). An **ability** is a current capability to learn that is based on both aptitude and experience. For example, a person might have an aptitude for sharpshooting because of excellent vision and a steady hand. The ability to shoot a rifle with precision, however, may only be present if enough experience with rifles has occurred so that the person knows how to hold, load, and fire the rifle. The ability to learn something includes not only aptitude but prior knowledge or experience. A person may have an aptitude to become a college student, i.e., possess a brain and nervous system capable of reaching college level thinking. The student may not currently, however, have the ability to perform at the college level if only the third grade in school has been completed.

VIEWS OF INTELLIGENCE

Theorists have different views of intelligence. They also disagree about the impact of environmental experience and heredity as determinants of a person's intelligence. Theories of intelligence, the role of heredity and environment in determining intelligence, and research support for heredity and environment each as the primary determinant of intelligence are discussed in this section.

Theories

What is the question concerning intelligence that has been debated for years?

The question has been debated for years as to whether intelligence is unified into a single general trait, whether intelligence is composed of a group or cluster of abilities, or whether a person's intelligence consists of many separate and independent abilities. Six explanations or theories of intelligence are presented here in the order in which they emerged.

What is meant by the *g* factor?

Spearman's *g* Factor. In 1904, Charles Spearman reasoned that because of high positive correlations between scores on such items as mathematical ability and mechanical ability, there must be a general level of intelligence responsible for the relationship. He called this general factor *g*. He further reasoned that this general intelligence is manifested in specific tasks that require varying levels of intelligence. Spearman viewed intelligence as consisting of one factor that could be measured on a continuum from low to high. Most measures of intelligence that produce a single score are built around this theory of a general intelligence.

How many factors of intelligence did Thurstone identify and what are they?

Thurstone's Primary Mental Abilities. In 1938, L. L. Thurstone identified seven factors of intelligence that he called primary mental abilities. Thurstone proposed that intelligence consists of numeric ability, word fluency, verbal meaning, memory, reasoning, spatial relations, and perceptual speed. He further proposed that each ability is different from the others and measurable on a separate continuum. For example, an individual may be high in numeric ability and low in word fluency. The measure of intelligence based on this view is composed of tests measuring each of these abilities. The intelligence score for a person is then derived from a composite or average of these tests.

Guilford thinks intelligence consists of how many factors?

Guilford's Structure of Intellect. In 1961, J. P. Guilford developed a model for the structure of human intellect that is three dimensional and provides for 120 distinguishable factors in intelligence. Guilford (1967) claims there is no evidence for a general factor of intelligence. Guilford's model (see Figure 8–3) proposes

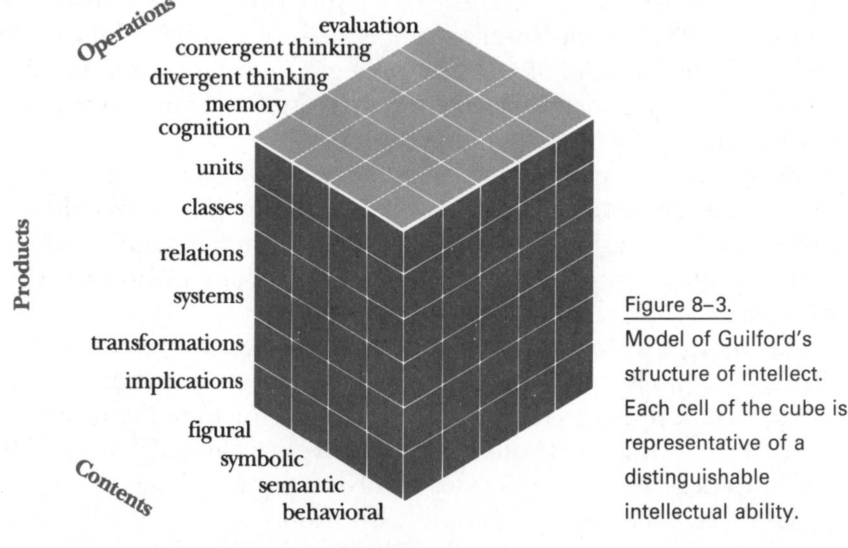

Figure 8–3.
Model of Guilford's structure of intellect. Each cell of the cube is representative of a distinguishable intellectual ability.

Note. From "Factorial Angles to Psychology" by J. P. Guilford, 1961, *Psychological Review, 68,* p. 6. Copyright © 1961 by American Psychological Association. Reprinted by permission of the author.

that one dimension consists of five kinds of operations (convergent thinking, divergent thinking, memory, evaluation, and cognition); another dimension consists of four kinds of content such as semantic (verbal) or symbolic (nonverbal) used in intellectual operations; and a third dimension consists of products or outcomes of the operations such as relations, units, or classes. Each of the 120 factors represents a unique intellectual ability. Guilford has identified and devised tests to measure most of the 120 factors theorized to make up intelligence.

What is the difference between Cattell's fluid and crystallized components of intelligence?

Cattell's Fluid and Crystallized Intelligence. Raymond B. Cattell (1971) proposed that there are two major theoretical components of intelligence: fluid and crystallized. **Fluid intelligence** is a general perceptual capacity that is dependent on the physiological functioning of the brain. It is determined by an individual's genetic endowment and represents an adaptive process. **Crystallized intelligence** reflects what has been learned through experience. It reflects cultural exposure and formal education and is composed primarily of knowledge and skills. It is the summation of all the particular perceptual skills acquired in specific fields. These two components of intelligence are usually correlated because a person's crystallized intelligence depends on fluid intelligence. The reason people who are the same in fluid intelligence may differ in crystallized intelligence is that there is a difference in the amount of their education or in the effort put into their schooling (Undheim, 1981). Fluid intelligence is believed to be fully developed by about 10 years of age and to begin to decline after age 20. Crystallized intelligence is believed to increase for many years, even after the end of formal schooling.

More recently, proponents of this theory suggest that crystallized abilities grow out of fluid abilities, resulting in the crystallized-fluid spectrum. Figure 8–4 is a diagram of the crystallized-fluid spectrum and some tasks that fall at different points on the spectrum.

Sternberg's Information Processing. Recently, research has shifted from abilities to information processing. Of primary concern is what happens to the information from the time the problem is perceived until a response is made. Robert Sternberg (1979) tried to understand the processes involved in intelligence by studying the differences in how people with widely varying intelligence test scores solve problems. He found that on certain sorts of problems people with higher intelligence take longer on encoding, the first step of information processing, than do people with lower in-

Maximum Adaptation or Transfer of Experience

A	Fluid Ability	block design embedded figures matrices scrambled sentences
B	Reasoning with Acquired Concepts	verbal analogies number series
C	General Educational Development	interpreting unfamiliar texts, tables, diagrams quantitative reasoning
D	Subject-Matter Proficiency	grammar computation
	"Crystallized" Achievements	factual knowledge

Maximum Direct Training

Figure 8–4.
The crystallized-fluid spectrum and some tasks that fall at different points on the spectrum.

Note. From *Essentials of Psychological Testing* (4th ed.) (p. 253) by L. J. Cronbach, 1984, New York: Harper & Row. Copyright © 1984 by Harper & Row. Reprinted by permission.

telligence. By more careful encoding, they can then do the later steps more quickly and efficiently. According to Sternberg's view, the general factor of intelligence proposed by Spearman may refer to the ability to realize ahead of time the type of problem to be faced and to recognize that careful encoding is necessary along with the strategies needed. Low intelligence scores seem to be related to this awareness. Support for this view also comes from the fact that most people learn a variety of strategies without any particular instruction, but people low in intelligence must have explaining and training to learn the strategies. When these strategies are taught to retarded persons, their performance improves on the particular task, but the strategies do not generalize to other tasks to improve their performance (Campione, Brown, & Ferrara, 1982).

To what does Sternberg think Spearman's *g* factor may refer?

Gardner's Multiple Intelligences. A broad view of intelligence derived from biological, psychological, and cross-cultural studies

Figure 8–5.
According to Gardner, a person has eight distinctly different intelligences, one of which is bodily kinesthetic intelligence (control of the body).

has been proposed by Howard Gardner (1983). According to Gardner (see Figure 8–5), a person has eight distinctly different and independent intelligences: spatial intelligence, linguistic intelligence, logical intelligence, mathematical intelligence, musical intelligence, intrapersonal intelligence (knowledge of self), interpersonal intelligence (knowledge of others), and bodily kinesthetic intelligence (control of the body). This theory attempts to dispel the assumption that verbal, spatial, logical reasoning, and mathematical abilities are more basic than other capacities. When speaking of intelligence and giftedness, people often fail to realize that different people have different gifts. Idiot savants are one source of support for this theory. **Idiot savants** are people who have an incredible, specific capacity such as the ability to draw, to remember music, or to compute numbers but who are otherwise retarded, sometimes with virtually no language ability.

Determinants

Which has the greater impact on intelligence, heredity or environment?

Psychologists agree that intelligence is determined by both heredity and environmental experience. The confusion and controversy is over the impact that each of these factors has in determining a person's degree of intelligence. The relationship of heredity and environmental experience to intelligence and research supporting each as the primary factor in the development of intelligence are discussed next.

What evidence is often used to support the view that heredity has a great impact on intelligence?

Heredity. R. C. Tryon (1940) experimented with selectively breeding rats according to their maze-learning ability. After several generations, he produced two groups of rats that were extremely different in maze-learning ability—a maze-bright group and a maze-dull group. Tryon's experiments with rats did not explain inheritance of intelligence in humans; however, the experiments did show that factors that influence intelligent functioning can be genetically transmitted from one generation to another, at least in rats.

What is meant by heritability of intelligence?

Heritability is a measure of how much trait variation in a population can be accounted for genetically. The heritability of intelligence for humans has been estimated to be as high as .85 (Ruch, 1984) and as low as .40 based on various populations studied. A basis for these estimates is the correlation or relationship between people having varied genetic similarities. The closer the genetic similarities, the higher the correlation of their measures of intelligence (Bouchard & McGue, 1981). For example, the correlation of

IQ scores between two groups of unrelated persons is .0; between parents and children or between siblings it is .50; and between identical twins it is .85 (see Figure 8–6).

Relationship	Correlation
Cousins	.15
Foster parent/child	.31
Parent/child	.40
Siblings	
reared apart	.24
reared together	.47
Dizygotic twins	
reared together	.60
Monozygotic twins	
reared apart	.72
reared together	.86

Figure 8–6. Strength of relationship (correlation) of measures of intelligence and genetic similarities.

Note. From "Familial Studies of Intelligence: A Review" by T. J. Bouchard, Jr. and M. McGue, 1981, *Science, 212,* p. 1056. Copyright © 1981 by the AAAS. Adapted by permission.

Environment. Correlational studies of the relationship between two groups of individuals with similar genetics but differing environments give support to the view that environment is an important aspect of intelligence. The correlation of the measures of intelligence for identical twins reared together is about .85 to .90; but for those reared apart the correlation is about .72. For siblings reared together, the correlation is about .47 to .50; but for siblings reared apart, the correlation is only about .24 (Bouchard & McGue, 1981). Differing environmental experiences are assumed to account for the difference in correlations because the two groups have the same genetic similarities.

Figure 8–7. Sensory stimulation through play, conversation, love, and attention has been found to be a factor in level of intelligence.

The role of environmental experience on the development of intelligence began to receive increased attention after children in an orphanage in Iowa were observed by H. M. Skeels (1938; 1942; 1966). Thirteen orphans who had been evaluated as retarded were placed in a building with retarded adults who were able to interact with the children and provide sensory stimulation through play, conversation, love, and attention. In 18 months, significant increases in intelligence test scores were noted compared with decreases in intelligence test scores in the control group that stayed in the orphanage (see Figure 8–7). The increase was from an average of 64 to an average of 92, and the decrease was from an average of 86 to an average of 61. The orphanage studies have been criticized as being poorly controlled; however, later and better controlled research studies also suggest a strong environmental influence on intelligence.

Children who were adopted and raised by families in a more affluent environment were found to have considerably higher measures of intelligence than would have been expected if they had remained in the impoverished environment into which they were born (Scarr & Weinberg, 1976). The earlier in life the children were adopted, the higher the intelligence measure tended to be.

Studies in physiological psychology also lend support to the role of the environment as a determinant of intelligence. In the prenatal period and early infancy, severe malnutrition has a damaging effect on brain development and therefore on intelligence (Kagan, Kearsley, & Zelazo, 1978). Also, nutrition can have an effect on brain operation and therefore on intelligence as was pointed out in chapter 2. Lowered oxygen intake has been found to affect verbal learning, verbal expression, short-term memory, and finger dexterity (West, 1984).

The possible range of values allowed by genetics for a characteristic is referred to as **reaction range** for that characteristic. The environment then influences the characteristic to some value within that reaction range. Figure 8–8 shows four generally accepted relationships of reaction ranges for intelligence. The research in general emphasizes the influence on intelligence of experiences early

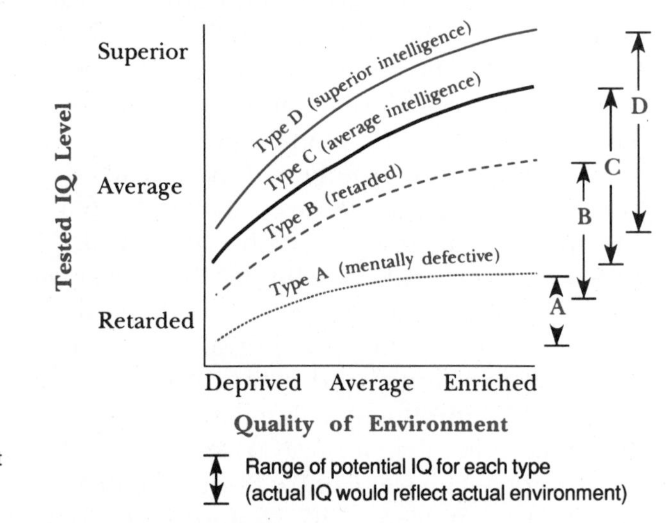

Figure 8–8. Hypothetical reaction range of measured intelligence for different types of individuals in different quality environments.

Note. From "Genetic Aspects of Intelligent Behavior" by I. I. Gottesman in *Handbook of Mental Deficiency: Psychological Theory and Research*, N. Ellis (Ed.) (p. 255), 1963, New York: McGraw-Hill. Copyright © 1963 by McGraw-Hill. Reprinted by permission.

in life. Heredity seems to set limits, but whether a person reaches that potential depends on environmental experience.

MEASUREMENT OF INTELLIGENCE

Some early history of intelligence testing, including a brief history of the two best known, individually administered intelligence tests, is provided in this section. Additionally, test evaluation is addressed, and a few tests used to evaluate aptitude and ability attributes of people in the workplace are reviewed. Finally, intelligence testing as applied in the world of work is discussed.

History

The history of intelligence testing dates back to the 1800s. Many different tests to measure intelligence have been devised including individually administered tests, group tests, and fair tests allowing for cultural differences. The best known individually administered tests, the Stanford-Binet and the Wechsler Intelligence Scales, are given special attention in the following discussion.

Figure 8–9.
Sir Francis Galton.

Early Contributors. In 1869, Sir Francis Galton (see Figure 8–9), Charles Darwin's cousin, had some ideas about classifying and measuring human qualities and abilities. Galton reasoned that intelligence was related to speed of perceptual-motor skills because information is acquired through the senses. He administered a battery of tests measuring such things as head size, reaction time, visual acuity, muscular power, and memory for visual forms; however, his tests never proved to be very useful. Galton was probably more preoccupied with measuring than anyone has ever been, and he pioneered some of the basic statistical concepts and set forth the idea that mental capacities can be quantitatively measured.

Who set forth the idea that mental capacities can be quantitatively measured?

Although the term *mental tests* was introduced by James McKeen Cantell in 1890, the testing of intelligence did not begin until 1904. Alfred Binet (see Figure 8–10) was commissioned by school authorities in Paris, France, to devise a way to differentiate between those students who were low in intelligence and those who were average and high in intelligence. The school officials wanted to identify those students who did poorly in school because they were of low intelligence and those who did poorly because of lack of motivation or poor instruction. The first test designed to measure a person's mental ability was developed by Binet, published, and used in Paris schools. The measure yields a score in the form of a mental age. For example, a child may be 10 years old chrono-

Figure 8–10.
Alfred Binet.

Figure 8–11.
Lewis Terman.

logically but function mentally as the average 6-year-old child does and have a mental age of 6; or a child who is six years old chronologically may function as the average 12-year-old child does and have a mental age of 12. The development and use of this test initiated a worldwide response, and Binet has become known as the father of intelligence testing.

What is meant by IQ?

In 1916 Lewis Terman (see Figure 8–11) of Stanford University translated, revised, and extended Binet's test, producing what is now called the *Stanford-Binet* test. This test has been revised four times, the most recent revision being in 1985. The test yields an **intelligence quotient (IQ),** which is a ratio of mental age to chronologic age multiplied by 100 to remove the decimal fraction. For example, an 8-year-old child with a mental age of 8 would have an IQ of 100 ($\frac{8}{8}$ x 100). An 8-year-old child with a mental age of 9 would have an IQ of 112 ($\frac{9}{8}$ x 100), or an 8-year-old child with a mental age of 6 would have an IQ of 75 ($\frac{6}{8}$ x 100). The Stanford-Binet tests from ages 2 through adulthood.

For what is David Wechsler known?

David Wechsler decided in the 1930s to develop a test that would place more emphasis on performance skills than was placed on these skills in Binet's test. Subtests of verbal skills such as vocabulary are scored separately from performance subtests such as picture completion and object assembly to yield a verbal IQ and a performance IQ. An overall IQ is derived by combining the scores from all the subtests such as vocabulary, picture completion, and object assembly. Wechsler developed three different tests—the Wechsler Preschool and Primary Scale of Intelligence (WPPSI), the Wechsler Intelligence Scale for Children (WISC), and the Wechsler Adult Intelligence Scale (WAIS). The latest revision of the WISC and WAIS was in 1981, and these scales are labeled the WISC-R and WAIS-R (see Figure 8–12). The Wechsler tests test from ages 5 through adulthood.

Figure 8–12.
A WISC-R Test Kit.

Types of Tests. The Stanford-Binet and Wechsler tests are the most widely used, individually administered tests of intelligence. These tests are expensive and time consuming to use because they are given to only one person at a time by a trained professional and require an average of about an hour for administration and another hour or so for preparation of the test results. Tests have now been developed to assess the intelligence of individuals in large groups simultaneously and to assess a variety of specific aptitudes and abilities. Paper-pencil intelligence tests that can be administered to large groups by nonprofessional testers were first developed for use during World War I—the Army Alpha test for literates and the Army Beta test for illiterates. Today, group tests are widely used (see Figure 8–13), and a proliferation of group tests are available for use.

Do some intelligence tests give an advantage to some individuals over others?

A criticism of many intelligence tests is that they may give an advantage to some individuals over others. For example, the IQ yielded may not be a fair score for a person who has a physical handicap such as deafness, who is mentally retarded, who has a specific learning disability in language such as dyslexia, who is of a different culture than the culture for which the test was designed, or who is too young to understand directions. A number of performance or nonverbal tests have been developed for use to minimize this problem, such as the following: the *Seguin Form Board* to test the mentally retarded; the *Bayley Scales of Infant Development*; the *Porteus Maze,* which consists of mazes that become more and more difficult; the *Progressive Matrices,* which consists of 60 designs to choose a part for the missing part; and the *Goodenough-Harris Drawing Test,* which consists of drawing a picture of a person and is scored according to such things as body parts represented, detail, and proportions rather than by artistic standards.

Figure 8–13.
Group intelligence tests (paper-pencil type) are widely used currently.

Recently, intelligence tests have been developed that add information-processing assessment to the traditional assessments. These tests assess the steps that a person uses to solve problems and to make decisions as well as those traditional things such as memory, reasoning, numeric ability, and vocabulary. Presently, there is little practical use for these tests (Heatherington & Parke, 1986). Neurometric tests are another type of intelligence test. These tests are administered by a computer that records and analyzes the brain waves. The person sits with the computer for a few minutes and listens to music or watches television programs. The test can differentiate the learning disabled from normals and measure such functions as concept organization, attention, word recall, spatial relations, and short-term memory as well as identify epileptics, people with brain tumors, and those who have the potentiality of having a stroke (Goleman, 1976). Should neurometric testing prove to be as accurate and as useful in diagnosing specific functions of the brain as early experiments have indicated, intelligence testing may become very simple.

Test Evaluation

Several things such as cost, time involved in administration, who the test is to be administered to, and the use to be made of the results of the test should be considered in evaluating an intelligence test. Three additional factors—reliability, validity, and standardization—that should receive special attention are discussed in this section.

What is meant by the reliability of a test?

Reliability. The **reliability** of a test is related to the consistency or stability of the measures. A scale measuring intelligence is like a scale measuring weight. If your scales show your weight to be 190 pounds, you step off and then get back on and the weight is shown to be 160 pounds, you step off and then get back on again and the weight is shown to be 150 pounds, the scales are not very reliable. Intelligence, like weight, is considered to be a rather stable trait; therefore, the intelligence test should yield consistent IQ scores for an individual. The reliability of a test is usually determined by a correlational study and reported as a correlation coefficient. The correlation coefficient expresses the relationship between test-retest scores, alternate forms scores, or split-half scores whereby a score on half the items may be correlated with a score from the remaining half. The higher the correlation coefficient, the more reliable the test score. For example, short tests, which take only a few minutes to administer, yield a test-retest reliability of around .80 or above. Some longer tests such as the Stanford-Binet, WAIS, or Army Classification Test yield reliabilities as high as .97.

How is the reliability of a test determined?

What is meant by the validity of a test?

Validity. The **validity** of a test is the extent to which the test measures what it is designed to measure. For example, a valid intelligence test would measure intelligence, not weight or reaction time. A measuring device may measure consistently and be very reliable but not be a valid or true measure. For example, weight scales may show an individual's weight to be 170 pounds each time weighed, but the scales may be set 20 pounds too high, the true weight really being 150 pounds. The validity of an intelligence test, the extent to which it truly measures intelligence, may be determined by whether the test is based on a sound theory. Validity of an intelligence test may be determined also by how well it correlates with some other intelligence test that already is known to have a high degree of validity. For example, if a large group of people are given some newly developed IQ test as well as the Stanford-Binet and their scores correlate .95, the newly developed test is considered to have high validity. If their scores correlate .30, it is considered to have low validity.

How is the validity of a test determined?

Another way to assess the validity of an intelligence test is to determine how well it predicts whether a person does what intelligent people are described as being able to do that less intelligent people cannot do well. The IQ test may be administered to a group of people going into a learning situation or into a job for which intelligence is a primary factor in the mastering of the material or the job. If those who score higher on the IQ test also achieve a higher level of mastery and those who score lower on the IQ test also achieve proportionately lower mastery, the test is said to have predictive validity.

How do standardized tests differ from tests that are not standardized?

Standardization. A **standardized test** is one that has been given to a large and representative sample of people and the distribution of their scores has been determined. **Standardization** is the process of obtaining the population distribution of scores for a test. The scores provide the test **norms**—standard performance at various points in the population distribution. These norms are used for comparison in determining if an individual's score is average, above average, or below average or for determining the percentage of the population that scores below the individual's score. If a test is not standardized, an individual's score cannot be interpreted in relationship to a population. If the standardization group is too small or not representative of the population, the interpretation may not be very valid. IQ tests are designed to yield an approximately normal distribution with 100 being the average or mean of the distribution. The standard deviation for different tests may vary. Figure 8–14 shows the classifications and the distribution of IQ scores expected among a large sample of people.

When using IQ tests, what shortcomings should be kept in mind?

Shortcomings. When using tests to measure intelligence, it is important to keep in mind that only a sample of behavior believed to reflect intelligence is considered. Behavior in the test situation

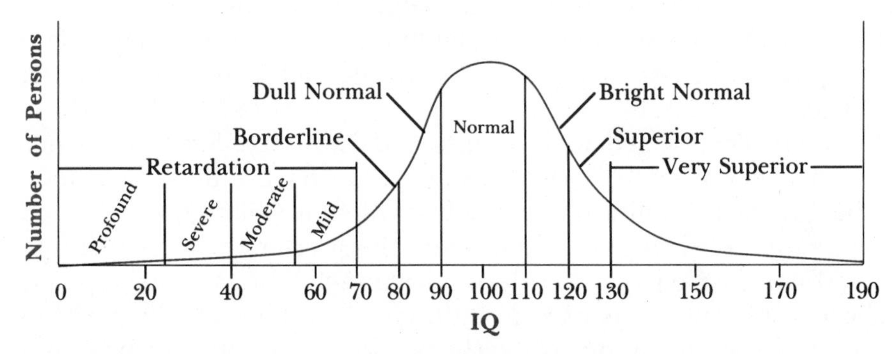

Note. Adapted from Fig. 5.1 of Matarazzo, J. D. *Wechsler's Measurement and Appraisal of Adult Intelligence 5th ed.* Copyright © 1937, 1941, 1944, 1958 by David Wechsler and © 1972 by the Williams and Wilkins Co. All rights reserved. Reproduced by permission.

Figure 8–14.
The classifications and the distribution of IQ scores expected among a large sample of people.

may be influenced by many factors other than factors of intelligence such as motivation and emotions of the person taking the test, the behavior and characteristics of the person administering the test, and environmental conditions such as noise level. Sometimes the test used may not be fair for an individual, may not be very reliable or valid, or may not have very good standardization as pointed out in the paragraphs on fair tests (page 271), reliability, validity, and standardization. Anyone using IQ test scores should consider that intelligence tests do not reflect aspects of intelligence such as creativity. The fact that IQ is a mathematical computation of mental age (as measured by one of these tests and compared with a norm group) divided by the chronologic age should also be considered. Some psychologists avoid the controversy in defining intelligence by defining it operationally as being what is measured on intelligence tests.

Figure 8–15. Personnel administrators often give IQ, achievement, aptitude, or ability tests to job applicants.

IQ Testing in the World of Work

Intelligence is a major characteristic that varies among people and often affects job performance. An employee's IQ may be a factor in the satisfaction derived from a job, in the length of time it takes to learn a job, in the amount of work produced, and in the performance of complicated tasks. The degree of intelligence of employees may make a difference in whether a firm has a profit or a loss. Therefore, psychological tests measuring intellectual abilities have been used extensively by personnel administrators to measure a job applicant's or an employee's IQ, achievement, aptitude, or ability in some area related to performance of a job (see Figure 8–15). A few of the aptitude and ability tests commonly used in business and industry are reviewed in this section. The relationship of IQ to satisfaction, success, and status in a job is also examined in this section.

What are some IQ tests frequently used in business and industry?

Some Tests Used in Business and Industry. Six intelligence tests frequently used in business and industry are described here. The Otis Self-Administering Tests of Mental Ability (World Book Company) consisting of 75 items and the shorter version consisting of 50 items called the Wonderlic Personnel Test are two popular, short intelligence tests used in industry. Test items involve vocabulary, sentence meaning, proverbs, analogies, number trends, and the like. The Thurstone Test of Mental Alertness (Science Research Associates) is a 20-minute assessment of intelligence based on quantitative and linguistic items. Trainability for industrial jobs may be assessed using the Adaptability Test (Science Research

Associates) for literates or the Purdue Non-Language Test, consisting of 48 geometric forms, for nonliterates. A longer, more reliable measure of intelligence is provided by the Civilian Edition of the Army Classification Test. This test contains 150 items and requires 40 minutes to take. Average IQ scores are available for 125 civilian occupations.

What are some multiple aptitude test batteries that are widely used in business and industry?

Dunnette (1976) lists the three multiple aptitude test batteries described below among the better known and more widely used ones for predicting work performance in organizational settings. The General Aptitude Test Battery (GATB) was developed by the United States Employment and Training Service for use in state employment offices. The factors currently measured by the GATB include numeric aptitude, verbal aptitude, spatial aptitude, form perception, clerical perception, motor coordination, finger dexterity, and manual dexterity.

The Differential Aptitude Tests (DAT) are used mostly for educational and vocational counseling of students in grades eight through twelve, but the DAT has come to be widely used in industry also. This battery of tests yields scores in verbal reasoning, numeric ability, abstract reasoning, clerical speed and accuracy, mechanical reasoning, space relations, spelling, and grammar.

Which test might be used to assess problem-solving ability?

The Employee Aptitude Survey (EAS) is a series of tests designed to measure problem-solving ability in a business environment. The EAS was developed primarily for use in industrial and organizational settings. The factors included might be regarded as basic components of intelligence: the ability to use words in thinking and communicating; the ability to handle numbers and work with numeric material; the ability to make rapid, accurate scanning movements with the eyes; the ability to perceive small detail rapidly and accurately within a mass of material; the ability to visualize objects in three-dimensional space; the ability to discover relationships and derive principles; the ability to produce words rapidly; and the ability to apply principles in order to arrive at a unique solution.

Is IQ a factor in whether a person finds a job satisfying and rewarding?

IQ and Job Satisfaction. Some people are very satisfied with their work and find their jobs so rewarding they look forward to going to work, seldom missing a day. Other people are not satisfied with their work and find their jobs unpleasant, boring, and frustrating, missing a day as often as they can. One factor in job satisfaction seems to be the degree of intelligence of the person performing the job in relation to the complexity of the job task. If a worker has too little intelligence or more than is required to perform the job, he or she may become dissatisfied. A high degree of intelligence may be an advantage in a complex job; but if a job is extremely simple, like stapling pages together all day, a low degree of intelligence might be an advantage. A person of low intelligence may be more satisfied and better able to perform some job functions than a person of high intelligence.

Figure 8–16. Formal schooling provides an opportunity for a person to become aware of individual strengths and weaknesses and make career choices that may enhance job satisfaction.

The upper limit of intelligence for a given occupation seems difficult to specify. A minimum or critical score is more easily established than an upper limit; however, the required intellectual ability of many occupations is not sharply defined by test scores. Sometimes there is a critical score below which workers are considered unsuitable for the job or a critical score above which workers tend to change jobs as soon as a promotion is available.

According to Guilford's and Gardner's views that a person has many different intelligences, job satisfaction may depend on whether a career choice matches abilities. If a person is constantly struggling to adjust to a job that is extremely difficult and if the person is constantly worried about failure, chances are the person is not very happy in the job. Working on a job that can be performed without a difficult struggle contributes to job satisfaction. Formal schooling provides an opportunity for a person to become aware of individual strengths and weaknesses and make career choices that may enhance job satisfaction (see Figure 8–16). For example, if mathematics is very difficult for a person, the idea of being an engineer, accountant, or mathematician might be abandoned. Or if a person has great difficulty in English courses, a career as an author might be dismissed.

Are IQ scores very good predictors of success in an occupation?

For what types of jobs may IQ scores have uses in predicting job success?

IQ as a Predictor of Success. IQ scores seem to be better predictors of academic achievement than of occupational success. Of course, IQ tests were originally developed to predict academic success, not success in an occupation. Intelligence tests are most likely to correlate with job success and prove to be a valid predictor of success in a given job that calls for verbal, numeric, and/or spatial aptitude or that requires skill learning to perform the job. Over the years, however, intelligence tests have tended to predict successful training for individuals in a variety of types of skilled work such as electrical workers, structural workers, process workers, machine operators, machinery workers, computing clerks, general clerks, and recording clerks. Intelligence tests have not been very valid predictors of success, however, for such manipulative and observational occupations as machine tenders, bench assembly workers, inspectors, packers, wrappers, and manual workers. Dexterity tests and perceptual tests have been better predictors of success in these areas (Ghiselli, 1966). The fact that more specialized achievement tests than IQ tests are given to adults for licensing for specific professions and entrance to higher education programs is evidence that IQ scores are not the best predictors of success in some occupations.

The basic task in personnel selection facing psychologists is devising effective procedures for choosing the applicants most likely to succeed in a given job. The following procedure does work; however, it is costly in terms of time, depends on large samples, and assumes that over the years both the jobs and the people who fill them will remain very much the same. The first step of the procedure is the job analysis in which the specific behaviors required for the performance of the job are determined. Following the job analysis, the traits and characteristics of persons believed most likely to succeed are described. The next task is to select employees and measure the variables (traits) believed to affect success. After a sufficient period of time, the performance of each selected employee is evaluated. The performance measures are then correlated with the measures of traits believed to affect performance. In this way, the strength of the relationship may be determined. The stronger the correlation, the more accurately success on the job can be predicted from the measured trait. Even if the relationship is strong, however, the initial findings should be **cross-validated,** which means the procedure should be repeated with another sample of applicants to see if the same results occur again. This is more likely to insure that the results have not been a chance or random occurrence. The final step then is to formulate specific recommendations regarding the selection of future personnel for the particular job. Although IQ scores have uses in predicting job success, it must be kept in mind that IQ scores do not explain all that is good and valuable about a person in relationship to job success.

What is the basic task in personnel selection facing psychologists?

What are the steps in the procedure for choosing applicants who are likely to succeed in a given job?

What is meant by saying the correlation of a performance measure and a measure of a trait such as IQ is cross-validated?

IQ and Occupational Status. People in occupations carrying high prestige such as lawyer, physician, or scientist tend to have higher IQ scores, whereas people in occupations of lower prestige tend to have lower IQ scores. In the normal range of IQ scores, 90 to 110 (see Figure 8–14), there is a relationship between IQ scores and status or prestige in society based on occupation, but this not a strong relationship. For example, on the average, teachers have higher IQ scores than auto mechanics and auto mechanics higher IQ scores than miners, but some miners have higher IQ scores than the average for teachers (see Figure 8–17). A correlation of

.50 has been estimated to exist between adult IQ scores and occupational status. Within an occupational group, IQ does not seem to relate to success (Jencks, Smith, Acland, Bane, Cohen, Gintis, Heyns, & Michelson, 1972). For example, attorneys or physicians who are considered more successful than other attorneys or physicians do not have significantly higher IQ scores. Income, often used as a criterion of success and status, is not very predictable from IQ scores.

Is the mean IQ score for males different from the mean IQ score for females?

Although there is no difference in the mean IQ scores of males and females, the proportion of women holding jobs in occupations of higher status is smaller than for men even though in recent years the proportion of women has been increasing. For example, surveys in the 1970s indicated that 97.8 percent of all practicing dentists were men (Coombs, 1975), and 99 percent of the dental assistants were women according to a personal communication from the Executive Director of the American Dental Assistants Association (Fernald & Fernald, 1978). It has been noted (Fernald & Fernald, 1978) that these distributions were apparently not based on differences in ability because women with intelligence compara-

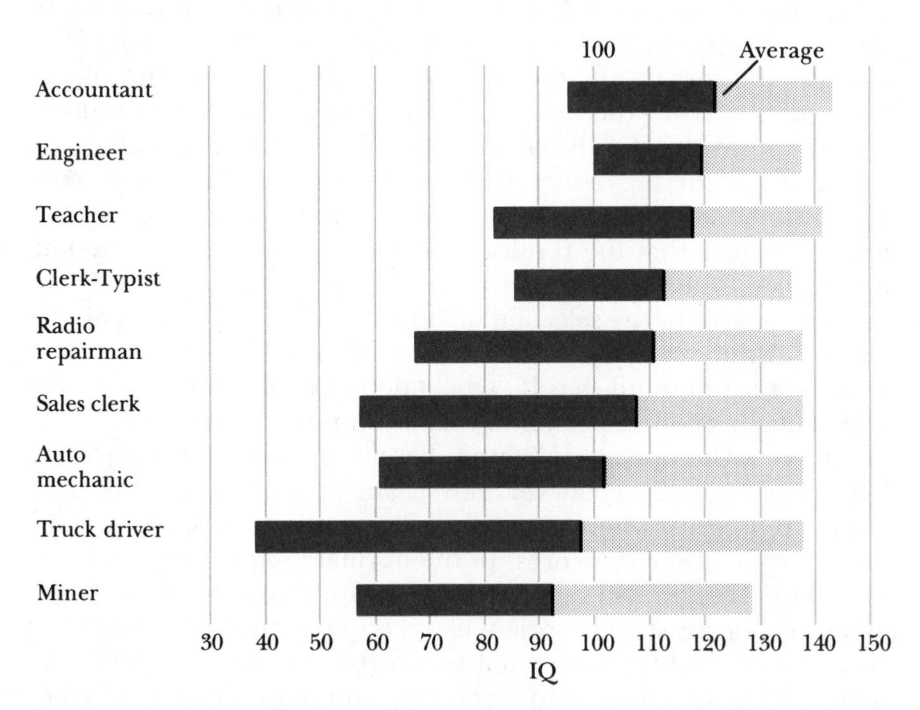

Figure 8–17.
Occupation and IQ.

Note. From *Psychology: The Study of Human Experience,* Copyright © 1985 by Robert E. Ornstein and the Institute for the Study of Human Knowledge. Reprinted by permission of Harcourt Brace Jovanovich, Inc.

ble to male dentists generally have more nimble fingers and show greater interest in cosmetics than male dentists. Thus, it would be expected that a greater number of females than males would perform in the dentist's role. Similar findings exist for some other highly prestigious occupations.

CREATIVITY

Do IQ tests assess creativity?

Although intelligence is a component of creativity, people with high IQ scores may be more or less creative than others. This suggests that intelligence is only a part of creativity. Because creative people tend to concentrate more on their work than on social approval, a high level of curiosity and motivation seem to be other components of creativity. And IQ tests, such as those discussed earlier in this chapter that have items with one clear-cut, generally accepted answer, assess intelligence that is different from the kind of intelligence required for creativity. In this section, the concept and expression of creativity are discussed.

The Concept of Creativity

Creativity appears to involve a thought process that is different from searching for knowledge to converge on one correct answer. Definitions of creativity have been offered, tests have been developed to assess creativity, and the stages in the creative process have been identified. An attempt is made here to clarify the concept of creativity through a discussion of these aspects of creativity.

Definition. Creativity appears to be a mix of several abilities and traits (Perkins, 1981); therefore, it is difficult to define. Creativity may be thought of as the ability to produce original and worthwhile solutions to problems—to respond uniquely and appropriately to problems that are large, medium, or small. Creativity may arise in solving problems in daily life, both on and off the job, as well as in trying to solve artistic or scientific problems.

What are the criteria of creativity?

Jackson and Messick (1968) defined creativity as consisting of four criteria: novelty, appropriateness, transcendence of constraints, and coalescence of meaning. An idea is novel if it is new or original, but to be a creative idea it must also be appropriate. For example, building the door in a room to go outside 3 feet up from the floor would be novel but not appropriate. An idea that transcends constraints goes beyond the traditional way of perceiving something familiar and gives a new perspective. For example, the person who first thought of accordionlike folding doors instead of the traditional hinged doors that swing open was able to transcend constraints. An idea that coalesces over time is an idea whose value becomes more obvious as time passes. Accordionlike doors continue to be used more and more. Piaget's view of intelligence proposed in the late 1920s, for example, was a creative idea; it was original, appropriate, and a nontraditional way of perceiving intelligence, and its value as a theory was not fully significant until recent years.

What additional type of thinking seems to be required for a person to be creative?

Divergent Thinking. Some research indicates that creativity requires divergent thinking (Guilford & Hoepfner, 1971), which was defined in chapter 7 as the type of thinking in which a person uses imagination to combine knowledge and experience in new ways to bring forth original answers or solutions. In divergent thinking, many possible combinations of existing elements may be generated to construct new answers.

Divergent thinking is unique in that it diverges from customary thought patterns. Creative thinking involves all styles of thought in varying combinations—logical, illogical (intuitive), inductive (going from specific facts to general principles), and deductive (going from general principles to specific situations). In addition, it includes fluency, flexibility, and originality. **Fluency** refers to the number of ideas or suggestions generated. **Flexibility** refers to the number of shifts from type or category of ideas or suggestions. For example, in generating ideas for uses of cardboard boxes, one category might be uses in play activities and another category might be household uses. **Originality** refers to the novelty or unusualness of the idea. For example, if 95 percent of the people who generate ideas for uses of cardboard boxes think of using them for making dollhouse furniture, even though they have never heard of using them for this, the idea is not rated as very original. If only 3 percent think of using them for this purpose, the idea is rated as highly original. Divergent thinking is the most widely used measure of creativity.

What is meant by fluency, flexibility, and originality?

What types of tests are used to measure a person's level of creativity?

Tests of Creativity. Tests of creativity are designed to determine how flexible, fluent, and original the person's thinking can be. Several tests have been developed to measure divergent thinking or creativity. One type of test requires the person taking the test to think of as many uses for an object as possible in a specified time. Another type of test requires the person taking the test to think of as many reactions as possible to some absurd question such as, What would be the results if people did not have to eat to live? or What would be the results if everyone in the world suddenly lost his or her ability to hear? Another type of test provides a word containing several letters of the alphabet, and subjects are asked to make as many words as possible by rearranging the letters. Another type of test presents simple drawings consisting of two or three lines and/or curves and instructs the subject to complete the drawing and make something meaningful from it (see Figure 8–18).

The Drawing-Completion Test of Creativity

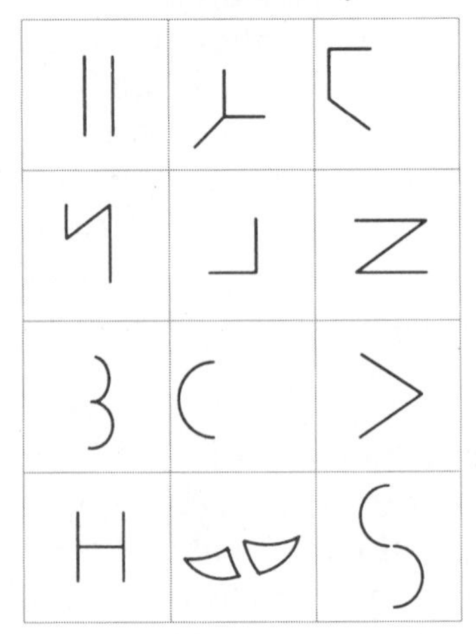

Average Person's Responses

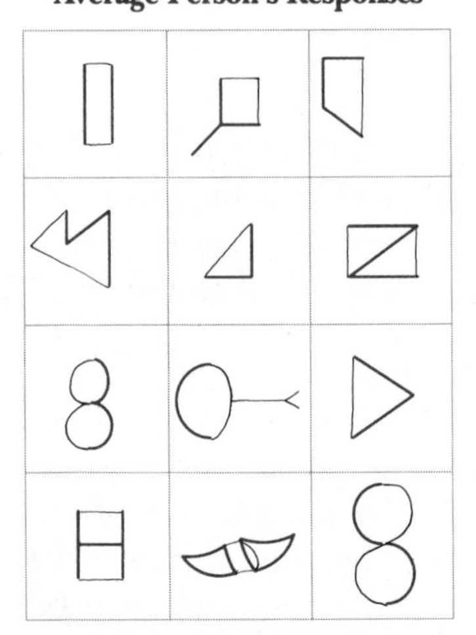

Creative Responses

Figure 8–18.
One type of creativity test and sample responses indicative of creativity versus noncreativity.

Note. From *Psychology: It's Principles and Meanings* by Lyle E. Bourne, Jr. and Bruce R. Ekstrand. Copyright © 1985 by CBS College Publishing. Reprinted by permission of Holt, Rinehart & Winston.

People may be high in both IQ and creativity, low in both IQ and creativity, high in IQ and low in creativity, or low in IQ and high in creativity. Research has shown that as a whole, people with higher intelligence measures tend to have higher measures of creativity, and people with lower measures of intelligence tend to have lower measures of creativity. However, this trend is not true at the upper end of the distribution of intelligence. Persons who have high measures of intelligence do not necessarily have high measures of creativity (Crockenberg, 1972), and often people who have only moderate measures of intelligence are highly creative.

How many stages appear as a common pattern in creativity?

Stages in the Creative Process. A sequence of stages appears as a common pattern in the process of generating a unique and appropriate solution to a problem. The first stage is preparation, during which time a person acquires all possible information that might relate to a problem. The second stage, called **incubation,** consists of the time during which the information that has been acquired is absorbed and assimilated. This stage appears to be inactive and unproductive; no conscious attention is given to the problem. But undoubtedly there is a lot of unconscious mental activity. Suddenly and unexpectedly a person may have insight into the problem, resulting in the conception of an idea that seems to be a solution. This stage is referred to as **illumination.** A final and very important stage is the verification of the idea by mentally or experimentally trying it out. Sometimes people get so excited during the illumination stage that they act immediately without going through the final stage of verifying the appropriateness of the idea.

What is meant by incubation and illumination in creativity?

Expression of Creativity

Whether the ability to be creative and engage in divergent thinking is innate or learned has been a question considered by psychologists and will be discussed in this section. Also, the expression of creativity in the workplace in terms of characteristics of the individual and of the organization is addressed.

Can creativity be learned?

Determinants of Creativity. Creativity at one time was considered by most people to be a kind of giftedness—an innate or inborn trait. Research has shown that environmental conditions may have an effect on creativity; however, much of what is known about creativity is based on preliminary research. It appears that at least some of the skills of divergent thinking are learned and can be taught or enhanced. Everyone has some creative thinking ability; it is a matter of degree, and some people have the ability to a higher degree than some other people.

Verbal and sequential skills of the left hemisphere of the brain are associated with convergent thinking, and the skills of the right hemisphere are associated with divergent thought. Eran Zaidel (1976) believes that up until approximately the time a child begins school or kindergarten, the two hemispheres of the brain are about equal in their abilities. The left hemisphere then seems to become more dominant in logic and reason with the development of language ability in that hemisphere. The right hemisphere then seems to take on creative and nonlogical abilities. During creative or divergent thinking, a person's right hemisphere seems to override the left hemisphere to become more dominant, and a person's thoughts seem to leave the world of logic and reason (Martindale, 1978).

Which half of the brain is associated with divergent thinking and thus creativity?

Carl Rogers (1961) described three conditions within the person and three conditions in the person's environment that tend to foster creativity. Holland (1981) summarized these conditions described by Rogers as follows:

What personality traits or conditions within a person foster creativity?

> The inner conditions fostering creativity are openness to experience, internal standards, and the ability to "toy" with ideas. A person who is open to experience is sensitive to things as they really are and does not jump to conclusions until all evidence is in. A person with internal standards strives to satisfy personal goals and expectations rather than someone else's. A person with internal standards decides what is good or bad on the basis of an internal standard of evaluation rather than on the basis of external standards established by others. A person with the ability to "toy" with ideas enjoys exploring new combinations of concepts and can see problems in fresh ways.
>
> The outer conditions fostering creativity are unconditional acceptance, absence of external evaluation, and empathetic understanding. Unconditional acceptance fosters creativity; people who are valued by those around them and accepted without reservations are more likely to be creative. The absence of external evaluation fosters creativity by permitting people to develop their own internal standards. Empathetic understanding fosters creativity; when people are truly understood by those around them, they are encouraged to be fully themselves. These conditions together provide the optimum climate for creativity. (p. 373)

What environmental or outer conditions foster creativity?

Creativity in the Workplace. Technically, an individual behaves creatively rather than being creative, and creativity is situational. A person may behave creatively in one situation as in the field of management and not in another situation as in the field of music. Overcontrol tends to inhibit the expression of creativity;

Do people behave more creatively in some situations than in other situations, or are people consistently creative or noncreative?

How do managers often inhibit creativity in the workplace?

thus, overcontrol in business and industry reduces creative behavior on the job. Often managers set up rigid systems, unvarying job procedures, and other means of control to the extent that employees are not encouraged to be creative; conformity rather than nonconformity is promoted. A person can be creative, however, without being a deliberate nonconformist.

What are some general characteristics of creative individuals?

Several general qualities have been cited by Meeker (1978) as characteristics of individuals who exhibit creative behavior. They are flexible; persistent at tasks of interest; impatient with routine or repetitive tasks; willing to take risks; imaginative; keenly aware of problems, people, and events; highly active and energetic; and high in verbal fluency. In addition, they exhibit a sense of humor; an unusual ability to synthesize, abstract, and organize; and an ability to come up with original ideas and expressions.

Psychologically unhealthy people are not as creative as well-adjusted, psychologically healthy people. If a person is preoccupied with anxieties, fear of punishment, fear of rejection (has constant concern with the impression being made on others or with other's opinions), or fear of criticism (has feelings of insecurity), creativity will be inhibited.

Some organizations function in such a manner as to foster creative behavior within the organization and are thus labeled creative organizations. DuBrin (1980) has listed some characteristics of creative organizations:

What are some characteristics of creative organizations?

1. A trustful management that does not overcontrol people.
2. Open channels of communication among members of the organization; a minimum of secrecy.
3. Considerable contact and communication between outsiders and the organization.
4. Large variety of personality types.
5. Willing to accept change, but not enamored with change for its own sake.
6. Enjoyment in experimenting with new ideas.
7. Little fear of the consequences of making a mistake.
8. Selects people and promotes them primarily on the basis of merit.
9. Uses techniques for encouraging ideas, such as suggestion systems and brainstorming.
10. Sufficient financial, managerial, human, and time resources to accomplish its goals.

SUMMARY

1. Intelligence has been defined as the ability to adapt, to solve problems, to learn, to understand and cope, to make appropriate responses, and to perceive.
2. Achievement is what a person has learned, whereas ability is a current capability to learn. Aptitude is thought of as an inborn capacity to learn.
3. In 1904, Spearman proposed that intelligence consists of a single, general ability. In 1938, Thurstone proposed that intelligence consists of a group of seven primary abilities. Later, Guilford proposed that there is no general intelligence, rather 120 distinguishable factors resulting from three dimensions of intelligence—operations, contents, and products.
4. More recent theorists have proposed that there are two components of intelligence—fluid (genetically determined) and crystallized (learned) (Cattell); that information processing, particularly encoding, is related to intelligence (Sternberg); and that intelligence is very broad, consisting of eight distinctly different intelligences (Gardner).
5. Research indicates that both environmental experience and heredity account for a person's intelligence. Heredity sets limits, and experience determines whether those limits are reached. Reaction range is the possible range of values allowed by a person's genetics.
6. Galton set forth the idea that mental capacities can be measured; then Binet developed the first measure of intelligence and the concept of mental age, which initiated the development of many different measures of intelligence and specific aptitudes, abilities, and achievements.
7. At Stanford University, Terman revised Binet's test and added the concept of Intelligence Quotient (IQ), which is a ratio of the mental age to the chronologic age multiplied by 100. Wechsler developed a similar test for children (WISC) and for adults (WAIS).
8. Group tests have been developed that can be administered to large numbers of individuals simultaneously by nonprofessional testers (paper-pencil tests). In addition, tests have been developed to provide a fair measure of IQ for individuals of a different culture than the culture for which the test was designed or for individuals with some handicap.
9. Test reliability (how consistently the test measures), validity (whether the test measures what it was designed to measure), and standardization (norms provided for interpreting a score) should be considered when attempting to measure intelligence.
10. Measures of intelligence do have some shortcomings in that they reflect only a sample of behavior, do not reflect all aspects of intelligence, and in some instances may not be fair for some individuals.

11. IQ tests, aptitude tests, ability tests, and achievement tests are frequently used in business and industry to assess characteristics of job applicants and employees.
12. Job satisfaction may be influenced by whether the employee has too little or too much intelligence for what is required for a given job and by whether the employee's specific abilities match the abilities required for a job.
13. IQ tends to predict success in a variety of skilled types of work that require learning and call for verbal, numeric, or spatial aptitude; but IQ has not been a very valid predictor of success in manipulative and observational types of occupations.
14. A procedure for choosing employees most likely to succeed in a given job involves doing a job analysis, describing characteristics hypothesized for success, measuring these characteristics, evaluating performance on the job, correlating the characteristics and performance measures, cross-validating, and using the highly correlated characteristics as characteristics for selection of future employees.
15. Occupations of higher status are associated with people who have higher IQ scores; however, status or success within an occupational group does not seem to be related to IQ. Income, which is most often used as a criterion of status or success, is not very predictive from IQ.
16. Creativity, the ability to produce original and appropriate responses, seems to require divergent thinking and to progress through a sequence of stages: preparation, incubation, illumination, and verification.
17. Creativity varies from low to high in people; however, most measures of intelligence call for convergent thinking and not for divergent thinking. Tests to measure creativity and divergent thinking have been developed.
18. The right hemisphere of the brain has been associated with creative thinking; however, research has shown that the environmental conditions of openness to experience, internal standards, ability to try out ideas, unconditional acceptance, absence of external evaluation, and empathetic understanding enhance the expression of creativity.
19. Overcontrol and poor psychological health inhibit creativity. Both individuals and organizations considered to be creative seem to have certain characteristics.

KEY TERMS AND CONCEPTS

Achievement
Aptitude
Ability
Fluid intelligence
Crystallized intelligence
Idiot savants
Heritability
Reaction range
Intelligence Quotient (IQ)
Reliability

Validity	Norms	Flexibility
Standardized test	Cross-validated	Originality
Standardization	Fluency	Incubation
		Illumination

QUESTIONS FOR REVIEW

1. What is intelligence, and what is the difference between aptitude, ability, and achievement?
2. How do the following theories of intelligence differ: Spearman's *g* factor, Thurstone's primary mental abilities, Guilford's structure of the intellect, Cattell's fluid and crystallized intelligence, Sternberg's information processing, and Gardner's multiple intelligences?
3. What is the research evidence for heredity and for environmental experience as determinants of intelligence?
4. Who were the early contributors to intelligence testing, and what were their contributions?
5. What three aspects of an intelligence test should be considered in evaluating its usefulness? Describe the aspects and identify shortcomings of intelligence tests.
6. Give the names and a brief description of the best known intelligence, aptitude, and ability tests used in business and industry.
7. How do IQ scores relate to job satisfaction, success, and occupational status?
8. How can psychologists use measurement of a trait or traits to choose applicants most likely to succeed in a given job?
9. What is creativity, how is it measured, and what are the stages in the creative process?
10. What are some internal conditions of the individual, external environmental conditions, and characteristics of the workplace that seem to enhance the development of creativity?

TEST YOURSELF

1. Intelligence is defined in terms of the responses available to an individual by ________________.
2. ________________ defined intelligence as the ability to adapt to the environment and to new situations and theorized that intellectual development occurs through a sequence of stages.
3. Achievement is the (a) same as intelligence (b) innate or natural capacity for performing or learning to perform some task (c) knowledge of a specific body of material including skills that a person has acquired through experience (d) current capability to learn that is based on both aptitude and experience.

4. J. P. Guilford proposed that intelligence is composed of ________________ factor(s), each representing a unique intellectual ability, rather than being composed of ________________ factor(s) as proposed by Thurstone or ________________ factor(s) as proposed by Spearman.
5. Idiot savants, people who have an incredible, specific capacity such as the ability to draw, remember music, or compute numbers but who are otherwise retarded, are one source of support for the theory of multiple intelligences. T or F
6. The importance of heredity on the development of intelligence was demonstrated by (a) Skeel's research with children in an orphanage in Iowa (b) research with identical twins (c) Scarr and Weinberg's research with children who were adopted and raised by families in a more affluent atmosphere than the one in which they were born (d) all of the above.
7. The fact that the correlation of IQ scores for identical twins is about ________________ compared with about ________________ for siblings and ________________ for two groups of unrelated persons is support for heredity as the primary determiner of intelligence.
8. Heredity seems to set limits on intelligence, and environmental experience seems to determine whether a person reaches that potential. T or F
9. IQ is the ________________ age divided by the ________________ age multiplied by ________________.
10. The first test designed to measure intelligence was the (a) Wechsler Intelligence Scale for Children (WISC) (b) Wechsler Adult Intelligence Scale (WAIS) (c) Binet, later known as the Standford-Binet (d) Otis Self-Administering Tests of Mental Ability.
11. The Wechsler Scales—WPPSI, WISC, and WAIS—are examples of tests designed to yield a fair score for a person who is of a different culture, deaf, or has dyslexia. T or F
12. The reliability of a test refers to how consistent or stable the measures derived from the test are. T or F
13. Which of the following is a series of tests designed to measure problem-solving ability in a business environment? (a) Employee Aptitude Survey (EAS) (b) Differential Aptitude Tests (DAT) (c) General Aptitude Test Battery (GATB) (c) Wonderlic Personnel Test
14. The degree of intelligence of a person in relation to the complexity of the task is not considered to be a factor in job satisfaction. T or F
15. IQ tests have been better predictors of success in such manipulative and observational occupations as machine tender, bench assembly worker, inspector, wrapper, and manual worker than dexterity tests. T or F
16. The first step of an effective procedure for choosing applicants most likely to succeed in a job is the (a) description of the traits and charac-

teristics of a person believed most likely to succeed (b) job analysis (c) cross-validation (d) measurement of the traits and characteristics believed to affect success.

17. When a performance measure is found to be strongly correlated with the measure of a factor believed to affect performance in a sample of workers and the procedure is repeated with another sample of workers also yielding a strong correlation, the initial findings are said to be (a) invalid (2) valid (c) cross-validated (d) standardized.
18. Income, often used as a criterion of success, is related to IQ. T or F
19. Research has shown that the ability to be creative and engage in divergent thinking is (a) innate or inherited, and environmental conditions can have little effect on it (b) at least partially learned, and particular conditions in the person's environment have an effect on it (c) related to the development of the left hemisphere of the brain (d) enhanced by the presence of external evaluation and rejection by society.
20. Empathetic understanding, unconditional acceptance, and absence of external evaluation provide an optimum climate for creativity. T or F

APPLICATIONS

A. In one family, there are four children—a set of identical twin girls 12 years of age, a male adopted child 14 years old, and a 10-year-old boy. The mother and father are well educated and have always spent a lot of time interacting with their children through play, conversation, love, and attention. The adopted child was born to parents with little formal education and who could have provided only an impoverished environment for him. He was only 4 months old at the time of adoption.

1. Which two children's IQ scores would you expect to be most similar? Why?
2. Do you think the adopted boy has a higher IQ than he would have had if he had not been adopted by this family? Why?
3. Do you think the 10-year-old boy's IQ score is likely to be more similar to one of the twin girl's IQ score or to the adopted boy's IQ score? Why?

B. The manager of Corporation A believes that most people must have detailed direction, be closely observed, and be threatened with punishment for failure to follow exact directives in order to be most efficient and productive on the job. Furthermore, it is the philosophy of the manager that employees prefer to be given detailed directives for functioning in their job and that few individuals have the capacity to be creative in solving problems.

The manager of Corporation B has some very different attitudes about workers. The Corporation B manager believes that if employees are given certain responsibilities or objectives to which they are committed, they will exercise self-direction and self-control and be even more efficient and productive on the job. Corporation B manager further believes that most employees have the capacity to exercise divergent thinking if encouraged to do so and can offer new ideas that may be profitable to the corporation.

1. Under which manager's leadership do you think the corporation will be more likely to be a creative organization? Why?
2. The employees' thinking likely will involve the right hemisphere of the brain more in which corporation?
3. Which employees (identify by personality traits) are likely to function better under the Corporation B manager?

SUGGESTIONS FOR FURTHER READING

Anastasi, A. (1982). *Psychological testing* (5th ed.). New York: MacMillan.

A very thorough text covering the general aspects of testing. This book discusses tests of intelligence, achievement, aptitude, and personality and the limits and extent of proper testing.

Buros, O. K. (Ed.) (1985). *The ninth mental measurements yearbook.* Highland Park, NJ: The Gryphon Press.

A yearbook containing descriptive lists of published tests in various areas including costs, publishers, and critical reviews.

Cronbach, L. J. (1984). *Essentials of psychological testing* (4th ed.). New York: Harper & Row.

A comprehensive coverage of the subject of psychological tests. Construction, reliability, validity, and types of tests are reviewed. Many sample test items are presented.

Gardner, H. (1983). *Frames of mind: The theory of multiple intelligences.* New York: Basic Books.

A view of intelligence that argues that people have eight different intelligences based on research in cognitive and physiological psychology. The mobilization of these intelligences for optimum benefit to a person and to society is also discussed.

Glaser, R., & Bond, L. (Eds.). (1981). Testing: Concepts, policy, practice, and research (Special issue). *American Psychologist, 36* (10).

The entire issue is devoted to testing and contains articles concerned with the use, misuse, history, and law regarding mental measurement. Also, the controversies over mental ability testing are summarized.

Loehlin, J. C., Lindzey, G., & Spuhler, J. N. (1975). *Race differences in intelligence.* San Francisco: W. H. Freeman.

A very thorough but sometimes rather technical review of the research regarding racial differences in IQ. This book gives an objective, balanced view of the issue.

Perkins, D. N. (1981). *The mind's best work.* Cambridge: Harvard University Press.

A book about creativity that maintains that everyone can think creatively and that it is a normal mental process.

Whimbey, A., & Whimbey, L. S. (1975). *Intelligence can be taught.* New York: Dutton.

Suggestions for increasing intelligence test scores are given, and the argument is made that many of the abstract skills that intelligence tests measure can be improved with training.

PART THREE

INDIVIDUALITY OF BEHAVIOR

CHAPTER 9

MOTIVATION

Objectives

When you have completed your study of chapter 9, you should be able to:

1. Define motivation.
2. Name and describe early philosophical views of the source or cause of human behavior.
3. Describe the current theoretical views of motivation.
4. Identify and describe primary and secondary motives.
5. Explain the concepts of unconscious and intrinsic motivation.
6. Describe the various techniques used to assess motivation.
7. Give the details of Maslow's hierarchy of needs theory.
8. Explain the basics of the VIE theory.
9. Name and describe other theories of motivation that may be used as tools for understanding everyday work performances of people.
10. Discuss motivation in relationship to marketing; the organizational problems of job satisfaction, absenteeism, and turnover; and organizational strategies.

Figure 9–1.
Why does an individual work? Why does an individual engage in a particular type of work?

Why do people behave as they do? Human behavior poses a basic question for psychology, and the answer to why a person behaves in a particular way has important applications in the world of work (see Figure 9–1). Why does an individual work or engage in a particular type of work? Why is one worker consistently absent and another rarely absent? Why does one have a high production rate and another a low production rate? Why is one dishonest and another honest? Why does one eat lunch and another skip lunch? Why does one join a union and another doesn't? Why does one pursue further education and another doesn't? Why does one resign to take a different job and another doesn't? Why does the same person behave differently at different times when in the same situation? The concept of motivation provides a partial explanation for this variability of behavior. This chapter is devoted to clarifying this concept and applying it in the world of work.

THE CONCEPT OF MOTIVATION

Why are involuntary behaviors easier to explain than voluntary behaviors?

Reflex (involuntary) behaviors do not require very elaborate explanations because a particular condition or stimulus moves a person to the action. For example, the eye will blink when a puff of air is directed to the eye, or a person will withdraw his or her hand if it touches a hot object. Most behaviors are not reflexive, however, and are explained indirectly as being the result of learning, thinking, or the physiological structure of the individual. If an internal cause of these behaviors could be located, a direct explanation could be made as in the explanation of reflex behaviors. Theoretical views of internal causes, such as the needs of people and the assessment of these needs, are discussed in this section.

Views

In defining motivation, what two characteristics are generally agreed on by psychologists?

Motivation is sometimes difficult to define because it must be inferred and cannot be observed directly. Psychologists generally agree on two characteristics and define **motivation** as the force that activates or causes behavior to occur and gives direction to behavior. Motivation is the internal source, cause, or explanation of voluntary behaviors—the forces and processes that initiate, maintain, direct, and influence the strength of a behavior. **Motives** are the specific needs, desires, and wants that motivate. The word *motive* comes from the Latin "movere," which means "to move or to activate." Literally a motive is whatever moves a person to action. Different views or theories exist about what activates and gives direction to behavior. In this section, philosophical origins of modern approaches to motivation and theories of motivation are discussed.

What is the literal meaning of motive, and what is the Latin word from which it came?

Philosophical Origins. From the earliest times, humans have attempted to explain their behavior by assigning it a source or cause. The topic was of great concern to early philosophers. Their speculations are significant because they laid the foundation for basic assumptions about human behavior and influenced modern theories of motivation.

Why are early philosophical views of human behavior significant?

Two basic philosophical assumptions exist about behavior. **Free will** is the assumption that humans freely choose their own behavior—that humans have control of their own destiny. The assumption of **determinism** proposes that every event, act, or decision is the consequence of prior physical, psychological, or environmental events that are independent of the human will. The humanistic approach to psychology assumes that individuals are free. Behaviorism and the more rigorous scientific approaches to psychology assume that an individual's behavior is caused or determined. When behavior is not predictable, such scientists assume that it is only because of a lack of knowledge. The dilemma is that humans want to believe that they have free will, but they desire predictability in dealing with others. The issue still is not settled.

What are the two opposing, basic, philosophical assumptions about human behavior?

Some early philosophical ideas that gave rise to the assumptions of free will and determinism and made a distinct imprint on the concept of motivation are rationalism, mechanism, hedonism, and dualism. **Rationalism** attributes a person's behavior to thought—conscious intention and reasoning, but rationalism cannot explain why a person reasons a particular way and chooses a particular behavior. Rationalism has both critics and supporters in psychology. The psychoanalytic viewpoint, for example, emphasizes the unconscious influences on people's thinking and behavior and downgrades rationality. Behaviorists do not believe there is an innate rational force in humans but that people may learn to think rationally (or irrationally) if trained and rewarded for doing so. The humanistic psychologist Carl Rogers has drawn the conclusion from his extensive study of humans in psychotherapy that the innermost core of human nature is rational.

What is the philosophy of rationalism?

René Descartes is considered to have been the father of the philosophy of mechanism. **Mechanism** attributes all natural events, including human behavior, to physical causes. This philosophy holds that the functioning of humans obeys laws of mechanics, and if the laws are known, behavior can be predicted. Behavior is viewed as being determined by forces beyond human control rather than as being chosen freely based on a conscious decision. The ancient idea of **hedonism** is an example of mechanistic philosophy because it attributed human behavior to pain and pleasure—people act to avoid pain and to seek pleasure.

What is the philosophy of mechanism?

What is the philosophy of hedonism?

The philosophy of **dualism** holds that human behavior is controlled by complex interactions of both the mind and the body, either of which may initiate behavior. Dualists assume that the mind guides behavior to satisfy bodily needs. God is the source of behavior, and behavior is instinctive; that is, humans have an inherited predisposition to behave in a particular way. In the late 1800s, instincts were viewed as the force that compels behavior. Darwin's theory of evolution represents an instinctive view of behavior. For example, people are compelled to gather in groups because of the "herd instinct" or to fight because of the "aggressive instinct." In 1932, E. C. Tolman (see Figure 9–2) put the idea of instincts into behavioral language when he defined instinct as wants or desires that are aroused by certain physiological conditions caused by some biological distress. A behavior must have a fixed outcome, but the behavior itself may vary. For example, the fixed outcome may be food intake, but the manner in which food intake occurs may vary. Thus, instinct came to be viewed as

What assumptions are made in the philosophy of dualism?

Figure 9–2.
E. C. Tolman.

changeable rather than mechanical in nature. As a result, behavior came to be viewed as a striving toward a biological goal. If the striving is hindered by an obstacle, it merely intensifies until the goal is finally achieved. Today, the term *drive* has replaced this view of instinct. Currently, **instinct** is used to designate unlearned, goal-directed behavior patterns that are universally unique to a particular species and are elicited by a particular environmental stimulus the first time the stimulus is presented. An example is nest building in birds. Birds have no previous knowledge of building nests and are not conditioned to build nests but do so instinctively. Instincts are found primarily in animals other than humans. Human behavior is usually either reflexive or learned.

Theories of Motivation. Researchers continue to try to explain human behavior, and a number of different theories exist today. Drive, incentives, needs, arousal, reinforcement, expectancy, and homeostasis are each theorized to be motivation—a source of human behavior.

"I'm hungry. I'm going to make myself a sandwich."

"I'm not hungry, but I just can't resist eating this apple pie."

Figure 9–3.
Hunger is a drive producing a desire for food (a pushing force); a table laden with food is an incentive to eat (a pulling force).

Drive, the force that compels behavior and that arises from physiological conditions that signify some biological distress, increases with increased deprivation and reduces when the biological need is satisfied. Drive has continued to receive widespread acceptance as motivation. One reason for this acceptance is the general belief that physiological research will disclose the source of behavior. Currently, however, the conclusion seems to be that drive cannot direct behavior; it can only provide the energy necessary for exhibiting a behavior. For example, the longer an organism is deprived of food, the higher the drive level for exhibiting food-seeking behaviors. But the consumption of food reduces the need for food, and the drive level for food-seeking behavior is lowered. The specific food-seeking behaviors cannot be explained by drive. Thus, the idea that there are two basic concepts of motivation—motivation as a pushing force (drive energizing behavior) and motivation as a pulling force (incentives giving direction to behavior)—dominates most psychologists' thinking about motivation.

Incentives are things in the environment that are perceived as having positive or negative value and that motivate approach or avoidance behavior because of some attribute of the stimulus itself. The sight of a friend or the threat of punishment motivate behaviors. Hunger is a drive producing a desire for food (a pushing force); a table laden with food is an incentive to eat (a pulling force) (see Figure 9–3). The most fundamental distinction between an incentive and a drive is that a drive is produced by a biological state whereas an incentive is produced by environmental states. In effect, the innate part of motivation is attributed to drive whereas the learned part is attributed to incentive. This external-internal model of motivation has implications for the practical control of behavior. For example, new associations can be learned in attempts to control smoking, eating, and fear reactions. Stimulus control of behavior is discussed further in chapters 11 and 12.

To what does the term *needs* refer?

Needs is a broader term than drive and refers to psychological (social or learned) needs as well as physiological needs. Psychologists agree that there are two kinds of energizing and directing forces—those that have a physiological basis and those that are acquired through environmental experience. The need to achieve and the need to be loved, recognized, and accepted by other people do not seem to have a physiological basis; however, they seem to be learned or acquired almost universally because they are learned from being with other people.

What is the arousal theory of motivation?

Recent evidence indicates that to think of a person as being more easily aroused by, more sensitive to, or more reactive to a stimulus is probably more accurate than to think of a person as having a higher drive level and thus being more energized than another person. **Arousal theory** is the view that behavior is a function of being aroused by a stimulus rather than a direct effect of deprivation. The level of arousal or activation of the organism may vary on a continuum from deep sleep to alertness to intense excitement. Theoretically, a person needs an intermediate level of stimulation and activation to function best. There is an optimum level of arousal in terms of both internal and external conditions. For example, hunger or thirst might be an internal stimulus or condition causing a person to be more sensitive to, reactive to, or aroused by an external condition such as the sight of food, the smell of food, or the presence of a kitchen or restaurant. As arousal or motivation increases, performance increases until the optimum point is reached; then, as arousal or motivation increases, performance decreases. The optimum level of arousal varies among different people for different tasks. Some people perform better at higher levels of arousal whereas others perform better at lower levels of arousal. Psychological tests are available to measure individual differences in need for stimulation. Also, the relationship between arousal (motivation) and performance varies for different tasks (see Figure 9–4). A very simple or boring task may be performed better at a higher level of arousal to avoid losing concentration or falling asleep. A complicated, difficult task involving logical reasoning

Does an increase in arousal (motivation) always increase performance?

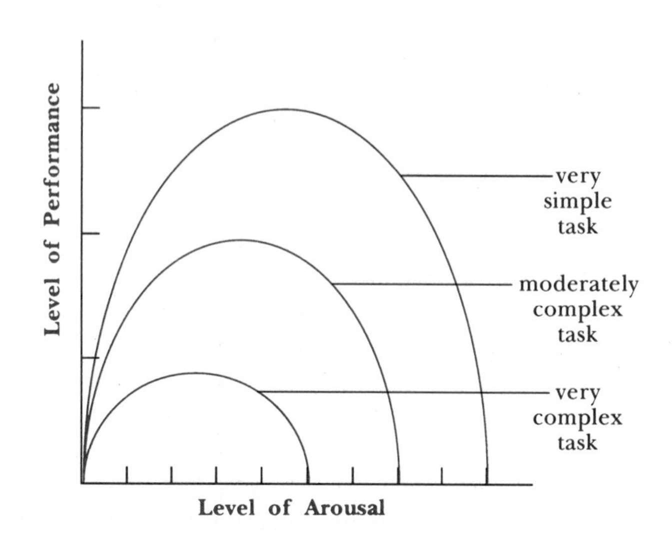

Figure 9–4.
Level of performance is a function of arousal or motivation. The optimum level of arousal or motivation for the best performance varies with the complexity of the task.

may be performed better at a lower level of arousal. Many contemporary psychologists reject the drive theory in favor of the arousal theory.

What is the assumption of reinforcement theory concerning motivation?

The **reinforcement theory** of motivation is based on the assumption that what is ordinarily called motivated behavior is simply learned behavior. This theory proposes one single source of behavior—reinforcement, which is a modern version of the ancient philosophical idea of hedonism. The concept of reinforcement as a source of behavior is presented in chapter 6 under the heading of operant conditioning. Learned associations account for an increase or a decrease in behavior.

Is thought the source of motivation?

Cognitive psychologists propose that the motivation behind a person's behavior is the deliberate, conscious choice to behave in a particular way in order to achieve an expected outcome of a believed value and that motivation is an interaction of forces—**expectancy theory.** Expectancy theory holds that people perform behaviors that are expected to result in receiving worthwhile rewards, in leading to desired goals, and in avoiding undesirable outcomes. This view has received considerable support from research and is applicable in practical situations as is pointed out later in this chapter.

What is meant by the concept of homeostasis?

Homeostasis is a central idea in biological psychology referring to the maintenance of biological equilibrium. Many behaviors occur automatically to maintain blood pressure, body temperature, glucose levels, and the condition of other chemical and metabolic processes that must remain within a certain range of values for life to continue. High temperatures may trigger perspiration, which cools the body, and cold may cause a person to shiver, which generates body warmth. But certain behaviors for restoring equilibrium, such as building a fire, putting on a coat to protect one's self from cold, and turning on an air conditioner to cool one's self are voluntary responses that are motivated by the physiological state and learning. The concept of homeostasis has been extended to include the need to maintain a psychological equilibrium such as the need for stimulation, for power, and for harmony or consistency. When conditions deviate too far from the optimum level, a person acts to restore the equilibrium. In an environment that is not stimulating enough, an organism begins to investigate, to explore, or to manipulate the surroundings in order to increase the stimulation. If the environment is too stimulating, a person may withdraw or begin to focus on only a part of the environment in order to reduce the stimulation. **Balance theory** holds that homeostasis or harmony needs to exist between facts, beliefs, feelings, attitudes, and behavior for psychological survival or well-being and that inconsistencies between any of these serve as an energizing force for responses to restore harmony. Harmony may be restored by changing either attitude, feeling, belief, or behavior or by rejecting information.

Motives

Motives or needs are classified as primary or secondary, intrinsic or extrinsic, conscious or unconscious. This section is concerned with specific primary and secondary motives or needs. Unconscious motivation, intrinsic motivation, and assessment of motives are also discussed.

What are primary motives?

Primary Motives. Needs that have a biological basis (drives) are called **primary motives.** Primary motives may be subdivided into those necessary for the survival of the individual, for the survival of the species, and for learning—the development of intelligence and attainment of knowledge. Individual survival needs include the need for food, fluids, air (oxygen), tolerable temperature, sleep and dreaming (discussed in chapter 5), and the need to be free from pain. Survival needs of the species include the sex drive to insure reproduction and the parental drive to insure adequate care of the young. Needs that promote survival by learning are referred to as **stimulus motives.** These motives include the need for sensory input, movement, exploration, curiosity, manipulation or touching of objects, and body contact—more global touching that includes people.

Which primary needs are related to individual survival? to species survival? to learning?

What structure in the brain is known to be a source of motivation for some of the primary drives?

The motivation for many of a person's behaviors can be traced to self-survival. The hypothalamus in the brain is sensitive to the chemistry and temperature of the blood and produces the desire for food, liquids, or temperature change (Davis, Gallagher, & Ladove, 1967; Epstein, Fitzsimons, & Simons, 1969). Some researchers believe that even a person's hunger for a specific food may be activated by some chemical imbalance in the blood (Davis, 1939). Pain is the signal system that activates voluntary behaviors that allow an individual to escape or avoid whatever is threatening him or her. If a person is in need of food, liquids, sleep and dreaming, air (oxygen), or temperature change, the internal condition activates behaviors that attempt to restore a physiological state of equilibrium.

What structure in the brain is known to play an important role in arousal?

Neural impulses in the brain are the source of different brain wave patterns related to different levels of arousal. Each of the senses—vision, hearing, smell, taste, and touch—may stimulate the reticular formation, which then arouses the higher brain centers. Different brain wave patterns differentiate the various levels of arousal as was pointed out in chapter 5. A desire for food, liquids, or any of the other individual survival needs may be activated by the environment or an external condition as well as by the internal physiological condition. A decrease in the involvement of purely biological factors and an increase in the environmental factors seems to occur the higher an organism is on the evolutionary scale.

Which tends to play a greater role in the human sex drive and parental drive, hormones or learning? in animals?

Drives related to survival of the species seem to be very powerful. Sexual behavior depends on a combination of hormones, involuntary mechanisms—particularly the hypothalamus reactions, and reactions to external stimuli, which are learned. In the sex drive and parental drive in lower animals such as rats, cats, or dogs, hormones appear to account primarily for the behavior, whereas in humans environmental stimuli play a greater role in the behaviors than do hormones. Humans have a more advanced development of the cortex of the brain that allows a greater ability to learn than do animals. The sex drive seems to differ from the individual survival drives in that it is not essential for self-survival and is not dependent on deprivation. Arousal of the drive is sought as actively as the reduction of the aroused drive; therefore, the sex drive motivates an unusually wide variety of behaviors, and almost any conceivable stimulus can come to be a source of arousal through association (conditioning). For example, a particular song, special perfume, candlelight, or soft music may become a stimulus for sexual arousal.

Although care and protection of the young in lower animals depends primarily on hormones, experience and learning play a greater role in the care and protection of young humans. Parenting behavior in humans is learned, and it consists of a complex set of motives and emotions (see Figure 9–5).

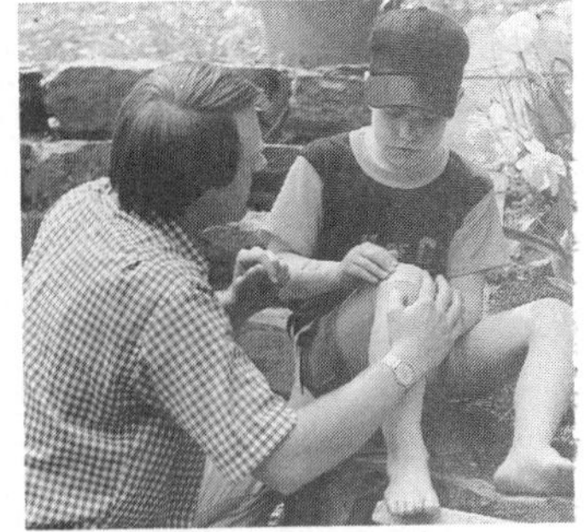

Figure 9–5.
Experience and learning play a greater role in the care and protection of young humans (parental drive) than do hormones.

A recent biological theory of motivation called **sociobiology** suggests that behavior is preprogrammed for one and only one function—to ensure the survival of the DNA molecules that make up one's genetic identity. All living organisms, including humans, are proposed to be designed to behave in such a way as to protect and propagate the genes. According to this theory, it is not the survival of the individual organism or the species that motivates behavior; it is the survival of the genetic material in the cells.

Stimulus motives (activity, sensory stimulation, manipulation, human body contact, curiosity, and exploration) apparently have a biological basis and are innately programmed. The need to move about and to be active seems to provide external stimuli to insure sensory stimulation. Experiments with sensory deprivation indicate that the need for sensory stimulation is so strong that in its absence visual images such as dots and geometric forms and eventually hallucinations begin to occur (Heron, 1957). Even during a sleep period when sensory stimulation is absent, involuntary mechanisms turn on dreaming, which provides stimulation of the brain. The need to manipulate—handle or touch objects—and the need to have global body contact with or touch other people seem to be related to the need to know something at the tactile level and the need to be soothed. Studies with baby monkeys separated from their mothers at birth indicate that a biological basis exists for the needs of cuddling and closeness. Without body contact, emotional, physical, social, and intellectual development are adversely affected. Curiosity and the desire to explore are activated by the new and unknown and are satisfied by knowledge. Exploration is a physical activity or search in space for knowledge of the unknown (see Figure 9–6). Curiosity is a mental activity, a search in the mind for answers to the unknown.

Figure 9–6.
Exploration is a physical activity or search in space for knowledge of the unknown. Curiosity is a mental activity, a search in the mind for answers to the unknown.

What are secondary motives?

Secondary Motives. Needs that have only a psychological (learned or social) basis are called **secondary motives.** Secondary motives include (a) the affiliation need or the need for love, acceptance, and approval from others; (b) the need to achieve or compare well with other people—the esteem need; (c) the need to be aggressive; (d) the need for security or the need to be free from fear; and (e) the need for consistency.

How does the affiliation need come to be learned?

During psychological development, each person acquires or learns certain needs, and these needs may be acquired in different strengths. For example, an infant's biological needs first are satisfied by people; then people become goal objects themselves. The child develops a need to be with people, to be accepted and approved of as a person by people, and to be loved by people. This need is referred to as the **affiliation motive.** The family, the first group with which an individual is associated, plays an important role in a person's need for affiliation. Children brought up to be dependent or who are raised with close family ties show stronger affiliation motives than those who are not.

How does the achievement need come to be learned?

If people in a child's life value and reward achievement, the child will develop a need to achieve in order to win approval. The **achievement motive** is the need to accomplish something important or valuable or to meet high standards in comparison to others. Fear also seems to be involved in achievement motivation. In addition to a need for success, a fear of failure or even a fear of success is a factor. Also, the incentive value of success or failure is involved. For example, if a task is so difficult that few people are able to accomplish it, then failure would have no negative incentive value because there would be no shame associated with failure. If the task is so easy that almost anyone can do it, then achieving success is not worth much and has little positive incentive. Research indicates a relationship between occupational choice and the need for achievement (McCelland, 1965). In a group of college graduates, 83 percent with high need for achievement went into occupations characterized by a high degree of risk, challenge, and decision making such as sales, management, or business ownership. Seventy percent of those who did not choose such an occupation had a low need for achievement.

To what does the term *aggression* refer?

How does the need to be aggressive come to be learned?

The **aggressive motive** is the need to behave in an aggressive manner. **Aggression** refers to any behavior consciously or unconsciously intended to inflict physical or psychological harm. If children observe people in their lives being aggressive as a means of achieving or gaining power over others, they may develop a strong need to be aggressive. Another view is that aggression is simply a result of frustration that is produced by the nonfulfillment of other needs. Freud proposed that people are born with a need to be aggressive and that aggression has a biological basis—that it is the result of a primary motive. According to this concept, the need to be aggressive is constantly generating energy that is released by an individual in small aggressive acts in order to maintain an equilibrium. If the energy is not released in small aggressive acts, it will build up greater tension and be released in more extreme aggressive acts. Research studies suggest, however, that the release of energy through aggressive acts tends to increase aggressive behaviors rather than decrease them (Lazarus, 1974); therefore, the view that the need to be aggressive is an innate characteristic is unpopular among the majority of psychologists today. In general, it is believed to be learned and is the result of a secondary need. Aggression is discussed further in chapter 13.

What is the Freudian view of aggression?

The **security motive** is the need to be free from fear. Fear can be attached to almost any stimulus—an object, a person, or a circumstance such as rejection or criticism, love, and failure. An individual learns a need to avoid or escape from whatever is causing the fear. Fears may be rational or irrational such as the fear of being in a room without windows, of driving over a bridge, or of riding in an elevator. Some people even have a fear of success. The motivation to avoid success has been associated primarily with females because our society has traditionally stereotyped women who achieve outside the home as being sexless, unfeminine, and cold; further, it has been assumed that a woman's need for affiliation is usually stronger than her need to achieve (see Figure 9–7). In a research study, Hoffman and Maier (1974) found that 65 percent of the female subjects gave responses that indicated a fear of success, but 77 percent of the male subjects also expressed this fear. Evidently, fear of success is a general kind of fear for many people, both male and female. Either the assumption of the origin of the fear in women is not correct, or the fear must originate from difference sources in males.

Figure 9–7.
Attitudes that keep women from pursuing their personal needs for achievement are changing, and more women are moving into management positions in the world of work.

Humans seem to have a need for consistency or agreement in their attitudes, beliefs, and behaviors. The tendency to change or reevaluate discrepancies in order to bring about agreement or balance is referred to as **cognitive consistency.** If a person behaves in a manner inconsistent with what is believed to be appropriate behavior or inconsistent with his or her feeling, disagrees with another person, or holds two conflicting attitudes, ideas, feelings, or opinions, the inconsistency usually makes the person so uncomfortable that he or she will do something to restore balance or agree-

What is cognitive dissonance, and how is it a source of motivation?

ment. The state of tension that is created in such a conflict is referred to as **cognitive dissonance** (Festinger, 1957). This dissonance motivates the person to engage in behavior that will reduce the conflict.

What are some behaviors people engage in to reduce cognitive dissonance?

In order to reduce dissonance, a person may use a number of different strategies. Some people may seek out information to support a belief that differs from another person's belief. Because new information may be in conflict with information or beliefs previously held, some people may avoid seeking information to avoid further dissonance. If new information is encountered that is inconsistent with information or beliefs previously held, some people find a way to deny or reject the information. If a person's behavior is inconsistent with what he or she believes to be appropriate behavior, either the behavior may be changed or the attitude may be changed to bring about consistency. Another way people reduce dissonance is to discredit the person who holds a conflicting attitude or belief. If information is received about a person that conflicts with the image held of that person, either the information will be rejected or the image of the person will change. Any time a decision is made between two conflicting alternatives, dissonance is present. Dissonance may be resolved after the decision is made by reevaluating the alternatives in a more biased manner in order to justify the decision.

How does intrinsic motivation differ from extrinsic motivation?

Intrinsic Motivation. Sometimes the activating force that causes a behavior to occur is intrinsic motivation rather than extrinsic motivation. **Extrinsic motivation** is the activation of behavior by the consequences of a behavior because of a need for such things as money, praise from other people, grades, good health, and awards. **Intrinsic motivation** is the activation of behavior by the behavior itself because of a need to demonstrate competence, to master the environment, to control desired outcomes, or to engage in an activity for its own sake. For example, a person may sing, play a musical instrument, dig in the garden, play video games, work crossword puzzles, or do other work simply because of the pleasure derived from it. People may seek out activities and challenges to demonstrate mastery. When a person has the belief that he or she can perform adequately, known as **self-efficacy,** an internal control is acquired that directs him or her to set goals and develop means of attaining them. Self-inefficacy has the opposite effect—apathy, despondency, and a feeling of being a victim of external forces (Bandura, 1982).

What are the behavioral results of self-efficacy and self-inefficacy?

Employers usually rely on extrinsic motivation rather than intrinsic motivation, thinking only in terms of needs that are satisfied by things such as money, prizes, and fringe benefits rather than needs that are satisfied by the work itself. Managers should consider that some employees may have a need to boost their feelings of competence, and whenever possible they should provide tasks that present a challenge and allow for self-direction. Influencing peoples' behavior by reward and punishment may be successful as long as the controls are present, but if they are removed the behavior may cease or drop in frequency. Research studies have shown, however, that sometimes imposing external rewards on an activity that is intrinsically motivated has the unexpected aftereffect of lowering intrinsic motivation for the activity (Deci, 1972; Lepper, Greene, & Nisbett, 1973). For example, if one reads just for the enjoyment of reading (intrinsic motivation) and then is paid money to read books, reading when the pay stops may become less frequent than it was prior to the application of extrinsic motivation.

What is sometimes the effect of imposing external rewards on an intrinsically motivated behavior?

Unconscious Motivation. Sometimes a person can analyze his or her own behavior and determine the source of motivation; however, very frequently the motive for a specific behavior is not consciously known to the person exhibiting the behavior. **Unconscious motivation** is not a particular kind of motivation; instead, it refers to any motive that moves a person without his or her knowledge or awareness of it as the cause of the behavior. Freud's view of unconscious motivation is probably the most extreme held by psychologists in that he viewed almost every act, regardless of how trivial, as derived from unconscious motives. Most psychologists agree that unconscious motives exist but not to the extent that Freud proposed. They prefer to think in terms of degree of awareness. For example, a person may be vaguely aware of the need to dominate others, the need for social approval, or the sex drive, but he or she may not completely be aware of the extent to which this need is dominating his or her behavior. Unconscious motivation is present in much of consumer behavior. A person may be unconscious of the causes of his or her behavior when buying certain products or a particular brand of that product. Some unconscious motivation may be a defense reaction by which a person psychologically protects himself or herself from reality. Knowledge of some needs might cause guilt feelings or anxiety. Sometimes motivations are unconscious simply because the motive is complex and derived from a combination of needs that the person cannot pinpoint.

How does unconscious motivation differ from conscious motivation?

Assessment. Because motivation is a theoretical concept and cannot be directly observed, a variety of techniques have been developed for measuring the strength of a need or motive. Techniques focus on observation of behavior, which is indicative of a motivational state. This observation may be in the form of direct observation, self-report, or projection into a stimulus situation.

In everyday life, people make observations in an unsystematic manner (see Figure 9–8). In addition, inferences are frequently made about people's motives such as the conclusion that a person did something because he or she was tired, jealous, wanted to make a particular person feel badly, or didn't want to lose another as a friend. Psychologists, however, use systematic ways of assessing motivation. In order to conduct scientific studies, several types of observation have been developed for measuring motivation. Because one function of motivation is the energizing of behavior, observers can expect that increased motivation will lead to increased restlessness and activity or performance; therefore, the general activity level may be measured as an indication of motivation level. Once a response has been learned to satisfy a motive, the rate of responding may be used to measure the strength of motivation. A highly motivated individual will sometimes endure a great deal of hardship in order to reach a desired goal; therefore, the stronger

"Every morning I try to analyze why I get out of bed and go to work."

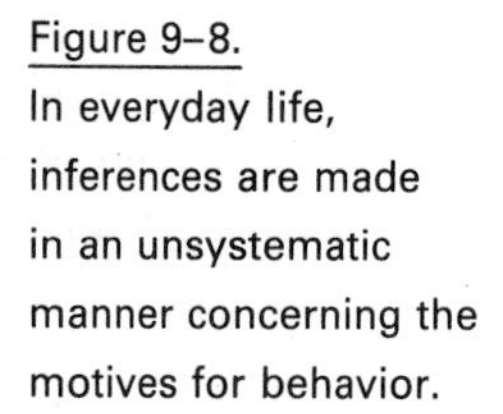

Figure 9–8.
In everyday life, inferences are made in an unsystematic manner concerning the motives for behavior.

How do psychologists assess motivation?

the motivation, the more pain a person will accept to satisfy the need for accomplishment. In most real-life situations, several motivations are operating at once, and behavior is generally determined by the stronger motivation; therefore, the relative strength of competing motives can be assessed just by observing what behaviors are exhibited.

Figure 9–9.
Self-report inventories are convenient to give and score and go below the surface appearance of the behavior to tap personal experience and feelings.

Psychologists may use standardized self-report inventories in which an individual gives information about his or her likes and dislikes and emotional reactions to certain situations. The self-report inventory is valuable in that it goes below the surface appearance of the behavior to tap the individual's own personal experience and feelings. Self-report inventories are convenient to give and score because observation of actual behavior or groups of raters of actual behavior are not required (see Figure 9–9). These inventories usually may be scored objectively. One disadvantage is that the person responding to the inventory may not give an accurate report and may not even be able to do so if the motives are unconscious.

What are some projection-type tests used to assess motivation?

Sometimes a person's motives are assessed in an indirect manner through use of tests whereby the person projects himself or herself into a stimulus situation. Projection of the self into the stimulus is the idea that because the stimulus has no inherent meaning, any meaning that is read into it will reflect the motives, emotions, conflicts, biases, and interests of the person providing the meaning. One of the most widely used tests of this type used for studying an individual's motivation is the Thematic Apperception Test (TAT), originally developed by H. A. Murray and Christina Morgan in the 1930s. This test assesses motivation as reflected in the content of stories created in response to certain standard pictures of objects and scenes. Twenty cards containing pictures of one or more human figures are shown to the subject. The subject is allowed enough time to make up a complete story for each picture. The story should include what has led up to the situation, what is happening, what the characters are doing, what their thoughts and feelings are, what is wanted and by whom, and what will happen or be done or what the outcome will be. Various scoring systems have been devised to assess the stories on their content, language, and themes—all of which are indicative of particular needs. For example, references to competition against a standard of excellence, unique accomplishment, achievement of a long-term goal, or strong effort for actions concerning the attain-

Figure 9–10.
Make up a story about this picture. Then analyze the story by relating each sentence to an appropriate need such as the need for achievement, the need for affiliation, and the need for power. Total the number of sentences that relate to each motive. This is similar to how the Thematic Apperception Test is used to assess motivation.

ment of achievement-related goals would count toward achievement motivation (see Figure 9–10). One picture in the series portrays a young, barefoot boy sitting alone in the doorway of a rustic building with only a small space around the doorway of the building in view. People with a strong affiliation motive may tell stories with themes of lonliness or abandonment, whereas people with a weak affiliation motive may tell stories with themes of happiness and secure relationships with others. For example, the boy may be on a camping trip with his family. This test is described further in chapter 11 in the section on personality assessment.

Other types of projection tests sometimes used to assess motivation are also described in chapter 11. These tests include free associations, open-ended sentences, drawings, and interpretation of ambiguous stimuli such as ink blots.

MOTIVATION IN THE WORKPLACE

What does the human resources approach to management attempt to do?

The functions served by work provide an opportunity for the application of motivation theory. Work serves the functions of reward, social status, self-esteem, and meaningfulness in life. A worker has an expectation of the type and amount of reward to receive. The workplace provides an opportunity for satisfaction of many needs such as affiliation, achievement or esteem, security, and power. Most business firms operate according to the philosophy that an employee is an investment. The employee has some knowledge, skills, and abilities (resources) that are an asset to the organization for certain conditions. Motivation may be a key factor in how much of the potential resource an organization realizes from an employee. The human resources approach to management attempts to account for the amount that has been invested in human resources and to determine how well these human resources are being used. For example, an accounting department may be using employees below their optimum level of skill, or the employees may not be motivated to perform at their optimum level of performance. The human resources approach proposes that not making maximum use of human resources is just as undesirable for a business firm as not making maximum use of economic resources. Some of the theories of motivation applicable in work settings are summarized in this section. The last part of this section is related to the application of the concepts of motivation to specific problems and situations encountered in the world of work.

Applicable Theories

Several theories of motivation specifically applicable to industrial and organizational settings will be reviewed in this section. Some of the theories may be used as tools for examining the needs people bring with them into organizations—needs that predispose them to behave in particular ways. Some may help a person understand how these individual predispositions and situational characteristics come together to produce particular ways of behaving on the job. Some may be used to increase the probability that employees will perform effectively. The different theories are not contradictory and in some cases may be quite complementary. Therefore, it is more important to decide which theory is most helpful in understanding a particular aspect of employee behavior rather than which theory is correct.

How may motivation theories be used in industrial and organizational settings?

Network of Three Basic Motives. One theory of motivation based on the work of several researchers consists of a network of three basic motives that identify patterns of behavior—the need for achievement, the need for affiliation, and the need for power (McClelland, 1961, 1962; Atkinson, 1964; Stringer, 1971). The need for achievement (**nAch**) is the need for success as measured against some internalized standard of excellence. People with a high need for achievement tend to seek and assume more personal responsibility, to take more risks, to set more challenging but realistic goals, to seek and use more feedback concerning the results of their actions, and to seek out more opportunities to enhance their desire to achieve (McClelland, 1961). Although they are competitive, they tend to avoid intense clashes, which may be a common occurrence for those with a need for power. They tend to choose people who are competent as working partners.

What are the three basic motives proposed to identify patterns of behavior in the workplace?

The need for affiliation (**nAff**) is the need for close interpersonal relationships and friendships with other people. People with a high need for affiliation tend to enjoy jobs that have many interactions with other people and find more satisfaction in warm relationships and friendships than in being powerful or in achieving (see Figure 9–11). In fact, such a person may avoid power because often people in positions of power must make decisions that alienate others. Employees with a high need for affiliation care very much what others think of them. Research on simple tasks has shown that people with a high need for affiliation perform better than people with a low need for affiliation. This is explained by the fact that people who have a high need for affiliation have a greater

Figure 9–11.
The workplace provides an opportunity for social interaction and the development of friendships that satisfy affiliation needs.

desire to please, to cooperate, and to be friendly (French, 1958). They tend to conform, to do what others do or what they think others would do, and to agree more with the judgment of others. People high in need for affiliation tend to choose friends as working partners and will not be motivated to affiliate with people who are extremely unpleasant and disliked. They will be motivated by a friendly request to cooperate and to help out for the common good, provided the request is from a person or group that has positive incentive value.

What are high nPow individuals like?

The need for power (**nPow**) is the need for direct control or influence over others or the need for control over the means of influencing others. People with a high need for power seek and enjoy work in which power, influence, or authority rests within the job. They may strive intensely for promotions, play organizational politics, and try to win arguments and persuade others.

Which two of the three basic needs are compatible? Which two are incompatible?

These three basic needs may exist in varying degrees in employees. Extremely high needs for both power and affiliation in an individual are somewhat incompatible. Extremely high achievement and power needs would be compatible, although the presence of one does not necessarily indicate the presence of the other. Recognizing the strength of these basic motives in the workplace can be helpful in the creation of the right kind of work climate.

Figure 9–12.
Abraham H. Maslow.

Maslow's Hierarchy of Needs. The American psychologist Abraham H. Maslow (see Figure 9–12) proposed a simple but very influential theory of motivation with the central theme that human needs are arranged in a hierarchy (Maslow, 1954, 1970). This theory places those needs with a physiological basis (primary motives) lowest in the hierarchy because they are the most basic and take priority over those needs that have a psychological basis (secondary motives). The secondary motives follow a specific order of priority with the order of the hierarchy being physiological needs first and then the need for safety, belongingness, esteem, and self-actualization. Maslow's proposed hierarchy is shown in Figure 9–13. A need higher in the hierarchy will become a motive of behavior if and only if the needs below it have been satisfied to a certain extent. Unsatisfied lower needs will dominate over unsatisfied higher needs. For the need highest in the hierarchy to become a motive for behavior, all the other needs below it must be somewhat satisfied. Only unsatisfied needs are motivating; therefore, when one need is satisfied, a higher need becomes a motive for behavior. Just as unsatisfied needs can move one down the hierarchy, satis-

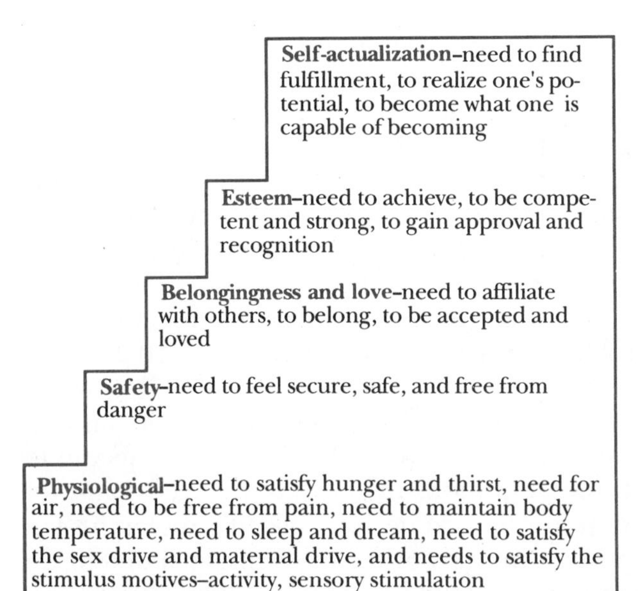

Figure 9–13. Maslow's hierarchy of needs.

fied needs open up higher needs. A person is constantly fluctuating from one need to the other due to temporary conditions and situations. For example, a person may be motivated to accomplish a task (achieve) but finally become hungry enough to stop to eat. Or a person motivated to achieve may become more motivated to seek love and acceptance (affiliation) following divorce.

What is a self-actualized person like?

The motivational life of a person may be described as a growth process—a climbing toward **self-actualization,** which is the need to find fulfillment in life, to realize one's potential, and to become what one is capable of becoming. Maslow formulated a list of 15 characteristics of self-actualized persons. Some of the characteristics include an effective perception of reality; self-acceptance and acceptance of others; being problem centered rather than ego centered; having a need for privacy and solitude at times; having a deep appreciation of the basic experiences of life; having an ability for very deep, satisfying interpersonal relations; being democratic in attitudes; having a good sense of humor that is philosophical and nonhostile; and being highly creative. Infants are dominated by physiological needs such as hunger and thirst, but young children add the need to feel secure and the need to be loved and accepted (safety and belongingness needs) to the physiological needs of infancy. Older children may be motivated by achievement (esteem) needs, but self-actualization needs do not arise until a person reaches adulthood. Because people are believed to progress through this hierarchy in a developmental fashion, many never reach the self-actualization stage of motivation. Among those who do, it remains a matter of degree. No one ever seems to reach a total state of self-actualization. To do so would be to enter an unending, satisfaction-saturated condition and so be left unmotivated for any new kind of action. Maslow discovered and studied people who seemingly had experienced a total state of self-actualization, but he found that rather than their motivation ending altogether, their motivation to live and act in a self-actualized fashion increased.

Maslow's theory is more philosophical than scientific, and research in organizations fails to support the theory. For example, the concept of need, the definitions of the specific needs, and the meaning of satisfaction are too vague for objective research. The need for power, important in the workplace, is not included in the hierarchy. Experimental studies fail to support the hypothesis that an increase in need satisfaction on a given level (safety, for example) causes the strength of that need to decrease and results in an increase in the strength of the next higher level need (belongingness). In fact, some research indicates that a high level of satisfaction may strengthen a need rather than diminish it (Dachler & Hulin, 1969). For example, success in meeting one's needs through popularity and acceptance may actually strengthen the need to belong. Success in acquiring power may create a desire for more power. Maslow's theory has received a great amount of attention, and in spite of the lack of research support, it has received a high degree of acceptance.

Figure 9–14.
Esteem needs may be satisfied when a manager polishes an employee's ego and causes him or her to feel more important.

The application of Maslow's theory to the motivation of people at work has important implications. Because managers attempt to influence human behavior, they need to consider what needs are relatively unsatisfied and thus can serve as motives. If an employee is not hungry or insecure, offering only rewards that are seen as food and security may not motivate the employee. If rewards in the form of social relations are ineffective in motivating work behavior, rewards that satisfy esteem needs such as fringe benefits, a new car to drive, a private office, or a prestigious-sounding title may be effective (see Figure 9-–14). If esteem needs are ineffective in motivating work behavior, providing opportunities for the individual to do what is personally satisfying, to realize his or her potential, and to be self-fulfilled will be the basis for motivation.

McGregor's Theory Y. Maslow's theory of motivation has influenced the theories of others. Douglas McGregor (1960) drew heavily on Maslow's theory and proposed that management by direction and control often fails to provide effective motivation of human effort toward organizational objectives. Management by direction and control can fail because the two methods are useless for motivating people whose physiological and safety needs are reasonably satisfied and whose affiliation, self-esteem, and self-actualization needs are dominant. McGregor believed that a theory of managing people based on motivation and human nature as an integrative view was needed. He proposed such a theory with the following assumptions and labeled it **Theory Y:**

What are the assumptions of McGregor's Theory Y?

1. The expenditure of physical and mental effort in work is as natural as play or rest.
2. External control and the threat of punishment are not the only means for bringing about effort directed toward achieving organizational objectives. People will exercise self-direction and self-control in the service of objectives to which they are committed.
3. Commitment to objectives is a function of the rewards associated with the achievement of those objectives.
4. The average human being learns, under proper conditions, not only to accept but also to seek responsibility.
5. The capacity to exercise a relatively high degree of imagination, ingenuity, and creativity in the solution of organizational problems is widely, not narrowly, distributed in the population.
6. Under the conditions of modern industrial life, the intellectual potentialities of the average human being are only partially fulfilled. (McGregor, 1960, pp. 47-48)

McGregor labeled the conventional management theory based on external direction and control **Theory X.** Theory X assumes that the average person naturally dislikes work and tries to avoid it and must therefore be coerced, controlled, directed, or threatened with punishment in order to be sufficiently motivated to work productively. Furthermore, it assumes that people prefer to be directed because they desire to avoid responsibility.

What are the assumptions of Theory X?

Some people seem to have developed qualities that fit the assumptions of Theory X because of environmental situations, but McGregor proposes that everyone has the potential for the behaviors and attitudes described in Theory Y and is capable of being intrinsically motivated. Attempts to use Theory Y assumptions to

With which employees will Theory Y or Theory X assumptions probably not work well?

manage employees who fit Theory X characteristics will probably fail. Likewise, management of those who fit the Theory Y characteristics with Theory X assumptions will probably result in a great deal of difficulty.

Critics of McGregor's theory point out that the behavioral characteristics of both Theory X and Theory Y represent extreme examples of motivation and human nature in the general population. In reality, very few people consistently demonstrate the characteristics of either theory. To view the characteristics of people on a continuum from the extreme of Theory X to the extreme of Theory Y would be more realistic (see Figure 9–15).

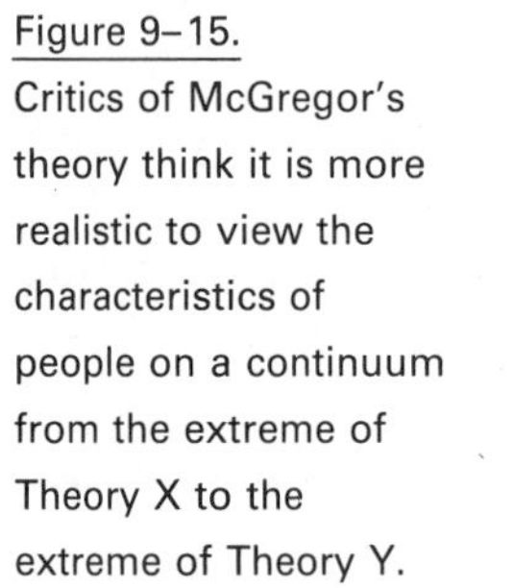

Figure 9–15.
Critics of McGregor's theory think it is more realistic to view the characteristics of people on a continuum from the extreme of Theory X to the extreme of Theory Y.

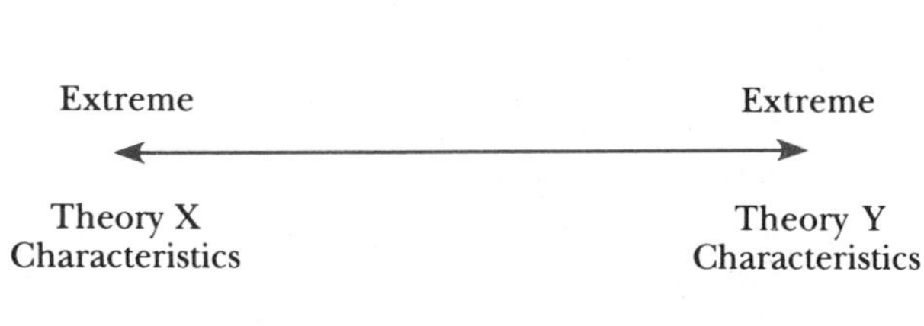

What are the two sets of needs or factors proposed by Herzberg, and what is the effect of satisfaction of each set?

Herzberg's Two-Factor Theory. Frederick Herzberg, a well-known industrial psychologist, was also influenced by Maslow, and he proposed a two-factor theory of motivation. Herzberg proposed that workers have two independent sets of needs that function differently (Herzberg, 1968). One set he called **hygiene factors** or maintenance factors, which are part of the job content but are external to the job itself. The situation in which the work is performed is an example of a hygiene factor. A favorable work environment, financial rewards, fringe benefits, relations with peers and supervisors, and company policies are also hygiene factors (extrinsic motivation). Herzberg concluded that when a person believes these factors to be inadequate, dissatisfaction occurs. But when a person believes these factors to be adequately present, they do not generate satisfaction or motivate to greater productivity. Hygiene factors are needs that must be satisfied merely to avoid worker dissatisfaction; however, these factors may attract a person to accept a job in an organization, help reduce turnover, prevent rebellion, or make it possible for a worker to be motivated.

Herzberg called the second set of job-related needs **motivation factors.** These factors occur at the time the work is performed and make the work itself rewarding (intrinsic motivation). Included in motivation factors are achievement, recognition, advancement, responsibility, growth possibilities, and enjoyment of the activity. Managers today are finding that recognition of employees for excellent work is a powerful influence on productivity (Cherrington & Wixom, 1983). When present, motivation factors lead to job satisfaction and increased productivity, but their absence rarely produces dissatisfaction. Figure 9–16 is a diagram of the relationships in Herzberg's theory. Probably the most controversial part of Herzberg's two-factor theory is that satisfaction and dissatisfaction are viewed as two separate and distinct variables rather than as opposite ends of a continuum of a single variable.

Motivational Force

← →

Force in a Dissatisfied Direction	No Force	Force in a Satisfied Direction
Hygiene factors absent	Hygiene factors present Motivation factors absent	Motivation factors present

Figure 9–16.
Herzberg's two-factor theory.

What do the *V*, the *I*, and the *E* stand for in VIE theory?

VIE Theory. Several psychologists have built on the theory of motivation that is based on the expectation or anticipation of reward, which involves information processing. V. H. Vroom (1964) is usually credited with development of the theory that has come be known as the valence-instrumentality-expectancy theory, or **VIE theory.** This is a theory of work motivation based on expectation of reward, perceived value of direct outcomes, and expected indirect or second-level outcomes. **Expectancy,** the anticipation or believed likelihood or probability that a reward will occur, energizes behavior. **Valence,** the perceived value of the outcomes, gives direction to behavior. Outcomes may be first-level outcomes, which are a direct result of the behavior such as receiving an award or certificate, or second-level outcomes, which are outcomes of first-level outcomes (indirect outcomes). Second-level outcomes of receiving an award might be being chosen over another applicant for a job, being invited to speak at a convention, or receiving praise from friends and relatives who see the award or certificate. **Instrumentality** is the belief that a behavior will achieve or secure second-level outcomes of value.

VIE theory assumes that the work behavior of an individual is the result of a deliberate, conscious choice in order to attain predetermined outcomes (see Figure 9–17). VIE theory further assumes

"I chose to work on this job because I expect a paycheck at the end of each week with which I can purchase a camera that I want and need very much."

Figure 9–17.
A worker makes a choice to work based on an expected reward, the value of that reward, and the instrumentality of that reward.

that the individual worker perceives a probability (see Figure 9-18) that a certain behavior will lead to particular outcomes of a particular value (see Figure 9–19) and also perceives a ratio between effort and reward for the self and effort and reward for others. A perception of inequity between a person's own ratio of effort to re-

Figure 9–18.
Expectancy: perceived probability of an outcome.

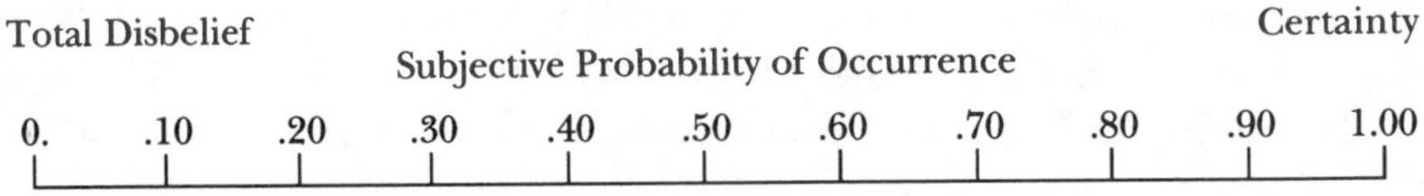

Total Disbelief — Subjective Probability of Occurrence — Certainty

0.	.10	.20	.30	.40	.50	.60	.70	.80	.90	1.00

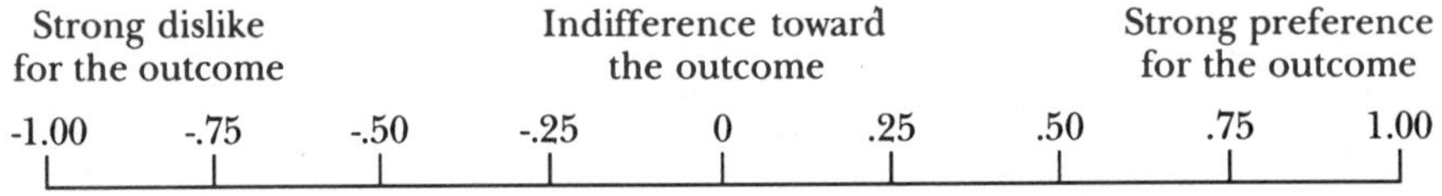

Strong dislike for the outcome			Indifference toward the outcome				Strong preference for the outcome	
-1.00	-.75	-.50	-.25	0	.25	.50	.75	1.00

Figure 9–19.
Valence: psychological value of the outcome.

ward and another person's ratio may lead to a greater expenditure of effort in order to increase the reward. Or the inequity between ratios may result in a withdrawal from the work situation. If a worker perceives his or her reward as excessive, he or she may continue to exert the same amount of effort for the reward or may decrease the amount of effort being exerted. The judging of the outcome of work in relationship to the effort with that of some reference group is not done by an absolute standard of comparison; it is in the eye of the beholder (Martin, 1982).

In VIE theory, both intrinsic and extrinsic rewards are recognized; however, neither is recognized as more desirable or more significant. What is important in VIE theory is expected outcomes that gain their valence or value from their relationship to the needs and values of the individual. For example, the outcome of working 7 days a week to meet a production quota by a particular deadline might be very valuable economically, but a person's internal value system may place a higher value on time spent with a family member or in religious activities. A primary determiner of expectancy may be an employee's perception of personal skills, talents, or abilities to accomplish a particular outcome. VIE theory is more complex than the previously mentioned theories because an individual is viewed as seeking a network of many interrelated outcomes rather than a single outcome, but it does seem to offer one of the best understandings of motivation. VIE theory is being given much attention by those concerned with behavior in organizations.

Application of Concepts

Explaining why a person behaves in a particular way has practical applications for organizations in improving marketing, decreasing absenteeism and employee turnover, increasing job satisfaction, increasing production, and building morale. Psychologists are often consulted by organizations and asked to make studies of human factors involved in these areas.

Marketing. Marketing is concerned with the buying and selling of products and services. Studying human behavior to learn the motive or motives causing a person to buy, who will buy, how many will buy, how much will be bought, and where the buying will occur

What is motivation research, and what are its uses in marketing?

is known as **motivation research,** which is extremely important in marketing. Motivation research tries to discover what needs, both conscious and unconscious, are involved in the choice of a product or service (see Figure 9–20) so that more effective appeals may be used in advertising. After a motive has been uncovered for selecting a product or service, questionnaires and field interviews may be used with representative samples to find how many people percentagewise have this specific motivation. Influences in buying, new markets, and direction for new advertising can be revealed through motivation research.

Figure 9–20. Motivation research identifies motives, perhaps unknown to the consumer, for buying a product.

Motivation research was popularized in the 1950s, and Vance Packard (1957) describes in his journalistic book *The Hidden Persuaders* many cases where results of studies were used by advertisers to manipulate consumers. Cars, for example, were found to be seen by many people as a symbol of status and adventure. Advertising then was focused on this motive. The motive for buying a convertible or a high-powered car may be quite different from the motive for buying a small, economical or conventional car, and thus the advertising may appeal to different motives.

What studies were the forerunner of the human relations movement, and what did the human relations movement stress?

Job Satisfaction and Organizational Problems. The interpretations of the studies conducted at the Hawthorne plant of the Western Electric Company that were discussed in chapter 1 under the heading *The Hawthorne effect* downgraded the role of economic incentives (money) on the grounds that workers' behaviors are influenced by social relationships. These interpretations shaped the trend of job satisfaction research, which later developed into the human relations movement. This movement stressed the importance of affiliation needs and the need for attention and recognition from others in productivity and job satisfaction. Because money is a generalized reinforcer and is associated with an almost unlimited number of things, the conditions under which it motivates varies; however, it is still considered to be a motive for working for practically every employee (Lawler, 1981).

Is money still considered to be a motive for working?

According to motivation theories, job satisfaction depends on whether personal needs, wants, desires, and expectations are fulfilled or satisfied on the job and on whether the job is compared favorably to some reference group. People have a tendency to avoid situations that are not satisfying, and consistently studies indicate that dissatisfied workers are absent more from their jobs and have greater turnover than employees who are satisfied (Atchison & Lefferts, 1972; Herzberg, Mausner, Peterson, & Capwell, 1957). Bass and Barrett (1972) suggested that perhaps absenteeism, which

How may dissatisfied employees indicate their dissatisfaction?

is temporary withdrawal, may be the easiest and least painful way for an employee to express dissatisfaction, especially because many companies give employees full pay when they are absent due to illness. Other actions such as tardiness, leaving early, and taking longer than authorized lunch or coffee breaks are also ways of temporarily avoiding the job situation.

Fulfillment of needs has been related to turnover in a study of needs of a group of workers who had quit their jobs compared with a matched group who had not quit. No difference was found in the needs and their strengths between groups; however, a significant difference was found in the degree to which their needs had been fulfilled (Ross & Zander, 1957).

Is there any relationship between job dissatisfaction and physical and mental health?

Research studies have found significant correlations between job satisfaction or dissatisfaction and such physical symptoms as fatigue, shortness of breath, headaches, and ill health (Burke, 1969/1970). A dissatisfied worker usually experiences more stress, thus producing biochemical changes that lead to physical symptoms. Also, significant correlations between job satisfaction and psychological well-being (mental health) have been found (Barrett, 1972; Kornhauser, 1965).

To be successful, should the supervisor or leader be employee oriented or production oriented?

A successful leader or supervisor has been defined in terms of productivity and employee satisfaction (Higgins, 1982). To be successful, the supervisor or leader must be employee oriented enough to maintain some degree of job satisfaction as well as production oriented enough to get the job done. A successful leader engages in both behaviors in varying degrees, stressing production and technical aspects of the job and viewing employees as the means of achieving the goals of the organization while also considering employees as human beings who may be intrinsically motivated and who have individual and personal needs.

What is Guion's definition of morale?

Morale is often discussed in the context of motivation; however, the word seems to have many meanings such as a feeling of happiness, satisfaction, or good personal adjustment; little conflict; many favorable attitudes; and cohesiveness—a "we feeling" that comes from finding personal need satisfaction with a group. Guion (1961) included all these meanings when he defined morale as the "extent to which an individual's needs are satisfied and the extent to which the individual perceives that satisfaction as stemming from his total job situation" (p. 303). Correlations found between morale and overall satisfaction suggest that morale may be a function of general satisfaction (Motowidlo & Borman, 1978). Another view proposes that high morale exists when an individual perceives a high probability of achieving both individual and group goals through a course of action and that whenever the individual perceives a considerable difference between group goals and personal goals, morale will suffer (Stagner, 1958). To raise morale within an organization, situations in which group and individual goals coincide to the greatest extent possible must be created.

What is one view of how to raise morale in an organization?

Motivational Strategies. A number of strategies or innovations such as flexible scheduling, job redesign, job enrichment, and goal setting have become popular in an effort to meet workers' needs. **Flexible scheduling** (see Figure 9–21), which allows workers to schedule their own 40-hour workweek within the time the organization is in operation, is a system that has been shown to decrease tardiness and absenteeism, increase productivity, and aid in retention of personnel (Chruden & Sherman, 1984). The 4-day workweek and **job sharing,** whereby two part-time employees perform a job normally performed by one full-time employee, have been instituted in some organizations in an effort to meet the needs of workers. Job satisfaction has been shown to be partly determined by the workers' perception of the degree to which the hours of work facilitate or interfere with valued off-the-job activities (Mott, Mann, McLoughlin, & Warwick, 1965).

"Now that both our jobs allow for flexible scheduling, we can take more family trips, have one of us home with the children most of the time, and plan our schedules to attend our community service club meetings."

Figure 9–21.
Such innovations as flexible scheduling and job sharing are a result of the recent trend for organizations to focus on the interrelationships between the world of work and the family, the community, and changing sex role definitions.

Job redesign is a procedure undertaken by some organizations to redesign jobs to make the work itself more rewarding, challenging, and meaningful to employees (Alderfer, 1976). In a job redesign experiment in the upholstery department at the Volvo automobile plant in Sweden, turnover that had been running 35 percent fell to 15 percent. The managing director of Volvo became convinced through the use of job redesign that a way must be found to create a workplace that meets the needs of the modern worker without adversely affecting productivity (Dowling, 1978).

Job redesign may take many forms. **Job enrichment,** the process of adding tasks of a managerial nature to a job, is a type of job redesign sometimes used to improve performance (Williams, DuBrin, & Sisk, 1985). In 1968 the Monsanto Chemical plant located in Pensacola, Florida, eliminated dull and dirty jobs by automation and made workers their own managers. The reported results indicated waste dropped to zero and production was up by 50 percent (*Work in America,* 1972). Using **job enlargement** in job redesign is the practice of adding tasks for variety and for task identity, which makes jobs more satisfactory for most people (Williams & Huber, 1986). Many firms are providing educational courses at the job site as well as implementing refund programs to pay for all or part of tuition costs for courses at schools outside the organization to meet the growth needs of workers. When **job rotation** is used in job redesign, it involves moving employees from job to job to keep the work from being as boring.

How does goal setting function to increase productivity and job satisfaction?

Goal setting is a strategy used to increase productivity and job satisfaction. Goal setting can aid in reducing discrepancies between what the environment offers, what is expected, and what is attained, which expectancy theory suggests is a factor in job satisfaction. Reaching defined goals most likely provides the employee with a greater sense of worthwhile contribution to the organization, a feeling of success, and reinforcement through some form of feedback. Evidence indicates that goal setting has a great impact on motivation (Latham & Steele, 1983). **Management by objectives (MBO)** is a managerial philosophy and technique whereby superiors and subordinates jointly identify goals, define each individual worker's responsibility in terms of individual goals, and use these goals as a guide for evaluating success on the job (Williams & Huber, 1986). Individual differences play an important role in goal setting. Research also indicates (Steers, 1975, 1976) that with clear and specific goals, individuals with high need for achievement perform tasks better, pursue goals no matter how much freedom they are given, and tend to prefer more difficult goals than individuals with low need for achievement. Identifying and effectively dealing with individual differences may determine whether flexible scheduling, a job redesign program, or goal setting will be a success or failure.

What is an MBO program?

SUMMARY

1. Motivation refers to the forces or processes that activate or cause behavior to occur and give direction to behavior, but different theories propose different sources of motivation. Motives are the specific needs, desires, and wants that motivate.
2. Two basic assumptions exist about behavior: free will, which assumes that humans freely choose their own behavior, and determinism, which assumes that behavior is the consequence of prior physical, psychological, or environmental events that are independent of the human will.
3. Philosophers have attributed behavior to conscious reasoning (rationalism), natural physical laws (mechanism), the desire for pleasure and avoidance of pain (hedonism), an interaction of mind and body (dualism), and instinct.

4. The source of motivation has been attributed to (a) drives, physiological needs brought about by biological distress; (b) incentives, learning that causes environmental stimuli to be a pulling force; (c) psychological (social or learned) needs, brought about by psychological (emotional or mental) distress; (d) arousal, sensitivity or reactiveness to a stimulus; (e) reinforcement, learned association between the behavior and the consequence of the behavior; (f) expectancy, the perceived probability of a consequence of a particular value; and (g) homeostasis, the need to maintain a balance or equilibrium.
5. Motives for behavior or needs are classifed as primary or secondary. Primary motives are those having a physiological basis and are necessary for survival—food, fluids, tolerable temperature, air (oxygen), freedom from pain, sleep and dreaming, sex, care of the young, sensory stimulation, activity, curiosity, exploration, manipulation, and human body contact.
6. Secondary motives are learned or acquired and have a psychological (emotional or mental) basis. The basic secondary motives are (a) affiliation, the need to be accepted by others; (b) achievement, the need to compare well with others in accomplishments; (c) aggressiveness, the need to inflict physical or psychological harm on others; (d) security, the need to be free from fear; and (e) cognitive consistency, the need for agreement or to be free from dissonance.
7. Motivation may be intrinsic, as when the satisfaction is in the behavior itself, or extrinsic, whereby the satisfaction is in the outcome of the behavior.
8. Motivation may be unconscious as well as conscious. A person may act to satisfy a need without being aware of the need that is the source of the behavior in order to protect the self from guilt feelings or anxiety or simply because recognition is too complex.
9. Motivation is assessed indirectly (a) by observing general activity levels, rates of responding, and endurance levels; (b) by self-report inventories; or (c) by projective-type tests such as the Thematic Apperception Test.
10. Various theories contribute to understanding motivation in the workplace, but no totally unifying theory of motivation applicable to work behaviors exists.
11. The need for affiliation (nAff), the need for achievement (nAch), and the need for power (nPow) are three basic, socially acquired motives that identify patterns of individual behavior important in the creation of the right kind of work climate for individual employees.
12. Maslow's theory of hierarchy of needs proposes a ranked order of priority for need satisfaction from physiological needs to safety to belongingness to esteem to self-actualization. Motivation is a general progression up the hierarchy; however, needs constantly fluctuate due to temporary conditions.
13. McGregor proposed an integrative view of managing people that

assumes that any person is capable of being intrinsically motivated (Theory Y). This view versus the traditional view that assumes an inherent lack of ambition that requires external direction and control (Theory X) has influenced management techniques.

14. Herzberg proposed that two factors exist in the work situation—hygiene factors external to the job itself, the satisfaction of which only avoids dissatisfaction, and motivation factors occurring at the time the work is performed, the satisfaction of which can produce job satisfaction and increased productivity.
15. VIE theory portrays behavior as being energized and directed by (a) valence, the believed values of the outcomes; (b) instrumentality, the ability of the first-level outcome to achieve other second-level outcomes of value; and (c) expectancy, the probability of the outcomes.
16. Motivation research to discover why people buy a particular product or service, who and how many will buy, and where and how much buying will occur has a practical application in marketing.
17. Satisfaction of needs seems to be a factor in organizational problems such as absenteeism, tardiness, turnover, physical and mental health, production, and morale of employees.
18. Some strategies that have been employed in organizations to enhance job satisfaction are (a) flexible scheduling, (b) job sharing, (c) goal setting, and (d) job redesign, which includes job enrichment, job enlargement, and job rotation.

KEY TERMS AND CONCEPTS

Motivation
Motives
Free will
Determinism
Rationalism
Mechanism
Hedonism
Dualism
Instinct
Drive
Incentives
Needs
Arousal theory
Reinforcement theory
Expectancy theory
Homeostasis
Balance theory
Primary motives
Stimulus motives
Sociobiology
Secondary motives
Affiliation motive
Achievement motive
Aggressive motive
Aggression
Security motive
Cognitive consistency
Cognitive dissonance
Extrinsic motivation
Intrinsic motivation
Self-efficacy
Unconscious motivation
nAch
nAff
nPow
Self-actualization
Theory Y
Theory X
Hygiene factors
Motivation factors
VIE theory
Expectancy
Valence
Instrumentality
Motivation research
Morale
Flexible scheduling
Job sharing
Job redesign
Job enrichment
Job enlargement
Job rotation
Management by objectives (MBO)

QUESTIONS FOR REVIEW

1. What philosophical views of human behavior influenced modern approaches to explaining behavior?
2. What is motivation, and what are the current theoretical views of motivation?
3. What are the primary motives, and how do they differ from secondary motives?
4. What are the basic secondary motives? Describe them.
5. How do intrinsic and extrinsic motivation differ, and how do conscious and unconscious motivation differ?
6. How are a person's motives assessed?
7. What are nAff, nAch, and nPow, and how can an understanding of these be useful in the workplace?
8. What are the basics of Maslow's, McGregor's, and Herzberg's theories? VIE theory?
9. How are motivation concepts applied in improving marketing and in alleviating some organizational problems?
10. What motivational strategies have been popular in an effort to meet workers' needs? Describe techniques.

TEST YOURSELF

1. Motivation is that hypothetical something within a person that ________________ and ________________ behavior.
2. Free will is the assumption (a) made by behaviorists (b) that humans freely choose their own behavior (c) that every event, act, or decision is the consequence of prior physical, psychological, or environmental events that are independent of the human will (d) all of the above.
3. Today the source of human behavior is attributed to (a) internal biological conditions (drives) (b) external environmental conditions (incentives) (c) instincts (d) both a and b.
4. Many contemporary psychologists reject the drive theory in favor of arousal theory. T or F
5. The optimum level of arousal for the best performance (a) is the highest possible level of arousal (b) is the lowest possible level of arousal (c) varies with the complexity of the task and among different people (d) varies among different people but remains constant for the tasks performed by a person.
6. Expectancy theory proposes that human behavior results from a deliberate, conscious choice to behave in a particular way based on the expected probability of outcomes or consequences of the behavior and the perceived value of the outcomes. T or F

7. Motives that have a biological basis are classified as ________________ motives, and ________________ motives are those that have a psychological or learned basis.
8. The factor or factors involved in achievement motivation seem(s) to be (a) the need for success (b) the fear of failure (c) the fear of success (d) all of the above.
9. The majority of psychologists today hold the view that the need to be aggressive is innate (inborn). T of F
10. The Thematic Apperception Test (TAT) is used to assess motivation as reflected in the (a) content of stories created in response to certain standard pictures (b) responses to a set of standardized questions (c) behavioral responses directly observed and evaluated according to general activity level, rate of responding, and the relative strength of competing motives (d) association of words and pictures.
11. Individuals with a high need for power (nPow) avoid playing organizational politics, arguing, and striving intensely for promotions. T or F
12. Individuals with a high need for affiliation tend to (a) enjoy jobs that have many interactions with other people (b) avoid power (c) care very much about what others think of them (d) all of the above.
13. In Maslow's hierarchy of needs, the order of priority from first or most basic to the last or highest is (a) self-actualization, safety, esteem, belongingness, physiological (b) physiological, esteem, belongingness, safety, self-actualization (c) physiological, safety, belongingness, esteem, self-actualization (d) none of the above.
14. Theory Y is a theory of management based on concepts of motivation proposed by (a) Frederick Herzberg (b) Abraham Maslow (c) Douglas McGregor (d) David McCelland.
15. According to Herzberg's two-factor theory, the satisfaction of hygiene factors results in (a) job satisfaction (b) job dissatisfaction (c) job satisfaction sometimes and job dissatisfaction other times (d) neither job satisfaction nor job dissatisfaction.
16. According to VIE theory, if the behavior of working overtime results in a promotion to the job of buyer that results in frequent travel to Europe, the travel to Europe would be called a ________________ of working overtime.
17. In VIE theory, valence is (a) the believed value of first-level and second-level outcomes (b) the believed ability of a first-level outcome to achieve or secure second-level outcomes (c) the belief that a particular behavior will lead to a particular first-level outcome (d) the believed probability of occurrence of a particular first-level outcome.
18. Motivation research is seldom used in marketing because it has proven to be of little benefit in discovering why a person buys a particular product or service because the motive for purchasing a product or service is so often unconscious motivation. T or F

19. Studies indicate that workers who do not have their needs satisfied or expectations fulfilled are more likely than those who do to (a) be absent more often from their jobs (b) quit their jobs (c) have more physical illness (d) all of the above.
20. If a job redesign strategy implemented by an organization in an effort to increase job satisfaction and thus reduce turnover, absenteeism, tardiness, and poor production is the addition of some tasks of a managerial nature to the job, the strategy is referred to as (a) job rotation (b) job enrichment (c) job enlargement (c) goal setting.

APPLICATIONS

A. A unit manager at the Zylo Corporation who supervises a large number of employees has noted that workers in the unit are being absent and tardy more and more frequently, and they are taking more and longer than authorized coffee breaks. The employees seem rather uninterested in their work and are just "making a day." Also, production is dropping off in the unit even though the same number of workers are still employed in the unit. Pressure is being placed on the manager to increase production and to keep production in the unit up to par with other units. In fact, the manager may lose the job as manager if this cannot be accomplished. After taking a night class concerned with motivation, the manager decides to try some motivational strategies.

1. If the manager decides to adopt an MBO philosophy and technique, what action would be taken?
2. If the manager decides to adopt a Theory Y philosophy and style of management, do you think it would be effective with all employees in the unit? Why?
3. If the manager takes action to motivate workers based on Herzberg's theory, would the focus be on intrinsic or extrinsic rewards? What are some specific factors the manager would probably focus on?

B. A department supervisor and the personnel department are in the process of selecting two present employees for promotions to fill two new jobs. For one of the jobs, they feel that an employee with a high need for affiliation would be more effective and better satisfied with the job. For the other job, they feel that an employee with a high need for achievement would be more effective and better satisfied with the job.

1. If the supervisor and the personnel department assess the motivation of the present employees informally (unsystematically), what are some characteristics they would look for in employees that would indicate a high need for achievement? a high need for affiliation?
2. If the supervisor and the personnel department decide to assess the motivation of the present employees formally (systematically) using the

TAT, describe the procedure for administering and scoring the test.
3. What would be some advantages of using a self-report inventory?

SUGGESTIONS FOR FURTHER READING

Deci, E. L. (1975). *Intrinsic motivation.* New York: Plenum.

A well-written book that combines many different concepts of intrinsic motivation. The role of cognition in motivation is also included. Key studies regarding effects of rewards on intrinsic motivation are presented.

Geen, R. G., Beatty, W. W., & Arkin, R. M. (1984). *Human motivation: Physiological, behavioral, and social approaches.* Newton, MA: Allyn and Bacon.

The latest theories and research findings are included in this very complete overview of motivation.

Maslow, A. H. (1970). *Motivation and personality* (2nd ed.). New York: Harper & Row.

This book is the most complete version of Maslow's general theory of motivation. It is a highly readable and systematic presentation of his views.

McClelland, D. C. (1985). *Human motivation.* Glenview, IL: Scott Foresman.

An excellent coverage of motivation that is up-to-date in regard to theories and research findings.

Packard, V. (1957). *The hidden persuaders.* New York: Pocket Books, Inc.

An intriguing book written for the average citizen that covers motivation research and unconscious motivation.

Petri, H. L. (1981). *Motivation: Theory and research* (2nd ed.). Belmont, CA: Wadsworth.

A book that presents and reflects the currently held views of motivation.

Spence, J. T. (Ed.). (1983). *Achievement and achievement motives.* San Francisco: W. H. Freeman.

Current research and thinking about achievement motivation is the focus of this book.

CHAPTER 10

EMOTIONS, STRESS, AND ADJUSTMENT

Objectives

When you have completed your study of chapter 10, you should be able to:

1. Define emotion in terms of its components.
2. Give support for the view that emotion is partially innate.
3. Explain how emotion is expressed nonverbally.
4. Describe the measurable dimensions of emotion and measurement techniques.
5. Briefly summarize several basic theories of emotion.
6. Describe tension, and identify symptoms of tension.
7. Describe some techniques for measuring emotional stress.
8. Identify and describe sources of psychological stress.
9. Differentiate between four types of conflict.
10. Cite several specific techniques useful in managing stress.

What would people be like if no emotion could be experienced?

People experience feelings such as fear, anger, sadness, guilt, happiness, joy, pleasure, and love. If people were incapable of feeling, life would be rather colorless and monotonous. Individuals would be more like computers or robots—able to behave but without feeling. Sometimes an emotion may be a very positive force, or an emotion may be a very negative force that overwhelms and destroys a person. Emotional states related to stress and how a person reacts to stressful events are unavoidable and, up to a point, may be beneficial. Intense emotional stress over an extensive period of time may have adverse effects. This chapter focuses on human emotion and emotional stress, which all people experience in their personal and work lives.

THE NATURE OF EMOTION

What do psychologists agree on about emotion?

Emotion involves many different feelings, sometimes called *affective states,* which constantly fill an individual's life. Although emotion is an abstraction like learning or motivation, psychologists tend to agree that it is composed of both physiological changes in the body and mental activity, may be expressed through behavior, and has three measurable dimensions. These dimensions are approach-avoidance, pleasantness-unpleasantness, and intensity. The various aspects of emotion, measurement of emotion, and various theories explaining emotion are discussed in this section.

Definition

How do many psychologists define emotion?

Though commonly experienced, emotion is not easy to define. Some psychologists make no attempt to define the concept, proposing that it is really too complex and subjective. Many other psychologists, however, believe that emotion is a combination of three aspects—physiological changes, feelings (affect), and expressive behavior. For example, fear may be associated with a pounding heart and increased blood pressure, a subjective feeling of some threat to well-being, and withdrawal from the situation. Pleasure may be associated also with a pounding heart and increased blood pressure, a subjective feeling that enhances well-being, and engagement in the activity. A person's behavior is motivated by feelings; she or he behaves in order to evade unpleasant states such as fear or guilt and to obtain pleasant emotional states such as happiness, love, pleasure, or joy. These three aspects of emotion—physiological changes, feelings, and expressive behavior—are examined separately in an attempt to define emotion more fully.

When a person experiences emotion, what happens in the body?

Physiology of Emotion. When people experience intense emotion, they are aware of some but not all of the changes in the body. Physiological psychologists indicate that the sympathetic part of the autonomic nervous system leading from the brain and spinal cord to the smooth muscles of the internal organs of the body, glands, and blood vessels is activated by emotion. As was pointed out in chapter 2, the sympathetic nervous system is the body's involuntary response to any kind of demand made on the body, whether it be physical, cognitive, or emotional, to enable the person to take action to adapt to environmental conditions. Activation of the sympathetic nervous system is often called the *flight or fight response* and affects many internal organs simultaneously as various chemicals are released into the bloodstream. The hormones epinephrine (adrenaline) and norepinephrine (noradrenaline) are secreted when the adrenal glands are activated by nerve impulses in the sympathetic nervous system. Epinephrine helps mobilize sugar in the blood to make more energy available to the brain and muscles and causes the heart to beat faster. Norepinephrine constricts the peripheral blood vessels and raises the blood pressure.

Which two hormones are especially important in the physiology of emotion?

The brain, primarily the cortex, is involved in perception and appraisal of stimuli that produce emotion, and it controls and directs the physiological responses. In the core of the brain is a complex group of structures known as the limbic system, which is related to emotion. The hypothalamus, included in this system, is

What system in the brain is especially related to emotion?

involved in activating the endocrine system to serve as a pathway to and from the cerebral cortex. Stimulation of certain points in the limbic system has produced great change in emotional behavior. For example, humans have experienced great pleasure when the posterior hypothalamus was stimulated or experienced rage or sexual sensations when other areas of the limbic system were stimulated (Delgado, 1969). The intensity of an emotion is related to the degree of physiological change in the body.

What is the role of mental activity in emotion?

Cognitive Component of Emotion. Emotion consists of a cognitive component as well as a physiological component. The cognitive component is based on mental activity referred to as information processing. Whether a person experiences fear, anger, love, or some other emotion depends on perception, appraisal of what is perceived, imagination, learning, and the recall of past experiences. Several people may witness the same scene and one of the group may perceive it as funny and experience humor. Another in the group may perceive it as a threatening situation and experience fear. Another in the group may perceive it as aggressive and experience anger. Whether a person is sad that the half-filled pitcher is half empty or happy that it is half full is a matter of perception. Cognition determines the kind and quality of emotion experienced.

How do people express emotion?

Why is verbal expression often inadequate in determining another person's emotion?

Expression of Emotion. People are constantly expressing emotion and monitoring other people's expression of emotion. Emotion may be expressed both verbally and nonverbally. Although people may be aware of their feelings and are willing to express verbally what they feel, they often find it hard to find words to describe their own emotions. In some situations when people have repressed or hidden their emotions in the unconscious part of the mind, they do not consciously know what emotions they really are experiencing. Consequently, the emotion cannot be verbally expressed. Sometimes the emotion is verbally minimized or denied entirely to avoid hurting another person or to conform to how a person believes he or she is supposed to feel. Sometimes a person verbally states the opposite of the emotion really felt. For example, a secretary fails to show up for work one day, and the office manager has a busy day trying to manage without any help. When the secretary comes to work the next day, the office manager may say, "I hope you enjoyed your day yesterday" rather than saying, "I am furious and hope you had a lousy day yesterday." Almost everyone at times, consciously or unconsciously, attempts to hide his or her emotions to protect the self-image or to conform to social expectations. Verbal expression of emotion is under the conscious control of the individual. For these reasons, determining another person's emotions based on verbal expression alone is considered to be inadequate. Because the physiological changes associated with emotions are not normally under the control of the individual, the expression of the emotion through facial display, body postures and gestures, vocal intonations, physical distance, and eye contact are usually more reliable expressions than verbal expressions.

What are some of the arguments used to support the view that facial expression as an indicator of emotion is partially innate?

Facial expression is an indicator of emotion that seems to be partially innate. Some psychologists believe that facial expressions are the key indicator of emotional experience. These psychologists believe that every basic emotion is accompanied by a characteristic facial pattern that occurs automatically as a result of hereditary programming (Izard, 1977). The various patterns are believed to be the product of evolution. Charles Darwin noted that most animals, including humans, share a common pattern of facial expressions. For example, they all bare their teeth in rage. Children who are born blind and deaf exhibit the same facial expressions for emotions as do children born without these defects. For example, they smile to express joy or raise their eyebrows to express surprise. Further evidence of universal facial expressions for the basic emotions is provided by Paul Ekman and his associates (1975). They showed photographs of six facial expressions to college students in five countries and found that the students in all countries accurately identified most of the emotions (see Figure 10–1).

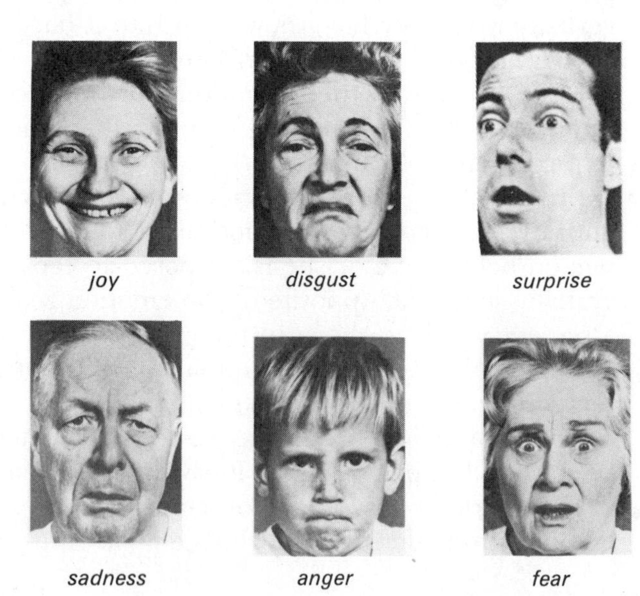

Figure 10–1.
Facial expressions of emotions.

The pupils of the eyes enlarge involuntarily whenever a person experiences emotion. Thus, a person may monitor the feelings of others through the eyes, usually unconsciously. For example, research studies have found that strangers with large pupils are usually perceived as being warmer, more attractive, or happier than those with smaller pupils, who are perceived as being less friendly and colder (Hess, 1975). A salesperson may unconsciously rely more on watching the eyes of prospective buyers to know what they really like than on what is verbally communicated. This is probably the basis for the expression sometimes used to describe a person experiencing happiness, "The eyes light up."

In an experiment studying facial expression, people were shown groups of three photographs similar to the group in Figure 10–2. Photograph *a* is a picture that has not been altered. Photograph *b* is composed of two right halves of the face shown in the original photograph. The right half is flipped over to form the left side. Photograph *c* consists of two left halves of the face shown in the original photograph. The left half is flipped over to form the right side. The left-face combinations were found to give the clearest, strongest expression of emotion (Sackeim, Gur, & Saucy, 1978). In chapter 2 it was pointed out that the right and left hemispheres of the brain are not equal partners. The left half of the brain, which controls the right side of the face and body, specializes in language and logic (the analytical brain). The right half of the brain, which controls the left side of the face and body, seems to be the feeling brain as well as the half that specializes in spatial relationships, form, and music. In view of this, a person should concentrate on the left side of the face and ignore the right side to perceive a stronger, clearer expression of the emotion the person is experiencing.

a

b

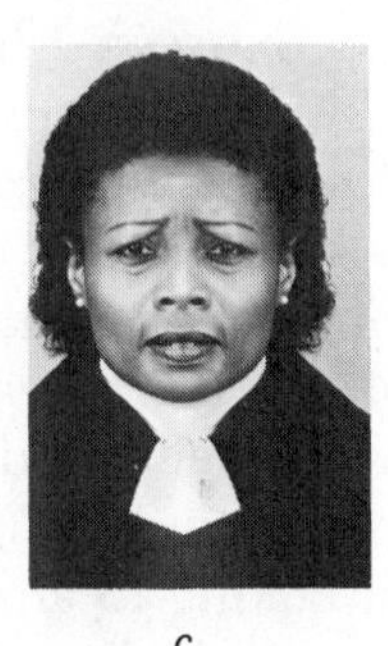
c

Figure 10–2. Three facial expressions of an emotion. Most people perceive photograph *c* as a clearer and stronger expression of the emotion.

Which side of the face gives a stronger, clearer expression of the emotion a person is experiencing?

Body postures and gestures as well as facial expression have been studied as nonverbal expressions of emotion. The study of body language (postures and gestures) has been made into a science called **kinesics** (Birdwhistell, 1952). When a person directly faces and leans toward another person, the emotion of interest and acceptance is indicated. The body of a person experiencing anxiety may be rather rigid and the back straight. A person who is feeling relaxed will likely be loose rather than rigid in his or her movements. When people are consciously trying to keep an emotion from showing in their faces, they are less conscious about their bodies, legs, feet, and hands, which may give cues. For example, a poker player may be able to avoid communicating a facial expression that would indicate the joy and excitement of having a good hand, but the player may unconsciously lean forward in expectancy of collecting the chips. Gestures such as a handshake, a slap on the back, a touch, and an embrace are expressions of feelings. Clenching the fist usually indicates anger; covering the eyes, shame or embarrassment; and rubbing the hands together, anticipation or excitement.

What is kinesics?

Emotions are also expressed by physical characteristics of the voice such as pitch, loudness, pauses, exclamations, stuttering, and voice inflections, all of which are referred to collectively as **paralanguage.** Screams may be indicative of fear; sobs of sorrow; laughter of joy; and groans of pain or unhappiness. A tremoring voice may be an expression of grief or great sorrow, a loud, high-pitched voice an expression of anger, and a normal or soft, high-pitched voice an expression of warm feelings. For example, the pitch of the voice is higher when talking to an infant than to an adult or when expressing love to an adult than when not engaging in love talk. Also, the pitch of the voice has been found to have a tendency to rise when a person is lying because a rise in the pitch of the voice is an expression of emotion (Freedman, Sears, & Carlsmith, 1978). Such physical characteristics of the voice are usually involuntary.

What is paralanguage?

Proxemics, the physical distance kept from a person, object, or event and the eye contact that is maintained, is another nonverbal expression of emotion. A standard distance seems to prevail that is appropriate for conversation with friends. This standard distance varies from culture to culture. Whenever someone stands closer than this standard distance, it indicates an approach emotion—perhaps aggression or affection. Whenever someone stands farther away than the standard distance, it indicates an avoidance emotion—perhaps fear or disgust.

How is emotion expressed by proxemics?

A psychological distance seems to be maintained through eye contact. Looking into a person's eyes seems to be like looking inside the person and seeing what's in the person's mind. As in physical distance, a standard or normal amount of time seems to prevail for eye contact. Gazing for a longer than standard time may indicate unusual dislike or hostility or unusual attraction as in love or sexual attraction. This sounds perplexing, but a person usually has no trouble distinguishing between a stare of love and a stare of hate. Gazing for less than a standard amount of time may indicate a fear of psychological closeness, guilt, negative thoughts, the desire to withdraw from the person, a general lack of interest as in depression, or a fear of people in general as in shyness. The more a person looks at another person, the more dominant, potent, or self-confident the person doing the looking appears (Argyle, Lefebvre, & Cook, 1974). Eye contact, then, expresses feelings of self-confidence as well as liking and hostility.

Measurement of Emotion

What is usually the basis for indirect and subjective assessments of people's emotions?

An individual's emotions are assessed constantly by the people with whom the individual has contact, and an individual is constantly assessing the emotions of others with whom she or he has contact. These assessments are indirect and subjective and usually are based on behavioral cues from verbal and nonverbal expression of emotion and on the situation in which the expression occurs. For example, if a person is observed to have tears streaming down the cheeks, it may be assumed that the person is sad. If the situation is also observed and it is noted that someone whom the person is very close to is in distress, this assumption is more likely to be correct. However, if it is noted that the person has just received some great honor, the assumption that the person is happy may be made; the tears are tears of joy. If it is noted that the person is in the kitchen cutting onions, the assumption that no emotion at all is being experienced may be made; the tears are a reflex response to irritation of the eyes.

On what three dimensions can emotion be measured?

Dimensions. Emotions can be described in terms of three dimensions, each of which is measurable: approach-avoidance, pleasantness-unpleasantness, and intensity. Because of variations in these dimensions, people respond differently to the same external situations in the same environment (Mehrabian, 1976). These dimensions may vary as a result of learning, as a result of variation in information processing, and as a result of innate differences.

The sensitivity of the autonomic nervous system and the size and activity of the endocrine glands seem to be two inborn differences that affect these dimensions.

What is the basis for measuring an emotion on the approach-avoidance dimension?

The degree to which the emotion causes a person to move toward or away from an object, person, or event is the basis for measuring an emotion on the approach-avoidance continuum. Generally, positive emotions such as love and pleasure cause approach reactions, and negative emotions such as fear and anxiety lead to avoidance reactions. Anger may also lead to approach reactions, but in an attacking and aggressive manner. Whether a person moves away from something or someone or whether a person moves toward something or someone depends on how the person feels about the self in relationship to the object, event, or person. If there is no hope of controlling the object, situation, or person, an individual may try to avoid it. But if there is hope of controlling, an individual may approach it. Thus, the emotion may be measured on the approach-avoidance continuum regardless of whether the emotion expressed is fear, anger, or liking. For example, one employee might like the management of Department X and ask for a transfer to that department. Another employee may not like the management of Department X and request not to be transferred to that department for fear of being fired from the job. Another employee might not like the management of Department X but would ask for a transfer to that department with the hope of battling it out and getting the management changed.

What is meant by positive and negative emotions, and can a person have a positive and a negative feeling about something simultaneously?

Probably the most obvious dimension used in measuring emotion is the degree of pleasantness-unpleasantness. Emotions are classified as positive or negative, the pleasant ones such as curiosity, humor, love, joy, and elation being positive and jealousy, hate, fear, anger, and grief being negative. A person's feelings may be described as a point on a continuum from extremely unpleasant or negative to extremely pleasant or positive. Sometimes an individual may have two different feelings associated with the same object, person, or event simultaneously. For example, an employee may experience mixed emotions concerning a promotion—joy over the raise received and also fear of performing the new tasks required.

What represents the intensity of an emotion?

The intensity of the emotion is the dimension represented by the level of physiological arousal. It is the degree to which the sympathetic division of the autonomic nervous system reacts. A person may be slightly irritated, angry, or in a rage. The intensity of the emotion is a function of the degree to which the person is physically stirred up or upset.

Physiological Measures. Activation of the sympathetic nervous system causes a wide variety of responses that may be measured to determine the intensity of the emotion. Some such responses that have been used in measurement are salivation, pupil enlargement, heart rate, blood pressure, respiration, resistance of the skin to the conduction of electricity known as **galvanic skin response (GSR),** temperature in body extremities such as the fingers, and vibration of the muscles controlling the vocal cords.

In ancient cultures, it was observed that emotional arousal was often associated with a dry mouth. People of these cultures determined if a person was guilty of something by giving the suspect a slice of bread and cheese or rice powder to chew. Those who could not swallow it or who spit it out dry were considered guilty. Fear of being found out and punished was believed to inhibit the flow of saliva.

How has the measurement of pupil enlargement often been used?

Devices for measuring pupil enlargement increasingly have been used in recent years as a measure of emotion (Hess & Polt, 1960). Pupil responses are often used to measure the interest value of advertisements. Pupil responses are also used in research studies concerned with sexual feelings in relationship to visual stimuli. Also, enlargement of the pupils is indicative that attention is elicited and mental activity is occurring.

The **polygraph,** commonly called a lie detector, is a modern attempt to measure changes in several physiological responses associated with emotion. The polygraph records changes in heart rate, blood pressure, respiration, and the galvanic skin response. The theory of lie detection is that lying produces feelings of guilt and fear of the truth being discovered. A polygraph test is sometimes used as part of a job application procedure to measure emotional responses to questions that may be of interest to the prospective employer such as questions about stealing or drug use (see Figure 10–3).

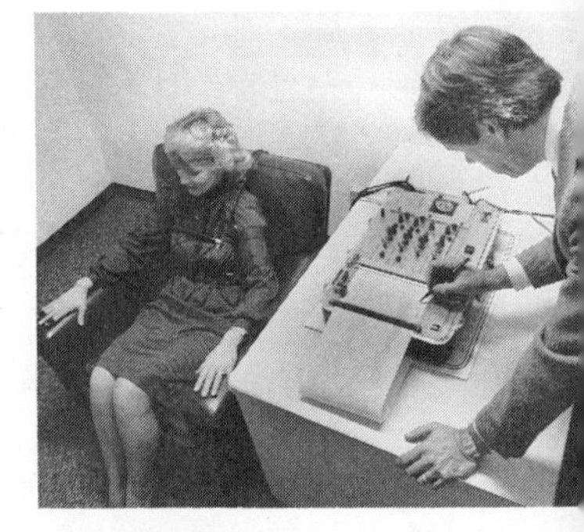

Figure 10–3.
A polygraph test is sometimes used as part of a job application procedure.

The **psychological stress evaluator** is a type of lie detector that will measure changes in a person's voice that are undetectable to the human ear. The activity of the sympathetic nervous system suppresses the vibration of the muscles controlling the vocal cords when a speaker is emotionally aroused. A device called a **voice stress analyzer** is used to replay the recording of a person's voice four times slower than the recorded speed and produce a voice printout in graphic form similar to the electroencephalogram (EEG) brain wave patterns. Voices may be recorded over the telephone, from radio or television, or from tape recordings without speaker knowledge as well as recorded in person. The speaker does not have to be hooked up to any equipment as with the polygraph. The polygraph and the voice stress analyzer give a fairly accurate indication of nervousness, tension, and anxiety; however, they do not always indicate guilt or lying.

Theories of Emotion

Various attempts have been made to explain emotion; however, most of the theories do not account for all three aspects of emotion—the physiological changes, the feelings, and the expressive behavior. In some theories, the physiological changes are thought to be the cause of the feeling. In other theories, the physiological changes are thought to be the result of the feeling. Still other theories propose an interaction of the three aspects of emotion. Some of the major theories of emotion are briefly reviewed for comparison. A summary of the major theories is provided in diagram form in Figure 10–4.

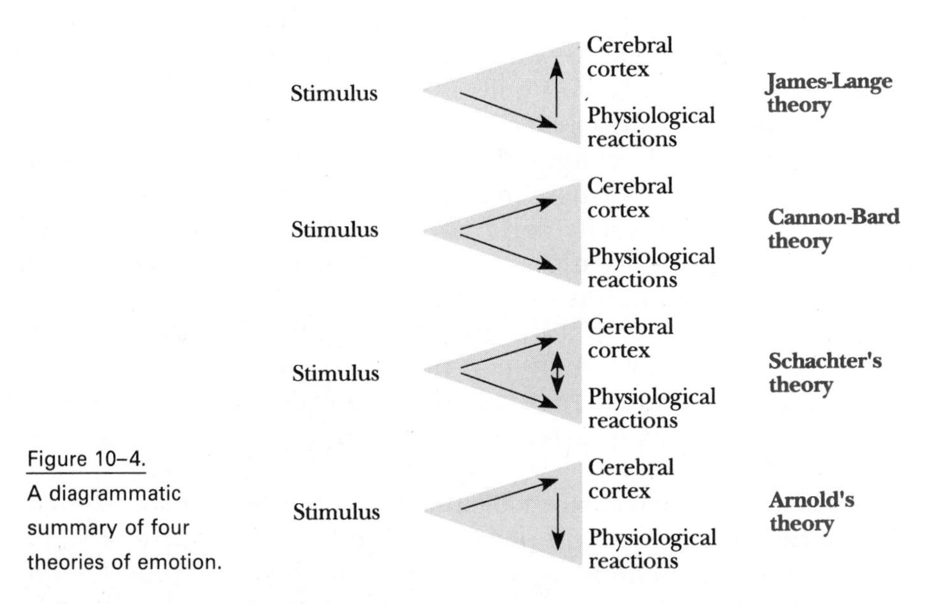

Figure 10–4. A diagrammatic summary of four theories of emotion.

Note. From Charles G. Morris, *Psychology: An Introduction,* 5/E, © 1985, p. 173. Adapted by permission of Prentice-Hall, Inc., Englewood Cliffs, New Jersey.

James-Lange Theory. William James (1884), the psychologist who was mentioned in chapter 1, and Carl Lange (1885/1922), a physiologist, proposed that a stimulus may produce a physiological change, and the sensation of this change is the emotion or feeling experienced. Specifically, this theory proposes that individuals feel sorrow as a result of crying, anger as a result of striking, fear because they retreat or tremble, happiness because they smile, or tickled because they laugh. Although most people think the reverse, that they cry because they are sorry, strike because they are angry, retreat because they are afraid, laugh because they are tickled, or smile because they are happy, the James-Lange theory does have some limited value today. This theory suggests that by acting a certain way a person may come to feel that way. Perhaps in some cases a person could overcome feelings of depression by engaging in pleasant activities or overcome fear by approaching the feared object rather than running away. In research with depressed and nondepressed people, a significant relationship was found between mood and the number and type of pleasant activities a person becomes involved in (Rehm, 1978). This theory may be illustrated by trying to keep a smiling face for a day and then trying to keep a sad face for a day to see if different feelings occur. In essence, the James-Lange theory proposes that the body responds first to a stimulus, and then the cognitive processes occur in the cortex based on the physiological responses.

Is body action the source of the feeling aspect of an emotion?

Cannon-Bard Theory. In 1927, Walter Cannon objected to the James-Lange theory, partially on the basis that the physiological arousal of one feeling is not different from the physiological arousal of other feelings. Cannon, with Philip Bard (1928), proposed that a stimulus triggers both physiological responses and psychological feelings simultaneously. According to this theory, the key brain structure that mediates the sending of messages simultaneously to the cortex for the cognitive component and to the autonomic nervous system for the physiological component is the thalamus. Research, however, has shown that the key brain structure mediating these two aspects of emotion is not the thalamus but structures in the limbic system. To summarize, the Cannon-Bard theory proposes that a stimulus activates both the cortex and the sympathetic nervous system simultaneously.

Are mediating structures present in the nervous system that simultaneously affect the psychological feeling and the physiological response to a stimulus?

Schachter's Theory. Neither the James-Lange theory nor the Cannon-Bard theory considered the role that such mental activities as thinking, evaluating, appraising, or interpreting can play in emotion. Cognitive psychologists offer theories proposing that emotion results from an interpretation of perceived physiological arousal and that previous experience directly affects the emotion. Research conducted by Stanley Schachter and Jerome Singer

Are perception and thinking interrelated so that each one affects the other?

(1962) has suggested that a stimulus produces an aroused state of the nervous system. This includes both the cerebral cortex in the central nervous system where perception or appraisal occurs and the autonomic nervous system where physiological changes are produced to adapt to the demand placed on the body. Perception or appraisal and arousal are interrelated, and thus, emotion is the result of both. If perceptions or appraisals can be changed, bodily changes are influenced; and if bodily changes can be changed, perception or cognitive appraisals of a situation are affected. For example, if a supervisor is angry because of a situation at home or a recent occurrence in a management meeting, a mistake made by a secretary may be perceived differently than when the supervisor is in a relaxed state. Also, if a mistake is perceived as nonthreatening and only involves the cost of retyping a page, the supervisor will not be aroused to anger as intensely as if the mistake is perceived as causing the company to lose a $100,000 contract or as threatening to the supervisor's ego by causing the supervisor to appear stupid.

How did Schachter demonstrate his theory?

Schachter supported this theory by demonstrating in an experiment that people aroused physiologically label the arousal depending on their perception of the situation (Schachter & Singer, 1962). Subjects in the experiment were aroused physiologically with an injection of adrenaline (epinephrine). Some were correctly informed as to the effects of the adrenaline and knew what to expect. Others were not informed or were incorrectly informed. Subjects were assigned a partner who had been instructed to be either euphoric and friendly or angry and resentful. When the subject had been correctly informed as to the effects of the injection, he or she was not as likely to experience emotion similar to the partner. When the subject was not informed or was incorrectly informed, she or he was more euphoric when with a euphoric partner and more angry when with an angry partner. Schachter believes that the situation a person is in when aroused gives clues as to the label for the emotion. Whether physiological arousal is labeled as happiness, love, hate, fear, anger, or grief depends on the situation and the person's perception or cognitive appraisal of the situation. To summarize, Schachter's theory proposes that the cognitive and physiological responses occur simultaneously in response to a stimulus, but the responses from the cerebral cortex also elicit physiological responses and these physiological responses in turn affect cognition.

Arnold's Theory. Magda Arnold (1960) emphasized appraisal or perception in her theory of emotion. Emotion is viewed as a tendency toward something that is appraised as good or away from something that is appraised as bad. Attraction and aversion are each accompanied by the pattern of physiological changes that prepares the body for action—approach or withdrawal. If a stimulus is appraised as neutral, these physiological changes are not elicited and there is no emotion. Appraisal of a stimulus is believed to occur almost instantaneously and precedes feeling, or affect. According to Arnold's theory, the feeling experienced and the physiological changes that lead to expressive behavior are both determined by the appraisal or perception that occurs in cerebral cortex processes. A business executive might see a person approaching and appraise the situation as good based on memories or imaginations of sales made; or the executive might appraise the situation as bad based on memories or imaginations of being robbed and mugged. In either case, the appraisal would produce a physiological response, and the business executive would experience a psychological feeling that would produce a direct action. Joy would produce approach and attempts to sell, anger would produce approach and physical or psychological assault, and fear would produce withdrawal and attempts to escape. To summarize, Arnold's theory proposes that the cerebral cortex responds first to a stimulus, and then the cognitive appraisal determines the feeling that elicits a physiological response.

Is a person's appraisal (perception and thinking) of a stimulus the source that elicits the physiological changes?

Plutchik's Theory. Robert Plutchik (1962, 1970, 1980) formulated a theory of innate emotion that defines eight primary emotions derived from evolutionary processes in terms of eight basic functions that are essential to the survival of the human species. All other emotions are believed to be varying intensities or mixtures of these primary emotions. Love, for example, is seen as a combination of joy and acceptance. Hostility or contempt is seen as a combination of anger and disgust (see Figure 10–5). Emotions across from each other on the wheel are opposites.

Plutchik associates each primary emotion with a basic function necessary for species survival such as reproduction, protection from dangerous things, and orientation to the environment. The basic functions necessary for species survival, the primary emotion with which each is associated, and an example of a higher and a lower intensity of each emotion are shown in Table 10–1.

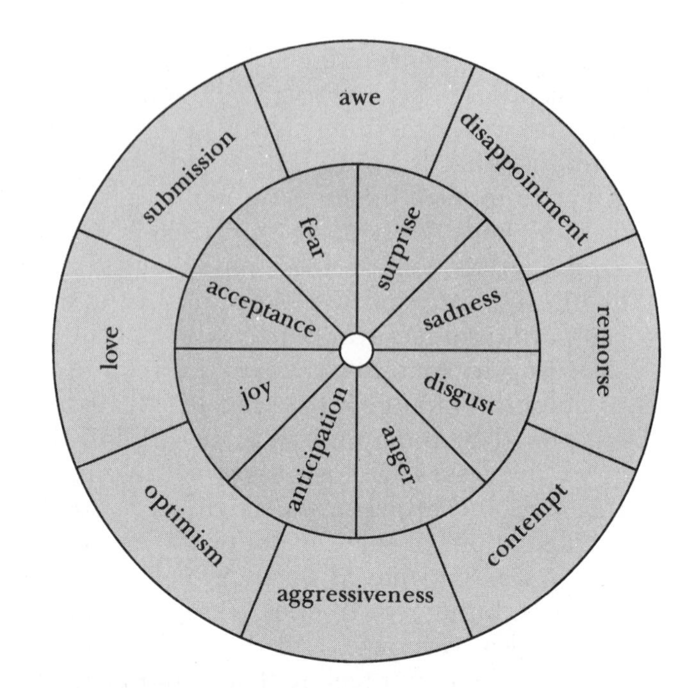

Figure 10–5.
Plutchik's eight basic emotions and the emotions formed by combinations of adjacent pairs.

Note. From *Emotion: A Psychoevolutionary Synthesis* (p.164) by Robert Plutchik, 1980, New York: Harper & Row. Copyright © 1980 by Harper & Row. Reprinted by permission.

What are the eight emotions believed by Plutchik to be innate?

The more recent theories of emotion indicate that emotion is more complex and that cognition plays a greater role than was originally believed. Therefore, the range of a person's emotions and the number of stimuli that produce emotions increases with physiological and cognitive development.

Function	Emotion	A Higher Intensity	A Lower Intensity
Protection	Fear	Terror	Apprehension
Destruction	Anger	Rage	Annoyance
Reproduction	Joy	Ecstasy	Pleasure
Deprivation	Sadness	Grief	Pensiveness
Incorporation	Acceptance	Interest	Attention
Rejection	Disgust	Loathing	Boredom
Exploration	Anticipation	Watchfulness	Readiness
Orientation	Surprise	Amazement	Distraction

Table 10–1
Primary emotions.

Note. From *Emotion: A Psychoevolutionary Synthesis* (p. 164) by Robert Plutchik, 1980, New York: Harper & Row. Copyright © 1980 by Harper & Row. Reprinted by permission.

EMOTIONAL STRESS

Stressors are the situations and events in a person's life that cause stress. Any situation that makes a special demand on the body produces **stress,** which is energy within the body produced to allow for action to cope with the situation, accomplish goals, or defend the self. If the body is injured, damaged, or diseased, special demands are made for healing of the injury, overcoming the damage, or conquering the disease. Heavy physical work, injury on the job, loss of sleep, poor nutrition, or illness might be sources of physiological stress for a worker. Psychologists are particularly concerned with psychological or emotional stress, demands that are placed on the body by the cognitive or mental processes. The body has mechanisms for adapting to or coping with both psychological and physiological stress. Of course, the stress may be so intense or prolonged that the mechanisms can no longer handle the stress. In this part of this chapter, attention is turned to tension, which is a result of stress, sources of stress, and techniques for managing stress.

Tension

What is the difference between stressors, stress, and tension?

Stressors, stress, and tension are all interrelated. Stressors produce stress, which in turn causes tension. **Tension** is the holding of stress in the muscles. In this section, an attempt is made to give the reader a better understanding of tension, to describe symptoms of tension, and to describe some stress measurement techniques.

Is tension always bad?

Understanding Tension. Because tension is the holding of energy in the muscles, some tension is necessary for an individual to function or act. All individuals who are alive experience some tension. Tension, therefore, is good up to a point. Tension has been defined (Woolf, 1974) as the condition of being strained or stretched. It is when the tension is present for too long or gets too intense that the body breaks down under strain. A string on a musical instrument, a string holding a package together, or the thread in a sewing machine might be used as an analogy of the function of tension. A certain amount of tension is necessary to get a job done satisfactorily. If the tension is too loose, the correct musical tone will not be produced, the package will fall apart, or the cloth will not be held together by the stitch. Too much tension will cause the string on the instrument or some part of the instrument to break. Likewise, too much tension will cause the string around the package to break or the contents of the package to be crushed, and too much tension will cause the thread in the machine to break or the material to pucker from the stitch. Too much tension also can cause physical pain. This may be demonstrated by clinching the hand into a very tight fist, tighter and tighter, and holding the clinch for 2 or 3 minutes. When the tension is released by letting the hand relax, the pain will go away. Much of a person's tension comes not from the problem or situation itself but from trying to resist or to hold on tightly. In order to function effectively, a person must manage stress so as to maintain just the optimum amount of tension.

What accounts for the fact that some people experience more tension than others?

Because of heredity, some individuals have a lower stress threshold for activation of the sympathetic nervous system and thus the production of energy and tension than do other individuals. Also, some individuals experience more stressors in their lives than do other individuals. Additionally, some individuals are better able to manage tension produced by stress than others because of predisposing factors and learning.

Hans Selye (1956), a medical researcher, coined the phrase **general adaptation syndrome** to represent the entire pattern of the sequence of physiological events that takes place during prolonged stress. He described three distinct stages of the general adaptation syndrome. The first stage, the alarm reaction, is the activation of the sympathetic nervous system. In this stage, physiological changes occur to handle the unusual situation. If the stress continues, thus continuing the activation of the sympathetic nervous system, the second stage, resistance, is reached. The body adapts to the physiological changes so that the person appears to be physiologically normal and does not experience symptoms such as increased breathing and increased rate of heartbeat. The body, however, is still under the influence of a hormone secreted by the pituitary gland that in turn stimulates the production of hormones of the adrenal gland. The increased production of these hormones weakens the body's defenses and causes the person to become more susceptible to infections. Thus, a person experiencing a great amount of stress over a long period of time may experience more illness than he or she would when not under such stress. If the person continues to experience the high level of stress for a long period of time, the pituitary gland and the adrenal gland finally will lose their ability to produce the increased amounts of the hormones and exhaustion, the third stage, begins. In this stage, the physiological processes begin to break down. If the stress continues, the eventual outcome will be death.

What are the three stages of the general adaptation syndrome?

How can a person tell when she or he is experiencing too much tension?

Symptoms of Too Much Tension. The way to tell whether too much stress and thus too much tension exists is to pay attention to the body. Some symptoms of too much stress are (a) feeling tired and exhausted much of the time, not only after a hard day's work but also at the beginning and in the middle of the day; (b) being bothered by seemingly minor health problems such as headaches, cramps in the legs, stiff neck, queasy stomach, or lower back pain; (c) having trouble sleeping, drinking or smoking too much, or taking too many pills; (d) avoiding contact or communication with other people or having trouble getting along with other people; (e) frequently losing control of the temper and staying irritable a great deal of the time; (f) worrying about mistakes or personal failures, real or imagined; (g) missing deadlines or forgetting appointments; (h) constantly worrying about time, always being in a hurry, and never feeling that the going is fast enough; (i) working late more often than usual because of not functioning well during the day; (j) feeling burned out, having given up on doing the job well, and often being tardy to work or absent from work; (k) experiencing little joy in life or actually suffering from depression.

What are psychosomatic illnesses?

Physical disorders that are the result of psychological stress are referred to as **psychosomatic illnesses.** Psychosomatic illnesses are real disorders, not imagined ones, and require medical attention. Some cases of ulcers, migraine headaches, asthma, high blood pressure, and heart disease are related to psychological stress. People who consistently exhibit excessive aggressiveness, competitive drive, impatience, and time urgency suffer twice as many heart-related deaths as people who are consistently calm and relaxed (Friedman & Rosenman, 1974). Herbert Benson (1975) of Harvard University has shown that prolonged stress can lead to high blood pressure, which can lead to diseases such as hardening of the arteries, strokes, and kidney malfunctions. Stress has also been shown to play a role in such diseases as arthritis, premenstrual syndrome, colitis, diabetes, and low blood sugar (Selye, 1976). Vulnerability to cancer and infectious disease has now been related to stress because stress is being found to play a role in the functioning of the immune system. "Behavioral immunology is mapping the connection between controlling stress and fighting disease" (Maier & Laudenslager, 1985, p. 44).

Can stress affect a person's immune system?

Measurement. Several objective techniques have been devised for measuring stress in the body. Thomas Holmes and Richard Rahe (1967) developed a scale to quantify the amount of stress a person experiences based on the impact of life experiences and the

Is a psychological measurement scale available to measure whether a person is experiencing mild, moderate, or major stress?

degree of adjustment involved in coping with the experience (see Table 10–2). The scale includes some common stressful events in people's lives from the most stressful down to the least stressful. The value of each life event that has occurred within the past 12 months is circled by the person taking the test, and then the values are totaled. A total of 150 to 199 units accumulated within a year indicates mild stress; 200 to 299 units indicates moderate stress; and 300 units and above indicates major stress. Holmes (1978) found that individuals who experienced a greater amount of stress ran a higher risk of physical illness or accidental injury. When major stress is indicated, the probability of having an illness or injury rises to about 80 percent compared with about a 30 percent probability with mild stress and a 50 percent probability with moderate stress. It is difficult, however, to predict stress-related illness because of the differences in individual reactions to stress.

Table 10–2
Scale of life-change units.

Life Event	Value	Life Event	Value
Death of spouse	100	Change in number of arguments with spouse	35
Divorce	73	Mortgage over $10,000	31
Marital separation	65	Foreclosure of mortgage or loan	30
Jail term	63	Change in responsibilities at work	29
Death of a close family member	63	Son or daughter leaving home	29
Personal injury or illness	53	Trouble with in-laws	29
Marriage	50	Outstanding personal achievement	28
Fired at work	47	Wife beginning or stopping work	26
Marital reconciliation	45	Begin or end school	26
Retirement	45	Change in living conditions	25
Change in health of family member	44	Revision of personal habits	24
Pregnancy	40	Trouble with boss	23
Sex difficulties	39	Change in work hours or conditions	20
Gain of new family member	39		
Business readjustment	39		
Change in financial state	38		
Death of close friend	37		
Change to different line of work	36		

Life Event	Value	Life Event	Value
Change in residence	20	Change in sleeping habits	16
Change in schools	20	Change in number of family get-togethers	15
Change in recreation	19	Change in eating habits	16
Change in church activities	19	Vacation	13
Change in social activities	18	Christmas	12
Mortgage or loan less than $10,000	17	Minor violations of the law	11

Note. Reprinted with permission from *Journal of Psychosomatic Research, 11,* T. H. Holmes and R. H. Rahe, "The Social Readjustment Rating Scale," Copyright © 1967, Pergamon Press, Ltd.

Biofeedback devices are available to give readouts of physiological responses to stressors such as galvanic response, blood pressure, brain wave patterns, and temperature in the hands. These devices range from simple devices such as a biofeedback card that can be carried in the billfold (see Figure 10–6) to very sophisticated and expensive electronic devices (see Figure 10–7).

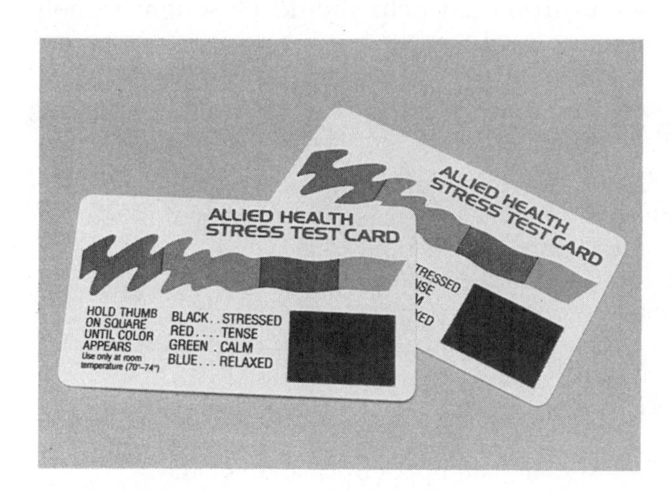

Figure 10–6.
Billfold-sized biofeedback cards similar to the above sketch are available to give a stress level reading to aid a person in stress control.

Is a psychological measurement scale available to measure a person's vulnerability to stress?

Psychologists Lyle H. Miller and Alma Dell Smith at Boston University Medical Center developed a test to measure vulnerability to stress (Wallis, 1983). A variety of self-report inventories have been developed such as the one developed by clinical psychologist William D. Brown (1983) to evaluate job-related stress. Statements such as "I dread Mondays," "If it weren't for money, I'd quit my

Figure 10–7. Sophisticated biofeedback machines are available such as the one pictured above that measures heart rate and blood volume pulse, a measurement of pulse amplitude at the fingertips caused by changes in the sympathetic nervous system.

job immediately," and "Those reporting to me do not seem especially loyal" are rated on a scale of 1 (strongly agree) to 5 (strongly disagree). The total of the ratings indicates whether the anxiety level is manageable, whether ways of lowering anxiety need to be explored, or whether professional help should be sought to help bring the anxiety under control.

HOW VULNERABLE ARE YOU TO STRESS?

Score each item on a scale from 1 (almost always) to 5 (never) according to how much of the time each statement applies to you.

____ 1. I eat at least one hot, balanced meal a day.
____ 2. I get 7 to 8 hours sleep at least 4 nights a week.
____ 3. I give and receive affection regularly.
____ 4. I have at least one relative within 50 miles on whom I can rely.
____ 5. I exercise to the point of perspiration at least twice a week.
____ 6. I smoke less than half a pack of cigarettes a day.
____ 7. I take fewer than five alcoholic drinks a week.
____ 8. I am the appropriate weight for my height.
____ 9. I have an income adequate to meet basic expenses.
____ 10. I get strength from my religious beliefs.
____ 11. I regularly attend club or social activities.
____ 12. I have a network of friends and acquaintances.
____ 13. I have one or more friends to confide in about personal matters.

____ 14. I am in good health (including eyesight, hearing, and teeth).
____ 15. I am able to speak openly about my feelings when angry or worried.
____ 16. I have regular conversations with the people I live with about domestic problems (e.g., chores, money, and daily living issues).
____ 17. I do something for fun at least once a week.
____ 18. I am able to organize my time effectively.
____ 19. I drink fewer than three cups of coffee (or tea or cola drinks) a day.
____ 20. I take quiet time for myself during the day.

____ TOTAL

To get your score, add up the figures and subtract 20. Any number over 30 indicates a vulnerability to stress. You are seriously vulnerable if your score is between 50 and 75, and extremely vulnerable if it is over 75.

Note. From "Vulnerability Scale" from the *Stress Audit,* developed by Lyle H. Miller and Alma Dell Smith, Boston University Medical Center. Copyright © 1983, Biobehavioral Associates, reprinted with permission.

Sources of Emotional Stress

What produces stress?

Any interaction between a person and the person's environment produces stress. Small and large amounts of stress constantly appear and disappear. Any emotion or feeling produces stress, whether the emotion is positive, such as love or joy, or negative, such as anger, hate, or grief. Anxiety, pressure, frustration, and conflict are sources of psychological stress that are given special attention in this section.

What is the psychoanalytic view of anxiety?

Anxiety. Anxiety is a psychological state characterized by apprehension, tenseness, dread, and foreboding. The causes of anxiety are usually not as specific as the causes of fear, and often the cause of the anxiety is not recognized by a person. The psychoanalytic view of anxiety proposes that anxiety is the result of internal, unconscious conflict resulting from evaluations and emotions of which a person is not aware. If the emotion conflicts with a person's conscious values or feelings of self-worth, anxiety develops; as a result, the person may unknowingly engage in particular behaviors to keep the emotion out of consciousness in order to lower the anxiety. These behaviors may become the source of even more anxiety. The original source of anxiety is still present, and even though unconscious it still produces physiological changes that occur in activation of the sympathetic nervous system. For example, an interior decorator may keep feelings of incompetency submerged in her or his unconscious mind by criticizing other interior decorators. This person may not be able to explain why she or he feels anxious or what it is he or she fears will happen. Various sources of the anxiety may be assumed that are not the true source. Anxiety seems to develop when an individual's perception or evaluation of a situation or an action called for and of his or her resources to handle it are not in balance. High levels of anxiety interfere with rational planning and effective performance and may contribute to failure, which in turn produces more anxiety and future failure.

What is the difference between trait anxiety and state anxiety?

Charles Spielberger (1966) distinguished between two types of anxiety. One type of anxiety, called **trait anxiety,** represents the general level of anxiety characteristically exhibited by an individual over time. This type is a relatively stable aspect of the personality. Some people seem to experience anxiety whether they are on the job, attending a party, going to school, or vacationing. They worry about many things and have a vague uneasiness about the outcome of events in general. The other type, **state anxiety,** refers to temporary situational anxiety. People who are generally free of anxiety may experience anxiety in a specific situation such as when taking a test, when making a speech before an audience, or when a robber is pointing a gun at them. The level of state anxiety is usually affected by the length and severity of the stressful event and by whether or not the stressful event is expected.

What is the difference between internal and external pressure?

Pressure. When a demand for a particular performance is made on a person and the person feels that the demand must be met, pressure occurs, which in turn produces stress. People set standards of behavior for themselves based on their ideals. If they do not meet these ideals, they hold themselves in low esteem. Therefore, they are under a lot of *internal pressure* to perform in accordance with these ideals in order to maintain their self-esteem. Internal pressure can be good and can bring great pleasure to a person when the ideal performance is accomplished. However, if a person's ideals are too difficult to achieve, internal pressure may be a source of extreme stress.

Demands to meet a particular standard of behavior are also made on a person by other people who are significant in his or her personal and work lives. Pressure from this source is referred to as *external pressure.* The general manager of Company X may demand that a project bid be submitted by a particular time in order to be considered. Or the president of Company Y may demand that an average number of projects be completed each day in order for the manager to remain in the position of manager. A new procedure may be demanded by the supervisor, and the employee must learn the procedure or resign from the job. Family members and close friends also may place demands on a person that are sources of external pressure and therefore stress.

What causes a person to experience frustration?

Frustration. When something or someone interferes with or prevents a person from reaching a goal that is important to him or her, the person experiences frustration, which in turn produces stress. The person must either give up the goal or overcome the barrier that is encountered in reaching the goal. Frustration is often a main source of stress on the job. Delays, lack of resources, losses, lack of ability (failure), and meaninglessness of the goal are five basic sources of frustration (Coleman & Hammen, 1974).

How do people with a low frustration tolerance and people with a high frustration tolerance respond to frustration?

Some people can tolerate more frustration than others. People with a low frustration tolerance may respond with anger and verbal or physical aggression to remove the barrier immediately. Or they may respond in counterproductive, defensive behavior, minimize the importance of achieving a goal, or deny the reality of the barrier. People with a high frustration tolerance are more likely to do something constructive to remove the source of the frustration. They may devise and initiate a systematic approach to remove the barrier, modify the goal to evade the barrier, or compensate by working to achieve some other goal.

What are four types of conflict that people experience?

Conflict. A common source of stress is conflict, which arises when a person is faced with incompatible motives, demands, opportunities, or goals. There is no complete solution to conflict. Decision making produces the stress. Kurt Lewin (1935) described four types of conflict in which approach represents an attraction or positive feeling and avoidance represents a withdrawal or negative feeling.

What are approach-approach conflicts?

In an **approach-approach conflict,** a person is simultaneously attracted to two equally attractive alternatives; however, the person cannot have or do both. This type of conflict is illustrated by the fable about the donkey who stood between two delicious bales of hay yet starved to death because he could not make a decision as to which bale of hay to eat. In the world of work, humans may have to choose or decide between equally attractive jobs, applicants to employ, meetings to attend, or contracts to accept.

What are avoidance-avoidance conflicts?

Avoidance-avoidance conflict involves making a decision between two equally unattractive alternatives. The person must face one of the unpleasant situations. These conflicts are more stressful to resolve than the approach-approach conflicts, and the individual is more likely to vacillate back and forth longer. As the person approaches making a choice and moves closer to one of the unattractive situations, more stress is experienced, and there is a tendency to back up and move toward the other unattractive situation to reduce the stress. But as the individual moves closer to it, more stress is experienced again, and the individual backs up and moves toward the other situation again. In this kind of conflict, many people simply wait for something to happen that will make the decision for them, or they try to find a way to avoid making the decision, thus prolonging the stress. This type of conflict might be illustrated when an employer has to either fire an employee or put up with the problem behavior of the employee.

What are approach-avoidance conflicts?

In an **approach-avoidance conflict**, a person has to decide whether to engage in a single activity, pursue a single goal, or take advantage of a single opportunity that has both desirable and undesirable characteristics or advantages and disadvantages. A shy person may have to decide whether to apply for a new job opening. Getting the job means an increase in salary, which is desirable, but getting the job also means having an interview with the company president, which is undesirable. The desire to approach increases in strength as a person gets nearer the goal. The desire to avoid also gets stronger as a person gets nearer the goal, but it increases at a faster rate than the desire to approach (see Figure 10–8).

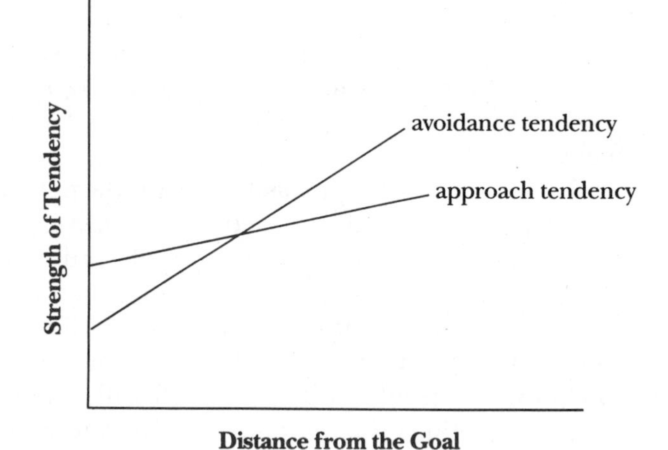

Figure 10–8. Diagram of approach-avoidance conflict.

Thus, the shy person may make preparations for the interview, but as the interview gets closer, the avoidance tendency strengthens faster than the approach tendency until the point is reached where avoidance is stronger. Then the appointment may be cancelled, or the shy person may turn around and walk away as the door to the interview office is approached. As the person retreats, the point may be reached at which the tendency to approach becomes stronger again. Then another appointment may be made. The vacillation back and forth prolongs the stress.

When a person must make a choice between two goals and each goal has desirable and undesirable characteristics, the conflict is more complex and produces even more stress than any of the previously mentioned types of conflict. Such conflict is referred to as **double approach-avoidance conflict.** For example, an employee may have to choose between the supervisor's request to work overtime and the spouse's request to go to a party. If the employee chooses to work overtime, the decision has the advantage of pleasing the supervisor and possibly providing a larger paycheck, but it also has the disadvantage of upsetting the spouse and possibly causing rejection by the spouse. If the employee chooses to attend the party, the decision has the advantage of pleasing the spouse but the disadvantage of upsetting the supervisor.

What is the most complex and stressful type of conflict?

Techniques for Managing Emotional Stress

Effective coping involves learning to use socially acceptable methods that can reduce the impact of stress, alter the environment to reduce the amount of stress, and change behavior so that less stress will be experienced. Humans begin to learn and use strategies for coping with psychological stress at birth. The strategies learned account for how a person characteristically behaves.

Defensive and Direct Coping. In general, a person learns to cope defensively or passively and directly or actively. When a person copes defensively or passively, he or she learns to use either unconscious processes or apathy, an extreme form of withdrawal. Neither may be very effective. Direct or active coping is action oriented—consciously taking action to alter the uncomfortable, stress-provoking situation. For example, a secretary who experiences stress when using the computer may cope actively by taking courses in night school to improve these skills. In direct or active coping, the source of the stress must be consciously recognized before action can be taken. Direct or active coping strategies are more

In the long run, are the defensive or passive strategies or the direct or active strategies more effective in coping with stress?

effective in the long run than defensive or passive strategies. In direct coping, of course, the action may consist of either constructive or destructive attempts to alter the stress-provoking situation. The secretary might take the action of smashing the computer and doing away with it. In situations of genuine helplessness where nothing can be done about the source of stress, action can only be taken to try to control the effects. In some situations, the most effective action may be to withdraw or physically escape the stress.

How do people with submissive, aggressive, and assertive personalities differ?

Being Good to the Self. Unmet physiological or psychological needs and negative feelings produce stress and tension. One technique to use to control the effects of stress and thus tension is to be good to the self so that the self is less vulnerable to stress. To be good to the self implies getting physical or primary needs met and also getting psychological or secondary needs met. People who have either very submissive or very aggressive personalities do not get their needs met. The goals of a submissive person seem to be to sacrifice the self to please others, to avoid conflict, and to avoid attracting attention. The person is subconsciously filled with fear of being disliked or rejected, which is also very stressful. A person with an aggressive personality, on the other hand, gets his or her needs met in ways that are hurtful and degrading to others, in ways that violate the rights of others, and by dominating others to insure winning by forcing others to lose. The resulting poor interpersonal relationships generate more stress. People who have assertive personalities, however, do get their needs met. Developing a more assertive personality whereby a person learns to express feelings and solve problems effectively is helpful in managing stress.

Being good to the self also implies providing enough pleasant feelings to at least balance the unpleasant feelings. Laughter as well as crying are natural tension reducers. Finding something in a situation to laugh about or imagining something humorous about the situation to laugh about can help to control the effects of stress.

Changing Perceptions, Attitudes, and Values. Another technique that can be used to control stress and manage tension is to perceive at least one positive thing about each life situation. Instead of perceiving only the bad aspects one can also perceive the good aspects of a situation. Actually, stress is a resource like money that can be spent on whatever, whenever, and whereever a person chooses. Sometimes it is helpful to examine values by arranging stressors in a hierarchy as to how important each is. The stressors can then be ranked as to how much energy is spent on each one and the rankings compared to see if the most energy is being spent on the most important stressors. Wasting or overspending energy on things not important is not effective coping.

Exercise and Relaxation. There are two proven ways to counteract excess stress. One way is through exercise and the other way is by relaxation. Stress produces tension to make action possible—a survival mechanism. If a person is stalked by a ferocious animal, the energy in the muscles is released either through running or fighting. Today neither fighting nor fleeing is the answer to most stressful situations. When the body is prepared for such a response, one good way to release the energy and thus the tension is through physical exercise. The best kind of exercises for this purpose are rhythmic exercises that use major muscles such as jogging, dancing, walking, swimming, aerobics, or bicycling.

What are two proven ways to counteract stress?

A person can learn also to relax to release the tension in the muscles. Using instructional tapes or an instructor as a guide is helpful in learning to relax. Relaxation techniques may include deep muscle relaxation, progressive relaxation, imagery of relaxing situations, daydreaming or taking a mental vacation, and meditation. Relaxation exercises always begin with breathing. When a person focuses on breathing, the basic rhythm of life, the breathing automatically slows. Dr. Herbert Benson's method of relaxation is presented in chapter 5.

To summarize managing tension, the acronym *triple A bc* (AAAbc) may be used (Tubesing & Tubesing, 1983). The first *A* is for alter, which implies removing the source of stress by changing something. The second *A* is for avoid, which implies removing the self from the stressful situation or figuring out how not to get there in the first place. The third *A* is for accept, which involves equipping the self physically and mentally for stress. The *b* stands for building resistance by increasing capacity to tolerate stress by practicing good health habits. The *c* stands for change—changing self-perception and perception of the situation.

What does *triple A bc* (AAAbc) stand for?

SUMMARY

1. Emotion has been defined as a combination of physiological changes, feelings (affect), and expressive behavior.
2. The physiological component of emotion is controlled by the responses of the sympathetic division of the autonomic nervous system

and determines the intensity of the emotion. The cognitive component is controlled by the thought processes.

3. The hormones epinephrine and norepinephrine are secreted by the adrenal glands and produce a host of biological changes in the body during emotional arousal.
4. Emotions are communicated verbally and nonverbally through (a) facial expressions (especially the left side of the face), which seem to be innate for basic emotions; (b) body postures and gestures, called kinesics; (c) paralanguage, physical characteristics of the voice; and (d) proxemics, the physical distance kept from a person and the eye contact that is maintained.
5. Emotion is usually assessed indirectly and subjectively by verbal and nonverbal behavior and by the situation; however, physiological responses such as pupil enlargement, heart rate, blood pressure, respiration, galvanic skin response, and voice vibrations may be measured objectively by devices such as the polygraph and the voice stress analyzer.
6. Emotions may be measured in terms of approach-avoidance, pleasantness-unpleasantness, and intensity; however, individuals may respond differently along these dimensions because of inborn differences and differences in what has been learned. And sometimes a person may have both pleasant and unpleasant emotions about a specific object, person, or event that exist simultaneously.
7. The James-Lange theory of emotion suggests that stimuli produce physiological changes in the body (the body responds first) and then the cognitive processes that produce the feeling (affect) occur.
8. The Cannon-Bard theory of emotion proposes that stimuli produce physiological changes in the body and thought processes in the brain simultaneously.
9. Schachter's cognitive theory of emotion also proposes that emotion is the result of physiological changes and the simultaneous appraisal of the stimulus; however, appraisal and arousal are interrelated, and a change in appraisal influences a change in arousal and a change in arousal influences appraisal.
10. Arnold's cognitive theory of emotion proposes that appraisal, which occurs first, determines the feeling (affect), which then elicits a pattern of physiological responses appropriate to the appraisal.
11. According to Plutchik, there are eight basic emotions that are innate and essential to survival of the human species: anger, joy, sadness, acceptance, disgust, anticipation, and surprise. All other emotions are varying intensities and/or mixtures of these.
12. Stress is energy in the body produced by any situation that places a special demand on the body (stressors), whether the demand is of a physiological nature or a psychological nature. Tension is the result of stress or energy being held in the muscles.

13. In order to function effectively, an optimum amount of tension must be maintained. Some tension is necessary for functioning, but too much tension hurts.
14. The general adaptation syndrome refers to the sequence of physiological events that takes place during prolonged stress. The alarm reaction, resistance, and exhaustion are the three stages that comprise the syndrome.
15. Psychosomatic illnesses are physical disorders such as stomach ulcers, migraine headaches, asthma, high blood pressure, and heart disease caused by psychological stress. Stress is being found to play a role in the functioning of the immune system and is now related to infectious diseases and disorders such as cancer and hardening of the arteries.
16. Stress and thus tension in the body may be assessed by paying attention to the body. Holmes and Rahe developed a scale of measurement based on impact of life experiences and the degree of adjustment involved in coping with the experience that determines whether the stress level is mild, moderate, or major for an individual. Biofeedback devices and self-report inventories are also available for assessment of stress.
17. Psychological stress is produced by any interaction between the person and his or her environment and includes mental activity, emotion, anxiety, pressure, frustration, and conflict.
18. Anxiety is characterized by apprehension, tenseness, dread, and foreboding, the source of which often is not as specific as the source of fear. Anxiety may be differentiated as trait anxiety, which is the general level of anxiety, and state anxiety, which is temporary situational anxiety. According to the psychoanalytic view, anxiety is the result of internal, unconscious conflict.
19. Pressure to meet a particular standard of behavior may be in the form of internal pressure—a standard set by self, or external pressure—a standard set by other people. Some pressure can be good, but too much pressure may be a source of extreme stress.
20. Frustration is the source of stress when something or someone interferes with or prevents an individual from reaching a goal. Individual differences exist in tolerance of frustration.
21. Conflict is the source of stress when an individual must make a decision between incompatible motives, demands, opportunities, or goals. Four types of conflict, from the lowest to the highest amount of stress produced, are (a) approach-approach, where a choice must be made between two equally attractive alternatives; (b) avoidance-avoidance, where a choice must be made between two equally unattractive alternatives; (c) approach-avoidance, which involves a decision as to whether to pursue a single activity or goal that has both desirable and undesirable characteristics; and (d) double approach-avoidance, which involves a choice between two activities or goals, each of which has advantages and disadvantages.

22. As a goal is approached, both approach and avoidance tendencies increase in strength, but the avoidance tendency increases faster than the approach tendency, which may account for changes in behavior and vacillation back and forth from one goal to another, prolonging the stress.
23. Coping with stress begins at birth and involves learning to use socially accepted methods to reduce tension, to alter the environment to reduce the amount of stress, and to change behavior so that less stress will be experienced. The coping methods learned may be defensive (passive) or direct (active).
24. Some behaviors that reduce tension or the stress that produces tension are (a) getting physiological and psychological needs met, (b) laughter and crying, (c) perceiving the positive rather than the negative aspects of a situation, (d) giving priority to stressors according to importance (value), (e) exercise, and (f) relaxation.
25. Managing tension may be summarized by the acronym *triple A bc* (AAAbc). The three *As* stand for avoid, alter, and accept, the *b* stands for building resistance, and the *c* stands for change.

KEY TERMS AND CONCEPTS

Kinesics
Paralanguage
Proxemics
Galvanic skin response (GSR)
Polygraph
Psychological stress evaluator
Voice stress analyzer
Stress
Stressors
Tension
General adaptation syndrome
Psychosomatic illnesses
Anxiety
Trait anxiety
State anxiety
Approach-approach conflict
Avoidance-avoidance conflict
Approach-avoidance conflict
Double approach-avoidance conflict

QUESTIONS FOR REVIEW

1. How is emotion defined in terms of its components?
2. What are some of the arguments used to support the view that facial expression as an indicator of emotion is partially innate?
3. Why are nonverbal expressions more reliable indicators of emotion than verbal expressions?
4. What three dimensions of an emotion can be described or measured, and what are some measurement techniques?
5. What is the central idea about emotion proposed by the James-Lange theory, the Cannon-Bard theory, Schachter's theory, Arnold's theory, and Plutchik's theory?

6. What is tension, and what are some symptoms of too much tension?
7. How is emotional stress sometimes measured?
8. What are some general sources of psychological stress?
9. How do the four types of conflict differ from each other?
10. How can a person cope with stress, and what are some specific strategies or techniques that may be used?

TEST YOURSELF

1. Many psychologists define emotion as a combination of (a) two aspects—physiological changes and feelings (b) three aspects—physiological changes, feelings, and expressive behavior (c) four aspects—heart rate, blood pressure, galvanic skin response, and respiration (d) five aspects—pupil enlargement, epinephrine, norepinephrine, perception, and appraisal.
2. An emotion can be measured in terms of the (a) approach-avoidance dimension (b) intensity and pleasantness-unpleasantness dimensions (c) pleasantness-unpleasantness dimension (d) approach-avoidance, intensity, and pleasantness-unpleasantness dimensions.
3. The physiological changes that occur during an emotional experience are produced by the (a) somatic nervous system (b) sympathetic nervous system (c) spinal cord (d) parasympathetic nervous system.
4. Epinephrine helps mobilize sugar in the blood to make more energy available to the brain and muscles and causes the heart to beat faster. T or F
5. Epinephrine constricts the peripheral blood vessels and raises the blood pressure. T or F
6. The ________________ system involved in emotion consists of a complex group of structures in the core of the brain that includes the ________________.
7. Verbal communication of emotion is considered to be inadequate because (a) people sometimes attempt to hide their emotions (b) people sometimes do not know what their emotions really are (c) sometimes words are inadequate to describe the emotion (d) all of the above.
8. The fact that most animals, including humans, share a common pattern of facial expressions and that children who are blind and deaf as well as people in various cultures exhibit the same facial expressions for emotions is evidence for the theory that facial expressions are (a) innate (b) learned (c) not communication of emotion (d) all of the above.
9. The ________________ half of the brain is believed to be dominant in controlling the muscles of the face and is considered to be the feeling brain; therefore, the ________________ side of the face gives the clearest, strongest expression of emotion.

10. Communication of emotion by voice intonations such as pitch, loudness, pauses, exclamations, and stuttering is called (a) proxemics (b) kinesics (c) paralanguage (d) nonlanguage.
11. The psychological stress evaluator has been developed to measure (a) heart rate, blood pressure, respiration, and the galvanic skin response (b) changes in a person's voice (c) size of the pupils of the eyes (d) the flow of saliva.
12. The theory of emotion that proposes that appraisal and bodily arousal are interrelated, that bodily arousal influences cognitive appraisal, and that cognitive appraisal influences bodily arousal is (a) the James-Lange theory (b) the Cannon-Bard theory (c) Arnold's theory (d) Schachter's theory.
13. The theory of emotion that proposes that a cognitive appraisal occurs first that then elicits a physical response is (a) the James-Lange theory (b) the Cannon-Bard theory (c) Arnold's theory (d) Schachter's theory.
14. According to Plutchik, ________, ________, ________, ________, ________, ________, ________, and ________ are basic emotions that are innate and serve a survival function.
15. Stress and tension in the right amounts are good. T or F
16. The third stage of the general adaptation syndrome is (a) the stage of exhaustion (b) the alarm reaction (c) the stage of resistance (d) activation of the sympathetic nervous system.
17. Psychosomatic illnesses are imagined illnesses. T or F
18. State anxiety refers to (a) temporary situational anxiety (b) the general level of anxiety characteristically exhibited by an individual over time (c) both a and b (d) any state of emotional arousal.
19. Deciding between two equally attractive alternatives is the (a) avoidance-avoidance type of conflict (b) approach-avoidance type of conflict (c) approach-approach type of conflict (d) double approach-avoidance type of conflict.
20. Two proven ways to counteract stress are through exercise and relaxation. T or F

APPLICATIONS

A. The president of the company, in a conference with the five managers, notices that one of the managers places the hand on the face partially covering the eye and then rubs the eye, a gesture that people often engage in when they refuse to accept something that is pointed out to them. When each manager is asked to respond to a question about what he or she did in a particular situation, the president notices that while answering one manager's face reddens slightly, a little chuckle of laughter comes forth, and the index finger is drawn across the face under the nostrils, behaviors that are characteristic of lying. The president also notices that another manager sits quietly without commenting during the presentation of the proposal but frowns slightly and picks lint from his trousers, indicative of disapproval but constraint from saying so.

1. What is the president of the company using to determine the managers' real feelings and honesty?
2. If the president of the company wants to get an idea in advance as to how well a proposal will be accepted before initiating it, do you think it is possible to tell from just presenting the proposal in a meeting where no verbal responses are made from the audience? Why or why not?

B. A group supervisor at Blank Corporation is aware that one of the employees in the group has been having a lot of problems at home during the past few weeks. Recently, this employee has been very irritable with co-workers, making more mistakes on the job than usual, forgetting some appointments, and taking aspirin for slight headaches and lower back pain. The company does have a gym available to employees for exercising before and after work and during lunch hours. The company also employs on a retainer basis a psychologist who is qualified to teach relaxation techniques.

1. Do you think the employee has too much tension? Why?
2. What would you suggest the supervisor do about the situation? Why?

SUGGESTIONS FOR FURTHER READING

Cooper, C. L. (1981). *The stress check.* Englewood Cliffs, NJ: Prentice-Hall.
An excellent review of the stress an individual experiences in life, especially in work situations.

Ekman, P. (1985). *Telling lies: Clues to deceit in the marketplace, politics, and marriage.* New York: Norton.
A nontechnical book on nonverbal communication of emotion and how nonverbal behaviors sometimes reveal an emotion a person thinks is disguised.

Lazarus, R. S., & Folkman, S. (1984). *Stress, appraisal, and coping.* New York: Springer.
A thorough, academic analysis of what stress is and how individuals react to stress.

Plutchik, R. (1980). *Emotion: A psychoevolutionary synthesis.* New York: Harper & Row.
A good, general overview of emotion, particularly the innateness of emotion.

Scheflen, A. E. (1972). *Body language and the social order.* Englewood Cliffs, NJ: Prentice-Hall.

Written by a leading authority in the science of kinesics, this book attends to how kinesic behavior is related to personal and individual feelings and to how it serves to control human behavior and to maintain the social order.

CHAPTER 11

PERSONALITY THEORIES AND MEASUREMENT

Objectives

When you have completed your study of chapter 11, you should be able to:

1. Describe the characteristics of a well-adjusted person.
2. Point out reasons why the personality of people who are in or will be in the workplace is important.
3. Describe personality differences among workers including Eysenck's two dimensions of personality.
4. Briefly summarize the basic features of Freud's theory.
5. Name several neo-Freudians, and point out the neo-Freudian's primary difference with Freud.
6. Briefly summarize Sheldon's body type theory and Allport's and Cattell's proposed traits.
7. Briefly summarize the basic features of Rogers' and Maslow's humanistic theories.
8. Discuss the social-cognitive perspective in terms of interaction, locus of control, and learned helplessness.
9. Name and describe techniques used in assessing an individual's personality.
10. Describe widely used objective and projective tests.

What is the meaning of the word *personality* as used by psychologists?

The word *personality* may bring to mind statements such as the following: "He really has personality." "She has a nice personality." "She has no personality." "He has a terrible personality." In all these statements, the word *personality* is used in the popular sense. Psychologists use **personality** to describe the characteristic way a person responds to other people, objects, or events in the environment. An individual's personality is a summation of the persistent behavior patterns that are unique to an individual; therefore, everyone has personality. Psychologists do not use the term in a judgmental way to indicate good or bad or use the word to mean charming. The purpose of this chapter is to describe personality in terms of adjustment, to explain how personality evolves, and to consider how personality is assessed.

PERSONALITY ADJUSTMENT

Personality adjustment is a continuing process as a person deals with the stresses of life. Little research has actually been concerned with the personalities of healthy, well-adjusted individuals although a great deal of scientific study has been devoted to maladjusted individuals. Personality adjustment seems to vary on a continuum from extremely maladjusted to extremely well adjusted. The degree of adjustment varies among individuals and may vary from time to time for an individual. What constitutes good mental health or, in other words, what characterizes the personality of well-adjusted individuals is discussed in this section.

Are people just well adjusted or maladjusted, or is there variation in the degree to which people are well adjusted or maladjusted?

Well-Adjusted Individuals

A number of different views or opinions exist as to what constitutes the personality of a well-adjusted person. Derlega and Janda (1978) emphasize that good mental health is not merely the absence of mental illness. In other words, there is more to being well adjusted than just not being maladjusted.

What characteristics are typical of well-adjusted people?

Characteristics. Certain well-defined skills are considered to be characteristic of well-adjusted people. However, a person does not have to possess all the characteristics to be considered well adjusted (Derlega & Janda, 1978). The more accurately a person can perceive or interpret reality and the less distorted the views of reality, the higher level of adjustment the person will be able to attain. The well-adjusted person seems to be very perceptive in evaluations of situations and other people. Personal motives do not unconsciously interfere very much with such evaluations. People who lack confidence and believe others dislike them or who have a great deal of guilt regarding their sexuality and view fairly innocent books, magazines, or movies as disgusting and shameful are allowing their personal motives to interfere with their evaluations of people and situations.

The more able a person is to profit from past experience and plan for the future, the better adjusted the person is likely to be. Well-adjusted individuals (a) seem to be primarily concerned with the present, (b) can achieve a better balance between the past, present, and future, and (c) thus, can realize a richer life. Although well-adjusted individuals remember, they do not brood over the past; and, although concerned with the future, they do not worry or become obsessed with it. They are able to find satisfaction in their present lives.

Figure 11–1.
A commitment to some form of work that is challenging and fulfilling characterizes most well-adjusted people.

Additionally, well-adjusted individuals are committed to some form of work and have the ability to be productive (see Figure 11–1). Adjustment also includes the capacity to feel and express a wide range of emotions. Well-adjusted people view themselves positively and are viewed positively by others. They are socially competent,

Figure 11–2.
Well-adjusted people are socially competent, feel comfortable in interacting with others, and are able to achieve intimacy in social relationships.

feel comfortable in interacting with others, and are able to achieve intimacy in social relationships (see Figure 11–2). They have the capacity to share their lives, to feel close to others, and to form deep friendships and love relationships. Maslow's characteristics of self-actualized persons listed on page 313 are considered to be characteristics of well-adjusted persons.

Comparison With Normal and Maladjusted Individuals. A person considered to be normal exhibits behaviors that are customary or commonly occurring in people. The literal meaning of *abnormal* is "away from normal," and abnormal behavior is considered to be behavior that deviates from normal behavior. It is sometimes difficult to differentiate whether behavior is normal or abnormal because of the matter of degree of deviation. Most often the degree of deviation is related to the amount of time spent engaging in a behavior, the frequency of occurrence of a behavior, or the condition under which a behavior occurs. The behavior of well-adjusted people is considered to be adaptive or normal. The behavior of maladjusted people is considered to be maladaptive or abnormal. Behaviors that create rather than solve problems or endanger life would be considered maladaptive. The maladjusted person unconsciously distorts perceptions and evaluations of reality. Oftentimes, a maladjusted person attempts to become a well-adjusted person and may seek help from a psychotherapist (see Figure 11--3). **Psychotherapy** is the term used for any attempt by a clinician to bring about desired personality or behavioral changes by applying particular psychological techniques. Psychotherapy has also been defined as "a corrective experience leading a person to behave in a socially appropriate, adequate, and adaptive way" (Bourne & Ekstrand, 1985, p. 55).

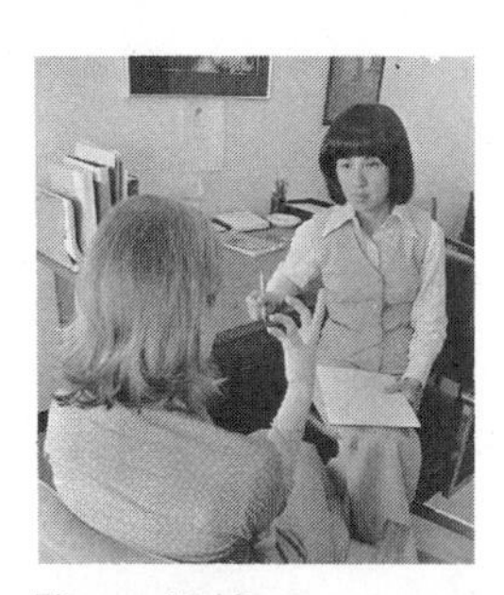

Figure 11–3.
People often seek the services of a clinician in an attempt to become more well adjusted.

Personality in the Workplace

A study of personality is appropriate, for a number of reasons, for those who are in or will be in a work situation. A number of these reasons are discussed in this section. Also, personality differences among workers and Eysenck's dimensions of personality receive attention here.

Why is personality important in the workplace?

Importance. Most knowledgeable people in the world of work agree that many employees who lose their jobs are dismissed because of personality characteristics rather than lack of skill or ability in general. Maladjustment may exist to such a degree as to interfere with performance and/or require treatment. Because people who are maladjusted have personality problems, they often create problems for supervisors and co-workers. In an extensive study conducted by Standard Oil Company of New Jersey, personality characteristics based on test scores and background information were correlated with measures of position level, salary history, and effectiveness rankings for 443 managers. Approximately half of the variation in managerial effectiveness was found to be related to personality characteristics (Laurent, 1966). The personalities of the individuals under a manager's supervision influence the style of leadership that works best for that manager. For example, a permissive or democratic leadership style seems to work better for people who are highly motivated, above average in intelligence, and well trained; however, people who have rigid, strict, or authoritarian personalities usually prefer a more direct or authoritarian style.

Personality has an impact on motivation and performance. J. M. Higgins (1982) proposes that an individual's view of the self, which is an important aspect of a person's personality, affects motivation and, in turn, performance. Well-adjusted individuals are likely to choose occupations that provide challenge, and they are more likely than maladjusted individuals to perform up to their real potential (see Figure 11–4). An individual's view of the self may be maintained, lowered, or enhanced in the workplace, and personality has an effect on this.

Figure 11–4. Individuals tend to work up to a level that fits their view of the self.

Personality Differences. Basic personality types have been found to exist for various occupational groups and for the manner in which members of an occupational group work. According to Holland (1981), overall, workers and professionals in different occupational groups as well as students preparing for different occupations have different personalities. Psychological tests, discussed later in this chapter, are available to use in comparing an individual's interests or personality with the interests and personality of individuals considered to be successful and contented in a particular occupation.

Holland (1972, 1973) proposes that occupations may be grouped according to six personality types. Table 11–1 lists and describes the personality types and lists a sampling of occupations associated with each personality type. The Vocational Preference Inventory (VPI) developed by J. L. Holland in 1965 is based on this theory that occupations can be described in terms of personality characteristics. The VPI is essentially a personality test that employs occupational item content. The 1985 revision is scored for 11 scales including Realistic, Investigative, Artistic, Scientific, Enterprising, Conventional, Self-Control, Status, Masculinity-Femininity, Infrequency, and Acquiescence. Research studies have shown that individuals tend to choose a career type that matches their personality type and that the closer the match, the greater the job satisfaction and the longer the individual will stay with the career (Cole, Whitney, & Holland, 1971; Holland, 1962, 1968). The VPI is a relatively inexpensive, reputable, interest (personality) inventory that

Personality Type	Description	Sample Occupations
Realistic	Likes work requiring physical strength; tends to avoid interpersonal and verbal types of work; prefers task problems that are concrete rather than abstract	Engineer, carpenter, architect, forester, machinist, printer agriculturist
Intellectual	Prefers tasks involving the intellectual processes such as thinking and comprehension; tends to avoid work activities that require domination and persuasion of people or close interpersonal contact; tends to be more introverted than extroverted	Physician, home economist, paramedic, anthropologist, veterinarian, biologist, medical radiographer
Social	Exhibits skill in interpersonal relations and chooses work situations requiring interpersonal relationships; prefers work activities that help other people such as teaching or therapeutic service; tends to avoid high stress, intellectual, problem-solving work activities	Minister, teacher, psychologist, counselor, dental assistant, nurse, social worker
Artistic	Tends to dislike structure, to be more introverted than extroverted, and to exhibit a high degree of femininity; expresses feelings and may act on impulse	Actor or actress, musician, photographer, artist, journalist, cosmetologist

Table 11–1
Holland's personality types and corresponding sample occupations.

Personality Type	Description	Sample Occupations
Enterprising	Desires power and status and likes work activities that involve manipulating and dominating others; tends to have good verbal skills	Attorney, salesperson, politician, manager, administrator, real estate agent, public relations worker, economist
Conventional	Prefers structure and order with rules and regulations governing the work activities; exhibits much self-control; identifies with power and status	Secretary, accountant, business teacher, clerk, data processing worker, financial advisor

Note. From *Introductory Psychology* by M. K. Holland, 1981, Lexington, MA: D. C. Heath & Co. Copyright © 1981. Reprinted by permission of D. C. Heath and Company.

yields a clear-cut profile and requires only about 20 to 30 minutes to administer.

Do all people who avoid goal setting have the same general type of personality?

Fred Massarik (1968) described two personality types in relationship to avoidance of goal setting. The **spontaneous type** includes people who respond unfavorably to the structure and restraints of goal setting because they feel that goal setting is unnecessary because they can achieve without setting formal goals. They respond with immediate and intentional purpose, seemingly guided by unconscious, long-range goals. The **anomic type** includes those persons who respond unfavorably to goal setting because they do not have inner standards and self-expectancies. They become frustrated with the interference goal setting creates with their spontaneity. The alienated and the drifter represent extreme examples of the anomic type. Being aware of the two personality types may help a supervisor better understand opposition to highly structured programs of planning and goal setting.

How do Type A people differ from Type B people?

Cardiologists Meyer Friedman and Ray Rosenman (1974) have differentiated two major personality types, Type A and Type B. Workers who exhibit the typical personality pattern of always hurrying and striving to accomplish too much, too quickly, too frequently are said to have a **Type A personality.** Type A personalities are characteristically restless, ambitious, and aggressive and are often referred to as workaholics. In the world of work, this personality type is usually admired; however, these individuals have been found to be prone to coronary heart disease. A person is said to have a **Type B personality** if he or she can relax and perform in a leisurely manner, realizing limitations.

Two major dimensions of personality, stability-instability (emotionality), which was labeled *neuroticism* prior to 1978, and extroversion-introversion, have been identified by Eysenck (1947, 1951). The dimension of **stability-instability** is related to emotional stability and refers to (a) changeability in mood; (b) sensitivity to emotional stress, tenseness, and anxiety; (c) tendency to worry; (d) concern about physical health; (e) tendency to feel guilty; (f) low self-esteem; and (g) feelings of fatigue. The dimension of **extroversion-introversion** is related to an individual's need to receive stimulation from the outside world. **Extroverts** are outgoing and tend to seek emotional stimulation in the form of social activities and exciting and adventurous events and sensory stimulation in the form of loud noises and colors (see Figure 11–5). **Introverts** are usually rather quiet and withdrawn (see Figure 11–6). Most individuals are probably **ambiverts,** a mixture of the two extremes, and vacillate from one extreme to the other in different situations. For example, a person in a supervisory position may be an introvert at a party but an extrovert (aggressive and outgoing) while supervising a crew of construction workers.

Figure 11–5. Extroverts are outgoing and tend to seek emotional stimulation in the form of social activities and exciting and adventurous events, and sensory stimulation in the form of loud noises and colors.

What are the effects in work situations of variations in Eysenck's two major dimensions of personality?

Research has shown stability-instability (emotionality) and extroversion-introversion to be important in a job environment. In general, an employee who is lower in the dimension of emotionality makes a better worker at all levels. In order to perform at a higher level on the job, a person must have good control over tension, anxiety, and emotional stress. DuBrin (1980) points out that the level of emotional arousal is related to job effectiveness. Job effectiveness increases when the optimum level of arousal is reached; however, optimum levels of arousal vary from person to person. One individual may need to be highly aroused in order to call on sales prospects, whereas another individual may be able to do so at a lower level of arousal. Individuals who are generally in a high state of emotional arousal do not need much pressure from the environment in order to perform a task, and they may even perform ineffectively if too much pressure is present from the environment. Understimulation is more apt to be a cause of job dissatisfaction and inadequate performance for extroverts than for introverts. Overstimulation is more likely to adversely affect job satisfaction and performance for introverts than for extroverts. Also, introverts are easier to condition. For example, introverts

Figure 11–6. Introverts are rather quiet and withdrawn.

would be more likely than extroverts to improve on getting to work on time when given a reward for doing so (Hamner & Organ, 1978).

THEORIES OF PERSONALITY

Many attempts have been made to describe how people establish the unique but fairly consistent pattern of behavior called personality. Personality theories can be grouped according to the approach used to explain how personality develops. Four perspectives—psychoanalytic, type and trait, humanistic, and social-cognitive—are briefly summarized in this section.

Psychoanalytic Perspective

According to Freud, what are the three components of an individual's personality?

Sigmund Freud (see chapter 1, page 16) and his followers focused on the unconscious part of the mind in their theories of personality. Collectively, these theories have come to be known as the psychoanalytic perspective. Freud's view of personality is the first formal theory of personality ever formulated; thus, many later theories are modifications. Freud's theory, defense mechanisms, and neo-Freudian views are discussed in this section.

Freud's Theory. Freud proposed that the personality is made up of three parts that continually interact with each other. The **id** is the unconscious part of the personality that operates to derive immediate pleasure. It is concerned only with immediate gratification of physiological needs. The id's way of thinking, called **primary process thinking,** may generate mental images and wish-fulfillment fantasies in the form of daydreaming or dreaming at night, but it cannot actually obtain the things needed and desired. The **ego** is the conscious part of the personality that is in contact with reality. It is responsible for the voluntary processes, perceives the needs of the individual, evaluates the environment, adapts to social norms, plans ahead, and finds ways to actually obtain the things needed and desired. The conscious mental activity of the ego is called **secondary process thinking.** The **superego** consists of the internalized values and moral standards, known as the conscience, and is sometimes conscious and sometimes unconscious. The id is the wants of the person, the superego is the shoulds of the person, and the ego is the doing of the functioning person. The id is the product of physiological needs, the ego is the product of the intellectual processes, and the superego is the product of socialization.

Internal conflicts between the physiological urges of the id and the internalized controls of the superego create anxiety or tension. The ego finds ways to control the anxiety level. This is what was referred to as coping in the earlier discussion of stress. The ego may use coping strategies consciously or unconsciously.

What are erogenous zones?

According to Freud, pleasure is derived from highly sensitive places on the body, such as the mouth or genitals, called the body's **erogenous zones.** Different erogenous zones become the source of pleasure as an individual progresses through childhood. This developmental part of Freud's theory is known as the **psychosexual stages** of development. Whether the pleasure needs are satisfied at each stage of development has major consequences for an individual's personality.

What personality traits result from unresolved conflict in the oral stage of development?

From birth to approximately age 1 or 2, the mouth is the principal erogenous zone—the *oral stage.* Gratification of the id comes through oral activities such as sucking or biting. If the id is not sufficiently satisfied for a child or unresolved conflicts arise during the weaning process, fixation may occur resulting in an oral personality, and as an adult such oral traits as smoking, biting the nails, chewing gum, overeating, or excessive talking may occur.

What personality traits result from unresolved conflict in the anal stage of development?

From approximately age 1 to age 3, the anus is the focus of sensation as voluntary control of the muscles related to the processes of elimination is gained—the *anal stage.* Holding back the process of elimination brings pleasure such as the feel of clean, dry clothing, and elimination brings pleasure as discomfort is relieved. During the toilet-training period, Freud theorizes that conflicts often arise from this struggle within the child and from the power struggle between the child and the parent. If the conflicts are unresolved, the result will be a desire to hold on to things (be a "pack rat") and ideas (be stubborn) and have a stingy, miserly, orderly, or obstinate adult personality—an anal personality.

What is probably the most controversial part of Freud's theory?

The focus of sensation changes to the sex organs when they are discovered between approximately age 3 to age 5, and both pleasure and anxiety are experienced—the *phallic stage.* Probably the most controversial part of Freud's theory is his idea that a child unconsciously feels sexual attraction for the parent of the opposite sex and then becomes jealous of the parent of the same sex, which creates anxiety. Freud called this the **Oedipus complex** for a boy and the **Electra complex** for a girl. The conflict is resolved by identification with the parent of the same sex. If identification with the same sex parent does not occur during this stage of development and identification with the opposite sex parent occurs, the adult personality may be characterized by jealousy and problems with heterosexual relationships.

Freud placed little emphasis on the *latency stage,* which includes the time from about age 6 to puberty, because he believed this to be a time when sexual impulses are dormant or repressed and no new conflicts occur. Unconscious coping strategies may be formed during this period to keep sexual impulses repressed if socialization produces guilt feelings, which in turn produce anxiety.

If all the other stages have been passed through successfully, an adolescent progresses toward heterosexual relationships and chooses a sexual partner—the *genital stage.* This genital stage with a renewed focus on sexuality continues through adulthood.

Freud first believed sex drives, which he called the *life instinct,* to be the motivating force for almost all behavior. Later, during World War I, he added aggressive drives as also a source of motivation. He called these drives the *death instinct.*

According to Freud, what two drives or needs are the motivating source of all behavior?

Defense Mechanisms. Freud also formulated the idea of a person using unconscious strategies called **defense mechanisms** to cope with anxiety. His daughter, Anna, is credited with identifying and describing specific strategies. The ego finds or learns ways early in childhood to control the anxiety level. These ways tend to be repeated because their use is reinforced whenever the anxiety is successfully reduced. They eventually come to constitute a person's personality, or in other words, the person's characteristic ways of responding to people, objects, or events in the environment. Defense mechanisms distort, falsify, or deny reality, and everyone uses them to a certain extent. The degree to which they are used is related to whether a person is considered to be well adjusted or maladjusted. If defense mechanisms are overused, they may prevent a person from coping directly and taking action to resolve conflicts. Unresolved conflict creates more anxiety and necessitates more use of the defense mechanisms. A vicious cycle is put in motion, and the distortions and denial of reality may reach serious proportions.

What are defense mechanisms, and what are some major defense mechanisms?

Some of the common defense mechanisms as described and illustrated in a work context by Williams (1978) are identified here. **Rationalization** is a form of self-deception in which a socially acceptable justification is developed to avoid having to face a nonacceptable view of oneself. For example, an executive fails because of poor business decisions but insists that the cause of failure was an unfavorable economy. **Fantasy** is inappropriate daydreaming. A management trainee who is frustrated by low status and unchallenging work, for example, daydreams about a future in the executive suite rather than creatively works to make such a future reality. A person using **projection** unconsciously rejects an unacceptable thought, desire, impulse, or emotion by blaming it on someone else. The executive who has ceased to be promoted because of nonperformance and projects the failure onto superiors by believing they block opportunities and favor other candidates illustrates the defense mechanism called projection. Aggression, discussed in a previous chapter, is a defense mechanism whereby the individual destructively attacks the real or imaginary source of frustration. Aggression may be expressed verbally in slander and gossip or physically in such behaviors as sabotage or fighting. **Displacement (scapegoating)** is behaving aggressively toward someone who cannot fight back as a substitute for aggression toward the source of frustration. For example, a supervisor who is angry at a superior may take it out on subordinates or family. **Overcompensation** consists of exaggerated and inappropriate behavior in some area of expertise as a means of handling an inadequacy in some other area. For example, an individual who feels ill at ease with people may talk too much or too loudly in a vain attempt to gain social acceptance. On a less extreme level, students who flunk out of school make up for feelings of shame by intensively applying themselves in a substitute career. Various forms of substitution can be wholesome forms of defense, except when they involve giving up too soon on a worthwhile initial objective or lowering self-expectations when the going gets rough. Repression, defined in a previous chapter, involves blotting out of consciousness ideas, memories, and feelings that cause conflict and tend to lower self-esteem. Repression is exemplified by supervisors who selectively forget their own errors and blunders, refuse to accept constructive criticisms of superiors, and thus are unable to make the behavioral changes required for effective performance. **Reaction formation** is a pendulum swing in the opposite direction from true desires or impulses as a means of maintaining self-control or self-respect. A highly ambitious manager whose career is stymied accepts defeat and becomes an extreme advocate of the stupidity of working hard and playing the upward mobility game. **Withdrawal,** physically and/or psychologically pulling away from people and conflict, is a frequently used defense mechanism. Withdrawal is exemplified by the shy individual whose protection is to be excessively quiet or by the manager whose reaction to departmental conflict is to avoid becoming involved—to act as though the conflict were nonexistent.

Figure 11–7.
Carl Jung.

Neo-Freudians. The prefix *neo* means new; therefore, **neo-Freudians** are "new Freuds." Although they accepted the basic ideas of Freud's theory in general, some of Freud's followers had views that differed from Freud's views, and they later established a theory of their own. Carl Jung (see Figure 11–7), Alfred Adler (see Figure 11–8), Karen Horney (see Figure 11–9), Erich Fromm, and Erik Erikson are well-known neo-Freudians. Erikson's theory was discussed in chapters 3 and 4. He proposed that the series of stages a person progresses through that are critical to personality development are social rather than sexual and that the stages encompass the entire life span.

Figure 11–8.
Alfred Adler.

Jung's primary difference from Freud was his belief that the unconscious mind exerts even more influence on the personality than Freud had theorized. Jung postulated that a person has a collective unconscious in addition to the personal unconscious consisting of a person's repressed thoughts and feelings that was postulated by Freud. The **collective unconscious** is an inherited unconscious common to all humans. It consists of a reservoir of representations of early ancestors' universal experiences—including various images of mother, spiritual concerns, and certain myths shared by people in different cultures. Jung's adult personality types are rational extroverts or introverts and irrational extroverts or introverts in contrast to Freud's classifications such as oral or anal personality.

Figure 11–9.
Karen Horney.

Adler and Horney, as well as Erikson, accepted that childhood is important in personality development and focused on social rather than sexual tensions. Adler proposed the source of anxiety to be feelings of inferiority. A child feels inferior to adults, and the striving for superiority and power shapes the personality. Horney contended that the helplessness of a child is the source of the anxiety, and a striving for security shapes the personality.

What are the five specific needs in accordance with which Fromm believes an individual's personality develops?

Fromm placed more emphasis on the ego, believing that it is the conscious striving for love and unity and for truth and justice, rather than unconscious strivings of sexual feelings, that is critical in personality development. According to Fromm, an individual's personality develops in accordance with the satisfaction of five specific needs that are purely human and have become embedded in human nature through evolution. These are the needs for relatedness, transcendence, rootedness, identity, and a frame of orientation. Relatedness is a universal love of people that implies mutual care and respect. Transcendence is becoming creative and rising above the animalistic nature. Rootedness is a feeling of brotherliness with other individuals. Identity is development of a mark of distinction to become a unique person with a personal identity—not the identity of another person or group. A frame of orientation is the development of a stable and consistent way of perceiving and comprehending the world—a philosophy of life.

Type and Trait Perspective

Theorists who define personality in terms of types and traits use a descriptive approach. They are concerned with describing and classifying rather than explaining personality. Hippocrates (460-377 B.C.) suggested that the human body consists of a brain and four humors (blood, black bile, yellow bile, and phlegm) that determine the characteristic behavior of the individual. He grouped people into personality types based on physical characteristics. Those with an imbalance of phlegm would be quiet, depressed, and withdrawn; those with an imbalance of black or yellow bile would be excited, noisy, or mischievous; and those with an imbalance of blood would go into angry rages. **Physiognomy,** the classification of personality traits based on facial features, proposed, for example, that people with large earlobes are generous, people with small earlobes are stingy, and people with small, beady eyes are sly and shifty. Although these classifications are not believed today, they are the basis for some expressions such as phlegmatic personality, meaning a dull and sluggish personality, and in a bad humor, meaning angry. Today personality classifications are usually based on characteristic behaviors and motives. Sheldon's body types, Allport's cardinal, central, and secondary traits, and Cattell's surface and source traits are discussed in this section.

Sheldon's Body Types. William Sheldon (1940) classified people into three personality types based on body build. **Endomorphs** are those who have soft, wide bodies with a larger proportion of the body weight than normal in the internal organs. **Mesomorphs** are those who have a firm bone structure and much accumulation of muscle. **Ectomorphs** are those who have a thin body with small bones (see Figure 11–10). Sheldon found a correlation between characteristic behaviors of people and body types. Endomorphs are typically sociable, slow moving, jovial, and fond of food. Mesomorphs are characterized as being action oriented, risk taking, adventurous, aggressive, and loud. Ectomorphs are usually sensitive,

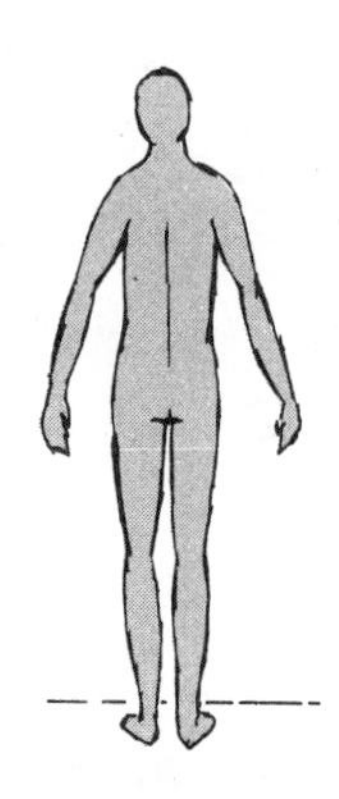
Ectomorph

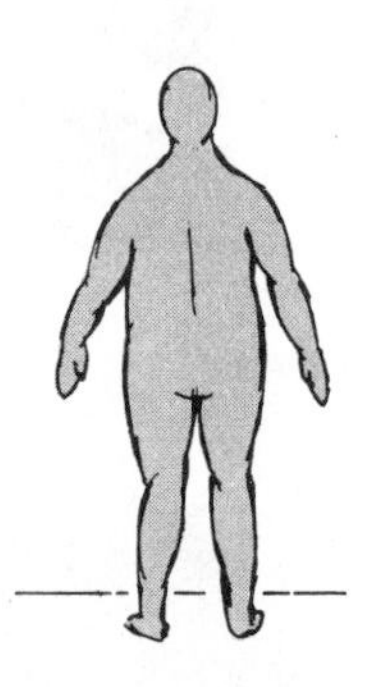
Endomorph

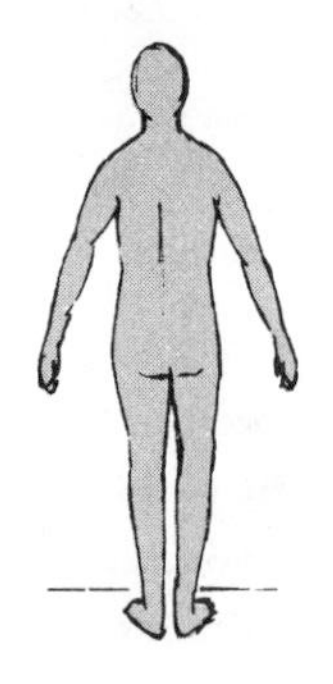
Mesomorph

Figure 11–10. Sheldon's three basic body builds.

quiet, restrained, and self-conscious, and they like privacy. Although a correlation has been found, such a small portion of the personality is accounted for by the body type that predicting personality based on body type is not very useful because so much error occurs.

Allport's Traits. Gordon Allport (see Figure 11–11) classified the thousands of human traits as cardinal, central, and secondary (Allport & Odbert, 1936). **Cardinal traits** are those that determine behavior in the most encompassing conditions, for example, the trait of being humanitarian. **Central traits** are more specific than cardinal traits but still are somewhat general such as the traits of being outgoing, cold, pessimistic, or efficient. **Secondary traits** are traits that are specific to certain circumstances such as being irritable while shopping, relaxed during the delivery of a speech, or happy when with a particular person. Allport also considered that some traits such as fear are commonly found in everyone to some extent. Other traits such as shyness and fear of people in general are unique to the individual. Allport's theory led to an interest in expressive behavior, the behavior displayed by a person that is a source of evidence concerning his or her personality. For example, a person may be classified as an extrovert or introvert or a Type A or Type B based on his or her actions.

Figure 11–11.
Gordon Allport.

Cattell's Traits. Raymond B. Cattell (see Figure 11–12), like Allport, grouped human traits into clusters (1957). He used a mathematical technique called **factor analysis** for analyzing the interrelationships of behavior data. The factor analysis allowed him to summarize large amounts of data relevant to many individuals and to group the related traits and classify them as personality factors. Using data from life records, subjects' answers to questions about the self, and standardized tests, Cattell grouped human behavior into about 35 trait clusters that he called **surface traits** because each trait is a summary of expressive behaviors that are related. For example, honesty is a surface trait that summarizes a group of many behaviors such as returning a lost billfold with all the money in it, telling parents the truth when questioned about something, or telling a potential buyer of your car all known problems. Cattell considered surface traits to be expressions of personality rather than the personality itself. He further used factor analysis to analyze the surface traits and obtained 16 **source traits** that represent underlying traits that enter into the determinination of multiple surface traits. Because he believes that surface traits are produced by the interaction of source traits, it is the source traits

Figure 11–12.
Raymond B. Cattell.

How do source traits differ from surface traits?

that have the most utility in accounting for behavior. Cattell developed a test in 1964 to measure the relative strengths of these 16 source traits, also called personality factors.

Humanistic Perspective

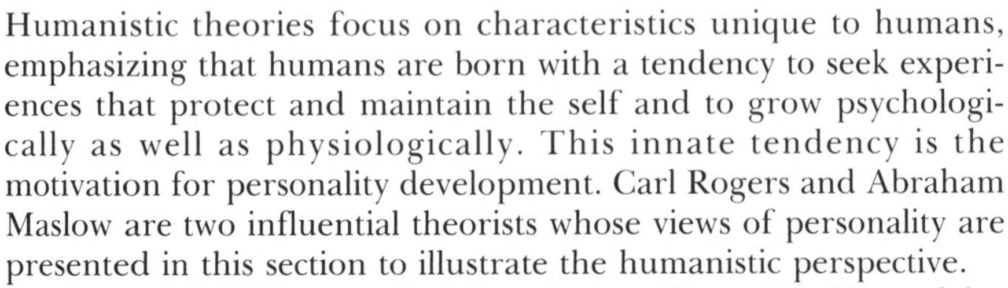

Humanistic theories focus on characteristics unique to humans, emphasizing that humans are born with a tendency to seek experiences that protect and maintain the self and to grow psychologically as well as physiologically. This innate tendency is the motivation for personality development. Carl Rogers and Abraham Maslow are two influential theorists whose views of personality are presented in this section to illustrate the humanistic perspective.

Figure 11–13.
Carl Rogers.

Rogers' Self Theory. Carl Rogers (see Figure 11–13) explains personality in terms of the self-concept, perceptions of the self, and the **actualizing tendency** of people, which is the tendency to engage in and value activities that satisfy their need to grow and to avoid those that hinder growth or are unpleasant (1961). The self, which is available to consciousness although not always conscious, is the primary structure of personality. The word *self* has come to have two meanings in psychology. One meaning, as used by Rogers, refers to the self as an object. It is a person's attitudes, feelings, perceptions, and evaluations—the person's organized, consistent image or system of conceptions—of himself or herself. The other meaning refers to the self as a doer. It is the group of psychological processes of the person such as thinking, remembering, and perceiving and is sometimes called the ego.

To what does Rogers refer with the word *self?*

As an infant experiences the world, the self is gradually separated from other things that exist in the environment, and the self-concept develops. The self-concept, as pointed out in chapter 4, consists of the perceptions of the physical image, of the abilities, and of the value or importance of the self. How people come to perceive themselves depends on their social experiences. For example, if a child's parents are warm and accepting, frequently giving praise, the child comes to perceive himself or herself as competent and likeable and develops a positive self-concept. However, if a child's parents are cold, rejecting, and constantly criticizing, the child develops feelings of inadequacy that lead to a negative self-concept. Also, internalized attitudes, values, and standards serve as a guide in the development of the self-concept. For example, if a student has the attitude that any grade less than an A is unacceptable and that student in a fair situation does not make an A, the

According to Rogers, what constitutes the self-concept?

student may become defensive and anxious because the self has been threatened. The student must either see the self as an unacceptable person, change the attitude, or perceive the experience in a distorted way through the use of defense mechanisms.

According to Rogers, what is the source of a maladjusted personality?

Rogers believes that personality is related to the level of discrepancy between a person's perception of the self (self-concept), the type of person one would like to be (the ideal self), and the type of person one really is (the real self). A person above average in intelligence who believes he or she is stupid yet must be smart enough never to make a mistake in order to be an acceptable or ideal person experiences anxiety. The lower the disparity, the less anxious and defensive the person will be. The higher the level of disparity, the more anxiety the person will experience, the greater the likelihood that defense mechanisms will be overused, and the greater the likelihood that a low or negative self-concept will be developed, all of which are characteristics of a maladjusted personality. In order to develop and maintain a positive self-concept, Rogers believes the following are essential: a warm and accepting environment, an understanding of the real self, and realistic ideals. He also believes that it is best if people in an individual's environment nurture psychological growth and the development of a well-adjusted personality by being genuine (open to their own feelings, self-disclosing, and without facades), accepting (unconditional positive regard), and empathic (sensing and reflecting the individual's feelings and meanings without being judgmental).

What does Rogers believe is essential in order to develop and maintain a positive self-concept?

Maslow's Hierarchy of Needs. Abraham Maslow explained personality in terms of differing motivations that are arranged in a hierarchy. The basis for a person behaving selfishly or violently may be because the person has not grown beyond the lowest motivating force of the hierarchy, physiological needs, or because he or she has reverted from a higher motivation back to the lower motivation. Maslow believes the progression to a higher motivating force is the result of a striving toward self-actualization. Although all the needs in the hierarchy are innate, those higher in the hierarchy are weaker than those that are lower. A need will direct action only when all of those below it have been satisfied to a certain degree. Maslow's hierarchy of needs theory and his concept of self-actualization are discussed in more detail in chapter 9.

The Social-Cognitive Perspective

Theorists who explain personality from the social-cognitive perspective build on the well-established theories of learning and cognition. They apply the principles of social learning theory and cognition and are particularly interested in stimulus control and what takes place between the stimulus situation and the response made by a person to deal with it. This perspective adheres to the idea that reinforcement, expectation, values, past experience, current emotion, and conditions of the situation all influence behavior. In this section, the interactionist view, locus of control, and learned helplessness are discussed.

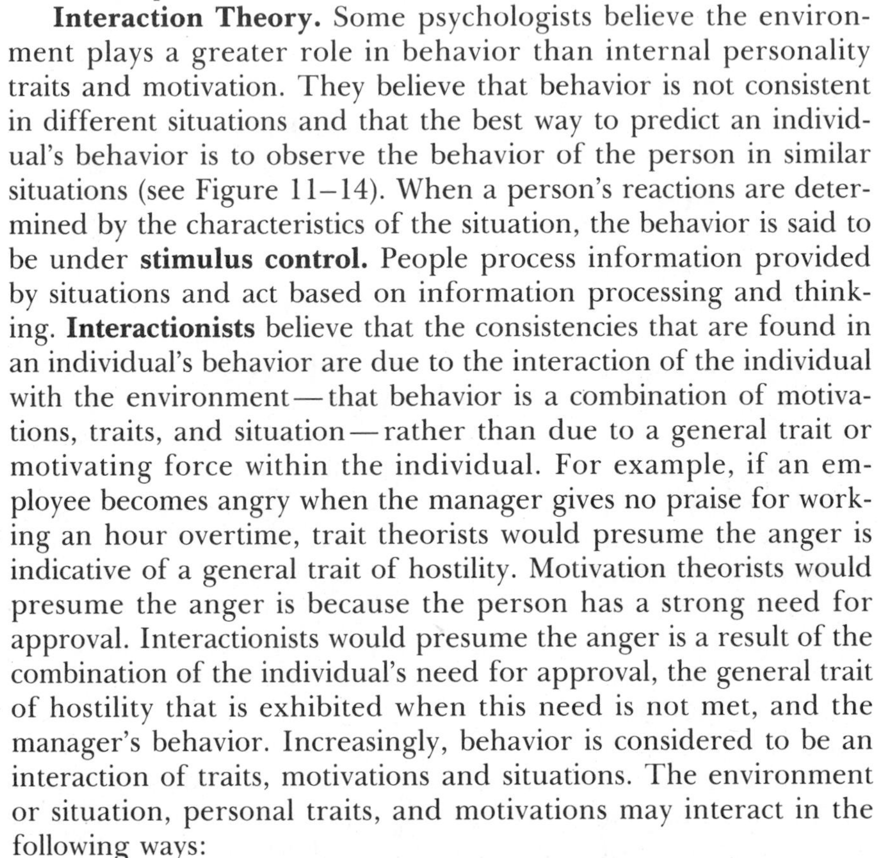

Interaction Theory. Some psychologists believe the environment plays a greater role in behavior than internal personality traits and motivation. They believe that behavior is not consistent in different situations and that the best way to predict an individual's behavior is to observe the behavior of the person in similar situations (see Figure 11–14). When a person's reactions are determined by the characteristics of the situation, the behavior is said to be under **stimulus control.** People process information provided by situations and act based on information processing and thinking. **Interactionists** believe that the consistencies that are found in an individual's behavior are due to the interaction of the individual with the environment—that behavior is a combination of motivations, traits, and situation—rather than due to a general trait or motivating force within the individual. For example, if an employee becomes angry when the manager gives no praise for working an hour overtime, trait theorists would presume the anger is indicative of a general trait of hostility. Motivation theorists would presume the anger is because the person has a strong need for approval. Interactionists would presume the anger is a result of the combination of the individual's need for approval, the general trait of hostility that is exhibited when this need is not met, and the manager's behavior. Increasingly, behavior is considered to be an interaction of traits, motivations and situations. The environment or situation, personal traits, and motivations may interact in the following ways:

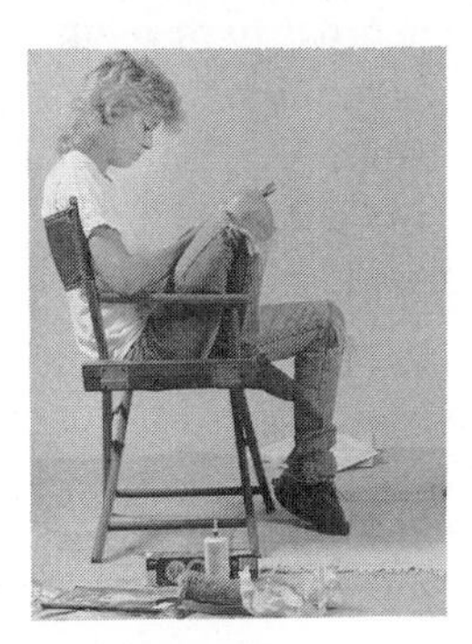

Figure 11–14. People's behavior depends to a large extent on the situation they are in.

1. Traits and motivations may influence an individual's interpretation of an event and thus the reaction.
2. An individual may choose the environment or situation.
3. An individual's behavior may create the situation for the reaction.

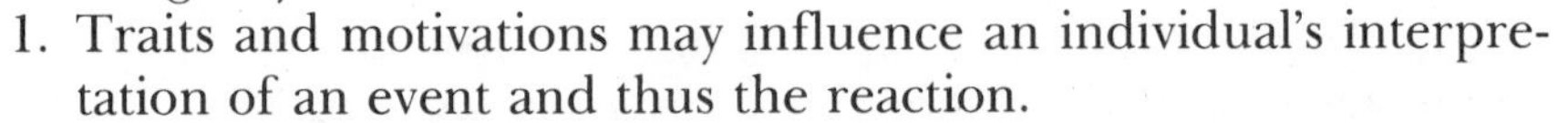

This interaction view of personality has spurred researchers to study the role of the environment in personal control and the self-concept. According to this view, the self-concept is shaped by interactions and not by innate, actualizing tendencies.

Personal Control Theory. Julian Rotter (1980) explains people's personalities according to how they attempt to control their environment. He believes that maladjustment originates in everyday relationhips with people and that expectation greatly influences a person's behavior. If a person's efforts are rewarded, the person will expect to be able to exert control over outcomes. If no consequence occurs as a result of a person's efforts, the person will not expect to be able to control outcomes. An important aspect of Rotter's theory is the concept of generalized expectancy whereby expectancy in a specific situation generalizes to other areas. For example, low expectation for success in learning math, based on environmental experience, may generalize to low expectation for success in getting a job or in developing friendships. Individuals with an **internal locus of control** perceive themselves as being the center of control in their lives. Individuals with an **external locus of control** perceive the center of control in their lives as being outside themselves. Internals are more likely than externals to attempt to improve their environment and be the agent for change. They believe they can effect change and expect to effect change. They are more likely than externals to see rewards as related to their own behavior and to be motivated to perform. They believe their skills can make a difference in the outcome of events. Externals, on the other hand, tend to believe that what they do will make no difference in the outcome. They are more likely to give up when they are hindered in meeting their goals and to see difficulties as threats. A number of studies have found that internals achieve more in school than externals (Findley & Cooper, 1983). Also, research studies indicate that internals are more independent and better able to delay gratification and cope with stress than externals (Lefcourt, 1982). A worker's reaction to the loss of a job, a supervisor's rating, or a promotion may be predicted based on whether the worker has an internal or an external locus of control. For example, a person who loses a job and has an internal locus of control may perceive the self as a factor in the job loss and believe he or she can make a difference in whether the next job obtained is lost. That person may do something to improve job skills or interpersonal relationships. A person who loses a job and has an external locus of control, however, may perceive the loss of the job as fate or as due to some condition beyond his or her control or to some other person's characteristics and make no effort to control loss of a job in the future.

What does Rotter believe the source of maladjustment to be?

How do individuals with an internal locus of control differ from individuals with an external locus of control?

How did Seligman demonstrate learned helplessness in the laboratory?

Martin Seligman (1975) and his associates have conducted much research to find how a person develops self-defeating expectancies that can affect subsequent behavior. In the classic study, dogs received many electric shocks while strapped in a harness to keep them from being able to escape or avoid the shock. The following day the dogs were placed so that they could learn to react to a warning signal within 10 seconds and avoid the shock. Dogs not previously shocked learned to avoid the shocks quickly, but approximately two thirds of those shocked the preceding day were unable to learn the avoidance behavior. Some had to be pushed in response to the warning signal 200 times before they learned how to avoid the shock. Those who had been shocked the preceding day appeared to passively accept the suffering. This phenomenon has been labeled **learned helplessness.** Later studies indicate that learned helplessness is stronger when the unavoidable shock occurs in an unpredictable manner (Overmier & Wiekiewicz, 1983). Similar studies with humans have demonstrated learned helplessness. Johnson (1981) suggests that if children who have early failures in school attribute the failure to their own inadequacies, learned helplessness develops. The reverse, learned mastery, has now been demonstrated (Volpicelli, Ulm, Altenor, & Seligman, 1983). When rats initially trained to press a lever to successfully escape shock were placed in a box in which they could not avoid shocks, they continued trying to escape the shocks for hundreds of trials. The demonstration of learned mastery is important because of the possibility of reversing learned helplessness, which produces fear and depression, reduces motivation, and interferes with learning (see Figure 11–15). It seems that for a child to experience success in school is not enough to prevent or reverse learned helplessness. The child must recognize that it is what he or she does that is the determining factor in the success. For example, a student who recognizes that he or she was successful in passing introductory accounting because of the time engaged in study will persist in increased and continued study time when faced with failure in a more advanced accounting class. The student who believes he or she passed introductory accounting because of the particular teacher will most likely be less persistent in increased and continued study time when faced with failure in a more advanced accounting class with a different teacher. A student who is unsuccessful in learning introductory accounting no matter how much time is spent in study develops learned helplessness and most

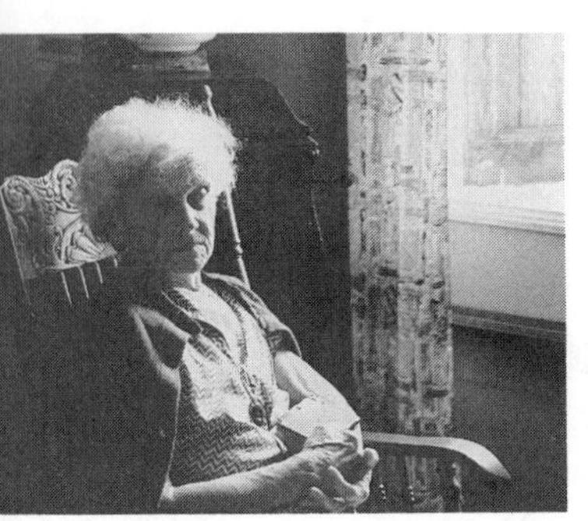

Figure 11–15.
People may learn to be helpless or depressed when they believe that no matter what they do they will be punished.

likely will not spend time in study in another accounting class with a different instructor that would result in successfully passing accounting.

PERSONALITY ASSESSMENT

People make informal assessments of other people's personalities all the time. Judgments are often made concerning traits and motivations based on observation, personal experience, or hearsay that are apt to be biased and unreliable. Reliable, unbiased measures of personality are more likely to be used by psychologists in diagnosing, treating, and researching and by personnel directors in hiring employees than by other people generally. In this section, the basic techniques used by professionals—observations, objective tests, and projective tests—are discussed.

Observations

Often the method used to assess an individual's personality is to directly observe his or her behavior in situations and his or her responses to questions in face-to-face interviews. The interview is the technique that has the longest record of use. The technique of direct, objective observation was initiated by the behaviorists. These two types of observations are addressed in this section.

Interviews. Freud used the interview technique to assess personality. He held long conversations or interviews with his patients and noted their comments and answers to questions. This technique is still widely used today in assessing personality. An interview consists of a conversation wherein the interviewer directs questions to the person being interviewed in order to evaluate the person's personality. The interviewer relies on nonverbal communications as well as verbal communications when making the evaluation. Although the success of this technique depends on the interviewer, most firms still rely heavily on the interview to assess personality for the purpose of selecting employees (see Figure 11–16). The validity of the interview technique is questionable because the interviewer may become too emotionally involved, because the interviewer's own personality may affect the evaluations, and because the interviewer may not be sensitive to nonverbal communications such as changes in pitch of voice. The interview does have an advantage over standardized tests in that it allows for specific questions pertinent to the individual and to the purpose of the assessment.

Figure 11–16. Most firms still rely heavily on the interview to assess personality.

Interviews differ according to the method used to obtain information. The primary difference is the amount of structure imposed by the interviewer. In the nondirective interview, the interviewer asks broad, general questions in order to avoid determining the course of the interview and influencing the remarks. The depth interview is somewhat more structured than the nondirective type, and the questions asked cover general areas. The patterned interview is highly structured and may consist of a set of detailed questions.

What are the major findings from research on interviewing?

Interviewing has been the subject of much research. Some of the major findings listed by Chruden and Sherman (1984) are as follows:

1. Interviewers form an immediate, usually subconscious, first impression within the first 5 minutes of the interview on the basis of appearance and actions. Information is then sought throughout the remainder of the interview to substantiate this first impression.
2. Interpersonal skills and motivation are probably best evaluated by the interview.
3. Structured interviews are more reliable than unstructured interviews.
4. The trait most validly evaluated is intelligence.
5. Unfavorable information influences the interviewer more than favorable information.
6. An interviewee is given a more extreme evaluation when preceded by an interviewee of opposing value.

These findings suggest that first impressions are indeed extremely important in interviewing for a job.

Direct Observation of Behavior. Often a person's behavior is assessed by observing his or her actions. If several observers report similar accounts of a person's behavior over a period of time, the assessment can be quite reliable. Direct observation of behavior consists of seeing the behavior or evidence of occurrence of the behavior and recording the data. The first step in direct observation is to precisely define the behavior to be observed. Vague terms like "lazy" should be replaced with specific responses that can be measured or counted such as "arrives late to work" or "completes fewer than five reports in a day." The next step is to observe the specified behavior and record the observation. The data collected over a period of time constitutes the assessment.

What is the first step in using direct observation of behavior as an assessment technique?

The data will probably be more reliable if it is collected without the person's knowledge. If two or more observers collect the data simultaneously, the assessment will be more reliable. Videotaped observations permit observation by any number of observers without the person being observed being aware of the observations. Sometimes assessors are too quick to type the personality of a person. Their observations may be based on too little data or may be biased by their own attitudes. If supervisors compare their perceptions of observed worker behaviors with others' perceptions, a higher level of objectivity will be effected.

What can increase the reliability of assessment by direct observation?

Objective Tests

Objective tests, sometimes called personality inventories, have been created by psychologists to measure a variety of traits, interests, and dimensions of personality. **Objective personality tests** usually are paper-and-pencil tests and are in the form of questions about the self (see Figure 11--17). An individual may be asked to indicate on an answer sheet how various statements about behaviors, opinions, and feelings relate to him or her. Questions such as "Do you frequently have headaches?" or "Do you make friends easily?" are often included on these tests. Sometimes a choice must be made from a list of several activities. For example, the individual may be asked, "Which activity in this group would you choose if you had to be engaged in one?" Or the individual may be asked, "What activity would you omit if you had to be engaged in all of the activities except one?" Sometimes individuals are asked to choose from a set of statements the one statement or those statements they feel best describe themselves.

Figure 11–17. Objective personality tests usually are paper-and-pencil tests and are in the form of questions about the self.

Validity and ethics sometimes present problems in objective testing. Individuals may fake answers or have unrealistic self-perceptions. The forced-choice type of test does reduce the possibility of falsifying answers. Asking personal questions pertaining to habits, attitudes about sex, or likes and dislikes are sometimes considered an invasion of privacy.

What are some aspects of the MMPI?

Minnesota Multiphasic Personality Inventory. The Minnesota Multiphasic Personality Inventory (MMPI) (Hathaway & McKinley, 1967) is the most widely used clinical objective personality inventory. It is a true-false test that contains 566 statements (Group Form) about the self. Responses to these statements yield 10 clinical scales that rate a person on traits used in clinical evaluations. These scales are listed and described in the box that follows. Four additional scales are validity indicators. For example, one of these is related to the indecisiveness of the individual based on the number of responses in the "can't say" category; another is related to attempts to falsify the outcome of the test by giving responses that would result in a favorable appearance. Carelessness, such as failure to answer a question, and answering the same or similar question inconsistently are also reflected in these validity scales. These scales are called Cannot Say, Lie, Infrequency, and Defensiveness. Four supplemental scales called Anxiety, Repression, Ego Strength, and McAndrew Addiction yield scores on additional traits.

MMPI CLINICAL SCALES

1. Hypochondriasis (Hs). Extreme and persistent concerns about one's physical health.
2. Depression (D). Poor morale, pessimism, feelings of hopelessness and sorrow.
3. Hysteria (Hy). Physical ailments that have no organic basis and feelings of sadness and lack of satisfaction.
4. Psychopathic deviation (Pd). Difficulty in forming satisfactory personal relationships and inability to anticipate the consequences of one's behavior.
5. Masculinity-femininity (Mf). Traditional masculine and feminine interest patterns.
6. Paranoia (Pa). Feelings of sensitivity, suspiciousness, persecution, and grandiosity.
7. Psychasthenia (Pt). Vague anxieties, insecurity, self-doubt, phobias, and obsessive-compulsive reactions.
8. Schizophrenia (Sc). Emotional isolation and poor reality contact, sometimes accompanied by hallucinations.
9. Hypomania (Ma). Hyperactivity, restlessness, distractibility, and unrealistic optimism.
10. Social introversion (Si). Shyness and feelings of uneasiness in and/or withdrawal from social situations. (Janda & Klenke-Hamel, 1982, p. 312.)

Note. From *Psychology: It's Study and Uses* (p. 312) by Louis Janda and Karin Klenke-Hamel, 1982, New York: St. Martin's Press.

What are some uses of the 16PF?

Sixteen Personality Factor Questionnaire. Cattell's Sixteen Personality Factor Questionnaire (16PF) is a test of normal, adult personality that measures levels of assertiveness, emotional maturity, shrewdness, self-sufficiency, tension, and 11 other primary traits. This test is based on 35 years of research and development and has been revised and improved several times since it appeared in 1949. The 16PF is frequently used in industry and business for selection, placement, and promotion of personnel by predicting such criteria as sales effectiveness, tolerance for routine, and length of time likely to remain with the company. It is also used by counselors and school psychologists in advising students and in identifying groups of students such as potential dropouts or drug users because it can test people 16 years old and up.

Which personality test is useful to individuals in making career choices?

Strong-Campbell Interest Inventory. The Strong-Campbell Interest Inventory (SCII) measures 23 basic areas of interest and compares the person's interests with the interests of people happily employed in a wide variety of occupations. It provides information useful to individuals in making career choices and to administrators in business and industry in making employment decisions.

Literally hundreds of objective personality tests are available. Only these three widely used ones have been described here for illustration.

Projective Tests

Projective tests use unstructured, vague, and ambiguous stimuli to obtain a response. The thoughts and perceptions that come to a person's mind are thought to reveal the conflicts, fears, fantasies, needs, and defenses that may be unknown to the person. It is believed that the person projects his or her personality into the stimulus and the response. Projective tests are used primarily in clinical situations because there is no one objective system for interpreting and scoring the test. A highly trained clinician is required to evaluate the responses. Different examiners may have only moderate agreement on the results unless they have been trained in the same system of scoring. Considerable time is usually needed to administer and interpret projective tests.

Rorschach Test. The classic Rorschach Test, developed in 1921 by Hermann Rorschach, uses 10 psychodiagnostic plates, which are inkblots formed by dropping ink on a piece of paper and then folding the paper to create a symmetrical design. Figure 11–18 is an inkblot similar to those used in the test. Each inkblot is different from the others and is printed on a separate card. Five are black and gray, three have several colors in some places on them, and two have some red places on them. For an example of how the test is scored, if a person taking the test sees ferocious animals or weapons in the blots, a need to be aggressive may be considered to

Figure 11–18. An inkblot similar to those used in the Rorschach Test to assess personality.

be present. The Rorschach Test is probably the best known and most widely used projective test although its reliability and validity are questioned. Because it evaluates basic personality structure and detects psychopathology of children, adolescents, and adults, it is used primarily in clinical settings for evaluation and treatment planning.

Figure 11–19. An example of a picture included in the set of pictures for the TAT.

Thematic Apperception Test. Another widely used personality projective test is the Thematic Apperception Test (TAT) described in chapter 9 as a test for motivation. This test consists of 31 pictures of one or more people in various positions and/or settings (see Figure 11–19). Twenty of the set are designated for use with women, 20 with men, 20 with boys, and 20 with girls, which makes the test appropriate for all individuals 10 years of age or older. The person taking the test is asked to make up a story about each of the 20 pictures describing the events that led up to the pictured scene, what is happening in the scene, and the outcome of the situation. The TAT reveals an individual's perception of interpersonal relationships and helps identify an individual's dominant motives, emotions, sentiments, conflicts, complexes, biases, and interests.

Other projective techniques sometimes used in assessing personality factors include word association tests wherein the person being tested says the first word that comes to mind after a standardized word is given by the test administrator. Sentence completion tests are sometimes used. In this type of test, a sentence is started and left incomplete to be completed by the person taking the test. Incomplete sentences might be such as "My father . . . " or "I like . . . " In other tests, the person being tested may be asked to draw a picture instead of responding verbally or in writing. Oftentimes a drawing of the self, of the family, or just a person is asked for.

SUMMARY

1. Personality is the characteristic or usual responses of a person to people, objects, or events in the environment—the persistent behavior patterns that are unique to an individual.
2. Theorists describe the personality of a well-adjusted person as being more than the absence of maladjustment. The well-adjusted person seems to have the ability to perceive reality accurately, to profit from experience, to have a commitment to some form of work, to form close or intimate social relationships, and to express a wide range of emotions.

3. The personality of people in the workplace is important because personality is related to success, management style that works best, motivation and performance, and the self-image.
4. Workers in different occupational groups have different personalities. Also, workers may be categorized as to whether they are spontaneous or anomic, Type A or Type B, extroverts or introverts, and stable or unstable.
5. Freud and neo-Freudians explain personality from a psychoanalytic perspective and focus on unconscious motivation. Freud explained personality in terms of (a) the interaction of the id, ego, and superego, (b) the use of defense mechanisms to reduce anxiety, and (c) the psychosexual stages of development. Some common defense mechanisms are rationalization, fantasy, projection, aggression, displacement, overcompensation, repression, reaction formation, and withdrawal.
6. Neo-Freudians Adler, Horney, and Fromm disagreed with Freud's proposed sexual and aggressive drives as the source of unconscious motivation for behavior. Adler proposed instead superiority; Horney proposed instead security; and Fromm proposed instead love and unity—all social needs.
7. In disagreeing with Freud, Erikson proposed social stages of development rather than sexual stages of development, and Jung proposed a collective unconscious in addition to Freud's proposed personal unconscious.
8. Using a type and trait perspective, Sheldon classified personality types according to body build—endomorph, mesomorph, and ectomorph; Allport identified cardinal, central, and secondary personality traits; and Cattell identified surface and source traits by using factor analysis.
9. The theories of Rogers and Maslow are representative of the humanistic perspective. Rogers explained personality in terms of the self-concept and the actualizing tendency. Maslow explained personality in terms of the actualizing tendency and a hierarchy of needs with self-actualization highest in the hierarchy.
10. The social-cognitive perspective builds on theories of learning and cognition. The interactionists view personality as the result of a combination of motivating forces, situations (environment or stimuli), and traits.
11. Personal control theory represents a social-cognitive perspective. Rotter explains personality in terms of whether the individual has developed an internal or external locus of control.
12. Another personal control theory is illustrated by the demonstration of how self-defeating expectancies develop and affect behavior resulting in what is called learned helplessness.
13. Observations, which include interviews and direct, objective observa-

tion of behavior, and objective and projective tests are basic techniques used to assess personality.

14. Interviewing, the first technique used to assess personality, depends on the interviewer for its success and validity. Nondirective, depth, and patterned interviews differ primarily in the amount of structure imposed by the interviewer.
15. Direct observation of behavior is usually somewhat reliable, especially when the behavior to be observed is precisely defined and two or more observers collect the data simultaneously.
16. Objective tests are usually paper-and-pencil tests in the form of questions to answer about the self. Three such tests that are widely used are (a) the MMPI, the most widely used objective test in clinical settings; (b) the 16PF, used in counseling and in business and industry for selection, placement and promotion of personnel; and (c) the SCII, used in making career choices because it compares an individual's interests with interests of people happily employed in a wide variety of occupations.
17. Projective tests use unstructured, vague, and ambiguous stimuli to obtain a response that is analyzed. The Rorschach Test, which uses inkblots, and the Thematic Apperception Test (TAT), which uses pictures, are two widely used projective tests. Word association and sentence completion tests are also types of projective tests.

KEY TERMS AND CONCEPTS

Personality
Psychotherapy
Spontaneous type
Anomic type
Type A personality
Type B personality
Stability-instability
Extroversion-introversion
Extroverts
Introverts
Ambiverts
Id
Primary process thinking
Ego
Secondary process thinking
Superego
Erogenous zones
Psychosexual stages
Oedipus complex
Electra complex
Defense mechanisms
Rationalization
Fantasy
Projection
Displacement (scapegoating)
Overcompensation
Reaction formation
Withdrawal
Neo-Freudians
Collective unconscious
Physiognomy
Endomorphs
Mesomorphs
Ectomorphs
Cardinal traits
Central traits
Secondary traits
Factor analysis
Surface traits
Source traits
Actualizing tendency
Stimulus control
Interactionists
Internal locus of control
External locus of control
Learned helplessness
Objective personality tests
Projective tests

QUESTIONS FOR REVIEW

1. What characteristics seem to differentiate the well-adjusted person from the maladjusted person?
2. Why is the personality of people who are in or will be in the workplace important?
3. What are some different personality types found in the workplace?
4. What are the highlights of Freud's theory?
5. Who were some of the neo-Freudians, and how did they differ from Freud?
6. What are the basic features of the theories proposed by Sheldon, Allport, and Cattell?
7. What are the basic features of the humanistic theories of Rogers and Maslow?
8. What is the interaction view of personality, locus of control, and learned helplessness?
9. How is personality assessed?
10. What are some widely used objective and projective tests? Name and describe them.

TEST YOURSELF

1. Psychologists use the word ________________ to describe the characteristic way a person responds to people, objects, or events in the environment.
2. Well-adjusted people (a) view themselves positively (b) view themselves negatively (c) are viewed positively by others (d) both a and c.
3. According to Eysenck, the two major dimensions of personality are ________________ and ________________.
4. In Freud's theory of personality, the ________________ is the unconscious part of the personality that operates to derive immediate pleasure.
5. In Freud's theory of personality, the ________________ finds ways to control the levels of anxiety and to obtain the things needed and desired.
6. The defense mechanism that involves behaving aggressively toward a substitute who cannot fight back rather than toward the real source of the frustration is called ________________.
7. According to Freud's psychosexual stages of development, the Oedipus complex for a boy and the Electra complex for a girl occur (a) between the approximate ages of 3 to 5 (b) between the approximate ages of 1 to 3 (c) from the age of puberty through adulthood (d) between age 6 and puberty.

8. Fromm, the neo-Freudian who placed greater emphasis on the ego than did Freud, believed personality develops in accordance with the satisfaction of five specific needs: ________________, ________________, ________________, ________________, and ________________.
9. Those individuals who have a body build consisting of much accumulation of muscle and a firm bone structure are classified as (a) sociomorphs (b) ectomorphs (c) endomorphs (d) mesomorphs.
10. Using a mathematical technique called factor analysis, Cattell grouped human traits into categories called cardinal, central, and secondary. T or F
11. ________________ was the personality theorist who proposed that the essentials for the development of a healthy personality are a warm and accepting environment that leads to a positive self-concept, an understanding of the real self, and realistic ideals.
12. Psychologists who believe that personality is a result of the combination of motivations, situations, and traits are referred to as (a) trait theorists (b) interactionists (c) situationists (d) socialists.
13. Individuals who tend to perceive the center of control in their lives as being outside themselves and believe that their environment determines the outcome of events rather than believing they can effect change are referred to as (a) internals (b) externals (c) Type As (d) Type Bs.
14. In learned helplessness, a passive acceptance of undesirable conditions and depression occur. T or F
15. Research studies indicate that interviewers form an immediate, usually subconscious, first impression within the first 5 minutes of the interview. T or F
16. The first step in using direct observation to assess an individual's behavior is (a) to observe the specified behavior (b) to precisely define the specified behavior (c) to record the observation (d) none of the above.
17. Objective personality tests usually are in the form of (a) direct observations of an individual's responses in specific situations (b) paper-and-pencil tests with questions for an individual to answer about the self (c) stories an individual is asked to make up about a picture (d) word associations with a word given by the person administering the test.
18. ________________ is the objective personality test most widely used in clinical evaluations and consists of 566 true-false statements, 10 clinical scales, and 4 scales related to the validity of the responses as well as 4 supplemental scales.
19. The Rorschach Test, probably the best known and most widely used projective test, consists of (a) 10 inkblots (b) 20 pictures (c) 566 true-false statements (d) 25 word associations.

20. Which of the following statements is true of projective tests? (a) They are used primarily in clinical situations. (b) A highly trained clinician is required to evaluate the responses. (c) Considerable time is needed for administration and evaluation. (d) all of the above.

APPLICATIONS

A. An employee who has worked for a firm for approximately a year is called and told by the boss, "I'm terminating your employment with the firm as of today. You will receive a check for the next 30 days as termination pay." Records indicate that the employee's production rate is above average. Records also indicate that many complaints from co-workers have been turned in concerning the ill manners and negative attitudes of the employee, who seems to constantly be in a fight with some co-worker. These problems have been discussed many times with the employee to no avail. The point has been reached that no one wants to work with this employee when two or more must work together to get a project done.

1. Do you think the employee was fired because of a lack of job skills or because of personality? Why?
2. What things about the case indicate that the employee is not well adjusted?

B. A manager of a firm seems to desire power and status, likes work activities that involve manipulating and dominating others, and tends to have good verbal skills. The manager is characteristically restless and ambitious, always hurrying and striving to accomplish much very quickly. The manager often wears bright-colored clothing, is very sociable, and engages in many exciting and adventurous activities during spare time.

1. Does the manager fit the personality that managers usually have, according to Holland? What is the personality type?
2. Would you type the manager as having a Type A or a Type B personality?
3. Would you type the manager as being an extrovert or an introvert?

SUGGESTIONS FOR FURTHER READING

Anastasi, A. (1982). *Psychological Testing* (5th ed.). New York: Macmillan.

A psychological testing textbook that contains one chapter on personality testing. Types of personality tests and specific tests are discussed.

Bandura, A. (1986). *The social foundations of thought and action: A social cognitive theory.* Englewood Cliffs, NJ: Prentice-Hall.

A good introduction to the social-cognitive perspective.

Hall, C. S., Lindzey, G., Loehlin, J. C., & Manosevitz, M. (1985). *Introduction to theories of personality.* New York: Wiley.

A revision of the classic textbook by Hall and Lindzey, *Theories of Personality,* that describes and evaluates the major theories of personality from Freud on through the social-cognitive theories.

Rogers, C. R. (1961). *On becoming a person.* Boston: Houghton Mifflin.
A philosophical and provocative book written for all who are interested in personality and psychological growth that sums up Rogers' beliefs.

Schultz, D. P. (1977). *Growth psychology: Models of the healthy personality.* Cincinnati: Van Nostrand Reinhold.
A short paperback book that presents seven prominent theorists' views regarding the healthy personality.

CHAPTER 12

PSYCHOLOGICAL DISORDERS AND TREATMENT

I. ABNORMALITY
- A. Diagnosis
  - 1. Labeling
  - 2. DSM-III
- B. Views
  - 1. Cognitive-Behavioral Model
  - 2. Organic Model
  - 3. Psychoanalytic Model
  - 4. Family or Systems Model
  - 5. Medical Model

II. CLASSIFICATION OF DISORDERS
- A. Neurotic Disorders
  - 1. Anxiety Disorders
  - 2. Somatoform Disorders
  - 3. Dissociative Disorders
  - 4. Psychosexual Disorders
- B. Psychotic Disorders
  - 1. Organic Mental Disorders
  - 2. Affective Disorders
  - 3. Schizophrenic Disorders
  - 4. Paranoid Disorders
- C. Personality Disorders
  - 1. Odd or Eccentric Personalities
  - 2. Dramatic, Emotional, or Erratic Personalities
  - 3. Anxious or Fearful Personalities

III. PSYCHOTHERAPY
- A. Insight Therapies
  - 1. Psychoanalysis
  - 2. Person-Centered Therapy
  - 3. Gestalt Therapy
  - 4. Group Therapy
- B. Behavior and Cognitive Therapies
  - 1. Behavior Modification
  - 2. Systematic Desensitization
  - 3. Aversion Therapy
  - 4. Assertiveness Training
  - 5. Self-Control and Self-Instructional Training
  - 6. Rational-Emotive Therapy
- D. Biomedical Therapies
  - 1. Chemotherapy
  - 2. Electroconvulsive Therapy
  - 3. Psychosurgery
  - 4. Aerobic Exercise

SUMMARY

KEY TERMS AND CONCEPTS

QUESTIONS FOR REVIEW

TEST YOURSELF

APPLICATIONS

SUGGESTIONS FOR FURTHER READING

Objectives

When you have completed your study of chapter 12, you should be able to:

1. Define abnormality in terms of diagnostic labeling.
2. Name and describe the latest official manual of psychological disorders used by clinicians and investigators to diagnose, communicate about, study, and treat various psychological disorders.
3. Briefly summarize different views proposed as the basis for abnormality.
4. Name and describe basic neurotic disorders as classified in DSM-III.
5. Name and describe basic psychotic disorders as classified in DSM-III.
6. Name and describe basic personality disorders as classified in DSM-III.
7. Name and describe commonly used insight therapies.
8. Define behavior modification, and name and describe a variety of techniques used in behavior modification.
9. Name and describe specific behavior and cognitive therapies in addition to techniques commonly used in behavior modification.
10. Name and describe different types of biomedical therapies.

Why do people seem to be especially curious about psychological disorders?

People seem to be especially curious about psychological disorders, which are referred to as abnormal behaviors, mental disorders, behavior disorders, mental illness, emotional disorders, or emotional illness. The reason for the fascination may be because most people have experienced the bewilderment and pain of a psychological disorder either through family members, friends, or self. Another reason may be because people without psychological disorders may see something of themselves in those people with psychological disorders because at times people without disorders feel, think, or act as those with psychological disorders act at times. The unusual behavior of those with psychological disorders is unusual just because it is more frequent, more intense, or for greater periods of time, or is displayed at more inappropriate times or under more inappropriate circumstances than that of those without disorders. For example, all people may cry, but if a person cries uncontrollably 50 percent of the time and even in happy settings for no known reason, the person may be considered to have a psychological disorder. All people may see, hear, feel, smell, or taste things that are not physically present when they are asleep and dreaming, but if a person sees, hears, feels, smells, or tastes things that are not physically present while in the waking state, the person may be considered to have a psychological disorder.

Managers, supervisors, and employees need to have some understanding of psychological disorders and treatment because approximately one person in ten can expect to be treated during his or her lifetime for some form of psychological disorder. This means that people with psychological disorders are often found in work environments, and because they have problems, they often are a problem for those who work with them. The psychological disorder may be the source of inefficiency in performance and poor social relationships. Dealing with a person with a psychological disorder as one would deal with a person without a psychological disorder may not be the best approach. Thus, it is important for supervisors and employees to be able to recognize symptoms of psychological disorders in order to make more appropriate decisions and to make referrals to someone who can provide professional help. This chapter focuses on psychological disorders and the classification and treatment of the disorders.

Why do managers, supervisors, and employees need to have an understanding of psychological disorders and treatment?

ABNORMALITY

Is each *person* considered to be either normal or abnormal? A common misconception is that *people* are classified. Actually, it is the *behaviors* of people that are classified. And whether a behavior is normal or abnormal is sometimes difficult to differentiate. Abnormal behavior literally means deviation from normal behavior. But what is normal behavior, and to what degree must the behavior deviate to be considered abnormal? In this section, the diagnosis of abnormal behavior and the different views of abnormality are discussed.

Diagnosis

No single, satisfactory criterion of abnormality or psychological disorder exists that specifies precise boundaries for the diagnosis of abnormal behavior. Most diagnosticians use one or more of a variety of criteria. Criteria used for labeling a behavior as a disorder, criticisms of labeling, and the DSM-III classification system are discussed next.

What different approaches have diagnosticians used to label a behavior as being abnormal?

Labeling. Some diagnosticians have used a statistical approach to label behavior that strays from the statistical average or from the majority as abnormal. However, using this definition alone, the high creativity of a person such as Albert Einstein would be considered abnormal. Clinical depression would not be considered abnormal because such a large percentage of people have this disorder at some point during their lifetime. Others have used cultural boundaries and expectations to diagnose whether or not a behavior is abnormal. But what is expected or commonly occurring behavior in one culture may not be customary or common in another culture. According to this criterion for labeling, there are no absolutes; whether or not a behavior is abnormal depends on the context of the culture in which the behavior occurs. Still others have defined abnormal behavior as behavior that deviates from ideal behavior or as behavior that negatively affects subjective feelings. According to this view, just about everyone exhibits some abnormality; it is just a matter of degree. Sometimes abnormal behavior is defined as behavior that is dysfunctional. But behavior that is functional in one environment may be dysfunctional in another environment. Or behavior that is functional for one person may be dysfunctional for another person. The legal criterion of insanity (abnormality) is whether or not the person is able to judge between right and wrong behavior and is able to exert control over his or her behavior (see Figure 12–1). Generally, psychologists diagnose behavior as abnormal according to several criteria. The more criteria the behavior fits, the more certain the diagnosis that the behavior is abnormal.

Figure 12–1.
The legal term for mental disorder is insanity, the criteria for which is whether or not the person is able to judge between right and wrong behavior and is able to exert control over his or her behavior.

The four criteria most frequently used to label a behavior as abnormal are the following:

1. The behavior is bizarre and extreme, such as hallucinations or delusions, uncontrolled violence, or even handwashing if performed repeatedly dozens of time a day for no rational reason.
2. The behavior disturbs or interferes with the well-being of the self or others, such as molesting a child, drunken driving, head banging, or endless, incoherent talking to others.
3. The behavior is inappropriate or is an excessive emotional display, such as panic, overwhelming happiness or unhappiness unwarranted by circumstances, or disabling, inappropriate guilt.
4. The behavior is an interference with daily functioning, such as excessive daydreaming, delusions, or inability to remember.

Why do some psychologists criticize the diagnosing of behaviors as abnormal?

Some psychologists criticize the diagnosing of behaviors as abnormal on the basis that diagnostic procedures are too unreliable. A behavior may be diagnosed differently by different clinicians. Another objection to labeling behavior as abnormal is the long-lasting psychological effect the labeling may have on how a person is regarded by others and how a person regards himself or herself. Szasz (1974) is critical of such labeling because he feels the labeling is just a method for disposing of those who behave in a way disapproved of by society—a form of punishment for nonconformity. An even more radical criticism is voiced by R. D. Laing (1967), who believes that the label of abnormal behavior is misleading because such behavior is really an act of heroism—a daring to leave the extreme world of logic and reason or explanation and to move into one's own mind.

What is the official classification system now used in this country for psychological disorders?

DSM-III. The *Diagnostic and Statistical Manual of Mental Disorders* (3rd ed.), referred to as **DSM-III,** is a manual of the official classification system currently used by diagnosticians in this country. Some background and history of DSM-III, its definition of a psychological disorder, and a general overview of its classification system are presented here.

The first official system used in this country for labeling abnormality came into use in 1840 and consisted of only one category. All psychological disorders were lumped together including the idiotic and the insane. Forty years later these disorders were subdivided into seven classifications: mania, melancholia, monomania, paresis, dementia, dipsomania, and epilepsy. Modern attempts in this country to label psychological disorders began with the first edition of the *Diagnostic and Statistical Manual of Mental Disorders* (DSM-I), developed in 1952 as an alternative to the sixth edition of the *International Classification of Diseases.* DSM-I replaced the outdated mental illness section of this publication. In 1967 the DSM-I was revised by 120 psychiatrists with a special interest in diagnosis. This revision became known as DSM-II and was adopted by the American Psychiatric Association as the official classification system. It was then accepted by the American Psychological Association and others throughout the country, giving clinicians and investigators a common language with which to communicate about psychological disorders. In 1974 the American Psychiatric Association appointed a task force consisting of a head and 14 advisory committees to develop DSM-III, which was finally published in 1980 after much field testing, controversy, and many drafts.

How is a mental disorder defined officially in DSM-III?

The definition given in DSM-III for a mental disorder is as follows:

> A clinically significant behavioral or psychological syndrome or pattern that occurs in an individual and that is typically associated with either a painful symptom (distress) or impairment in one or more important areas of functioning (disability). In addition, there is an inference that there is a behavioral, psychological, or biological dysfunction, and that the disturbance is not only in the relationship between the individual and society. (When the disturbance is limited to a conflict between an individual and society, this may represent social deviance, which may or may not be commendable, but is not by itself a mental disorder.) (DSM-III, 1980, p. 6)

On how many dimensions and on what dimensions are mental disorders evaluated?

In DSM-III, evaluation of a disorder consists of five axes or dimensions. On Axis I, an evaluation of the major mental disorders is made and includes such disorders as depression, paranoid schizophrenia, phobias, senility, multiple personality, and sexual masochism. On Axis II, an evaluation of personality disorders is made and includes personalities such as dependent, antisocial, narcissistic, and compulsive. Also, Axis II includes specific developmental disorders such as deficits in reading, language, and articulation. On Axis III, an evaluation of physical disorders and conditions is made such as the presence of diabetes, high blood pressure, and allergies. On Axis IV, the psychosocial stressors are evaluated as none, minimal, mild, moderate, severe, extreme, catastrophic, or unspecified (no information). On Axis V, the highest level of adaptive functioning achieved by the individual during the previous year is evaluated as superior, very good, good, fair, poor, very poor, or grossly impaired.

Mental disorders are grouped into how many and what classifications?

More than 200 specific, distinguishable disorders and conditions, grouped in a logical and consistent manner into 18 categories in Axis I and Axis II, are included in DSM-III. Some of these specific disorders are distinguished later in this chapter. The V Codes are not discussed because they are not really mental disorders; however, they often are the focus of attention or treatment and need to be distinguished in the classification system. Examples of V Codes are academic or occupational problems, bereavement, marital problems, parent-child problems, and malingering (pronounced *mah LING ger ing*), which is the gross exaggeration of physical or psychological symptoms for such purposes as avoiding work or evading criminal prosecution. The 18 general classifications (DSM-III, 1980, pp. 15-19) are the following:

1. Disorders usually first evident in infancy, childhood, or adolescence
2. Specific developmental disorders
3. Organic mental disorders
4. Substance use disorders
5. Schizophrenic disorders
6. Paranoid disorders
7. Psychotic disorders not elsewhere classified
8. Affective disorders
9. Anxiety disorders
10. Somatoform disorders
11. Dissociative disorders
12. Psychosexual disorders
13. Factitious disorders
14. Disorders of impulse control not elsewhere classified
15. Adjustment disorders
16. Psychological factors affecting physical conditions
17. Personality disorders
18. V Codes for conditions not attributable to a mental disorder

Sixteen of these classifications are recorded on Axis I and only two (#2 and #17) are recorded on Axis II.

Views

What are the popular views of the source of psychological disorders?

Theorists have different views as to the cause or explanation of psychological disorders. The explanation of abnormality influences the treatment of the disorder and has important implications for society at large and for individuals with disorders. The cognitive-behavioral, organic, psychoanalytic, family or systems, and medical models are some of the popular viewpoints today.

Cognitive-Behavioral Model. Learning theorists (behaviorists) propose that behavior is learned; therefore, abnormal behavior is explained as being the result of learning. Deviant behaviors are not believed to be symptoms of an underlying condition but instead have simply been conditioned by environmental experiences or learned by observation. Although these theorists recognize that biological factors may be an explanation for some abnormal behavior, learning is believed to be the major explanation for psychological disorders. They believe that inappropriate behaviors may be decreased in frequency of occurrence and more appropriate behaviors may be learned through the use of operant and classical conditioning and modeling techniques. Association of stimuli, delivery of reinforcing and punishing consequences, and provision of a model are frequently used treatment techniques. The expanded version of this view, which includes covert or unseen behaviors such as thinking, memory, perception, and information processing, is referred to as the **cognitive-behavioral model.** This view holds that abnormal behavior is primarily a result of environmental experience and maladaptive thinking, and treatment focuses on learning new, underlying thought patterns and behaviors through use of behavior modification techniques, processes of rational thinking, and observation of a model.

Organic Model. According to the **organic model** of psychological disorders, the basis for the disorders is in the biochemical or physiological processes. Researchers have found a physiological basis for many psychological disorders. As was pointed out in chapter 2, various concentrations of particular chemical substances in specific areas of the brain are associated with various behaviors. Also, the electrical stimulation of certain areas of the brain is associated with different behaviors. In chapter 3, heredity was noted as being the basis for some abnormal behaviors due to abnormalities in the genes and chromosomes. Treatment based on this model may include the administration of drugs, surgery, shock treatments, diet control, exercise, or administration of vitamins and minerals.

Psychoanalytic Model. The **psychoanalytic model** of psychological disorders was developed by Freud. He proposed that the condition causing a behavioral disorder is due primarily to anxiety, guilt, and other psychological disturbances that can occur in early childhood. For example, Freud believed the severe mental disorder called *schizophrenia* (pronounced *SKIZ o FRE ne ah*) to be the result of a psychological disturbance in the first 2 years of life. The most important aspect of this view is that psychological disorders are symptoms of underlying conflicts that are probably repressed and unconscious to the individual. Treatment involves bringing into consciousness the repressed and unconscious conflicts through psychoanalysis using such techniques as probing memories of early childhood, dream analysis, and free association.

Family or Systems Model. According to the **family or systems model,** psychological disorders are seen as arising from an entire family setting rather than from an individual. An individual's abnormal behavior is viewed as a symptom of psychopathology within the family and not as a product of the individual alone. Treatment based on this model involves the entire family as a system and the patterns of functioning and communicating in the family (see Figure 12–2) because it is believed that a disturbed family creates one disturbed person within the family to enable the other members of the family to function. When the disturbed member is helped, the entire family may experience chaos and be forced to develop new patterns of relating and communicating to each other.

Figure 12–2. Treatment of a disturbed member of a family would include the entire family if the treatment is based on the family or systems model.

Medical Model. The **medical model** of psychological disorders is based on both the organic and psychoanalytic models. Theorists who accept this view propose that people who have psychological problems are sick and are therefore no more responsible for their disorder than people who exhibit abnormal body temperature from a physical illness such as measles or who hobble from a broken leg. This view has greatly influenced clinical psychology and psychiatry as can be seen in the medical terminology used by psychologists and psychiatrists. For example, they speak of mental illness rather than mental health; the "doctors" have "patients" with a psychological "illness" treated with "therapy" in mental "hospitals"; when the patients respond, they are "cured." When anyone refers to people who have psychological disorders as being sick, he or she is demonstrating an acceptance of this view. The DSM-III is based on this view. For the specific, distinguished disorders, the essential features (symptoms or syndrome), associated features (symptoms), age at onset, course, impairment, complications, predisposing factors, prevalence, sex ratio, familial pattern, and differential diagnosis are addressed just as in a physician's medical handbook on physiological disorders.

CLASSIFICATION OF DISORDERS

The more than 200 psychological disorders classified in DSM-III constitute too many to discuss individually in detail in this chapter; therefore, only a few of the disorders will be discussed briefly. There are no general categories in DSM-III labeled *neurotic disorders* and *psychotic disorders.* The behaviors previously listed in these categories in DSM-II are now separated into more specific categories. The more specific categories that comprise neurotic, psychotic, and personality disorders are discussed in this section.

Neurotic Disorders

What are some general features of neurotic disorders?

People with neurotic disorders are in contact with reality and maintain basic control over their thoughts and feelings. They deal ineffectively with the problems of living and thus experience much stress and anxiety. Defense mechanisms are used excessively as coping strategies, and because the defense mechanisms merely repress the stress and anxiety from consciousness rather than remove the source of the stress and anxiety, more and more stress and anxiety are experienced. Such a great amount of the person's energy is used up in repressing the stress and anxiety that new, more effective behaviors are not learned. Neurotic behaviors are extremely persistent because of the reinforcing consequence of relief from tension or anxiety provided by the defense mechanism and also because of the reinforcement received from significant people in the life of the person with neurotic behaviors in the form of sympathy, attention, and support. Neurotic behaviors are extremely difficult to change. Examples of neurotic behaviors are described in the following paragraphs.

What are four specific psychological disorders that are classified as anxiety disorders?

Anxiety Disorders. Phobic disorders, panic disorder, generalized anxiety disorder, and obsessive-compulsive disorder are included in the category of anxiety disorders. **Phobias** are persistent and irrational fears of specific objects, activities, or situations that result in a compelling desire to avoid the dreaded object, activity, or situation. The fear is recognized as unreasonable and unwarranted. Phobias may be learned according to the principles of classical conditioning. For example, an individual who has an extreme, unrealistic fear of riding in elevators may have had a frightening experience in a small, closed place that was repressed, perhaps in early childhood, and conditioning and generalization occurred so that any similar stimulus now elicits fear. Or the fear may be displacement. Fear of angry feelings toward a loved one such as a parent, child, or spouse may be substituted with a fear of elevators to keep the anger repressed and prevent the person from acting directly on the anger.

The essential features of *panic disorder* are unpredictable, recurrent panic attacks marked by the sudden onset of intense apprehension and fear or terror, sometimes accompanied by feelings of impending doom. Attacks usually last only a few minutes. During an attack, the person may experience chest pain, heart palpitations, choking or smothering sensations, dizziness, sweating, hot and cold flashes, and fear of dying or going crazy. A person experiencing such attacks often becomes reluctant to be alone or in public places.

Generalized anxiety disorder is characterized by persistent anxiety and tenseness that is generalized and not associated with anything in particular and has a duration of at least one month. The specific manifestations of the anxiety may vary in different individuals, but generally there is (a) motor tension such as trembling, muscle aches, fidgeting, or jumpiness; (b) autonomic hyperactivity such as upset stomach, sweating, tingling in hands or feet, lump in the throat, or diarrhea; (c) apprehensive expectation such as worry or anticipation that something bad will happen to self or others; and (d) vigilance and scanning such as being impatient, having difficulty in concentrating or sleeping, and being easily distracted.

The essential elements of *obsessive-compulsive disorder* are either (a) the repetitious performing of a behavior according to certain rules or in a stereotyped fashion even though the individual desires to stop performing the behavior (a **compulsion**) or (b) the presence of recurrent, persistent thoughts, ideas, or images that are not voluntarily produced and are not suppressed when suppression is attempted (an **obsession**). Additionally, the compulsion or obsession must be a source of distress to the individual and not due to another disorder. This disorder seems to result from the individual repressing anxiety by cognitive means such as filling the mind with constant, trivial thoughts or by behavioral means such as staying busy so that anxiety-provoking thoughts or behaviors are avoided. This may be a learned coping strategy or, according to psychoanalytic theory, it may be a symbolic reaction. For example, a compulsion to wash one's hands may be related to guilt feelings about something.

What are four specific psychological disorders that are classified as somatoform disorders?

Somatoform Disorders. Sometimes an individual learns to displace anxiety by expressing it through physical symptoms, causing somatoform disorders. The physical symptoms present are real, but no organic cause of them can be found. The person is not conscious of the anxiety that is the source of the physical disability; therefore, the person is not consciously trying to convince others that something is physically wrong. Also, the person cannot bring the symptoms under voluntary control. Four somatoform disorders, somatization (pronounced *so MAH ti ZA SHUN*), hypochondriasis (pronounced *HI po kon DRI ah sis*), conversion, and psychogenic pain, are described here.

In *somatization*, there is a pattern of vague, recurring physical complaints. The person usually has a long medical history that involves many physicians, a variety of physical disorders, unnecessary surgery, and the use of much medication. A similar disorder, *hypochondriasis,* involves a preoccupation with one's physical health.

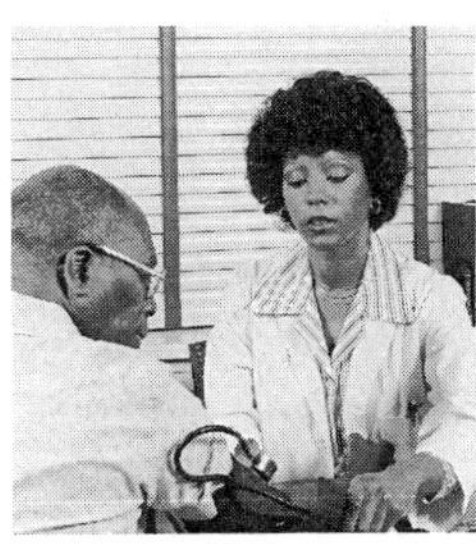

Figure 12–3.
When a person has a needless preoccupation with his or her health, distorts the meaning of aches and pains, imagines aches and pains, and constantly complains of ill health even though a physician can seldom find anything physically wrong, the behavior is diagnosed as hypochondriasis.

The person typically overreacts. For example, every small symptom is interpreted as a symptom of a serious disease, and the person rushes to a doctor (see Figure 12–3). Or when people with this disorder read or hear about the symptoms of a particular illness, they may believe that they have those symptoms and will visit a physician. The meaning of normal aches and pains may be distorted, aches and pains may be imagined, and complaints of ill health are constant even though a physician can seldom find anything physically wrong.

When a person reduces anxiety by displacing the anxiety to a part of the body and then inactivating that part of the body, the response is called *conversion.* Blindness, deafness, and paralysis that have no physical cause are examples. Psychoanalytic theory suggests that the physical symptom is related to some traumatic past experience. After seeing someone murdered, a person might lose his or her sight; or a person might lose all feeling in one hand if that hand has been used in a way that brings about guilt and accompanying anxiety. This form of coping with anxiety is not as common today as in Freud's day. People are more knowledgeable of the physiological functioning of the body, and this coping strategy is not as likely to be used.

Psychogenic pain consists of feeling pain for which there is no physical basis in some part of the body. The pain is not faked; it is actually felt. Learning theorists propose that reinforcement may motivate the pain. The individual may be receiving some benefit such as workmen's compensation, care and attention, or the privilege of evading some disliked task.

What are four specific psychological disorders classified as dissociative disorders?

Dissociative Disorders. In dissociative disorders, the part of the person's personality that is the source of the anxiety seems to be separated from the rest of the personality and repressed. *Psychogenic amnesia,* one type of dissociative disorder, is a sudden inability to remember important personal information that is not due to an organic disorder. Often associated with psychogenic amnesia is *psychogenic fugue,* the sudden, unexpected travel of a person to some place away from home with the assumption of a new identity and an inability to recall the previous identity. After recovery, there is no recollection of events that occurred during the time away from home with the new identity. In *multiple personality,* a new identity arises that allows the person to repress the old identity. Rather than having only one identify, the person may be dominated by one or more alternative identities at various times as a way to cope with anxiety. The transition from one personality or identity to the other is sudden and often associated with stress, and usually the original personality has no knowledge or awareness of the existence of the other personalities. The subpersonalities may not know each other or may be constant companions. Another dissociative disorder is *depersonalization.* With depersonalization, the person suddenly feels changed or different in a strange way. People with this disorder may feel they are outside their bodies, that their actions are mechanical, that they are dreaming, or that their extremities have changed in size.

What are three types of psychosexual disorders?

Psychosexual Disorders. Three groups of psychosexual disorders are gender identity disorders, disorders associated with paraphilias, and psychosexual dysfunctions. In *gender identity disorders,* the individual has feelings of discomfort and inappropriateness about his or her anatomical sex. Also, the disorder is characterized by persistent behaviors generally associated with the other sex. Transsexualism is one such disorder. The individual may additionally have a wish to be rid of his or her genitals and live as a member of the other sex and may be uncomfortable wearing the clothes of his or her own sex, a condition that leads to cross-dressing. The diagnosis of transsexualism is made only if the condition has been continuous for at least 2 years and is not due to another mental disorder or genetic abnormality.

The essential feature of disorders associated with **paraphilias,** unusual or bizarre acts or imagery necessary or preferred for sexual excitement, is that the imagery or acts involve either (a) use of nonliving objects or nonhumans for sexual arousal or (b) insistent and involuntary repetitive sexual activity with humans that involves real or simulated humiliation or suffering or nonconsenting partners. Paraphilias interfere with the achievement of a loving sexual relationship. Paraphilias may involve use of children, animals, or corpses and engagement in activities such as exposure of genitals to unsuspecting strangers, observation of unsuspecting people who are naked or engaging in sexual activity, aggression including the inflicting of physical and/or psychological pain, urination, and lewd telephone talk.

Psychosexual dysfunctions are disorders in the desire or responses that characterize the sexual response cycle—the appetitive phase, the excitement phase, the orgasm phase, or the resolution phase. The disorder is not diagnosed as psychosexual dysfunction if the cause is a physical disorder, medication, or another mental disorder. Dysfunction occurs commonly in mild forms and under temporary conditions; therefore, it is considered to be a psychosexual dysfunction only when it is a typical behavior pattern and occurs in an extreme form.

Psychotic Disorders

What are some general features of psychotic disorders?

The main distinction between neuroses and psychoses is that in psychoses the individual loses contact with reality. Fantasy and actuality sometimes cannot be differentiated; thus, these disorders involve severe, abnormal behaviors in that the person cannot function in the real world. Perception, thinking, and feeling seem to be guided more by internal stimuli than external stimuli. Typical symptoms of psychoses are hallucinations, the perception of things that are not really there; **delusions**, belief in things that are not true; inappropriate emotion, a feeling that does not match the external situation; and withdrawal, the regard of self as alien to the external world. A person may have psychotic episodes that vary in intensity and in length of time. No person is usually psychotic 24 hours of every day. Some theorists propose that the withdrawal from or loss of contact with reality sometimes is an unconscious strategy for coping with stress and anxiety. Psychoses include organic mental disorders, affective disorders, schizophrenic disorders, and paranoid disorders.

What constitutes an organic mental disorder?

Organic Mental Disorders. Any disturbance in the brain that results in producing disordered mental activity that is either transient or permanent and the cause of the disturbance is either known or presumed is classified as an organic mental disorder. The causes of brain disturbance may be aging of the brain, the ingestion of a substance, or some physical disease. Syndromes of organic mental disorders may be relatively global cognitive impairment, relatively selective areas of cognitive impairment, delusions and hallucinations, organic affective disorders consisting of manic or depressive episodes, marked personality change, intoxication, impairment of short- and long-term memory, and withdrawal. The specific classification is made according to the cause agent and the syndrome. For example, a specific classification might be alcohol intoxication. Substance abuse disorders, unhealthy patterns of drug, chemical, or alcohol consumption, are often interrelated to organic mental disorders. If a drug is prescribed by a physician and taken for legitimate reasons or is consumed for recreational

What constitutes a substance abuse disorder?

purposes without any complications of the use, the use is not classified as a psychological disorder by the DSM-III system.

Affective Disorders. Affective disorders have as a common denominator a disturbance in mood not due to an organic mental disorder. The mood disturbance is a prolonged and penetrating emotional state that affects the whole person—feelings, outlook, attitude, self-regard, activity level, trends in thinking, and homeostatic balance. In affective disorders, the person seems to fail to use a strategy to repress feelings and maintain his or her normal mood range.

The depressions include *major depression* (the full syndrome and the one discussed here), *dysthymic disorder* (a chronic, partial syndrome), and *atypical depression* (an atypical syndrome). Major depression is characterized by lower than normal moods consisting of such symptoms as listlessness, brooding, fatigue, feelings of worthlessness, slowing of the thought processes, anxiety, and profound sadness and loneliness (see Figure 12–4). Psychotic depressions are differentiated from normal depressions, which are

How is psychotic depression different from normal depression?

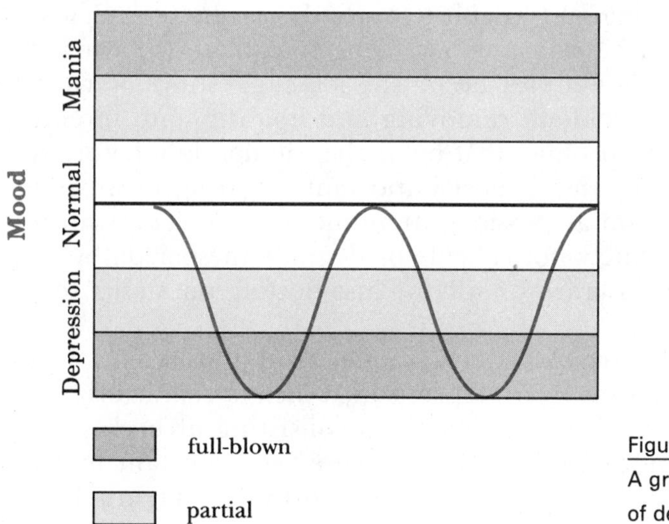

Figure 12–4.
A graphic illustration of depression.

associated with some event in a person's life, in that psychotic depressions fail to disappear in a normal amount of time, gradually get worse, or are not associated with any event in the person's life. Various explanations for depression have been proposed. There is

Figure 12–5.
About 80 to 94 percent of suicides are estimated to be associated with depression, which is characterized by such symptoms as brooding, listlessness, fatigue, feelings of worthlessness, slowing of the thought processes, anxiety, and profound sadness and loneliness.

some evidence that biochemical factors or heredity play a role. Psychoanalytic theory proposes that the person has guilt and the depression is self-punishment, or that the person has anger toward someone or some situation but cannot express the anger and takes it out on himself or herself instead. Learning theory suggests that depression is a result of learned helplessness. When a person repeatedly experiences failure or perceived failure, the person comes to believe he or she has no control over the successes and failures in life.

Suicides are linked to depression. At least 80 to 94 percent of suicides (Schotte & Clum, 1982) are estimated to be associated with depression (see Figure 12–5). Although about 70 to 80 percent of those individuals who commit suicide have threatened or given some warning signals within 3 months prior to the act, most people with suicidal thoughts will not act on them. Suicide thoughts are not uncommon in people under great stress. Although a few of those individuals who take their own life are out of touch with reality (psychotic with hallucinations and delusions), most are not out of touch with reality. When one is confronted with a person considering suicide, asking and listening to why he or she feels that way and to how she or he plans to do it, being empathetic (showing that you understand how upset he or she is), suggesting alternative solutions to the problem, removing and holding onto intended weapons, getting a promise that he or she will not do it before seeing or calling you, and—most important—getting professional consultation as soon as possible oftentimes can prevent a suicide. One should absolutely not ridicule or degrade the person by indicating he or she is crazy or silly or just putting on an act to get attention.

When confronted with a person considering suicide, how could you possibly prevent a suicide?

Another affective disorder is *mania,* the opposite end of the emotional continuum from depression, which is characterized by higher than normal mood elevations consisting of high spirits, clowning, feelings of superiority, tirelessness, constant motion, unnatural warmth, and abnormal generosity (see Figure 12–6). *Bipolar disorder,* formerly called manic-depressive psychosis in DSM-II, is a combination of depression and mania. With this disorder, a person may suddenly change back and forth from extremely lower than normal moods (depression) to extremely higher than normal moods (mania) (see Figure 12–7). The manic behavior seems to be a defense against the depression and continues until exhaustion occurs and allows for a return to the depression.

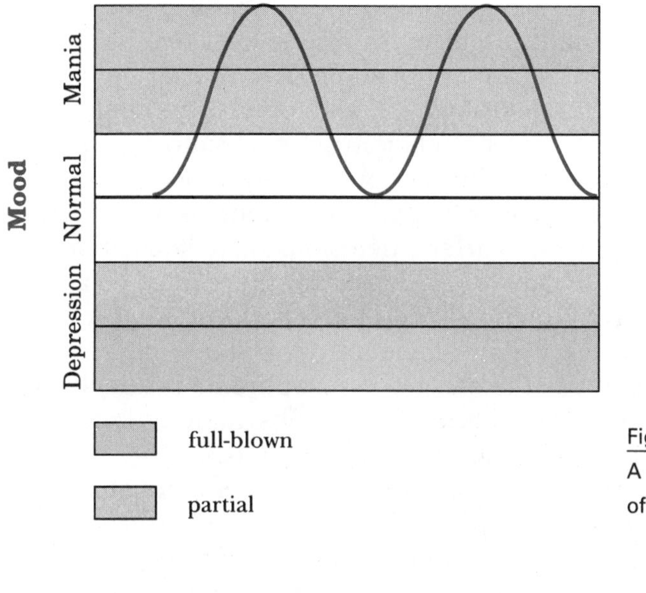

Figure 12–6.
A graphic illustration of mania.

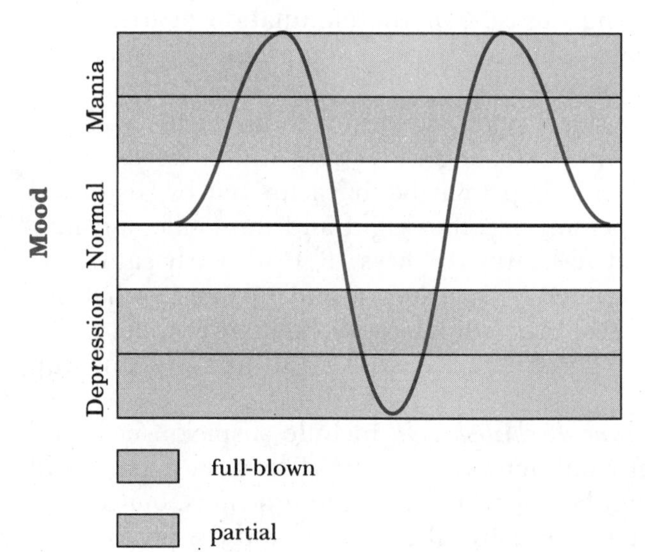

Figure 12–7.
A graphic illustration of bipolar disorder.

What are the general features of schizophrenia?

Schizophrenic Disorders. Schizophrenic disorders are serious illnesses. No single symptom determines the diagnosis; therefore, several types are described. There may be disturbances in communication, thought content, perception, affect, identity, vitality, social interaction, and motor behavior. Emotional distress may also be present. Usually some event in the person's life triggers the development or activation of the disorder. The onset may be sudden, but typically there is a gradual developmental period. For a disorder to be diagnosed as schizophrenia, at least one of the following symptoms must be present at some time during the illness: (a) bizarre delusions; (b) delusions that are about such things as the body, grandness of the self, or religion; (c) persecutory or jealous delusions accompanied by hallucinations of any type; (d) auditory hallucinations; and (e) incoherent speech content accompanied by blunt, flat, or inappropriate affect, delusions or hallucinations, or any grossly deranged behavior. Additionally, there must be a deterioration in adaptive function, presence of symptoms for more than 6 months, and exclusion of mental retardation and organic mental disorder. Because the onset of schizophrenia is usually during adolescence and early adulthood, onset of symptoms before the arbitrary age of 45 is a criterion to be considered.

What are four types of schizophrenia, and what are the distinguishing features of each type?

A complete diagnosis of schizophrenia includes a designation of the type. *Disorganized schizophrenia,* formerly called *hebephrenic schizophrenia* in DSM-II, consists of behavior that may be childish or immature. Inappropriate silliness and giggling, a refusal to wear clothes or to use eating utensils, or the elimination of urine and feces at inappropriate times are typical symptoms. Incoherence may be present, but there is a lack of delusions. This type seems to represent the coping strategy of regression to an earlier stage of development as a means of dealing with stress and anxiety.

Catatonic schizophrenia is primarily characterized by disturbed motor activity. The person becomes rigid and immobile and may remain motionless for hours or days. People with catatonic schizophrenia may be mute or in a stupor and remain in whatever position they are placed. According to psychoanalytic theory, this type represents the handling of hostility and anxiety through immobility.

Symptoms of *paranoid schizophrenia* include suspiciousness and delusions along with hallucinations. The disorder of paranoid schizophrenia may not be apparent in first interactions, but usually the fear of persecution gradually takes control and the person may become hostile and aggressive toward anyone who does not agree with his or her delusions. One or more of the following delusions dominate in paranoid schizophrenia: delusions of grandeur—the person is some great or grand person; delusions of persecution—the person believes others are attempting to do him or her harm or get something he or she has; delusions of reference—the person believes everything others do is in reference to him or her; or delusional jealousy—the person is suspicious of a rival or of one believed to enjoy an advantage. Hallucinations with persecutory or grandiose content may be present. Individuals with this disorder are often extremely religious and use their religious beliefs to deny and keep hostility and desires repressed.

Undifferentiated schizophrenia includes several or all of the symptoms of schizophrenia and is not differentiated in a clear-cut way as the other types are differentiated. The person may be incoherent, may exhibit bizarre or chaotic behavior at times, and may have hallucinations and delusions. Undifferentiated schizophrenia is used as the diagnosis when the criteria for one of the other types are not met.

How do paranoid disorders differ from paranoid schizophrenia?

Paranoid Disorders. Paranoid disorders are distinguished by the fact that they do not have all the symptoms to meet the criteria for another psychotic disorder. These disorders feature only an organized delusion in an otherwise more or less intact person. Hallucinations are not present. Only delusions of persecution or reference or delusional jealousy are present, and the delusions are plausible. They cannot be the bizarre or physically impossible delusions that may characterize schizophrenia. The delusion must be present for at least a week. All specific paranoid disorders must meet these criteria. *Paranoia* is the most commonly diagnosed paranoid disorder. It features a highly specific, persistent, persecutory delusion or delusional jealousy that persists for at least 6 months. The delusion commonly involves the spouse, a family member, a supervisor or employer, or remote enemies such as foreigners or political groups.

What is the most commonly diagnosed paranoid disorder?

Personality Disorders

When are personality traits diagnosed as a personality disorder?

As was pointed out in chapter 11, personality traits are relatively stable over a wide range of situations and include patterns of behaving, thinking, relating, and feeling. When the personality traits are rigid, inflexible, maladaptive, distressful, or a source of impairment in functioning socially or occupationally, a diagnosis of personality disorder may be given. Often personality disorders are accompanied by disorders of mood. There are three basic clusters of personality disorders—odd or eccentric; dramatic, emotional, or erratic; and anxious or fearful—each of which includes several specific personality disorders. Multiple diagnoses of personality disorders may be made if a person meets the criteria for more than one of the disorders.

What are the three basic clusters of personality disorders?

What are three specific personality types and the distinguishing features of each that are classified as odd or eccentric personality disorders?

Odd or Eccentric Personalities. The odd or eccentric cluster includes paranoid personality, schizotypical personality, and schizoid personality. Individuals with a *paranoid personality* demonstrate unwarranted suspiciousness and mistrust of people, super sensitivity, and restricted expression of emotion. The diagnosis is *schizotypical personality* when an individual's communication, action, or thinking is strange or odd but not as bizarre or deviant as schizophrenia. A *schizoid personality* is indicative of individuals who are not motivated and who do not have the capacity to form relationships with other people to become emotionally involved with other people. Individuals with a schizoid personality do not demonstrate oddities or strangeness in their behaving, thinking, or perceiving—the primary difference between this personality and the schizotypical personality.

What are four specific personality types and the distinguishing features of each that are classified as dramatic, emotional, or erratic personality disorders?

Dramatic, Emotional, or Erratic Personalities. The personality disorders forming the cluster referred to as dramatic, emotional, or erratic personalities are histrionic, (pronounced *HIS tre ON ik*), borderline, narcissistic (pronounced *NAR si SIS tic*), and antisocial personalities. *Histrionic personality* is characterized by "overly dramatic and reactive behavior which can include emotional outbursts, craving for excitement, drawing attention to oneself, and dramatic self-presentation. The interpersonal relationships of these individuals are often shallow, and individuals with such personalities appear to be vain, egocentric, dependent, and manipulative" (Webb, DiClemente, Johnstone, Sanders, and Perley, 1981, p. 127). Features of *borderline personality* include (a) chronic feelings of emptiness, (b) an intolerance of being alone, (c) emotional instability, especially the ability to control anger, (d) impulsive and self-damaging behaviors, (e) identity disturbances, and (f) intense interpersonal relationships. *Narcissistic personality* is the diagnosis when the individual (a) has a grandiose sense of self-importance, (b) has a constant need for attention and admiration, (c) has a lack of empathy, (d) fantasizes ideal love and unlimited success, (e) exploits others, (f) overreacts, and/or (g) is indifferent to criticism or defeat. People with *antisocial personality* chronically violate the rights of others in overt behavior. The pattern typically begins before the age of 15 and continues into adulthood during which time there is no 5-year period without antisocial behavior.

Anxious and Fearful Personalities. The cluster of personality disorders labeled anxious and fearful includes the avoidant, dependent, compulsive, and passive-aggressive personalities. In *avoidant* *personality*, fear of rejection is the source of avoidance of desired close relationships. An individual with avoidant personality typically wants guarantees of uncritical acceptance, has low self-esteem, and is socially isolated even though he or she desires affection from others. *Dependent personality* is a personality in which the individual typically allows another person or other persons to assume responsibility for major aspects of his or her life. Individuals with this disorder even avoid having to rely on the self at all costs and lack self-confidence. Persons with *compulsive personality* are stubborn or indecisive because they are trying to make the perfect decision. They tend to be perfectionistic, rigid, extremely conventional, very serious and preoccupied with details and order, and dedicated to work to the exclusion of relationships with other people—somewhat similar to the Type A personality described in chapter 11. A *passive-aggressive personality* consists of extreme procrastination, intentional inefficiency, and use of forgetfulness as an excuse for failure to act when more effective and assertive behavior is possible.

What are four specific personality types and the distinguishing features of each that are classified as anxious and fearful personality disorders?

PSYCHOTHERAPY

Psychotherapy was defined in chapter 11 as any attempt by a clinician to change a behavior disorder by applying particular techniques. The techniques employed by a clinician to change behavior depend on the theory of personality development and the theoretical model of abnormal behavior the therapist accepts. Techniques or therapies may be grouped as insight, behavior and cognitive, or biomedical therapies. A few therapies of each of these types are described in this section.

What is psychotherapy?

Insight Therapies

Many therapy techniques are based on the assumption that behavior disorders can be remedied if the individual with the disorder gains insight into his or her problem. Gaining insight involves gaining knowledge that the disorder exists, knowledge of what led to the disorder, and/or knowledge of the feelings and conflicts that are below the level of conscious awareness in order to identify and label them. These forms of psychotherapy are also based on the assumption that for effective change in behavior, the self-knowledge must be accurate. Psychoanalysis, person-centered therapy, gestalt therapy, and group therapy are examples of insight therapies examined here.

What is the goal of and what techniques are used in psychoanalysis?

Psychoanalysis. The goal of psychoanalysis is to bring repressed feelings and sources of anxiety and stress into consciousness in order to enable a person to reevaluate those feelings and sources of anxiety to resolve the conflict. The goal is to have the individual reexperience feelings associated with a memory and to achieve insight. Freud developed several techniques to help a person reexperience feelings that are painful psychologically and to overcome resistance to insight. One such technique that Freud found useful was hypnosis. He also used free association to break though the defenses in a more gradual process than with the process of hypnosis. In free association, the client assumes a comfortable position, typically lying on the couch, and talks about anything that comes to mind (see Figure 12–8). The analyst watches for the surfacing of important repressed material at the verbal level and resistance to recalling or talking about the material by blanking out, making accusations that the analyst is too demanding or is inconsiderate, or forgetting appointments when it seems that threatening material may be uncovered in that session. Occasionally the analyst makes remarks and offers interpretation to aid in the gradual process of self-insight and self-discovery. Psychoanalysis also may include dream analysis. Unconscious impulses are thought to be expressed in dreams and are likely to be displaced onto objects and situations that are symbols of the unconscious wishes. In psychoanalysis, attention is paid to responses made by the client to the analyst because it is believed that feelings will generalize and be displaced or transferred to the therapist.

Figure 12–8. Freud's office in London containing the couch that his patients used.

What is the goal of and what techniques are used in person-centered therapy?

Person-Centered Therapy. Person-centered therapy is based on Carl Roger's theory of the development of the self-concept. The goal of this technique is to help the person develop a more realistic self-concept, increase his or her sense of self-worth, and gain strength to face the repressed conflicts and feelings. In other words, the goal is to help the person gain accurate insight into the self. This therapy is also called *nondirective therapy* because the therapist listens without judgment or interpretation and does not direct the client toward certain insights. The therapist uses **active listening**—echoing, restating, and clarifying what the person has said and acknowledging the feelings expressed—to provide a psychological mirror that helps clients see themselves more clearly. The therapist also aids the insight process by providing an accepting environment that allows the person to let down his or her defenses and see the self more accurately. An accepting environment is provided by the therapist showing **unconditional positive regard**

(respect for the person as an important human being with unique values and goals), **empathetic understanding** (accurately reflecting the person's experiences and feelings), **genuineness** (honesty in the relationship with the person), and **congruence** (a fit between the feelings and the behavior toward the person). The therapist also serves as a model to the client.

What are the goals of and what are planned exercises used in gestalt therapy?

Gestalt Therapy. Gestalt therapy was developed by Fritz Perls in the 1950s and 1960s and has no connection with the Gestalt theory of perception with the exception of the concept of whole. The aims of Gestalt therapy are to provide insight into how conflicting parts of the personality create distress and to make people whole (the meaning of *gestalt*) by breaking through their defenses. Emphasis is placed on becoming aware of current feelings and behavior, unlike psychoanalysis, which explores the past. The therapist is highly directive, unlike person-centered therapy in which the therapist is nondirective, and leads the client through planned exercises.

Exercises may consist of training the client to speak in the first person and in the present tense or having the person move back and forth between two chairs, assuming the role of the self in one and the role of another person such as parent, spouse, or child in the other chair. In another exercise, the client carries on a dialogue between two conflicting parts of his or her personality such as between the dominant side and the submissive side, the nice side and the nasty side, or the approach side and the avoidance side. Exercises in attending to body language are conducted. Clients are instructed in noticing things such as furrowed brow, folding of arms, change in pitch of voice, or shuffling of feet. Sometimes the client is asked to argue the view directly opposed to his or her expressed view. The purposes of these exercises are to help clients recognize impulses they have been denying, to broaden their perspectives, to heighten their awareness of the elements of conflict, and to gain insight.

Figure 12–9.
In group therapy, a person receives more feedback than in individual therapy.

Group Therapy. Many forms of group therapy such as encounter groups and family therapy are used in a wide variety of settings. The basic assumption in group therapy is that the disorder is related to an inability to communicate, to relate to others, and to perceive accurately. The goal of group therapy is to provide feedback (see Figure 12–9). A person may find out his or her problem is not unique, may find out how she or he affects others, may find needed encouragement to try out new behaviors, may find fulfillment through helping another person in the group, and may find a safe and accepting environment in which to try out new behaviors. Some advantages of group therapy are that (a) it is more economical to treat several clients simultaneously than separately, (b) improvement by a group member provides hope for others, and (c) appropriate behaviors receive more reinforcement than just reinforcement from the therapist. A form of group psychotherapy called *transactional analysis* that provides individuals with the tools for improving the way they communicate with people is described in the section on communication in chapter 14.

Behavior and Cognitive Therapies

In general, how do behavior therapies and cognitive therapies attempt to change behavior?

Behavior therapies attempt to change abnormal behavior directly by applying laws and principles of learning theory. Cognitive therapies attempt to change behavior disorders indirectly by altering the client's perceptions and thinking. Increasingly, the cognitive viewpoint is being incorporated in behavior therapies, a reason for discussing the two types of therapies in the same section. The behavior and cognitive therapies that receive attention here are the general behavior modification techniques, systematic desensitization, aversive conditioning, assertiveness training, rational-emotive therapy, and self-instructional training.

What is behavior modification, and what are some of the techniques generally used in behavior modification?

Behavior Modification. Behavior modification, the systematic application of learning theory laws and principles to bring about desired behavior changes, was discussed in chapter 6. Behavior modification is an umbrella term for a wide variety of behavior therapy techniques. Operant conditioning, the use of positive reinforcement, is commonly used to increase the frequency of a desired response by delivery of a reinforcing consequence or to decrease the frequency of an undesirable response by removal of a reinforcing consequence. The operant conditioning technique of shaping is also frequently used to help an individual develop a desired behavior. Many psychiatric wards and hospitals use token economies in which some type of token, such as a plastic chip, is given as a consequence of a desired behavior. These chips may then be used by the patients to purchase amenities such as a private room, access to television, or special foods. The biofeedback technique is used to provide feedback about specific physiological responses to stimuli such as blood pressure or brain wave pattern to enable an individual to modify his or her biological state. Biofeedback is often used to give feedback related to the state of anxiety to help a person learn how to relax. Because behaviors may be learned by watching the behavior of other people, providing models of people displaying appropriate and adaptive responses is often used as a technique for teaching better coping strategies to an individual with behavior disorders.

Classical conditioning, the association of a stimulus with another stimulus that brings forth a particular response whereby the stimulus associated with it comes to bring forth the same or a similar response, is frequently used by therapists in helping an individual modify a behavior. Classical conditioning is used (a) to change an inappropriately negative emotional response to a neutral or positive response or (b) to change an inappropriately positive emotional response to a negative response (see Figure 12–10).

Figure 12–10.
If every time a person who responds negatively emotionally to cooked carrots also experiences a stimulus that elicits a positive emotion, such as an expression of love or a compliment, classical conditioning may occur and cooked carrots come to be associated with expression of love or compliments and elicit a neutral or more positive emotional response.

Systematic Desensitization Therapy. Desensitization is a technique used to help a person overcome a conditioned fear response. The client is taught relaxation techniques and then constructs a **stimulus anxiety hierarchy** that lists stimuli or activities related to a particular fear that range from a least or no anxiety-producing one to the one that is most anxiety provoking. Then the client is asked to imagine the first stimulus in the hierarchy, and the therapist may even vividly describe the stimulus to the client. The client practices relaxation while imagining until there is no anxiety. Then the therapist and client move to the next step in the hierarchy and do the same thing. When progression through the hierarchy has been completed in this manner, a progression through the hierarchy takes place with the real stimulus or activity rather than an imagination of it. This therapy technique may be applied to a wide variety of phobias and anxiety-producing situations including speaking in public, riding in elevators, being alone, being in a crowd, or engaging in sexual intercourse. A very simple hierarchy for fear of snakes is given in the box that follows.

Sample Anxiety Hierarchy for Snake Phobia

1. The letter *S*.
2. The word *snake*.
3. A funny cartoon drawing of a snake.
4. A realistic drawing of a snake.
5. A photograph of a snake.
6. A real snake 25 feet away.
7. A real snake 2 feet away in a cage.
8. A real snake 2 feet away not in a cage.
9. Touching a real snake with the finger tip.
10. Holding and stroking a real snake.

What is aversion therapy?

Aversion Therapy. Although aversion therapy is available and is used quite frequently, it is a very controversial therapy. In aversive therapy, a painful (aversive) stimulus is paired with a behavior or an impulse that is self-defeating for the purpose of making the goal behavior unappealing. This technique is sometimes used to make smoking a cigarette, drinking alcohol, using a paraphilia for sex arousal, or engaging in self-injurious behavior less appealing. An example of aversion therapy is the development of a taste aversion to alcohol. Tasting alcohol may be paired with a substance producing nausea and vomiting until conditioning occurs and the taste of alcohol comes to produce nausea and vomiting and is aversive to the individual rather than desirable.

What is the goal of assertiveness training and what are the techniques used to accomplish the goal?

Assertiveness Training. Assertiveness training is a type of therapy used to help people with aggressive or submissive personalities become more assertive. The goal of assertiveness training is to help the individual function more effectively in society—to decrease anxiety, to enhance social skills, to express genuine feelings, to be able to say no to unreasonable requests, and to stand up for legitimate rights. Assertiveness training usually consists of (a) pointing out irrational beliefs such as it is terrible to make a mistake or to be disapproved of by another person, (b) observing a model, and (c) role playing or behavior rehearsal. Specific responses to accomplish specific goals are taught. For example, a specific response that is taught for use in refusing a request is "broken record." Broken record consists of repeating the same statement each time a request or argument is made such as saying to an insurance salesman, I understand, but I have no need for insurance at this time. No matter what the salesman says or asks, the statement is repeated. This keeps the client from getting emotionally aroused and frustrated about what to say, about the appropriateness of the answer, about having to answer questions, about lack of conversational skills or lack of skills to win an argument, and about giving in to a request to which he or she really does not want to give in.

What do self-control and self-instructional training involve?

Self-Control and Self-Instructional Training. Mentioned previously in chapter 6 in the discussion of application of learning principles, self-control and self-instructional therapy involve training a client in techniques whereby he or she chooses the goal behavior, does the monitoring and recording, plans the strategies, and directs language toward the self, making comments or suggestions and telling stories of possible consequences of a behavior in order to modify behavior. Some specific strategies sometimes used are (a) restriction of the stimulus field such as not smoking while driving to reduce the frequency of smoking; (b) avoidance of powerful stimuli that trigger old responses such as avoiding window shopping to reduce the behavior of making unnecessary purchases; (c) stimulus control such as going to a library to increase the likelihood of studying; (d) response prevention such as cutting up credit cards to avoid using them; (e) engaging in competing behavior such as grasping something firmly in the hand to avoid nail biting; (f) creating imaginary horror stories about the consequence of a behavior to reduce the frequency of a behavior; and (g) creating imaginary rewards for a behavior to increase the frequency of the occurrence of the behavior.

Figure 12–11.
Albert Ellis.

Rational-Emotive Therapy. Rational-emotive therapy dates back to the mid-1960s when Albert Ellis (see Figure 12–11) decided that an aggressive approach (verbal attack) works best in getting a client to break through defenses, to confront his or her thinking, and to develop more rational patterns of perceiving and thinking. Irrational thoughts or assumptions are believed to be the source of abnormal functioning. Therefore, the goal of rational-emotive therapy is to point out the false beliefs, to get the client to see what is wrong with this belief and what the consequences of this irrational thinking are in terms of relationships with others and self-perceptions, to enable the client to separate rational from irrational thoughts, and to accept reality. Ellis believes that an individual preferably should take three steps to modify or change behavior: (a) realize that some of his or her beliefs are false, (b) realize that the false beliefs are the source of his or her disturbance, and (c) practice to break old habits of thought and behavior. Techniques most often used by rational-emotive therapists include (a) persuasion to show by logic and reason the falseness of the belief, (b) showing people how to attack their self-defeating ideas while unconditionally accepting themselves, (c) modeling to demonstrate new ways of thinking and behaving, (d) humor to show the absurdity of the belief or behavior, (e) role playing of more rational behaviors to learn that clients can behave in a more rational manner, and (f) activity homework assignments (based on systematic desensitization described earlier) to do what clients irrationally fear.

What is the goal of rational-emotive therapy?

What three steps does rational-emotive therapy assume an individual must take to change behavior, and what techniques are used to take a person through the steps?

Biomedical Therapies

What are four major types of biomedical therapies?

Biomedical therapies are based on the assumption that a physiological disorder is the source of the abnormal behavior. Biomedical therapies include such treatment techniques as chemotherapy, electroconvulsive therapy, psychosurgery, and aerobic exercise.

What does chemotherapy involve?

Chemotherapy. In psychotherapy, the term *chemotherapy* refers to the use of any type of drug to modify or control behavior (see Figure 12–12). In the field of medicine, chemotherapy refers to the treatment of cancer with particular drugs. In psychotherapy, drugs used to modify or control behavior might involve the prescribing of vitamins or minerals such as the naturally occurring chemical called lithium that is widely used in the treatment of bipolar disorder, antianxiety drugs (minor tranquilizers), antidepressant drugs, and antipsychotic drugs (major tranquilizers) that reduce delusions and hallucinations. Use of drugs in the treatment of psychological disorders has greatly reduced the use of psychosurgery and electroconvulsive therapy and the confining of individuals in mental hospitals. As pointed out in chapter 5, antianxiety drugs (minor tranquilizers) work primarily by depressing the activity of the central nervous system. Valium, an antianxiety drug, has been estimated to be one of the most widely prescribed drugs in the world (Caplan, Abbey, Abramis, Andrews, Conway, and French, 1983). People suffering from clinical depression seem to have an imbalance in brain chemicals. Antidepressant drugs act on these chemicals and relieve the symptoms of depression in up to 80 percent of all cases (Scarr & Vander Zanden, 1987). Antipsychotic drugs are used in the treatment of schizophrenia because they tend to eliminate hallucinations, delusions, and paranoid symptoms. Studies comparing the use of the most popular antipsychotic drugs, the phenothiazines (pronounced *FE no THI ah zeens*), with other forms of therapy suggest that these drugs are the most effective form of treatment now available for schizophrenia (Davis, Schaffer, Killian, Kinard, & Chan, 1980).

Figure 12–12. Chemotherapy is the use of drugs to modify or control behavior.

What is ECT?

Electroconvulsive Therapy. Popularly known as electric shock treatment, electroconvulsive therapy (ECT) is one of the most controversial of the biomedical treatments although it has proved to be effective in the treatment of depression. Exactly how it works is not known; however, research with animals has demonstrated that it produces changes in the brain's chemistry (Sackeim, 1985). Much of the controversy is concerned with the temporary and/or permanent loss of some memory or brain damage although less than 1 percent of patients who receive ECT report memory impairment. Because of the controversy, ECT is usually used as a last resort after patients fail to respond to drug treatments or as treatment for cases in which suicidal tendencies require prompt and immediate attention. ECT works faster than drug treatments. The procedure for ECT involves passing an alternating 110-115 volts of electricity across the patient's temples for a fraction of a second after the patient has been given a sedative and injected with a muscle relaxant. A convulsion much like an epileptic seizure occurs for about a minute; however, the patient experiences no discomfort because of the medications given prior to the treatment. Typically, treatment involves repetition of the procedure about three times a week for 2 to 4 weeks.

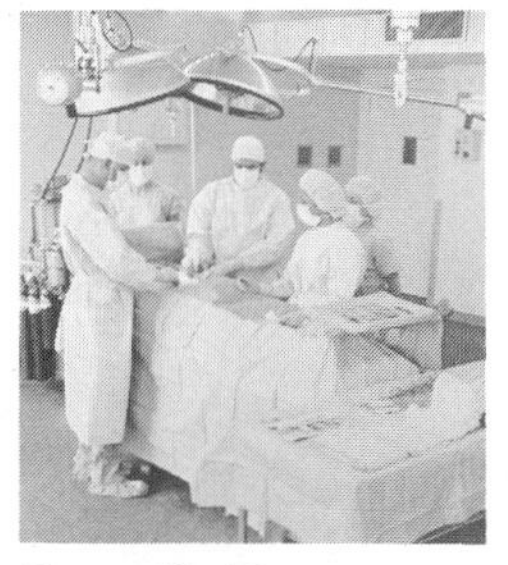

Figure 12–13. Surgery on the brain is one type of biomedical therapy for psychological disorders.

Psychosurgery. Psychosurgery, involving surgery on the brain, is another one of the biomedical treatments of psychological disorders (see Figure 12–13). The controversial **prefrontal lobotomy** in which the connections of the frontal lobes of the brain to the emotional areas of the brain are surgically severed was frequently used during the 1940s and 1950s to treat psychological disorders. This operation was used to reduce extremely violent behaviors and severe psychotic disturbances such as hallucinations. Prefrontal lobotomy is rather rare today because many who had this surgery later showed brain dysfunction to the point of having little or no intelligence. Chemotherapy is helping to make this type of surgery obsolete. Another type of surgery is used in severe cases of epilepsy when chemotherapy is not effective. This psychosurgery involves the severing of the corpus callosum of the brain, which connects the two hemispheres of the brain. The surgery prevents electrical overactivity from spreading from one hemisphere of the brain to the other. This "split-brain" surgery and the psychological side effects were discussed in chapter 2 in boxed material.

What are two types of psychosurgery?

Figure 12–14. Studies have shown that exercise that improves heart and lung functioning is associated with lower levels of both anxiety and depression.

Aerobic Exercise. Aerobic exercise, sustained exercise (see Figure 12–14), is a new type of biomedical therapy that seldom has any negative side effects or risks, involves only natural behaviors, and does not require a surgeon or a prescription from a physician. Studies have shown that exercise that improves heart and lung functioning is associated with lower levels of both anxiety and depression. After obtaining a depression score for a large group of women students, McCann and Holmes (1984) randomly assigned one group of mildly depressed students to participate in aerobic exercise, another group to participate in relaxation exercise, and another group to receive no treatment. Depression scores obtained after 10 weeks indicated that those participating in aerobic exercise had become significantly less depressed than either of the other two groups. Figure 12–15 is a graph of the results of the experiment. There are still many questions to be answered, however. How much exercise is needed for the most desirable effects? Will sustained exercise prevent depression and anxiety? How do the physical changes that occur from exercise affect an individual's psychological state?

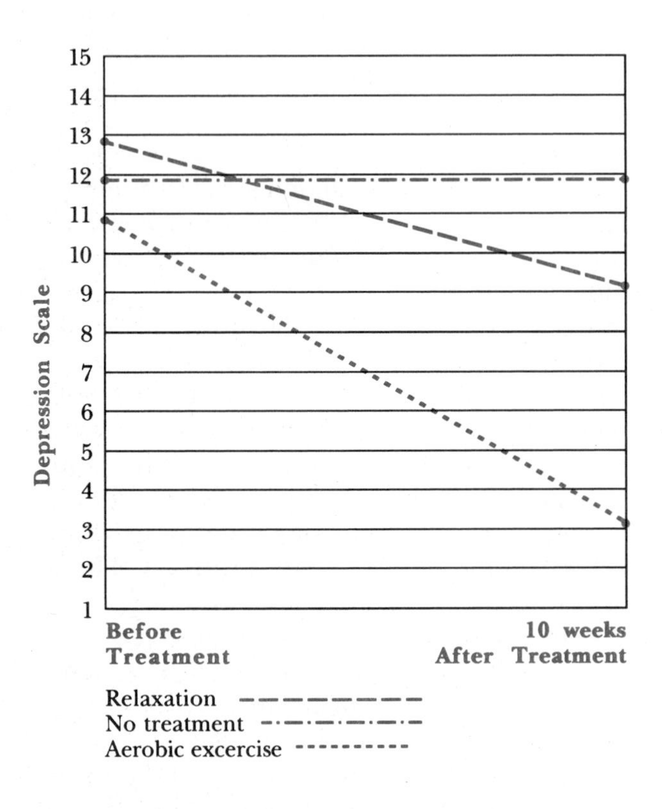

Figure 12–15.
A graph of the relationship found between aerobic exercise and depression in a research study.

What reasons have been theorized by psychologists for the decrease in depression in people engaging in aerobic (sustained) exercise?

Some psychologists reason that the decrease in depression in people engaging in sustained exercise is due to increased production of neurotransmitters such as endorphins and norepinephrine, whereas others reason that the exercise burns off anxiety-creating chemicals such as lactic acid. Still others reason that the decrease in depression is a side effect of sounder sleep because of increased muscle relaxation or of higher self-esteem because of a sense of accomplishment (Ledwidge, 1980; Mihevic, 1982).

There are many types of psychotherapies in use today, and only a few of the techniques have been described. Much controversy exists over which type of therapy is most effective. Perhaps it is better to think, as Paul (1967) suggested, in terms of "what treatment, by whom, is most effective for this individual with that specific problem, and under which set of circumstances" (p. 111). In general, behavior therapies seem to be better for treating phobias, family therapy for marriage problems, group therapy for interpersonal relationship problems, cognitive therapies for mild depression, and chemotherapy for severe depression or schizophrenia. People need to become informed consumers of psychological services.

SUMMARY

1. Abnormal behavior has been defined from a statistical, a cultural, an ideal, a functional, and a legal approach; however, diagnosis is generally made according to several criteria, and the more criteria the behavior fits, the more certain is the diagnosis. The criteria frequently used are whether the behavior is (a) bizarre and extreme, (b) disturbing to the well-being of the self or others, (c) inappropriate or excessive, and (d) dysfunctional.
2. The official classification system currently used by diagnosticians in this country is in the *Diagnostic and Statistical Manual of Mental Disorders (3rd ed.)*, referred to as DSM-III and published by the American Psychiatric Association in 1980. In this system, more than 200 specific disorders are distinguished and grouped into 18 general classifications.
3. Theorists have different views as to the cause of psychological disorders and thus different treatments. The major views are (a) the cognitive-behavioral model based on learning and thinking, (b) the organic model based on physiological processes, (c) the psychoanalytic model based on unconscious conflicts, (d) the family or systems model based on psychopathology within the family, and (e) the medical model based on the idea that the disorder is an illness.
4. The anxiety disorders include phobic disorders (persistent and irrational fear of a stimulus), panic disorder (unpredictable, recurrent anxiety attacks), generalized anxiety disorder (persistent anxiety not associated with anything in particular), and obsessive-compulsive disorder (repetitious, involuntary occurrence of a thought or a behavior that the individual desires to suppress).
5. The somatoform disorders include somatization (a pattern of vague, recurring physical complaints), hypochondriasis (needless preoccupation with one's physical health), conversion disorder (displacement of anxiety to a part of the body), and psychogenic pain disorder (feeling pain for which there is no physical basis).

6. The dissociative disorders include psychogenic amnesia (a sudden inability to remember), psychogenic fugue (sudden, unexpected travel to some distant place accompanied by assumption of a new identity and inability to recall previous identity), multiple personality (emergence of more than one identity), and depersonalization (suddenly feeling changed or different in a strange way).
7. The psychosexual disorders include gender identity disorders whereby the individual feels discomfort about his or her anatomical sex and persists in behaviors associated with the other sex. Transsexualism is an example of such a disorder. Also included are paraphilias, unusual or bizarre acts or imagery necessary or preferred for sexual excitement, and psychosexual dysfunctions, disorders in the desire or responses that characterize the sexual response cycle.
8. Organic mental disorders include any disturbance in the brain that results in disordered mental activity, the cause of which is known, such as aging of the brain, ingestion of a substance, or a disease.
9. Affective disorders, disturbance in mood not due to an organic mental disorder, include depression, mania, and bipolar disorder, a sudden change back and forth from depression to mania.
10. Schizophrenic disorders include disturbances in communication, thought content (delusions), perception (hallucinations), affect, identity, vitality, social interactions, and motor behavior and a deterioration in adaptive functioning. The four distinguishable types are (a) disorganized (regression to an earlier stage of development), (b) catatonic (disturbed motor activity usually characterized by immobility), (c) paranoid (suspiciousness, delusional jealousy, and/or delusions of grandeur, persecution, and reference along with hallucinations), and (d) undifferentiated (several or all symptoms and not meeting the criteria for one of the other types).
11. Paranoid disorders are distinguished by delusions that are plausible and that persist for at least a week without hallucinations in an otherwise intact person. Paranoia, the most commonly diagnosed paranoid disorder, features a highly specific, persistent for at least 6 months, delusional jealousy or persecutory delusion commonly involving the spouse, a family member, a supervisor, an employer, or a remote enemy.
12. Personality disorders are grouped into three basic clusters: (a) odd or eccentric including paranoid, schizotypical, and schizoid personalities; (b) dramatic, emotional, or erratic including histrionic, borderline, narcissistic, and antisocial personalities; and (c) anxious and fearful including avoidant, dependent, compulsive, and passive-aggressive personalities.
13. Psychoanalysis is an insight therapy that uses techniques such as hypnosis, free association, dream analysis, and unconscious responses made by the client to bring unconscious conflict into consciousness.

14. Person-centered therapy is an insight therapy that does not direct the client toward certain insights but allows insight to occur and a more realistic self-concept to develop by providing active listening and an accepting environment consisting of unconditional positive regard, empathetic understanding, genuineness, and congruence.
15. Gestalt therapy is an insight therapy that directs the client (a) to see how conflicting parts of the personality create distress and (b) to become whole by having the client do exercises such as role playing, dialogue, attending to body language, and arguing opposing views.
16. Group therapy uses feedback from members of the group as well as the therapist to help a client gain insight and increased ability to communicate, relate to others, and perceive more accurately.
17. Behavior modification therapy is the systematic application of learning theory laws and principles including classical and operant conditioning and the use of reinforcement, shaping, token economies, biofeedback, and modeling.
18. Systematic desensitization therapy is a behavior and cognitive therapy that uses relaxation, construction of a stimulus anxiety hierarchy, imaging, and presentation of stimuli to help a client overcome a conditioned fear response.
19. Aversion therapy is a controversial behavior therapy in which a painful or aversive stimulus is paired with the behavior or impulse that is pleasurable but self-defeating until conditioning occurs and the behavior or impulse comes to be aversive to the client.
20. Assertiveness training is a behavior and cognitive therapy aimed at helping a client function more effectively in society by (a) decreasing anxiety, (b) enhancing social skills, (c) expressing feelings, (d) being able to say no, and (e) standing up for legitimate rights.
21. Self-control and self-instructional training involve training a client in techniques whereby he or she chooses the goal behavior, does the monitoring and recording, plans the strategies, and talks to the self to control behavior.
22. Rational-emotive therapy is a cognitive therapy that uses persuasion, logic and reasoning, modeling, humor, role playing, and systematic desensitization to help people overcome their self-defeating ideas and to get a client (a) to realize that certain beliefs are false, (b) to realize that the false beliefs are the source of the disturbance, and (c) to practice to break old habits of thought and behavior.
23. Chemotherapy is a biomedical therapy that involves the administration of drugs such as antianxiety drugs, antidepressant drugs, and antipsychotic drugs to modify behavior.
24. Electroconvulsive therapy (ECT) is a biomedical therapy that is controversial but effective in the treatment of depression that involves the passing of an alternating 110-115 volts of electricity across the patient's temples for a fraction of a second.

25. Psychosurgery is a biomedical therapy that involves surgery on the brain such as prefrontal lobotomy and "split-brain" surgery.
26. Aerobic (sustained) exercise is a biomedical therapy that involves only natural behaviors and has been found to be associated with lower levels of both anxiety and depression.

KEY TERMS AND CONCEPTS

DSM-III
Cognitive-behavioral model
Organic model
Psychoanalytic model
Family or systems model
Medical model
Phobias
Compulsion
Obsession
Paraphilias
Delusions
Active listening
Unconditional positive regard
Empathetic understanding
Genuineness
Congruence
Stimulus anxiety hierarchy
Prefrontal lobotomy

QUESTIONS FOR REVIEW

1. What is meant by the diagnostic label *abnormal,* and what is the official definition for a mental disorder that is currently used in this country?
2. How are disorders evaluated and categorized in DSM-III, and what is the historical background of DSM-III?
3. What are the various current and popular views or models of abnormality?
4. What DSM-III general categories of psychological disorders and specific disorders within the categories were previously labeled neurotic disorders in DSM-II? Differentiate between the specific disorders.
5. What DSM-III general categories of psychological disorders and specific disorders within the categories were previously labeled psychotic disorders in DSM-II? Differentiate between the specific disorders.
6. What are the DSM-III types of personality disorders and the specific personalities included within the types? Describe the specific personalities.
7. What are the goals and techniques of the major insight therapies?
8. What is behavior modification, and what are some of the techniques used in behavior modification?
9. What are the processes involved in the behavior and cognitive therapies called systematic desensitization, aversion therapy, assertiveness, self-control and self-instructional training, and rational-emotive therapy?
10. What are the major types of biomedical therapies, and what are some effects and controversies associated with them?

TEST YOURSELF

1. Psychologists diagnose behaviors as abnormal according to several criteria, and the more criteria the behavior fits the more certain the diagnosis. T or F
2. The official classification system currently used by diagnosticians in this country for diagnosing behavior disorders is in the (a) sixth edition of the *International Classification of Diseases* (b) second edition of the *Diagnostic and Statistical Manual of Mental Disorders* (c) third edition of the *Diagnostic and Statistical Manual of Mental Disorders* (d) *Eighteen Category System* developed by the American Psychological Association in 1974.
3. The view that proposes that a psychological disorder is an illness and the person with the disorder is no more responsible for his or her disorder than a person with a physical disorder is known as the (a) organic model (b) medical model (c) cognitive-behavioral model (c) family or systems model.
4. Phobias are classified as (a) anxiety disorders (b) somatoform disorders (c) affective disorders (d) dissociative disorders.
5. ________________ are unusual or bizarre acts or imagery necessary or preferred for sexual excitement and may involve children, animals, or corpses and activities such as exposure of genitals to unsuspecting strangers, observation of unsuspecting people who are naked or engaging in sexual activity, aggression—including the inflicting of physical and/or psychological pain, and lewd telephone talk.
6. The main distinction between neuroses and psychoses is that in neuroses the individual loses contact with reality. T or F
7. ________________, a disorder in which the individual may suddenly change back and forth from listlessness, profound sadness, loneliness, or feelings of worthlessness to a wild, violent, or extremely elated mood, was formerly called ________________ in the DSM-II.
8. Psychotic depressions are depressions that (a) fail to disappear in a normal amount of time (b) gradually get worse (c) are not associated with any event in the person's life (d) all of the above.
9. The type of schizophrenia that features regression to an earlier stage of development and consists of childish, immature, and inappropriate behavior and incoherence without delusions is now called ________________ schizophrenia but was formerly called ________________ schizophrenia in DSM-II.
10. Paranoid schizophrenia, which involves suspiciousness and delusions along with hallucinations, may not be apparent in first interactions. T or F
11. A specific delusional jealousy or persecutory delusion in an otherwise intact person that involves the spouse, a family member, a supervisor, or an employer and persists for at least 6 months without hallucina-

tions would be diagnosed as (a) paranoid schizophrenia (b) schizoid personality (c) paranoia (d) paranoid personality.

12. When a person's communication, action, or thinking is strange or odd but not necessarily bizarre or deviant, his or her personality is labeled (a) schizotypical (b) schizoid (c) histrionic (d) antisocial.
13. When a person has a grandiose sense of self-importance, constant need for attention and admiration, lack of empathy, and fantasies of ideal love and unlimited success and/or overreacts, exploits others, and is indifferent to criticism or defeat, the diagnosis is (a) histrionic personality disorder (b) narcissistic personality disorder (c) schizotypical personality disorder (d) borderline personality disorder.
14. Antisocial personality disorder typically begins before the age of 15 and continues into adulthood. T or F
15. Borderline personality disorder is the label for personalities that are questionable as to whether there is really a disorder because they are usually considered not to be a disorder but the person believes he or she has a disorder. T or F.
16. Extreme procrastination, intentional inefficiency, and use of forgetfulness as a failure to act when more effective and assertive behavior is possible is labeled (a) avoidant personality disorder (b) dependent personality disorder (c) passive-aggressive personality disorder (d) Type A personality disorder.
17. In person-centered therapy, the therapist uses the technique of ______________, is ______________, and provides an accepting environment by showing ______________ ______________ ______________, ______________ ______________, ______________, and ______________.
18. An advantage of group therapy is that (a) it is more economical to treat several clients simultaneously than separately (b) improvement by a group member provides hope for others (c) appropriate behaviors receive more reinforcement than just reinforcement from the therapist (d) all of the above.
19. Systematic desensitization therapy consists of (a) the construction of a stimulus anxiety hierarchy (b) relaxation training (c) imaging stimuli (d) all of the above.
20. A therapy that uses an aggressive approach consisting of verbal attack, persuasion, and humor to show the absurdity of a belief or behavior is known as (a) rational-emotive therapy (b) assertiveness training (c) aversion therapy (d) none of the above.

APPLICATIONS

A. Carmen Flores, a beautiful, successful, 34-year-old interior designer, is brought to the clinic by Antonio, her 37-year-old husband, a rather prominent attorney. Antonio laments that for the past 3 years his wife has made increasingly shrill accusations that he is unfaithful to her. He declares that he has done everything in his power to convince her of his innocence, but there is no shaking her conviction. A careful examination of the facts reveals that there is actually no evidence that Antonio has been unfaithful. When asked what her evidence is, Carmen becomes somewhat vague and mysterious, declaring that she can tell by such things as a faraway look in his eyes.

Carmen is absolutely sure that she is right and considers herself highly insulted to be told that she is imagining the disloyalty. Antonio reports that for the last year Carmen has been increasingly bitter, creating a kind of cold war atmosphere in the household. Militantly entrenched against Antonio and refusing to show him any affection except at social gatherings, Carmen seems intent on giving the impression socially that they have a good relationship. However, after they are alone, the coldness reenters the picture. Carmen has actually physically assaulted Antonio on occasion, but her account obscures the fact that she initiated the assault. Carmen's description of the tussle actually begins with the point where Antonio attempted to interrupt her assault by holding her arms. Carmen declares that she will never forgive him for holding her down and squeezing her arms, and her account makes it appear that she was unfairly pinned down by Antonio.

Carmen experiences no hallucinations; her speech is well organized; she interprets proverbs with no difficulty; she seems to have a good command of current events; and generally she displays no difficulty with thinking, aside from her conviction of the disloyalty. Carmen describes herself as having a generally full and effective life, with a few close friends, and no problems except those centering on her experience of unhappiness in the marriage. Antonio reports that Carmen is respected for her skills but that she has had difficulties for most of her life in close relationships with friends. She has lost a number of friends because she seems always to be intolerant of differences in opinion. Carmen reports that she does not want to leave the marriage, nor does she want to have her husband leave her; instead, she is furious about the injustice, and she demands that it be confessed and redeemed (Webb, DiClemente, Johnstone, Sanders, & Perley, 1981, pp. 80-81).

1. Would you classify Carmen as having a psychological disorder? Why?
2. What specific label would be appropriate for the behavior of Carmen? Why?

B. A 30-year-old male is brought to the emergency room of a local hospital by the police because of an injury incurred during a fight at the loading dock where he works. Questioning by the police revealed that he arrived in town last week and got a job at the loading dock; however, he does not recall any details of his life prior to this time. When the police ran a description check on him, they found that he fit the description of a missing person who disappeared 2 weeks ago from a town about 800 miles away. A visit by the missing man's wife confirmed that he was indeed her husband, Kunio Nitobe. A physical exam showed no evidence of any drug abuse or brain damage from head trauma or disease. His wife did state that he had been under a lot of pressure and experiencing many problems and much stress in connection with his job with a large corporation in their hometown. The case study revealed no previous psychological or serious physiological problems.

1. Would this psychological disorder be considered a psychotic disorder, a neurotic disorder, or a personality disorder, and in what general classification would the disorder be included?
2. What specific label would be appropriate for this disorder? Why?

Note. From *DSM-III Training Guide* (pp. 80-81) by L. J. Webb, C. C. DiClemente, E. E. Johnstone, J. L. Sanders, and R. A. Perley, 1981, New York: Brunner/Mazel. Copyright © 1981 by Brunner/Mazel. Adapted by permission.

SUGGESTIONS FOR FURTHER READINGS

American Psychiatric Association (1980). *Diagnostic and statistical manual of mental disorders* (3rd ed.). Washington, DC: Author.

The official classification system for psychological disorders used in the United States.

Belkin, G. S. (1980). *Contemporary psychotherapies.* Chicago: Rand McNally.

Various methods of psychotherapies are discussed. Principles and procedures related to the various methods are identified in the discussion.

Coleman, J., Butcher, J. N. & Carson, R. C. (1984). *Abnormal psychology and modern life* (7th ed.). Glenview, IL: Scott, Foresman.

A balanced presentation of abnormal behavior that emphasizes no particular approach or theory. This is one of the most widely used textbooks in the field of abnormal psychology.

Endler, N. S. (1982). *Holiday of darkness.* New York: Wiley-Interscience.

A prominent psychologist's interesting account of an experience with depression.

Sarason, I. G., & Sarason, B. R. (1984). *Abnormal psychology* (4th ed.). Englewood Cliffs, NJ: Prentice-Hall.

A basic and authoritative abnormal psychology text.

Snyder, S. H. (1980). *Biological aspects of mental disorder.* New York: Oxford University Press.

A book that points out the relevance of the findings in the fields of biochemistry, genetics, and pharmacology to the study of behavior disorders.

Webb, L. J., DiClemente, Carlo C., Johnstone, E. E., Sanders, J. L., and Perley, R. A. (Eds.). (1981). *DSM-III training guide.* New York: Brunner/Mazel.

A concise, practical guide to DSM-III that helps an individual develop expertise in using the system by explaining coding procedures, distinguishing the categories and specific disorders, and providing case vignettes.

PART FOUR

SOCIAL BEHAVIOR

CHAPTER 13

ATTITUDES AND SOCIAL RELATIONSHIPS

Objectives

When you have completed your study of chapter 13, you should be able to:

1. Define attitude, belief, opinion, prejudice, discrimination, value, stereotype, and the three components of an attitude.
2. Explain how attitudes are formed.
3. Explain how attitudes can be assessed, and name and describe four attitude scales.
4. Discuss four approaches used in attempts to change attitudes.
5. Identify sources of prejudice, ways of reducing prejudice, and laws that attempt to eliminate discrimination in the workplace.
6. Describe the Asch experiments, Milgram's experiment, techniques used, and factors involved in conformity, compliance, and obedience as means of persuading a person to behave in a particular way.
7. Identify factors influencing altruism and attribution, and describe the fundamental attribution error.
8. Identify factors that affect affiliation, liking, and loving.
9. Describe two kinds of romantic love, name and define the stages in the human sexual response cycle, and cite ways in which sexual behavior is sometimes manifested in the workplace.
10. Cite bases of aggression and research findings related to TV and pornographic violence.

What are the concerns of social psychology?

Social psychology is the area of psychology concerned with how an individual's behavior is influenced by other people and how other people are influenced by an individual's behavior. Social psychology is also concerned with the behavior of people within groups. Humans are social creatures who exist within a social environment that affects their behavior and is affected by their behavior. Much of a person's time on a job is spent in social interaction with people. An individual's social environment at work may consist of a circle of friends, a section of employees, a department of people, a larger group called a division, or the entire organization as well as people outside the organization such as customers or clients. The focus of this chapter is on (a) attitudes, important determiners of behavior; (b) behavior change through use of persuasion and obedience to authority; and (c) social interactions, specifically helping and perceiving causes for actions, attraction, sex, and aggression.

ATTITUDES

The study of attitudes has been of primary interest to social psychologists. Attitudes reflect social influences and are a major source of an individual's behavior. The nature of attitudes, changing attitudes, and prejudice are discussed in this section. Changing people's attitudes is an important means of behavior control in our society because a person cannot be forced to purchase a particular product, vote for a particular politician, like or dislike a particular person, or work for a particular goal. Sometimes persuasion and obedience to authority are used to change a person's behavior. Prejudice and the resulting discrimination are also current concerns in our society.

The Nature of Attitudes

Attitudes consist of various aspects that can be broken down into component parts. Attitudes develop; they are formed as a person develops emotionally, cognitively, behaviorally, and socially. Sometimes a person is said to have a good attitude or a bad attitude toward some person, object, idea, or situation. Sometimes a person is told to change or improve his or her attitude. Attitudes can be assessed. In this chapter, attitudes are defined, theories explaining how attitudes develop are discussed, and methods that have been devised to assess attitudes are described.

"I'm not going to enjoy this new project because I know already I'm not going to like working with a female supervisor."

Figure 13–1. Attitudes dispose a person to think, feel, and act in a particular way.

Components of Attitudes. An **attitude** is usually defined as a person's disposition to think, feel, and act either positively or negatively toward a person, idea, object, or situation. Attitudes are relatively long lasting and consist of a combination of emotional, intellectual, behavioral, and social aspects (see Figure 13–1). Beliefs, opinions, values, prejudices, and discrimination are special aspects of attitudes. A **belief** is based on factual information not involving feeling, emotion, likes and dislikes that is accepted as being true although the information may be true or false. An **opinion** is similar to a belief; however, the factual evidence supporting an opinion is weaker than the evidence supporting a belief. For example, based on the age stated on an application form, an employer may have a belief that the job applicant is under 21 years of age. If the applicant is seen in the waiting area and there is no other information about the applicant's age, the employer may have an opinion that the applicant is under 21 years of age.

Prejudice is an attitude a person holds toward some members of a group of people that favorably or unfavorably predisposes the same attitude toward all members of the group. Prejudice involves prejudging an individual without reasonable evidence such as judging an applicant to be irresponsible because the applicant's age is under 21. **Discrimination** is an action taken based on a prejudice. Discrimination would be demonstrated if the applicant is not hired for the job because of age even though he or she may be the best qualified applicant.

Values involve what two things?

Values are attitudes about the worth of things based on the positive or negative feelings associated with them. Values involve both thinking and feeling. For example, one employee may value a large, comfortable desk chair more highly than do other employees in the office if the chair prevents a backache for that employee or if it is a status symbol to that employee because of his or her low self-esteem.

What are the components of an attitude?

An attitude is characterized by three components: cognitive, affective, and conative. The *cognitive component* of an attitude is the belief or opinion held about a person, object, idea, or situation. The cognitive component consists of mental activities such as perception, memory, and thinking. Often the beliefs and opinions that accompany attitudes are not true or are only partially true. The *affective component* of an attitude is the feeling a person has toward the other person, object, idea, or situation. People may like, dislike, love, hate, fear, respect, or have positive or negative feelings in general toward something or someone. The *conative component* of an attitude is the action or response tendency. The response may be to approach or to avoid the person, object, idea, or situation. The conative component of an attitude consists of any directed effort toward action. To illustrate these component parts of an attitude, a person is said to have a favorable or positive attitude toward a new marketing concept if he or she believes the information that provides support for the concept (cognitive component), likes or has positive feelings about the concept (affective component), and votes in favor of a proposal to incorporate the concept into the company's present marketing strategies (conative component).

What are the theories explaining how attitudes are formed?

Attitude Formation. Attitudes are not inherited; they are acquired. How people acquire attitudes has been of interest to psychologists for many years. Theories explaining how attitudes are acquired may be classified as emotional, cognitive, behavioral, and social. According to emotional theory, attitudes are primarily acquired through the process of learning and begin to be formed in infancy. The affective (feeling or emotional) component of an

Figure 13–2.
Information, life-styles, social patterns, and values are presented to people through mass media.

attitude is learned through the processes of classical conditioning as explained in chapter 6. For example, if a salesperson dresses attractively, the positive appearance may become associated with the product he or she is selling so that the buyer develops a positive attitude toward the product. Likes, dislikes, and fears are often the result of associations formed in early childhood experiences.

Cognitive theory holds that information comes from many sources during a person's lifetime to form the beliefs, opinions, perceptions, memories, emotions, and thoughts that make up the cognitive component of attitudes. Important sources of information are parents, other family members, peers, significant people such as teachers and famous people, television, books, newspapers, and other forms of mass media. Information, life-styles, social patterns, and values are presented to people through mass media (see Figure 13–2). The fact that children become attracted to television at an early age suggests the possibility for the strong influence of the mass media over attitude formation.

Behavior theory explaining the development of attitudes is based on the concept of cognitive dissonance discussed in chapter 9 and later in this chapter. This is the idea that the behavior, feeling, and cognitions of the person have a tendency to be consistent to avoid the uncomfortableness of dissonance. Therefore, the behaviors that a person engages in are important factors in the formation of his or her attitudes. For example, a person who "takes" things home from the workplace such as small tools, paper clips, or paper may develop a different attitude about such practices than if he or she does not take things home. Or a person who attends religious services regularly may develop a different attitude about church than if he or she does not attend. Also, attitudes may be shaped by the consequences of the behaviors of a person—operant conditioning. For example, a creative attitude may develop if a worker is praised and reinforced for exhibiting creativity in a job situation, but a creative attitude will probably not develop if the worker is criticized and punished for exhibiting creativity. Children identify with parents and act the way parents do by responding positively and negatively to the same things and situations. Parents reward and punish children for expressing (the conative component) certain attitudes.

Learning by observation of a model, or according to social theory, is the basis for the development of many of a person's attitudes. Parents serve as models for their children. Most frequently these attitudes formed early in life through observation remain with a person throughout his or her life (see Figure 13–3). As children grow older and begin school, peers and adults other than their parents begin to serve as models for the formation of attitudes and are thus a strong social influence on attitudes. During adolescence, the influence of the peer group on attitude formation and the resulting behavior are quite dramatic. The impact of peer influence on attitudes is also very strong among college students who are exposed to many and varied attitudes.

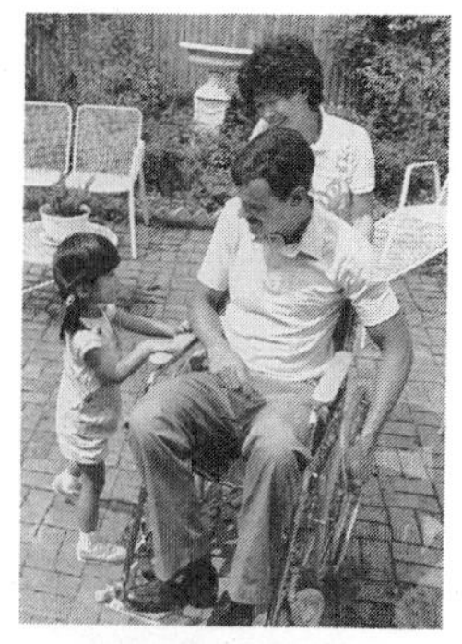

Figure 13–3.
Attitudes are often acquired in early childhood through modeling, punishment, and reward and may remain with a person throughout life.

Assessment. Numerous methods have been devised by psychologists to measure attitudes. The assessment of attitudes involves identifying the attitudes a person holds, determining the strength of individual attitudes, and determining whether the attitude is positive or negative. Frequently, employers have an interest in measuring an employee's or a potential employee's attitudes toward various job-related aspects such as transfers, travel, promotions, shift work, or particular groups of people. Manufacturers may have an interest in assessing consumers' attitudes, and politicians often have an interest in assessing voters' attitudes. The self-report method is the method most commonly used in measuring attitudes. This method involves asking the person to report how he or she feels about some person, object, idea, or situation; how he or she behaves in circumstances involving particular people, objects, ideas, or situations; and what his or her beliefs are concerning certain things. Usually a list of possible answers is provided that will indicate the strength and direction (positive or negative) of the attitude.

The self-report method yields an attitude score. Four types of scales that use this method have been developed to assess attitudes. The Thurstone attitude scale is attributed to the work of Thurstone and Chave (1929). Statements ranging from extremely favorable to extremely unfavorable about a person, object, idea, or situation are listed in random order. Each statement has previously been assigned a scale value that is used to determine an attitude score. The respondent must check those statements with which he or she agrees.

How does a Thurstone scale assess attitudes?

On a Guttman attitude scale (Guttman, 1950), respondents indicate the strongest statement they are willing to endorse in a series of successively more extreme statements. The statements are arranged along an attitude dimension so that anyone accepting a more extreme item would accept all of the preceding ones. The

How does a Guttman scale assess attitudes?

following is an example of an item of this type that might be used in assessing an attitude toward a particular ethnic group:

1. I would not mind living in the same city with a person of this particular ethnic group.
2. I would not mind living on the same street with a person of this particular ethnic group.
3. I would work beside a person of this particular ethnic group.
4. I would have a person of this particular ethnic group in my home to visit.
5. I would marry a person of this particular ethnic group.

A lot of time is required to construct Guttman scales, and consequently, this method is not widely used.

How does a Likert scale assess attitudes?

A Likert scale (Likert, 1932) is another type of attitude scale that consists of a series of statements to which the respondent indicates the extent of his or her agreement or disagreement on a five- or six-point scale as illustrated below:

The supervisor is fair in work load assignments.

1 Strongly disagree
2 Disagree
3 Undecided
4 Agree
5 Strongly agree

An individual's score is determined by totaling the numeric values of his or her responses to the statements. This is the simplest attitude scale, and it has consistently been found to be more reliable and less time consuming to construct than the Thurstone or Guttman scales.

How does a semantic differential scale assess attitudes?

A semantic differential scale (Osgood, Suci, & Tannenbaum, 1957) presents a series of adjectives and their antonyms. The respondent rates an item along a scale between the adjective and its antonym. For example, to assess someone's attitude toward a supervisor, some of the adjectives and their antonyms might be as follows:

Fair	1	2	3	4	5	6	7	Unfair
Pleasant	1	2	3	4	5	6	7	Unpleasant
Strong	1	2	3	4	5	6	7	Weak

Typically, a person, object, idea, or situation is rated between many adjective pairs, perhaps 15 or 20, and the numeric values of the ratings are totaled to determine an attitude score.

Can attitudes be more accurately assessed from actions than from self-report measures?

Some psychologists believe that attitudes can be more accurately ascertained from actions or behaviors than from verbal statements or self-report measures. What a person says is not always consistent with what he or she does. A study conducted by Zanna, Olson, and Fazio (1980) suggests that the strength of the relationship between behavior and reported attitude varies from person to person according to the personality of the person.

Whether the person is field independent or field dependent, or in other words, the degree to which a person's behavior is guided by situational cues, affects the relationship between actual behavior and verbal statements. For example, managers who are guided more by their own thoughts and feelings than by situational facts and who have strong negative feelings toward a particular ethnic group are more likely to allow their negative feelings to influence the decision to avoid giving a promotion to a person of this particular ethnic group. However, managers who have strong negative feelings toward a particular ethnic group but are guided more by the situation than by their own feelings are more likely to be aware of their feelings and to make the promotion of a person of this particular ethnic group contingent on situational facts such as supervisor rating or production quotas. People who are guided more by their thoughts and feelings than by situational facts are likely to show more consistency between reported attitudes and behavior. Those people who are guided more by the situation than by their feelings are likely to show less consistency between reported attitudes and behavior because they do not allow their attitudes to influence their behavior to the extent that others do.

Changing Attitudes

Do attitudes change?

Although attitudes are relatively enduring, they can and do change. Attempts to change attitudes or to change a person's behavior by changing his or her attitude generally focus on changing one of the components: cognitive, affective, or conative. The creation of dissonance, the creation of fear, and the provision of new information are techniques sometimes used that are discussed in this section. Also, the relationship between an individual's personality and attitude change is discussed.

What constitutes dissonance?

Dissonance. The three components of an attitude are usually consistent with each other. Because people seem to have a need for consistency, if any one of the three components is changed, dissonance or inconsistency can be created. Dissonance, which was discussed briefly in chapter 9, occurs (a) when a person has feelings that are inconsistent with the behavior and/or beliefs, (b) when the beliefs are inconsistent with the behavior and/or feelings, or (c) when the behavior is inconsistent with the feelings and/or beliefs. For example, dissonance would be experienced by an employee who feels uncomfortable working with a person of a particular ethnic group but also believes he or she should work with all people no matter what their ethnic affiliation and who does work with the person. Dissonance is so uncomfortable that the person is usually motivated to eliminate the dissonance by establishing consistency. Sometimes consistency is established by changing the other components to be consistent with the component that has already been changed and thus the attitude is changed. For example, the person who has uncomfortable feelings working with the person of another ethnic group but who engages in the behavior may experience a change in feelings and cease to be uncomfortable.

Is dissonance always created by new, conflicting information?

New, conflicting information, reinforcement, choice, and justification are factors that play a role in the creation of dissonance. A person's beliefs may be changed by the presentation of new, conflicting information. This new information does not always result in changing beliefs, however. It may be regarded as unreliable; new facts may be sought to refute the new information; or the person may deny the inconsistency of the information and rationalize or minimize it in such a way that discrepancy, the source of dissonance, is avoided.

What are some conditions that affect whether beliefs and feelings will change to match a behavior?

Dissonance may be created by changing a person's behavior through the use of reinforcement. Once a behavior is changed and there is conflict between beliefs and feelings and the new behavior and the person receives reinforcement or a reward for the behavior, the belief or feeling is less likely to change. This is because the behavior can be rationalized as being engaged in for the reward. If there is little or no reward for the behavior, then the beliefs and feelings are more likely to change because the behavior cannot be rationalized as being engaged in for the reward (see Figure 13–4). Also, if the conflicting behavior occurs by choice rather than by force or pressure, the beliefs and feelings are more likely to change. When the behavior is forced or pressured, the person can rationalize the source of the behavior as being outside the self and thus little dissonance occurs. Likewise, if a person has a very good reason for a behavior that is in conflict with his or her beliefs and feelings, the beliefs and feelings are less likely to change. If the behavior cannot be justified, the beliefs and feelings are more likely to change.

Fear. Arousal of fear can be a useful technique for changing attitudes (see Figure 13–5). Slight to moderate fear arousal has been found to be effective in changing attitudes; however, if fear is aroused out of proportion to the actual situation and a person becomes too fearful, denial of the danger may be used as a defense mechanism, in which case fear arousal is not very effective as a means of attitude change. In the classic study of fear arousal as a means of attitude change (Janis & Feshbach, 1953), three groups of high school students were exposed to messages that emphasized the importance of dental care and were designed to arouse varying degrees of fear. The group that had high fear arousal and was shown horrible pictures of rotten teeth and infected gums reported fewer changes in their dental care behaviors than either of the other two groups. One of the other groups was exposed to a less threatening message that gave the information without such horrible pictures, and the other group received information on dental care in a nonthreatening manner.

Figure 13–4.
A person who holds a neutral attitude and signs a petition may later acquire an attitude that agrees with the position of the petition to resolve dissonance.

Figure 13–5.
Slight to moderate fear arousal has been found to be effective in changing attitudes; however, if fear is aroused out of proportion to the actual situation and a person becomes too fearful, denial of the danger may be used as a defense mechanism and fear arousal would not be very effective as a means of attitude change.

Is high fear arousal an effective way to change attitudes?

Later research has shown that high fear arousal can be more effective in changing attitudes than low fear arousal (Dabbs & Leventhal, 1966). These conflicting findings were explained when an experiment on attitude change was conducted that coupled fear arousal with specific suggestions on how to change the behavior (Leventhal, 1970). A message that aroused greater fear generated more intentions to stop smoking but was not effective in actually reducing the number of cigarettes smoked unless specific suggestions on how to change the behavior were also given in the message. Merely giving specific suggestions on how to change without any fear arousal, however, was not as effective in producing change as giving specific suggestions with fear arousal.

What factors related to the communicator determine the effectiveness of new information in changing attitudes?

New Information. The introduction of new information is another method for changing attitudes. An individual's social environment constantly provides new information. Several factors determine how effective new information will be in changing attitudes. These factors include credibility, attractiveness, and power of the communicator. If the source of the information is perceived as being especially knowledgeable, objective, and trustworthy, the new information is more likely to be internalized. When the communicator of the new information is liked, is perceived as being similar to the self, and is perceived as attractive, the information will probably be accepted in order to identify with the source or maintain a relationship with that person. The more power a communicator of new information has to reward a person for accepting the new information or to punish a person for rejecting the new information, the more likely the person is to change his or her attitude. A person with a low self-image who is more ego defensive than a person with a high self-image will be less likely to accept the credibility, attractiveness, and power of the communicator and less likely to change an attitude based on new information.

What factors related to the message determine the effectiveness of new information in changing attitudes?

The characteristics of the message also may be a factor in attitude change. Printed material is usually more effective with people of higher socioeconomic status than with people of low socioeconomic status. Face-to-face communication is usually more effective than other forms of communication (see Figure 13–6). A review of the literature on attitude changes (McGuire, 1969) indicates that a message is more likely to change attitudes if the following conditions exist:

1. The message begins with material that is agreeable rather than disagreeable to the person.
2. The intent to change attitude is not made obvious.

3. The conclusions to be drawn are made clear.
4. Both sides of the issue are presented.
5. The side of the issue that is intended to change the person's attitude is presented second.
6. The discrepancy between the position of the message and the person's view is only moderate rather than extreme.
7. The message is only moderately frightening rather than extremely frightening.

According to Chaiken and Eagly (1983), if a communicator is especially likable, he or she is likely to be more persuasive in changing attitudes in face-to-face or video presentations; however, if he or she is not likable, the use of written messages will probably be more effective in changing attitudes than face-to-face or video messages.

Figure 13–6.
Face-to-face communication is usually more effective than other forms of communication.

Personality Factors. The personality traits of an individual seem to be a factor in attitude change. Some people's attitudes seem to change much easier than other people's attitudes. In some cases, a change in attitude may have been because the person was open-minded and intelligent. In other cases, it may have been because the person was gullible or had low self-esteem. A highly intelligent person is likely to understand new information and not to hold on to a belief or opinion because of insecurity about his or her intelligence.

What are some explanations for the fact that some people's attitudes change easier than others?

An individual who feels inadequate as a person and has low self-esteem is more likely to change his or her attitudes than someone with higher self-esteem (Eagly, 1980). Obviously, if a person does not think very highly of the self, he or she will not put much value on his or her beliefs, feelings, and behaviors. When people with low self-esteem find their beliefs, feelings, and behaviors challenged, they may give them up without much hesitation. People with low self-esteem lack confidence in their own judgment. A person's feeling of competence with regard to a specific something is related to the ease with which attitudes regarding that specific something may be changed. For example, most likely it will be harder to change a teacher's attitude toward a particular teaching program than to change a painter's attitude toward the teaching program. Likewise, it will most likely be harder to change a painter's attitude than a teacher's attitude toward a brand of paint.

Figure 13–7.
Salespeople often entertain prospective customers just prior to attempting to sell their products or services because a person is more likely to change attitudes when in a good mood.

The general mood of a person is a factor in attitude change. When people are in a good mood, they are more likely to change attitudes. Salespeople often entertain prospective customers just prior to attempting to sell their products or services (see Figure 13–7). In one research study, subjects who were provided pleasant background music during a persuasive message were influenced more than those not experiencing the pleasant background music (Galizio & Hendrick, 1972).

Which attitudes are most resistant to change?

Sometimes attitudes change frequently and easily; however, research indicates that some attitudes are very resistant to change. Attitudes that have been formed early in life and attitudes to which the person is highly committed do not change much with time (Freedman, Sears, & Carlsmith, 1981). This points out the significance of early experiences and motivation (goals) in the development and maintenance of attitudes and thus behavior.

Prejudice

Prejudice, defined earlier in this chapter as an attitude a person holds toward some members of a group of people that favorably or unfavorably predisposes the same attitude toward the whole group, is usually thought of as being an unfavorable attitude. However, a person may be prejudiced in favor of a particular group. Discrimination is the behavior that expresses the prejudice. **Stereotyping** is the assigning of identical characteristics to all members of a group and holding on to the stereotype even when faced with conflicting information. Stereotyping seems to be the primary element of prejudice.

What theories have been offered to explain the development of prejudice?

Sources of Prejudice. A number of theories have been proposed to explain the development of prejudice. Some historians suggest that prejudice may have its origin in years of conflict between groups. Often economic factors are important in generating conflict. A group may be stereotyped as inferior to justify exploitation of the group or exploitation of the resources of the group. This may be the source of some prejudice, but it cannot explain all prejudice.

Why is a person theorized to come to believe his or her in-group is superior to the out-group?

One group of theorists advanced the idea that people have an in-group or reference group with which they identify and an out-group that is not considered their own. The out-group has some characteristics that set it apart from the reference group or in-group. According to this theory, a person comes to believe his or her in-group is superior to the out-group because (a) it is the source of his or her satisfactions and (b) its members are more similar to the person. The characteristics that set the out-group apart from the in-group come to be more than just a means of developing group solidarity and cohesiveness and become the source of prejudice.

Another popular theory explaining the source of prejudice is that prejudice is the result of displaced aggression. A person or group of people become a **scapegoat** for the frustrations of the prejudiced individual or group. *Scapegoat* is the biblical term for a live goat over whose head all the sins of the children of Israel were confessed and that was then sent into the wilderness, symbolically bearing their sins. Psychologists use the term *scapegoat* to mean a person or group bearing the blame for others. In prejudice, a person or group displaces anger, hostility, and frustration onto a another person or onto a group that is smaller, less powerful, and less threatening than other groups. Individuals or groups that are more likely to become scapegoats are those that are readily available, have previously been scapegoats, have no power to strike back, and are easily identified by their physical appearance (Allport, 1944).

Psychologists have not been able to explain all prejudices with a unified theory. Some psychologists believe the personality of the individual who is prejudiced may have much to do with explaining the source of prejudice. This belief is based on research that indicates that people who are prejudiced against one minority group also tend to be prejudiced against other minority groups and even imaginary groups that do not exist (Adorno, Frenkel-Brunswik, Levinson, & Sanford, 1950). Prejudice seems to be a personality trait that generalizes to many situations rather than being related to just one specific situation.

Reducing Prejudice. Although prejudice can probably never be eliminated, psychologists have identified some methods of reducing it. Experiments have shown that sometimes the prejudice is reduced by increased contact with the group against whom the prejudice is held. Sometimes, however, the prejudice may be increased with more contact if anger and competitiveness prevail. The nature and quality of the contact seem to be the determining factors. Although sometimes increased contact may help a person see that his or her beliefs are not true and may change them, it is clear that just contact alone is usually not sufficient to reduce prejudice.

Figure 13–8.
Integrated classrooms need to foster equal status and cooperation to be most successful in reducing prejudice.

Five main conditions need to be present along with the contact before prejudice can be reduced (Cook, 1978). First, the members of the two groups need to see each other in situations of equal status (see Figure 13–8). Even when the contact is congenial, if the members of one group are of lower status, such as in job status or

Figure 13–9.
The success of males and females in nontraditional jobs aids in reducing stereotypes of abilities of males and females.

education, the contact will most likely continue the stereotypes and prejudice.

Second, the members of the two groups need to become personally acquainted with each other. Often members of prejudiced groups may have frequent contact without really getting to know each other personally. If the contact does not bring about a knowledge of each other as individuals—knowing about each other's personal lives and inner feelings—assumptions will probably continue to be made on the basis of group membership, and prejudice will not be reduced.

A third condition for reducing prejudice is for the contact to involve individuals who violate the stereotype. If the contact is with an individual who happens to have a stereotypical characteristic, the prejudice will not be reduced, only strengthened. For example, actually encountering men and women who are successful in nontraditional occupations is a condition for reducing stereotyping of abilities of males and females (see Figure 13–9).

The fourth and fifth conditions for reducing prejudice seem to be social support and cooperation. Social support of the contact from family, friends, the law, custom, or just an atmosphere that favors equality, fair treatment, and the contact itself is needed to reduce the prejudice. A situation wherein the prejudiced members of two groups must cooperate with each other to attain a common goal is a powerful factor. Mutual cooperation seems to produce a feeling of rapport or comradeship that can break through the prejudice. When cooperation is vital for survival, either physically, psychologically, or economically, it is difficult for a person to hold prejudices toward people with whom he or she is engaged in the struggle.

Sometimes prejudice resulting from scapegoating can be reduced by improving the emotional well-being of the prejudiced person and changing the person's coping strategy to a more satisfactory one. This might be accomplished through some form of psychotherapy. Because child-rearing practices involving punishment are considered by some psychologists to be the origin of scapegoating, changing child-rearing practices to less physically abusive techniques may reduce scapegoating, which in turn would reduce some prejudices.

What are some laws banning discrimination?

Discrimination. Although prejudices may exist in the workplace, there are federal laws administered by the Equal Employment Opportunity Commission (EEOC) banning discrimination by an employer, manager, supervisor, or employee representing an employer. The most comprehensive law is Title VII of the Civil Rights Act of 1964. Title VII prohibits discrimination in employment on the basis of race, color, religion, sex, or national origin. Discrimination against persons because of their being in the 40 to 70 age range is illegal under the Age Discrimination in Employment Act. The Equal Pay Act prohibits unequal wages for equal (or very similar) work because of sex. Discrimination against the physically handicapped is illegal under the Rehabilitation Act of 1973; however, this law only applies to those firms holding at least $2,500 worth of contracts with federal government agencies.

In addition to the above mentioned laws, there are several Presidential Executive Orders requiring employers with government contracts to take affirmative action for minorities, women, handicapped persons, and Vietnam veterans. Failure to meet these requirements may result in the cancellation of contracts and denial of future business with the government.

Many states have laws banning discrimination on the same bases as federal laws with agencies to enforce them. Most of these state laws prohibit physical handicap discrimination whether or not the employer does business with the federal government.

Discrimination in business is sometimes very subtle, disguised under "business reasons." However, sometimes only a visual investigation is necessary to reveal that there are no women or blacks or members of other ethnic groups in certain positions, or that women and members of certain ethnic groups are found in only certain positions such as clerical or maintenance positions. A thorough investigation of personnel records can provide evidence that discrimination on the basis of sex, race, or national origin has occurred in hiring and possibly in promotions. Other forms of discrimination can be revealed through an investigation of a company's personnel records. Discrimination in business is an example of the effect of attitudes, specifically prejudice, on behavior.

PERSUASION AND BEHAVIOR CHANGE

Often persuasion is used to get a person to express a desired behavior. In persuasion, strong pressures are applied to change or obtain a particular behavior using people's disposition to conform to norms, ability to feel guilt, and respect for authority. Pressures to behave a particular way are usually applied by persuading the person that the behavior is necessary to avoid violation of socially accepted standards, by causing the person to feel guilty, and by ordering or commanding the desired behavior. In this section, conformity, compliance, and obedience are discussed as means of persuading a person to behave in a particular way.

Conformity

What is conformity?

Conformity is behavior exhibited by a person in order to be in accordance with the norms or standards of society. Most people acquire a strong disposition to conform during childhood. Conformity is reinforced with praise, approval, and acceptance. Nonconformity is punished by criticism, disapproval, and rejection. The classic experiments demonstrating conformity and factors influencing conformity are discussed in this section.

What was the first formal demonstration of conformity?

The Asch Experiments. Solomon Asch (1952) was the first to demonstrate experimentally that the technique of showing a person that behavior change is necessary to avoid violation of socially accepted norms or standards is highly effective in modifying behavior. Subjects in his experiment were asked to decide which of three lines matched a given line in length (see Figure 13–10). Unknown to the subjects, Asch placed seven other people in the experiment who had been previously told what response to make each time. On the first few trials, these seven other people gave correct responses. Then they unanimously began giving incorrect responses. The subjects were faced with responding according to their own perceptions and going against the group or going along with the group. The study indicated that about 75 percent of the subjects conformed at least once to the incorrect answer given by the group. Most people find it less anxiety arousing to contradict evidence received by their own senses than to publicly disagree with the judgments of many other people.

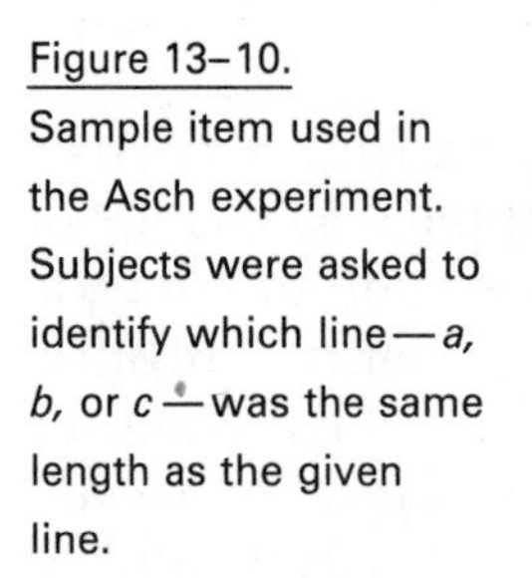

Figure 13–10. Sample item used in the Asch experiment. Subjects were asked to identify which line—*a*, *b*, or *c*—was the same length as the given line.

What are some factors that have been found to influence conformity?

Influencing Factors. Many different experiments have been conducted since the Asch experiments that support Asch's findings and identify some of the factors influencing conformity. Two factors that are especially significant are the size of the influencing group and whether the individual has any social support—an ally. The larger the group of people who behave that way, the greater the pressure to conform and the more likely that behavior is to occur. For example, a child may persuade a parent to change his or her stand on some rule by convincing the parent that everyone else's parents see it another way. The more allies or social support a person has for not conforming, the less pressure experienced and the less likely the behavior will be changed. For example, if the parent knows two or three other parents who stand as he or she does on the rule and they "stick together," the parent being pressured will be less likely to change even though the majority of parents do not stand that way on the rule. Early studies indicated that sex is a factor in conformity with females being more likely to conform than males. However, a later study (Sistrunk & McDavid, 1971) found males to be more conforming than females on "feminine" items with which the males were unfamiliar and females to be more conforming than males on "masculine" items with which the females were unfamiliar. (See paragraph beginning bottom page 141.) No difference in the degree of conformity was found between males and females on neutral items that were equally familiar to both sexes.

Compliance

What is compliance?

Often a person can be persuaded to behave in a particular manner just by being asked or requested to exhibit the behavior. When a person submits to a direct request to behave in a particular way, the means of persuasion is called **compliance.** People seem to have a tendency to want to please other people in order to be liked, loved, or approved of by them, especially if they have a strong need for affiliation. This strong disposition to please is acquired during childhood as is the strong disposition to conform. In this section, techniques used to obtain compliance and characteristics of the requestor that facilitate obtaining compliance are the primary focus.

What techniques are used to cause a person to feel guilty and to comply with a request?

Techniques Used. Getting a person to comply with a direct request involves causing the person to feel guilty if he or she does not comply. A person usually feels guilty when he or she does something that harms or hurts another person, even psychologically, especially if the harm was unintentional. A guilty person then tries to make amends by doing something good, helpful, or pleasing for the person harmed. If a person can be convinced that he or she has done harm or has hurt the requestor, the person is more likely to comply with the request than if he or she does not feel that harm or hurt has occurred. This is why crying, playing the role of the martyr, or just looking sad and forlorn are effective techniques for persuading a person to behave as requested and to "get your own way." Also, when a person is in a good mood, compliance is more likely to occur than when that person is in a bad mood.

Does the mood of an individual affect whether he or she complies with a request?

A person tends to feel guilty if he or she does not comply with a friend's request or the request of a person who has bestowed a favor. Therefore, a technique a requestor may use for getting a person to feel guilty and comply with a request is to get the person to like or feel obligated to him or her. This may be done by the requestor increasing his or her own attractiveness to another person, agreeing with the views and opinions of the person, or doing favors for the person. People in sales who are in the business of persuading people to exhibit a particular behavior—buy their product or service—are trained to dress attractively, give small gifts, take prospective customers to lunch or dinner, and buy them drinks.

How may a requestor get a person to feel obligated to comply with a request?

A person usually feels guilty about stopping something he or she has been doing for a person or refusing to do something that seems so trivial. Therefore, a technique frequently used to obtain compliance with a request is to build up to the request by making small or trivial requests. Once a person has complied with a small or trivial request, the chances are much greater that the person will comply with a larger request. People in sales, for example, often ask customers to accept some literature, or they ask for just one minute of their time. If the customer can be persuaded to agree to such a small request, the chances are much greater that the person can be persuaded to comply with the larger request to purchase the product or service. The reverse of this technique is also effective in obtaining compliance with a request. If a request for a large response—much larger than the request for which compliance is desired—is made first and the request is refused, when the request is made for a much smaller response, the person is then more likely to feel guilty about not complying and comply with the request for a smaller response. For example, if a person is asked to

What two types of requests made prior to the request for the desired behavior increase the probability that the desired behavior will occur?

donate 8 hours of time, refuses, and is then asked to donate just one hour—the amount really desired—the chances are greater that the person will comply with the request for one hour of time than if he or she had just been asked initially for the one hour. This technique is often used in collective bargaining or in settlement of claims.

The Requestor. Characteristics of the requestor have an effect on compliance. The credibility or believability of the message sent preceding the request is an important factor. The more expertise the requestor has, the more credible he or she is perceived to be and the more likely compliance with his or her request will occur. This is the reason that in medicine commercials on TV the person delivering the message and making the request to purchase and use the product may be a dignified person in a white coat looking like a pharmacist or physician.

What characteristics of the requestor have an effect on compliance?

The sincerity of the requestor is another important characteristic in obtaining compliance with a request. The clearer a requestor can communicate in the message preceding the request that he or she really believes what is being said, the more likely that compliance with the request will occur. This is why in TV commercials the requestor is often shown personally using the product. Also, a message may be perceived as more sincere if it is overheard rather than directed toward the person to whom the request is to be made. It seems that there is less suspect that the one delivering the message is deceptive or has ulterior motives. This is why often in TV commercials the message is presented by the audience merely overhearing a conversation rather than by the requestor looking directly at the TV audience and giving information.

What are two techniques often used in TV commercials to increase the perceived sincerity of the requestor?

Studies have shown that the rate of the requestor's speech may also be a factor in compliance. Within limits, a fast-talking requestor is more likely to be viewed as being more knowledgeable and objective than a slow-talking requestor. Therefore, people are more likely to be persuaded to comply with a request when the message delivered by the requestor is spoken at a fast rate than a slow rate.

Obedience

Respect for authority is shown by obeying the orders and commands of the authority figure. Most people learn very early in life to obey the orders and commands of those who are more powerful or who have more authority in order to avoid punishment (see

Figure 13–11.
Most people learn very early in life to obey the orders and commands of those who are more powerful or who have more authority in order to avoid punishment.

Figure 13–11). Thus, ordering and commanding are often used to persuade a person to behave in a particular way. When a person behaves in a particular manner because of an order or command given by another person, the behavior is said to be **obedience.** In this section, the power or authority of the commander is discussed as a factor in obedience. Also, the role of modeling in obedience is discussed.

Power of the Commander. Obtaining the desired behavior of a person by simply ordering or commanding the person to behave in a particular manner is effective if the individual doing the ordering or commanding has enough power or authority to inflict punishment for failure to carry out the orders or commands. Otherwise, commands may not produce obedience; they will only produce anger and hate directed toward the person doing the commanding. If the person doing the ordering or commanding is a powerful authority figure such as a company president, supervisor, military officer, parent, or teacher, he or she may be able to successfully influence behavior by ordering or commanding because of the respect generally afforded individuals in that position.

Can a relatively powerless source of authority obtain obedience to orders just from giving the appearance of authority?

Research studies also have indicated that a relatively powerless source of authority can obtain obedience to orders just from giving the appearance of authority. This is blind, unquestioned obedience to authority. Stanley Milgram (1963) first tested this blind, unquestioned obedience to authority by having an experimenter order a subject to deliver electrical shocks of higher intensity each time another subject made an error. The second subject was actually an actor pretending to be receiving the shocks so that the real subject believed he or she was delivering shocks. If the subject found the task disturbing as the shocks became more intense and wanted to stop, the experimenter, using strong authoritative tones, ordered the subject to continue. The ordering became increasingly stronger each time the subject tried to stop. Total obedience to the final 450-volt shock was obtained from 65 percent of the subjects. This study and further experiments indicate that many people have a tendency to obey the commands of a person who gives the appearance of authority even when the commands do not make sense and are inhumane. It seems that the obeyer rationalizes that the commander is responsible for his or her behavior rather than assuming responsibility for his or her own behavior.

Does exposure to disobedient models affect obedience?

Modeling. Another factor in obedience seems to be the degree to which the person given the commands has been exposed to disobedient models. If the person to be persuaded has been exposed primarily to obedient models, he or she is more likely to obey. If the person to be persuaded has been exposed primarily to disobedient models, he or she is more likely to disobey. Most leaders know that one or a few disobedient followers set an example for others, causing the number of disobedient followers to be likely to increase. Classroom teachers know that if one child is allowed to defy the authority of the teacher, others may follow suit. If a person's childhood consisted of an authoritarian parent that everyone in the family obeyed, that person is more likely to obey commands than a person whose childhood consisted of models who were disobedient to an authoritarian parent.

SOCIAL INTERACTIONS

People help one another. People infer motives and intentions for others' behavior. People affiliate with, like, love, and have sexual relationships with other people. People also inflict harm on other people. In this section, the focus is on helping and perceiving others, interpersonal attraction, and aggression.

Helping and Perceiving Others

Two important aspects of social interactions are willingness to help others and the perception of others' motives for behavior. Helping others is important because it is related to the welfare of people. The motives ascribed for a person's behavior are important because these determine behavior associated with that person and are the basis for predictions of how the person is likely to behave in the future. Altruism and attribution are the topics discussed here.

What is altruism?

Altruism. People often help other people. Sometimes help given another person is really for self-gain. An employee may volunteer to help the boss install a burglar alarm system because promotion on the job depends on how much the boss likes him or her. This type of helping behavior is based on the principle, You scratch my back, and I'll scratch yours. **Altruism** is helping behavior that is not linked to self-gain—behavior that is exhibited without expectation of any recognition or reward in return except perhaps the good feeling that comes from the behavior itself. Charitable contributions made anonymously or to strangers might be examples of altruism.

What are some factors that influence altruism?

Several factors have been found to influence altruism. A person in a good mood is more likely to behave altruistically than a person who is in a neutral or bad mood (Isen & Levin, 1972). The greater a person's fear of embarrassment, the less likely he or she is to exhibit altruism. When other people are present to observe, individuals who score high on need for approval are more likely to act in an altruistic way than those who score low on need for approval (Satow, 1975). The clearer it is that a person really has a genuine need for help, the higher the probability that the person will render aid. The more a person feels that his or her values and personality are similar to the values and personality of the person needing help, the more likely he or she will behave in an altruistic manner. Additionally, the more personal responsibility the person feels, the more likely he or she is to help. As the number of passive bystanders increases, the less likely it is that one of them will help. This is discussed in more detail in chapter 14 in the discussion of bystander apathy. And finally, people have been found to be less altruistic in noisy places than in quiet places (Mathews & Canon, 1975). The most plausible explanation given for this finding is that the noise distracts the attention of the person from the need.

What is attribution?

Attribution. The process of ascribing (attributing) causes for people's behavior is referred to as **attribution**. Attribution theorists look for the causes of behavior. Fritz Heider (1958) proposed that people tend to attribute the behavior of a person to one of two basic causes: (a) disposition — something internal such as a personality trait, the person's deliberate effort, or the person's physiological state, and (b) situation — something external such as a social situation, someone else's actions, or luck. The classic point of view is that people act according to their basic personality. Milgram's experiment, concerned with obedience to authority, and the experiment on bystander apathy described in chapter 14 caused some psychologists to swing radically toward the situation view. Attribution theory has generated much research during the last few years (Harvey & Weary, 1984). Most psychologists today agree that the cause of people's behavior is not totally dispositional and not totally situational but rather an interaction between the two.

Why is attribution important?

Attribution processes are important because whether a person likes or dislikes another person and how a person behaves toward another person depend primarily on the perceived cause of the person's behavior. For example, if a person bumps into you, you will feel and act differently toward that person if you believe the person is blind, was pushed into you by another person, or fainted than if you believe the person bumped into you deliberately or because of carelessness.

What do people tend to rely on in making assumptions as to why a person behaved in a particular way?

In making assumptions as to why a person behaved or is behaving in a particular way, people tend to rely on whether the behavior is distinctive, similar to the behavior of other people, and consistent. For example, if an employee who seldom becomes angry does become angry about a situation that upsets most people, the employee's behavior is more likely to be attributed to the particular situation. If the employee usually becomes angry about the situation even though most people do not, the employee's behavior is more likely to be attributed to his or her own personality or temperament.

Research studies indicate that most people tend to overestimate the dispositional factors and underestimate the situational factors. This tendency is known as the **fundamental attribution error.** For example, marriage counselors commonly hear disputes between spouses in which one spouse explains his or her own behavior by citing circumstances and then accuses the other spouse of acting a particular way because of selfishness, inconsiderateness, repressed hostility, thoughtlessness, or some other negative personality trait. When a person sees other people behave in a manner he or she doesn't like or can't understand, the temptation seems to be very strong to attribute the behavior to personality characteristics (disposition). Once this attribution is done, the person seems to unconsciously give enough cues to the other person to provoke the expected behavior—self-fulfilling prophecy. In assigning causes for behavior, people usually do not make enough allowances for roles, for pressures, and for differences in experience.

Several reasons for the fundamental attribution error occurring in the majority of people have been offered. First, a person knows his or her own situations and influences and doesn't know others' situations and influences; therefore, it is easier to assign dispositional factors than to look for hidden situational reasons. The other person can protect his or her ego by attributing failure to situation and success to the self. Second, the behavior of a person naturally gets more attention than the context in which the behavior occurs (the situation). A third reason is thought to be because typically the person's behavior is observed in only a limited number of situations.

Figure 13–12.
Attraction is the process by which people are drawn together in friendships and in romantic love.

Interpersonal Attraction

Attraction is the process by which people are drawn together (see Figure 13–12). Most people seem to seek out other people and to want to affiliate with people. A person may like being with people in general, may like some people better than other people, may have friends, may love some people, and may have a romantic or sexual relationship with a person of the opposite sex. In this section, some of the factors that contribute to affiliation, liking, and loving are pointed out, and the sexual relationship is discussed.

What two factors have the most powerful impact on affiliation, liking, and loving?

Affiliation, Liking, and Loving. Several factors affect affiliation, liking, and loving. Proximity has a powerful impact. Although physical proximity does not always result in liking and loving, researchers have found that being in close proximity leads to liking more often than it leads to disliking. It seems that if social rewards can be obtained close by, there is no need to put forth the effort to seek further. The rewards can be obtained at a lower cost when they are close in proximity. After togetherness, the next most powerful factor in affiliation, liking, or loving is similarity. People tend to be attracted to other people who are similar in many different ways. The similarities may be in such factors as age, physical appearance, personality characteristics, educational level, occupation, status, intelligence, political preferences, or religious preference. It seems that it is rewarding to a person to be agreed with because agreement increases self-confidence, makes communication easier than when there is disagreement, causes a person to assume he or she is or will be liked (which sets the stage for self-fulfilling prophecy), and provides a basis for engaging in joint activities.

Why is a person sometimes attracted to a person with an opposite trait?

Two other influences on affiliation, liking, and loving are complementary traits and reciprocity. Sometimes a person is attracted to a person with an opposite trait, not merely because of the different trait but because the different trait can supply a lacking quality—the two are complementary. Usually in this type of attraction, there are some similarities. People seem to have a natural tendency to be attracted to those people who like them—to reciprocate. Most people have several different friends to meet a variety of needs. Friendships seem to develop first based on proximity, then based on similar characteristics, then based on role relationships such as co-workers, and then based on similar attitudes and values (Houston & Levinger, 1978).

Sexual Relationships. Romantic love seems to be of two types. **Companionate love** is a loving friendship that consists of deep affection and attachment, appreciation, respect, trust, loyalty, emotional intimacy, and close acquaintance. **Passionate love** consists of a highly emotional state that is often a confusion of feelings such as anxiety and relief, altruism and jealousy, tenderness and sexual aggression, and elation and forlornness. Liking and loving often lead to romantic love, marriage, and a sexual relationship (see Figure 13–13). The link between love and sex depends to a large extent on the sexual values of the people involved. Many dating men and women believe the sexual relationship strengthens their love and commitment, but many others believe their love will remain just as strong or stronger without sex.

Figure 13–13.
Liking and loving often lead to romantic love, marriage, and a sexual relationship.

What are the stages in the sexual response cycle?

William Masters and Virginia Johnson (1966) broke down the traditional taboo and legitimized the study of the sexual response cycle under laboratory conditions. They found four phases or stages in the sexual response cycle: (a) *excitement* (bodily sexual arousal), (b) *plateau* (peak of bodily sexual arousal), (c) *orgasm* (release of the sexual tension), and (d) *resolution* (return to the pre-excitement state). The Masters and Johnson study and the many scientific studies in a number of different areas of sexuality that have followed have dispelled myths and provided a body of knowledge in the area of sexual relations, both psychologically and physiologically. A few psychologists today are specialized in the area of human sexual relations.

How is sex sometimes manifested in the workplace?

Little research has been conducted on sex in the workplace. But because of the women's movement and concerns about sexual harassment of women at work, more is being learned about it. In a book titled *Sex and the Workplace,* Barbara Gutek states, "Sex is manifested in various ways at work, from sexual relationships between workers to flirtatious conversations, pictures and posters, jokes, and styles of dress. Over 80 percent of workers report some kind of 'social-sexual' experience on the job. Even more important, such experiences can be—and are—a problem for workers and for organizations" (1985, p. ix). Gutek further surmises that because many managers, human resources professionals, consultants, and other decision makers do not fully understand sexuality in the workplace, the problem is often ignored, sometimes resulting in employees being demoralized, a healthy work environment being disrupted, or job satisfaction being reduced.

Aggression

Sometimes human social interactions consist of physical or verbal behavior that hurts or destroys another person either physically or psychologically. This type of behavior is called aggression and was defined earlier in chapter 9. Aggression, which may be directed against property as well as people, is usually an expression of anger or hostility. Violence is the most extreme form of aggression. The bases of aggression and TV and pornographic violence are addressed in this section.

What are some factors that may play a role in aggression?

Bases of Aggression. Many factors play a role in aggression. As was pointed out in chapter 2, part of the limbic system in the brain is involved in aggression and can be a basis for aggression. Hormonal imbalance, perhaps brought about by a pituitary tumor, or brain disease has sometimes been found in individuals exhibiting senseless brutality toward other people. Males, in general, tend to be more aggressive than females. This trend is found in both humans and animals and is believed to be partly due to the early influence of the sex hormones on the brain. Aggression in humans is far more complex than in animals. In animals, aggression is primarily under the direct control of the hormones, whereas in humans many other factors such as learning, emotion, motivation, memory, and thinking interact with the influence of the hormones.

What is the frustration-aggression hypothesis, and what revisions has it undergone?

Freud theorized that aggression originates internally as an instinctive drive. About 20 years later the **frustration-aggression hypothesis** that aggressive behavior is the result of frustration brought about by external factors began to prevail. More recently, the roles of thinking and perception in aggression are being recognized. How a person thinks and perceives an external event may determine the extent of the frustration and thus the aggressiveness of the response. Because of the threat of punishment, aggression is often displaced onto a safer target than the source of the frustration. For example, an employee may be frustrated by the supervisor and displace aggression onto co-workers. A child may be frustrated by the parents and displace the aggression onto the pet or siblings. A spouse may be frustrated by the other spouse and displace the aggression onto the children. The frustration-aggression hypothesis has recently undergone another revision, and many psychologists now believe that aggression is an interaction between emotional states and environmental conditions. Frustration merely creates a readiness for aggressive behavior. The presence of a weapon or scapegoat, seeing aggressive behavior exhibited by others, or experiencing intense, hostile emotions are examples of conditions that have been associated with aggression.

Most psychologists now believe that aggression is learned through experience, and any kind of aversive experience, not just frustration alone, produces a general state of emotional arousal that leads to aggressive behavior. Whether aggressive behavior occurs depends on whether aggressive behavior has been rewarded in the past and whether aggressive behavior has been observed as well as observed to be rewarded in other people. Further, psychologists today believe that aggressive behavior can occur without emotional arousal if a person believes aggression will lead to a desired outcome or if aggression is the norm for the behavior of the other people in the individual's environment. It seems a person feels pressure to conform to the norm behavior even if the norm behavior is aggressive.

What is the belief of most psychologists today concerning aggression?

TV and Pornographic Violence. Because of the explanations of aggression, there is much concern about the aggressive actions portrayed on television and in pornography. From cartoons, drama, comedy, and news, people learn that violence commonly occurs and is rewarded, clean, fun, and more appropriate for males than females. Well-controlled research studies have shown that both children and adults are more prone to act aggressively soon after viewing violence, are more likely to tolerate aggression in others, and are less likely to intervene or take action when others are behaving aggressively than when they have not recently viewed violence. One study, conducted over a 10-year period, found that the number of violent TV programs watched in the third grade correlated significantly with aggressive behavior in the eleventh grade. However, a correlation was not found between aggressive behavior in the third grade and a preference for watching violent TV programs in the eleventh grade (Eron, Huesmann, Lefkowitz, & Walder, 1972).

What are the findings from research studies concerned with viewing violence?

Research studies indicate that exposure to pornographic violence contributes to violence by men against women. In general, studies find that men are sexually aroused by aggressive-erotic films, that there is an increase in the amount of aggression exhibited toward women after viewing such a film, that men become more accepting of such myths as women really enjoy being sexually dominated after viewing pornographic violence, and that men have more fantasies of rape after viewing aggressive-erotic materials. Although there seems to be a clear link between TV and pornographic violence and violent behavior in our nation, our constitution guarantees freedom that includes the right to portray violence.

What are the findings from research studies concerned with viewing pornographic violence?

SUMMARY

1. Attitudes, a person's disposition to think, feel, and act either positively or negatively toward a person, idea, object, or situation, are acquired in a social environment and are assumed to be important determinants of behavior.
2. Beliefs, opinions, prejudices, discrimination, and values are aspects of attitudes, which are characterized by three components—cognitive, affective, and conative.
3. Attitudes may be acquired through learning by identification with parents, peers, and other significant people and by classical and operant conditioning. Learning of attitudes begins in infancy, and the mass media is an important influence also on the formation of attitudes.
4. The attitudes a person holds, along with the strength and direction (positive or negative) of the attitudes, may be assessed through use of attitude scales such as a Thurstone scale, a Guttman scale, a Likert scale, and a semantic differential scale, and through the observation of behavior.
5. Although relatively enduring, attitudes may change when dissonance, inconsistency existing between the components of an attitude, is created. Some sources of dissonance are conflict between behavior and beliefs and feelings or new information that conflicts with beliefs.
6. Arousal of fear is one technique sometimes used to change attitudes. New information may result in a change of attitude depending on the credibility, attractiveness, and power of the communicator and whether the message is printed or presented face-to-face and meets certain conditions.
7. Some personality characteristics that seem to be factors in attitude change are intelligence, general mood, and self-esteem.
8. Prejudice is an attitude toward a group of people that predisposes a person favorably or unfavorably toward the whole group. Discrimination is the behavior that expresses the prejudice, and stereotyping is the assigning of identical characteristics to all members of a group.
9. Some theorists believe prejudice has its source in conflict between groups; some believe in-groups are the source; some believe scapegoating is the source; and some believe personality is the source.
10. Sometimes prejudice can be reduced through contact, particularly if the following conditions prevail: equal status, personal acquaintance, violation of stereotypes, social support, and cooperation.
11. A person may be prejudiced, but laws prohibit discrimination in employment situations. Sometimes discrimination in business is very subtle, disguised under "business reasons."
12. Requesting (compliance), ordering or commanding (obedience) and showing that the behavior change is necessary to avoid violation of

socially accepted standards (conformity) are techniques often used to change an individual's behavior.

13. Conformity to socially accepted standards is learned during childhood, and most people find it anxiety arousing to disagree with socially accepted standards. The Asch experiments demonstrated conformity.
14. A person is more likely to comply with a request if he or she can be made to feel guilty and if he or she likes the person making the request. Thus crying, playing the role of a martyr, looking sad and forlorn, and giving compliments and doing favors are often effective techniques for obtaining compliance with a request. Also, making a small, trivial request first and getting compliance increases the likelihood of compliance with a larger request, and making a large request first and getting rejection increases the likelihood of compliance with a smaller request.
15. Obedience to an order or command may be obtained if the person doing the commanding has the power to inflict punishment for failure to obey or is an authority figure, and if the person being commanded has been exposed primarily to obedient models.
16. Milgram's study and further experiments indicate that many people have a tendency to obey the commands of a person who merely gives the appearance of being an authority figure—blind, unquestioned obedience to authority—particularly if they do not perceive themselves as responsible and have not been exposed to many disobedient models.
17. Altruism, helping behavior that is not linked to self-gain, has been found to be influenced by mood of the person, fear of embarrassment, need for approval, the clearness of a genuine need for help, similarity of personality and values, feeling of responsibility for the person, and noise level.
18. Attribution, the process of ascribing causes to people's behavior, is important because it determines whether a person likes another person and how a person behaves toward another person. The cause of a person's behavior may be attributed to disposition (something internal) or to situation (something external); however, research indicates a tendency to overestimate the dispositional source and underestimate the situational source—the fundamental attribution error.
19. Factors that have been found to affect affiliation, liking, and loving are proximity, similarity, complementarity, and reciprocity.
20. Romantic love may consist of companionate love and/or passionate love. Masters and Johnson identified four stages in the sexual response cycle (excitement, plateau, orgasm, and resolution).
21. Sexual behavior may be manifested in various ways at work from sexual relationships between workers to flirtatious conversations, pictures and posters, jokes, and styles of dress.

22. Aggression, physical and/or verbal behavior that hurts or destroys and may be directed toward people or property, is sometimes related to hormonal imbalance or brain disorder, frustration, emotional states, environmental conditions, learning by reinforcement and observation, and pressure to conform.
23. Violence, the most extreme form of aggression, is portrayed on TV and in pornography. Research studies have shown that both children and adults are more prone to act aggressively after viewing violence and that exposure to pornographic violence contributes to violence by men against women.

KEY TERMS AND CONCEPTS

Attitude
Belief
Opinion
Prejudice
Discrimination
Values
Stereotyping
Scapegoat
Conformity
Compliance
Obedience
Altruism
Attribution
Fundamental attribution error
Companionate love
Passionate love
Frustration-aggression hypothesis

QUESTIONS FOR REVIEW

1. What is the definition of attitude, belief, opinion, prejudice, discrimination, value, and stereotype? What are the three components of an attitude?
2. How are attitudes formed?
3. How are attitudes assessed? Describe four scales.
4. What approaches are used in attempts to change attitudes?
5. What are some sources of prejudice, how can prejudice be reduced, and what laws have been made to attempt to eliminate discrimination in the workplace?
6. What are the classic experiments that demonstrated conformity and obedience, what techniques are used, and what factors need to be considered in using conformity, compliance, and obedience as means of persuading a person to behave in a particular way?
7. What factors influence altruism and attribution, and what is the fundamental attribution error?
8. What factors affect affiliation, liking, and loving?
9. How does companionate love and passionate love differ, what are the stages in the human sexual response cycle, and how is sex sometimes manifested in the workplace?
10. What are the bases or sources of aggression, and what are the research findings concerning TV and pornographic violence?

TEST YOURSELF

1. A person's values are a product of the worth of something and how positively or negatively he or she feels about that something. T or F
2. The action or response tendency or any directed effort toward action is the (a) cognitive component of an attitude (b) affective component of an attitude (c) conative component of an attitude (d) all of the above.
3. Attitudes begin to be formed (a) as a person reaches adulthood (b) in infancy (c) in late childhood (d) about the time a child reaches school age.
4. The ________________ scale is the attitude scale that measures the strength and direction of an attitude by having respondents choose the strongest statement they are willing to endorse in a series of successively more extreme statements.
5. The basic assumption of dissonance theory is that the need (a) to be free from fear can be the motivation for attitude change (b) for cognitive dissonance can be the motivation for attitude change (c) for cognitive consistency can be the motivation for attitude change (d) for new information can be the motivation for attitude change.
6. Beliefs and feelings are more likely to change than they would otherwise (a) if a person freely chooses to behave in a manner that conflicts with his or her beliefs and feelings (b) if a person receives little or no reward for behaving in a manner that conflicts with his or her beliefs or feelings (c) if a person cannot justify the behavior that conflicts with his or her beliefs and feelings (d) all of the above.
7. In the study of three groups of high school students who were exposed to messages that emphasized the importance of dental care, the group that had high fear arousal reported (a) fewer changes in their dental care behaviors than a group exposed to a less threatening message (b) more changes in their dental care behaviors than a group exposed to a less threatening message (c) approximately the same number of changes in their dental care behaviors than a group exposed to a less threatening message (d) conflicting results with fewer changes the first time but more changes the second time.
8. Compared with other forms of communication used to change an attitude, face-to-face communication is usually (a) less effective (b) more effective (c) neither more nor less effective (d) more effective only when the communicator is perceived as being attractive.
9. Prejudice is an attitude toward a group of people that (a) favorably predisposes a person's attitude toward each individual member of the whole group (b) unfavorably predisposes a person's attitude toward each individual member of the whole group (c) favorably or unfavorably predisposes a person's attitude toward each individual member

of the whole group (d) has no effect on a person's attitude toward each individual member of the whole group.

10. Assigning identical characteristics to all members of a group is referred to as (a) in-grouping (b) stereotyping (c) scapegoating (d) discrimination.
11. ________________ seems to be an especially powerful condition, along with contact, for reducing prejudice.
12. The most comprehensive federal law banning discrimination in employment situations is (a) the Equal Pay Act (b) Title VII of the Civil Rights Act of 1964 (c) the Age Discrimination in Employment Act (d) the Rehabilitation Act of 1973.
13. When a person changes his or her behavior because of being made to feel guilty for not behaving as requested, that person is demonstrating (a) conformity (b) compliance (c) obedience (d) manipulation.
14. ________________ was the first to study blind, unquestioned obedience to authority and found that people have a tendency to obey the commands of a relatively powerless person who gives the appearance of being an authority figure even when the commands do not make sense or are inhumane.
15. Whether a person obeys a command seems to be related to how much (a) the person perceives the self as being responsible for the harm (b) the person has been exposed to disobedient models (c) power or authority the one doing the commanding has to inflict punishment for failure to carry out the orders or commands (d) all of the above.
16. ________________ is helping behavior that is not linked to self-gain and may be affected by such things as mood of the person, fear of embarrassment, need for approval, clearness of need for help, similarity of values and personality, and noise levels.
17. The fundamental attribution error is that most people tend to overestimate the situational factors when attributing causes to people's behavior. T or F
18. The two most powerful factors in affiliation, liking, and loving are ________________ and ________________.
19. Romantic love may be of the ________________ love type or the ________________ love type, and the sexual response cycle consists of the ________________, ________________, ________________, and ________________ stages.
20. Well-controlled research studies have shown that both children and adults are more prone to act aggressively and to tolerate aggression in others after viewing violence than before viewing violence. T or F

APPLICATIONS

A. Alberto Sanchez is employed by a cleaning supplies distributor as a salesperson. Alberto calls on the purchasing agents of firms and attempts to persuade them to purchase the cleaning supplies. Sometimes Alberto takes the purchasing agent to lunch or dinner and gives the purchasing agent free samples of the products for personal use before asking for the order. Alberto is always careful to dress neatly and attractively when making calls. While pointing out the features of the products and making a request for a purchase, Alberto talks rapidly.

1. What method of persuasion and what technique is Alberto using?
2. Why does Alberto try to talk fast while discussing products and requesting a person to buy?
3. Why does Alberto always dress neatly and attractively?

B. Mary Adams, an attorney who employs two secretaries and a paraprofessional in her office, sometimes has to deal with mistakes in actions or inappropriate behavior and errors made by her employees that she attributes to carelessness, ignorance, or a deliberate intention to avoid more work. When she herself exhibits any inappropriate behavior or makes a mistake, she tends to attribute the mistakes to misinformation from another person, lack of sufficient time, or interruptions.

1. What is Mary's tendency to overestimate or attribute mistakes made by her employees to disposition and to overestimate or attribute her own mistakes to situation called?
2. Why does Mary have this tendency?

SUGGESTIONS FOR FURTHER READING

Allport, G. W. (1954). *The nature of prejudice*. Reading, MA: Addison-Wesley.

This book is considered to be a classic and provides thorough coverage of the topic of prejudice.

Aronson, E. (1984). *The Social Animal* (4th ed.). New York: Freeman.

Several topics in the field of social psychology are presented in a witty manner in this introductory book.

Baron, R. A., & Byrne, D. (1987). *Social psychology: Understanding human interaction* (5th ed.). Boston: Allyn and Bacon.

A textbook in social psychology that is a comprehensive introduction to human interaction covering topics discussed in this chapter as well as other topics.

Berscheid, E., & Walster, E. H. (1978). *Interpersonal attraction* (2nd ed.). Reading, MA: Addison-Wesley.

A short but comprehensive and readable summary of attraction.

Kelley, H. H., Berscheid, E., Christensen, A., Harvey, J. H., Huston, T. L., Levinger, G., McClintock, E., Peplau, L. A., & Peterson, D. R. (1983). *Close Relationships*. New York: Freeman.

Both the internal and external factors that play a role in intimate relationships are discussed by specialists in the field.

Liebert, R. M., Sprafkin, J. N., & Davidson, E. S. (1982). *The early window: Effects of television on children and youth* (2nd ed.). New York: Pergamon Press.

One of the most comprehensive texts published on the effects of television.

Milgram, S. (1974). *Obedience to authority.* New York: Harper & Row.

Milgram's discussion of the findings from his classic experiment, the ethical issues related to the experiment, and the problem of obedience to authority.

Shaver, K. G. (1985). *The attribution of blame: Causality, responsibility and blameworthiness.* New York: Springer-Verlag.

A comprehensive theory of assignment of blame as an explanation of responsibility.

CHAPTER 14

GROUP PROCESSES

Objectives

When you have completed your study of chapter 14, you should be able to:

1. Explain why groups form and how individuals come to be members of groups, the sequence of group formation, and positions, roles, and status in a group.
2. Explain how the presence of a group affects an individual's performance, decision making, helping of others, assuming of responsibility, and personality.
3. Cite factors and conditions that affect group performance.
4. Explain what groupthink is, and cite some techniques that may be used to prevent it.
5. Describe the directional patterns, the basic structures of communication in groups, and the informal communication links.
6. Summarize the theory of transactional analysis, and use the terminology of the theory.
7. Contrast three approaches to the study of leadership.
8. Describe three basic styles of leadership.
9. Explain leadership effectiveness in terms of style and idiosyncrasy credit.
10. Summarize the contingency theory of leadership.

In social interaction, groups form that have a great influence on behavior of individuals, communication occurs in the groups, and leaders of the groups emerge. Understanding group processes is important to understanding human behavior. For most people, much of the time spent working on a job is spent interacting with other people and in groups. Social psychologists refer to a **group** as a collection of individuals who interact with each other, share some common identity, and share some common goals or desires. A number of people merely standing or sitting near each other would not be considered a group. A group may be composed of as few as two people or any number up to a huge crowd. Group processes will be examined in this chapter with the primary focus on the formation, influence, and performance of groups, communication within groups, and leadership.

What constitutes a group?

What are the two basic purposes served by the formation of a group?

GROUPS

Most groups come into existence to serve one of two basic purposes. Some groups form to serve people's social needs, and some groups form to accomplish a task. Other groups serve both a social function and a task-oriented function. Social groups form to provide enjoyment (see Figure 14–1). Task-oriented groups form to accomplish some goal. The task may be anything—perhaps to widen a road, select an employee, operate an effective mailing system, or build a profitable business. In this section, group formation, group influence on individual behavior, and group performance are discussed.

Figure 14–1.
Most groups come into existence to serve one of two basic purposes. A task-oriented group may form to accomplish a task. A socially oriented group may form to provide enjoyment.

Group Formation

Groups form, people are members of groups, and groups have structure. The reasons for group formation, conditions for membership, formation process from the standpoint of developmental sequence, and group structure including position, roles, status, and norms are discussion topics.

Reasons for Formation. Groups may form for any number of reasons. Most often a group is formed to achieve a goal that can only be accomplished, or more easily accomplished, by the interaction of two or more people. It would be impossible for a single individual to simultaneously perform all the tasks that are necessary for a space flight, for example. A house could be built more easily by group members combining their knowledge and skills in carpentry, electricity, plumbing, and roofing than by a single individual who would have to master all these skills in order to build the house.

Festinger's social comparison theory (Festinger, 1954) offers another explanation for the formation of groups. The social comparison theory proposes that people are attracted to groups that contain individuals similar to themselves because such groups supply information or feedback that enables people to compare or evaluate their own opinions, attitudes, and abilities.

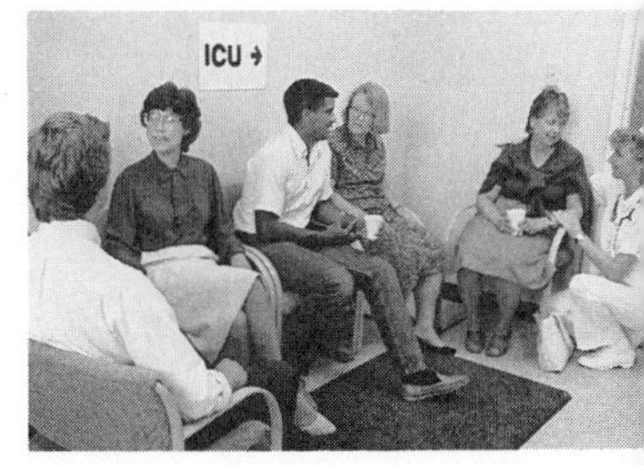

Figure 14–2.
A reason for the formation of some groups is to provide support to individuals who are experiencing or anticipating stress.

A third reason for the formation of some groups is to provide support to individuals who are experiencing or anticipating stress (see Figure 14–2). This reason for the formation of groups is supported by experimental studies that demonstrate that a greater percentage of people choose to wait with others rather than to wait alone when they are anticipating a very painful electric shock (Schachter, 1959). These experiments also demonstrated that a greater percentage of people choose to wait with people who are also going to experience the shocks rather than with people who are not anticipating them.

Groups also may form to satisfy people's needs such as emotional needs, esteem needs, status needs, or recreational needs. People have so many different needs (such as reduction of tension, companionship, reduction of boredom, or need for reassurance) that all of them cannot be listed here. Sometimes groups form to satisfy members' needs to seek or share information or to share the same interests or concerns. People seem to have a basic need to belong to or affiliate with other people and thus form groups.

What is the social exchange theory?

The social exchange theory proposes that people join a group because being a member of the group is a means to an end. Being a member of the group yields rewards that are greater than the costs of not being a member of the group (Thibaut & Kelley, 1959). Furthermore, whether a person remains in a group or joins another depends on the rewards received in that group compared with the previous group.

What are the two conditions under which a person may be a member of a group?

Conditions for Membership. More than likely, a person will belong to many groups. Why people join groups or belong to groups is of interest to social psychologists. An individual may be a member of a group through one of two conditions related to choice. Sometimes one has no choice about being a member of a group; he or she may be automatically conscripted into a group. For example, a worker might be a member of the Building II group merely because he or she works in that building. Or a worker might be a member of the group of female employees of a business firm as a result of being a female. Or an employee may be in the group comprising the electrical department because of the nature of the work he or she performs. A person is born into some groups such as a family, a race, or a nationality.

On the other hand, sometimes a person is a member of a group because he or she chooses to join the group; membership is acquired or achieved voluntarily. For example, a worker may choose to join the group attending the annual company picnic or the group subscribing to Plan A insurance or the group taking the air traffic controller course.

What are the phases and the developmental sequence of a group?

Formation Process. From the standpoint of developmental sequence, a group is viewed as having different structures depending on its developmental phase. The process of group formation has been described as a four-phase sequence (Rosenfeld, 1976). In the first phase, called the **orientation phase,** the members of the group are getting acquainted. Early in this phase there may be a general feeling of discomfort accompanied by some anxieties and uncertainties. Through interaction, the members confirm or change expectations of the activities of the group and the rewards rendered by membership in the group. Also, through interaction, the members learn what behaviors are tolerated and expected by other members of the group and assess the goals and emotional atmosphere of the group. If a member continues through this phase, the general feelings of discomfort, anxiety, and uncertainty subside and a feeling of belonging is experienced. During the second phase of group formation, called the **conflict phase,** members' individual personalities and needs begin to clash. Members may begin to experience anger, hostility, and aggression toward each other and particularly toward the leader. Members may have to give up some of their individual wants, desires, and needs for the benefit of the group as a whole. This compromising and reaching of agreements characterizes the **balance phase.** By the end of this phase, positions and roles are established, harmony exists in interpersonal relations, and members are working competently and enthusiastically to accomplish common goals.

Sometimes groups disband, which is called the **parting phase.** Groups may fluctuate back and forth between the conflict phase and the balance phase and continue to exist; however, a group may dissolve when the balance stage cannot be reached following a conflict stage. Divorce would be an example of the dissolving of a group. Sometimes a group's existence is limited by time or situation. For example, a group may be formed to campaign for a political candidate and then disband following the election. Or a grievance committee may be formed to function for one year and may disband and be replaced by a new group at the end of the year.

What is meant by group position, group role, and group status?

Structure. When groups form, there is some organizational structure that may be formal or informal. An understanding of the structure of groups is necessary to understanding the effect of groups on individual behavior. The structure of a group is often viewed from the standpoint of the position, roles, and status of individual members and norms of the group. **Group position** refers to a specific slot occupied by an individual in a group. The behavior displayed by an individual in a particular position is referred to as **group role. Group status** refers to the group's evaluation of the contribution of particular roles to the welfare of the group (Harari & Kaplan, 1982). In some groups, particularly in work situations, positions and roles may be clearly defined. But in other groups, positions, roles, and status emerge as members of the group interact and come to behave in a systematic way. Sometimes a position may be defined; however, the role or behavior to be exhibited by the person in that position may not be clearly defined. When role confusion exists, the individuals concerned often experience anxiety and stress.

Because people are members of many groups, an individual has multiple roles. A person may compete for a position because that role is valued higher than another role. The position of president is higher in status than vice president, and the role of a committee chairperson is higher than that of a committee member. Being a member of the middle social class is higher in status than being a member of the lower social class.

To what does the term *group norm* refer?

Members of a group demand that another member conform to the rules and standards and exhibit attitudes agreed upon by the members of the group. The term **group norm** refers to these rules, standards, and attitudes with which members are expected to comply and that serve as a basis for the evaluation of the behavior of a member. A group may be viewed in terms of its norms because group behavior depends on the norms probably more than any other aspect. Members of a group have a tendency to think and behave similarly—a basis for stereotyping. If members of a group do not have similar attitudes and feelings, the group enters a conflict phase. Through continued interaction, the members' attitudes and behaviors become more similar and the group enters a balance phase. The following boxed material illustrates the effect of norms on individual behavior.

GROUP NORMS

Williams and Huber (1986) provide the following examples to illustrate how norms express the collective values of members of a group and provide guidelines that ensure the successful achievement of the goals of the group.

Group A consists of 15 employees who work in a chemical plant. The nature of their jobs provides little chance for promotion. They rotate over three shifts and are primarily involved in loading ships with pelletized fertilizer. The following norms are of central importance to this group:

1. One employee shall not exert so much effort that other employees appear to be unproductive by comparison.

2. When an employee is unable to perform well because of a hangover or fatigue, others will cover for that individual; however, abuse of the sick-day privilege will not be tolerated.
3. Employees will not discuss with management anything derogatory about another group member.
4. Employees will not express favorable attitudes toward management and the company in general.

The norms of Group A stand in stark contrast to those of Group B. Group B consists of 11 people in an information-processing center of the same plant in which the Group A employees work. Each looks forward to promotion into a higher position. Promotion decisions are usually made on the combined basis of seniority, competence, and ability to adopt a managerial perspective. Group B reflects a need for nondestructive, internal competition. The following are among its most obvious norms:

1. Taking the initiative with executives in order to be selected is taboo.
2. It is never permissible to make remarks or stimulate rumors that may interfere with a peer's promotion, even though the remarks or rumors are true.
3. Poor productivity and poor quality work from anyone capable of high performance is unacceptable because it reflects negatively on the group.
4. An employee does not recommend friends or acquaintances to fill vacancies unless they fit the model required to maintain the favorable image the group enjoys. (p. 158)

Group Influence on Individual Behavior

People often behave differently in the presence of a group than they behave when alone. Being in the presence of a group affects individual behavior in a number of different ways. Social facilitation, shift toward polarization, deindividuation, and bystander apathy are some of the ways individual behavior is affected by the presence of a group that are described in this section.

What is the social facilitation phenomenon?

Social Facilitation. In general, the presence of a group increases the rate or level of individual performance—a phenomenon called **social facilitation.** There seems to be an increased motivation to perform. Researchers have found (Zajonc, 1965) that the presence of others engaged in a similar activity increases the motivational level and the anxiety level of the individual (see

Figure 14–3). Under conditions of increased motivation, people who generally perform effectively perform even better. This increased arousal results in faster working and greater productivity for a person than when the individual is less motivated or less aroused. However, if a person should happen to be more highly motivated or experience an anxiety level higher than his or her optimum level, performance may not improve and may even decrease. Sometimes an individual may have so much fear of evaluation from those present that he or she becomes extremely anxious.

Figure 14–3.
Researchers have found that the presence of others engaged in a similar activity increases the rate or level of individual performance.

What is the shift toward polarization?

Shift Toward Polarization. An individual may shift to a more extreme position when making a decision in the presence of a group than when making a decision alone. In other words, an individual is usually more willing to make riskier decisions as a member of a group than when alone—the **risky-shift phenomenon.** Also, an individual is willing to make an even more conservative decision when in a group than when alone—the **stingy-shift phenomenon.** This tendency of people to shift to a more extreme position when making decisions in the presence of a group is called the **shift toward polarization** (Lamm & Myers, 1978).

What are the conditions for the shift toward polarization to occur?

Mere presence of a group does not seem to be the only condition required for the shift to occur. Research on this shift toward polarization indicates that two additional conditions must be present: group discussion and the expression of different initial opinions. A consistent finding in research (Wrightsman, 1977) is that group decisions made following discussion and the expression of different initial opinions will usually be more extreme in the same direction as the average preferences of the individual group members prior to the discussion (see Figure 14–4). When most members of a group are leaning toward taking a risk, the group takes an even riskier position than the average degree of risk that the individual members are willing to take. When most members of a group are leaning toward being conservative, the group takes an even more conservative position than the average conservativeness of the individual members. Once an individual participates in a group decision that is more extreme than his or her initial position, that individual retains a more extreme position than his or her initial position.

What explanations for the shift toward polarization have been offered?

Several explanations for the shift toward polarization have been offered. One explanation is that increased familiarity with the issues occurs during discussion, and the strength of the information that emerges in the discussion is the source of the shift. Maybe those group members who support extreme views simply provide more information favoring their views. This explanation has not received much research support and, therefore, is not a widely accepted theory. Another explanation is that members of a group who dare to have more extreme views initially also tend to be more dominant and exert more influence over other group members than those who are less daring and, thus, less dominant (Marquis, 1962). Research findings have not consistently supported this explanation either. A third explanation is that there is a **diffusion of responsibility**—no one individual is responsible for the decision of the group. When a single individual decides on a course of action that ends in failure, that individual alone bears the total responsibility for the failure. If, however, a course of action decided on by a group ends in failure, the responsibility for the failure is shared among all the members of the group. Fourth, the shift toward polarization is explained by some psychologists in terms of social value (Brown, 1965). Because our culture values daring behavior, most people want to be at least as daring as the average person and usually perceive themselves as being daring. When they realize through group discussion that their positions are not as daring as they had perceived them to be, they are willing to shift to a position that will fit their perceived self-image. In other words, when the group norm is learned through discussion, group members conform to the new perception of the norm. This theory seems to have the most research support.

Figure 14–4.
If each member of a committee holds a mildly liberal view, the committee decision will most likely be very liberal. If each member of the committee holds a mildly conservative view, the committee decision will most likely be very conservative.

What is meant by the term *deindividuation?*

Deindividuation. When a person feels submerged in a group, that person does not feel that he or she is responding as an individual. That person loses his or her distinctive personality and adopts a perceived group personality. The individual sets his or her own personality aside. This phenomenon is referred to as **deindividuation** and is most often explained by the diffusion of responsibility theory and by identification. A group identification rather than an individual identification exists. As a member of the group, the person may have a feeling of anonymity as an individual. A deindividuated person loses his or her inhibitions. The person is more likely to express emotions and behave affectionately, show joy or sorrow, behave aggressively, or release feelings of anger and hostility (Zimbardo, 1969). People have a tendency to act differently in a group setting than when they are alone (see Figure 14–5). Mob behavior can partly be explained by the deindividuation phenomenon. The larger the group, the more the members become deindividuated.

Figure 14–5.
Mob behavior can partly be explained by the deindividuation phenomenon.

What accounts for the phenomenon of bystander apathy?

Bystander Apathy. Logically, a person may reason that if a group of people is present in a time of need, help is more likely to occur. Often, however, a person in need of help is ignored by bystanders or passersby. Research suggests that the presence of a group actually inhibits rather than facilitates helping (Latané & Darley, 1970). Several factors such as diffusion of responsibility, modeling, deindividuation, and fear seem to account for this phenomenon called **bystander apathy.** Because of the diffusion of responsibility that exists in a group, individual members of a group of bystanders may not feel a personal responsibility to help. Additionally, the presence of others who are not helping sets the norm for the behavior of the other members of the bystander group. Usually a member of a group conforms to the norms of the group. Deindividuation decreases the likelihood that members of the group will feel guilty about not helping. When deindividuated, a member of a group loses his or her inhibitions for behaving in an unacceptable manner. Fear of embarrassment seems to increase with the number of people present who could observe any attempts at assistance and any blunders that are made. Thus, the presence of a group affects helping behavior also in that there is a relationship between the number of people who are present when a call for help is made and the likelihood that assistance will be offered (see Figure 14–6).

Figure 14–6.
A relationship has been found to exist between the number of people who are present when a call for help is made and the likelihood that assistance will be offered.

Group Performance

The efficiency of a group compared with the efficiency of a person working alone has been studied by psychologists. The findings are relevant to behavior in work situations. Logically, a person may reason that a group of people would be more efficient and thus more productive than a single individual. Two heads are better than one is an axiom often quoted and is often the basis for forming committees. However, in some situations, a group effort may be less efficient than a person working alone. Some factors that affect the efficiency of group performance and the type of thinking that occurs within a group that affects group performance are discussed in this section.

What factors affect the efficiency of a group?

Factors Affecting Group Efficiency. Several factors such as the size of the group, the nature of the task, the composition of the group, the climate in which the group functions, and the style of leadership affect the efficiency of the performance of a group. The size of the group has been shown to affect group performance; however, different ideas exist about what is the ideal size. Studies of group size and performance have led to some conclusions. The larger the group, the greater the possibility for interpersonal conflict. Smaller groups have been shown to be more creative, to express more ideas, to have a higher level of morale, and to need less supervision (Harari & Kaplan, 1982). **Parallel coaction tasks** are tasks in which each member of the group is involved in a completely separate function and works independently but parallel. In parallel coaction tasks, the larger the size of the group, the more work that gets done. In tasks that require group interaction and cooperation, larger groups may accomplish more than smaller groups, but not always. A person seems to work less when there are many to do the work (see Figure 14–7). A member of a group is not always aware that individual effort is decreased with an increase in the size of the group.

Figure 14–7.
As more people become available for a collective task, the effort of each individual usually declines. Each of these people would probably push harder if the others were not helping.

Even though increasing the size of the group may produce a gain in efficiency when interaction and cooperation are required, a point will finally be reached where no further gain is made by increasing the size of the group. For example, one person working alone might require 4 hours to complete a task, and two people cooperating as a group may be able to complete the task in 1 hour (2 hours of total work time required), producing as much in half the time. Three people cooperating on the task as a group may be able to complete the task in 40 minutes (2 hours of total work time required), but there is no change in the total hours of work required to complete the task. The task may be completed in 30 minutes by increasing the size of the group to 10 (5 hours of total work time required), but one more hour of work time would be used than for one person working alone to complete the task, which would be a decrease in production efficiency. The principle of least group size states that the optimum group size for the performance of tasks requiring group interaction is the minimum number of individuals required to make available to the group all the requirements for performance of the task.

What is the principle of least group size?

The composition of the group also affects performance. Groups composed of individuals who are compatible in terms of needs, beliefs, age, sex, seniority, marital status, or other characteristics show higher morale and productivity than groups composed of individuals who are not compatible. A high degree of satisfaction and productivity is often displayed in groups composed of friends. Sometimes, however, in groups composed of friends, socializing may interfere with performance. Of course, the abilities of the members of the group as well as the sex of the members affect the performance of the group. In a research study comparing the performance of all-male groups, all-female groups, and mixed-sex groups, the mixed-sex groups performed better than the same-sex groups when incompatibility on variables other than sex were controlled by random sampling (Hoffman & Maier, 1961).

The climate in which a group functions affects the productivity of the group. One example of a work climate is the type of leadership under which productivity occurs. One study compared the effects of the leadership climate on productivity by using three groups of 10-year-old boys as subjects (Lippit, 1940). Each group was supervised by an adult leader. In one group, the leader was dictatorial, gave personal criticism, and did not actively participate with the group except when giving instructions. In another group, the leader acted more like a member of the group than an authority figure, held group discussions to aid in decision making, allowed members some freedoms such as choosing a working partner, gave praise, and gave criticism objectively—a participative type of leadership. In the third group, the leader just did not function. Complete freedom was given, and the members were neither praised nor criticized. Each type of leadership was rotated from one group of boys to another group every 6 weeks for a specified period of time. Productivity was highest with the groups functioning in a dictatorial climate but only when the leader was present. Also, members of such groups tended to be either destructive and hostile or meek and submissive. In the climate in which the leader did not function and complete freedom was given, production was lowest and there was little satisfaction and a lot of horseplay. In the climate in which the leader acted more like a member of the group than an authority figure, held discussions, allowed some freedoms, and gave praise, the production was steady, even when the leader was not present, and members tended to be friendly and content.

How does the leadership climate in which a group functions affect productivity?

The general leadership style, classified by whether the leader is task oriented or social/emotional oriented, affects group perfor-

How do task- and social/emotional-oriented leadership styles differ?

mance (Bales, 1970). A task-oriented leadership style is all business, and the concern is for getting the job done quickly and efficiently. Social/emotional-oriented leaders are concerned with getting the job done, but their primary concern is to maintain a climate of friendliness among members of the group and to foster good feelings. On a short-term basis, the task-oriented leadership style is usually more productive; however, on a long-term basis, the social/emotional leadership style is usually more productive.

What is meant by the term *groupthink?*

Groupthink. One of the advantages of a group decision is that the expertise necessitated by a decision that requires specialized information is more likely to be available in a group. Likewise, the biases, prejudices, and unconscious motives of some individuals may be counteracted by the insights of others in a group. Psychologist Irving Janis (1972) made a study of disastrous group decisions and argues that group decision making may be inefficient. **Groupthink** is the term Janis uses to describe the type of thinking that occurs when people make decisions as a cohesive group based on a compulsion to maintain unanimity and each other's approval to the extent that critical, realistic thinking does not occur. In a cohesive group, members concede to the needs of the group rather than to the satisfaction of individual needs; the satisfaction of individual needs puts the group in a conflict stage. Group cohesiveness was found to be the major factor in groupthink (Janis, 1972). The more cohesive a group, the greater the members' tendency to rationalize or intellectualize the decisions of the group. Rationalizing or intellectualizing by members of the group results in the illusion that the group is invulnerable and should not be influenced by outsiders. Also, the more cohesive the group, the more pressure that may be applied on dissenting members to conform. Individual members of such groups are not likely to take positions in decision making that would threaten the unity of the group. This may lead to inferior and often disastrous decisions.

How may groupthink be prevented?

A number of suggestions have been made for preventing groupthink (Janis & Mann, 1977). They are the following:

1. Group leaders should encourage and reinforce the expression of doubts, fears, objections, or criticisms as an accepted part of a member's role in the group.
2. Group leaders should refrain from stating their own opinions first. The leader may divide the group into several small subgroups to reach tentative decisions, and then have a discussion on the differences in ideas and decisions reached in the small groups.

3. Qualified outsiders' opinions should be brought into the group. The outsiders may meet with the group, or members of the group may be encouraged to seek opinions from outsiders they know and whose judgments they value.
4. At least one member of a group should be assigned the role of devil's advocate to challenge the majority's decision.
5. After a decision has been made, the group should hold a "second chance" meeting to reevaluate and voice any afterthoughts or misgivings and to reaffirm the decision.

COMMUNICATION

Communication is an important aspect of group processes because it is the means of social interaction (see Figure 14–8). Individuals, usually leaders, speak for groups, and individual members within a group communicate with each other. The positions people hold in groups, the roles they play in groups, and the power they have to influence groups depend considerably on their ability to communicate. Achieving effective communication in groups is not easy. Large firms usually have flowcharts that clearly specify how and with whom members of the group are to communicate. In small and informal groups, role relationships usually determine the communication patterns. Patterns of group communication and transactional analysis, a system for analyzing the transactions (basic units of communication) in individual-to-individual relationships, are described in this section.

Figure 14–8. Communication is an important aspect of group processes because it is the means of social interaction.

Patterns of Group Communication

Patterns of communication provide an index of the distribution of power and status in groups, determine operational efficiency, and are an important factor in the morale of the group members. Communication patterns in groups may be classified according to directional flow, basic structure, and whether the communication link is a formal one or an informal one.

What is a downward, an upward, and a horizontal communication?

Directional Patterns. In organized groups, messages may flow downward, upward, or horizontally. Downward communication involves conveying messages from higher level positions to lower level positions. For example, a department supervisor may convey a message from the division supervisor to his or her subordinates. A building contractor giving a performance evaluation to a construction crew supervisor would be another example of a downward communication. Upward communication is the sending of messages from a lower level position to a higher level position. Examples of upward communication are the reporting of the malfunctioning of a machine to the supervisor and the supervisor reporting employee misconduct to the president of the firm. Horizontal communications consist of the exchange of information among employees at the same position level. Some people may be better at communicating in one direction than another. For example, a person may communicate well with his or her supervisor (upward), especially if motivated to advance to a higher job level. The same person, however, may not communicate as well with his or her peers (horizontal) or with lower level employees (downward).

Some communication problems that may interfere with these directional patterns of communication are fear of reprisal in giving upward communications to supervisors and the fact that, in downward communications, employees often take directions from their supervisors as an indication of displeasure with their work. Sometimes the unavailability of the supervisor hinders upward communication. The grouping of employees into different departments, buildings, or shifts particularly hinders horizontal communication (Sharma, 1979).

What are four basic communication structures in a group?

Basic Communication Structures. One of four basic communication structures seems to exist in any group regardless of whether the group is small or large, formal or informal. Generally, the more a basic structure allows a person to communicate with other people in the group, the greater the satisfaction that person will experience in the group (Leavitt, 1951). Also, the person at the center of the basic communication structure is named more frequently by the members of the group as the leader. Structures that are more centralized seem to be more effective when the operations are simple enough that the one person at the center can handle the directing. When the operations are very involved and complex and demand too much of the one person at the center, less centralized structures seem to be more effective.

The four basic structures of communication in groups are the wheel, the *Y*, the circle, and the chain (see Figure 14–9). The wheel communication structure is the most tightly centralized of the structures. In this pattern, all communication is channeled through one person. Communication flows from the hub of the wheel (the one person through which all communication is channeled), down the spokes (the members of the group), and back up the spokes to the hub. The wheel is the most typical structure and usually is the

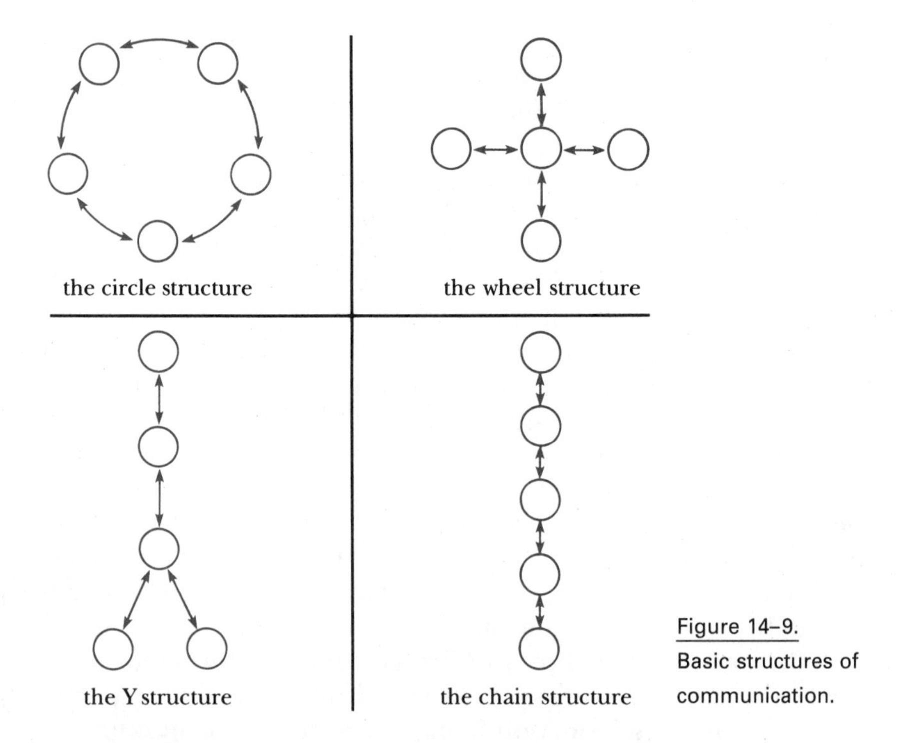

Figure 14–9.
Basic structures of communication.

most efficient for small groups. A wheel structure is illustrated in the football huddle with the quarterback representing the hub. Communication in the *Y* communication structure starts with one person and branches out like an inverted *Y*. The branches of the *Y* may branch out to form other inverted *Y* structures. The *Y* is the most typical structure of large groups, and it is usually the most efficient. Although less centralized than the wheel, it is still tightly centralized. The *Y* structure is illustrated in a group with a president, a vice president who reports to the president, directors of sales, manufacturing, and finance who report to the vice president, and several department heads who report to the directors. In the circle communication structure, all members of the group tend to be equal, and communication circulates through the group. Although not the most efficient for problem solving, the circle pattern is especially effective in discussion groups. The circle is the least centralized of the basic structures. No person controls communication more than another person. The chain communication structure is often less effective than other structures because a person only communicates with the people next to him or her, and the people on either end of the chain communicate with only one other person. If a group is seated in a straight line and messages are sent back and forth from a person in the group to another person in the group by way of the line, a chain communication structure is being used.

What are two common ways messages get transmitted informally to group members?

Informal Communication Links. Messages get transmitted to group members in many informal ways that are not designated on a flowchart or according to a structured pattern. Two common ways are through the grapevine and through an information hub (DuBrin, 1981). A source of information that comes by bypassing someone in the official structure of communication is referred to as the **grapevine.** Research indicates that information travels faster by the grapevine than through formal communication systems and that the higher a person's position in the group's structure of communication, the more information he or she receives through the grapevine. Although the information transmitted through the grapevine is not always correct, neither is the information transmitted through official patterns (Sutton & Porter, 1968). Rumors usually travel by way of the grapevine.

Usually one individual in a group gets more information than others. Such a person comes to be relied on to know everything and is known as an **information hub.** A person may be an information hub because of his or her position or role in the organization. For example, the secretary or social friend of the person in the center of the wheel communication structure would be an information hub. Sometimes a sympathetic listener who hears a lot or a very knowledgeable person who learns a lot by being consulted can be an information hub.

Transactional Analysis

What is transactional analysis?

Transactional analysis, a theory of communication, is based on the premise that people can learn to understand themselves and other people and to improve their interpersonal relations by analyzing the basic units of communication in individual-to-individual relationships. The concept was originated by Eric Berne (1961) for use as a psychotherapy technique to help people improve their lives. Transactional analysis is also a theory of communication that provides the supervisor, the subordinate, the customer, the salesperson, the employer, and the employee with the tools for improving the way they communicate with people both on and off the job. A knowledge of transactional analysis and its characteristic terms will help a person understand why he or she says certain things and why other people say the things they do.

Strokes and Stamps. Transactional analysis is based on the reinforcement principle of motivation—the fact that people need to be recognized and need to maintain a positive self-image, good self-concept, and high self-esteem. Any communication that recognizes an individual's existence such as "Good morning, Pat" is called a **stroke.** Different types of strokes may be given. For example, a positive stroke causes a person to feel good about himself or herself, and a negative stroke causes a person to feel badly about the self. A **discount** is either a stroke that is less positive than it should be or a stroke not delivered. For example, a worker may be ignored when he or she arrives on the job site or when he or she completes a task. Or the person may not be given full credit for something when full credit is due. Mixed strokes have both positive and negative aspects such as in the following: "That's an excellent rate of responding (positive stroke) for a person as slow as you (negative stroke)."

What are some types of strokes?

A feeling that is collected from a stroke is called a **stamp.** Stamps build up over a period of time. In other words, people collect stamps. Good feelings are gold stamps and bad feelings are brown stamps. There are different kinds of stamps for different specific feelings such as red stamps for anger and yellow stamps for cowardice. Everybody collects stamps; however, because it seems that most people have a tendency to give more negative strokes than positive strokes, more brown stamps are collected. People also seek out situations to increase their stamp collections if they are trying to collect a particular kind of stamp. The stamps a person collects are "cashed in" whenever enough have been collected and the person is ready to do so. Doing favors, giving compliments, rewards, or promotions, and working overtime are examples of some ways employees cash in gold stamps. Being tardy or absent, stealing, having an accident, and quitting a job are examples of some ways employees may cash in brown stamps. In order to improve human relations on the job or anywhere else, a person must stop collecting brown stamps (negative feelings) or any color of negative stamp such as red stamps (anger) and also must avoid giving any negative colored stamps to anyone who is trying to collect them. The way to prevent the cashing in of brown stamps is to not have any to be cashed in.

What are some types of stamps?

How are gold stamps and brown stamps "cashed in"?

A person who works and communicates with others on a job especially needs to become aware of the kinds of strokes co-workers try to get and give. People have a tendency to trade stamps. If a person gives negative strokes and thus brown stamps,

How may human relations be improved using transactional analysis?

that person will most likely receive negative stamps in return. If a person gives positive strokes and thus gold stamps, that person will most likely receive positive strokes in return. If a person discounts (does not stroke), negative strokes will be received in return because people usually prefer a stroke of some kind to nothing at all and react negatively to not receiving a stroke. The implication is that positive strokes must be given for any performance if human relations are to be improved. If positive strokes are not given for good performance, the good performance will cease and poor performance will replace it. People seeking negative strokes will give negative strokes and play psychological games to get them. Another condition for improving human relations is to avoid playing psychological games (described in a later paragraph) with those individuals who are using psychological games to get negative strokes and to avoid giving a negative stroke in return for a negative stroke. Poor performance must be stroked in some way other than negatively for it to cease, such as through the use of extinction or through the use of reinforcement to shape more satisfactory performance.

What are three categories of life scripts?

Life Scripts. A person's general attitudes about life begin to be formed in infancy and are important in determining the behavior or personality of that person throughout his or her lifetime. According to the theory of transactional analysis, people (or groups, such as a family or work organization) have **life scripts** that consist of the affective element of the attitudes held by the person concerning such things as success, work, sex, love, education, and religion. Life scripts, usually unconscious to the person, are lifetime plans that are like the script for a play. They are written before they are acted out. Life scripts are differentiated into three general categories: (a) the *winner,* who communicates openly, honestly, and easily and gets along well with other people; (b) the *loser,* who plays games, does not communicate openly, honestly, and easily, and does not get along well with other people; and (c) the *nonwinner,* who sometimes communicates openly, is sincere, and sometimes gets along well with others but very often does not. It is estimated that approximately 25 percent of a person's life script is determined between the ages of 6 and 20 (Higgins, 1982). Relationships are sought with other individuals in groups such as in marriage, social groups, and work groups to obtain specific kinds of strokes to play out life scripts. These unconscious lifetime plans usually do not change unless there is some environmental condition that causes the life script to be rewritten.

Life Positions. Self-esteem is the attitude or feeling a person has about the self. A person also has an attitude or feeling about people in general. Transactional analysis proposes that there are four **life positions,** attitudes or feelings about the self and others, that a person may hold and act out: (a) I'm not OK—You're OK (the position of the very young child and often the position of subordinates), (b) I'm OK—You're not OK (the position of prejudiced or angry individuals); (c) I'm not OK—You're not OK (usually the position of losers and individuals who are a menace to society); and (d) I'm OK—You're OK (the position of well-adjusted individuals and the position of winners). Most people have a position that tends to prevail throughout their later childhood and adult life, and as with life scripts, a life position is the basis for many interactions with people. A person seeks strokes to support his or her life position. Life positions have a tendency to persist; however, they may shift under certain environmental conditions.

What are four life positions a person may hold?

Ego States. An individual's personality is viewed in transactional analysis as consisting of three parts or ego states—the Parent, the Adult, and the Child (see Figure 14–10). The **Parent ego state** consists of values, opinions, dos and don'ts, shoulds and should nots, and stored memories of statements and actions of parents and authority figures. The Parent ego state is the criticizer and/or nurturer. The Parent ego state has a place in a worker's personality, but if it becomes too dominant in interactions with others, problems in human relations may arise.

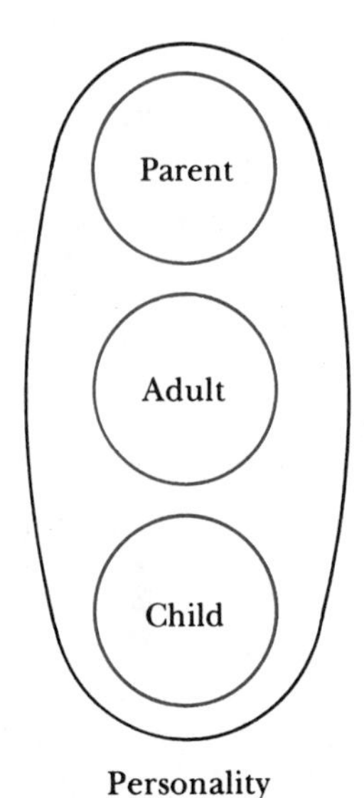

Personality

Figure 14–10.
Ego states of the personality according to transactional analysis theory.

The **Adult ego state** consists of the knowledge, logical reasoning, rational thinking, and information processing of the individual. The Adult is the manager of the Parent and Child states. The Adult state is the decision maker, the builder of self-esteem, and the problem solver. The Adult may dominate in well-adjusted individuals, but not to the extent that the Parent and the Child states are excluded.

The **Child ego state** is made up of the feelings about everything the person has experienced and the person's current feelings. Feelings, of course, trigger behaviors. The source of openness, manipulation, spontaneity, sensuality, affection, creativity, happiness, rebellion, intuition, and hostility is in the Child ego state. The Child is the manipulator, the adapter to demands of authority and power by use of defense mechanisms learned to survive childhood, and the expresser of the healthy, natural, spontaneous emotions.

According to transactional analysis, what is the source of a maladaptive personality?

When an individual communicates with another person, he or she speaks or acts from one of the ego states. Understanding which ego state expressions are coming from and are directed toward will help a person communicate more effectively, respond more appropriately to others, and recognize a maladaptive personality. A maladaptive personality is one in which an ego state is overly dominant or exists in too small an amount. Diagrams of some maladaptive personalities are shown in Figure 14–11.

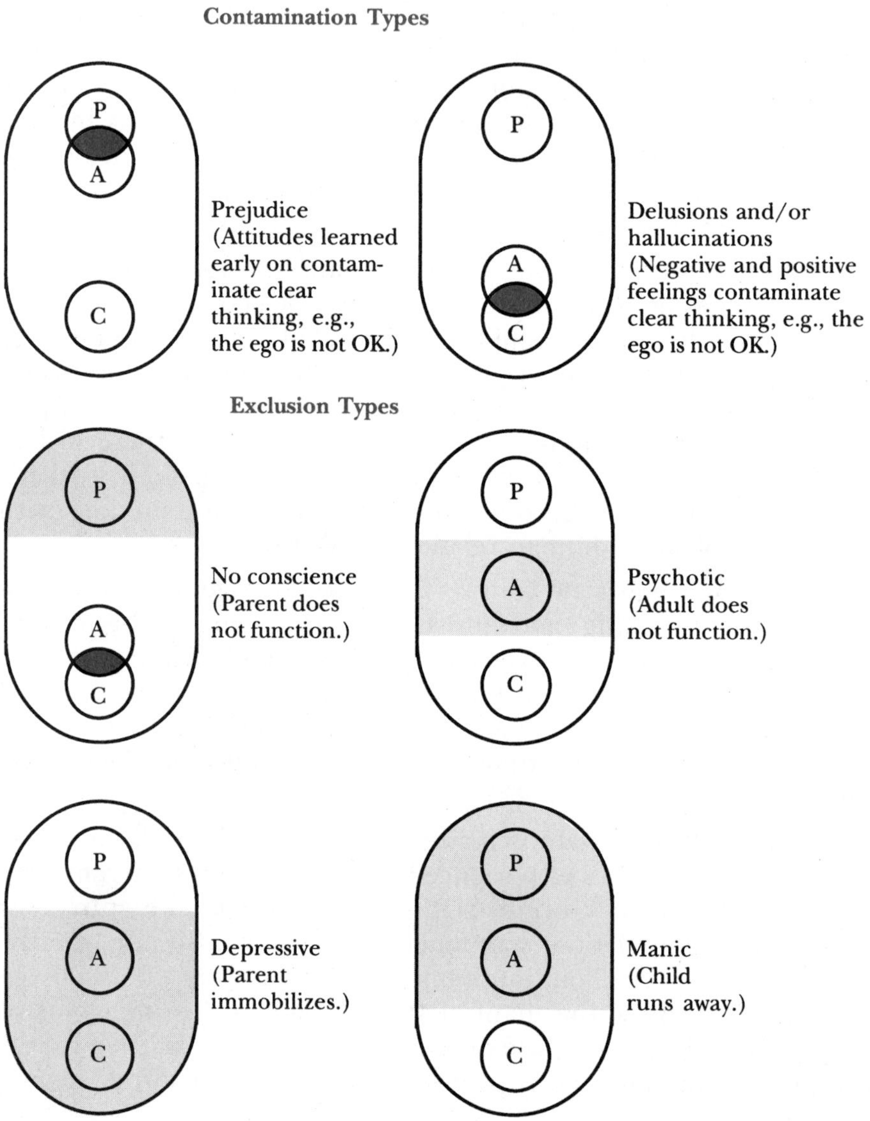

Contamination Types

Prejudice
(Attitudes learned early on contaminate clear thinking, e.g., the ego is not OK.)

Delusions and/or hallucinations
(Negative and positive feelings contaminate clear thinking, e.g., the ego is not OK.)

Exclusion Types

No conscience
(Parent does not function.)

Psychotic
(Adult does not function.)

Depressive
(Parent immobilizes.)

Manic
(Child runs away.)

Figure 14–11.
Diagrams of some maladaptive personalities based on transactional analysis theory, which proposes that functional and content differences of the ego states account for personality differences.

Transactions. Analyzing the structure of social interaction is basic to using transactional analysis to improve communication. A social interaction that consists of a statement or stimulus directed toward a person and that person's response is a **transaction.** Three basic types of transactions may occur: (a) complementary, (b) crossed, and (c) ulterior (see Figure 14–12). In **complementary transactions,** sometimes called parallel transactions, the response is sent back to the same ego state from which the stimulus was received and is sent from the same ego state to which the stimulus was sent. For example, one person may say to another person, "You shouldn't drink so much coffee" and the reply may be one of obedience, "Ok, I'll start drinking only one cup each morning for breakfast." The comment came from the Parent and was directed to the Child. The reply came from the Child and was directed to the Parent. Thus, the transaction was a complementary one. This type of transaction may go on indefinitely.

What are three basic types of transactions?

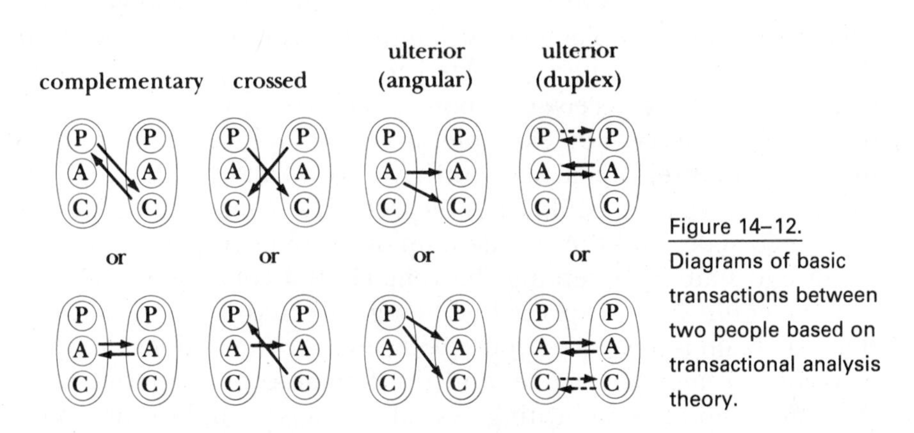

Figure 14–12. Diagrams of basic transactions between two people based on transactional analysis theory.

In **crossed transactions,** the response does not come back to the ego state from which the stimulus was sent, nor does it come back from the ego state the stimulus was directed toward. If the reply to the preceding statement had been, "Well, you shouldn't put so much salt on your food," a crossed transaction would have occurred. The reply came from the Parent, not the Child it was directed to, and was directed to the Child, not the Parent from which it came. In crossed transactions, disagreement is present and either conversation on the topic ends or Child-to-Child negative complementary transactions occur. A crossed transaction may be used to stop psychological games. For example, an employee may ask a supervisor for an evaluation of a task just completed, making the request from the Adult ego state and directing it to the Parent ego state, unconsciously trying to hook the supervisor into giving a criticizing response (a negative stroke). If the supervisor does not respond back from the Parent ego state with a "you should have" (a complementary transaction) but instead responds from the Adult ego state with an objective evaluation and praise for all the aspects of the task that are well done (a crossed transaction), the employee lost at the game. Eventually, if the supervisor continues to respond with a crossed transaction, the asking for an evaluation of tasks just completed may cease.

What are two types of ulterior transactions?

Ulterior transactions are complementary transactions or messages with a hidden meaning. In **duplex ulterior transactions,** the words have unspoken meanings that are understood by both the sender and receiver. The hidden meanings may be conveyed through body language, social context, or tone of voice. In **angular ulterior transactions,** the message sent can be interpreted by the receiver as being directed toward either of two different ego states. Consequently, a complementary transaction is more likely to occur than when the message is directed to only one ego state because whichever one the receiver responds back from, the response will be complementary. For example, a male employee may say to a female employee, "That new outfit you're wearing today is really sharp!" The remark could be interpreted as being directed to the Adult ego state, and the female employee could respond from the Adult ego state by accepting the remark as a compliment. Or the remark could be interpreted as being directed to the Child ego state to obtain a feeling response with sexual connotations or anger to receive a negative stroke, and the female could respond from the Child ego state indicating sexual feelings or indicating anger aroused by the remark.

What are psychological games?

Psychological Games. A game consists of a set or series of ulterior transactions that occurs repeatedly, has a predetermined end, and has well-defined psychological strokes. A game may be either of two types. In one type, a person manages to get another person to give him or her a negative stroke. In the second type, a person tricks others into letting him or her give them negative strokes. A con is part of both types of games, but a con will not succeed unless it can hook into a weakness. All games are not completely undesirable, but all are time-consuming and wasteful, involve deceitful communication, and lower someone's self-esteem. Games cause poor communication and hide real feelings. To improve communication, games should not be played. An effective technique to help a person stop playing games is for the person to become aware of the games he or she becomes involved in and then prevent the initiator of the game from giving or receiving a negative stroke. Workers will benefit from becoming aware of the games they and those they work with play.

What are ways in which people may spend their time in social interaction?

Time Structuring. People spend their time in physical activities, in mental activities, and in social interactions. In social interaction, time may be spent in the following five ways:

1. *Intimacy* is time spent with another person communicating openly, expressing genuine feelings, and developing a growing relationship in an atmosphere that is free of games.
2. *Games* are time spent communicating with another person in a deceitful way (as in ulterior transactions) in order to obtain positive or negative strokes.
3. *Pastimes* are times spent in transactions that have no particular meaning and literally pass the time. They intuitively let an individual know with whom he or she can be intimate or play games.
4. *Rituals* are time spent in stylized exchanges that require no thought to be performed such as "How are you" and the reply "I'm fine." They are programmed by tradition and custom.
5. *Withdrawal* is time spent in any process or activity that avoids communicating with others. Withdrawal may include daydreaming, sleeping excessively, or watching television excessively.

LEADERSHIP

Progress does not come from traits and abilities but from the organization that humans impose on themselves by creating groups. The creation and maintenance of organization depends "more on the quality of leadership than any other single event" (London, 1978, p. 573). A leader has been defined in many ways; however, a leader is generally defined as the "group member who has the most influence on the other group members" (Seidenberg & Snadowsky, 1976, p. 426). The concern in this section is with approaches to studying leadership and leadership effectiveness.

Approaches to the Study of Leadership

What are three approaches to the study of leadership?

Three approaches to the study of leadership in formal groups have emerged: (a) the trait approach, which is concerned with the traits or characteristics of the leader; (b) the style approach, which focuses on methods and techniques used; and (c) the situational approach, which looks at the influence of environmental factors. The question is whether traits, styles, situations, or a combination of these produces leaders (see Figure 14–13).

Figure 14–13.
Do traits, styles, situations, or a combination of these produce leaders?

Trait Approach. The trait approach to studying leadership was popular at one time; however, this approach has practically vanished because it does not explain much about why relationships between some traits and leadership occurred. For example, research studies have shown leaders, compared with others, to be taller, more attractive in physical appearance, more domineering, more confident, more extroverted, more intelligent, and better adjusted psychologically (Gibb, 1969). The primary problem with this approach has been that individual traits do not predict who will become a leader, and a specific trait may not be found in leaders of all groups and situations. Intelligence, dominance, verbal fluency, and adjustment are traits found in leaders that are common to more groups and situations than other traits. **Charisma** seems to refer to some magnetic quality that has the mysterious ability to draw people to a person and to allow that person to control them. Many people associate charisma with leadership, but the term is too elusive to define objectively enough for research.

How do authoritarian, participative, and permissive styles of leadership differ?

Style Approach. The basic styles that have been identified as being used by leaders are autocratic or authoritarian, democratic or participative, and laissez-faire or permissive. Authoritarian leaders centralize the power in themselves, make the decisions for the group, and do not allow the members of the group to participate in the decision-making process. With this type of leadership, members of the group become increasingly dependent on the leader, and the leader becomes indispensable to the group. Participative leaders share their power with other members of the group and allow decisions to be made by the consensus of the group. Although the participative leader has as much power as an authoritative leader, the power is used differently; it is used to obtain input from the group members. Participative leaders function in the interest of the group rather than in their own best interests. Laissez-faire or permissive leaders, on the other hand, have power over the group but they do not exercise it. They are passive and allow the members of the group to make their own decisions.

Because the laissez-faire or permissive style cannot be considered as true leadership, leadership styles fall on a continuum somewhere between extremely authoritarian and extremely democratic. The positions along the leadership continuum are as follows:

1. The leader decides and then announces decisions to the group.
2. The leader decides and then persuades the group to accept and support his or her decisions.
3. The leader presents ideas to and encourages questions from the group regarding a decision.
4. The leader presents tentative ideas subject to change by the group.
5. The leader presents alternatives from which the group makes a decision.
6. The leader establishes boundaries within which the group selects alternatives and makes a decision.

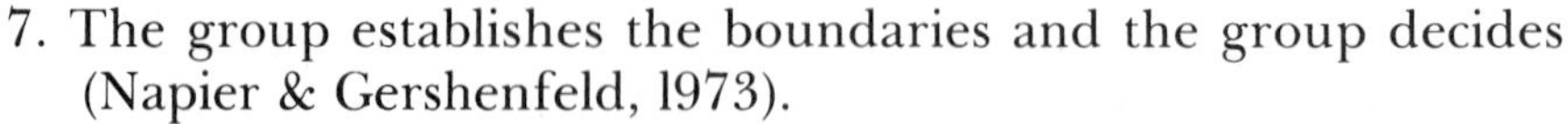

7. The group establishes the boundaries and the group decides (Napier & Gershenfeld, 1973).

What is the basic assumption of the situational approach to studying leadership?

Situational Approach. The basic assumption in the situational approach to studying leadership is that special skills and competence appropriate to the goals of the group identify the leader. In other words, the particular task and particular situation determine the leader—a person emerges as a leader by happening to be in the right place at the right time. According to this theory, a person may be a leader in one group or at one time and a follower in another group or at another time. One situation that seems to be a factor related to the emergence of a leader is how much control the person has on the flow of communication—the more centralized the person's position in the communication structure, the more likely the person is to become a leader.

Informal Group Leadership. Sometimes leadership in informal groups is studied. Although no one is usually assigned to a leadership position in informal groups and members of informal groups may not even be aware of leader-follower relationships, most groups have one person who plays an influential role in the activities of the group. Even in small groups of friends or in a family, one person in the group often acts as the leader. A leader may emerge in small groups spontaneously as immediate needs arise, and when the immediate need vanishes, the person's position as a leader may vanish with it.

Figure 14–14. Informal leaders often emerge such as when a worker who has highly specialized knowledge or skill comes to be respected as the authority on certain matters.

In work situations, informal group leaders often emerge. Williams and Huber (1986) point out some major roles played by informal group leaders: the representative to management, the technical expert, the information source, the enforcer, the tension reducer, and the crisis manager. A worker who has good communication skills and a great deal of self-confidence and courage may emerge to represent a group to management. A worker who has highly specialized knowledge or skill may come to be respected as the authority on matters of his or her expertise. (see Figure 14–14). One worker may have privileged information needed by the group and may be looked to for direction. Sometimes a co-worker in a group needs to be chastised and a behavior change effected. A member of the group may voluntarily come forth and use persuasion or muscle and thus come to be elevated in respect by the group. Sometimes a person's skill in reducing conflict in the group results in that person coming to be recognized as a key person. This person who emerges as a leader in the group may be the comic, philosopher, or human relations expert. A member of an informal group may emerge as a leader in some specific crisis situation such as when the group is threatened by some outside source.

Leadership Effectiveness

Several theories have been proposed to explain the effectiveness of those in leadership positions. The theories that are discussed in this section include those related to the style of leadership, the banking of idiosyncrasy credits, and contingencies.

Leadership Style. Leadership style refers to the pattern or constellation of leadership behaviors that characterize a given leader (Williams & Huber, 1986, p. 437). Usually a leader feels more comfortable using one particular style than using other styles. Also, a leader tends to be relatively consistent in the use of one particular style. Sometimes one style is more effective in a particular situation than another style; therefore, the effectiveness of a particular leader varies from one situation to another.

An autocratic or authoritarian style of leadership has a tendency to foster negative feelings in members of the group. These negative feelings may be expressed openly in rebellious behaviors such as overt hostility and the destruction of property, may be repressed through the use of defense mechanisms such as denial, or may be expressed in indirect ways such as dropping out of the group. Charismatic leadership is a variation of the authoritarian style in which the leader thinks of the self as having superior attributes and expects subordinates to show reverence and personal loyalty as well as obedience. The actual quality of the leader's decisions are never put to the test to determine whether they are inferior. Paternalism is another variation of the authoritarian style in which the leader assumes the role of a father responsible for the welfare of the children (the subordinates). Fringe benefits and welfare programs are expressions of this style of leadership, which ultimately result in reducing employees to the role of dependents and which can be withdrawn anytime employees fail to comply with demands of the leader.

What are two variations of the authoritarian style of leadership?

The democratic or participative style of leadership has a tendency to lead to greater satisfaction, motivation, and cohesiveness among members of the group than do other styles of leadership, which in turn leads to greater achievement. In some situations, however, such as when a quick decision is needed, the participative style may be less efficient.

In general, what are the results of participative and permissive leadership?

In general, the result of laissez-faire leadership, sometimes called free-reign or permissive leadership, is often chaos as various members attempt to lead in various directions. And, in general, groups under an authoritarian style of leadership, compared with groups under a participative style, have been found to make fewer errors, require less communication, and require less time to complete a job, all of which facilitate production.

Leadership styles are also classified as task oriented or social/emotional oriented. The task-oriented leader is concerned with efficiency and moving the group toward a goal, while the social/emotional-oriented leader is interested in reducing tension and building morale. If a leader plays both of these roles, he or she will be more effective than if only one of the roles is played.

What is the idiosyncrasy credit theory of leadership effectiveness?

Idiosyncrasy Credit. Idiosyncrasy credit is the label for the followers' perceptions of the leader—the sum total of positive impressions. One theory of leadership effectiveness suggests that effectiveness is related to the idiosyncrasy credit the leader builds up (Hollander, 1958). Positive impressions accrue to the leader through helping the group accomplish its goals and by conforming to the expectations or norms of the group. The leader loses credits by deviating from the norms of the group or by failing to accomplish the goals of the group. The more idiosyncrasy credit the leader builds up, the more effective he or she can be. This is because surplus credits allow the leader to deviate from the group norm and fail to accomplish a goal without reducing the followers' perceptions of the leader to the extent of rejection. The theory explains why some leaders can engage in idiosyncratic behavior and still be perceived as effective leaders by the members of the group.

Contingency Theory. Fred Fiedler (1967) proposed a contingency theory of leadership effectiveness. This theory views effective leadership as contingent on situational favorability—the degree to which the followers accept the way the leader uses power. Situational favorability is determined by three factors: (a) the degree of liking between the leader and followers (the more positive the personal feelings, the more favorable the situation); (b) the degree to which the task is structured (the higher the structure, the more favorable the situation); and (c) the leader's power (the stronger the power, the more favorable the situation).

What constitutes a favorable leadership situation for a leader?

In this theory, leadership style is defined as the extent to which a leader is task oriented versus relationship (social/emotional) oriented, and a relationship is considered to exist between the degree of esteem held for the least preferred co-worker (LPC) and leadership style (referred to as an LPC score). An LPC score is determined for the leader by having the leader rate the person liked least among all the people ever worked with. The least preferred co-worker is rated according to a list of bipolar adjectives. For example, one adjective might be *organized* to be rated on a scale from strong to weak. Research studies by Fiedler indicate that leaders who describe least preferred co-workers in favorable terms (high LPC) are relationship (social/emotional) oriented, and leaders who describe least preferred co-workers critically (low LPC) are task oriented. The higher the LPC score, the more the leadership style tends to be permissive, relaxed, nondirective, and concerned with group needs. The lower the LPC score, the more the leadership style tends to be autocratic or authoritarian and task oriented. Low-LPC leaders are more effective in either highly favorable or highly unfavorable situations; however, high-LPC leaders are more effective in moderately favorable situations. Although the assumption is usually made that years of experience as a leader are related to leadership effectiveness, this condition was not found by Fiedler to be a factor. The primary strength of the contingency theory is the specification of the conditions under which leaders will be most effective. Based on this theory and the research support for it, the conclusion has been drawn that no leader is effective in all situations.

How does Fiedler test to determine whether a leader is task oriented or relational (social/emotional) oriented?

SUMMARY

1. A group is a collection of individuals who interact with each other and share something in common. Most groups that come into existence serve a task-oriented and/or a socially-oriented function.
2. Some explanations for the formation of groups are that groups form to achieve a goal, to allow self-evaluations of the members, to provide emotional support, and to satisfy an unlimited number of needs such as the reduction of tension and boredom and the need for companionship.
3. Membership in some groups is conscripted—the members have no choice—and membership in some groups is acquired or achieved voluntarily.
4. The four-phase developmental sequence of group formation is the orientation phase, the conflict phase, the balance phase, and the part-

ing phase. The structure of a group may also be described by the positions, roles, and status of the members and by the norms of the group.

5. Being in the presence of a group has been found to cause an individual (a) to increase performance (social facilitation) and, because of diffusion of responsibility, to shift to a more extreme position in decision making (the risky-shift and stingy-shift phenomena); (b) to lose his or her distinctive personality (deindividuation); and (c) to be less willing to help in a time of need (bystander apathy).
6. Group performance has been found to be related to such factors as size, composition, climate, groupthink, and whether the task is a parallel coaction task or an interaction task. Groups are composed of members who are compatible or similar in some ways. On a short-term basis, groups that function under a dictatorial leadership are usually more productive. On a long-term basis, groups that function under a participative type of leadership are usually more productive.
7. Groupthink, the term for ineffective decision making in very cohesive groups that is thought to occur because of the compulsion to maintain unanimity and each other's approval, may be prevented if the group leader recognizes it and encourages such things as internal disagreements, outside opinions, and reevaluations.
8. Patterns of communication in a group provide an index of the distribution of power and status in the group. Communications flow upward to higher levels, downward to lower levels, and horizontally to peers.
9. The basic communication structures that may exist in a group, in the order of degree of centralization, are the wheel (the most centralized), the *Y*, the chain, and the circle. When operations are not too involved and complex for one person to handle, the more centralized structures seem to be the most effective; otherwise, the less centralized structures seem to be the most effective.
10. The grapevine and information hubs may transmit messages by bypassing someone in the official communication structure and thus make information travel faster.
11. Transactional analysis, a theory of communication explaining social interaction between individuals, uses unique, catchy terms to describe the principles. A stroke represents any communication that gives a person recognition; stamps are the feelings one gets from strokes. Stamps are collected, cashed in, and traded, and gold stamps (positive feelings) are better to give and to receive than brown stamps (negative feelings) for improving human relations.
12. According to transactional analysis, a person acts out the life script of either a winner, a loser, or a nonwinner based on unconscious attitudes formed early in life. Life scripts may explain many communications between individuals.

13. According to transactional analysis, how a person feels about the self and about other people in general determines a person's life position that may be any one of four positions: (a) I'm not OK—You're OK; (b) I'm OK—You're not OK; (c) I'm not OK—You're not OK; or (d) I'm OK—You're OK. Life positions may explain many communications between individuals.
14. According to transactional analysis, an individual's personality consists of three ego states—the Parent, the Child, and the Adult. Transactions (communications between two people) may be sent from any one of the ego states to any one of the ego states of the other person.
15. In complementary transactions, there is no conflict because the response is sent to the same ego state from which the message was received and the response is sent from the same ego state that received the message.
16. Crossed transactions produce conflict and occur when the response does not come back to the ego state that the message was sent from nor does it come back from the ego state the message was directed toward.
17. Ulterior transactions are complementary transactions with hidden meanings that are understood by both the sender and receiver (duplex) or messages that can be interpreted as being directed toward either of two different ego states (angular).
18. A psychological game is a set or series of ulterior transactions that a person uses repeatedly and that has a predetermined end and well-defined psychological payoffs (strokes). A game cons a person into giving the initiator a negative stroke or into letting the initiator give the person a negative stroke.
19. One of the ways people spend their time is in social interaction, which may be of several types: intimacy, games, pastimes, rituals, or withdrawal, which is avoidance of social interaction.
20. A leader is the member of a group who has the most influence over the other members of the group, either formally or informally. Three different approaches have emerged to study leadership: the trait approach, the style approach, and the situational approach.
21. Authoritarian, participative, and permissive styles of leadership have been identified. An authoritarian style has a tendency to foster negative feelings in members of the group whereas the participative style tends to lead to satisfaction, motivation, and cohesiveness. The permissive style often leads to chaos.
22. One leadership theory proposes that a leader can be more effective if he or she builds up more idiosyncrasy credit. The contingency theory of leadership effectiveness views effective leadership as contingent on (a) the degree of situational favorability, which consists of the degree of liking, task structure, and power; and (b) leadership style, which is determined by a score derived from rating the least preferred coworker (LPC).

KEY TERMS AND CONCEPTS

Group
Orientation phase
Conflict phase
Balance phase
Parting phase
Group position
Group role
Group status
Group norm
Social facilitation
Risky-shift phenomenon
Stingy-shift phenomenon
Shift toward polarization
Diffusion of responsibility
Deindividuation
Bystander apathy
Parallel coaction tasks
Groupthink
Grapevine
Information hub
Transactional analysis
Stroke
Discount
Stamp
Life scripts
Life positions
Parent ego state
Adult ego state
Child ego state
Transaction
Complementary transactions
Crossed transactions
Ulterior transactions
Duplex ulterior transactions
Angular ulterior transactions
Charisma
Idiosyncrasy credit

QUESTIONS FOR REVIEW

1. Why do groups form and individuals become members of groups, and what is (a) the sequence of group formation, (b) group position, (c) group role, (d) group status, and (e) group norm?
2. How does the presence of a group affect an individual's performance, decision making, helping of others, assuming of responsibility, and personality?
3. What are some factors and conditions that affect group performance?
4. What is groupthink, and how may it be prevented?
5. In a group, what are the three directional patterns of communication, the four basic structures, and two common informal communication links?
6. What is transactional analysis, and what are strokes and stamps, the three life scripts, the four life positions, the three ego states, transactions (complementary, crossed, and ulterior), psychological games, and five ways time may be spent in social interaction?
7. What three approaches to the study of leadership have emerged, and how do they differ?
8. What are three basic styles of leadership, and how do they differ?
9. How does the style of leadership and idiosyncrasy credit affect leadership effectiveness?
10. Who proposed a contingency theory of leadership effectiveness, and what is the theory?

TEST YOURSELF

1. A group, as defined by psychologists, consists of (a) a few people merely standing or sitting near each other (2) two or more people who interact with each other, share some common identity, and share some common goals or desires (c) a crowd of people merely standing or sitting near each other (d) both a and c.
2. Groups come into existence to serve the group members' social needs and/or to accomplish a task or goal. T or F
3. An individual may be a member of a group under the condition of (a) being conscripted into the group (b) acquiring membership (c) achieving membership (d) all of the above.
4. The second of the four-phase developmental sequence in the process of group formation is the ________________ phase.
5. The norms of a group consist of the (a) collective attitudes of the members (b) behaviors agreed upon by members (c) collective values of the members (d) all of the above.
6. The phenomenon of social facilitation refers to the (a) increase in individual performance as a result of being in the presence of a group (b) decrease in individual performance as a result of being in the presence of a group (c) increase in anxiety experienced as a result of being in the presence of a group (d) increase in motivation beyond the individual's optimum level of performance as a result of being in the presence of a group.
7. The shift toward polarization refers to the ________________ and the ________________ phenomena.
8. The deindividuation phenomenon is most often explained by (a) the diffusion of responsibility theory and identification (b) the emotional well-being of the person in the group (c) the fear of embarrassment that seems to increase with the size of the group (d) all of the above.
9. An explanation for the phenomenon referred to as bystander apathy is (a) fear of embarrassment (b) diffusion of responsibility (c) presence of others who are not helping sets the norms or model for behavior (d) all of the above.
10. In general, smaller groups express more ideas, are more creative, and need less supervision than larger groups. T or F
11. The principle of least group size states that the optimum group size for the performance of tasks requiring ________________ ________________ is the least number of individuals required to make available to the group all the requirements for performance of the task.
12. In a study with 10-year-old boys, the authoritarian style of group leadership resulted in steady production even when the leader was not present, and the members of the group tended to be friendly and content rather than hostile or meek and submissive. T or F

13. Groupthink is the term used to describe the type of thinking that occurs when people make decisions as a cohesive group resulting in an (a) efficient decision because more specialized information is available to the group (b) inefficient decision because of a compulsion to maintain unanimity and each other's approval to the extent that critical, realistic thinking does not occur (c) efficient decision because biases and prejudices of some individuals may be counteracted by the insights of others in the group (d) efficient decision because the unconscious motives of some individuals may be counteracted by the insights of others in the group.
14. The ________________ is the communication structure that is the most typical and usually the most efficient structure for small groups.
15. ________________ ________________ is a theory of communication and a technique developed by Eric Berne to help people understand themselves, understand other people, and improve interpersonal relations.
16. In transactional analysis, stamps are recognition and reinforcement, and strokes are feelings. T or F
17. In transactional analysis, the life position of the prejudiced person is (a) I'm not OK—You're not OK (b) I'm OK—You're not OK (c) I'm OK—You're OK (d) I'm not OK—You're OK.
18. In transactional analysis, the ________________ ego state consists of values, opinions, dos and don'ts, shoulds and should nots, and stored memories of statements and actions of parents and authority figures.
19. Research studies have shown that (a) individual traits predict who will become leaders (b) a few specific traits are found in leaders of all groups (c) leaders, compared with others, are taller, more attractive in physical appearance, more intelligent, more domineering, more confident, and better adjusted psychologically (d) all of the above.
20. The label for the sum total of positive impressions or favorable perceptions that followers have for their leader is referred to as (a) situation favorability (b) charisma (c) LPC score (d) idiosyncrasy credit.

APPLICATIONS

A. Lucus and Jane both work at the Mayday Plant. Lucus' group leader gives instructions in a commanding way, personally criticizes and belittles subordinates when a mistake is made or a project is not completed on schedule, and observes from the office, having little contact with the people being supervised except to give instructions and check to see that the instructions are followed. Lucus' group leader is all business and is mainly concerned with getting jobs done quickly and efficiently. Jane's group leader is quite different and often calls the group together to discuss some matter and to make a group decision on how to handle a situation. Although mistakes are pointed out and workers are instructed on how to correct mistakes, when a worker does a job especially well, recognition and praise are given. Jane's group leader spends much time socializing and getting to know personally the people being supervised, is friendly with subordinates, and allows subordinates some freedom of choice such as freedom to chose a working partner.

1. Would you classify the leadership style of Lucus' group leader as authoritarian, participative, or permissive? as task oriented or social/emotional oriented?
2. Would you classify the leadership style of Jane's group leader as authoritarian, participative, or permissive? As task oriented or social/emotional oriented?
3. Which group leader do you think will be more productive on a short-term basis? On a long-term basis?

B. One day at work Anita and John recorded the following comments and the responses made by co-workers:

Transaction 1. Where is the Johnson file?
It's in the top drawer on the left.

Transaction 2. I'm so excited, my daughter just made the drill team.
That's great! My daughter was on the drill team all four of her high school years.

Transaction 3. You must do things as I tell you to.
You are always telling me what to do.

Transaction 4. Why don't you stop giving me this job to do? I hate it! (angrily)
Well, I'm tired of hearing that from you. (angrily)

Transaction 5. I think the artwork on this project is excellent.
You obviously don't know much about art.

Transaction 6. Go and clean up the tool room.
It doesn't need cleaning yet. I'll do it when I decide I want to.

Transaction 7. Why don't we go to my place and work on this project? (man to woman) (Hidden meaning is maybe something exciting will happen.)
Sure! Sounds like a great idea! (Hidden meaning is the hope that something exciting will happen.)

1. What ego state is each of the comments coming from, and what ego state is each of the comments directed toward? Diagram each transaction.
2. What ego state is each of the responses coming from, and what ego state is each of the responses directed toward?
3. What type of transaction(s) is(are) 1-3? 4-6? 7?

SUGGESTIONS FOR FURTHER READING

Berne, E. (1967). *Games people play.* New York: Grove Press.

Many psychological games that people play are described and illustrated in this book.

Harris, T. (1969). *I'm OK, you're OK.* New York: Harper & Row.

An easy-to-read presentation of the theory of transactional analysis.

James, M., & Jongeward, D. (1971). *Born to win: Transactional analysis with gestalt experiments.* Reading, MA: Addison-Wesley.

Numerous examples are given in this book on transactional analysis. Experiments and exercises are included to help the reader understand and apply the principles of transactional analysis.

Janis, I. L. (1982). *Groupthink: Psychological studies of policy decision.* (2nd ed.). Boston: Houghton Mifflin.

A recent book about groupthink that includes a discussion of the Watergate cover-up.

Jongeward, D. (1976). *Everybody wins: Transactional analysis applied to organizations.* Reading, MA: Addison-Wesley.

A book that shows how the principles of transactional analysis can be applied in the world of work and how transactional analysis can be used as a training tool in industry.

Lindzey, G. & Aronson, E. (Eds.). (1985). *Handbook of social psychology* (3rd ed., Vols. 1 & 2). New York: Random House Distributed by Erlbaum.)

Nearly 2000 pages of an authoritative overview of social psychology.

Shaw, M. E. (1980). *Group dynamics: The psychology of small group behavior* (3rd ed.). New York: McGraw-Hill.

The reader is provided with a comprehensive review of what is known about groups. Issues and problems in the study of groups are identified.

APPENDIX

STATISTICS

Objectives

After completing the study of the appendix, you should be able to:

1. Define common statistical terms.
2. Organize a set of data into a rank distribution, an ungrouped frequency distribution, and a grouped frequency distribution, and prepare graphs for the set of data in the form of a histogram and a frequency polygon.
3. Determine the mean, median, mode, range, variance, and standard deviation for a set of data.
4. Determine the percentage of scores in a set of data that fall 1, 2, or 3 standard deviations above or below the mean of the set of data, and determine the score for a set of data that is representative of 1, 2, or 3 standard deviations above or below the mean.
5. Prepare a scattergram for a set of data consisting of two variables, and determine whether a strong or weak relationship exists and whether the relationship is positive or negative.
6. Give the logic of hypothesis testing.

Statistics as a method may be subdivided into two categories: (a) *descriptive statistics**, concerned with describing the data collected and presenting it in a convenient, usable, and understandable form; and (b) *inferential statistics,* concerned with drawing conclusions and making inferences about populations based on sample data taken from a *population.*

DESCRIPTIVE STATISTICAL PROCEDURES

Research studies usually involve a large number of observations presented in numeric form that represent a characteristic or a phenomenon. A collection of these observations is the *data,* often called scores. Because of the large number of observations, some organization and summarization of the data is needed in order to describe the data collected.

Distributions

What are three kinds of distributions that may be prepared for a set of data?

The first step in providing a description of a set of data might be to organize the data by preparing a **rank distribution,** an arrangement of the scores in a hierarchical order from highest to lowest.

**Terms defined previously in chapter 1 are in italics.*

An arrangement referred to as a *frequency distribution* consists of grouping all identical scores together (an ungrouped frequency distribution) and determining the number of scores that are identical, or grouping together all scores that fall into a particular category such as 70 through 74 (a grouped frequency distribution) and determining how many times (frequency) items of data fall into that category. This makes the data more meaningful and manageable. See Table A–1 for an example.

Graphs

The researcher might want to prepare a graph of the data to get an idea of the shape of the distribution and to see if the scores are evenly distributed or concentrated heavily in certain parts of the distribution such as near the middle or near the upper or lower end. Seeing the distribution can enhance understanding. A **histogram** is a type of bar graph in which the frequencies associated with the scores composing a set of data are represented in terms of the lengths of the bars. The area of a bar is directly proportional to the frequency it represents. The scores are plotted along the horizontal axis and the frequencies along the vertical axis (see Figure A–1). A **frequency polygon** is a line graph in which the frequencies associated with the scores composing a set of data are plotted as points and connected. A frequency polygon is shown in Figure A–2.

What is a histogram?

What is a frequency polygon?

Measures of Central Tendency

A *measure of central tendency* is a representative point or score for a set of data that tends to be near the middle of the score range. The measure of central tendency may relate to the average value of the scores, the value of the score that is in the middle position when the scores are in rank order, or the most commonly occurring score.

The familiar arithmetic average obtained by totaling all the items of data and dividing that number by the number of items of data is one measure of central tendency known as the *mean.* The mean may be obtained for any set of observations that can be added and divided. Some data such as supervisor ratings on a scale of 1 through 5 or data in the form of agree, disagree, or undecided as responses to a question cannot be described by a mean.

How is the mean obtained for a set of data?

The **median** is a measure of central tendency based on the rank distribution. The median is the point or score below which half (50

What is the median for a set of data?

Rank Distribution	Ungrouped Frequency Distribution (Category size = 1)		Grouped Frequency Distribution (Category size = 3)	
	Score	**Frequency**	**Score**	**Frequency**
90				
88				
87				
87	90	1	90–92	1
86				
86	89	0	87–89	3
85				
85	88	1	84–86	9
85				
85	87	2	81–83	13
84				
84	86	2	78–80	7
84				
83	85	4	75–77	2
83				
83	84	3		
83				
83	83	5		
82				
82	82	4		
82				
82	81	4		
81				
81	80	3		
81				
81	79	2		
80				
80	78	2		
80				
79	77	0		
79				
78	76	1		
78				
76	75	1		
75				

Mean = 2888 ÷ 35 = 82.5
Median = 83
Mode = 83
Range = 90 − 75 = 15

Data collected: The following scores were made on a work sample test taken by 35 applicants. (A minimum amount of data is used for illustration. In practice, one would need to have many more scores in the sample.)

83, 86, 84, 83, 87, 83, 82, 78, 85, 90, 75, 81, 78, 85, 80, 79, 85, 88, 81, 76, 85, 80, 79, 80, 81, 81, 83, 84, 82, 83, 86, 84, 82, 87, 82

Table A–1
Organizing data.

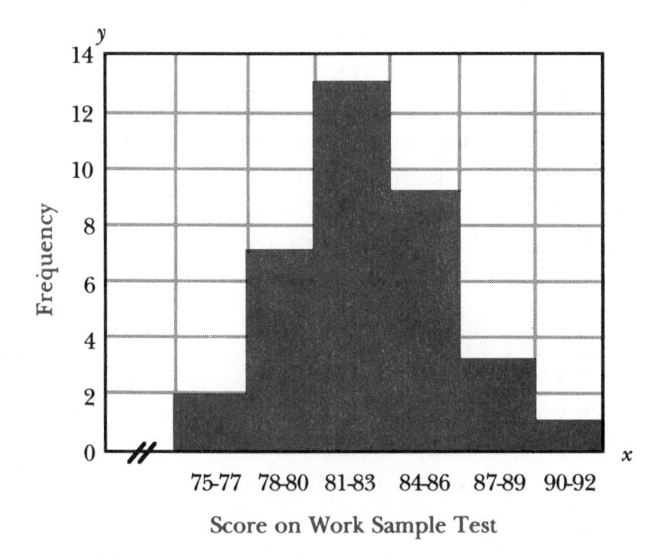

Figure A-1.
A histogram for the grouped frequency distribution in Table A-1.

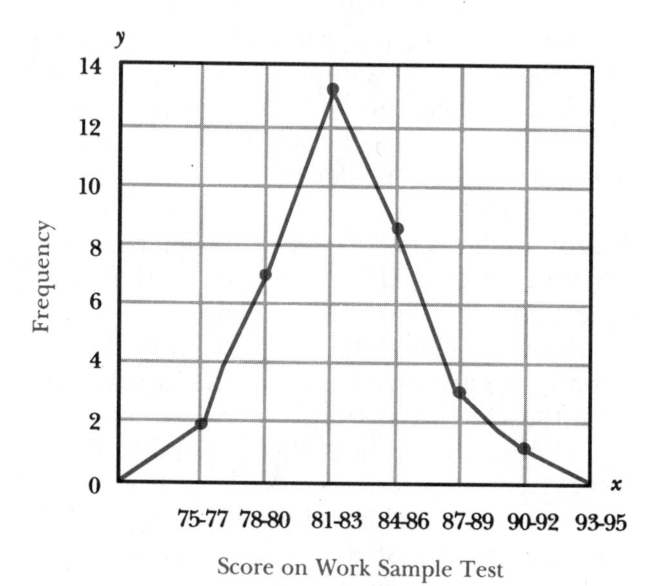

Figure A-2.
A frequency polygon for the grouped distribution frequency distribution in Table A-1.

percent) of the items of data fall when they are arranged in rank order. For an odd number of items of data, the median will be the score that falls in the middle and has an equal number of scores above it and below it. For an even number of items of data, the median will be the average of the two middle scores. The median may be calculated from a frequency distribution by use of a mathematical formula.

What is the mode for a set of data?

The **mode,** another measure of central tendency, is the score occurring most frequently and may be determined by inspecting the frequency distribution. Oftentimes a set of data is bimodal or multimodal. The mode is the only measure of central tendency that can express data such as responses categorized as strongly agree, agree, undecided, disagree, or strongly disagree. The mean, median, and mode are given for the data in Table A–1 on page 514.

Measures of Variability

A *measure of variability* describes the spread of the observations or scores around the central tendency. A measure of variability is needed to indicate whether the terms of data are widely scattered or whether they cluster closely around the mean. If the variation is small, all individual scores will cluster around the mean; if the variation is large, some individual scores may be very different from the mean and there is less assurance that the mean is representative of a score in the distribution. For example, if the value of each of the items of data is 7, the mean will be 7 and the measure of variability will be 0. If the mean is 7 and the scores range from 6 to 8, the measure of variability will be smaller than if the mean is 7 and the scores range from 1 to 25.

Is the range a stable measure of variability?

A number of different methods may be used for determining a measure of the degree of variability. The *range,* which is the difference between the highest and the lowest item of data, is the simplest measure of variability to calculate. Because only the two extreme items of data or scores are used to determine its value, the range tends to vary with the size of the sample, and it is not as stable as measures of variability that reflect the dispersion of the scores between the two extremes.

How is the variance of a set of data calculated?

The **variance** is a measure of variability that reflects the dispersion of the scores composing a set of data that is calculated by determining how much each score deviates from the mean of all the scores, squaring each deviation, and then finding the average of the squared deviations. The *standard deviation* is the square root of the variance. The greater the variability of the scores from the mean, the greater the standard deviation will be. The variance is a measure of variability in square measure, whereas the standard deviation is a measure of variability in the original unit of measure. Expressing the variation in the same unit of measure as the data is advantageous because then the measure can be added to or subtracted from the mean. Thus, the position of a particular score may be expressed as a particular number of units (standard deviations) above or below the mean. Variance and standard deviation are very useful measures of variability because each score in the distribution is considered rather than only two of the scores considered as in the range. Table A–2 illustrates the calculation of the variance and standard deviation for the work sample scores given in Table A–1 for the data collected.

How is standard deviation as a measure of variability advantageous over variance?

Standard Normal Curve

The **standard normal curve** is a theoretical, bell-shaped, symmetrical curve (frequency polygon) that represents the distribution of scores for any population. If the sample selected to be observed is representative of the population, the set of scores (data) will be normally distributed, and a graph of the distribution will resemble somewhat the standard normal curve. The graph will show more cases falling near the mean and fewer cases falling near the very high and very low scores. The graph of the distribution of scores for a sample is a frequency polygon (see Figure A–2).

What does the standard normal curve represent, and how is it shaped?

The standard normal curve is divided into uniform, linear distances on each side of the mean (standard distances or deviations). These standard distances, however, do not represent equal percentages of the total area under the curve and, therefore, do not represent an equal percentage of the total number of cases falling within that linear distance. The average amount of the spread of the scores or data across each of the uniform, linear distances for a sample is whatever the standard deviation value is computed to be. Figure A–3 shows the standard normal curve. Based on the sample data given in Table A–1 and a standard deviation of 3.28 as given in Table A–2, the statement could be made that approximately 68 percent of all subjects taking the work sample test will score between 79.22 and 85.78—in other words, between one standard deviation above and one standard deviation below the mean. The statement could also be made that approximately 95 percent of the population of applicants will score between two standard deviations above and below the mean—in other words, between 75.94 and 89.06. An applicant who scores 92.34 scores three standard deviations above the mean. See the diagram in Figure A–4.

Does each standard deviation from the mean represent the same percentage of cases?

Score	Mean of Scores	Difference	Difference Squared
90	82.5	7.5	56.25
88	82.5	5.5	30.25
87	82.5	4.5	20.25
87	82.5	4.5	20.25
86	82.5	3.5	12.25
86	82.5	3.5	12.25
85	82.5	2.5	6.25
85	82.5	2.5	6.25
85	82.5	2.5	6.25
85	82.5	2.5	6.25
84	82.5	1.5	2.25
84	82.5	1.5	2.25
84	82.5	1.5	2.25
83	82.5	.5	.25
83	82.5	.5	.25
83	82.5	.5	.25
83	82.5	.5	.25
83	82.5	.5	.25
82	82.5	−.5	.25
82	82.5	−.5	.25
82	82.5	−.5	.25
82	82.5	−.5	.25
81	82.5	−1.5	2.25
81	82.5	−1.5	2.25
81	82.5	−1.5	2.25
81	82.5	−1.5	2.25
80	82.5	−2.5	6.25
80	82.5	−2.5	6.25
80	82.5	−2.5	6.25
79	82.5	−3.5	12.25
79	82.5	−3.5	12.25
78	82.5	−4.5	20.25
78	82.5	−4.5	20.25
76	82.5	−6.5	42.25
75	82.5	−7.5	56.25
		Total	376.75

Variance = 376.75 ÷ 35 (number of scores) = 10.76

Standard Deviation = $\sqrt{10.76}$ = 3.28

Table A–2
Variance and standard deviation.

Correlations

Sometimes the data collected are paired measures, making it possible to determine the **correlation**—the relationship between the

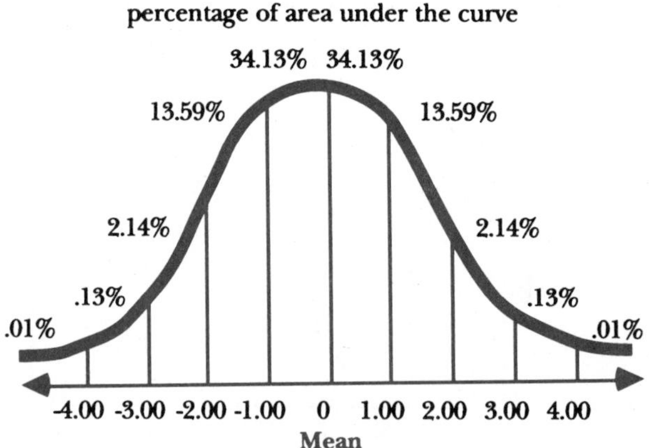

Figure A–3.
The standard normal curve.

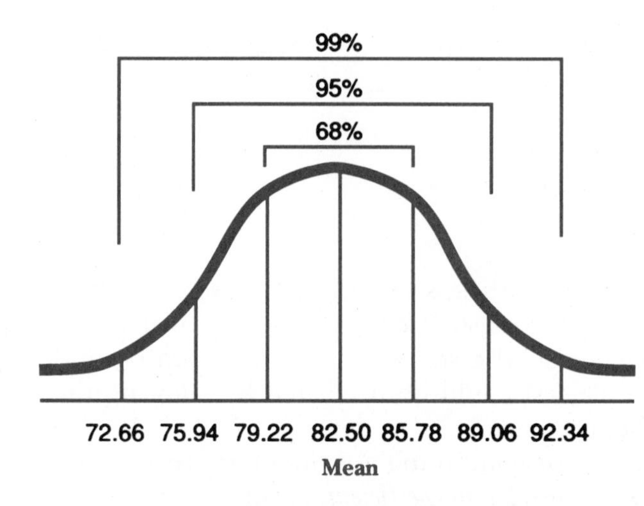

Figure A–4.
Work sample test scores comparable to 1, 2, or 3 standard deviations above or below the mean.

variables. For example, the data in Table A–1 might also include the number of months of work experience the subject has on the job as well as the score on the work sample test. Some sample scores paired with number of months of work experience are listed in Figure A–5.

What constitutes a positive relationship and a negative relationship?

If higher work sample scores are associated with more experience and lower scores are associated with less experience, a positive relationship (correlation) is said to exist. If the lower work sample scores are associated with more experience and the higher work

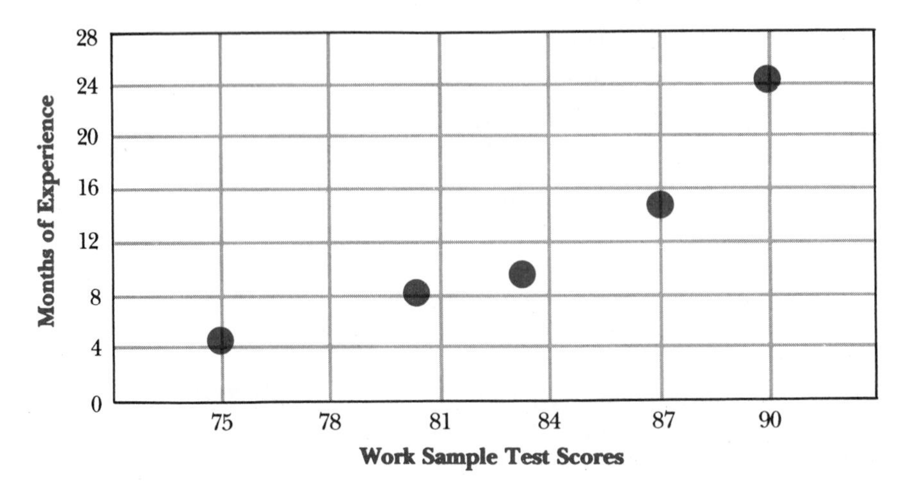

The following data were collected on five applicants. (A minimum of data are used for illustration. In practice more data would be collected.)

Applicant	Work Sample Test Scores	Months of Experience
B. Jones	90	24
T. Arnold	83	9
J. Mound	75	4
S. Dickens	80	8
J. Doe	87	15

Figure A–5.
A scattergram for a set of paired measures.

sample scores are associated with less experience, a negative relationship (correlation) is said to exist. If either a positive or negative correlation is found to exist, the score that an applicant would make on the work sample test could be predicted by knowing the number of months of experience.

What values may a correlation coefficient be?

Formulas are available for computing a numeric representation of the correlation, called a *correlation coefficient.* A correlation coefficient may range from 0 to +1.00 or from 0 to -1.00. The plus or minus sign indicates the direction of the relationship (positive or negative), and the numeric value indicates the degree of the relationship. The higher the degree of the relationship, the more accurately one variable in the pair can be predicted from the other known variable.

What is a scattergram?

A visual representation (graph) of the correlation can be prepared in the form of a **scattergram,** a two-dimensional plot of points with each point representing the paired measurements on the two variables. Figure A–5 shows a scattergram of the relationship between work sample test scores and months of experience for five applicants, and Figure A–6 shows scattergram patterns for several correlation coefficients. A lower-left-to-upper-right pattern represents a positive correlation; an upper-left-to-lower-right pattern represents a negative correlation; and an undifferentiated or circular pattern indicates no relationship. The closer the pattern approaches a straight line, the higher the degree of relationship.

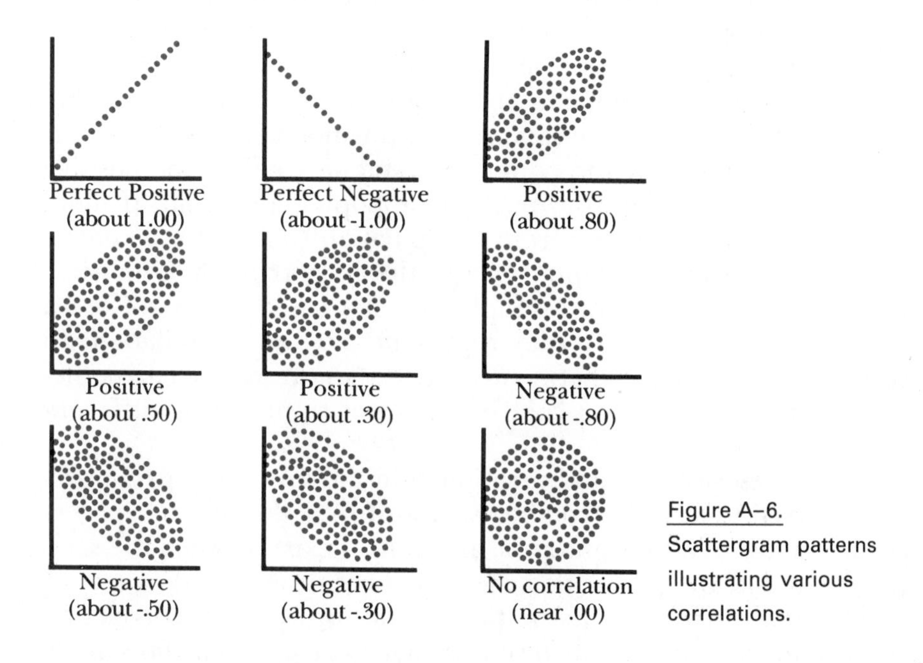

Figure A–6. Scattergram patterns illustrating various correlations.

INFERENTIAL STATISTICS

The logic and methods of inferential statistics are more complex than the logic and methods of descriptive statistics, which is concerned with making assumptions about or estimating population characteristics from sample data, testing hypotheses, and drawing conclusions about the truthfulness or falseness of hypotheses. Inferential statistics involves using formulas to determine how large a sample is needed for a given level of accuracy, to estimate the mean and standard deviation of populations, and to test hypotheses. Randomization in selection of subjects for data collection is crucial to using many of the formulas. Also crucial in inferential statistics is selecting the proper formula to test a hypothesis. Some formulas are used to test hypotheses when large samples are used, and other formulas are used when the set of data is from a small sample. Particular formulas are used for particular types of data such as categorical, rankings, numeric without an absolute zero (interval data), or numeric with an absolute zero (ratio data).

On what is the logic of hypothesis testing based?

The logic of hypothesis testing is based on the laws of probability and chance. Theoretically, if the means of all possible samples that could be drawn from a population could be plotted as a frequency polygon (line graph), one would have a standard normal curve that represents the means of all the possible samples that could be drawn from a population, the mean of which is the true population mean. Because only one sample is drawn from which to obtain data to represent the population, the researcher hypothesizes that the mean of the sample drawn is not significantly different from the mean of the population (the mean of all the possible samples that could be drawn), the true population mean. If more than one sample is drawn from a population such as for a control group and an experimental group, the researcher hypothesizes that the means of the two samples are not significantly different from each other because they represent the same population. In studies of relationships between variables, the researcher hypothesizes that the correlation coefficient is not significantly different from 0.

What are null hypotheses?

Hypotheses of the kind mentioned in the preceding paragraph are referred to as null hypotheses. A **null hypothesis** is a hypothesis that states that no significant differences exist between the sample mean and the population mean, between the means of two or more samples from the same population, or between correlation coefficients and 0. Any differences that exist between the sample mean and the estimated population mean, the two or more sample means from the same population, or a sample correlation coefficient and 0 that are within the area on the standard normal curve that would include 95 percent of the cases (not more than approximately 2 standard deviations from the mean or from 0) are considered to be caused by chance and are not considered to be significant differences. The null hypothesis would be accepted or retained when this occurs. Only if the differences are great enough to be in the area on the standard normal curve that would include the most extreme 5 percent of the cases (further than approximately 2 standard deviations from the mean or from 0) does the researcher usually reject the null hypothesis. If the null hypothesis is rejected, the difference is considered to be great enough that it is unlikely to be a chance difference—in other words, the difference is considered to be significant. The conclusion is then drawn that the sample is not representative of that population, that a difference this great between two samples is caused by the variation in the independent variable rather than chance, or that a relationship does indeed exist between two variables.

What are the levels used to reject a null hypothesis?

The decision about the point that must be reached to reject the null hypothesis is arbitrary; however, it must be made before the set of data is collected. The customary points are the 5 percent level or the 1 percent level. When a researcher rejects a null hypothesis at the 5 percent level, there is a 5 percent probability that the conclusion is wrong and a 95 percent probability that the conclusion is correct. Sometimes a researcher will not reject a null hypothesis unless the difference is significant at the 1 percent level and there is only a 1 percent probability that the conclusion is wrong and a 99 percent chance that the conclusion is correct. Of course, there is a greater probability of making another type of error—concluding that the differences are only chance differences when in fact they are not.

Inferential statistical procedures involve determining probabilities of chance and deciding whether to reject or retain null hypotheses to support research hypotheses. Psychology is a science because it employs scientific methods to investigate behavior, to interpret the information collected from the investigation, and to draw conclusions about behavior based on information collected.

SUGGESTIONS FOR FURTHER READING

Brightman, H. J. (1986). *Statistics in plain English.* Cincinnati: South-Western Publishing Company.

A book that is a self-teaching text written for anyone who has difficulty understanding statistics.

Clark, C. T., & Jordan, E. W. (1985). *Introduction to business and economic statistics* (7th ed.). Cincinnati: South-Western Publishing Company.

A text for an introductory course in statistics that is a complete treatment of the basic principles of statistics.

ANSWERS

TO TEST YOURSELF AND APPLICATIONS

CHAPTER 1

Test Yourself

1. Exorcism
2. A
3. B
4. Empirical
5. B
6. Consumer
7. Educational
8. D
9. Germany, 1879
10. Introspection
11. William James
12. Psychoanalytic
13. T
14. B
15. Alertness
16. B
17. Control
18. B
19. C
20. 5

Applications

A. 1. Experimental group, 3.0; control group, 0.
   2. Experimental.
   3. Industrial and organizational.
   4. Independent variable, stress seminar; dependent variable, change in number of units produced.

B. 1. Clinical psychology.
   2. Psychoanalytic.
   3. Psychoanalysis.

CHAPTER 2

Test Yourself

1. Neurons
2. A
3. Thalamus
4. Hypothalamus
5. Right; language; analytical
6. D
7. Occipital
8. Pituitary
9. B
10. B
11. Synaptic
12. Sympathetic; autonomic
13. Reticular activating
14. T
15. A

16. Neuro-modulators
17. T
18. F
19. Adrenal; epinephrine; norepinephrine
20. C

Applications

A. 1. Yes, biological rhythms.
   2. Yes, air around large bodies of water usually contains more negative ions, which has been found to be associated with elevations in mood.
   3. No, alcohol depresses the central nervous system rather than stimulating it.
   4. Left for Jack; right for Bindra.

B. 1. Yes, because he does not seem to be getting foods rich in choline such as eggs, meats, fish, liver, cereals, and legumes.
   2. No, because caffeine in coffee is a stimulant, and he does not seem to need further stimulation; in fact, he is probably overstimulating the central nervous system.
   3. No, because his adrenal glands would probably become trained to react to stress more efficiently, and he would function better, be ill less often, and save time in the long run.
   4. Yes, he could eat more high-carbohydrate foods and a lot of turkey, and also he could drink a glass of warm milk just before retiring.

CHAPTER 3

Test Yourself

1. C
2. Meiosis
3. XY
4. Down's syndrome
5. C
6. Dominant
7. T
8. B
9. Teratogens
10. T
11. Babinsky
12. F
13. D
14. D
15. Doubled; five
16. F
17. B
18. Crying, gurgling and cooing, babbling, phonemes, morphemes, syntax
19. D
20. A

Applications

A. 1. Yes, because both Bob and Ann could possibly be carriers of a recessive red- or blonde-hair gene even though they have dark brown hair.

2. Bob's sperm will determine whether they have a boy or a girl. A sperm with an X chromosome will produce a girl; a sperm with a Y chromosome will produce a boy. If the child is a boy, it is very much more likely that he will be color blind than if the child is a girl.
3. No, because there is evidence that alcohol and nicotine in cigarettes can be teratogens.
4. An extra chromosome with the 21st pair resulting in 47 chromosomes rather than the normal 46 in the body cells would cause Down's syndrome.

B. 1. No, because according to Erikson, children who emerge from the first year with a firm sense of trust in people and in their own ability to make things happen are those with parents who respond predictably, reliably, and lovingly to the child's needs.
2. Sarah will most likely develop a dependent personality and be somewhat shy and reserved rather than develop the trait of independence and of feeling confident to take actions and make decisions based on her own thinking.
3. She will double her height by age 2. (5′6″)
4. Contrast and movement; touch; seeing and hearing.

CHAPTER 4

Test Yourself

1. D.
2. D
3. B
4. D
5. B
6. A
7. Sensorimotor, preoperational, concrete operational, formal operational
8. A
9. T
10. F
11. Peer interaction
12. Conventional; good-boy/good-girl; approval (praise)
13. Solitary, onlooker, parallel, associative, cooperative
14. D
15. F
16. C
17. A
18. A positive concept of self
19. B
20. A

Applications

A. 1. Level II—conventional level, because they are reasoning in terms of being liked and approved of by others, abiding by the rules, keeping everybody happy, and maintaining good will. They are judging right behavior to be what they think a group of which they are a member expects from them and would approve.

2. Stage 3—good-boy/good-girl, because they are reasoning right behavior to be what they think will make them look good to a group whose approval they value.
3. Stage 4—maintaining social order, because they are reasoning in terms of following the rules, upholding the law, and legal responsibility.

B. 1. Bill.
2. Marcie.
3. Bill and Gertie. Bill, because he is coping with anger by making another person look less capable and less important. By belittling others and making others hurt like he does, his perception of himself is higher in relationship to others. Gertie, because by continuing to stay in a position to be hurt and frightened, obviously she doesn't feel important enough or valuable enough to be protected. Unconsciously, she must feel she does not have qualities that would cause others to like her if she feels others like her only for what she does for them and thinks she will not be admired or liked if she does not hold the piece of machinery.

CHAPTER 5

Test Yourself

1. D
2. D
3. Fovea
4. Cones
5. C
6. D
7. F
8. T
9. D
10. C
11. A
12. T
13. Constancy
14. D
15. B
16. C
17. Stage 1 with REM
18. F
19. B
20. D

Applications

A. 1. Yes. The influence would be the halo effect.
2. Vi most likely really did not perceive the perfume odor strongly because of adaptation. The constant stimulation of her smell receptor cells caused them to become less sensitive and would raise the threshold for transduction. Also, it is

possible that her sense of smell might not have the same stimulus threshold because of some hereditary condition.

B. 1. Yes, Pert most likely really did dream more because of the tendency to make up for lost dream time—a particular amount seems to be needed.
   2. Directed consciousness; flowing consciousness; daydreaming; altered—detachment from awareness of stimuli and events of everyday life; Stage 1 with REM.
   3. No, daydreaming is a variety of the normal awake state. No, the majority of a person's waking state is spent in flowing consciousness.
   4. No, Pert probably is really more efficient. Studies of deep relaxation confirm this.

CHAPTER 6

Test Yourself

1. A
2. Classical
3. Classical; stimulus
4. Extinction
5. Stimulus generalization
6. C
7. T
8. Negative reinforcement
9. F
10. Shaping
11. D
12. D
13. Premack
14. Intrinsic
15. D
16. T
17. F
18. Bandura; modeling; identification
19. D
20. C

Applications

A. 1. Yes. Classical conditioning.
   2. Stimulus generalization.
   3. Liking. The particular type of ring.

B. 1. A reinforcing consequence for being on time because (a) punishment is not as predictable (does not follow the law as reliably) as reinforcement; (b) undesirable side effects are less likely to occur; (c) a socially acceptable behavior is being learned, whereas punishment would only be suppressing an unacceptable behavior and no learning or growth is occurring; and (d) reinforcement is more humane.
   2. Alternate response (they can't be late if on time) and self-monitoring and recording.
   3. Be sure the reinforcement is received only if employees arrive to work by the specified time; provide the reinforcement

immediately on arrival; provide a large enough quantity of the reinforcement to be worth the effort to be on time; and be sure the reinforcement is something the employees are deprived of enough to really want. Also, the size or amount of reinforcement might be given in proportion to how much before starting time arrival occurs. In addition, if the reinforcement is given every time the employee arrives on time, the behavior change (learning) will occur faster.

4. Intermittent—variable ratio.

CHAPTER 7

Test Yourself

1. A
2. B
3. Short-term
4. Semantic; episodic
5. C
6. B
7. Engram
8. F
9. Proactive inhibition
10. T
11. T
12. F
13. F
14. T
15. D
16. Motor representation, images, concepts, language
17. F
18. Convergent and divergent
19. Set
20. D

Applications

A. 1. The student should study about one hour each day during the week because distributed practice has been found to lead to superior retention.

2. The student should read over and study the whole unit each session because a more intelligent person can probably use the whole method more effectively than a person of lower intelligence; the whole method is more effective if distributed practice rather than massed practice is used; and the whole method tends to be more effective for learning meaningful and highly organized material.

3. Yes, because overlearning facilitates remembering.

B. 1. No. Ebbinghaus found that percentage of recall varies according to method used for measurement.

2. Free recall was the method of measurement used with Group 1. Serial recall was the method of measurement used with Group 2. Recognition was the method of measurement used with Group 3.

3. Yes, because of the serial position effect.
4. Lower, because Ebbinghaus found memory to be a function of time.

CHAPTER 8

Test Yourself

1. Behaviorally oriented psychologists
2. Piaget
3. C
4. 120; 7; 1
5. T
6. B
7. .85; .50; .0
8. T
9. Mental; chronologic; 100
10. C
11. F
12. T
13. A
14. F
15. F
16. B
17. C
18. F
19. B
20. T

Applications

A. 1. The identical twins. Correlational studies have shown identical twins to have a higher positive relationship between their IQs than any other two groups of individuals—.85.
2. Yes, because Scarr and Weinberg found in their research study that children who were adopted and raised by families in a more affluent environment had higher measures of intelligence than would have been expected if they had remained in the impoverished environment into which they were born, particularly if they were adopted early in life.
3. One of the twins. Correlational studies have shown that siblings' IQs have a higher positive correlation than unrelated persons—.5 compared to .0.

B. 1. Corporation B. The manager's beliefs are more likely to lead to the corporation having more of the characteristics of creative organizations than are the Corporation A manager's beliefs.
2. Corporation B. Creative thinking (divergent thinking) seems to occur in the right hemisphere of the brain.
3. Those who are psychologically healthy and not preoccupied with anxieties, fear of rejection, fear of punishment, or insecure and thus have a fear of criticism because creativity will be more inhibited in them.

CHAPTER 9

Test Yourself

1. Activates or energizes; directs
2. B
3. D
4. T
5. C
6. T
7. Primary needs; secondary needs
8. D
9. F
10. A
11. F
12. D
13. C
14. C
15. D
16. Second-level outcome
17. A
18. F
19. D
20. B

Applications

A. 1. The superiors and subordinates jointly would identify goals, define each worker's reponsibilities in terms of individual goals, and use these goals as a guide for evaluating success on the job.

2. No, because some people seem to have developed qualities that fit the assumptions of Theory X (dislike of work and desire to avoid responsibility) because of environmental situations even though they have the potential for the behaviors and attitudes described in Theory Y. Using Theory Y assumptions to manage employees who fit Theory X characteristics will usually fail.

3. Intrinsic rewards. The manager would probably focus on such specific factors as giving recognition, providing responsibility, and providing growth possibilities.

B. 1. nAch—that they seek and assume more personal responsibility, take more risks, set more challenging but realistic goals, seek and use more feedback concerning the results of their actions, seek out more opportunities to enhance their desire to achieve, and are more competitive but avoid intense clashes than do other employees. nAff—that they enjoy interactions with other people, have warm relationships and friendships, and care about what others think of them more than do other employees.

2. Twenty cards containing pictures of one or more human figures with very few plot hints are shown to the employees. The employee is allowed enough time to make up a complete story for each picture. The story is to include what has led up to the picture scene, what is happening, what the characters are doing, what their thoughts and feelings are, what is

wanted and by whom, and what will happen or be done or what the outcome will be. The story is analyzed sentence by sentence by relating each sentence that can be classified to an appropriate need such as the need for achievement, the need for affiliation, and the need for power, and then the number of sentences that relate to each motive are totaled.

3. They are convenient to give and score because they are paper-pencil type tests that are scored objectively. Also, the individual's own personal experience and feelings can be tapped.

CHAPTER 10

Test Yourself

1. B
2. D
3. B
4. T
5. F
6. Limbic; hypothalamus
7. D
8. A
9. Right; left
10. C
11. B
12. D
13. C
14. Fear, anger, joy, sadness, acceptance, disgust, anticipation, surprise
15. T
16. A
17. F
18. A
19. C
20. T

Applications

A. 1. Nonverbal communication, specifically kinesics.
   2. Yes, because facial display, kinesics, and proxemics are even more reliable indicators of a person's feelings than verbal communication.

B. 1. Yes, because the irritability, mistakes, forgetting, headaches, and lower back pain are symptoms of too much tension.
   2. Try to persuade the employee to get involved in an exercise program and to go to the company psychologist for training in how to relax because exercise and relaxation are two proven ways to counteract excess tension.

CHAPTER 11

Test Yourself

1. Personality
2. D
3. Stability-instability
4. Id
5. Ego

6. C
7. A
8. Relatedness, transcendence, rootedness, identity, frame of orientation
9. D
10. F
11. Carl Rogers
12. B
13. B
14. T
15. T
16. B
17. B
18. Minnesota Multiphasic Personality Inventory (MMPI)
19. A
20. D

Applications

A. 1. Personality. The employee had a production record above average and there had been numerous complaints from co-workers. Discussions with the employee had not resulted in any improvements.

2. Did not profit from past experience. Not viewed positively by others. Not socially competent. Did not form close friendships.

B. 1. Yes. Enterprising.

2. Type A.

3. Extrovert.

CHAPTER 12

Test Yourself

1. T
2. C
3. B
4. A
5. Paraphilias
6. F
7. Bipolar disorder; manic-depressive psychosis
8. D
9. disorganized; hebephrenic
10. T
11. C
12. A
13. B
14. T
15. F
16. C
17. Active listening; nondirective; unconditional positive regard, emphathetic understanding, genuineness, congruence
18. D
19. D
20. A

Applications

A. 1. Yes. The behavior meets one or more of the four criteria most frequently used to label a behavior as a psychological disorder; namely, bizarre and extreme such as a delusion, disturbance with the well-being of the self or others (the husband), and inappropriate or excessive emotional display (actual physical assault of the husband).

2. Paranoia. The criteria for other psychoses are not met, the criteria of a plausible delusional jealousy is met, and the time frame covers more than 6 months (3 years.)

B. 1. A neurotic disorder; dissociative disorder.

2. Psychogenic fugue. Unexpected travel to a place away from his home, the assumption of a new identity, and inability to recall the previous identity.

CHAPTER 13

Test Yourself

1. T
2. C
3. B
4. Guttman
5. C
6. D
7. A
8. B
9. C
10. B
11. Cooperation
12. B
13. B
14. Stanley Milgram
15. D
16. Altruism
17. F
18. Proximity; similarity
19. Companionate; passionate; excitement; plateau; orgasm; resolution
20. T

Applications

A. 1. Compliance; (1) Causing the purchasing agent to feel guilty by not complying with the request to purchase specifically by bestowing favors and by increasing his attractiveness in order to be liked. (2) Putting the prospective buyer in a good mood with food and drink (lunch or dinner). (3) Increasing credibility (appearing more knowledgeable and objective) by speaking at a fast rate.

2. To appear more knowledgeable and objective.

3. To be liked more by the prospective buyer.

B. 1. Fundamental attribution error.

2. Because she doesn't know all the situations and influences of her employees, to protect her own ego, and the behavior of the employees elicits more attention than the context in which the behavior occurs.

CHAPTER 14

Test Yourself

1. B
2. T
3. D
4. Conflict
5. D
6. A

7. Risky-shift; stingy-shift
8. A
9. D
10. T
11. Group interaction
12. F
13. B
14. Wheel
15. Transactional analysis
16. F
17. B
18. Parent
19. C
20. D

Applications

A. 1. Authoritarian; task-oriented.
2. Participative; social/emotional-oriented.
3. Lucus' group leader; Jane's group leader.

B. 1.

	From	To
(1)	Adult	Adult
(2)	Child	Child
(3)	Parent	Child
(4)	Child	Parent
(5)	Adult	Adult
(6)	Parent	Child
(7)	Adult (Child)	Adult (Child) Hidden

2.

	From	To
(1)	Adult	Adult
(2)	Child	Child
(3)	Child	Parent
(4)	Child	Parent
(5)	Parent	Child
(6)	Parent	Child
(7)	Adult (Child)	Adult (Child) Hidden

Diagram

(1) P P
A⇄A
C C

(2) P P
A A
C⇄C

(3) P P
A A
C C

(4) P P
A A
C C

(5) P P
A A
C C

(6) P P
A A
C C

(7) P P
A⇄A
C⇄C

3. Complementary; crossed; ulterior (duplex).

GLOSSARY

Ability. A current capability to learn that is based on both aptitude and experience.

Accommodation. An adaptation process whereby existing action patterns and thought structures (schemes and operations) are modified in order to adapt to new situations.

Acetylcholine. The first chemical substance (neurotransmitter) released by neurons to be identified as an excitatory neurotransmitter.

Achievement. The knowledge and skills that a person has acquired through experience or learning.

Achievement motive. The need to accomplish something important or valuable or to meet high standards.

Active listening. Echoing, restating, and clarifying what a person has said and acknowledging the feelings expressed to provide a psychological mirror that helps the person see himself or herself more clearly.

Activity theory. The theory that assumes that activity is the essence of life and that aging people should maintain activities and work responsibilities for as long as possible for best adjustment to aging.

Actualizing tendency. The tendency of people to engage in and value activities that satisfy their need to grow and to avoid those that hinder growth or are unpleasant.

Adaptation. The innate ability of an organism to adjust to the environment such as when the cells in sense organs become less sensitive by being exposed to a constant level of stimulation.

Adrenal glands. Endocrine glands located near the kidneys that release several hormones into the bloodstream, particularly epinephrine (adrenalin) and norepinephrine (noradrenalin) during stress, resulting in a number of important changes in the body that prepare it for action.

Adult ego state. In transactional analysis, the part of the personality that consists of the knowledge, logical reasoning, rational thinking, and information processing of the individual.

Afferent neuron. A cell in the nervous system, sometimes referred to as a sensory neuron, that receives input directly from cells in the sense organs.

Affiliation motive. A learned need to be with people, to be accepted by some people, and to be loved by people.

Ageism. Discrimination, prejudice, or stereotyping on the basis of age.

Aggression. Any behavior consciously or unconsciously intended to inflict physical or psychological harm.

Aggressive motive. The need to behave in an aggressive manner—to inflict harm.

Altered states. Induced states of consciousness, i.e., states that do not occur spontaneously and must be deliberately evoked.

Alternate states. States of consciousness that occur naturally that are different from the normal awake state such as sleep and dreaming and the state between sleep and awake.

Altruism. Helping behavior that is not linked to self-gain—without expectation of any recognition or reward in return except perhaps the good feeling that comes from the behavior itself.

Ambiverts. Individuals who are a mixture of extroversion and introversion and vacillate from one extreme to the other in different situations.

Amplitude. The height or magnitude of a sound wave, which is the primary determiner of the loudness of the sound.

Androgens. Hormones secreted primarily by the male sex glands (testes) that stimulate the reproductive organs to mature and trigger the development of secondary sex characteristics such as beard growth.

Androgyny. A self-concept that allows a person to engage in both feminine- and masculine-stereotyped traits.

Angular ulterior transaction. A message with a hidden meaning that can be interpreted by the receiver as being directed toward either of two different transactional analysis ego states.

Anomic type. The term for people who respond unfavorably to goal setting because they do not have inner standards and self-expectations and because they become frustrated with the interference with their spontaneity.

Anxiety. A generalized feeling of apprehension, tenseness, dread, and foreboding with causes that are usually not as specific as the causes of fear.

Applied psychology. Practical application of knowledge of psychology to current problems.

Approach-approach conflict. Conflict resulting from a situation in which a person is simultaneously attracted to two equally attractive alternatives.

Approach-avoidance conflict. Conflict resulting from a situation in which a person has to decide whether to engage in a single activity, pursue a single goal, or take advantage of a single opportunity that has both desirable and undesirable characteristics or advantages and disadvantages.

Aptitude. An innate or natural capacity for performing or learning to perform some task.

Arousal theory. The view that behavior is a function of being aroused, more sensitive to, or more reactive to a specific stimulus rather than a direct effect of deprivation.

Assimilation. An adaptation process whereby existing action patterns and thought structures are applied to new situations.

Attachment. An emotional tie or bond (affection) that develops between a person and another specific individual—a psychological need for the physical presence and emotional support of that individual.

Attitude. A person's disposition to think, feel, and act either positively or negatively toward a person, idea, object, or situation.

Attribution. The process of ascribing (attributing) causes to people's behavior.

Autonomic nervous system. The division of the peripheral nervous system that serves the involuntary muscles and regulates the activities of the internal body organs such as the heart, stomach, and glands.

Avoidance-avoidance conflict. Conflict resulting from a situation in which a person must make a decision between two equally unattractive alternatives or unpleasant situations.

Awareness level. The division or level of consciousness that includes those things noted and kept track of by a person.

Axon. A long, slender, tubelike fiber ranging in length from a few thousandths of an inch to 2 or 3 feet extending away from the main body of a neuron.

Balance phase. The third phase of a four-phase developmental sequence in the process of group formation that involves members giving up some of their individual wants, desires, and needs for the benefit of the group as a whole and that is characterized by compromise and agreement.

Balance theory. The belief that homeostasis or harmony needs to exist between facts, beliefs, feelings, attitudes, and behavior for psychological survival or well-being and that inconsistencies between any of these serve as an energizing force for responses to restore harmony.

Behavior. Any activity or movement of an organism in response to a specific stimulus or set of stimuli whether or not the activity is mental, physical, internal, or external.

Behavior modification. The application of learning theory to modify or change people's behavior—either individual or group behaviors.

Behavioral medicine. The application of learning theory to the treatment and prevention of illness.

Behaviorism. A view that defines psychology as the study of behavior focusing on the relationship between stimuli and responses and emphasizing objectivity and the empirical approach.

Belief. One aspect of an attitude that does not involve feeling, emotion, likes, or dislikes and may be true or false but is accepted as fact.

Biofeedback. A method of training people to regulate internal physiological states such as heart rate, blood pressure, brain wave pattern, glandular and muscular activity, and temperature using electronic recording devices that provide immediate feedback, usually in visual or auditory form.

Biorhythms. Biological cycles such as emotional, intellectual, and physical cycles that are believed by some scientists to begin at birth, rise and fall at different rates, and have a small but significant part of the explanation of human behavior.

Blind spot. The place on the retina where the optic nerve is located that has neither rods nor cones and is therefore insensitive to light rays.

Bystander apathy. Failure on the part of passersby to intervene when help is needed due to the presence of a group, which inhibits rather than facilitates helping behavior.

Cardinal traits. Allport's term for the characteristics of people that determine behavior in the most encompassing conditions such as the trait of being humanitarian.

Case study method. A method of studying behavior by conducting an intensive investigation of a single case that results in a large amount of information.

Central nervous system. The division of the nervous system that consists of the brain and spinal cord.

Central traits. Allport's term for the characteristics of people that are more specific than cardinal traits but are still somewhat general such as the traits of being outgoing or pessimistic.

Cerebellum. A lobed structure consisting of two hemispheres that is attached to the brain stem in the hindbrain and is involved in the control of motor behavior, especially balance and coordination.

Cervix. The necklike lower end of the uterus opening into the vagina of the female.

Cesarean section. The surgical removal of the baby from the uterus through an incision in the abdominal wall.

Charisma. An elusive term that refers to some magnetic quality that has the mysterious ability to draw people to a person and to allow that person to control them.

Child ego state. In transactional analysis, the part of the personality that consists of the feelings about the person's past experiences and the person's current feelings and is the source of openness, manipulation, spontaneity, sensuality, affection, creativity, happiness, rebellion, intuition, and hostility.

Chromosomes. Complex structures in the cell nucleus composed of thousands of genes threaded together like strings of beads.

Clairvoyance. Perception of an event too remote to have come through the senses such as perception of an automobile accident 1,000 miles away.

Classical conditioning. A form of learning based on associations. When a new event is paired with an event that brings forth a particular behavior, the new event becomes a signal for the event that is bringing forth the behavior and also comes to bring forth the behavior.

Clinical psychology. An area of psychology concerned with helping individuals achieve psychological well-being and with diagnosing and treating psychological disturbances.

Closure rule. The patterning principle whereby missing pieces of a familiar pattern are automatically filled in.

Cognitive consistency. The tendency to change or reevaluate discrepancies in order to bring about agreement or balance.

Cognitive dissonance. The state of tension that is created when there is inconsistency among an individual's attitudes, beliefs, feelings, and/or behaviors.

Cognitive-behavioral model. The expanded version of behavior therapy, based on learning theory, that includes covert or unseen behaviors such as thinking, memory, perception, and information processing.

Cognitive psychology. A newer approach to the study of human behavior that is based on the view that the mind is an information-processing center and that emphasizes the role of memory and the thought processes in explaining behavior.

Collective unconscious. An inherited unconscious proposed by Jung as an addition to Freud's personal unconscious that is common to all humans and consists of a reservoir of representations of early ancestors' universal experiences.

Common sense assumptions. Ideas one holds to be true without any proof that they are true.

Common-fate rule. The

patterning principle whereby parts are grouped as a single whole if they move together.

Companionate love. A loving friendship that consists of deep affection and attachment, appreciation, respect, trust, loyalty, emotional intimacy, and close acquaintance.

Complementary transactions. In transactional analysis, responses sent back to the same ego state from which the message was received; sometimes called parallel transactions.

Compliance. The act of submitting to a direct request to behave in a particular way.

Compulsion. The repetitious performing of a behavior according to certain rules or in a stereotyped fashion even though the individual desires to stop performing the behavior.

Computerized axial tomography. A method of computing images in three dimension of a basic structure such as the brain based on X-ray photographs—commonly referred to as a CAT scan.

Conception. The union of male and female gametes, a sperm and an ovum, marking the beginning of a new organism.

Concepts. Categories for representing or classifying environmental stimuli according to common characteristics that allow a person to identify a new stimulus and guide action in a new situation.

Concrete operational stage. The third stage in Piaget's theory of intellectual development, the period from about 6 or 7 to 11 years of age, during which the child develops the capacity to reason and solve problems in a logical manner and to conserve.

Conditioned response. A response that is learned; that is, a response that is brought forth by a conditioned or learned stimulus.

Conditioned stimulus. A previously neutral stimulus that, through association with an unconditioned stimulus or another conditioned stimulus, comes to bring forth a response similar to the one brought forth by the stimulus with which it is associated.

Cones. Cells located on the back layer of the retina of the eye that respond to differences in wavelength of light rays and light intensity and are involved in color vision.

Conflict phase. The second phase of a four-phase developmental sequence in the process of group formation during which members' individual personalities and needs begin to clash.

Conformity. The act of behaving a particular way in order to be in accordance with the norms or standards of society.

Congruence. A fit between the feelings and the behavior toward a person, a condition that is considered to be a part of an accepting environment for that person.

Conserve. In Piaget's theory of intellectual development, the ability to recognize that the quantity (mass, volume, length, number, etc.) of a substance does not change despite a change in appearance if nothing is added or subtracted.

Constancy principles. Interpretative rules for judging occurrences that involve stabilizing processes that provide a standard, dependable way of interpreting events rather than following the movements.

Consumer psychology. A specialty branch of psychology that studies the dynamics underlying the purchase and consumption of particular products or brands and the utilization of particular services.

Continuity rule. The patterning principle of grouping continuous contours together.

Continuous schedules. Schedules of reinforcement in which the consequence follows the response every time it occurs.

Control group. In an experiment contrasting two groups, the group that does not receive the experimental treatment.

Conventional morality. Level II in Kohlberg's theory of moral development when moral value resides in what is conventional or typical or the rules of society.

Convergent thinking. The type of thinking used to retrieve from long-term memory answers or previous solutions to bring together or converge information related to a problem.

Corpus callosum. The large mass of nerve fibers that connects the two cerebral hemispheres of the brain and allows the two sides of the brain to communicate with each other.

Correlated reinforcement. Reinforcement in which the quantity of reinforcement varies in proportion to the quantity or intensity of the response.

Correlation. The relationship between two or more variables.

Correlation coefficient. A numeric representation of the relationship that exists between two variables.

Correlational method. A scientific method of studying behavior that involves an investigation of the relationships between measurable events.

Counseling psychologist. A psychologist who may or may not have a doctoral degree and who works primarily with people who have less serious problems—perhaps problems associated with educational and vocational choices or individual and family adjustment problems.

Critical periods. A particular time in the developmental process during which an environmental condition will have a greater effect on behavior than at other times.

Cross-validated. The condition whereby the initial findings of a relationship between a performance measure and a trait or characteristic measure such as IQ believed to affect performance have been found in a repeated study with another sample.

Crossed transactions. In transactional analysis, transactions in which the response does not come back to the ego state from which the message was sent nor does it come back from the ego state the message was directed toward.

Crystallized intelligence. The component of intelligence theorized by Cattell to reflect what a person has learned through experience and which is believed to be able to increase for many years, even after the end of formal schooling.

Data. Observations in numeric form, often called scores, that represent a characteristic or a phenomenon.

Defense mechanisms. Unconscious coping strategies that a person uses to control the anxiety level.

Deindividuation. The phenomenon in which an individual sets his or her own personality aside, becomes submerged in a group, and has a group identification rather than an individual identification.

Delusions. Beliefs held by a person that are not true.

Demonology. One of the earliest explanations of behavior—the belief that spirits possess a person's body and direct a person's behavior.

Dendrites. The short, delicate, branchlike extensions that protrude from the main cell body of a neuron to receive messages or impulses from neighboring cells and conduct that information to the main cell body.

Dependent variable. The variable that is measured in an experimental study in order to observe the effect of the manipulation of the independent variable.

Depolarization. The state of a neuron when the balance of electrical charges between the interior and the exterior of the cell is altered and the cell's interior is positive with respect to the exterior.

Depressants. Drugs that reduce or depress central nervous system functioning.

Descriptive statistics. The part of statistics that is concerned with describing the data collected and presenting the data in a convenient, usable, and understandable form.

Determinism. The assumption that every event, act, or decision is the consequence of prior physical, psychological, or environmental events that are independent of the human will.

Developmental psychology. The specialized area of psychology concerned with the growth and development of a person from the beginning of life until death and the behavior and behavioral changes characteristic of each period of development.

Dichromats. Those individuals who have one type of cone missing, either the red-green cones or the blue-yellow cones, and therefore do not perceive color normally.

Difference threshold. The minimum level of energy change required for a stimulus difference to be detected such as a change in brightness, loudness, temperature, taste, or pressure.

Diffusion of responsibility. The phenomenon that, in a group, no one individual is responsible for the actions of the group.

Discount. In transactional analysis, a stroke that is less positive than it should be or a stroke not delivered.

Discrimination. An action taken based on a prejudice.

Discriminative stimulus. The situation or setting in which a response is emitted.

Disengagement theory. The theory that assumes that as people grow older, withdrawal from society is natural and has psychological benefits.

Displacement (scapegoating). A defense mechanism whereby aggressive behavior is directed unconsciously toward someone who cannot fight back as a substitute for aggression toward the source of frustration.

Distributed practice. A method of learning that involves practicing or repeating what is to be learned in short periods of time with rest periods intervening.

Divergent thinking. The type of thinking that uses imagination and combines knowledge and experience in new ways to bring forth new, unusual, or unheard-of answers or solutions; creative thinking.

Dominant gene. The gene in a pair that predominates over the other gene in the pair to influence the development of a particular characteristic.

Dopamine. A now well-known inhibitory neurotransmitter thought to be related to a mental illness known as schizophrenia that is taken back into the knobs on the terminal branches after being released.

Double approach-avoidance conflict. Conflict resulting from a situation in which a person is faced with a choice between two goals, each of which has desirable and undesirable tendencies.

Down's syndrome. A form of mental retardation produced by the presence of an extra chromosome on the 21st pair.

Drive. The term referring to the force that arises from physiological conditions that signify some biological distress and thus compels behavior.

DSM-III. The *Diagnostic and Statistical Manual of Mental Disorders* (3rd ed.), published by the American Psychiatric Association, which is a manual of the official classification system for psychological disorders used in the United States.

Dualism. The philosophy that human behavior is controlled by complex interactions of both the mind and the body, either of which may initiate behavior. This philosophy is based on the assumption that the mind guides behavior to satisfy bodily needs, that God is the source of behavior, and that behavior is instinctive.

Duplex ulterior transactions. In transactional analysis, complementary transactions with hidden meanings that are understood by both the sender and receiver.

Echoic memory. The sensory image or impression of a sound that is held for 3 or 4 seconds making it possible for an individual to rehear information, almost like an echo even if attention is elsewhere.

Eclectic. An approach used by psychologists whereby the psychologist selects from the many theories and approaches available and uses what seems to fit the situation rather than relies on one approach only.

Ectomorphs. Individuals who have a thin body with small bones.

Educational psychology. The specialized area of psychology concerned with increasing the efficiency of learning in schools and with studying behavior in educational settings.

Efferent neuron. A cell in the nervous system, sometimes referred to as a motor neuron, that carries messages out from the brain and spinal cord to muscle cells that control outward, external movements as well as to the smooth muscles that control glands and internal organs.

Ego. The conscious part of the personality that is in contact with reality and that is responsible for the voluntary processes, perceives the needs of the individual, evaluates the environment, adapts to social norms, plans ahead, and finds ways to actually obtain the things needed and desired.

Electra complex. Freud's term for the conflict and anxiety experienced by a girl during the phallic stage of development as she unconsciously feels sexual attraction for her father and becomes jealous of her mother, the resolution being identification with the mother.

Electrons. Negative charges of electricity that are present in all atoms.

Embryo. The early formation of the human young from the time of attachment to the uterus (about 2 weeks after conception) until all specialization of cells has occurred and all major organs and structures have their beginning formation (about 8 weeks after conception).

Empathetic understanding. The accurate reflection of a person's experiences and feelings; a condition that is considered to be a part of an accepting environment for that person.

Empirical approach. The pursuit of knowledge through observation and

experimentation—
a method that deals with information that is available to the senses and can be validated and confirmed by other individuals.

Empiricism. The philosophy that behavior is determined, not chosen, and that relationships exist between stimuli and responses.

Encoding. The process of coding, translating, and entering information into the memory system for immediate or later use.

Endocrine glands. The ductless glands of the body that empty secretions called hormones and in some cases peptides directly into the bloodstream, bringing about a widespread and immediate effect on behavior.

Endomorphs. Individuals who have soft, wide bodies with a larger proportion of the body weight than normal in the internal organs.

Endorphins. Opiatelike substances naturally produced in the body and released into the bloodstream acting as neuromodulators to control pain.

Engineering psychology. A subdivision of industrial and organizational psychology that specializes in the discovery and application of information about the relationship between human behavior and machines, tools, jobs, and work environments.

Engram. A general term for a persistent structural change in the brain caused by stimulation of living neural tissue; the physical representation of memory in the brain.

Episodic memory. The part of long-term memory that consists of the chronologic record of a person's personal experiences; sometimes said to be like a person's diary or autobiographical record.

Equilibrium. The sense of balance or an awareness of body position that makes it possible to maintain an upright posture.

Erogenous zones. Highly sensitive places on the body such as the mouth or genitals.

Estrogens. Hormones secreted primarily by the female sex glands (ovaries) that play a role in the development of the reproductive organs and secondary sex characteristics such as breast development.

Existentialism. A loosely organized view of psychology that is more philosophical and less scientific than other views and that stresses human existence in the here and now—immediate experience.

Exorcism. Techniques used during the time period when demonology was the primary explanation for aberrant human behavior in an attempt to drive evil spirits out of people.

Expectancy. The anticipation or believed likelihood or probability that a reward will occur as a result of a particular behavior.

Expectancy theory. The belief that people perform behaviors that are expected to result in receiving worthwhile rewards, in leading to desired goals, and in avoiding undesirable outcomes.

Experimental group. In an experiment contrasting two groups, the group that is subjected to a change in an independent variable.

Experimental method. A scientific method of investigation that seeks to define cause-and-effect relationships through the manipulation of certain variables.

Experimental psychology. An area of psychology in which rigorous research methods are used to experimentally investigate basic psychological processes in the study of behavior, usually in laboratory settings.

External locus of control. The perception of a person that the center of control in his or her life is outside the self.

Extinction. The weakening and eventual disappearance of a response when a learner no longer associates the new stimulus with the old stimulus that elicits the response (in classical conditioning) or no longer associates the consequence with the response (in operant conditioning).

Extrasensory perception (ESP). The controversial theory that stimulation of the brain for perception can come in some way other than through the known sensory channels.

Extrinsic motivation. The source of behavior that comes from the consequence of the behavior because of a need for such things as money, food, praise, grades, good health, or awards.

Extrinsic reinforcers. Tangible things that are satisfying consequences and reinforce a behavior.

Extroversion-introversion. One of the two major dimensions of personality proposed by Eysenck that is related to the individual's need to receive stimulation from the outside world.

Extroverts. Individuals who are outgoing and tend to seek emotional stimulation in the form of social activities and exciting, adventurous events and sensory stimulation in the form of loud noises and colors.

Factor analysis. A mathematical technique for analyzing the interrelationships of behavior data that allows a summary of large amounts of data relevant to many individuals and groups and the classification of factors.

Family or systems model. The view that psychological disorders arise from an entire family setting rather than from an individual; thus, an individual's abnormal behavior is a symptom of psychopathology within the family and not a product of the individual alone.

Fantasy. A defense mechanism whereby the individual daydreams inappropriately and unconsciously to escape reality.

Feature analysis. A theory of perception that explains perception as an active, hypothesis-testing process in which a person seems to abstract features of the signal or neural impulse and to compare them with patterns stored in long-term memory.

Fetus. The developing human young from the beginning of the 9th week after fertilization until birth.

Field dependent. A cognitive style whereby an individual tends to make global judgments and is more influenced by the field or immediate environment than by factual analysis.

Field independent. A cognitive style whereby an individual tends to make judgments analytically and to disregard environmental information that may affect the judgment.

Figure-ground rule. The tendency to perceive a figure with a defined contour and boundary as being in front of a ground that flows around the figure.

Fixed interval schedule. An intermittent schedule of reinforcement in which a reinforcer follows the response only after a set period of time.

Fixed ratio schedule. An intermittent schedule of reinforcement in which a reinforcer follows the response only after a set number of responses has occurred since the last reinforcer was given.

Flexibility. The shifting from type or category of ideas or suggestions to another type or category so that the greater the number of shifts the more flexible the thinking.

Flexible scheduling. A procedure that allows workers to schedule their own 40-hour workweek within the time the organization is in operation.

Fluency. The total number of ideas or suggestions generated so that the greater the number generated the more fluent the person.

Fluid intelligence. The component of intelligence theorized by Cattell to reflect a general perceptual capacity that is dependent on the physiological functioning of the brain and is determined by an individual's genetic endowment.

Forebrain. The upper portion of the brain, above the midbrain, that includes such structures as the neocortex, corpus callosum, thalamus, and hypothalamus. The lower part controls hormonal release, autonomic nervous functions, and emotional and motivational processes, whereas the upper part is associated with consciousness.

Forensic psychology. A specialty branch of psychology concerned with the application of knowledge of human behavior in legal matters.

Formal operational stage. The fourth and last stage in Piaget's theory of intellectual development that may occur between the ages of 11 and 15 and is characterized by the ability to do abstract thinking, to consider all possible combinations of events in problems presented, and to exclude those that are irrelevant.

Fovea. An area on the retina of the eye where the cones are most concentrated and is thus the area where vision is sharpest when the image is projected on the retina.

Free recall. A method of measuring memory in which an individual is given a list of items to learn and then recall at a later time in any order.

Free will. The assumption that humans freely choose their own behavior and have control of their own destiny.

Frequency. The number of cycles of a sound wave that arrive per second.

Frequency distribution. An arrangement of a set of data that consists of grouping together all scores that fall into a particular category.

Frequency polygon. A line graph in which the frequencies associated with the scores composing a set of data are plotted as points and connected.

Frontal lobes. The large front portion of each hemisphere of the neocortex lying behind the forehead.

Frustration-aggression hypothesis. The theory that aggressive behavior is the result of frustration brought about by external factors.

Functional fixedness. A type of set in which a person fixes in the mind the function of an object to the point that thinking of another function for the object may be difficult.

Functionalism. The view of James that psychologists should study the functioning of the mind because the mind consists of the abilities to feel, to make decisions, and to adapt to an environmental situation.

Fundamental attribution error. The tendency to overestimate dispositional factors and underestimate situational factors.

Galvanic skin response (GSR). Changes in the resistance of the skin to the condition of electricity.

Gametes. Male sperm or female ova, cells that contain 23 single chromosomes.

General adaptation syndrome. A phrase coined by Hans Selye to represent the entire pattern of the sequence of physiological events that takes place during prolonged stress.

Generalized conditioned reinforcers. Reinforcers such as money or approving smiles that are associated with many different reinforcers; therefore, ineffectiveness from overuse does not usually occur.

Genes. The basic units (carriers) of heredity that are composed of DNA molecules and are located on the chromosomes.

Genetic engineering. The modification of an individual's hereditary makeup through manipulation of the genetic materials.

Genuineness. Honesty in the relationship with a person; a condition that is considered to be a part of an accepting environment for that person.

Gestalt. A German word meaning form, pattern, or whole.

Gestalt psychology. The view that human behavior should be studied as an organized whole rather than as separate individual parts with emphasis on form, patterns, or wholes in perception.

Glial cells. Nonexcitable cells in the nervous system that surround, protect, and nourish neurons, seeming to play a role in the growth of neurons and neural pathways and in the metabolism of the nervous system.

Gonads. The sex glands, the testes in the male and the ovaries in the female, that secrete hormones related to the maturation of the reproductive organs and the development of secondary sex characteristics.

Grapevine. A source of information that comes by bypassing someone in the official structure of communication for a group.

Group. A collection of individuals who interact with each other, share some common identity, and share some common goals or desires.

Group norm. A standard with which members of a group are expected to comply and against which the behavior of members is evaluated.

Group position. The specific slot occupied by an individual in a group.

Group role. The behavior displayed by an individual in a certain position in a group or the expected behavior of an individual in a certain position in a group.

Group status. An evaluation of the contribution of particular roles to the welfare of the group.

Groupthink. The term coined by Janis to describe the type of thinking that occurs when people make decisions as a cohesive group based on a compulsion to maintain unanimity and each other's approval to the extent that critical, realistic thinking does not occur.

Hallucination. An unrealistic sensory experience; the perception of things that are not really there in the environment.

Hallucinogens. Drugs that usually produce changes in a person's ability to receive and interpret sensory information, resulting in distorted perceptions and hallucinations.

Halo effect. A distorted perception in which a favorable impression of an individual is created by one favorable characteristic that overshadows to other characteristics so that virtually everything the individual does is judged in a favorable light.

Hawthorne effect. The phenomenon that the attention given to participants during an experimental research project may have an effect on the responses of the participants.

Hedonism. The ancient philosophical idea that behavior is determined by the desire to avoid pain and the desire to seek pleasure.

Heritability. A measure of how much trait variation in a population can be accounted for genetically.

Hindbrain. The lower part of the brain below the midbrain that merges with the spinal cord and includes such structures as the medulla, pons, and cerebellum.

Hippocampus. A brain structure that is a part of the limbic system and seems to be related to learning, remembering, and recognizing novelty.

Histogram. A type of bar graph in which the frequencies associated with the scores composing a set of data are represented in terms of the lengths of the bars.

Homeostasis. A central idea in biological psychology that refers to the automatic maintenance of equilibrium of life-sustaining processes such as blood pressure and body temperature that has been extended also to apply to maintaining a psychological equilibrium.

Hormones. Chemicals secreted by the endocrine glands directly into the bloodstream that function as neuromodulators to have an effect on behavior.

Humanism. A newer view of human behavior that postulates that people have an inborn tendency to grow and improve and that emphasizes subjective experience and psychological needs in explaining the uniqueness of a person's personality.

Hygiene factors. Factors that are part of the job content, such as financial rewards, fringe benefits, or company policies, but that are external to the job itself. Herzberg proposed that these factors must be satisfied to avoid worker dissatisfaction, but that they do not generate satisfaction or motivate greater productivity.

Hypnosis. An induced passive state of consciousness in which there is increased responsiveness to suggestions and commands.

Hypothalamus. A structure in the forebrain that functions as a thermostat to maintain the needed balance for the body for survival and plays an important role in motivation and emotion.

Hypothesis. A belief, hunch, tentative statement, or explanation that has not been proven or disproven.

Iconic memory. A visual image, or icon, held in the sensory register no more than 1 or 2 seconds.

Id. The unconscious part of the personality that operates to derive immediate pleasure, being concerned only with immediate gratification of physiological needs.

Identification. Unconscious modeling of others' behavior, such as their ways of coping with stress or their sex role behavior, and the unconscious internalizing of others' values, attitudes, and feelings.

Idiosyncrasy credit. The sum total of positive impressions in the followers' perceptions of a leader.

Idiot savants. People who have an incredible specific capacity such as the ability to draw, remember music, or compute numbers but who are otherwise retarded, sometimes with virtually no language ability.

Illumination. The third stage in the process of creativity when suddenly and unexpectedly the person has insight into the problem, resulting in the conception of an idea that seems to be a solution.

Illusion. A misleading or invalid perception of reality brought about by the reliability of the patterning and stabilizing principles.

Imitation. The conscious modeling of others' behavior.

Incentives. Things in the environment that are perceived as having positive or negative value and motivate approach or avoidance behavior because of some attribute of the stimulus itself.

Incubation. The second stage in the process of creativity that consists of the time during which the information that has been acquired is absorbed and assimilated through unconscious mental activity.

Independent variable. The variable in an experimental study that is manipulated by the experimenter while all other variables are held constant.

Industrial and organizational psychology. An area of psychology that specializes in applying psychological principles in work-related situations and in conducting research to expand knowledge of behavior applicable in organizational settings.

Inferential statistics. The part of statistics concerned with drawing conclusions and making inferences about populations based on samples taken from a population.

Information hub. An individual in a group who gets more information than others in the group because of his or her position or role in the organization or social position.

Insight learning. Learning that occurs in the thought processes and includes both learning sets and insight—a sudden awareness of how a problem can be solved without any trial and error preceding it or a sudden awareness or knowledge of a fact from inference without any direct input preceding it.

Instinct. An unlearned, goal-directed behavior pattern that is universally unique to a particular environmental stimulus the first time the stimulus is presented.

Instrumentality. In VIE theory, the belief a person has that a behavior will achieve or secure second-level outcomes (outcomes that are a result of first-level outcomes) that are of value.

Intelligence quotient (IQ). The ratio of the mental age to the chronologic age multiplied by 100.

Interactionists. Theorists who believe that the inconsistencies that are found in behavior are due to the interaction of the individual with the environment—that behavior is a combination of motivations, traits, and situation.

Intermittent schedules. Schedules of reinforcement in which the consequence follows the response some of the time but not every time.

Internal locus of control. The perception of a person that the center of control in his or her life is within the self.

Interneurons. Neurons, sometimes referred to as association neurons, that carry messages to and receive messages from other neurons in the brain and spinal cord.

Interval schedules. Intermittent schedules of reinforcement in which a reinforcer follows the response only after a specific period of time has elapsed since the last reinforcer was given.

Intrinsic motivation. The source of behavior that comes from the behavior itself because of a need to demonstrate competence, master the environment, control desired outcomes, or engage in an activity for its own sake.

Intrinsic reinforcers. Internal feelings of satisfaction such as feelings of competence, achievement, or self-actualization that a person gets from performing a particular behavior.

Introspection. The method used by the structuralists to investigate the contents of the mind by asking a person to describe his or her feelings or conscious awareness of the stimulus presented.

Introverts. Individuals who are usually rather quiet and withdrawn.

Ions. Particles formed when a neural atom or group of atoms loses or gains one or more electrons.

Job enlargement. A form of job redesign that involves the practice of adding tasks for variety and task identity.

Job enrichment. A form of job redesign that is the process of adding tasks of a managerial nature to a job.

Job redesign. A procedure employed by some organizations to redesign jobs to be more challenging, rewarding, and meaningful in an effort to fulfill employees' intrinsic needs.

Job rotation. A form of job redesign in which employees are moved from job to job to keep the work from being as boring.

Job sharing. The performance of a job by two part-time employees that is normally performed by one full-time employee.

Kinesics. The science of body language—the study of body postures and gestures.

Kinesthetic sense. The sense that enables one to be aware of the movements and positions of different body parts.

Law. A theory that is generally accepted, very strongly supported, and somewhat precise.

Learned helplessness. The development of self-defeating expectancies that leads to passive acceptance of undesirable conditions and depression.

Learning sets. Specific approaches that have been learned that may be used in solving new but similar problems or learning new but similar tasks with a common underlying principle.

Levelers. Individuals with a cognitive style whereby they tend to see new stimuli as very similar to what has been previously presented and to simplify the grammatical structure of verbal materials in recall.

Life positions. In transactional analysis, the four positions a person may hold and act out as a result of attitudes or feelings about the self (self-esteem) and others, one of which tends to prevail throughout a person's later childhood and adult life.

Life scripts. In transactional analysis, unconscious lifetime plans based on attitudes concerning such things as success, work, sex, love, education, or religion that will be acted out like the script of a play.

Limbic system. An interconnection of several structures in the center core of the brain, including parts of the thalamus, hypothalamus, and the hippocampus that is related to motivation and emotion, especially aggression, and includes the pleasure centers of the brain.

Local circuits. Tiny areas on neurons where weak electrical interactions between branches of dendrites from neurons may occur even though stimulation is not of a sufficient strength to cause depolarization of the cell.

Logical error. A type of distorted perception of others in which one has a tendency to see different traits as belonging together when they logically do not.

Logos. A word that comes from a Greek word meaning knowledge, study of, or wisdom.

Long-term memory. In the structural approach to explaining memory, the information that is held in the third level or the storage system that holds it relatively permanently.

Love. As defined by Rubin (1970), an attitude held by one person toward another consisting of three components—attachment, caring, and intimacy.

Magnetic resonance imaging. A method of computing an image based on magnetic fields and radio frequencies, used mostly as a brain scan that shows the presence and location of certain chemical elements—commonly referred to as MRI.

Management by objectives (MBO). A managerial philosophy and technique whereby superiors and subordinates jointly identify goals, define each individual worker's responsibility in terms of individual goals, and use these goals as a guide for evaluating success on the job.

Massed practice. A method of learning that involves practicing what is to be learned from start to finish in one long, unbroken time interval.

Maturation. The control that genes exert over the unfolding of biological events from conception to death.

Mean. The familiar arithmetic average obtained by totaling all the items of data and dividing by the number of items of data.

Measure of central tendency. A representative point or score for a set of data that tends to be near the middle of the score range.

Measure of variability. A numeric representation of the spread, dispersion, or deviation of the scores in a set of data.

Mechanism. Ren Descartes' view that human behavior is attributable to physical causes and can be predicted according to the laws of mechanics.

Median. A measure of central tendency based on the rank distribution—the point or score below which half (50 percent) of the items of data fall when they are arranged in rank order.

Medical model. A view of psychological disorders, based on both the organic and psychoanalytic models, that people who have psychological disorders are sick and are no more responsible for their disorder than people who exhibit physical disorders such as abnormal temperature from measles or hobbling from a broken leg.

Meditation. A technique for detaching the self from awareness of the stimuli and events of everyday life that activate the sympathetic nervous system and for achieving a state of deep relaxation, inner peace, and heightened self-awareness.

Medulla. The structure in the lowest part of the brain adjoining the spinal cord that controls reflex behaviors involved in breathing, heart rate, and the maintenance of an upright posture.

Meiosis. A special two-step process of cell division that occurs in the maturation of reproductive or germ cells in which four daughter cells (gametes) each receive only 23 single chromosomes instead of the 23 pairs that were in the parent cell.

Memory. The process of preserving information for later use—the persistence of learning over time.

Mesomorphs. Individuals who have a firm bone structure and much accumulation of muscle.

Midbrain. The structure in the brain located near the center of the brain that has many functions but plays a major role in hearing and seeing.

Mitosis. The method of cell division in which the two daughter cells each receive identical genetic material (23 pairs or 46 chromosomes) to that of the parent cell.

Mode. A measure of central tendency that is the score in a set of data that occurs most frequently.

Monochromats. Those individuals who have two types of cones missing, both the red-green cones and the blue-yellow cones, and therefore do not perceive color normally.

Moral development. The process of internalizing standards of right and wrong—of internalizing a culturally defined set of rules whereby behaviors are personally classified as good or bad, acceptable or unacceptable.

Morale. A word sometimes used to mean degree of happiness or general satisfaction; more specifically, the degree to which a person's needs are satisfied and the degree to which the satisfaction is perceived as stemming from the total job situation.

Morpheme. A meaningful unit of sound.

Motivation. That which activates or causes behavior to occur and gives direction to behavior—the internal source (forces and processes) of behavior.

Motivation factors. Factors of a job that occur at the time the work is performed and make the work rewarding in and of itself. Herzberg proposed that these factors lead to job satisfaction and increased productivity, but that their absence rarely produces dissatisfaction.

Motivation research. The study of why people buy products and services in an attempt to try to discover the unconscious motives, attitudes, and preferences involved in the purchase.

Motives. The specific needs, desires, and wants that motivate. Literally, a motive is whatever moves a person to action.

Myelin sheath. Fatty nodules that cover the axons of some neurons, serving as a sheath to insulate the fiber of the axon and speed up the transmission of a message as it jumps over the shielded places.

nAch. In the network of three basic motives theory, the *need for achievement*—the need for success as measured against some internalized standard of excellence.

nAff. In the network of three basic motives theory, the *need for affiliation*—the need for close interpersonal relationships and friendships with other people.

Naturalistic method. A scientific method of collecting evidence to test hypotheses that involves the careful observation and recording of behavior in a natural setting with as little interference by the investigator as possible.

Needs. A broad term that refers to the learned or psychological needs of an individual as well as the physiological drives of the body for survival.

Negative reinforcement. A consequence of a behavior that is reinforcing because the behavior either removes, provides escape from, or prevents the occurrence of an aversive discriminative stimulus and thus increases the frequency of occurrence of the behavior.

Neo-Freudians. "New Freuds" or those who accepted the basic ideas of Freud's theory in general but who had some distinctly different views.

Neocortex. The cerebral cortex or simply cortex of the brain that is the mass of cell bodies and unmyelinated axons of neurons that covers the two hemispheres of the brain that form an unbrella over the structures in the center of the brain.

Neonatal. The time of life from birth up to about 2 weeks old.

Nerve. A bundle of axons from many neurons, much like a telephone cable that consists of many wires, that carries impulses between body parts and the central nervous system.

Neuromodulators. Chemical substances produced and secreted into the bloodstream (sometimes from neurons as a special type of neurotransmitter and sometimes from various other places in the body) that interact with neurotransmitters and affect the way they function.

Neurons. The specialized cells

of the nervous system.

Neurotransmitters. Chemical substances released by a neuron into the synaptic area that bind or lock into receptor sites on the receiving neuron to stimulate it.

Neutral stimulus. A person, place, event, or object that does not bring forth a specific response.

Nonconscious level. A low level of consciousness that includes awareness of and information of the automatic internal events such as the heart beating or the blood circulating.

Nonsense syllable. A vowel between two consonants that together do not form a meaningful word, such as BAX, JUP, HEB, or LOM.

Norepinephrine. A neurotransmitter that seems to play a role in the body's response to stress.

Norms. The average or standard performance of a representative group at various points in the distribution that provides the comparison for determining if an individual's performance is average, above average, or below average.

nPow. In the network of three basic motives theory, the *need for power*—the need for direct control or influence over others or the need for control over the means of influencing others.

Null hypothesis. A hypothesis that states that no significant differences exist between the sample mean and the population, between the means of two or more samples from the same population, or between correlation coefficients and zero other than chance differences.

Obedience. The act of carrying out an order or command authorized by another person.

Objective personality tests. Inventories, usually paper-and-pencil tests, in the form of questions about the self.

Observational (social) learning. A type of learning that expands on operant conditioning and focuses on modeling whereby a person learns to do something by watching someone else do it.

Obsession. The persistent, repetitious, involuntary occurrence of thoughts, ideas, or images even though the individual desires to suppress them.

Occipital lobes. The large lump or area at the back of each of the two hemispheres of the cortex that receives and interprets impulses from the eyes.

Oedipus complex. Freud's term for the conflict and anxiety experienced by a boy during the phallic stage of development as he unconsciously feels sexual attraction for his mother and becomes jealous of the father, the resolution being identification with the father.

Operant conditioning. A type of learning that occurs when a randomly or spontaneously emitted behavior becomes associated with the consequence or effect the behavior has on the environment and increases or decreases in frequency according to whether the effect is desirable or undesirable.

Operants. The spontaneous behaviors that an organism is capable of emitting such as pressing, pecking, turning, making a sound, or moving body parts.

Operational definitions. Objective definitions of stimuli and behaviors that allow for reliable or consistent measurement of them.

Operations. In Piaget's theory, thought structures that enable the individual to adapt to the environment, to act and think in a particular way.

Opinion. A belief that an individual may hold even though the factual evidence available to support the belief is weak.

Organic model. The view that the basis for psychological disorders is in the biochemical or physiological processes.

Orientation phase. The first phase of a four-phase developmental sequence of group formation during which the members of the group are getting acquainted and confirming or changing expectations of the activities of the group and the rewards rendered by membership in the group.

Originality. The novelty or unusualness of an idea.

Ovaries. The female sex glands that release hormones, primarily estrogens and progesterones, related to development and function of reproductive organs, development of secondary sex characteristics, and pregnancy, childbirth, and nursing of the newborn infant.

Overcompensation. A defense mechanism whereby exaggerated behavior is expressed in an area of competency unconsciously as a means of handling inadequacy in some area.

Overlearning. A learning procedure that refers to the continuation of practice or repetition of what is being learned beyond the point when the material has been learned.

Ovum. The female reproductive cell called an egg that may develop into a new organism when fertilized by a sperm.

Pancreas. An endocrine gland located near the stomach that secretes two hormones that work against each other to control the level of sugar in the blood.

Paralanguage. A form of nonverbal communication of emotion by physical characteristics of the voice such as pitch, loudness, pauses, exclamations, stuttering, and voice inflections.

Parallel coaction tasks. Tasks in which members of the group work separately and independently but parallel.

Paraphilias. Unusual or bizarre acts or imagery necessary or preferred for sexual excitement involving use of children, animals, or corpses and activities such as exposure of genitals to unsuspecting strangers, observation of unsuspecting people who are naked or engaging in sexual activity, aggression including the inflicting of physical and/or psychological pain, and lewd telephone talk.

Parapsychologists. Those psychologists who study paranormal or beyond normal happenings such as extrasensory perception occurrences.

Parasympathetic nervous system. A subsystem of the autonomic nervous system that is activated in the normal maintenance of life support functions.

Parathyroids. The endocrine glands embedded in the thyroid that release a hormone that controls the calcium and phosphate levels in the blood related to excitability of the nervous system.

Parent ego state. In transactional analysis, the part of the personality that consists of values, opinions, dos and don'ts, shoulds and should nots, and stored memories of statements and actions of parents and authority figures—the criticizer and/or nurturer.

Parietal lobes. The lumps or large areas of the cortex located at the top of the hemispheres between the frontal lobes and the occipital lobes that are involved in the integration of sensory input.

Parting phase. The fourth phase of a four-phase developmental sequence of group formation that involves the disbanding or dissolving of the group either from failure to reach a balance phase following a conflict phase or because of a limited existence due to time or situation.

Passionate love. A highly emotional state that is often a confusion of feelings such as anxiety and relief, altruism and jealousy, tenderness and sexual aggression, and elation and forlornness.

Peptides. Chemical substances such as endorphins that consist of varying lengths of chains of amino acids produced naturally in the body and released into the bloodstream from various parts of the body that act as neuromodulators to control various behavioral systems.

Perceptual learning. A type of cognitive learning that increases one's ability to extract information from the environment as a result of practice or experience with environmental stimulation.

Perceptual organization. The processes of perception that are the bases for patterning or putting together large amounts of information quickly and integrating the elements into meaningful wholes.

Perceptual set. A perceptual expectancy that prepares a person to perceive in a particular way as a result of prior experiences, suggestions, and motivations.

Perinatal. The period of birth that includes from shortly before, during, and immediately after birth.

Peripheral nervous system. The division of the nervous system that consists of all the nerves that carry messages to and from the brain and spinal cord and that go out to all parts of the body.

Person perception. An individual's perception of another person.

Personality. The characteristic way a person responds to other people, objects, or events in the environment—a summation of the persistent behavior patterns that are unique to an individual.

Personnel psychology. The study of individual differences in performance of employees, methods to assess such differences, and the application of principles of psychology to management and employee training.

Phobias. Persistent and irrational fears of a specific object, activity, or situation that are recognized as being unreasonable and unwarranted and result in a compelling desire to avoid the dreaded object, activity, or situation.

Phonemes. The smallest distinguishable units of sound that are used in a language.

Physiognomy. The classification of personality traits based on facial features that is not believed today but is the basis for some expressions used today.

Physiological psychology. An area of psychology in which behavior is studied as a function of physical changes in the body, especially in the brain, the nervous system, and the biochemistry of the body.

Pitch. How high or low a sound is as determined by the frequency of the sound waves.

Pituitary gland. An endocrine gland located in the brain that produces peptides and many hormones that control the timing and amount of growth of the body and that control the other endocrine glands.

Placebo. An inert substance that has no physical power to affect a person but may psychologically produce the expected effect.

Placenta. An organ developed in the uterus by the fertilized ovum to permit the exchange of nutrients and waste products between the mother and the developing child.

Polarization. The state of a neuron when the electrical charges of the cell's interior and exterior are stable; the state of a neuron when it is at rest, neither receiving nor transmitting a message.

Polygenic. Characteristics of a person such as intelligence, temperament, or personality that are influenced by a variety of genes operating in a complex interaction.

Polygraph. A device commonly called a lie detector that measures or records changes in heart rate, blood pressure, respiration, and galvanic skin response — physiological responses associated with emotion.

Pons. The mass of nerve fibers positioned above the medulla that connects the higher and lower levels of the brain and the two hemispheres of the cerebellum.

Population. The total set of all possible cases from which a sample is selected.

Positive reinforcement. A consequence of a behavior that is the delivery of something that pleases, rewards, or satisfies the person and increases the frequency of the occurrence of the behavior.

Positron emission tomography. A method of generating a computer image of the brain based on the emission of positrons that detect where a radioactive form of glucose goes while the brain performs — commonly referred to as a PET scan.

Postconventional morality. Level III in Kohlberg's theory of moral development when moral value resides in principles that underlie the laws and conventions of a society and conformity by the self rather than in rules and obedience to authority.

Postnatal. The time of life after birth.

Precognition. Perception of a event before it occurs.

Preconscious level. The level of consciousness that consists of stored knowledge and memories that can become conscious as needed.

Preconventional morality. Level I in Kohlberg's theory of moral development when moral value resides in external happenings, in actions, or in needs in relationship to the self.

Prefrontal lobotomy. Brain surgery in which the connections of the frontal lobes of the brain to the emotional areas of the brain are surgically severed.

Prejudice. A favorable or unfavorable attitude toward some members of a group of people that predisposes the same attitude toward all members of the group.

Premack principle. The principle demonstrated by Premack that a behavior that occurs often can be used as a reinforcer of a behavior that occurs less frequently.

Prenatal. The time of life before birth.

Preoperational stage. The second stage in Piaget's theory of intellectual development, the period from approximately 2 to 7 years of age, during which the child becomes increasingly able to represent objects and events symbolically.

Primary motives. Needs that have a biological basis and are necessary for survival.

Primary process thinking. The id's way of thinking.

Primary reinforcers. Reinforcers that are effective in increasing a behavior by satisfying a biological need. They may lose their effectiveness due to overuse but, subsequently, may regain their effectiveness after a period of deprivation.

Primary sex characteristics. Physical structures of a person essential to reproduction such as the ovaries and vagina in the female and the testes and penis in the male.

Principle. A law incorporated into a more general and extensive statement that applies to a large range of instances.

Proactive inhibition. The interfering effect of previous learning upon the recall of information learned more recently.

Progesterones. Hormones secreted by the ovaries of the female that create the menstrual cycle and prepare the female body for pregnancy, childbirth, and nursing of the newborn infant.

Programmed instruction. A teaching technique based on the operant conditioning principle of shaping whereby an individual is presented with small segments of information that move the individual closer and closer to the final object of the course of study.

Projection. A defense mechanism whereby an unacceptable thought, desire, or impulse is unconsciously rejected by blaming it on someone else.

Projective tests. Tests that use unstructured, vague, and ambiguous stimuli to obtain a response and require a highly trained clinician to evaluate the responses.

Proxemics. Nonverbal communication of emotion exhibited by the physical distance kept from a person or event and the eye contact that is maintained.

Proximity rule. The patterning principle whereby parts seem separate or grouped together depending on how close they are together.

Psyche. A word that comes from a Greek word meaning mind, life, spirit, or soul.

Psychoanalysis. Therapy based on the psychoanalytic approach to explaining behavior that attempts to bring repressed feelings and sources of anxiety into the patient's consciousness.

Psychiatrists. Medical doctors who have followed their medical school training with 3 to 5 years of specialized schooling in psychological disorders.

Psychoanalytic model. The view developed by Freud that psychological disorders are due primarily to anxiety, guilt, and psychological disturbances in early childhood and are symptoms of underlying conflicts that are probably repressed and unconscious to the individual.

Psychoanalytic psychology. An approach to explaining human behavior through the unconscious processes that places particular emphasis on conflicts and anxieties that have their roots in early childhood experiences.

Psychoanalyst. A therapist—counselor, psychologist, or psychiatrist—whose approach to treatment is based on psychoanalytical theory.

Psychokinesis. The ability to influence a physical object or event through thought rather than through the muscular system.

Psychological amnesia. An extreme form of unconscious blocking out of memories (repression) whereby all memory of personal events is blocked out.

Psychological stress evaluator. A device that is a type of lie detector that will measure changes in a person's voice that are undetectable to the human ear.

Psychology. The scientific study of behavior and mental processes and the application of knowledge gained through that study.

Psychosexual stages. The stages a child passes through (oral, anal, phallic, latency, genital) according to Freud, based on different erogenous zones becoming the source of pleasure as progression through childhood occurs.

Psychosomatic illnesses. Physical disorders such as some cases of ulcers, migraine headaches, asthma, high blood pressure, and heart disease that are the result of psychological stress.

Psychotherapy. The term used for any attempt by a clinician to bring about desired personality or behavioral changes by applying particular psychological techniques.

Puberty. The period of time from the beginning of development of the primary and secondary sex characteristics in early adolescence until the physiological achievement of sexual maturity; on the average a period of about 2 years from age 10 or 11 to age 12 or 13.

Punishment. An aversive consequence that follows the occurrence of a response that is either physiologically or psychologically unpleasant to the person and decreases the occurrence of that response.

Pure psychology. Theoretical psychology—theories, laws, and principles.

Pygmalion effect. Tendency of an individual to act, perhaps unconsciously, in such a manner as to insure the expected outcome.

Randomization. The process of selecting by chance (randomly selecting) a sample of subjects in such a way that each member of the population has an equal chance of being selected.

Range. The amount of variation between the highest and the lowest items of data.

Rank distribution. An arrangement of the scores in a set of data in a hierarchical order from highest to lowest.

Ratio schedules. Intermittent schedules of reinforcement in which a reinforcer follows a response only after a certain number of responses have been emitted.

Rationalism. The philosophical idea that attributes a person's behavior to thinking—conscious intentions and reasonings.

Rationalization. A defense mechanism whereby a person unconsciously develops a socially acceptable justification as a form of self-deception to avoid having to face a nonacceptable view of oneself.

Reaction formation. A defense mechanism whereby a person unconsciously swings in the opposite direction from true desires or impulses as a means of maintaining self-control or self-respect.

Reaction range. The possible range of values allowed by a person's genetics for some characteristic.

Receptor sites. Places or parts on a neuron that respond to stimulation or "take up" a substance, allowing it to have an impact on the neuron.

Recessive gene. The gene that when paired with a dominant gene does not produce an effect in development; it defers to a dominant gene.

Recognition method. A method of measuring retention of memory by determining the percentage of material learned that can be recognized using measurement tools such as multiple-choice tests.

Reflex. An automatic response to a stimulus that is innate such as the eye blink in response to a puff of air or the knee jerk in response to a tap on the knee.

Reinforcement theory. The assumption that reinforcement is the source of behavior and that what is ordinarily called motivated behavior is simply learned behavior.

Relearning method. A method of measuring memory based on percentage of savings in terms of amount of time and number of trials necessary to recall previously learned material.

Reliability. The degree to which a test produces consistent or stable measures for an individual on different occasions.

REM sleep. A stage of sleep during which dreaming occurs that is characterized by rapid eye movements.

Repression. The unconscious blocking out of memories that may be unpleasant, emotionally disturbing, or in conflict with the belief system; the psychoanalytic explanation for forgetting.

Response. Any behavior—body movements, glandular secretion, or mental activity—that is a result of stimulation.

Response discrimination. The process that occurs when two or more similar but physically different responses are emitted in a particular situation and one response is reinforced and maintained while the other responses are extinguished.

Response generalization. The emission of a response to a stimulus or in a particular situation that is similar but slightly different from the response originally learned.

Reticular activating system. A system in the brain extending through the hindbrain and into the center core of the brain that consists of a netlike bundle of neurons that regulates levels of awareness and serves as an arousal system to activate large areas of the higher parts of the brain.

Retina. The area at the back of the eyeball that contains the receptor cells that are activated by light rays.

Retrieval. The process of locating information in long-term memory storage and bringing it into consciousness.

Retrieval cue. Any stimulus that helps retrieve a memory.

Retroactive inhibition. The

interfering effect of later learning upon the recall of information learned just prior to or previously.

Reverberating circuit. A relatively permanent structural change in the brain formed as sensory information travels in the form of a neural impulse from one cell to the next until a full round or circuit is made; the circuit may be repeated when triggered by a cue.

Ribonucleic acid (RNA) molecules. Molecules that control the production of protein similar to the way genetic information is encoded in deoxyribonucleic acid (DNA) molecules.

Risky-shift phenomenon. The fact that an individual is usually willing to make riskier decisions as a member of a group than when alone.

Rods. Receptor cells on the retina of the eye that are sensitive to brightness or differences in light intensity and are involved in night vision.

Sample. The set of subjects selected from a population to represent the population in a scientific study.

Scapegoat. A person or group bearing the blame for others as in displaced aggression.

Scattergram. A two-dimentional plot of points with each point representing the paired measurements on the two variables.

Schemes. In Piaget's theory, action patterns that enable a person to act in a particular way to adapt to the environment.

Secondary motives. Needs that an individual has that have only a learned or psychological basis such as the need for achievement or for affiliation.

Secondary process thinking. The conscious mental activity of the ego.

Secondary reinforcers. Conditioned or learned reinforcers that gain their effectiveness from association with other reinforcers such as a smile, which a person may associate with friendly conversation, or a good grade, which a person may associate with acquiring a desired job. They may lose their effectiveness from either overuse or extinction.

Secondary sex characteristics. Physical characteristics of a person related to sex but not part of the reproductive system such as body hair or breast tissue.

Secondary traits. Allport's term for traits that are specific to certain circumstances such as being irritable while shopping.

Security motive. The need to be free from fear.

Self-actualization. In Maslow's theory of motivation, the need highest in the hierarchy, which is the tendency of an individual to realize his or her maximum potential.

Self-concept. The perception an individual has of his or her capacities and abilities.

Self-efficacy. The belief by a person that he or she can perform adequately, which leads to internal control, goal setting, and the development of means of attaining goals.

Self-esteem. The perception an individual has of his or her value or importance and significance to other individuals.

Self-image. The perception an individual has of his or her physical and personality characteristics.

Semantic memory. The part of long-term memory that consists of information, facts, and general, nonpersonal knowledge; sometimes said to be like the person's dictionary or encyclopedia.

Semantics. The relationship between sound and significance; the formation of concepts or word meanings.

Sensorimotor stage. The first stage in Piaget's theory of intellectual development, the period from birth to approximately 2 years of age, during which the child learns relationships between sensations and motor responses—the stage that occurs prior to the development of language.

Sensory memory. In the structural approach to explaining memory, information held in the first level or storage system where it is stored in the sensory registers.

Serial recall. A method of measuring memory in which an individual is given a list of items to learn and then recall at some later time in the order learned.

Serotonin. A now well-known inhibitory neurotransmitter related to sleep and activities associated with sleep such as dreaming and insomnia.

Set. A habit or predisposition to respond in a certain way to solve a problem because of experience.

Sex-linked characteristics. Characteristics that are determined by the pair of X and Y chromosomes containing the genes that determine sex.

Sexuality. The whole of an individual's sexual behavior including the gender concept (gender identity, sex-role stereotyping, and sex-role behavior), biological development of primary and secondary sex characteristics, sexual arousal, and response to sexual arousal for reproduction.

Shaping. Creating a new behavior by reinforcing closer and closer approximations of the desired or target behavior.

Sharpeners. Individuals with a cognitive style whereby they tend to notice differences quickly and accurately between new stimuli and stimuli previously presented and to recall details of verbal material (stories).

Shift toward polarization. The tendency of people to shift to a more extreme position when making decisions in the presence of a group.

Short-term memory. In the structural approach to explaining memory, information held in the second level or storage system where it is held in the present consciousness.

Significant difference. A difference between groups in some measurable characteristic that is great enough that it is unlikely that the difference is due to chance factors.

Similarity rule. The patterning principle in perception whereby similar patterns are grouped together.

Social facilitation. The phenomenon that the presence of a group increases individual performance.

Social learning. A type of learning which expands on operant conditioning and focuses on modeling, whereby a person learns to do something by watching someone else do it.

Social psychology. The specialized area of psychology that deals with behavior of people in groups such as families or peer groups and focuses on such topics as interpersonal relationships and attitudes.

Sociobiology. A recent biological theory of motivation that suggests that behavior is preprogrammed for one and only one function—to ensure the survival of the DNA molecules that make up one's genetic identity.

Somatic nervous system. A division of the peripheral nervous system that consists of the spinal nerves and cranial nerves such as the auditory nerve and the optic nerve.

Source traits. The traits obtained by Cattell by analyzing the surface traits that represent the underlying traits that enter into the determination of multiple surface traits—the ones that have the most utility in accounting for behavior.

Sperm. The male reproductive cell that when united with an ovum may produce a new organism.

Spontaneous recovery. The reappearance of a conditioned response after a lapse of time following extinction.

Spontaneous type. Individuals who (a) respond with immediate and intentional purpose, seemingly guided by unconscious, long-term or life-long goals and (b) respond unfavorably to goal setting because they feel that goal setting is unnecessary because they can achieve without it.

Stability-instability. One of the two major dimensions of personality proposed by Eysenck that is related to emotional stability and refers to (a) changeability in mood; (b) sensitivity to emotional stress, tenseness, and anxiety; (c) the tendency to worry; (d) concern about physical health; (e) the tendency to feel guilty; (f) low self-esteem; and (g) feelings of fatigue.

Stamp. In transactional analysis, a feeling that is obtained from a stroke.

Standard deviation. A measure of variability that considers every score in the set of data and is calculated by taking the square root of the variance.

Standard normal curve. A theoretical, bell-shaped, symmetrical curve (frequency polygon) that represents the distribution of scores for any population.

Standardization. The process of obtaining a distribution of scores for a test from a large sample of people to provide the comparison for determining if an individual's score is average, above average, or below average and for determining the percentage of the population that scores below the individual's score.

Standardized test. A test that has scores available from a large representative sample of people to provide the comparison for determining if an individual's score is average, above average, or below average or for determining the percentage of the population that scores below the individual's score.

State anxiety. Anxiety that is experienced temporarily in a specific situation.

Statistics. A body of scientific methods consisting of mathematical ways of handling data and deciding whether a difference in behavior is attributable to independent variables rather than to chance factors. Also, a collection of numeric facts that have been gathered through observation or from other numeric data such as averages, tables, and graphs.

Stereotyping. The assigning of identical characteristics to all members of a group and maintaining the stereotype even when faced with conflicting information.

Stimulants. Drugs that increase activity in the central nervous system and have the capacity to increase arousal and alertness, elevate mood, and combat tiredness and sleepiness.

Stimulus. Any physical event, either internal such as a pain or thought, or external such as something heard, seen, felt, or smelled.

Stimulus anxiety hierarchy. A list of stimuli or activities related to a particular fear that range from a least or no anxiety-producing one to the one that is most anxiety provoking.

Stimulus control. The control of a person's reactions by the characteristics of the situation.

Stimulus discrimination. Learning to differentiate or recognize differences between similar stimuli and to respond differently to similar stimuli.

Stimulus generalization. The principle that when a new stimulus comes to be associated with a stimulus that already elicits a particular response, any stimulus similar to that new stimulus may also elicit the response, even if direct conditioning has not occurred.

Stimulus motives. Needs that cause an individual to seek out environmental stimulation that promotes learning, including the need for activity, sensory input, exploration, curiosity, manipulation, and human body contact.

Stimulus thresholds. The minimum levels of energy required for transduction to occur.

Stingy-shift phenomenon. The fact that an individual is usually willing to make a more conservative decision when in a group than when alone.

Storage. The process of holding learned information in the memory system.

Stress. Energy produced within the body by any situation, physical or psychological, to allow for action to cope with the situation, accomplish goals, or defend the self.

Stressors. The situations and events in a person's life that cause stress.

Stroke. In transactional analysis, any communication that recognizes one's existence, whether the communication is verbal or nonverbal.

Structuralism. An early view held by Wilhelm Wundt and his followers that the structure of the mind could be discovered by analyzing conscious sensory experience and reducing it to its basic elements.

Subliminal perception. Unconscious perception of weak, below threshold stimulations in the subconscious part of the mind.

Superego. The internalized values and moral standards of an individual, sometimes conscious and sometimes unconscious, known as the conscience.

Superstitious behavior. A relationship between a response and reinforcement that occurs when reinforcement follows the response by chance and the reinforcement is not contingent on the response.

Surface traits. The 35 traits proposed by Cattell that represent a summary of expressive behaviors that are related.

Survey method. A self-report method of studying behavior in which questions are usually prepared to which answers are obtained through direct interviews, by mail, or by telephone, usually to investigate such behaviors as the attitudes, feelings, or opinions of large groups of people.

Sympathetic nervous system. The subsystem of the autonomic nervous system that is activated in emergency situations, in emotional experience, and in times of stress whether the stress is physical or mental in nature.

Synapse. The small space that separates one neuron from another neuron, and where the neurons communicate, generally the space that separates the terminal branch of one neuron from the dendrites of the next neuron.

Syntax. The rules or grammar of the language.

Telepathy. Perception of another person's thoughts.

Temporal lobes. The lumps or large areas on each side of the two hemispheres of the neocortex devoted primarily to hearing.

Tension. The holding of stress in the muscles, defined in the dictionary as the condition of being strained or stretched.

Teratogens. Agents or influences that cause physical defects or have negative effects on the embryo and/or fetus during prenatal development.

Terminal branches. Small fibers that extend from the end of an axon of a neuron, each of which has a knob on the end from which chemical substances (neurotransmitters) are released.

Testes. The male sex glands that release hormones, primarily androgens, that play a role in the maturation of reproductive organs and the development of secondary sex characteristics.

Thalamus. A structure in the forebrain that functions as a relay station for messages coming in from the sense organs and directs the messages to particular areas of the brain.

Theory. A tentative, satisfactory explanation of a phenomenon based on present knowledge.

Theory X. McGregor's label for the theory of managing people based on external direction and control.

Theory Y. McGregor's label for the integrative theory of managing people based on concepts of motivation and human nature and the assumption that everyone is capable of being intrinsically motivated.

Thyroid gland. An endocrine gland located near the neck area that secretes a hormone that regulates the rate at which energy is produced and used by the body.

Timbre. The quality or texture of a sound, which is determined by a complex pattern of overtones produced by accompanying sound waves that are different multiples of the basic frequency.

Time-out/response cost. A punishing consequence that is the delay for some period of time, the removal, or the prevention of occurrence (giving up) of some pleasant discriminative stimulus.

Trait anxiety. The general level of anxiety characteristically exhibited by an individual over time.

Transaction. In transactional analysis, a social interaction that consists of a message directed toward a person and that person's response.

Transactional analysis. A theory of communication based on the premise that people can learn to understand themselves and other people and to improve their interpersonal relations by analyzing the transactions or basic units of communication in individual-to-individual relationships.

Transduction. A process whereby energy received from the environment is translated at the sense organ level and relayed to the peripheral nervous system.

Trichromats. Those individuals who have all three kinds of cones and therefore have normal vision.

Type A personality. An individual who exhibits the typical personality pattern of always hurrying and striving to accomplish too much, too quickly, too frequently.

Type B personality. An individual who can relax and perform in a leisurely manner, realizing limitations.

Ulterior transactions. In transactional analysis, social interactions of the complementary type that have an unspoken or hidden meaning.

Unconditional positive regard. Respect for the person as an important human being with unique values and goals, a condition that is considered to be a part of an accepting environment for a person.

Unconditioned response. A behavior brought forth by an unconditioned (unlearned) stimulus; a reflex response.

Unconditioned stimulus. A phenomenon that always brings forth a specific response, even the first time it is presented; a reflex response.

Unconscious level. The level of consciousness that contains information that is not available to conscious awareness but is conscious at some level because it can affect behavior, dreams, mannerisms, and speech as in slips of the tongue.

Unconscious motivation. Any motivation for behavior that comes from a motive that moves a person without his or her knowledge or awareness of it as the cause of the behavior.

Uterus. The organ in the female in which the young develops.

Valence. In VIE theory, the

value an individual places on the outcome or outcomes of behavior.

Validity. The extent to which a test measures what it is designed to measure.

Values. Attitudes a person has about the worth of things based on the positive or negative feelings associated with them.

Variable. Any characteristic, attribute, or event that may vary in amount when measured or that may be present or absent.

Variable interval schedule. An intermittent schedule of reinforcement in which a response is reinforced after a variable time period has elapsed since the last reinforcer was given.

Variable ratio schedule. An intermittent schedule of reinforcement in which a response is reinforced after a variable number of responses have been emitted since the last reinforcer was given.

Variance. A measure of variability that reflects the dispersion of the scores composing a set of data that is calculated by determining how much each score deviates from the mean of all the scores, squaring each deviation, and then finding the average of the squared deviations.

VIE theory. A theory of work motivation based on expectation of reward, perceived value of outcomes, and expected indirect or second-level outcomes of value (instrumentality).

Voice stress analyzer. A device used to replay the recording of a person's voice four times slower than the recorded speed and produce a voice printout in graphic form similar to the electroencephalogram (EEG) brain wave patterns.

Withdrawal. A defense mechanism whereby an individual physically and/or psychologically pulls away from people and conflict.

Zygote. The cell produced by the union of a sperm and an ovum; the fertilized ovum.

REFERENCE LIST

Adorno, T. W., Frenkel-Brunswik, E., Levinson, D. J., & Sanford, R. N. (1950). *The authoritarian personality.* New York: Harper & Row.

Ainsworth, M. D. S. (1972). Attachment and dependency: A comparison. In J. L. Gewirtz (Ed.), *Attachment and dependency.* Washington, DC: Winston.

Alcoholics shrinking brain. (1981, February 7). *Science News,* p. 87.

Aldefer, C. P. (1976). Change processes in organizations. In M. D. Dunnette (Ed.), *Handbook of industrial and organizational psychology.* Chicago: Rand McNally.

Allport, G. W. (1944). *ABC's of scapegoating.* New York: Anti-Defamation League of B'nai B'rith.

Allport, G. W., & Odbert, H. S. (1936). Trait-names: A psycho-lexical study. *Psychological Monographs, 47*(1, Whole No. 211), 1-171.

American Psychiatric Association (1980). *Diagnostic and statistical manual of mental disorders* (3rd ed.). Washington, DC: Author.

Amoore, J. E., Johnston, J. W., Jr., & Rubin, M. (1964). The stereochemical theory of odor. *Scientific American, 210*(2), 42-49.

Apgar, V. A. (1953). A proposal for a new method of evaluation of the newborn infant. *Current Research in Anesthesia and Analgesia, 32,* 260-267.

Argyle, M., Lefebvre, L., & Cook, M. (1974). The meaning of five patterns of gaze. *European Journal of Social Psychology, 4,* 125-136.

Arnold, M. B. (1960). *Emotion and personality* (2 vols.). New York: Columbia University Press.

Asch, S. E. (1952). *Social psychology.* New York: Prentice-Hall.

Asher, S. R., Oden, S. L., & Gottman, J. M. (1977). Children's friendships in school settings. In L. G. Katz (Ed.), *Current topics in early childhood education* (Vol. 1). Norwood, NJ: Ablex.

Atchison, T. J., & Lefferts, E. A. (1972). The prediction of turnover using Herzberg's job satisfaction technique. *Personnel Psychology, 25,* 53-64.

Atkinson, J. W. (1964). *An introduction to motivation.* Princeton, NJ: Van Nostrand.

Atkinson, R. C., & Shiffrin, R. M. (1968). Human memory: A proposed system and its control processes. In K. W. Spence & J. T. Spence (Eds.), *The psychology of learning and motivation: Advances in research and theory* (Vol. 2). New York: Academic Press.

Atkinson, R. C., & Shiffrin, R. M. (1971). The control of short-term memory. *Scientific American, 225*(2), 82-90.

Ausubel, D. P., & Youssef, M. (1965). The effect of spaced repetition on meaningful retention. *Journal of General Psychology, 73,* 147-150.

Baddeley, A. D., & Hitch, G. (1974). Working memory. In H. G. Bower (Ed.), *The psychology of learning and motivation* (Vol. 8). New York: Academic Press.

Bales, R. F. (1970). *Personality and interpersonal behavior.* New York: Holt, Rinehart and Winston.

Bandura, A. (1965). Influence of models' reinforcement contingencies on the acquisition of imitative responses. *Journal of Personality and Social Psychology, 1,* 589-595.

Bandura, A. (1977). *Social learning theory.* Englewood Cliffs, NJ: Prentice-Hall.

Bandura, A. (1982). Self-efficacy mechanism in human agency. *American Psychologist, 37*(2), 122-147.

Bard, P. A. (1928). A diencephalic mechanism for the expression of rage with special reference to the sympathetic nervous system. *American Journal of Physiology, 84,* 490-515.

Barrett, G. V. (1972). Research models of the future for industrial and organizational psychology. *Personnel Psychology, 25,* 1-17.

Barrow, G., & Smith, P. A. (1979). *Aging, ageism, and society.* St. Paul, MN: West.

Bass, B. M., & Barrett, G. V. (1972). *Man, work, and organizations.* Boston: Allyn and Bacon.

Bee, H. (1981). *The developing child* (3rd ed.). New York: Harper & Row.

Begley, S. (1983, February 7). How the brain works. *Newsweek,* pp. 40-47.

Bem, S. L. (1975, September). Androgyny vs. the tight little lives of fluffy women and chesty men. *Psychology Today,* pp. 58-62.

Benson, H. (1975). *The relaxation response.* New York: Morrow.

Benson, H., Kotch, J. B., Crassweller, K. D., & Greenwood, M. M. (1977). Historical and clinical considerations of the relaxation response. *American Scientist, 65,* 441-445.

Berezin, N. (1980). *The gentle birth book: A practical guide to Leboyer family-centered delivery.* New York: Simon & Schuster.

Berne, E. L. (1961). *Transactional analysis in psychotherapy.* New York: Grove Press.

Birdwhistell, R. L. (1952). *Introduction to kinesics.* Louisville, KY: University of Louisville Press.

Bottomley, P. A., Hart, H. R., Jr., Edelstein, W. A., Schenck, J. F., Smith, L. S., Leue, W. M., Mueller, O. M., and Redington, R. W. (1984, February). Anatomy and metabolism of the normal human brain studied by magnetic resonance at 1.5 tesla. *Radiology, 150,* 441-446.

Bouchard, T. J., Jr., & McGue, M. (1981). Familial studies of intelligence: A review. *Science, 212,* 1055-1059.

Bourne, L. E., Jr., & Ekstrand, B. R. (1985). *Psychology: Its principles and meanings* (5th ed.). New York: Holt, Rinehart and Winston.

Bower, G. (1981, June). Mood & memory. *Psychology Today,* pp. 60-69.

Brent, R. L. (1980). Radiation teratogenesis. *Teratology, 22,* 251.

Brim, O. G., & Kagan, J. (1980). *Constancy and change in human development.* Cambridge, MA: Harvard University Press.

Brown, R. W. (1965). *Social psychology.* New York: Free Press.

Brown, W. D. (1983, August 26). Job anxiety. *The Houston Post,* pp. 1E and 5E.

Bryden, M. P. (1973). Auditory-visual and sequential-spatial matching in relation to reading ability. *Child Development, 43* (3), 824-832.

Budzynski, T. (1977). Biofeedback and the twilight states of awareness. In G. Schwartz & D. Shapiro (Eds.), *Consciousness and self-regulation.* New York: Plenum.

Bugelski, B. R. (1971). *The psychology of learning applied to teaching* (2nd ed.). Indianapolis: Bobbs-Merrill.

Burke, R. J. (1969/70). Occupational and life strains, satisfaction and mental health. *Journal of Business Administration, 1* (2), 35-41.

Buss, A. H., & Plomin, R. A. (1975). *A temperament theory of personality development.* New York: Wiley.

Campione, J. C., Brown, A. L., & Ferrara, R. A. (1982). Mental retardation and intelligence. In R. J. Sternberg (Ed.), *Handbook of human intelligence.* Cambridge: Cambridge University Press.

Cannon, W. B. (1927). The James-Lange theory of emotions: A critical examination and an alternative theory. *The American Journal of Psychology, 39,* 106-124.

Caplan, R. D., Abbey, A., Abramis, D. J., Andrews, F. M., Conway, T. L., & French, J. R., Jr. (1984). *Tranquilizer use and well being: A longitudinal study of social and psychological effects.* Ann Arbor: Institute for Social Research, University of Michigan.

Carlson, N. (1980). *Physiology of behavior* (2nd ed.). Boston, MA: Allyn and Bacon.

Cattell, R. B. (1957). *Personality and motivation structure and measurement.* London: Harrap.

Cattell, R. B. (1971). *Abilities: Their structure, growth, and action.* Boston: Houghton Mifflin.

Chaiken, S., & Eagly, A. H. (1983). Communication modality as a determinant of persuasion: The role of communicator salience. *Journal of Personality and Social Psychology, 45,* 241-256.

Cherrington, D. J., & Wixom, B. J., Jr. (1983). Recognition is still a top motivator. *Personnel Administration, 28* (5), 87-91.

Chruden, H. J., & Sherman, A. W., Jr. (1984). *Managing human resources* (7th ed.). Cincinnati: South-Western.

Cole, N. S., Whitney, D. R., & Holland, J. L. (1971). A spatial configuration of occupations. *Journal of Vocational Behavior, 1,* 1-9.

Coleman, J. C., & Hammen, C. L. (1974). *Contemporary psychology and effective behavior.* Glenview, IL: Scott, Foresman.

Collins, A. M., & Quillian, M. R. (1969). Retrieval time from semantic memory. *Journal of Verbal Learning and Verbal Behavior, 8,* 240-247.

Colt, E. W., Wardlaw, S. L., & Frantz, A. G. (1981). The effect of running on plasma B-endorphin. *Life Science, 28,* 1637-1640.

Combs, A. W., & Snygg, D. (1959). *Individual behavior.* New York: Harper and Brothers.

Cook, S. W. (1978). Interpersonal and attitudinal outcomes in cooperating interracial groups. *Journal of Research and Development in Education, 12,* 97-113.

Coombs, J. A. (1975). *A nationwide study of women in United States dental schools,* Doctoral dissertation. Cambridge, MA: Harvard University.

Coon, D. (1983). Manual with test bank to accompany *Essentials of psychology: Exploration and application* (3rd ed.). New York: West.

Corballis, M. C., & Beale, I. L. (1976). *The psychology of left and right.* Hillsdale, NJ: Erlbaum.

Cotman, C. W., & McGaugh, J. L. (1980). *Behavioral neuroscience.* New York: Academic Press.

Craik, F. I. M., & Lockhart, R. S. (1972). Levels of processing: A framework for memory research. *Journal of Verbal Learning and Verbal Behavior, 11,* 671-684.

Craik, F. I. M., & Watkins, M. J. (1973). The role of rehearsal in short-term memory. *Journal of Verbal Learning and Verbal Behavior, 12,* 599-607.

Crockenberg, S. B. (1972). Creativity tests: A boon or boondoggle for education. *Review of Educational Research, 42,* 27-45.

Cronbach, L. J. (1984). *Essentials of psychological testing* (4th ed.). New York: Harper & Row.

Dabbs, J. M., Jr., & Leventhal, H. (1966). Effects of varying the recommendations in a fear-arousing communication. *Journal of Personality and Social Psychology, 4,* 525-531.

Dachler, H. P., & Hulin, C. L. (1969, March). A reconsideration of the relationship between satisfaction and judged importance of environmental and job characteristics. *Organizational Behavior and Human Performance, 4*(4), 252-262.

Davis, C. M. (1939). Results of self-selection of diets by young children. *Canadian Medical Association Journal, 41,* 257-261.

Davis, H. P., & Squire, L. R. (1984). Protein synthesis and memory: A review. *Psychological Bulletin, 96,* 518-559.

Davis, J. D., Gallagher, R. L., & Ladove, R. (1967). Food intake controlled by a blood factor. *Science, 156,* 1247-1248.

Davis, J. M., Schaffer, C. B., Killian, G. A., Kinard, C., & Chan, C. (1980). Important issues in the drug treatment of schizophrenia. In *Special report: Schizophrenia 1980.* Washington, DC: U. S. Government Printing Office.

Deci, E. L. (1972). Intrinsic motivation, extrinsic reinforcement, and inequity. *Journal of Personality and Social Psychology, 22,* 113-120.

Deese, J. (1958). *The psychology of learning.* New York: McGraw-Hill.

Delgado, J. M. R. (1969). *Physical control of the mind.* New York: Harper & Row.

Derlega, V. J., & Janda, L. H. (1978). *Personal adjustment.* Morristown, NJ: Silver Burdett.

Dienstebier, R. A. (1982). Aerobic exercise, catecholamines, and temperament. *SASP Newsletter, 8*(6), 29-30.

Di Vesta, F. J., & Thompson, G. G. (1970). *Educational psychology: Instruction and behavioral change.* New York: Appleton-Century-Crofts.

Dowling, W. F. (1978). Job redesign on the assembly line: Farewell to blue-collar blues. In D. R. Hampton, C. E. Summer, & R. A. Webber, *Organizational behavior and the practice of management* (3rd ed.). Glenview, IL: Scott, Foresman.

DuBrin, A. (1980). *Effective business psychology.* Reston, VA: Reston.

DuBrin, A. (1981). *Human relations: A job oriented approach* (2nd ed.). Reston, VA: Reston.

Dunnette, M. D. (1976). Toward fusion. In M. D. Dunnette (Ed.), *Handbook of industrial and organizational psychology.* Chicago: Rand McNally.

Eagly, A. H. (1980). Recipient characteristics as determinants of responses to persuasion. In R. E. Petty, T. M. Ostrom, & T. C. Brock (Eds.), *Cognitive responses to persuasion.* Hillsdale, NJ: Erlbaum.

Ebbinghaus, H. (1885). *Uber das Gedachtnis* (On Memory). Leipzig: Duncker & Humblot.

Ekman, P. (1975, September). The universal smile: Face muscles talk every language. *Psychology Today,* pp. 35-36.

Elias, M. F., Elias, P. K., & Elias, J. W. (1977). *Basic processes in adult developmental psychology.* St. Louis: Mosby.

Epstein, A. N., Fitzsimons, J. T., & Simons, B. (1969). Drinking caused by the intracranial injection of angiotensin into the rat. *Journal of Physiology* (London), *200,* 98P-100P.

Erikson, E. H. (1963). *Childhood and society* (2nd ed.). New York: Norton.

Eron, L. D., Huesmann, L. R., Lefkowitz, M. M., & Walder, L. O. (1972). Does television violence cause aggression? *American Psychologist, 27,* 253-263.

Eysenck, H. J. (1947). *Dimensions of personality.* London: Kegan Paul.

Eysenck, H. J. (1951). The organization of personality. *Journal of Personality, 20,* 101-117.

Fernald, L. D., & Fernald, P. S. (1978). *Introduction to psychology* (4th ed.). Boston: Houghton Mifflin.

Fernald, L. D., & Fernald, P. S. (1985). *Introduction to psychology* (5th ed.). Dubuque, IA: Wm. C. Brown.

Ferster, C. B., & Skinner, B. F. (1957). *Schedules of reinforcement.* New York: Appleton-Century-Crofts.

Festinger, L. (1957). *A theory of cognitive dissonance.* Evanston, IL: Row, Peterson.

Festinger, L. A. (1954). A theory of social comparison processes. *Human Relations, 7,* 117-140.

Fiedler, F. E. (1967). *A theory of leadership effectiveness.* New York: McGraw-Hill.

Findley, M. J., & Cooper, H. M. (1983). Locus of control and academic achievement: A literature review. *Journal of Personality and Social Psychology, 44,* 419-427.

Flavell, J. H. (1982). On cognitive development. *Child Development, 53,* 1-10.

Fletcher, J. C. (1981). The fetus as patient: Ethical issues. *Journal of the American Medical Association, 2467,* 772-773.

Fowler, C. A., Wolford, G., Slade, R., & Tassinary, L. (1981). Lexical access with and without awareness. *Journal of Experimental Psychology: General, 110,* 341-362.

Frazier, D. (1977, July 25). Industry finding value in charting biorhythms. *The Houston Post,* p. 14A.

Frazier, K. (1984-85). Gallup youth poll finds high belief in ESP, astrology. *The Skeptical Inquirer, 9,* 113-114.

Freed, W. J., Cannon-Spoor, H. E., Krauthamer, E., Hoffer, B. J., & Wyatt, R. J. (1983). Catecholaminergic brain grafts: A behavioral, histochemical, and biochemical comparison of substantia nigra and adrenal medula grafts. *Psychopharmacology Bulletin, 19,* 305-307.

Freedman, J. L., Sears, D. O., & Carlsmith, J. M. (1978). *Social psychology* (3rd ed.). Englewood Cliffs, NJ: Prentice-Hall.

Freedman, J. L., Sears, D. O., & Carlsmith, J. M. (1981). *Social psychology* (4th ed.). Englewood Cliffs, NJ: Prentice-Hall.

French, E. G. (1958). Effects of the interaction of motivation and feedback on task performance. In J. W. Atkinson (Ed.), *Motives in fantasy, action and society.* New York: Van Nostrand.

Friedman, M., & Rosenman, R. H. (1974). *Type A behavior and your heart.* New York: Knopf.

Gage, F. H., Bjorklund, A., Stenevi, U., Dunnett, S. B., & Kelly, P. A. T. (1984). Intrahippocampal septal grafts ameliorate learning impairments in aged rats. *Science, 225,* 533-536.

Galizio, M., & Hendrick, C. (1972). Effect of musical accompaniment on attitude: The guitar as a prop for persuasion. *Journal of Applied Social Psychology, 2,* 350-359.

Gardner, H. (1983). *Frames of mind: The theory of multiple intelligences.* New York: Basic Books.

Ghiselli, E. E. (1966). *The validity of occupational aptitude tests.* New York: Wiley.

Gibb, C. A. (1969). Leadership. In G. Lindzey & E. Aronson (Eds.), *Handbook of social psychology* (2nd ed.). Reading, MA: Addison-Wesley.

Gibson, E. (1969). *Principles of perceptual learning and development.* New York: Appleton-Century-Crofts.

Goleman, D. (1976, May). A new computer test of the brain. *Psychology Today,* pp. 44-48.

Gottesman, I. I. (1963). Genetic aspects of intelligent behavior. In N. Ellis (Ed.), *Handbook of mental deficiency: Psychological theory and research.* New York: McGraw-Hill.

Grasha, A. F. (1978). *Practical applications of psychology.* Cambridge, MA: Winthrop.

Guilford, J. P. (1961). Factorial angles to psychology. *Psychological Review, 68,* 1-20.

Guilford, J. P. (1967). *The nature of human intelligence.* New York: McGraw-Hill.

Guilford, J. P., & Hoepfner, R. (1971). *The analysis of intelligence.* New York: McGraw-Hill.

Guion, R. M. (1961). Some definitions of morale. In E. A. Fleishman (Ed.), *Studies in personnel and industrial psychology.* Homewood, IL: Dorsey.

Gutek, B. A. (1985). *Sex and the workplace.* San Francisco: Jossey-Bass.

Guttman, L. (1950). The problem of attitude and opinion measurement. In S. A. Stouffer, et al. (Eds.), *Measurement and prediction.* Princeton, NJ: Princeton University Press.

Hall, E., Perlmutter, M., & Lamb, M. (1982). *Child psychology today.* New York: Random House.

Hammer, W. C., & Organ, D. W. (1978). *Organizational behavior: An applied psychological approach.* Dallas: Business Publications.

Hansel, C. E. M. (1980). *ESP and parapsychology: A critical reevaluation.* Buffalo, NY: Prometheus.

Harari, H., & Kaplan, R. M. (1982). *Social psychology: Basic and applied.* Monterey, CA: Brooks/Cole.

Harris, A. C. (1986). *Child development.* St. Paul, MN: West.

Harvey, J. H., & Weary, G. (1984). Current issues in attribution theory and research. In *Annual Review of Psychology, 35.* Palo Alto, CA: Annual Reviews.

Hathaway, S. R., & McKinley, J. C. (1967). *The Minnesota multiphasic personality inventory* (rev. ed.). New York: Psychological Corporation.

Heatherington, E. M., & Parke, R. D. (1986). *Child psychology* (3rd ed.). New York: McGraw-Hill.

Hebb, D. O. (1949). *The organization of behavior.* New York: Wiley.

Heider, F. (1958). *Psychology of interpersonal relations.* New York: Wiley.

Helms, D. B., & Turner, J. S. (1976). *Exploring child behavior.* Philadelphia: W. B. Saunders.

Hepner, H. W. (1973). *Psychology applied to life and work.* Englewood Cliffs, NJ: Prentice-Hall.

Herbst, A. B. (1981). Diethylstilbestrol and other sex hormones during pregnancy. *Journal of Obstretics and Gynecology, 58,* 355.

Heron, W. (1957). The pathology of boredom. *Scientific American, 196*(1), 52-56.

Herzberg, F. (1968, January-February). One more time: How do you motivate employees? *Harvard Business Review, 46*(1), 53-62.

Herzberg, F., Mausner, B., Peterson, R., & Capwell, D. F. (1957). *Job attitudes: Research and opinion.* Pittsburgh: Psychological Service of Pittsburgh.

Hess, E. H. (1975). The role of pupil size in communication. *Scientific American, 233*(5), 110-119.

Hess, E. H., & Polt, J. M. (1960). Pupil size as related to interest value of visual stimuli. *Science, 132,* 349-350.

Higgins, J. M. (1982). *Human relations: Concepts and skills.* New York: Random House.

Hilgard, E. R. (1973). A neodissociation interpretation of pain reduction in hypnosis. *Psychological Review, 80,* 403-419.

Hilts, P. J. (1974). *Behavior modification.* New York: Harper's Magazine Press.

Hintzman, D. S. (1974). Theoretical implications of the spacing effect. In R. L. Solso (Ed.), *Theories in cognitive psychology: The Loyola symposium.* Hillsdale, NJ: Erlbaum.

Hobson, J. A., & McCarley, R. W. (1977). The brain as a dream state generator: An activation-synthesis hypothesis of the dream process. *American Journal of Psychiatry, 134,* 1335-1348.

Hoffman, L. R., & Maier, N. R. F. (1961). Quality and acceptance of problem solutions by members of homogeneous and heterogeneous groups. *Journal of Abnormal and Social Psychology, 62,* 401-407.

Holland, J. L. (1962). Some explorations of a theory of vocational choice: I. One- and two-year longitudinal studies. *Psychological Monographs, 76*(26, Whole No. 545).

Holland, J. L. (1968). Explorations of a theory of vocational choice: VI. A longitudinal study using a sample of typical college students. *Journal of Applied Psychology Monograph, 52*(1, Pt. 2).

Holland, J. L. (1972). The present status of a theory of vocational choice. In J. M. Whiteley & A. Resnikoff (Eds.), *Perspectives on vocational development.* Falls Church, VA: American Personnel and Guidance Association.

Holland, J. L. (1973). *Making vocational choices: A theory of careers.* Englewood Cliffs, NJ: Prentice-Hall.

Holland, M. K. (1981). *Introductory psychology.* Lexington, MA: D. C. Heath.

Hollander, E. P. (1958). Conformity, status, and idiosyncrasy credit. *Psychological Review, 65,* 117-127.

Holmes, T. H. (1978). Life situations, emotions, and disease. *Psychosomatics, l9,* 747-754.

Holmes, T. H., & Rahe, R. H. (1967). The social readjustment rating scale. *Journal of Psychosomatic Research, 11,* 213-218.

Holzman, P. S., & Gardner, R. W. (1960). Leveling, sharpening, and memory organization. *Journal of Abnormal and Social Psychology, 61,* 176-180.

Hothersall, D. (1985). *Psychology.* Columbus, OH: Charles E. Merrill.

Houston, T. L., & Levinger, G. (1978). Interpersonal attraction and relationships. In P. Mussen & M. Rosenzweig (Eds.), *Annual Review of Psychology.* Palo Alto, CA: Annual Reviews.

Hurvich, L. M., & Jameson, D. (1974). Opponent processes as a model of neural organization. *American Psychologist, 29,* 88-102.

Hyden, H. (1969). Biochemical aspects of learning and memory. In K. Pribram (Ed.), *On the biology of learning.* New York: Harcourt Brace Jovanovich.

Isen, A. M., & Levin, P. F. (1972). The effect of feeling good on helping: Cookies and kindness. *Journal of Personality and Social Psychology, 21,* 384-388.

Izard, C. E. (1977). *Human emotions.* New York: Plenum.

Jackler, R. (1986, August 10). AIDS babies' numbers growing. *The Houston Post,* pp. 1A, 26A.

Jackson, P. W., & Messick, D. (1968). Creativity. In P. London & D. Rosenhan (Eds.), *Foundations of Abnormal Psychology.* New York: Holt, Rinehart and Winston.

Jacobs, P. A., Brunton, M., Melville, M. M., Brittain, R. P., & McClemont, W. F. (1965). Aggressive behaviour, mental sub-normality, and the XYY male. *Nature, 208,* 1351-1352.

James, W. (1884). What is an emotion? *Mind, 9,* 188-205.

Janda, L. H., & Klenke-Hamel, K. E. (1982). *Psychology: Its study and uses.* New York: St. Martin's Press.

Janis, I. L. (1972). *Victims of groupthink.* Boston: Houghton Mifflin.

Janis, I. L., & Feshbach, S. (1953). Effects of fear-arousing communications. *Journal of Abnormal and Social Psychology, 48,* 78-92.

Janis, I. L., & Mann, L. (1977). *Decision making.* New York: Free Press.

Jencks, C., Smith, M., Acland, H., Bane, M. J., Cohen, D., Gintis, H., Heyns, B., & Michelson, S. (1972). *Inequality: A reassessment of the effect of family and schooling in America.* New York: Basic Books.

Johnson, D. L. (1981). Naturally acquired learned helplessness: The relationship of school failure to achievement behavior, attributions, and self-concept. *Journal of Educational Psychology, 73,* 174-180.

Kagan, J., Kearsley, R. B., & Zelazo, P. R. (1978). *Infancy: Its place in human development.* Cambridge: Harvard University Press.

Keasey, C. B. (1971). Social participation as a factor in the moral development of preadolescents. *Developmental Psychology, 5*(2), 216-220.

Kendrick, C., & Dunn, J. (1983). Sibling quarrels and maternal responses. *Developmental Psychology, 19*(1), 62-70.

Kimble, D. P. (1977). *Psychology as a biological science.* Glenview, IL: Scott, Foresman.

King, N. J., & Montgomery, R. B. (1980). Biofeedback-induced control of human peripheral temperature. A critical review of the literature. *Psychological Bulletin, 88,* 738-752.

Kinsbourne, M. (1982, April). Hemispheric specialization and the growth of human understanding. *American Psychologist, 37,* 411-420.

Klatzky, R. L. (1975). *Human memory: Structures and processes.* San Francisco: W. H. Freeman.

Klatzky, R. L. (1980). *Human memory: Structures and processes* (2nd ed.). San Francisco: W. H. Freeman.

Kleitman, N. (1963). *Sleep and wakefulness.* Chicago: University of Chicago Press.

Klonoff, H. (1974). Effects of marijuana on driving in a restricted area and on city streets: Driving performance and physiological changes. In L. L. Miller (Ed.), *Marijuana: Effects on human behavior* (pp. 359-397). New York: Academic Press.

Kohlberg, L. (1959). *The development of modes of moral thinking and choice in the years 10 to 16.* Unpublished doctoral dissertation, University of Chicago.

Kohlberg, L. (1969). Stage and sequence: The cognitive-developmental approach to socialization. In D. A. Goslin (Ed.), *Handbook of socialization theory and research.* Chicago: Rand McNally.

Kohler, I. (1962). Experiments with goggles. *Scientific American, 206*(5), 62-72.

Kolata, C. (1982). Food affects human behavior. *Science, 218,* 1209-1210.

Kornhauser, A. (1975). *Mental health of the industrial worker.* Huntington, NY: Krieger.

Krueger, A. (1978). Ions in the air. *Human Nature, 1*(7), 46-53.

Kubler-Ross, E. (1969). *On death and dying.* New York: Macmillan.

Kunst-Wilson, W. R., & Zajonc, R. B. (1980). Affective discrimination of stimuli that cannot be recognized. *Science, 207,* 557-558.

Laing, R. D. (1967). *The politics of experience.* New York: Pantheon.

Lamm, H., & Myers, D. G. (1978). Group-induced polarization of attitudes and behavior. In L. Berkowitz (Ed.), *Advances in experimental social psychology (Vol. 11).* New York: Academic Press.

Lange, C. G. (1922). *The emotions* (English Translation). Baltimore: Williams & Wilkins. (Original work published 1885)

Langway, L. (1983, March 28). Bringing up superbaby. *Newsweek,* pp. 62-68.

Larin, H. M. (1982). Drug and obstetric medication effects on infant behavior as measured by the Brazelton Neonatal Behavioral Assessment Scale. *Physical and Occupational Therapy in Pediatrics, 2*(1), 75-84.

Latan, B., & Darley, J. M. (1970). *The unresponsive bystander: Why doesn't he help?* New York: Appleton-Century-Crofts.

Latham, G. P., & Steele, T. P. (1983, September). The motivational effects of participation versus goal setting on performance. *Academy of Management Journal, 26*(3), 406-417.

Laurent, H. (1966). EIMP applied to the International Petroleum Co. *Standard Oil of New Jersey Technical Report.*

Lawler, E. E. (1981). *Pay and organizational development.* Reading, MA: Addison-Wesley.

Lazarus, R. S. (1974). *The riddle of man.* Englewood Cliffs, NJ: Prentice-Hall.

Leavitt, H. J. (1951). Some effects of certain communication patterns on group performance. *Journal of Abnormal and Social Psychology, 46,* 38-50.

Leboyer, F. (1975). *Birth without violence.* New York: Alfred A. Knopf.

Ledwidge, B. (1980). Run for your mind: Aerobic exercise as a means of alleviating anxiety and depression. *Canadian Journal of Behavioural Science, 12,* 126-140.

Leeper, R. W. (1935). A study of a neglected portion of the field of learning: The development of sensory organization. *Pedagogical Seminary and Journal of Genetic Psychology, 46,* 41-75.

Lefcourt, H. M. (1982). *Locus of control: Current trends in theory and research.* Hillsdale, NJ: Erlbaum.

Lepper, M. R., Greene, D., & Nisbett, R. E. (1973). Undermining children's intrinsic interest with extrinsic reward: A test of the 'overjustification' hypothesis. *Journal of Personality and Social Psychology, 28,* 129-137.

Leventhal, H. (1970). Findings and theory in the study of fear communications. In L. Berkowitz (Ed.), *Advances in experimental social psychology* (Vol. 5). New York: Academic.

Lewin, K. (1935). *A dynamic theory of personality* (D. K. Adams & K. E. Zener, trans.). New York: McGraw-Hill.

Liebeskind, J. C., & Paul, L. A. (1977). Psychological and physiological mechanisms of pain. *Annual Review of Psychology, 28,* 41-60.

Likert, R. A. (1932). A technique for the measurement of attitudes. *Archives of Psychology, 1* (1, Whole No. 140), 5-55.

Lippit, R. O. (1940). An experimental study on the effect of democratic and authoritarian group atmospheres. *University of Iowa Studies in Child Welfare, 16*(3), 43-195.

Livant, W. P. (1962). Grammar in the story reproductions of levelers and sharpeners. *Bulletin of the Menninger Clinic, 26,* 283-287.

London, P. (1978). *Beginning psychology* (rev. ed.). Homewood, IL: Dorsey Press.

Lynch, G., & Baudry, M. (1984). The biochemistry of memory: A new and specific hypothesis. *Science, 224,* 1057-1064.

MacLeod-Morgan, C. (1982). EEG lateralization in hypnosis: A preliminary report. *Australian Journal of Clinical and Experimental Hypnosis, 10*(2), 99-102.

Maier, S. F., & Laudenslager, M. (1985, August). Stress and health: Exploring the links. *Psychology Today,* pp. 44-49.

Marcel, A. (1983). Conscious and unconscious perception: Experiments on visual masking and word recognition. *Cognitive Psychology, 15,* 197-237.

Marquis, D. G. (1962). Individual responsibility and group decisions involving risk. *Industrial Management Review, 3,* 8- 23.

Martin, J. (1982, Winter). The fairness of earnings differentials: An experimental study of the perceptions of blue-collar workers. *The Journal of Human Resources, 27*(1), 110-122.

Martindale, C. (1978). Creativity, consciousness and cortical arousal. *Journal of Altered States of Consciousness, 3,* 69-87.

Maslow, A. H. (1954). *Motivation and personality.* New York: Harper & Row.

Maslow, A. H. (1970). *Motivation and personality* (2nd ed.) New York: Harper & Row.

Massarik. F. (1968). Today as an integrating factor. In C. Buhler & F. Massarik (Eds.), *The course of human life: A study of goals in the humanistic perspective.* New York: Springer Publishing Company.

Masters, W. H., & Johnson, V. E. (1966). *Human sexual response.* Boston: Little, Brown.

Matarazzo, J. D. (1972). *Wechsler's measurement and appraisal of adult intelligence* (5th ed.). Baltimore: Williams & Wilkins.

Mathews, K. E., Jr., and Canon, L. K. (1975). Environmental noise level as a determinant of helping behavior. *Journal of Personality and Social Psychology, 32,* 571-577.

McCann, I. L., & Holmes, D. S. (1984). Influence of aerobic exercise on depression. *Journal of Personality and Social Psychology, 46,* 1142-1147.

McClelland, D. C. (1961). *The achieving society.* Princeton, NJ: Van Nostrand.

McClelland, D. C. (1965). Achievement and entrepreneurship. *Journal of Personality and Social Psychology, 1,* 389-392.

McClelland, D. C., & Atkinson, J. W. (1948). The projective expression of needs: 1. The effect of different intensities of the hunger drive on perception. *Journal of Psychology, 25,* 205-222.

McCormick, D. A., & Thompson, R. F. (1984). Cerebellum: Essential involvement in the classically conditioned eyelid response. *Science, 223,* 296-299.

McConnell, J. V. (1974). *Understanding human behavior* (2nd ed.). New York: Holt, Rinehart and Winston.

McGeoch, J. A., & Irion, A. L. (1952). *The psychology of human learning.* New York: Longmans Green.

McGlone, J. (1980). Sex differences in human brain asymmetry: A critical survey. *The Behavioral and Brain Sciences, 3*(2), 215-263.

McGrath, M. J., & Cohen, D. B. (1978). REM sleep facilitation of adaptative waking behavior: A review of the literature. *Psychological Bulletin, 85*(1), 24-57.

McGregor, D. M. (1960). *The human side of enterprise.* New York: McGraw-Hill.

McGuire, W. J. (1969). The nature of attitudes and attitude change. In G. Lindzey & E. Aronson (Eds.), *The handbook of social psychology* (2nd ed., Vol. 3). Reading, MA: Addison-Wesley.

McKean, K. (1984, February). New parts for damaged brains. *Discover,* pp. 68-72.

Meeker, M. (1978). Measuring creativity from the child's point of view. *The Journal of Creative Behavior, 12*(1), 52-62.

Mehrabian, A. (1976). *Public places and private spaces: The psychology of work, play, and living environments.* New York: Basic Books.

Melzack, R., & Wall, P. D. (1965). Pain mechanisms: A new theory. *Science, 150,* 971-979.

Mihevic, P. M. (1982). Anxiety, depression, and exercise. *Quest, 33,* 140-153.

Milgram, S. (1963). Behavioral study of obedience. *Journal of Abnormal and Social Psychology, 67,* 371-378.

Miller, L. K. (1975). *Principles of everyday behavior analysis.* Monterey, CA: Brooks/Cole.

Miller, N. E. (1985, February). Rx: Biofeedback. *Psychology Today,* pp. 54-59.

Miller, N. E., & Brucker, B. S. (1979). A learned visceral response apparently independent of skeletal ones in patients paralyzed by spinal lesions. In N. Birbaumer & H. D. Kimmel (Eds.), *Biofeedback and self-regulation.* Hillsdale, NJ: Erlbaum.

Miller, N. E., & DiCara, L. (1967). Instrumental learning of heart rate changes in curarized rats: Shaping and specificity to discriminative stimulus. *Journal of Comparative and Physiological Psychology, 63,* 12-19.

Mintun, M. A., Raichle, M. E., Kilbourn, M. R., Wooten, G. F., and Welch, M. J. (1984). A quantative model for the *in vitro* assessment of drug binding sights with positron emission tomography. *Annals of Neurology, 15,* 217-227.

Morgan, C. T., King, R. A., & Robinson, N. M. (1979). *Introduction to psychology* (6th ed.) New York: McGraw Hill.

Morris, C. G. (1979). *Psychology: An introduction* (3rd

ed.). Englewood Cliffs, NJ: Prentice-Hall.

Morris, C. G. (1985). *Psychology: An introduction* (5th ed.). Englewood Cliffs, NJ: Prentice-Hall.

Motowidlo, S. J., & Borman, W. C. (1978). Relationships between military morale, motivation, satisfaction, and unit effectiveness. *Journal of Applied Psychology, 63,* 47-52.

Mott, P. E., Mann, F. C., McLoughlin, Q., & Warwick, D. P. (1965). *Shift work.* Ann Arbor, MI: University of Michigan.

Myers, D. G. (1986). *Psychology.* New York: Worth.

Napier, R., & Gershenfeld, M. (1973). *Groups: Theory and experience.* Boston: Houghton Mifflin.

Nickerson, R. S., & Adams, M. J. (1979). Long-term memory for a common object. *Cognitive Psychology, 11,* 287-307.

Oakley, R. (1983). *Drugs, society, and human behavior* (3rd ed.). St. Louis: C. V. Mosby.

Ojemann, G. A. (1983). Prospects for further brain-stimulation studies during neurosurgical operations under local anesthesia. In M. Studdert-Kennedy and D. Poplin (Eds.), *Psychobiology of language.* Cambridge, MA: MIT Press.

Olton, D. S. (1977). Spatial memory. *Scientific American, 236*(6), 82-98.

Ornstein, R. (1985). *Psychology: The study of human experience.* New York: Harcourt Brace Jovanovich.

Osgood, C. E., Suci, G. J., & Tannenbaum, P. H. (1957). *The measurement of meaning.* Urbana: University of Illinois Press.

Overmeier, J. B., & Wielkiewicz, R. M. (1983). On unpredictability as a causal factor in "learned helplessness." *Learning and Motivation, 14,* 324-337.

Packard, V. (1957). *The hidden persuaders.* New York: Pocket Books, Inc.

Paivio, A. (1974). Language and knowledge of the world. *Educational Researcher, 3*(9), 5-12.

Parten, M. B. (1933). Social play among preschool children. *Journal of Abnormal and Social Psychology, 28,* 136-147.

Paul, G. L. (1967). Strategy of outcome research in psychotherapy. *Journal of Consulting Psychology, 31,* 109- 119.

Pennock, G. A. (1930). Industrial research at Hawthorne. *Personnel Journal, 8,* 296-313.

Perkins, D. N. (1981). *The mind's best work.* Cambridge, MA: Harvard University Press.

Phillips, J. L., Jr. (1975). *The origins of intellect: Piaget's theory* (2nd ed.). San Francisco: W. H. Freeman.

Piaget, J. (1952). *The origins of intelligence in children* (M. Cook, Trans.). New York: International Universities Press. (Original work published 1936)

Pines, M. (1980, December). The sinister hand. *Science, 80,* 26-27.

Plutchik, R. (1962). *The emotions: Facts, theories, and a new model.* New York: Academic Press.

Plutchik, R. (1970). Emotions, evolution, and adaptive processes. In M. B. Arnold, (Ed.), *Feelings and emotions: The Loyola symposium.* New York: Academic Press.

Plutchik, R. (1980). *Emotion: A psychoevolutionary synthesis.* New York: Harper & Row.

Premack, D. (1965). Reinforcement theory. In D. Levine (Ed.), *Nebraska symposium on motivation* (Vol. 13). Lincoln, NE: University of Nebraska Press.

Pylyshyn, Z. W. (1973). What the mind's eye tells the mind's brain: A critique of mental imagery. *Psychological Bulletin, 80*(1), 1-24.

Qualls, P. J., & Sheehan, P. W. (1981). Electromyograph biofeedback as a relaxation technique. A critical appraisal and reassessment. *Psychological Bulletin, 90*(1), 21-42.

Rathus, Spencer. (1981). *Instructor's guide to accompany psychology.* New York: CBS Publishing.

Reed, S. K. (1982). *Cognition: Theory and applications.* Monterey, CA: Brooks/Cole.

Rehm, L. P. (1978). Mood, pleasant events, and unpleasant events. *Journal of Consulting and Clinical Psychology, 46,* 854-859.

Rimland, B. (1983). The Feingold diet: An assessment of the reviews by Mattes, by Kavale, and Forness and others. *Journal of Learning Disabilities, 16*(6), 331-333.

Roffwarg, H. P., Muzio, J. N., & Dement, W. C. Ontogenetic development of the human sleep-dream cycle. *Science, 152,* 604-619.

Rogers, C. R. (1961). *On becoming a person: A therapist's view of psychotherapy.* Boston: Houghton Mifflin.

Rosenfeld, L. (1976). *Now that we're all here: Relations in small groups.* Columbus, OH: Merrill.

Rosenthal, R., & Jacobson, L. (1968). *Pygmalion in the classroom.* New York: Holt, Rinehart & Winston.

Ross, I. C., & Zander, A. (1957). Need satisfactions

and employee turnover. *Personnel Psychology, 10,* 327-338.

Rotter, J. B. (1980). Interperson trust, trustworthiness, and gullibility. *American Psychologist, 35* (1), 1-7.

Rubin, Z., & McNeil, E. B. (1985). *Psychology: Being human.* New York: Harper & Row.

Ruch, J. (1978). A study of self-hypnosis with implications for other self-control procedures. In F. H. Frankel & H. S. Zamansky (Eds.), *Hypnosis at its bicentennial: Selected papers* (pp. 131-144). New York: Plenum.

Ruch, J. (1984). *Psychology: The personal science.* Belmont, CA: Wadsworth.

Ruopp, R., Travers, J., Glantz, F., & Coelen, C. (1979). *Children at the center. Final report of the National Day Care Study (Vol. 1).* Cambridge, MA: ABT Associates.

Sachs, M. L. (1984). The runner's high. In M. L. Sachs and G. W. Buffone (Eds.), *Running as therapy: An integrated approach.* Lincoln: University of Nebraska Press.

Sackeim, H. A. (1985, June). The case for ECT. *Psychology Today,* pp. 36-40.

Sackeim, H. A., Gur, R. C., & Saucy, M. C. (1978). Emotions are expressed more intensely on the left side of the face. *Science, 202,* 434-436.

Satow, K. L. (1975). Social approval and helping. *Journal of Experimental Social Psychology, 11,* 501-509.

Scarr, S., & Vander Zanden, J. (1987). *Understanding psychology* (5th ed.). New York: Random House.

Scarr, S., & Weinberg, R. (1976). IQ test performance of black children adopted by white families. *American Psychologist, 31,* 726-739.

Schachter, S. (1959). *The psychology of affiliation.* Stanford, CA: Stanford University Press.

Schachter, S., & Singer, J. E. (1962). Cognitive, social, and physiological determinants of emotional state. *Psychological Review, 69,* 379-399.

Schardein, J. L. (1980). Congenital abnormalities and hormones during pregnancy: A critical review. *Teratology, 22,* 251.

Schotte, D. E., & Clum, G. A. (1982). Suicide ideation in a college population: A test of a model. *Journal of Consulting and Clinical Psychology, 50,* 690-696.

Seamon, J. G., Brody, N., & Kauff, D. M. (1983). Affective discrimination of stimuli that are not recognized: Effects of shadowing, masking, and cerebral laterality. *Journal of Experimental Psychology: Learning, Memory, and Cognition, 9,* 544-555.

Segall, M. H., Campbell, D. T., & Herskovits, M. J. (1966). *The influence of culture on visual perception.* New York: Bobbs-Merrill.

Seidenberg, B., & Snadowsky, A. (1976). *Social psychology: An introduction.* New York: Free Press.

Seligman, M. E. P. (1975). *Helplessness: On depression, development, and death.* San Francisco: Freeman.

Selye, H. (1956). *The stress of life.* New York: McGraw-Hill.

Selye, H. (1976). *The stress of life* (rev. ed.). New York: McGraw-Hill.

Senden, M. V. (1960). *Space and sight* (P. Heath, Trans.). New York: Free Press.

Sharma, J. (1979). Organizational communications: A linking process. *The Personnel Administrator, 24* (7), 35-39, 43.

Sheldon, W. H., Stevens, S. S., & Tucker, W. B. (1940). *The varieties of human physique: An introduction to constitutional psychology.* New York: Harper & Brothers.

Shepard, R. N., & Metzler, J. (1971). Mental rotation of three-dimensional objects. *Science, 171,* 701-703.

Sistrunk, F., & McDavid, J. W. (1971). Sex variable in conforming behavior. *Journal of Personality and Social Psychology, 17,* 200-207.

Skeels, H. M. (1938). Mental development of children in foster homes. *Journal of Consulting Psychology, 2,* 33-43.

Skeels, H. M. (1942). The study of the effects of differential stimulation on mentally retarded children: A follow-up report. *American Journal of Mental Deficiencies, 46,* 340-350.

Skeels, H. M. (1966). Adult status of children with contrasting early life experience: A follow-up study. *Monographs of the Society for Research in Child Development, 31* (3), 1-65.

Skinner, B. F. (1948). 'Superstition' in the pigeon. *Journal of Experimental Psychology, 38*, 168-172.

Skinner, B. F. (1953). *Science and human behavior.* New York: Macmillan.

Slaby, R. G., & Frey, K. S. (1975). Development of gender constancy and selective attention to same-sex models. *Child Development, 46,* 849-856.

Snyder, S. H. (1977). Opiate receptors and internal opiates. *Scientific American, 236*(3), 44-56.

Snyder, S. H. (Interviewed by D. Goleman.). (1980, June). Matter over mind: The big issues raised by newly discovered brain chemicals. *Psychology Today*, pp. 66-76.

Sperry, R. (1982). Some effects of disconnecting the cerebral hemispheres. *Science, 217,* 1223-1226, 1250.

Spielberger, C. D. (1966). The effects of anxiety on complex learning and academic achievement. In C. D. Spielberger (Ed.), *Anxiety and behavior.* New York: Academic Press.

Stagner, R. (1958). Industrial morale: 2. Motivational aspects of industrial morale. *Personnel Psychology, 11,* 64-70.

Stapp, J., & Fulcher, R. (1981). The employment of APA members: *American Psychologist, 36*(11), 1263-1322.

Stapp, J., & Fulcher, R. (1983). The employment of APA members: 1982. *American Psychologist, 38*(12), 1298-1320.

Steers, R. M. (1975). Task-goal attributes, *n* achievement and supervisory performance. *Organizational Behavior and Human Performance, 13,* 392-403.

Steers, R. M. (1976). Factors affecting job attitudes in a goal setting environment. *Academy of Management Journal, 19,* 6-16.

Stephan, W., Berscheid, E., & Walster, E. (1971). Sexual arousal and heterosexual perception. *Journal of Personality and Social Psychology, 20*(1), 93-101.

Stepney, R. (1983, September). Why do people smoke? *World Press Review, 30,* 56.

Sternberg, R. J. (1979). The nature of mental abilities. *American Psychologist, 34,* 214-230.

Stevens, C. F. (1979). The neuron. *Scientific American, 241*(3), 55-56.

Stringer, R. A., Jr. (1971). Achievement motivation and management control. In G. W. Dalton & P. R. Lawrence (Eds.), *Motivation and control in organizations.* Homewood, IL: Irwin-Dorsey.

Stuss, D. T., & Benson, D. F. (1984). Neuropsychologic studies of the frontal lobes. *Psychological Bulletin, 95,* 3-28.

Super, D. E. (1957). *Psychology of careers: An introduction to vocational development.* New York: Harper & Brothers.

Sutton, H., & Porter, L. W. (1968). A study of the grapevine in a governmental organization. *Personnel Psychology, 21,* 223- 230.

Szasz, T. S. (1974, December). Our despotic laws destroy the right to self-control. *Psychology Today,* pp. 20-29, 127.

Taskin, D. P., Calvarese, B. M., Simmons, M. S., & Shapiro, B. J. (1978). Respiratory status of 74 habitual marijuana smokers. Presented at the annual meeting of the American Thoracic Society, Boston.

Thibaut, J. W., & Kelley, H. H. (1959). *The social psychology of groups.* New York: Wiley.

Thompson, R. F., Berger, T. W., & Madden, J., IV. (1983). Cellular processes of learning and memory in the mammalean CNS. *Annual Review of Neurosciences, 6,* 447-491.

Thurstone, L. L., & Chave, E. J. (1929). *The measurement of attitude.* Chicago: University of Chicago Press.

Tinkelberg, J. R., & Darley, C. F. (1975). Psychological and cognitive effects of cannabis. In P. H. Cornell & N. Dorn (Eds.), *Cannabis and man.* New York: Churchill Livingstone.

Tobias, S. (1979). Anxiety research in educational psychology. *Journal of Educational Psychology, 71,* 573-582.

Tolman, E. C. (1932). *Purposive behavior in animals and men.* New York: Appleton-Century-Crofts.

Travers, R. M. (1972). *Essentials of learning* (3rd ed.). New York: Macmillan.

Troll, L. E. (1975). *Early and middle adulthood: The best is yet to be — maybe.* Monterey, CA: Brooks/Cole.

Tryon, R. C. (1940). Genetic differences in maze-learning abilities in rats. In *39th Yearbook, Part I.* National Society for the Study of Education. Chicago: University of Chicago Press.

Tubesing, N. L., & Tubesing, D. A. (Eds.). (1983). *Structured exercises in stress management* (Vol. 1). Duluth, MN: Whole Person Press.

Tulving, E. (1972). Episodic and semantic memory. In E. Tulving & W. Donaldson (Eds.), *Organization of memory.* New York: Academic Press.

Turkington, C. (1986, March). Alcohol abuse linked to levels of serotonin. (Research News) *APA Monitor,* p. 18.

Undheim, J. (1981). On intelligence: IV. Toward a restoration of general intelligence. *Scandinavian*

Journal of Psychology, 22(4), 251-265.

Vandenberg, S. G. (1967). Hereditary factors in normal personality traits. In J. Wortis (Ed.), *Recent advances in biological psychiatry* (Vol. 9). New York: Plenum.

VanRijn, P. (1973). *Instructor's manual to accompany psychology: Its principles and meanings.* Hillsdale, IL: The Dryden Press.

Volpicelli, J. R., Ulm, R. R., Altenor, A., & Seligman, M. E. P. (1983). Learned mastery in the rat. *Learning and Motivation, 14,* 204-222.

Vroom, V. H. (1964). *Work and motivation.* New York: Wiley.

Wallis, C. (1983, June 6). Stress: Can we cope? *Time,* pp. 48-52.

Watson, D. (1978). *Psychology: What it is/how to use it.* San Francisco: Canfield Press.

Watson, J. B., & Rayner, R. (1920). Conditioned emotional reactions. *Journal of Experimental Psychology, 3,* 1-14.

Webb, L. J., DiClemente, C. C., Johnstone, E. E., Sanders, J. L., & Perley, R. A. (Eds.). (1981). *DSM-III training guide.* New York: Brunner/Mazel.

Wechsler, D. (1975). Intelligence defined and undefined: A relativistic appraisal. *American Psychologist, 30,* 135-139.

Weingartner, H., Rudorfer, M. V., Buchsbaum, M. S., & Linnoila, M. (1983). Effects of serotonin on memory impairments produced by ethanol. *Science, 221,* 472-474.

West, J. B. (1984, February). Human physiology at extreme altitudes on Mount Everest. *Science, 223,* 784-788.

Williams, J. C. (1978). *Human behavior in organizations.* Cincinnati: South-Western.

Williams, J. C., DuBrin, A. J., & Sisk, H. L. (1985). *Management and organizations* (5th ed.). Cincinnati: South-Western.

Williams, J. C., & Huber, G. P. (1986). *Human behavior in organizations* (3rd ed.). Cincinnati: South-Western.

Wilson, E. O. (1975). *Sociobiology: The new synthesis.* Cambridge, MA: Harvard University Press.

Witelson, S. F. (1976). Sex and the single hemisphere: Specialization of the right hemisphere for spatial processing. *Science, 193,* 425-427.

Woolf, H. B. (Ed.). (1974). *The Merriam-Webster Dictionary.* New York: Pocket Books.

Wrightsman, L. S. (1977). *Social psychology in the seventies* (2nd ed.). Monterey, CA: Brooks/Cole.

Zaidel, E. (1976). Auditory vocabulary of the right hemisphere following brain bisection or hemidecortication. *Cortex, 12,* 191-211.

Zajonc, R. B. (1965). Social facilitation. *Science, 149,* 269-274.

Zanna, M. P., Olson, J. M., & Fazio, R. H. (1980). Attitude-behavior consistency: An individual difference perspective. *Journal of Personality and Social Psychology, 38,* 432-440.

Zimbardo, P. G. (1969). The human choice: Individuation, reason, and order versus deindividuation, impulse, and chaos. In W. J. Arnold & D. Levine (Eds.), *Nebraska symposium on motivation* (Vol. 17). Lincoln: University of Nebraska Press.

Zimbardo, P. G. (1985). *Psychology and life* (11th ed.). Glenview, IL: Scott, Foresman.

ACKNOWLEDGMENTS

Figure 1–2. The Picture Cube/Frank Siteman
Figure 1–5 The Picture Cube/Nancy Bates
Figure 1–7. American Red Cross
Figure 1–8. USDA Photo
Figure 1–10. The Bettmann Archive, Inc.
Figure 1–11. The Bettmann Archive, Inc.
Figure 1–12. The Bettmann Archive, Inc.
Figure 1–14. The Bettmann Archive, Inc.
Figure 1–16. The Picture Cube/D. Judith Sedwick
Figure 1–17. The Bettmann Archive, Inc.
Figure 1–18. The Picture Cube/Frank Siteman
Figure 1–19. H. Armstrong Roberts
Figure 1–21. H. Armstrong Roberts
Figure 1–24. Courtesy of NCR Corporation
Figure 2–4. E. R. Lewis, Univesity of California, Berkeley
Figure 2–10. © Richard Hutchings, Science Source/Photo Researchers
Figure 2–22. Peter Arnold, Inc.
Figure 2–24. Photo courtesy of Celanese
Figure 2–25 Virginia State Travel Service
Figure 2–26. Elizabeth Wilcox, Photo Researchers, Inc.
Figure 3–2. USDA Photo
Figure 3–10. March of Dimes Birth Defects Foundation
Figure 3–14. Good Samaritan Hospital, Cincinnati, Ohio
Figure 3–15. The Christ Hospital, Cincinnati, Ohio
Figure 3–17. University of Cincinnati Medical Center
Figure 3–18. Photo by Bob Ohr for The Christ Hospital, Cincinnati, Ohio
Figure 3–25. The Picture Cube/Robert V. Eckert, Jr.
Figure 3–28. William Vandivert, courtesy of *Scientific American*
Figure 3–30. Good Samaritan Hospital, Cincinnati, Ohio
Figure 3–31. HUD
Figure 3–32. H. Armstrong Roberts
Figure 3–34. H. Armstrong Roberts
Figure 4–1. H. Armstrong Roberts
Figure 4–5. H. Armstrong Roberts
Figure 4–7. The Picture Cube/Jeffrey Dunn
Figure 4–8. New England Memorial Hospital Public Relations Department
Figure 4–9. The Bettmann Archive, Inc.
Figure 4–14. Photo courtesy of Big Toys
Figure 4–16. Scott Paper Company, Philadelphia, Pennsylvania
Figure 4–19. H. Armstrong Roberts
Figure 4–20. USDA Photo
Figure 4–22. The Picture Cube/Nancy Bates
Figure 4–25. Courtesy of Abbott Laboratories
Figure 6–7. The Picture Cube/Ken Robert Buck
Figure 6–12. The Picture Cube/David S. Strickler
Figure 7–1. The Bettmann Archive, Inc.
Figure 7–8. H. Armstrong Roberts
Figure 7–12. H. Armstrong Roberts
Figure 8–1a. Huffy Corporation
Figure 8–1b.U. S. Chess Federations/Bruce Helm
Figure 8–2. The Picture Cube/Sandra Johnson
Figure 8–5. Trans World Airlines
Figure 8–7. H. Armstrong Roberts
Figure 8–9. The Bettmann Archive, Inc.
Figure 8–10. The Bettmann Archive, Inc.
Figure 8–12. From the Wechsler Adult Intelligence Scale-Revised. Copyright © 1981 by the Psychological

Corporation. All rights reserved.
Figure 8–13. The Picture Cube/Martha Stewart
Figure 8–16. The Picture Cube/Sarah Putnam
Figure 9–1a. Pennsylvania Power & Light Company
Figure 9–1b. McDonald's Corporation
Figure 9–5. Peter Arnold, Inc./James H. Karales
Figure 9–6. Florida Division of Tourism
Figure 9–12. The Bettman Archive, Inc.
Figure 10–1. Photos by Edward Gallob
Figure 10–3. The Picture Cube/David S. Strickler
Figure 11–1 AT&T Company
Figure 11–2. H. Armstrong Roberts
Figure 11–3. The Picture Cube/Frank Siteman
Figure 11–7. The Bettmann Archive, Inc.
Figure 11–8. The Bettmann Archive, Inc.
Figure 11–9. The Bettmann Archive, Inc.
Figure 11–15. H. Armstrong Roberts
Figure 11–17. The Picture Cube
Figure 11–19. Harvard University Press
Figure 12–1. H. Armstrong Roberts
Figure 12–3. H. Armstrong Roberts
Figure 12–5. H. Armstrong Roberts
Figure 12–8. Reuters/Bettmann Newsphotos
Figure 12–9. The Picture Cube/David S. Strickler
Figure 12–12. H. Armstrong Roberts
Figure 12–13. Courtesy of Johnson & Johnson
Figure 13–5. American Cancer Society
Figure 13–8. Monkmeyer Press Photo Service/David S. Strickler
Figure 13–9. AT&T Company
Figure 13–12. USDA photo by Jack Schneider
Figure 13–13. Monkmeyer Press Photo Service/Mimi Forsyth
Figure 14–4. Richard Younker
Figure 14–5. UPI/Bettmann Archive
Figure 14–6. Ulrike Welsch
Figure 14–13. (Golda Meir) UPI/Bettmann Newsphotos; (Martin Luther King) UPI/Bettmann Newsphotos; (Margaret Thatcher) Reuters/Bettmann Newsphotos; (Ronald Reagan) UPI/Bettmann Newsphotos

NAME INDEX

U

V

W

X, Y, Z

SUBJECT INDEX

A

B

C

D

E

F

G

H

J

K

L

M

N

O

P

S